A CHEQUERED BRILLIANCE

A CHEQUERED BRILLIANCE

The Many Lives *of*
V.K. KRISHNA MENON

JAIRAM RAMESH

PENGUIN
VIKING
rint of Penguin Random House

VIKING

USA | Canada | UK | Ireland | Australia
New Zealand | India | South Africa | China

Viking is part of the Penguin Random House group of companies
whose addresses can be found at global.penguinrandomhouse.com

Published by Penguin Random House India Pvt. Ltd.
4th Floor, Capital Tower 1, MG Road,
Gurugram 122 002, Haryana, India

First published in Viking by Penguin Random House India 2019

Copyright © Jairam Ramesh 2019

All rights reserved

10 9 8 7 6 5 4

The views and opinions expressed in this book are the author's own and the
facts are as reported by him which have been verified to the extent possible,
and the publishers are not in any way liable for the same.

ISBN 9780670092321

Typeset in Bembo Std by Manipal Technologies Limited, Manipal
Printed at Replika Press Pvt. Ltd, India

www.penguin.co.in

'A volcano has been extinguished.'

—*Indira Gandhi on the death of Krishna Menon*

'But the glow of the lava which poured out so copiously and brilliantly from it . . . would long remain in the memories of men and annals of history.'

—*K.P.S. Menon on the death of Krishna Menon*

A Note on Names of People and Places

I have retained the names of people and places as they were referred to during Krishna Menon's time.

Name in Book	Current Name
Bombay	Mumbai
Calcutta	Kolkata
Simla	Shimla
Poona	Pune
Trivandrum	Thiruvananthapuram
Palghat	Palakkad
Tellicherry	Thalassery
Midnapur	Medinipur
Calicut	Kozhikode
Cochin	Kochi
Bangalore	Bengaluru
Madras (state)	Tamil Nadu
Madras (city)	Chennai
Orissa	Odisha
NEFA	Arunachal Pradesh
Peking	Beijing
Chou En-lai	Zhou Enlai
Mao Tse-Tung	Mao Zedong
Ceylon	Sri Lanka
Abyssinia	Ethiopia
Burma	Myanmar
Malaya	Malaysia

Contents

The Post-1947 Years

Part V

A First Word

This is a book on one of India's most compelling, consequential and controversial political personalities. He has been referred to at various times as Rasputin, Mephistopheles, Lucifer, Svengali, Evil Genius, The World's Most Hated Diplomat, Sombre Porcupine, The Formula Man and other colourful images. He was both admired and admonished for over three decades.

He was first 'discovered' in Madras sometime in 1916 or 1917 by the extraordinary Irishwoman Annie Besant, who had made India her home, but it was his avatar as Jawaharlal Nehru's soulmate, sounding board and envoy between 1935 and 1964 that earned him a permanent place in India's twentieth-century history.

He spent twenty-three years in London agitating and making the case for India's freedom with political parties and parliamentarians, trade unions, universities, the media, literary and cultural personalities and all sorts of civic organizations across the UK. In that period he was also the editor of a number of well-known books published in the mid-1930s and helped establish the highly regarded publishing imprint Pelican Books.

He had a key role to play in making the Korean armistice possible in 1953 and in contributing to a political settlement on Vietnam, Cambodia and Laos in 1954. He was very active in defusing tensions between the US and China in 1955.

He figured constructively in the negotiations to end the Suez Canal crisis in 1956 but drew criticism for his stance on the Soviet invasion of Hungary that took place almost at the same time.

He holds the record for having made the longest speech at the United Nations (UN) in 1957, running into some eight hours spread over two days and defending India's case on Kashmir. The speech was not only exhaustive but was evidently so exhausting that he collapsed soon after making it and required medical attention in order to resume.

He finds significant mention in histories of the negotiations over nuclear disarmament, the struggle against colonial rule in Africa, the emergence of Cyprus, the campaign against apartheid in South Africa and the crisis in Congo. Out of power and in the political wilderness between 1963 and 1974, he became a crusader for world peace and the abolition of war.

He was seen as the architect of India's liberation of Goa from Portuguese rule in 1961, which earned plaudits at home but drew intense criticism in the West. He continues to be held chiefly responsible for India's military debacle in the war with China a year later. He was forced to resign as India's defence minister in November 1962 but grew in stature subsequently. His reputation was redeemed to a large extent by the dignified manner in which he handled his ejection from the pinnacle of power.

He spent three decades crusading against the British rule in India, but after the transfer of power was accomplished, he strongly advocated India remaining in the Commonwealth. He was a municipal councillor for a long time in London and almost became an MP in the UK House of Commons. Upon his death, seven of his British friends, all distinguished men and women in their own right, issued a statement calling him 'a good Britisher and a true Indian'.

His two elections as a Lok Sabha MP from North Bombay in 1957 and 1962 made global headlines and his campaigns drew film stars, literary figures and eminent professionals. Denied a ticket in 1967, he quit the Congress after a three decade-long association and returned to Parliament in 1969 and 1971 as an independent supported by the communist and other left parties.

He had an uncanny ability to make instant enemies—and there were many of them. Even so, he had a legion of acolytes and admirers. He evoked strong criticism for his style even as he was grudgingly applauded for his substance. He hobnobbed with presidents and prime ministers of different countries, many of whom found him brilliant but exasperating.

Many years after his death, buildings and roads were named after him and statues erected in India. In 2008, the South African government recognized his contributions to the ending of apartheid, and five years later, the Bangladesh government honoured him for his role in the emergence of that country. A plaque marking the place where he stayed and a bust of him as well can be found in London.

This man is V.K. Krishna Menon, at once both cantankerous and charming, a man well-endowed with both eccentricities and capabilities that make him a continuing field of excavation.

In the Nehruvian era, there was an age of V.K. Krishna Menon. This book recalls that age.

* * *

Over the past quarter of a century, substantial new material in which Krishna Menon figures prominently has become available in archives in different countries, including India, the US, the UK, Canada, Sweden, Russia, France, China and Australia. Krishna Menon's own papers, humungous as they are, were made available to the public only in early 2019. Till the mid-1990s, just thirty-one volumes of the *Selected Works of Jawaharlal Nehru* had been published and those too had not been excavated meaningfully. Since then another sixty-five volumes have appeared. A careful reading of them is required to understand the evolution of twentieth-century India. They provide a window into the mind of the architect of the modern Indian nation-state. For a quarter of a century beginning 1935, the largest part of Nehru's correspondence, barring that with his daughter, was with Krishna Menon, in which the two shared their innermost thoughts on important issues and the personalities of the day and bared their souls to each other.

This new biography does not intend to eulogize Krishna Menon for his numerous contributions nor castigate him for his many sins. It is, instead, meant to be a clinically objective narrative of his chequered life, based almost entirely on contemporary documentary evidence. I narrate a complex tale letting the written materials speak for themselves. Krishna Menon is an eminently fit subject for what has been called 'psychohistory'. I have refrained from tilling that field and have stuck mostly to what the archives tell us. This is not a judgemental undertaking; it is, instead, what I could call a pretty straightforward narrative biography. As far as possible, I have kept myself out of the story. Krishna Menon's proponents have spun many legends, just as his detractors have propagated many myths. Neither approach does full justice to the man and his mix of contradictions and brilliance. My task has been to pierce through the legends and the myths, the embellishments and the exaggerations and present the man as he was—erratic, insecure, frequently acerbic in speech, very often supercilious in silence; but always arresting and compelling. He could never be ignored and always stood out, warts and all.

The truth regarding Krishna Menon is without doubt much more complex than what has been written about him thus far; and it is this that makes his life even more noteworthy and worth revisiting. And because of who he was and what he did and his unique relationship with Nehru, Krishna Menon's kaleidoscopic life also sheds light on the extraordinary times in which he lived and illuminates the forces that shaped those turbulent decades.

The Pre-1947 Years

1

The Vengalil Family

Vengalil Krishnan Krishna Menon was born on 3 May 1896[1] in his mother's ancestral home, Vengal, in the historic city of Calicut, where the Portuguese explorer Vasco da Gama had landed in May 1498. Krishna Menon would play a crucial role in ending the Portuguese rule in India over four and a half centuries later. Vengalil was the *taravad* or matrilineal joint family to which he belonged. Taravad was a unique social institution characteristic of the Nair community of what is now Kerala.

Krishna Menon belonged to a wealthy landed family. He grew up till his early teens in nearby Tellicherry, the English East India Company's first settlement on the Malabar coast. This was the town in which E.K. Janaki Ammal—later to be India's first woman scientist of repute—was born in November 1897. She would get to know Krishna Menon well in London in the 1940s and would write to him on 9 August 1954 when he was at the height of his global fame:

> I was looking through an old file and came across a letter of yours and when I read it I could not but help saying to myself, 'He has more than justified my faith and hopes in him'. This is to let you know that your role as a great Asian is just beginning . . .

Krishna Menon had seven siblings, of whom two older sisters turned out to be quite remarkable in their own right. His eldest sister, V.K. Chinnammalu Amma, born in 1890, was reportedly proficient in many languages including Sanskrit, Latin and French and taught in girls' schools in Coimbatore, Madras and other places. She was a very early firebrand feminist. A century ago in October 1919, she was to write an article in a publication brought out by the Theosophical Society in which she highlighted the strengths of the matriarchal system but also spoke about the need to reform it further:[2]

> . . . The position of women in Malabar is an effective answer to critics who say that the Women in India cannot rise beyond the level of household drudges. Remove the obstacles that lie in the way of their progress—early marriage, enforced and despised widowhood, etc. and give them their birthrights—equal rights of property, freedom to determine their own future and proper educational facilities and the Women of India will be, as they were in times of yore, one of the greatest glories of our Great Land.

Five years later, she waxed eloquent on women in ancient India:[3]

> . . . If there exists the impression that the ideal of women's freedom is alien to India, which has been sanctified by the lives of women in ancient times like Maitreyi, Gargi, Draupadi, Kunti and Gandhari, it is produced by sheer blindness. In Sanskrit *sahadharmacharini* ['partner in the performance of Dharma'] is the synonym of *bharya* [wife] . . . In India centuries ago, our ancestor Manu said that, 'wherever women are worshipped, the Gods rejoice' . . . For that precept to become meaningful, the women of India will have to wake from their long slumber and live in full awareness of being citizens of India. Only then will our Nation reach that exalted position that it richly deserves.

An extremely independent-minded and almost 'eccentric'[4] Chinnammalu Amma distanced herself from the family in the mid-

1930s. She wrote to Krishna Menon on 4 February 1937, when she was teaching at the Government Girls School in Coimbatore:

> I have been wanting to write to you about family affairs for some time but I mislaid your letter and did not know the address. A few days ago I saw the address of the India League in the Fleet Street Annual. I think your address is the same.
>
> . . . I wish to separate from my family . . . In the event of your deciding to give me some compensation, it may be less delicate for you if I offer my terms. I am willing to take Rs 1000 and go away. I do not want lands or property in any shape. This is my only condition so far as compensation is concerned. If it is deemed that this amount is too high I am open to bargaining—in fact will take any amount given.
>
> Be certain of one thing alone. The separation must take place. That admits of no doubt. Please do not treat this letter as a matter of no consequence. You are the person to whom I have to communicate my decision. I am asking for no personal favour.
>
> Yours affly,
> V.K. Chinnammalu Amma
>
> PS: Please reply only to the business side of this letter and leave questions of sentiment aside.

J. Devika, a leading scholar at the Centre for Development Studies, Thiruvananthapuram, has translated Chinnammalu Amma's writings in Malayalam into English. I asked her opinion of this somewhat brutal letter. Her response minced no words:[5]

> Her [V.K. Chinnammalu Amma's] invisibility is perhaps what should be written about. Women may have talent, excellent education, and a sense of belonging to the public, but they rarely scale the heights that their brothers do. That is a tragic feature of Kerala's achievements. In many families, including my own, women of that generation excelled, like many men in their families.

But they ended up either as housewives or school teachers, or in some such tiny niche, while the men went on to becoming national figures. The best they often did was find a job to sustain themselves.

Look at the clarity with which she expresses herself, is it not reminiscent of Menon's discourse itself—clear, forthright, non-sentimental? And where did she end up with all her talents, her polyglot brilliance?

Chinnammalu Amma, however, did keep up some contact with Krishna Menon for, on 6 February 1957, he wrote to her from New York:

. . . This is only a brief note to acknowledge your letter. I am in the throes of the debate on Kashmir which is so very exacting. I want to write to you, when I am with myself and not with these affairs . . . Please feel and think we all love you very much and we also know that we must pay regard to your views and your well-being. So please take care of yourself and do not worry . . . Please keep well and think kindly of people, even if they do not understand or appear to be what you wish them to be.

This letter was written just a few days after Krishna Menon had given his famous eight-hour speech at the UN on Kashmir spread over two days. This marathon oration was to make him a national hero. Chinnammalu Amma must have been following the speech closely, because nine years earlier she had written an article in a noted Madras-based publication of those times. The article was called 'Sheikh Muhammad Abdullah' and is one of the early public appreciations of the Kashmiri leader by any Indian writer. Quoting Gandhi, who told the dithering Maharaja of Kashmir in 1947 that 'the will of the people of Kashmir is the supreme law in Kashmir', she ended the article by noting:

The proceedings at the U.N.O. [United Nations Organisation] on the Kashmir question are still inconclusive. But one thing is certain. The gospel of communal harmony insisted upon by her leader [Sheikh Abdullah] will bring Kashmir to her cherished goal of a free, secular, democratic Government, serving as an example to both India and Pakistan.[6]

In April 1957, a democratically elected communist government came to power in Kerala. Although she had distanced herself from her family, a worried Chinnammalu Amma wrote to Prime Minister Nehru on 26 June 1957, introducing herself as Krishna Menon's eldest sister, quoting extracts from a letter she had received from her younger sister V.K. Janaki Amma and then asking the Prime Minister a pointed question:

The Govt of Kerala is a communist one. Only 5 acres of land will be given to a person. This will be law very soon. Compensation will be nominal. Many families are changing into companies for fear of this law. No one of us have derived any benefit from the family property, but still it would be a great pity to lose [it] . . . What father gave us is ours . . .

I should like to know whether such revolutionary changes are going to take place in Kerala. You as the head of the Central govt ought to know Kerala has not been banished from India I hope. Please give me the information.

Three weeks later, on 17 July 1957, Nehru replied after having her concerns examined:

Whatever legal rights you have in your land and property cannot be taken away from you. Even if some kind of a company is formed, you will presumably get your due share. Under our Constitution, I do not see how any compensation given can be merely nominal.

I do not of course know what kind of land policy the Kerala Government is going to follow . . . They have stated, however, that they will follow our Constitution . . .

I therefore suggest you need not be apprehensive. I cannot of course guarantee what might happen in the future but it is very unlikely that your rights will suffer.

As it turned out, a reluctant Nehru was finally persuaded by his colleagues to dismiss the democratically elected communist government in Kerala in July 1959 taking recourse to Article 356 of the Constitution, the very first time this provision was to be used. His daughter, Indira Gandhi, then the Congress president, played a pivotal role in this decision. As far as I have been able to make out, Krishna Menon appears not to have objected to her decision with any great conviction. It is possible that he was less than supportive of the communist government because of its radical land-reform policies, which would have meant his family losing a few thousand acres of land. It is ironical that many years after his death, a prominent minister of this government, V.R. Krishna Iyer, would be the president of the Krishna Menon Memorial Society for almost two decades. Krishna Iyer would hold on to the view that Krishna Menon had nothing to do with the dismissal of the communist ministry in Kerala in 1959 but there is no clinching evidence available in support of such an unequivocal view.

Another sister, who was a year older than Krishna Menon, V.K. Janaki Amma, was to become his constant emotional support for over half a century till her death in 1963. They were extremely close. The two siblings wrote to each other regularly over a period of almost four decades, and if there was one person Krishna Menon trusted implicitly and with whom he shared his thoughts freely on various matters—personal and professional—it was Janaki Amma. His letters from London in the late 1920s speak of plans to return to India and start schools along with her. These plans, however, never fructified. A number of his women friends too got to know her well, and on at least two occasions, Janaki Amma chided him for not marrying them. She may also have contributed to Krishna Menon's finances in the late 1920s and early 1930s without the knowledge of their father who regarded his son as a big disappointment for not becoming a lawyer and returning to India. When their father passed away in 1935, Krishna Menon would execute a power of attorney in Janaki Amma's name for his share of the inheritance. By all accounts she was a formidable lady, which can be gauged by this letter of 28 September 1935 sent to the district magistrate of Malabar in Calicut:

I have the honour to request you to issue the license enclosed herewith in my name. For the license holder, Mr. K. Krishnan Kurup, my father, is no more and the estate, for which the protection of which the license was issued, is in my possession . . .

The entreaty was for a gun licence. Janaki Amma was an expert swimmer and a crack shot, whereas both swimming and shooting were pastimes alien to her brother. Nonetheless, Janaki Amma indulged Krishna Menon in one of his curious beliefs—strange because he considered himself a progressive, socialist and rationalist. Krishna Menon was fixated on astrology. When he was about to depart as high commissioner in the UK, he had written to Janaki Amma in a mood of extreme depression. On 16 June 1952, at his request, she sent him a nine-page letter based on a dissection of his horoscope:

. . . I got a good astrologer from Feroke [part of Calicut]. He says that during this period [15-4-52 to 6-7-52] you will be mentally agitated and although there is no danger of your being unbalanced mentally or even getting irritated outwardly still there is no chance of your being highly mentally worried. According to the horoscope this is all due to yourself and from no outward cause—you imagine things and then worry yourself—that is what the astrologer said . . . About marriage this period is a probable time too . . . You will marry only an outside India person and she won't be a Hindu. If you marry she will be very devoted to you and . . . there is chance of your having one son also . . .

The astrologer attributed the cause of Krishna Menon's troubles then to the position of the moon and Mars and predicted that with the impending movement of the planets, he would find another job later in the year. But he continued to be dispirited, and on 22 June 1953, Janaki Amma wrote again to her brother, who was then in New York leading India's delegation to the UN. He had also just been elected to the Rajya Sabha and had asked her to consult another astrologer:

. . . I am sending you one more reading. I am sorry I could not send this earlier. This man I am told is a very competent man. But on paper one really looks just as the other. I shall send you some more next week . . .

The man who looked into the horoscope said that he would answer questions if we ask him. If you can send me some questions, I shall get the answer and send it to you . . .

Janaki Amma had two daughters—Janaki and Madhavi.[7] Nehru's first epistolary contact with this side of Krishna Menon's family took place when he sent a handwritten letter to Madhavi from Allahabad on 2 October 1940:

My sister [Vijaya Lakshmi Pandit] showed me your letters to her. I want to tell you also that I shall be happy to have you as our guest here. Your uncle, Krishna Menon, spoke to me about you when I was in England last and I have been wanting to meet you and your mother since then. I hope I am not taken away and made unapproachable.

A year later, on 21 September 1941, Nehru wrote to Krishna Menon:

I had a letter from your sister some days ago. She told me that her daughter was coming to Allahabad to be interviewed by some examiners. My sister has written to her that we shall be very happy indeed to have her daughter stay with us in Allahabad.

On 24 December 1955, Nehru, accompanied by the then chief minister of Madras, K. Kamaraj, visited Janaki Amma in her home in Calicut. Krishna Menon was away in New York when Nehru and Kamaraj called on his sister. Janaki Amma had wanted Krishna Menon to be present when she had been told of the visit. She cabled her brother, who replied:

Cannot leave New York before 22nd. Regret unable to arrive there for 24th. Express regret to Prime Minister and request him to accept such limited facilities as we have and overlook inconveniences.

There is a hilarious account of those few hours in Nehru's own words, sent to his personal secretary on 27 December 1955:

I do not know what instructions are sent to places which I visit on my tours . . . People have been told that I should have meals after the European style and that various kinds of meat are necessary . . . When I arrived at Calicut and reached Krishna Menon's house, I found that there was much consternation at the prospect of my having to be provided with plenty of meat . . . The house is vegetarian and they were unhappy about this. Worse still, the District Magistrate sent four chickens to be slaughtered and cooked. The lady of the house was completely upset at this idea. Fortunately, I came in time to prevent this outrage on her sentiment and I asked specially for a Malayali vegetarian meal. A very good dinner was given to me which I enjoyed . . .

I am not a vegetarian but I do not eat much meat at any time and often I do not eat it at all at home. Therefore there is not only no need for laying stress on meat, but I would much rather not have it when I am touring and require light meals. The only instruction that should be sent is that I am prepared to eat anything provided the meal is a light one and there are no chilies or spices in it . . .

K. Kamaraj, Janaki Amma and Nehru, Calicut, December 1955

In the 1940s, Madhavi worked for the *National Herald*, the newspaper started by Nehru in 1938, and she and Indira Gandhi were in regular touch with each other. On 9 October 1974, three days after her uncle's death, Madhavi was to write to the Prime Minister from her home in Madras:

> My uncle liked you as much as he liked us and for me it was a sharing of a great personal loss with you. He and my children shall always look up to you for guidance and we are sure that you will choose to be with us . . .

Two months later, it was Indira Gandhi's turn to write to Madhavi:

> Your daughter Janaki came to see me for a brief moment on Divali day . . . I should like to have her over to my house occasionally on holidays but I do not know if this would appeal to her. Young people are so independent minded these days and I would like her to feel obliged to come even if she does not want to . . . I am writing to you so that you ascertain her wishes. I have already told her that she should feel free to phone and come over but we can also send the car if she needs it.

Janaki Amma was also instrumental in deepening Krishna Menon's interest in the Theosophical Society, whose headquarters had been shifted from New York to Madras in 1886. The Society aimed for the 'universal brotherhood of humanity' and 'encouraged the study of comparative religion, philosophy and science'. In 1907, a sixty-year-old Annie Besant became its president. She was one of the most charismatic personalities of the pre-Gandhi phase of the Indian freedom movement. She had come to acquire a great influence particularly on upper-caste, educated Indians, who were very impressed by the fact that a fiery Irish lady had made India her home, was extolling the virtues of Hindu culture and was agitating for India's freedom from British rule. A thirteen-year-old Nehru was initiated into the Society by Annie Besant herself and was tutored for about three years by Ferdinand T. Brooks, a young Theosophist. One of Nehru's noted, if somewhat controversial, biographers was to write that 'later in life only one other man ever got as close to Nehru as Ferdinand Brooks had, his alter ego (or dark side) V.K. Krishna Menon'.[8]

Krishna Menon's father, Krishnan Kurup, died in June 1935. A few months before his death Krishnan Kurup was to receive a poignant letter dated 30 May 1935 from his son in London. It was a description of his professional life thus far, but was also full of self-recrimination, which throws much light on the troubled father–son relationship:

> This letter is at least two years late . . . I manage to earn a scanty living and to keep up the things in which I have rightly or wrongly got entangled . . . I was called to the Bar last summer . . . The man with whom I work . . . is very good to me especially as he has discovered rather at first to his surprise that ability is not the monopoly of the white skin . . .
>
> I had two briefs in the Privy Council which comes to me independent of the solicitors . . . I did want to write to you about this as I joined the Inns of Court and became a lawyer largely to please you as I know that it has been one of the disappointments of your life that I did not become a lawyer but merely a man with nothing particular to do . . . I have to do other things as writing and editing . . . to keep myself and to find money for other things. I of course carry on the Indian work as before . . .
>
> I am anxious to hear from you and I always think of you mostly with a guilty conscience but always with gratitude and love . . . Try to forgive me for all that I have not been to you and others for whom I have a responsibility. I am conscious of it all the time especially when I realize each moment of my life how much I owe to those who had the sole burden for me for 22 years . . .

Tellicherry has certainly produced numerous Menons as well as a number of Krishna Menons. But could Tellicherry have produced two V.K. Krishna Menons? This question arises because in early 1931, the famed British publisher George Allen & Unwin brought out a book called *A Theory of Laughter*. The cover page reads:

A THEORY OF LAUGHTER
WITH SPECIAL REFERENCE TO
COMEDY AND TRAGEDY

by

V.K. KRISHNA MENON, M.A.

LONDON
GEORGE ALLEN & UNWIN
MUSEUM STREET

The preface to the book ends thus:

KRISHNA MENON

TELLICHERRY
April, 1930

Now, Krishna Menon had been in the UK since 1924 and was to return to India for the first time, by all accounts, only in late 1932. So if our V.K. Krishna Menon had come to India only in late 1932, why did he say 'Tellicherry, April 1930' in the book? Or is it that all his biographers and his family members are mistaken, and he actually came to India much earlier? Strangely, there is no mention whatsoever of this book in his vast archive. Krishna Menon also never mentioned it in the biographical descriptions of himself that he prepared in the 1930s. The only evidence in his archive is that in 1930 Krishna Menon hoped Cambridge University Press would publish his MA thesis, forbiddingly titled:

The Psychology of Reasoning Being an Experimental Study of the Mental Processes Involved in Reasoning together with A Historical Outline of Philosophical, Psychological and Logical Theories on 'Reason' and 'Reasoning' from Early Times to the Present Day

It is *possible* that the author of a potential book with this title could also be the author of a book called

A Theory of Laughter with Special Reference to Comedy and Tragedy

The Theory of Laughter immediately drew a mildly positive review in the British *Journal of Mental Science* but was forgotten till 1995 when it found favourable mention in a book on Mark Twain, whose author told me:[9]

> I see Menon's work as an early and useful complication of Bergson and Freud, and a call for us to loosen those knots a bit in thinking about what comic outbreaks are and can do. Menon called laughter 'mental hopping,' and though the phrase never caught on, he was trying to name an important psychological and existential condition: of momentary or provisional liberation from constrictive habits of mind, from culturally imposed or inflected assumptions about the relative intellectual or moral weight of experience. I'm not convinced that theories of laughter have improved much beyond that insight in the past eighty-odd years—so in that way, Menon was, and still is, ahead of his time.

Alas, the mystery of the book will remain. A Scotland Yard report of 26 November 1930 mentions a Vadaka Karampat Krishna Menon—another V.K. Krishna Menon—as 'a prominent member of the Commonwealth of India League'.[10] But this was the first and last time such a person was mentioned in police reports on the League. Could he have been the author? That is indeed probable. But can we overlook the fact that the George Allen & Unwin archive at the University of Reading in the UK has papers relating to this book under 'Vengalil Krishnan Krishna Menon' and the British Library too has the book under this name?

And the confusion caused by the name 'Menon' continues. A biography of Stalin by the well-known Medvedev brothers[11] has this account of his last few days:

1–2 March 1953: eyewitness accounts

Visitors were admitted to the Kremlin office for the last time on the evening of 17 February 1953. From 8 to 8:30 p.m., Stalin received [a] delegation from India led by the Indian ambassador, Krishna Menon. At 10:15 Bulganin, Beria and Malenkov arrived . . .

The Indian ambassador to the Soviet Union who called on Stalin was not Krishna Menon but K.P.S. Menon, who was born in Ottapalam, some 100 kilometres from the former's place of birth.

Too many Menons would confuse the Americans as well. Ten days before India gained independence on 15 August 1947, a bewildered American embassy wrote to MI5, the domestic British security and intelligence agency:

On December 16 1946 you gave this office certain information on V.K. KRISHNA MENON which was passed on to our State Department.

The Daily Express carried an article on 19 June 1947 giving an account of S. KRISHNA MENON's death. At that time we supposed S. KRISHNA MENON was the same as V.K. KRISHNA MENON, because of his affiliation with the Indian Civil Service. After noting the government appointment just made of V.K. KRISHNA MENON [as India's High Commissioner to the UK], we are aware that our assumption was incorrect.

Can you give us any particulars on S. KRISHNA MENON— was he related to V.K. KRISHNA MENON? Any information you can send would be greatly appreciated.

Exactly on the day India became free, MI5 replied:

Sricant KRISHNA MENON was born on 24.11.96, came to the U.K. from India about 1921 and has been employed for some time as a Clerical Office in the Office of the High Commissioner for India in London. He died on 18.6.47. He is no relation to V.K. KRISHNA MENON, the High Commissioner for India Designate. The name MENON is very common in Madras . . .

Notes

1. In some accounts, Krishna Menon's year of birth is given as 1897. I have gone by family accounts.
2. *Stri-Dharma*, the official organ of the Women's Indian Association, Madras, vol. 1, no. 8 October 1919.
3. Devika (2005).
4. A description used by her grandniece Janaki Ram.
5. An email correspondence dated 18 February 2019.
6. 'Sheikh Muhammed Abdullah', *Swatantra*, 22 May 1948.
7. There were three Janakis in Krishna Menon's closest circle: V.K. Janaki Amma, his sister; her daughter V.A. Janaki; and her granddaughter Janaki Sastri, later Janaki Ram.
8. Wolpert (1996).
9. Michelson (1995) and email correspondence dated 30 November 2018.
10. All intelligence agency and Scotland Yard files on Krishna Menon are at the British Library, London.
11. Medvedev and Medvedev (2003).

2

Annie Besant's Protégé (1918–30)

After completing school in Calicut, Krishna Menon came to Madras in mid-1915 to study at the famed Presidency College. He was admitted thanks to his father's friend M.A. Candeth, who was then a professor of history at the college. Candeth had been a contemporary of Nehru at Cambridge. Forty-six years later, in December 1961, one of Candeth's sons would lead the Indian Army in liberating Goa from the Portuguese rule, an operation masterminded by the then defence minister of India—Krishna Menon.

At Presidency College, Krishna Menon quickly made a mark and won a scholarship and two prestigious awards. The first of these in 1915 was a prize named after Prof. Gustav Oppert given for excellence in the study of Sanskrit. The second was in 1918 when he received a prize named after Prof. E.H. Elliot for excellence in the study of the English language and literature. But he was at the same time caught up in political activities in the city that were orchestrated by Annie Besant and aimed at securing 'Home Rule' for India. He unfurled the flag of the Home Rule League that she had founded in 1916 on the flagstaff of the college building. This could have got him into serious trouble with the authorities but 'he was let off with a warning' with Candeth yet again intervening on his behalf.

It was also perhaps through Candeth that Krishna Menon met a sparkling lecturer of philosophy at Presidency College,

S. Radhakrishnan. The two would have a 'long acquaintance of over fifty years' but rarely see eye to eye on national and international issues. It was only in April 1951 that Krishna Menon, then India's high commissioner in the UK, and Radhakrishnan, then India's ambassador in Moscow, finally agreed on something—namely, getting wheat from the Soviet Union to tide over a food crisis in India. The world-famous philosopher would go on to become President of India in May 1962 and play a key role in Krishna Menon's resignation from Nehru's cabinet six months later.

Krishna Menon may have encountered Annie Besant for the first time sometime in late September 1917. This was after she had returned to Madras to a rousing welcome from her 'house arrest' in the hill station of Ootacamund. Her incarceration had resulted in a twenty-eight-year-old Nehru's first available piece of public writing. This 'Letter to the Editor' by him appeared in *The Leader* on 21 June 1917:

> *Qui Deus vult perdere prius dementat* [Those whom the gods wish to destroy, they first make mad]—so said the wise men of old and we are seeing the proverb justify itself in our ancient land . . . with my sorrow at the treatment accorded to Mrs. Besant is mingled joy and gladness that this day has come. For madness has fallen on the bureaucracy and this is the surest presage of their coming fall. Home Rule has come and we have but to take if we stand up like men and falter not.

Even some high-ranking officials of the British government felt the impact of Annie Besant's magnetic personality. Edwin Montagu, the secretary of state for India, was in India during November 1917–May 1918 and maintained a diary of his travels. He recorded, after his visit to the famous Elephanta Caves near Bombay:[1]

> . . . The Elephanta Caves are interesting on a small scale, with very nice carvings in the rock of the life of Shiva. I particularly liked that Shiva who cut his wife into fifty-two pieces, only to discover that he had fifty-two wives! This is really what happens to the Government of India when it interns Mrs Besant . . .

Conventional wisdom has it that Nehru's public life started with his association with Mahatma Gandhi. Actually, it had started with Annie Besant like it would do for Krishna Menon. Through her, Krishna Menon also got intimately involved with the Boy Scouts movement.

Krishna Menon got his bachelor of arts degree in economics, history and political science in 1918, the same year that Annie Besant served as the first woman president of the Indian National Congress. She had taken over that position on 26 December 1917. Krishna Menon joined the Law College in Madras on his graduation but that was only to please his father. He never completed this course and, having joined the Theosophical Society in 1918, spent the next six years spreading its message as well as that of the Boy Scouts movement in Madras, Cochin and Calicut. For

Krishna Menon as a Boy Scout, circa 1919

a while he also taught at the National University in Madras started by Annie Besant, with Rabindranath Tagore as its first chancellor.

Annie Besant has the unique distinction of having two 'Krishnas' as her protégés. The first and earlier one was Jiddu Krishnamurti, who was to become a world-famous philosopher but who broke with the Theosophical Society and her plans for him as the World Teacher in August 1929. Almost simultaneously, the other Krishna—Krishna Menon—also left Annie Besant, ostensibly on the grounds that she did not support complete independence for India as was being demanded by a younger generation of Congressmen, most notably Nehru. But both the Krishnas continued to write to the formidable lady, always addressing her as 'Dearest Mother' and signing off as 'Your loving son'.

In fact, the two Krishnas got to know each other well and maintained their friendship till the political Krishna passed away in 1974. Krishna Menon was to be influenced greatly by the seer in his views, particularly in regard to education. On 25 September 1926, he wrote to his sister Janaki Amma at great length, expounding his own personal philosophy as it were but showing that he was clearly in thrall to Jiddu Krishnamurti, who was referred to as 'Krishnaji' in the Theosophical Society circles:

> . . . The world has to become receptive for the World Teacher. This does not mean everyone should be persuaded to join the Star of the Theosophical Society. They are forms of work. That is all. We have to speak boldly but gently of what we know to be true. We have to bring Krishnaji nearer to everyone and make the world understand what he stands for. He stands for the great idea of what he calls The Kingdom of Happiness—We have to start by being perfectly happy ourselves . . .
>
> Next then there is the practical side of work . . . What little any one does is so much done—Clean houses, clean streets, clean bodies and minds these are all wanted . . . We have to fight social evils. Untouchability, cruelty to servants and animals, and women. We have to fight against dirt and misery. We have to fight against all evil customs . . . Begin each day afresh. Forget all past prejudices, antagonisms and our opinions about other people. I should take each one as they are . . . Make Hinduism more real . . . Krishnaji's great appeal has been to rise above limitations . . .

Two years later, on 12 August 1928, he wrote again to his sister:

> . . . I had another talk with Krishnaji . . . Remember Krishnaji does not ask for any belief . . . He is asking us all to doubt everything. You will understand his point of view when you hear him. It makes life all so different. . .

Soon after Jiddu Krishnamurti's break with the Theosophical Society, Krishna Menon was to write to Janaki Amma from London on 16 August 1929:

> . . . I suppose you know that the Order of the Star has been dissolved. There will be only business organisations . . . The Malayalam Star

Publications Ltd. should I think be formed. Its work will be the
issue of the bulletin which will contain all of Krishnaji's talks every
month, the translation and sale of his books and also the sale of the
English books in the Malayalam area.

Annie Besant had planned that Krishna Menon would get some
experience in the UK before coming back to Madras to teach at the
National University. With her financial support, Krishna Menon set
sail for the UK in July 1924. Dr George Arundale, an Englishman who
had made India his home and would succeed her as president of the
Theosophical Society, accompanied him. The year 1924 thus marked
Krishna Menon's passage to England; it happened just about the time
that E.M. Forster's acclaimed *A Passage to India* was published, which
would cause such great convulsions in London and elsewhere.

Dr Arundale had Krishna Menon installed as a history teacher
in St Christopher's School in the English town of Letchworth, and
the plan was to have him stay in the UK for no more than a year.
But Krishna Menon ended up staying in that country for almost
three decades. St Christopher's is still going strong. It was started
in 1915 with the initial sponsorship of the Theosophical Society.
Through Dr Arundale, Krishna Menon was also to become part of
the Theosophical Society network in England. He was well-regarded
as a teacher but lasted just a year at the school.

In 1925 the London School of Economics beckoned, and he
moved there. He also joined the Independent Labour Party (ILP),
which had been founded in 1893 seven years before the Labour
Party came into being. Krishna Menon was to get very close to the
Labour Party leaders by 1932, by which time he was also its active
member. But he cut his teeth in British politics in the ILP, which
was part of the Labour Party, though it took more radical positions,
especially on India. By the early 1920s itself the ILP had, for instance,
recognized 'the full right of the Indian people to self-government and
self-determination' and asserted that 'should India choose to belong
to the British group of nations, it must be on the basis of equality and
freedom'. Two particular ILP members would play an important role
in Krishna Menon's life.

The India-born Fenner Brockway and Krishna Menon would have a particularly turbulent relationship over the next few decades. Half a century later in June 1967, Brockway would reminisce:[2]

> . . . I quarreled with Krishna partly because I thought the India League was too much under Communist control and partly because when I and others stood out against the Labour Government's suppression of the Congress in 1929–31. At the end of that Government he invited on the executive of the India League Labour MPs who had never criticized the Government's attitude to India . . . Now I was wrong . . . I have to say this in fairness to Krishna—when I went back to India recently [early 1967] he was the first to come and see me. I appreciated that gesture of his very deeply.

Brockway was six months short of his centenary when he passed away in April 1988. In January 1989, the Government of India conferred the Padma Bhushan on him posthumously.

H.N. Brailsford was considered to be among the finest left-wing journalists of the first half of the twentieth century. He was a vociferous critic of British imperialism, and his book *Rebel India* in 1931 had excited Krishna Menon no end. The two were ideological kindred spirits till the late 1930s but fell out on the issue of Stalin, whom Brailsford denounced. When Krishna Menon was appointed high commissioner to the UK in August 1947, Brailsford would write to no less a man than Gandhi himself on the day India gained independence:

> At the risk of seeming to interfere, may I say a word about Krishna? I have known him for many years. I never myself had any disagreement or personal unpleasantness in my dealings with him. I respect him for his devotion and hard work . . . He seems to create round himself an atmosphere of suspicion and intrigue. He split the Indian community in London and for many years it gave a painful exhibition of disunity . . . He is a man of first-rate ability in certain directions, but his gift is not for dealing in a friendly and trustful way with others—whether as equals or subordinates.

There is a little story, typical of the web Krishna Menon wove, behind
how I got hold of this letter. I found it in the British intelligence files
declassified in 2007. It figures as an enclosure to a letter written on
21 October 1954 by Alexander Clutterbuck, the UK high commissioner
in New Delhi, to Sir Seville Garner of the Commonwealth Relations
Office in London. After dissecting Krishna Menon's personality as he
saw it, Clutterbuck told Garner:

> . . . Walter Crocker [Australia's high commissioner in India] gave
> me the other day something that H.N. Brailsford wrote to Gandhi
> about him in 1947. I enclose this in case you have not seen it.
> It seems to me to hit him off admirably . . .

After leaving Letchworth in mid-1925, Krishna Menon came to
London and got involved with the Commonwealth of India League
that had just been launched by Annie Besant. He also came to the
attention of the prominent Theosophist, suffragist and supporter
of progressive causes Muriel de la Warr. She died in 1930 but not
before giving Krishna Menon opportunities to speak in her famed
garden parties on self-determination for India. She may well have
contributed to the emergence of Krishna Menon the public speaker.
And it is most probably through her that he got to know George
Lansbury, the Labour Party leader with whom he would have much
to do till the mid-1930s.

The Commonwealth of India League was meant to replace
another of Annie Besant's creations called 'Home Rule for India
British Auxiliary' that was established in 1914. The League's single-
point objective was Dominion Status for India. Dominion Status
meant different things to different people but everyone agreed that
it certainly involved Indians gradually ruling over India, with the
King of England remaining as the supreme authority as in the case
of other Dominions such as Australia, Canada and New Zealand.
Initially, the pivot of the League was in Manchester but gradually,
Krishna Menon made London its hub and opened branches in many
other cities of the UK. In 1928 Krishna Menon became one of
the two secretaries of the League, the only Indian in the five-man

body that actually ran the organization on a day-to-day basis. The treasurer then was H.S.L. Polak, who had been one of Gandhi's key associates in South Africa.

One of Krishna Menon's earliest public appearances was in Bristol on 19 June 1928, where he spoke at a Theosophical Society discussion meeting on the 'The Problem of Justice' as viewed by different religions. The next day, the *Western Daily Press* reported on his speech:

> . . . Krishna Menon (Madras) spoke for Hinduism the oldest religion represented. To the Hindu, he said, the problem of justice was answered by the belief in the law of karma, the law of cause and effect. The Hindu faith taught that man was the author of his own fate, each individual was the architect of his own destiny and with this belief the element of injustice disappeared. Coupled with this belief in the law of karma was the belief in reincarnation or rebirth.

But such speeches on Hinduism were going to be few and far between, and from 1929 onwards he would lecture only on India and its freedom. On 30 March 1929, the *West Middlesex Gazette* would report:

> One of the most animated debates . . . took place at the Ealing Society last week when Mr. V.K. Krishna Menon put a motion 'That India should be granted Dominion Status' . . . Mr. Krishna Menon put his case in a well-informed and forceful style . . . He spoke with such animation that he swayed his listeners considerably and when the motion was put in the meeting, it was lost only by the narrow majority of 1. Some of the voting, as may be imagined, was dictated by the heart than by the head.

He was doing many other things as well. On 19 August 1929, he wrote to his sister Janaki Amma:

> . . . I am asked to stay here till next summer with a view to carrying on Indian propaganda on a large scale. I have to edit

The Indian News which is a tiny little fortnightly paper and to
organize the work of the Commonwealth of India League. In the
meanwhile I am finishing my doctorate at the university though it
is very unlikely that I shall be successful in doing that. I may also sit
for my law finals in the meantime. There are also various other odd
jobs that take up all the time one can find. I have told Dr. Besant
that even if I have to stay here after next year I would like to return
to India for a short span and she has agreed . . .

He would speak often in Bristol, and on 27 September 1929, the
Times of India carried this report:

REFORMS FOR INDIA
GRANT OF FULL DOMINON STATUS URGED

LONDON, September 26

Presiding over the Women's Delegate Conference on Indian
Affairs at Bristol under the auspices of the local branch of the
Commonwealth of India League, Mrs. William Graham, wife of
the President of the Board of Trade, said she was convinced that
India was not getting justice . . .

Mr. Krishna Menon declared that Reforms without responsibility
had proved a failure. The only solution lay in granting of Dominion
Status.

The Conference unanimously adopted a resolution urging the
Government to take immediate action for granting Dominion
status to India.

A short while later, Krishna Menon was invited to speak by the
Theosophical Society at Bournemouth. On 29 November 1929, he
informed Maud Morris, who had invited him, that 'he was absolutely
useless as a propaganda lecturer for the Theosophical Society' and
suggested India–related topics instead. The next thing we know is
that a conference was held at the Bournemouth Labour Hall on

23 March 1930, and it passed a resolution that urged upon 'H.M. [His Majesty's] Government to follow a policy of conciliation and cooperation with India and the early introduction into Parliament a measure for conferring the status of a fully self-governing Dominion'.

On 23 May 1930, one Ernest Baker of the Lewisham district branch of the ILP wrote to Doreen Young of the Commonwealth of India League. The letter reveals something about Krishna Menon's personal morality:

> I have written to Mr. Menon personally for the excellent lecture at our meeting last night when he undoubtedly impressed a large number of people profoundly . . .
>
> One thing in connection with last night's meeting is worrying. Mr. Menon would accept no payment to cover his expenses. Will you please let me know what these expenses were so that I may satisfy my conscience on this score . . .

Twenty-three years later when he was beginning to hit the headlines in the US, Audrey Pong nee Layton would write to him on 30 August 1953 from Ann Arbor in Michigan:

> Just a line to renew acquaintance. I have seen your picture in the newspaper more than once, and have intended to write. Do you remember Audrey Layton and Doreen Young? Two good-for-nothing girls who didn't know enough English history to pass the London matriculation in 1927. I lost track of Doreen Young years ago, but I am living just outside Ann Arbor. My husband is Chinese . . . I should love to hear from you, and better still have you come to stay for a few days. My husband joins me in extending a cordial welcome.

We don't know if Krishna Menon ever got in touch with Pong, but Doreen Young continued to be active in India League activities, married S.A. Wickramasinghe, the founder of the Communist Party of Ceylon, and became a member of Ceylon's Parliament in 1952.

There is a general belief that Krishna Menon became dissatisfied with the League's limited objective of Dominion Status, particularly after the forty-year-old president of the Indian National Congress, Nehru, gave the call for *purna swaraj* or complete independence at its historic session at Lahore in end-December 1929. The session had taken place at Bradlaugh Hall, named after Charles Bradlaugh, with whom Annie Besant had had an intimate association before she became fascinated by the Theosophical Society and India. However, the dissatisfaction does not seem to have been a sudden event because very soon after Nehru's historic declaration, Krishna Menon wrote to Annie Besant on 17 January 1930:

Dear Mother:

I am sending under separate cover a letter to *New India* about the work here and asking for support. I feel very strongly that at the present juncture that we should be able to watch Indian affairs and to bring pressure to bear on this country. If we do not give it, the only people in the field, it seems to me, will be the anti-Indian elements of either extreme.

The League work has grown and the organization has also begun to demand all one's time and energy. I have not been able to read a book or go to college for some months now. As it is we have to work later hours and over the weekends.

I am carrying the whole burden of the *Indian News* . . . All the work on it is voluntary and I am glad to say that some of my English friends from the University are giving me their time and help on the editorial side . . . Miss Jane Tarlo a graduate of the London School of Economics who is helping me with The Indian News has written an article on the Naval Conference. I thought you would like it for *New India* . . .

Kindly let me know if there is anything you wish me to do here.

Respectfully & Affectionately,

Your Son
Krishna

Jane Tarlo was one of the many young, educated and gifted British women who would be mesmerized by Krishna Menon's personality and volunteer their services for political activities concerning Indian independence. She would later have a brief career in the British silent film industry.

The article which he sent Annie Besant was to appear in *New India* on 27 March 1930 and is worth quoting at some length for the light it sheds on Krishna Menon's activities in the late 1920s:

HOME RULE FOR INDIA
THE NEED FOR PROPAGANDA IN BRITAIN
BY V.K. KRISHNA MENON

I would like to draw the attention of Indian leaders, through *New India*, to the urgency of a well-directed campaign in England for granting Dominion Status to India at the present juncture . . .

I have been associated with propaganda for India in Great Britain through the Commonwealth of India League and a little fortnightly paper the *Indian News* . . . The League has organized hundreds of meetings through its many Branches in the country; these are active right through the year. We keep up a steady and even minute pressure by writing to the provincial and local papers; our Branches bring up the problems of India before the local M.P., and we now-a-days are able to get good attendance at our 'Delegates Conferences'. The men and women who come to these Conferences return to report to their own organisations; thus in addressing hundred people and discussing Indian matters with them we are really speaking to an audience ten or twenty or even fifty times that number. The *Indian News* is a very useful weapon. It is kept up in order that Indian leaders may have an organ that they can use. It is not a paper that is intended for the well-educated few, but at the same time its importance lies in the fact that it is read by M.P.s and others in positions of responsibility. This little paper circulates between four and five thousand copies. If we had enough money we could increase the circulation to about three to four times its present size . . .

I would like to ask my countrymen through *New India* to support our work here, so that we shall be able to speak with strength that that support gives us. We hope that when the time comes, there will be at hand machinery that our leaders will find useful.

Southampton Independent Labour Party.

A CONFERENCE

WILL BE HELD AT THE

ADYAR HALL, 32, Carlton Crescent, SOUTHAMPTON, On SATURDAY, 26th APRIL, 1930.

SUBJECT:

"DOMINION STATUS FOR INDIA,"

TO BE OPENED BY

Mr. V. K. Krishna Menon, M.A., B.Sc.

(Secretary, Commonwealth of India League).

Chair to be taken at 3 p.m. by MR. T. A. PITT
(Chairman, Southampton I.L.P.).

TEA will be served at 4.30 p.m. at a charge of 9d. DISCUSSION TO FOLLOW.

The Report of the Simon Commission on India will be published shortly after Easter and the question of India is consequently of special importance.

All Labour, Trade Union, Co-operative and other bodies are invited to send delegates and notification should be sent on the attached form, together with delegation fee of sixpence per delegate. Please state if tea is required.

Members (other than delegates) of the above bodies are also invited to attend (admission sixpence).

GILBERT WHITE, *Hon. Secretary.*

To GILBERT WHITE, 106, Percy Road, Southampton.

Name of Organisation ....

The following have been appointed as delegates to the Conference on 26th April, 1930:—

Name...   Name...
Address..   Address...

Name...   Name...
Address..   Address...

Please provide teas for ....delegates.

....Secretary.

Krishna Menon at Independent Labour Party (ILP), UK, 1930

Even as late as mid-1930, Krishna Menon was still wedded to Dominion Status for India. On 26 June 1930, he moved a resolution at a meeting of the council of the Commonwealth of India League:

> The Commonwealth of India League urges on the H.M. [His Majesty's] Government its considered opinion that to secure a fair chance of success for the Round Table Conference it is essential that the Conference
>
> (1) should be regarded as a free Conference called to reach an agreement on the establishment of Dominion Status and not as a stage in the Inquiry inaugurated by the Statutory Commission;
> (2) should treat the Report of the Statutory Commission as merely part of the material before the representatives of the Conference and not as the basis for discussion.

This resolution was seconded by none other than Annie Besant. The British government had just announced that the first Round Table Conference on India would be organized in November 1930. The Statutory Commission mentioned in Krishna Menon's resolution is known as the Simon Commission, which came to India in 1928 to assess the implementation of the Montague–Chelmsford Reforms of 1919, designed to give Indians a greater degree of self-government. The Simon Commission was boycotted by the Indian National Congress on the grounds that it did not have any Indian as a member and was met with strong protests when it visited India. One member of the Simon Commission was to get to know Krishna Menon well in the late 1930s and would, as Prime Minister, play an important role in making India free in August 1947—Clement Attlee. Attlee was, however, to be quite wary of Krishna Menon right through their relationship.

The Commonwealth of India League
203, STRAND, W.C. 2

India To-day

A PUBLIC MEETING

will be held at the

Friends Meeting House

EUSTON ROAD, LONDON, N.W. 1

On FRIDAY, the 4th JULY, at 7.45 p.m.

(Doors open at 7 15 p.m.)

Chairman—
PETER FREEMAN, M.P.
(Chairman, The Commonwealth of India League)

Speakers—
C. F. ANDREWS, M.A.
Sir ALBION BANERJI, C.S.I., C.I.E.
Dr. ANNIE BESANT
FENNER BROCKWAY, M.P.
DAVID S. ERULKAR
JAMES MARLEY, M.P.
V. K. KRISHNA MENON, M.A., B.Sc.
B. SHIVA RAO, M.A.
Rt. Hon. V. S. SRINIVASA SASTRI, P.C.

Tickets : Reserved, 2/6 ; Unreserved, 1/-
A FEW FREE SEATS

In view of the Simon recommendations and the grave
situation in India, the meeting is of the utmost interest and
importance. The seating capacity of the hall is limited and
very early booking is advised. All enquiries to the Commonwealth of India League, 203, Strand, W.C.2.

Blanchard Field, Printer, 198, Blackfriars Road, S.E.

Annie Besant, Krishna Menon and others speaking on India's independence,
London, 1930

In late 1929 and early 1930, the influential British weekly the
Spectator ran hard–hitting editorials supporting India's cause and

demand for self-determination. This was an achievement for Krishna Menon who, along with Mahatma Gandhi's Quaker associate, Horace Alexander,[3] had spent many hours persuading its editor, Evelyn Wrench, to support Dominion Status for India. To be fair, Wrench did not need much convincing because, seven years earlier, he had taken a progressive position on India and was an admirer of Gandhi at that time. Even so, the fact that he lent his voice unequivocally to 'self-determination for India' was quite a watershed event. Later in the year, on 13 September 1930, in the run-up to the First Round Table Conference, Krishna Menon wrote in the *Spectator*:

> . . . If the British Government proposes to proceed with the Conference it should do so and risk the failure or win glory for itself on its own responsibility. The temptation, however, would be to add to the Conference all the elements that bring to it weight, influence and prestige. It is conceivable that the Government may arrange for the Conference to be opened by His Majesty the King . . . It would be unwise and a regrettable blunder to involve the Crown in any manner, where it could by the fact of its association with such a move become the subject of acute hostility in India . . .

The First Round Table Conference was held in London between 12 November 1930 and 13 January 1931. Gandhi had launched the Civil Disobedience Movement prior to the start of the conference, and the Indian National Congress boycotted it. Consequently, the conference proved to be a damp squib and had minimal impact. A few months earlier on 6 September 1930, the council of the Commonwealth of India League, with Annie Besant present, had passed three resolutions all moved by its chairman, Peter Freeman, who was a Labour Party member of the British House of Commons. These resolutions were carried unanimously. The 'memorandum circulated for information' to the members after this meeting has this written in hand:

Issued by V.K. Krishna Menon as Secretary of the League.

And what do these resolutions that, in many ways, represented the last hurrah for the League, say? The first reads:

> The Commonwealth of India League considers that the terms put forward by the Indian Congress leaders . . . constitute a reasonable basis for negotiations, and the League urges H.M. Government to endeavour to reach an agreement with India on these lines.

The second is worded identically and is directed at the Labour Party:

> The Commonwealth of India League considers that the terms put forward by the Indian Congress leaders constitute a reasonable basis for negotiations, and urges the Labour Party to press the H.M. Government to endeavour to reach an agreement with India on these lines.

The third resolution looks inward and says:

> The Council of the Commonwealth of India League accepts the terms of the Indian National Congress leaders as a basis on which the immediate policy and propaganda of the League should be concentrated . . .

At the end of the 'memorandum for information' there is this directive to Krishna Menon and his fellow-secretary, T.H. Redfern:

> The Council directed the Secretaries to issue Speakers' Notes at intervals of not less than a fortnight and that instructions should be placed on the minutes book.

At the meeting, an eighty-three-year-old Annie Besant appears not to have protested but later events showed that these resolutions had a devastating effect on her. Soon after they were passed, miffed at being omitted from the list of leaders invited by the British government to the First Round Table Conference, she resigned from her beloved Commonwealth of India League. On her resignation, Redfern issued a 'Memorandum' on 1 October 1930:

> The resignations from the Commonwealth of India League of Dr. Besant and Mr. H.S. L. Polak are causing some astonishment among League members who are entitled to expect information concerning some misunderstandings which have arisen . . .
>
> Although it is not practicable to embrace all who consider themselves friends of India in one organization (such an attempt would savour of Carlyle's facetious suggestion of a Society for the Amalgamation of Heaven and Hell), there is no sufficient reason for any division amongst us . . .
>
> . . . Among those whom work to make it possible for India to take her place as a Self-governing Dominion of her free choice, it is not unreasonable to hope for mutual understanding of our differing views on points of tactics, and for the necessary adjustments to make common policy feasible and successful.

Redfern's hopes that somehow Annie Besant would be mollified were soon to be belied. On 19 June 1931, Fenner Brockway, then on the Executive Committee of the League, wrote to the famous British mathematician-philosopher Bertrand Russell:

> Dear Bertie:
>
> I hear my friends Krishna Menon and Mrs. Nehru have been to see you to urge that you should accept nomination for the Chairmanship of the Commonwealth of India League. I hope very much you will agree. The League used to be moderate and theosophist. It has completely evolved from that mental mess and is now very rapidly moving to the left. It has recently endorsed the Indian National Congress position and following that I joined it and became a member of its executive.
>
> The Chairmanship would not involve detailed work. Menon is a capable secretary . . .

The 'Mrs Nehru' mentioned by Brockway to Russell was Rameshwari Nehru, wife of Jawaharlal Nehru's cousin. She was the first of the extended Nehru family who would be dazzled by Krishna Menon, although her son—B.K. Nehru—would later be strongly allergic to him. Rameshwari was an early activist on women's issues and was one of the founders of the Indo-Soviet Friendship Society in the 1950s, with which Krishna Menon would also be intimately associated.

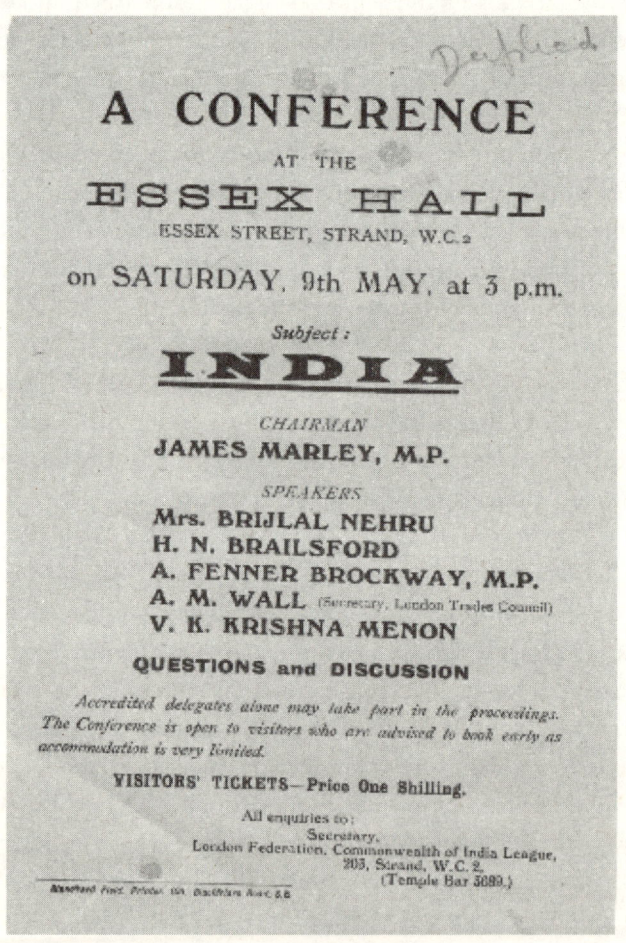

Commonwealth of India League meeting with Rameshwari Nehru, Krishna Menon and others, London, May 1930

Ten days later, Russell, accepting Brockway's offer, wrote the first of his many letters to Krishna Menon:

> . . . I am happy to be associated with the Commonwealth of India League and much honoured to have been elected as Chairman. I very much regret having to be away for the next six months but after my return I shall hope to take a due part in the work of the League, with whose objects I have most hearty sympathy . . .

Gandhi came to the UK on 12 September 1931 for the Second Round Table Conference. The Commonwealth of India League played a major role in setting up a 'Gandhi Reception Committee 1931', with over thirty leading British public personalities as members and Krishna Menon as its secretary along with John Fletcher of the Society of Friends.

Gandhi outside the Quaker Friends House, London, September 1931.
Krishna Menon at extreme left (in suit).

Krishna Menon edited a slim volume called *Notes on Gandhi* that 'were prepared to offer a simple handbook on the ideas and concepts of a complex man'. For the first time, wrote one of Krishna Menon's biographers, 'Englishmen read the essence of Gandhi's moral testament',[4] which would appeal to anybody with even a passing knowledge of Christ and his teachings. He ended the notes with a little-known self-deprecatory quote of Gandhi's:

> This Mahatma I must leave to his fate. Though a non-cooperator I shall gladly subscribe to a bill to make it criminal for anyone to call me a Mahatma and to touch my feet . . .

There was a reception for Gandhi at the Quaker headquarters on Saturday, 12 September 1931, and two days later Polak wrote to Krishna Menon:

> My dear Krishna:
>
> You must have had a lot of cursing from some of us so perhaps I may write to tell you how glad I am that all your efforts resulted successfully on Saturday. All these things being discipline of the soul, the experience will have been a most valuable one for you . . .

The reception had been a grand success although there had been quite a number of regrets including this one that came just as the function was about to start:

> The Marques of Linlithgow regrets that owing to absence in Scotland, he is prevented . . . to accept the kind invitation of the Gandhi Reception Committee to welcome Mahatma Gandhi on his arrival in London. The invitation in question only reached Lord Linlithgow today.

Five years later, Linlithgow would be viceroy in India and have much to do with Gandhi, and in the early 1940s, he would develop a visceral hatred of Krishna Menon.

Apart from being exposed to Gandhi face-to-face for long hours, Krishna Menon also got to know a key member of Gandhi's entourage—Madan Mohan Malaviya—very well. Malaviya was one of India's most respected figures and had been president of the Congress a year before Annie Besant. Although not a Theosophist, he counted himself as an admirer of the lady for her doughtiness and her appreciation of Hindu culture. Krishna Menon wrote to Malaviya on 12 December 1931 when he was still in London, beseeching for financial support for his propaganda activities:

> Before you go away I want to tell you that I am sincerely grateful to you for your appreciation of what little we have been able to do here. We are fortunate in having the benefit of your advice and appreciation . . .
>
> My own view about educating opinion here is that we must get the Labour Party and their leaders irrevocably committed and enthusiastic in our cause. I know the movement and the people from inside and I am not at all happy about the official policy. However, we have friends, and the influence and pressure of the movement which we are educating is bound to tell.
>
> If the paper in the new form materializes we shall be able to include a few intellectuals among our supporters . . . We are very grateful to you for the assistance you have given us and we will make every effort to raise money here. What I want to request you is that you should secure for us the funds for one of the larger items which causes us not a little anxiety. If you could finance us to the extent of our rent, which is 135 pounds, it would relieve us of a major burden and enable us to carry on.
>
> I am giving time to this work here. I hope you will do me the favour of asking me to give this up when the time arrives and you begin to feel that I can be of better service in India than here . . .

Malaviya was to be one of Krishna Menon's most important financial benefactors for the next few years. He not only arranged for funds to be transferred from India for the activities of the India League through his contacts with Indian businessmen like

G.D. Birla, but also arranged for Krishna Menon to write regularly for publications like the *Hindustan Times* that enabled a steady income stream, which, in turn, sustained the India League. Malaviya had been impressed with Krishna Menon, and on 6 March 1932, the veteran Congress leader's son Govind would write to him:

> You are doing good work. Particularly the meetings and demonstrations you organized. Father was glad to know of it all and sends you his congratulations. We trust you to carry on the work as vigorously as possible.

Swallowing his prejudices, Krishna Menon collaborated with the Quakers, particularly Agatha Harrison, for making the Gandhi visit a big success. She took great pride in his later achievements. Krishna Menon was to pay handsome tributes to her when she died suddenly in October 1954 while attending an international conference on Indo-China, in which he played an important role. But in the early 1930s, Krishna Menon was impatient with the 'tepid sentimentalism' of the Quakers and their friends like C.F. Andrews. For their part, Gandhi's English admirers warned him against 'extremists' like Krishna Menon who, they believed, would be detrimental to India's interests in the UK, where the Conservatives were then gaining in strength.

During Gandhi's eighty-four-day sojourn in the UK, the Executive Committee of the Commonwealth of India League met on 12 November 1931 and unanimously recommended that the object of the League should be reworded as to read 'support the claim of India for Swaraj'. It also recommended that the name of the League be amended as to read 'India League'. Krishna Menon was present at that meeting and ensured the resolution was adopted without any dissent. On 4 December 1931, the vice chairman of the Commonwealth of India League, J.F. Horrabin, a Labour Party MP, wrote, for the first time, to the president of the Indian National Congress a letter that naturally Krishna Menon had drafted:

During the last eleven weeks the Commonwealth of India League has had the very great privilege of close contacts [with] Mahatma Gandhi . . .

The Executive Committee of the League has recommended to its Council that the object of the League should be reworded so as to bring it into line with its policy and its support of the cause of Indian independence. Along with the change of the object to 'complete Swaraj' it is also recommended that our name shall be changed into 'The India League'. The League supports the Congress cause but remains an independent organization, in the main British in its constitution . . .

. . . We hope that the Congress will recognize in the League a useful instrument, which in no way committing the Congress, is willing to be of service . . . We are satisfied that Mahatma Gandhi is fully cognizant of our position . . . and are very proud that he has agreed to take this message himself from us to the Congress . . .

A few months earlier, the League had wanted to expand its footprint beyond the British Isles and made a serious attempt to establish itself in the US. On 19 August 1931, Horrabin had addressed a letter to a number of American organizations thus:

The deep and widespread interest in the Indian question among the people of the United States and the consequent need for correct and reliable information about India and her demand for freedom was recently discussed by the executive committee of the Commonwealth of India League. The League regards the informing of enlightened American opinion to be of primary importance and has therefore decided to spare the services of its secretary for a period of approximately three months, February, March and April 1932 for lecture work in America.

Mr. Krishna Menon is an Indian himself and is devoting his energies to the organization of opinion, both parliamentary and public, in this country. He is a most effective speaker both at

public meetings and at conferences or groups. His brilliant career
at the university gives him the knowledge of international politics
so essential in the interpretation of the implications of the Indian
problem.

However, this visit of Krishna Menon did not materialize. He
would try again in 1940 to go to the US but those plans too did
not fructify. It was only in 1946 that he would first set foot there,
a country where he was to be both loved and loathed in equal
measure.

Annie Besant died in Madras on 30 September 1933. Rich
tributes were paid to her by many in India and England. Krishna
Menon attended a memorial meeting in her honour in London. He
was to later recall to her biographer Arthur Nethercot that 'when she
walked out on the [Commonwealth of India] League, she was old,
highly emotional and easily offended'. Nethercot, who interviewed
Krishna Menon in 1957 for his masterly two-volume biography,[5] had
this to say:

> He [Krishna Menon] played down the idea that there had really
> been a serious split among the leaders of the League about policy,
> though most of them felt that a more aggressive programme was
> called for by the pressure of the opposition . . . C.P. Ramaswamy
> Aiyar[6] . . . told me that Krishna Menon, whom he regarded as
> a thorough patriot dedicated to what he considered India's best
> interests and not to his own, had been growing more bitter against
> England for some time because of the failure of the Labour Party
> to redeem its promises, and at the end could no longer go along
> with his sponsor and discoverer [Annie Besant] in her insistence
> that India remain with the Empire. He thus influenced the League
> to a new orientation.

Over four decades later, on 6 October 1976, one of his closest friends,
the British Labour leader Michael Foot, delivered the second Krishna
Menon Memorial Lecture in New Delhi after Jenny Lee—whose
husband, the late Aneurin (Nye) Bevan, had been a stalwart of the

Labour left—had launched the series earlier in the year. In the course of the lecture, Foot remarked:[7]

> . . . Mrs Besant fought for India's freedom in India while Krishna Menon worked for India's freedom in Britain . . . We gave you Annie Besant and you gave us Krishna Menon who spoke to us in a language that we could understand . . .

Annie Besant made one more lasting contribution to Krishna Menon's life. His intimate association with her and the Commonwealth of India League ensured that beginning sometime in 1927, British intelligence and police agencies started monitoring his activities closely and started maintaining dossiers on him. This was to continue till well after India's Independence. The surveillance would become particularly intense from the mid-1930s, when Krishna Menon was suspected of being a communist and when he was virtually in daily touch with top leaders of the Communist Party of Great Britain (CPGB) such as Harry Pollit, James Klugmann, Ben Bradley and the Palme Dutt brothers—Rajni and Clements.

Krishna Menon made his debut in the Scotland Yard records as early as on 28 December 1927:

V. KRISHNA MENON

V. Krishna MENON . . . who hails from Madras and is a research student at the London School of Economics, holds extreme political views and is anti-British in conversation. He is about 32 years [of] age and is about 5 feet 9 inches in height. He has stated that he has been in this country for the past three years, and that when he returned to India he would not secure a Government situation but would seek an appointment where he could do 'political work'.

Two years later on 4 December 1929, Scotland Yard brought to the notice of the authorities an article he had written in the *Bradford Pioneer*.

India: A New Chapter

Hope for the Future

By V.K. Krishna MENON

It began thus:

> As an Indian deeply concerned with the developments and
> implications of Indian policy, I would like to express my relief
> and hopefulness in finding that a genuine effort has at last been
> made to end the deadlock in the Indian situation. I am not unduly
> optimistic, nor do I think India's struggle for freedom is far from
> over. But I am glad that the real struggle in which a sense of tact_
> will play a part has at last begun.
>
> India has shown great political sagacity in laying greater stress
> on the Conference than on the declaration. Her boycott of the
> Simon Commission has borne fruit, her constructive efforts which
> produced the Nehru Report can now find further fields of political
> expression and be instrumental in the winning of Swaraj. In a
> sense, the comparative fearlessness with which India is accepting
> Britain's invitation is a very significant sign. Those of us who know
> our country see in it strength. India is no longer afraid that she will
> be tricked out of freedom.

As it turned out, Krishna Menon's optimism was completely
misplaced. A few months later on 28 May 1930, New Scotland Yard
reported:

V.K. KRISHNA MENON

> V.K. Krishna Menon, M.A. B.Sc (Econ) attended as representative
> of the Birmingham College Educational Society a meeting of the
> Coventry Trades Council held. . . . on the evening of the 15th May,
> at which 25 delegates were present.
>
> MENON did so for the purpose of giving facts about India,
> the working conditions there, etc. He said that the Indians would

be quite content if not interfered with. They were peace-loving people, but what was now greatly irritating them, as it had done for such a lengthy period, was the fact that nearly the whole of their existence was spent in labouring under the vilest of conditions—he quoted instances.

At times, the informant of New Scotland Yard couldn't get Krishna Menon's name right and hence this report of 24 May 1933:

VRISHNA KRISHNU KRISHNA MENON

Vrishna Krishnu Krishna MENON is writing and speaking against the treatment, and in particular the food, given to the political prisoners in India. He has written letters on this subject to the Press.

That Krishna Menon was being tracked on a daily basis is evident from another Scotland Yard Report of 1 August 1934 but clearly, British authorities continued to have problems with his name:

VRISHNA KRISHNU KRISHNA MENON

Vrishna Krishnu Krishna MENON has been appointed by John Lane (The Bodley Head), ltd, Vigo Street, W., the publishers as their reader of manuscripts on India.

Thus British security agencies went to great lengths to keep tabs on Krishna Menon. In 1986, quite extraordinary disclosures were to be made by a Joan Miller,[8] who was recruited by British intelligence to inform on those considered subversive. Miller wrote that Krishna Menon was 'unhinged on the British and the way they'd mishandled affairs in India' but admits that she did not get very far with him because of 'different temperaments'. But she pointed to another recruit, simply called 'Helen', who was successful in not only providing information on Krishna Menon but also ensnaring him romantically for a very short period. It is impossible to verify this claim but it certainly adds an element of further spice into Krishna Menon's life.

Notes

1. Montagu (1930).
2. Fenner Brockway Oral History Archive, Nehru Memorial Museum and Library.
3. Carnall (2010).
4. Chakravarty (1997).
5. Nethercot (1963).
6. Eminent lawyer and administrator and one of Annie Besant's closest colleagues, known mostly for his tenure as Divan of Travancore.
7. *India Weekly*, 14 October 1976.
8. Miller (1986).

3

'Chronic' at the LSE (1924–34)

Even before he had left for the UK with George Arundale in mid-1924, Krishna Menon had enrolled at the London School of Economics (LSE). Just the previous year, another Indian destined to change the course of Indian history in profound ways and justifiably become an icon—B.R. Ambedkar—had completed his doctorate in economics there. Krishna Menon was to remain associated with that venerable institution for almost a decade, which led Frida Laski, wife of Harold Laski, his mentor in this phase of his life, to remark that 'Krishna was a chronic [perpetual student] at the LSE'.

Krishna Menon got a BSc degree in economics with first-class honours in 1927, specializing in the history of political ideas. He then moved to University College, London (UCL), from where he received his MA in industrial psychology. Charles Spearman, a very well-known English psychologist, was to give Krishna Menon this testimonial on 5 June 1931:

I have great pleasure in giving this testimonial to Mr. V. Krishna Menon. He has been working in the laboratory under my charge for the past three years. At the end of the first two of these he has obtained the degree of M.A. with a research of unusual excellence. And throughout his work has been of this high standard. I regard him a man of exceptional ability and equally

47

exceptional energy. Unless I am very mistaken, he is destined to
become of a man of mark.

This was high praise coming from a fellow of the Royal Society and
a man who is well known to students of statistics even today.

After getting his degree, Krishna Menon went back to 'haunt
the LSE' and registered for his doctorate there. He was enrolled for
three years as an 'external student' with permission to attend the
institute for supervision under Harold Laski. He never completed
the doctorate but was awarded the MSc (Econ) degree in early
1935, with a thesis on 'Research on English Political Thought in the
Seventeenth Century'. The entries in his record reveal the following:

1929/30: Prof. Laski: 'Is now doing political work'
1930/31: No report
1931/32: Prof Laski: Mr. Menon is engaged in other activities.

It is clear that Krishna Menon was a presence at the LSE in one
form or another from 1924 until 1934, a feat perhaps unique in the
school's history. Indeed, in his archive there is an official testimonial
dated 24 August 1934 from the Registrar of the LSE that reads:

THIS IS TO certify that VENGALIL KRISHNAN KRISHNA
MENON was registered as a regular student of the London School
of Economics from October, 1924, to June, 1934.

In September 1934 ,he applied for further registration to complete
his PhD but LSE's director William Beveridge refused his request as
he had already been registered for so many years above the normal
course. But Beveridge pointed out that as he had already a first degree
as an internal student, Krishna Menon was entitled to sit for the MSc
(Econ) examination, which is what he did in December 1934.

Beveridge appears to have believed that Krishna Menon was
a communist and was simply interested in spreading propaganda
among the students at the LSE in favour of Indian independence.
Beveridge considered this unacceptable in an academic institution.

That Krishna Menon was allergic to Beveridge is clear from a letter Frida Laski wrote to the former on 11 September 1931, a day before the reception to Gandhi at the Quaker headquarters. She wanted Krishna Menon to invite some more people and started by saying:

> . . . You will possibly not like these names, but I have got past the point of converting sympathisers, I want to get others along . . .

and went on to suggest a few names starting with 'Sir William Beveridge, LSE'.

Many years later, one of Krishna Menon's greatest admirers Marie Seton set out to write his biography, but it was never published. Much of the material she collected for her book, however, is neatly preserved in his archive. Seton approached Beveridge for an interview, and he responded on 4 June 1958 when Krishna Menon was at the pinnacle of global prominence:

> I have today your letter of 2nd June as to possible material for your proposed life of Krishna Menon.
>
> I am afraid that I can only disappoint your hope of hearing anything from me about him. There is really nothing that I would like to say about him, and I have in fact a remote recollection of him now.

Beveridge was seventy-nine years old and Seton was jogging him for his recollection of events that had taken place a quarter of a century earlier. Perhaps Beveridge genuinely did not remember anything about Krishna Menon. But one person who did remember something about the Beveridge–Krishna Menon tension was Harold Wilson, the former prime minister of Great Britain, who, in the course of his Nehru Memorial Lecture in London on 2 November 1978, reminisced:

> My own personal connection with India and Nehru was largely due to yet another who delivered this lecture before me, Krishna Menon. I first came to know Krishna through Beveridge, with

whom I used to work. Beveridge used to describe Krishna as the perpetual student, because long after he had finished his academic course he remained on year after year at the London School of Economics. Whether Beveridge knew it or not, and I suspect he did, Krishna was in fact using the School as his base, and just perhaps doing a little odd work from time to time, while exerting his influence in every possible way towards India's independence.

Although Krishna Menon never completed his doctorate, he got a glowing testimonial from Laski on 5 May 1934:

I am glad to recommend Mr. V.K. Krishna Menon for the post of tutor to the L.C.C. [London County Council]. His work at the School of Economics was brilliant. I have kept in the closest touch with him since that time. His knowledge of political science is wide and his interest profound. I regard him as a man of the highest integrity of character. I am convinced that he has exactly the qualities required for a successful teacher.

Of course, Krishna Menon never became a teacher, although by 1933 he had also got a diploma in education from the University of London to add to his long string of academic qualifications. Education would remain his abiding passion till the very end. One of his close friendships would be with Maria Montessori who would spend seven years in India from 1939 onwards, developing her ideas on schooling in collaboration with the Theosophical Society.

The biggest benefit to Krishna Menon from his decade-long association with the LSE was undoubtedly Laski. Through the eminent don, who had one foot in academics and the other in politics, he became friendly with many leading lights of the Labour Party, of whom Arthur Greenwood, Clement Attlee, Stafford Cripps and Nye Bevan were the most prominent. Laski's mentorship also opened doors to Krishna Menon in the media fraternity and in left-wing intellectual circles.

Laski was Krishna Menon's intellectual guru in many respects and provided both financial and intellectual support to his

India League for a fifteen-year period beginning 1932. Krishna Menon became an integral part of the Laski family, and on 26 June 1935 Frida Laski wrote to him after getting to know that he had been hospitalized:

Dear Krishna:

I am glad to learn you have gone away to receive proper attention. I am sure it is the best thing for you & I know you will be wise and let people treat you. We want you to get back to good health with the least possible delay. You are a vital part of the Indian movement and we can't afford to have you away ill; so please be quick and get back to work and do everything the doctors tell you and that will be the shortest way to health . . .

Diana [Laski's daughter] is off to the sea with some of the students.

The previous month, on 22 May 1935, Diana Laski had sent a handwritten card to Krishna Menon:

Will you come to my party on Tuesday next, May 28th at 8.30 at 5 Addison Bridge Place?

Letters such as this one make his omission from Frida Laski's memoirs quite intriguing. Records of the Commonwealth of India League also reveal that she attended its meetings and took an active part. She was a member of the Executive Committee of the India League, which replaced the Commonwealth of India League in early 1932. However, Krishna Menon does form an important part of Harold Laski's masterly biography, co-authored by a noted American political scientist and a British MP.[1] Laski was always very supportive of Krishna Menon. In the mid-1930s, the professor recommended his student for an academic position at Andhra University in Waltair, of which S. Radhakrishnan was then vice-chancellor. And on 1 February 1936, Laski would send a message to Krishna Menon:

This is merely a note to say that I think you and your colleagues surpassed yourselves in that meeting on Monday night. In common, I am sure, with all who were concerned in it, I owe you a real debt of gratitude . . .

The meeting had been organized by the India League in honour of a visiting Nehru. Laski was later to recall his association with the closest of all his students while speaking at the Indian Independence anniversary celebrations in London on August 1949:

I do not know how many times I have gone to meetings that I did not want to attend, have made speeches that I did not want to make, have written articles that I had no time to write, because I was under this grim control of this irrepressible embodiment of the will of India to be free. I look back and what I owe Krishna Menon for having made me attend as a member of his army is a debt that I can never repay.

India League pamphlet with contributions from Gandhi, Nehru and
Krishna Menon and foreword by Harold Laski, 1935

Laski passed away relatively young, on 24 March 1950. According to the unpublished notes of Marie Seton, Krishna Menon, who was then India's high commissioner to the UK, was 'the last person to see Harold Laski alive. He telephoned H.L. Beales [the eminent historian at the LSE and Labour Party intellectual] and burst into tears.' Four days later, wrote Laski's biographers, 'Krishna Menon made available the Indian embassy's Rolls Royce for the funeral.' A year later, he co-founded with the LSE a Harold Laski Society and, in 1954, supported the launch of the Harold Laski Institute of Political Science in Ahmedabad by P.G. Mavalankar, son of the first speaker of Lok Sabha.

Three fellow students of Krishna Menon at the LSE invite special attention.

The first was B.K. Nehru, son of Jawaharlal Nehru's cousin, who joined the LSE in 1929 but was not impressed by Krishna Menon at all.[2] He and Krishna Menon were to be at daggers drawn through the 1950s when the former was seen to be close to the Americans and the latter was considered a closet communist.

The second was Michael Straight, an American whose parents had founded the well-known magazine *New Republic*. In 1983, Straight was to publish his memoirs[3] in which he described his Indian friend as 'a Hindu with an arrogant manner and cavernous eyes' and as 'a perpetual student in a perpetual rage' who 'fought on every issue' with the result that 'every issue was inflamed by his venom'.

The third was Minoo Masani, who played an important role in Krishna Menon's life, in a positive way in the 1930s and 1940s but in a very negative manner thereafter.[4] Masani was an uncompromising socialist in the 1930s but did an ideological somersault after that. In 1956, he would describe Krishna Menon as 'a violent anti anti-Communist without being a Communist himself'.

In the mid-1930s and early 1940s, Krishna Menon collected around himself, as volunteers for the India League, very many young Indian men and women who were studying in the UK. But during his decade-long time at the LSE he does not seem to have had great success in radicalizing Indian students there. On the contrary, Indian students at the institution avoided being seen with him, lest they antagonize Beveridge. Tarlok Singh, later to join the Indian Civil Service (ICS) and become a distinguished administrator with much to do with Krishna Menon in the 1950s, wrote to him as secretary of the LSE Students Union on 23 November 1933:

> While appreciating to a considerable extent the objective of your scheme, we now feel that we have no place for your plans for the simple reason that our interest in politics is not acute enough to permit us to make active participation in it. For unless that is what the scheme implies, it is meaningless. We have so many immediate objectives in view that we can ill-afford to spare time for matters extraneous to them.

The scheme that Krishna Menon had proposed to the LSE Students Union was to host a meeting of the India League.

Notes

1. Kramnick and Sheerman (1993).
2. Nehru (1997).
3. Straight (1983).
4. Masani (1977).

Agitator, Editor, Lawyer, Councillor (1934–47)

Agitator

By the beginning of 1932, the Commonwealth of India League had ceased to exist, and in its place arose the India League. Formally, the India League came into being on 27 January 1932, and Bertrand Russell became its chairman. There were a number of other eminent British public figures also to be closely associated with it. But the man who was to run the India League single-handedly for the next decade and a half was Krishna Menon.

When the India League came into existence, there were at least five other non-official organizations already in place, each claiming to advocate India's interests in the UK.[1] Very often, these organizations were in conflict with each other, not only because of personality clashes but also because of the desire of each to be the 'sole spokesman' for Indian interests. The policy of the Indian National Congress towards them was summed up by Nehru in his letter to Fenner Brockway of 20 August 1931:

> . . . As you know the London branch of the Congress has been disaffiliated . . . We have had bitter experiences of our branches

and our Committee [Congress Working Committee] is against all
foreign commitments.

But within five years, this was to change entirely because of the
special relationship that Nehru and Krishna Menon would establish
with each other beginning November 1935.

The *India Review* was a fortnightly sixteen-page broadsheet on
'Indian Life, Literature, Politics and Affairs' started by Krishna Menon
in January 1932 with substantial financial support mobilized by Madan
Mohan Malaviya. This was in addition to the fortnightly *India News*
that he was already bringing out. The *India Review* was to soon make
its presence felt. Two young Indians, later to achieve fame as authors,
helped him bring it out—K.S. Shelvankar and Mulk Raj Anand.[2]

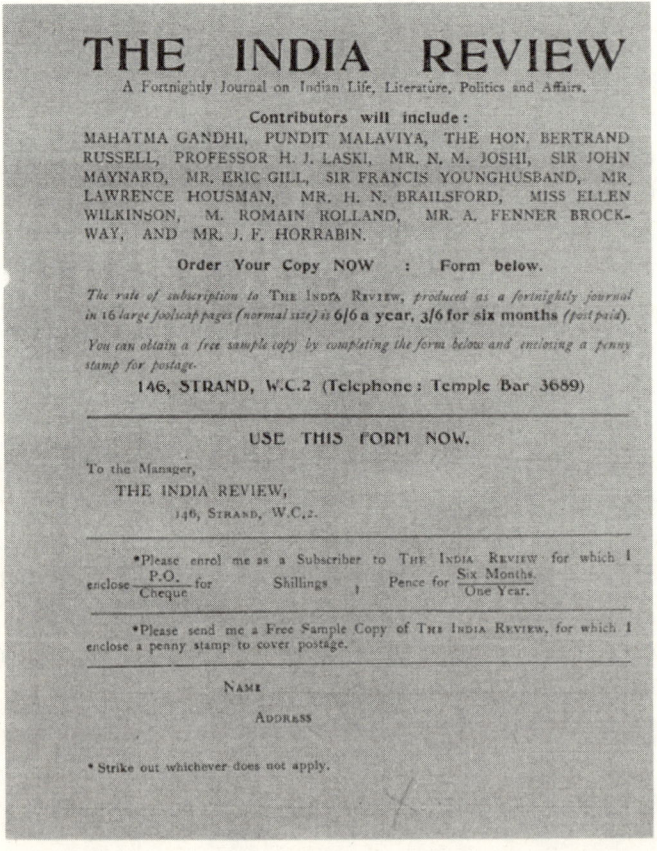

India League announcement for the India Review, *early 1932*

The inaugural issue featured an article by Gandhi, and the 27 February 1932 issue carried an Urdu poem of Muhammed Iqbal in translation:

Hejaz in Silence has to anxious ears proclaimed
That God's Old compact with desert dwellers shall be reordained.
The lion which sprang from the wilds and shattered Rome,
The angels say, shall be reborn in its old home.
O ye who in Western lands reside, learn God's home is not a business concern,
The gold you think is pure, soon shall impure turn.
A suicide's death awaits your civilization,
A slender bough to rest a nest is no safe position.
In angry seas where storms and furies rage, the ant shall ride;
Contemptible, but safe, in a frail-leaf caravan it shall stride.

But a few months later in its 15 October 1932 issue, it also carried this letter from a spirited reader, obviously an Englishman:

. . . I am, Sir, an Imperialist. I am sincerely convinced that the departure of the British from India would involve grave dangers not only to the welfare of the Indian people but also to world peace and prosperity. I am a regular reader of the 'India Review' not because I accept its opinions—they are, in fact, an anathema to me—but because it gives the 'other side'. If I cannot accept its attitude, I can at least admire its consistency with which it puts the case for self-determination . . . Mr. Winston Churchill is free from humbug. But the Government's constitutional scheme is hypocritical and perhaps—from the point of view of those, like myself, who desire to keep the British empire intact, highly dangerous.

I hope you will find space for this letter, for I doubt if any Conservative newspaper will publish it. I enclose my card and beg to remain,

INDIGNANT CONSERVATIVE
Blackpool October 7, 1932

The Indian National Congress had been founded in 1885 and had never missed its annual session. It was to do so for the first time in nearly half a century in 1932, the year when Ramsay McDonald was British prime minister. The British authorities prohibited it. Krishna Menon would write in the 16 April 1932 issue of the *India Review,* bringing to light something that was unknown to almost everybody in both Britain and India:

> It is one of the ironies that among the few Britons who was marked out by India for the greatest honour she can confer—the presidency of the Congress-was Mr. Ramsay McDonald. The Congress elected Mr. McDonald in 1911 as its President not because he had at that time any influence on British policy or even the distant hope of becoming Prime Minister but because he in those days, of long ago appeared to India to cherish ideals of liberty and progress, to stand for the downtrodden and the weak and to be able to speak and understand the language of those who yearned to be free. Today the Government of Mr. McDonald aims at the complete suppression of the Congress by any means open to an autocratic government in its dealings with a subject people . . . Incidentally if Mr. McDonald had been able to accept the presidency of the Congress in 1911, which he was prevented from doing owing to domestic reasons, he would still be a member of the All India Congress Committee, an unlawful body.

Krishna Menon sought contributions from a diverse set of people for the *India Review.* He reached out to one of India's most prominent politicians who was to change its history and geography in the next decade, but who was then in self-imposed exile in London. He wrote to M.A. Jinnah on 19 April 1932:

Dear Mr. Jinnah:

I wonder whether you would be willing to write an article for the 'The India Review' for our number appearing on the 14th of May . . .

We should also like to leave the choice of the subject to you but, if we may make a suggestion, we should say your views of the prospects of success of the 'dual policy' or on the next step to be taken when the Committees return would be very useful. Alternatively, we should appreciate an article either surveying the present position, or giving views of the future.

We feel that in view of your place in Indian public life you could consider our request a legitimate one and give us the benefit of your views during this notable phase of Indian constitutional development.

Jinnah replied three days later:

I am in receipt of your letter of the 19th. I wonder whether it would be convenient to you to come and see me next week say Tuesday or Wednesday between 4 to 5 pm at my chambers as I would like to have your ideas as to what you really want me to write about.

Nothing, however, came of this exchange. In a later letter to Mountbatten, Krishna Menon would refer to Jinnah as the 'Fuhrer'.

Among the earliest initiatives of the new India League was a submission of a detailed memorandum to the Joint Council of the Labour Party and its affiliate, Trade Union Congress. It went out on 17 March 1932 under the name of its vice chairman, J.F. Horrabin, MP, and Krishna Menon:

The India League ventures to approach the Joint Council of the Labour Party and the Trade Union Congress with the suggestion that it should consider the present position in India, and make a declaration that might serve to rally opinion in this country, and at the same time to convince Indians that they are not wholly without support . . .

It is not generally not recognized how wanton and unprovoked is the present repression, for the struggle was deliberately precipitated by Lord Willingdon's refusal to discuss the situation with Mr. Gandhi.

May we recall to you in the barest outline what is going on:

(1) Some twenty thousand persons were in prison by the end of January for non-violent offences . . .

(2) Most of the leaders of the Nationalist Movement, e.g. Mr. Sen Gupta, Abdul Gaffar Khan and of course, Mr. Gandhi himself, were imprisoned or deported without trial.

(3) Villages are subject to collective fines imposed by executive officials without judicial process.

(4) Trials before special tribunals are held in camera and at these secret sittings a suspect may be sentenced to death in his absence.

(5) Coercive ordinances originally devised to deal with terrorism have been extended to districts . . .

(6) The Air Force is being used in the North West Frontier Province to bomb villages . . .

(7) The complete muzzling of the press in India removes the usual check of publicity on the conduct of officials and police . . .

We would ask the Joint Council to receive a deputation consisting of Mr. Bertrand Russell, Mr. H.N. Brailsford, Mr. H.J. Laski, Mr. J.F. Horrabin and our Secretary [Krishna Menon], who will urge on the Council the desirability of a definite stand.

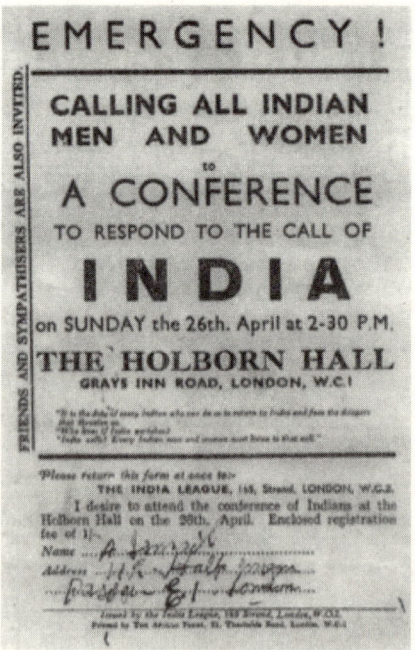

India League protest meeting against ordinances in India, London, 1932

Four days later, Krishna Menon approached the Labour Party leader George Lansbury. Lansbury, an admirer of Annie Besant, had earlier been chairman of the predecessor organization to the Commonwealth of India League and was among the few in the Labour Party then who genuinely cared for Indian self-determination. Krishna Menon wrote on 21 March 1932:

> I enclose herewith [a] copy of the letter sent to the Joint Council as suggested by you.
>
> I have received this morning a reply from Mr. W. Gillies of the Labour Party, a copy of which I also enclose.
>
> It does not appear from this letter that our Memorandum and request will come up before the Joint Council this week since Mr. Gillies says it has been 'handed over to the Party'.
>
> I should be glad to have your advice as to what we should do.

Krishna Menon would write regularly to Lansbury, who took a paternal interest in him. On 26 January 1932, Krishna Menon had asked the Labour leader to not extend his party's cooperation to the Third Round Table Conference being planned by the British government:

> By participating . . . the Labour party, it seems to us, is cooperating with a Government which is carrying out a coercive policy in India. The most effective form of protest that the party could make against the repression would be the withdrawal of such cooperation. It would convince India of the goodwill of the Labour party and also, perhaps prove a restraint on India officials.

The Labour Party did not heed Krishna Menon's request. But that did not stop him from wishing Lansbury on his seventy-third birthday on 21 February 1932, in a language that reflected the affection that marked their relationship. After greeting him on behalf of the India League thus:

> We would like to join with the many thousands of people who are thinking of you today with affectionate esteem and wish you many happy returns of the day.
>
> We are glad to feel that your voice is still raised as earnestly as ever in the cause of peace and freedom and against exploitation and suppression.

Krishna Menon added in his own hand:

> May I add a word of my personal greeting and express the good
> wishes and gratitude of my people to you in these times and always.

*Four British stalwarts of the India League. Harold Laski, George Lansbury, Bertrand Russell
and J.F. Horrabin. Sketch by Horrabin, 1932. Some years later, Horrabin would do the
illustrations for Nehru's* Glimpses of World History.

After submitting the memorandum to the Labour Party and
the Trade Union Congress, the India League decided to send a
four-member delegation to India to prepare a report on conditions
prevailing in the country. Krishna Menon wrote to Malaviya on
2 April 1932:

> The opinion of our friends here is that the India League should
> send out a deputation of two or three people including at least
> one prominent member of the House of Commons . . . This
> matter is being discussed at our next meeting and if we agree we
> shall propose to make an appeal both in India and here for funds
> to do this.

Krishna Menon's contacts with Malaviya were soon to attract the attention of Scotland Yard, which reported on 30 April 1932:

The attached is a copy of a telegram sent by V.K. Krishna MENON to the Press Times, Delhi which was stopped a day or so ago by the telegraph authorities in Delhi on the score of being objectionable. Krishna MENON is presumably the editor of India Review, published as you know by the India League (formerly the Commonwealth of India League) in London. The Press Times Delhi may be the Hindustan Times with which I believe MALAVIYA is connected. I was not aware that V.K. Krishna MENON was the representative of the Hindustan Times in this country but I do know that he has interested MALAVIYA financially in the India League.

The intercepted telegram was Krishna Menon's letter to the *Hindustan Times* containing the resolution on India to be moved shortly by Lansbury at the Labour Party's annual conference:

. . . This Conference reaffirms its belief in the right of the Indian peoples to choose the form of the Government which they consider to be in harmony with their national aspirations and profoundly regrets that the Government should have abandoned the policy of consultations and conferences with the representatives of all sections of the Indian people with the view of establishing this right in the most effective and certain manner . . .

On 2 August 1932, the members of the first-ever India League delegation were informed by its vice chairman that they were being

sent for the purpose of collecting first hand information about the state of affairs of India and the trend of opinion there, and make a report on its return to this country. It is hoped that this report will serve as a basis for more intensive education of public and Parliamentary opinion in this country.

The team comprised Monica Whately, Ellen Wilkinson, Leonard Matters and Krishna Menon. Whately was an active member of the Labour Party. Wilkinson and Matters had been Labour Members of Parliament, and Matters was also the London correspondent of *The Hindu*. The British intelligence report on the delegation referred to Krishna Menon as

> a journalist in Britain of somewhat extreme political tendencies. He was secretary of the India League and although quite presentable was a 'fellow traveller' of the communists indulging in diabolical political position on Indian and international politics.

Most of the funding for the delegation was arranged for by Malaviya. This was to be strenuously denied for long by Krishna Menon but the evidence appears incontrovertible—the Indian industrialist G.D. Birla provided financial support at Malaviya's instance. The group set sail from Venice on 5 August 1932 and was to be in India for eighty-three days. It went to ten of the eleven provinces of British India and spent time in villages, towns and cities meeting people from all walks of life. By its own reckoning, 'the average mileage per member covered by the delegation is approximately 12,000 (within India)'.

The delegation travelled to some places in India as a foursome. It had split up into two teams—one comprising Whately and Matters and the other Wilkinson and Krishna Menon—which then separately visited different parts of the country. Wilkinson's most recent biographer writes:[3]

> [T]he fact that she and Menon moved in similar circles and shared a keen appreciation for literature doubtless eased their relationship as travelling companions. So too would their temperamental similarities. Menon, like Ellen was passionately committed to social reform. But, like Ellen, he was 'not inclined to circumscribe his vision by the directions of particular discourse or a dogma', preferring a pragmatic focus on ends not means. He was also an attractive and charismatic figure whose company provided a welcome distraction from her recent heartbreak.

Krishna Menon and Wilkinson met Gandhi on 25 September 1932 in Yerwada Jail in Poona. He had been on a fast since the afternoon of 20 September 1932, undertaken in protest against the British government's decision to conduct elections by having separate electorates not only by religion but also by caste. This was an anathema to Gandhi, who believed it would lead to the disintegration of India. Gandhi's fast had awakened the conscience of large sections of Hindu society, and on 24 September 1932, the historic 'Poona Pact' had been signed by 'caste Hindus' such as Malaviya and C. Rajagopalachari on the one side and representatives of what were then called 'Depressed Classes' led by Dr B.R. Ambedkar on the other. The pact provided for quotas for these 'Depressed Classes' in legislatures and also threw upon temples across the country to all Indians, irrespective of caste. Gandhi gave Krishna Menon and Wilkinson a 'message for Great Britain', which was then published exclusively by the *Daily Herald* in London:[4]

Every day of the fast seems to be conclusive evidence of the hand of God in it. Even I with my boundless faith in God and His mercy was not prepared for this great awakening against untouchability. That some of the great temples should have spontaneously admitted the 'untouchables' without restriction is to me a modern miracle . . .

The Cabinet decision was to me a timely warning from God that I was asleep when He was knocking at the door and waking me up. The settlement arrived at is to me but the beginning of the work of purification . . . I do not want the British Cabinet to come to any hasty decision . . . If they have not realized the true inwardness of the Agreement, they must summarily reject it, but if they have, they will not alter one word or comma of it, but they will implement every condition that is implied in the great settlement which the so-called untouchables and the so-called touchables have arrived at with all their heart and with God as their witness.

The very next day, that is, on 26 September 1932, the British government accepted the terms of the Poona Pact. Strangely, Krishna Menon's final report prepared after the delegation returned to London

makes no mention of any conversation with Gandhi, although there
is a fairly detailed account of the encounter of Whately and Matters
with Willingdon, who rejected the idea that Gandhi was a saint of
any kind and called him 'a shrewd politician'.

The India League group returned to London and made its initial
report to 'a great meeting' in Kingsway Hall on 26 November 1932.
Bertrand Russell chaired the meeting, and present in the audience
were Laski and another British politician who would, in the years
to come, become intimately associated with Indian affairs—Stafford
Cripps. Lansbury was also there. All through 1933, Krishna Menon
spoke on his delegation and its findings to audiences—small and
large—in different cities such as London, Manchester, Bristol and
Birmingham. He also wrote a 'Letter to the Editor' in the well-
circulated left-wing *New Statesman & Nation*. The editor, Kingsley
Martin, and his wife, Dorothy Woodman, through her organization
Union of Democratic Control (UDC), were both active supporters
of the India League. The letter started thus:

> In 1932 nearly a hundred thousand persons were sent to prison in
> India for political reasons. The number includes men, women and
> children. The Ordinances and the Indian Penal Code which later
> a British administrator called 'Britain's grim gift to India' rendered
> all these arrests, 'trials' and imprisonments legal enough. They
> make even the detention in prison camps of several thousands of
> young men and some women without trial, and without statement
> of charges, under heavy armed guard, also legal. In Germany we
> should call them Concentration Camps . . .

The letter, soon to be widely noticed, was provocative and pungent.
It forced Martin to add this comment of his own:

> The author of this letter was one of a group of English and Indian
> men and women who recently spent several months in investigating
> conditions in India on behalf of the India League. We have usually
> refrained from publishing stories of the Ordinance regime in India
> owing to the great difficulty in substantiating them. Mr. Menon,

who has lived for some years in this country and whose opinions are of a moderate nature, tells us that he is able and willing to fully substantiate every statement in his letter and that a full report of The India League delegation's experience in India will be published shortly . . . Ed.

Woodman, on her part, had moved a resolution at the Labour Party conference at Edmonton in February 1933, at which Krishna Menon also spoke. The resolution, reflecting what he said, asserted

the right of the Indian people to self-determination and independence

and called on the British government to

grant full self-government to India as soon as possible and summon a constituent assembly elected by universal franchise and commissioned to draw up a constitution.

The British establishment was trying its best to stop the publication of the India League delegation's final report. But news of the impending indictment of British rule in India was spreading, and on 26 October 1933, Horace Alexander wrote to Krishna Menon:

I am so glad your report will soon be out. Such a large and well-documented volume ought to provide splendid ammunition for throwing (non-violently!) at Churchill, Hoare and Co. . . .

Finally, a small company called Essential News published the 554-page *The Condition of India* in March 1934. The voluminous report, with a characteristically punchy foreword by Bertrand Russell, was prepared almost single-handedly by Krishna Menon. It excoriated British rule in India in painstaking detail and ended by suggesting:

. . . The way out is in recognizing and in helping the fulfillment of self-determination . . . The principle of self-determination, in our view, can be implemented only through a Constituent

Assembly . . . consisting of representatives who have the mandate
of their constituents . . . It is essential that the representatives
should be elected on adult franchise, or as near adult franchise as
possible . . . The Constituent Assembly would appoint a delegation
to negotiate with His Majesty's Government on all points on which
such negotiation is necessary and the agreement reached would
become the subject of legislation by the British Parliament . . .

While he was writing up the delegation's report, Krishna Menon
also launched a spirited campaign against the British government's White
Paper on India, which was presented in Parliament in March 1933.

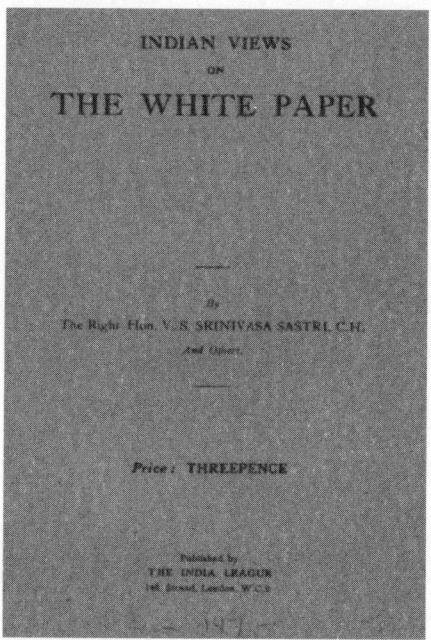

India League pamphlet, 1933

The India League propagated the views of V.S. Srinivasa Sastry, a man
Gandhi hugely respected in spite of their differing political outlooks.
Interestingly, Sastry's biographer was to write three decades later[5] that
he was against the idea of a constituent assembly because 'Indians could
not compose their communal differences' but also pointed out:

[T]he idea of a Constituent Assembly had been mooted by Mr. V.K. Krishna Menon on behalf of the India League of London and had been supported by some of the most prominent members of the British Labour Party.

Most of the Congress leaders in India were under arrest and hence, no formal opinion was forthcoming from them. But almost all other sections of Indian political opinion expressed their dismay and Krishna Menon published a pamphlet in which he added his own attack under the title 'Broken Pledges'. He ended it by quoting an ex-viceroy (Irwin), who in a confidential dispatch stated:

> . . . I do not hesitate to say that both the Governments of England and India appear to me, up to the present moment unable to answer satisfactorily the charge of having taken every means in their power of breaking to the heart the words of promise they had uttered to the ear . . .

This, more than anything else, was the most stinging riposte to the White Paper.

The Condition of India, in many ways, represents Krishna Menon's most outstanding achievement in some two decades of agitation and protest by the India League. The book was promptly banned in India by this notification:

Finance Department
(Central Revenue)

Notification
Customs
New Delhi the 29th March 1934

No. 17: In exercise of the powers conferred by section 19 of the Sea Customs Act, 1878 (VIII of 1878), the Governor General in Council is pleased to prohibit the bringing into British India of any copy of (a) the book entitled 'Condition of India' being the report of the Delegation sent to India by the India League, in 1932 published by Essential News, 65 Portland Place, London W.I. or (b) any translation, reprinting or other document containing substantial reproductions of the matter contained in the said book.

G.S. Hardy
Joint Secretary to the Govt. of India

But the ban was applicable only in India. A year later on 16 October 1935, Nehru would write to Krishna Menon from Switzerland that the book had been sent to him and 'even a hasty glance has shown that this is a very useful publication'. The book was criticized in mainline newspapers, most scathingly in *The Times,* the universally acknowledged voice of the British establishment. When he died in October 1974, it was to carry a long and handsome tribute to Krishna Menon. But forty years earlier, it had this to say about the book:

> . . . The writers of this report fail to comprehend that nationalism in India is not the monopoly of the Congress Party and that the Congress party was not the sole exponent of Indian people as a whole . . .

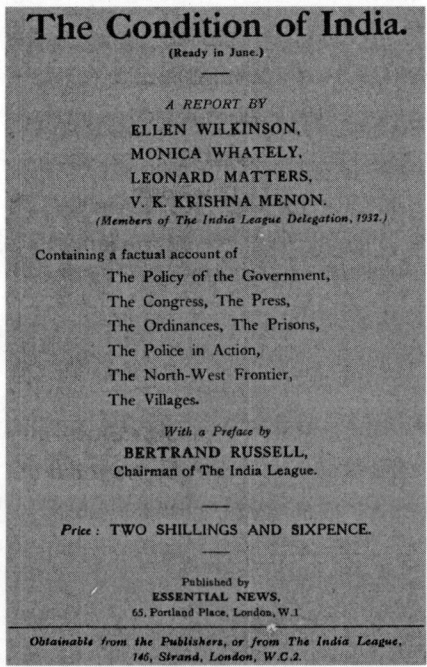

Publication announcement of the Condition of India, *India League, early 1934*

Three years later, sometime in mid-July 1935, Wilkinson was to write to Krishna Menon's sister Janaki Amma in Calicut:

> I was sorry to hear from Krishna of the sad news of the death of your father. I have the most vivid recollection of him . . . It must have been a great comfort to him and to you as I know it has been to Krishna that his son was able to see him once before he died.
>
> Krishna has not been very well lately. He does not want me to tell you this, but I do think that that would be fair to you. However, he has now gone into the country with friends, and he will soon be quite well again. Please do not be anxious. The doctor says that there is nothing organically wrong with him, but he has been working very hard lately and London in the summer is a very tiring place to live. One day it is bitterly cold, and the next day there is a heat-wave. But Krishna has been very well looked after by all his friends, and we soon expect to see him among us, ordering us about, and telling us what slackers we are, in his best style.
>
> I have often thought of you, and that lovely home of yours in which you gave me such charming hospitality. I hope that you are well yourself, and your daughter. Give her my love . . . I remember the hot discussions we had about literature when I was in Madras. It seems all so long ago, and yet might have been yesterday.
>
> I wonder whether we shall ever meet again. I do hope so, so that we can have a really long talk. I think as I am writing of that view across the garden from the window and water where the village women washed their clothes, and the palms and rain. It was all so marvellous . . .

A year after *Condition of India* came out, Wilkinson co-authored, with a noted German scholar Edward Conze, a well-received book called *Why Fascism?* that argued that 'the rise of the Nazis in Germany was because of the failure of social democratic forces and the Communist left to capture the imagination of the working class'. The book was edited by Krishna Menon. Wilkinson also wrote fiction, and she sent him one of her novels with a short note that is unfortunately undated but was probably written sometime in 1936:

[A]s you seemingly are able to get me to produce works—when my own publisher can't.

She was close to Nehru as well and remained an indefatigable champion of India's freedom till her untimely death in 1947, when she was education minister in Attlee's cabinet.

Through the latter half of the 1930s, Reginald Sorensen was a pillar of the India League as one of its parliamentary secretaries. In July 1967, he was interviewed in London by B.R. Nanda for the oral history archives of the Nehru Memorial Museum and Library. Sorensen went down memory lane in that conversation and spoke of Krishna Menon as well:

Nanda: When you were working for the India League during the years 1936–39, before the war, how was the Labour Party's mind working?

Sorensen: The India League was suspect in certain quarters, very suspect indeed partly because of Krishna Menon . . . because of his frequent association with Communists and secondly because of liability to irascibility . . . Nevertheless Menon's arguments were perfectly valid which was 'We are a non-party organization and therefore I don't mind who helps us, Conservative, Labour, Liberal or Communist' . . .

Nanda: How did Mr. Krishna Menon impress you?

Sorensen: Oh in those days he was a very slim, fiery-eyed young man with eyes like burning spheres. Even in those days he had an extraordinary volubility—electric and arresting in the extreme, but physically very sparse . . .

Nanda: Do you recall the activities of those days?

Sorensen: . . . during 1929–31 we had an India League group in the House of Commons. When I went back in 1935 we reconstructed it. I was the Parliamentary Secretary . . . From that time onward, Krishna Menon and I were very closely cooperating in meetings, conferences, producing memoranda and questions in the House . . . He would come to me and say 'Why not ask this question'. I asked hundreds of questions . . . from 1935 right onwards to 1945.

A fine example of this 'questions-raising' activity of Krishna Menon in the House of Commons would be provided in a letter that Nehru would write to him on 25 November 1936:

> There is another urgent matter. I enclose a note (from Govind Ballabh Pant) on the method of voting prescribed by the U.P. Government. It is a perfect scandal, and meant to give every advantage to the big zamindars and to drag on their tenants. It is a matter of considerable importance to us in this province . . . You can well imagine that with this device anything can be done in the elections. There is no doubt that ordinarily our candidates are bound to win given fair play. It is this fair play that is lacking . . . I wonder if it is possible for you to do anything at the other end in Parliament and elsewhere. Our case is exceedingly strong but this does not carry us far in India. Any way I wish you try. The time is short and the matter is urgent.

A couple of days letter came Krishna Menon's response:

> . . . The question of coloured boxes in the U.P. has been the subject of questions in the [House of] Commons and very unsatisfactory answers were returned. It was taken up again with [R.A.] Butler [secretary of state for India] by Miss Wilkinson . . . I understand that the powers here are unwilling to interfere. The matter however is to be raised again and again in the House of Commons . . .

Editor

In mid-1933, a perpetually financially strapped Krishna Menon signed up to be a freelance editor with two well-known publishing houses in London: the first being Selwyn and Blount and the other John Lane The Bodley Head. The second assignment was to be especially noteworthy but the first was no less important. As general editor, his task was to identify authors and topics and work with them till the book was finally published.

With Selwyn and Blount, Krishna Menon launched the 'Topical Books Series'. In his own words:

> The books in this series will deal with problems and personalities of topical interest . . . Each book in this series will be written by an author whose analysis and opinions will bear the impress of knowledge and experience as well as of courageous thought.
>
> The series is not planned to propagate any set of dogmas or opinions but will be based on a careful choice of the most significant problems and appropriate writers to deal with them. Each book will have its own character but the SERIES under a general editorship ensures for all of them a uniqueness which the circumstances of our day both enable and demand.

The very first book in this series was Lansbury's memoirs, *My England*. Lansbury was then leader of the Opposition in the House of Commons and a widely loved Labour leader. *Why Fascism?* by Ellen Wilkinson and Edward Conze too was part of this series. Krishna Menon achieved a feat by getting four young Oxford men to contribute to *Young Oxford and War,* which was a book based on the famous 'King and Country' debate that took place at the Oxford Union in February 1933 on the resolution 'that this House will not in any circumstances fight for its King and Country'. Krishna Menon took pains to ensure that all points of view got prominent place in the volume. One of the Oxford students who contributed to the book became one of Krishna Menon's strongest supporters and closest friends—Michael Foot who led the Labour Party in the 1980s. And the Indian who was secretary of the Oxford Union when the debate took place ended up becoming one of Krishna Menon's vociferous critics in the 1950s as the publisher of the Bombay tabloid *Current*—D.F. Karaka.

In early July 1933, Krishna Menon also signed up to be an editor with the well-known publishing house John Lane The Bodley Head. The three directors of this enterprise were Allen Lane, John Lane's nephew, Lindsay Drummond, and Ronald Boswell. Krishna Menon came on board as the general editor of a series of books called 'Twentieth Century Library'. This series 'was to consist of volumes each of which would deal with a problem in the context of a changing civilisation'. Twenty books by well-known authors were to be edited by Krishna Menon and published in 1934 and 1935.

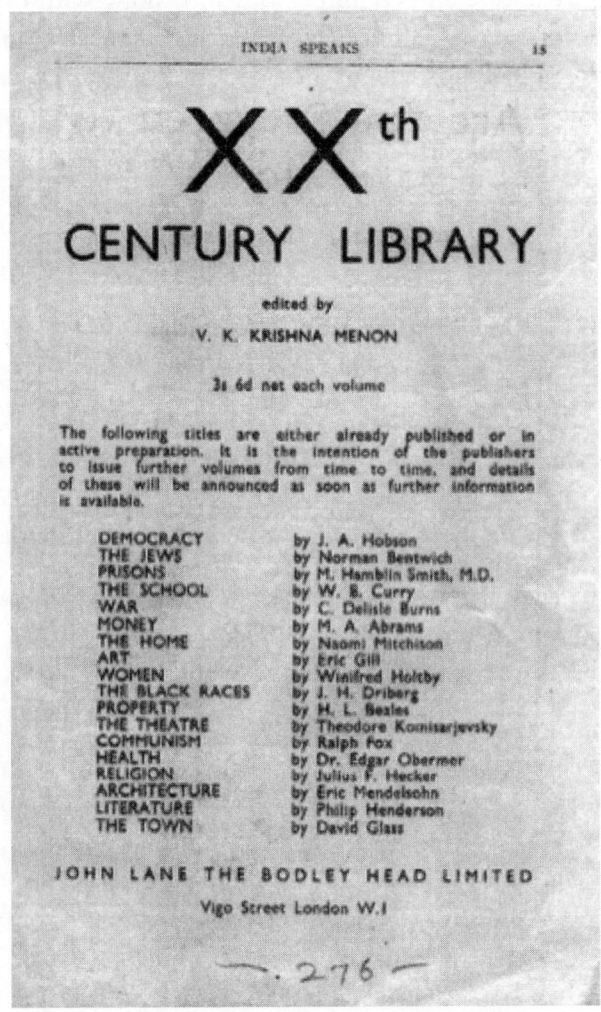

INDIA SPEAKS 15

XXth
CENTURY LIBRARY

edited by

V. K. KRISHNA MENON

3s 6d net each volume

The following titles are either already published or in active preparation. It is the intention of the publishers to issue further volumes from time to time, and details of these will be announced as soon as further information is available.

DEMOCRACY	by J. A. Hobson
THE JEWS	by Norman Bentwich
PRISONS	by M. Hamblin Smith, M.D.
THE SCHOOL	by W. B. Curry
WAR	by C. Delisle Burns
MONEY	by M. A. Abrams
THE HOME	by Naomi Mitchison
ART	by Eric Gill
WOMEN	by Winifred Holtby
THE BLACK RACES	by J. H. Driberg
PROPERTY	by H. L. Beales
THE THEATRE	by Theodore Komisarjevsky
COMMUNISM	by Ralph Fox
HEALTH	by Dr. Edgar Obermer
RELIGION	by Julius F. Hecker
ARCHITECTURE	by Eric Mendelsohn
LITERATURE	by Philip Henderson
THE TOWN	by David Glass

JOHN LANE THE BODLEY HEAD LIMITED

Vigo Street London W.I

276

The first series of books edited by Krishna Menon at John Lane The Bodley Head

Krishna Menon also tried to interest a third publishing house, J. M. Dent & Sons, to agree to his proposal to edit a series of volumes on the 'The Inheritance of the Nineteenth Century' but that attempt did not succeed. However, the rejection letter from the publisher congratulated him for the 'The Twentieth Century Library' he was doing for John Lane The Bodley Head which 'were beautifully produced and had very solid stuff'.

In 1936, Lane set up Penguin Books and, along with Boswell and Krishna Menon, also announced the launch of Pelican Books, which was to be the non-fiction side of the Penguin venture. That was when the Lane–Krishna Menon relationship was amicable and mutually beneficial. On 23 June 1936, Lane wrote to his Indian editor:

> I am sending you some suggestions received from a man who came to see me the other day on which I would like to have your opinion . . .

A few days later on 5 July 1936, Krishna Menon was to write to Lane:

> Mr. Beales, Mr. Williams and I met yesterday and had a long discussion about the ideas and scheme for the Pelican books. I arranged that we have a meeting with you (as you desired) on Monday at 12.

After the idea of Pelican Books had taken shape, Lane guided Krishna Menon on 18 September 1936:

> I am enclosing herewith the sort of letter you might write to Bernard Shaw. As you may remember, I have already approached Messrs Constable with a view to this author's work and for this reason I don't want to go above their heads personally. However, it is perfectly in order for you to do so without mentioning my name.

The letter that Krishna Menon sent George Bernard Shaw soon thereafter was to launch a revolution in publishing:

> You may have seen an announcement in the Press recently to the effect that Penguin books are shortly launching their new venture

Pelican books which, while similar in format and to be sold at the same price as Penguin books, will aim at slightly more serious public.

As one of the editors of the new series I am approaching you to ask whether you would consider the inclusion of some of your work preferably *The Intelligent Women's Guide to Socialism*. I may add that among the first ten volumes will be Sir James Jean's *Mysterious Universe,* H.G. Wells's *Short History of the World* and Olaf Stapledon's *Last and First Man.*

The first and last book edited by Krishna Menon in the Pelican series

The Pelican series, with Krishna Menon drawing up most of the list of books and functioning as general editor, produced many evergreen bestsellers. But the Lane–Krishna Menon relationship began to sour sometime in late 1937, and by the end of that year he was issued a termination notice by Lane, effective mid-June 1938. Lane was very frustrated with Krishna Menon's pace of editing work on the manuscripts that were being sent to him. The relationship deteriorated to such an extent that the two were communicating with each other largely through their respective solicitors during most of 1938. Finally they met and on 24 November 1938, Krishna Menon wrote perhaps his last letter to Lane:

I must say I was rather surprised at some of the things you said but at
the same time I appreciate very much your frankness in the matter.

I shall be glad if you will come to definite arrangements as soon
as possible so that all matters are cleared up.

The 'definite arrangement' that Lane made soon thereafter was Krishna
Menon's quick exit from Pelican. Lane's most recent biographer has
this to say about the parting:[6]

> Both complained of poor communications with Lane grumbling
> that he had not heard for months from Menon about which titles
> he proposed to take on, and Menon complaining that Lane had not
> been in touch about the contractual negotiations for these books;
> but the truth of the matter was that Lane, mercurial and easily
> bored, found that austere and unconvivial Menon far from [a]
> kindred spirit, and was happy to freeze him out. Menon lectured
> him for an hour in a Soho restaurant in a low monotone, and
> Lane, who could neither hear nor understand what he was trying
> to say, finally lost patience and called him a 'bottleneck' at which
> Menon, ill, under-nourished and overworked, felt bruised and
> isolated. He complained that Lane never returned his calls or kept
> him informed, and seemed to inhabit 'a world which paralyses all
> action and makes decent people feel they don't fit in with things'.

The very last Pelican classic that Krishna Menon edited was Sigmund
Freud's *Totem and Taboo,* which had originally come out in 1913 but
that was reissued as a Pelican paperback in 1940.

Before Lane and Menon went their separate ways, they, along
with Boswell, had ensured the publication and distribution of the
first of Nehru's international bestsellers: his autobiography. In an
interview with Marie Seton twenty years later, Lane was to recall
that Krishna Menon's impact on him was 'enormous'. He told her
that 'Krishna Menon had the idea of publishing for the masses—the
best books at the cheapest price'. Lane admitted that 'Krishna Menon
imbued him with his own enthusiasm for publishing with ideas and
that he awakened his social conscience'.

Having published Nehru, Krishna Menon was to make an attempt at getting Gandhi as well to write a book to be published by John Lane. He wrote to Mahadev Desai, Gandhi's secretary, on 5 August 1936, requesting Gandhi for a book on pacifism or non-violence, saying:

[I]n the present international situation people are seeking various methods of resistance to war and the idea of non-violence is beginning to have appeal though limited in this country.

But that book by Gandhi did not materialize for a somewhat unusual reason as this communication of 28 August 1936 from Desai reveals:

. . . Please thank John Lane for their invitation to Gandhiji to write a book on non-violence. His hands are too full to permit him to undertake an effort of that kind. I almost think that he can never settle down to prepare a book or treatise on any of the theories he has taught and lived. He must go on making experiments all his life, leaving it to others to study them and their results and to base treatises on these studies. He can direct a movement by means of regular articles containing detailed instructions but he cannot successfully play the role of a writer. I do not think it is in his line.

Lawyer

On 19 November 1934, Krishna Menon was called to the bar after having enrolled in the Middle Temple four years earlier while being a student simultaneously at the LSE and University College London. Initially, he worked in the chambers of Samuel Lincoln. Lincoln was to later tell Marie Seton:

. . . of all the pupils I have had, he [Krishna Menon] was the most thorough in research and argued points of law with exactitude . . . I remember when he used to cross-examine, he was always very careful in framing his phrase. And then there was a long pause. He was born for the profession and if he hadn't gone to Nehru he would have made a name for himself in India as a barrister.

Lincoln was also to recall that Allen Lane of Penguin Books settled the dispute with Krishna Menon in late 1938 with a payment of 125 pounds—a princely sum then for anyone but especially so to someone struggling to make ends meet. Krishna Menon's solicitor absconded with the money, and when Lincoln advised him to prosecute, Krishna Menon's reaction was

> What do I want with money? My needs are few. Let us be merciful, the man has a wife and children.

This incident, reflective of Krishna Menon's disdainful attitude to money matters, which was to get him into serious trouble when he was high commissioner, is confirmed in Lane's biography as well.

Krishna Menon was never much of a lawyer in England. His political activities left him with no time whatsoever to take on too many cases. Between 1936 and 1941, he worked with Denis Pritt, a Labour Party MP and also a lawyer who took on political cases. Thereafter, for six years he took up some cases of Indians who came on appeal to the Privy Council. He also became a member of the Haldane Society, later to be called the Haldane Club, which was 'an organization of Socialist lawyers' in which Stafford Cripps, Pritt and Clement Attlee were prominent figures.

PROPOSAL FOR THE BAR.

To The Under Treasurer,

I have seen Mr. *Krishna Menon* and have satisfied myself that he is a fit and proper person to be called to the Bar, and I hereby propose him for Call in *Michaelmas* Term, 1934

MASTER OF THE BENCH.

....

This Form must be signed and sent to the Under Treasurer, Middle Temple, London, E.C.4, before the ....

Krishna Menon's recommendation for being called to the Bar, signed by Stafford Cripps, London, 1934

Two cases with which Krishna Menon was associated deserve special mention. The first was that of Udham Singh, who had shot dead Sir Michael O'Dwyer on 13 March 1940 in London. O'Dwyer had been the governor of Punjab when the infamous Jallianwala Bagh massacre had taken place in Amritsar twenty-one years earlier. Krishna Menon had, at first, condemned Singh's act in keeping with the sentiments of top leaders of the Congress back home but then changed his mind after they had changed theirs, sensing Singh's popularity in India. He muscled his way to be the junior counsel to St John Hutchinson in Singh's defence team, conscious of its publicity value.[7] The trial lasted exactly two days, and Krishna Menon appears to have been eloquent by his silence. The execution took place soon thereafter on 31 July 1940.

O'Dwyer had, interestingly, a much earlier Laski connection as well, a fact Krishna Menon would have been only too well aware of. In 1922, Sir Sankaran Nair, a noted Indian jurist, had written a book accusing O'Dwyer of terrorism and culpability in the Amritsar killings. O'Dwyer sued Nair for libel and, as Laski's biographers write, 'For five weeks from 1 May to 6 June 1924 and for five hours a day, Laski was one of the twelve special jurors.'[8] He was also the only one to reject O'Dwyer's petition. It is this case that 'marked the real beginning of his [Laski's] commitment to the cause of Indian independence'. Laski's commitment to India thus began just when Krishna Menon landed in England for the first time.

Almost three decades after Singh's execution, the famous Indian movie star Balraj Sahni would write to Krishna Menon on 29 November 1969:

A group of Indians settled in the UK are out to make a film on Udham Singh the terrorist revolutionary who shot Sir Michael O' Dwyer of Jallianwala Bagh. It is a progressive effort, which is being wholeheartedly supported by Hrishikesh Mukherjee who is directing the picture, myself and several other friends. My son [Parikshat Sahni] is to play the role of Udham Singh.

The bearer, a namesake of mine, is the organizer of the group. He tells me that you defended Udham Singh and therefore he will need your permission for portraying you as a character in the film. I am sure you will have no objection and will also give the producer your valued suggestions.

Alas, for a variety of reasons, this film never got made.[9] Balraj Sahni passed away in 1973. Subsequently, however, two films on the subject would get made: *Jallianwala Bagh* released in 1977 and *Udham Singh* in 1999. Neither would have any reference to Krishna Menon.

The second case was that of Jiwan Lal Gauba, who had been held in contempt of the Lahore High Court by its chief justice in 1936. The case took on political overtones and a serious attempt was made by Gauba and his German-born wife, Elizabeth, to petition the Privy Council, for which Krishna Menon approached Cripps and Walter Monckton. The matter was to drag on and finally on 21 May 1938, Cripps told Krishna Menon:

> I have now heard from Walter Monckton and I gather nothing is to be done in the way of appealing in the Gauber [Gauba] matter. We must now resort to political activities if you want to accomplish anything.

Elizabeth Gauba was to become great friends with Krishna Menon, sharing a common passion for education—she would start a school in New Delhi where Indira Gandhi's two sons studied for a while. The paths of Walter Monckton and Krishna Menon crossed again a decade later when Monckton was advising the Nizam of Hyderabad who, for over a year following Indian Independence, dilly-dallied on acceding to the Indian Union, toying with the idea of being an independent country. Monckton was defence secretary in the UK government when the Suez Canal crisis erupted in late 1956, a crisis that Krishna Menon helped defuse.

It was a piece of historical irony that when Krishna Menon was high commissioner in London, the Privy Council's jurisdiction over India ceased as the Supreme Court of India became functional from 28 January 1950. The Privy Council would hear its last case from

India in December 1949, and the formal ceremony marking the transition from it to the Supreme Court was held in London on 6 February 1950. The London *Times* reported two days later:

> Mr. Krishna Menon said it was a historic occasion and marked another stage where two peoples had agreed, and they welcomed the position whereby the transference of functions and authority to India has been through harmonious agreement. The two countries had not only set themselves an example but that might in some way serve the world by giving a lead in the peaceful settlement of disputes.

In 1959, Krishna Menon was to be largely responsible for the establishment of the Indian Society of International Law. The Society's building next to the Supreme Court was named after him in 1994, and his bust greets visitors to it. He resumed his legal career in the Supreme Court of India in right earnest when he was in political oblivion from January 1963 and was involved in a couple of important cases, which continue to be cited.

Borough Councillor

While he was editing and keeping the India League going, Krishna Menon got involved in local politics. In November 1934, he was elected as a Labour Party councillor from Ward 4 in the St Pancras Borough of Greater London. It was for a three-year term but he ended up serving for fourteen years. This was his first experience in elected office, and in it he 'gave leadership to the white man— both in peacetime and in war'. The borough had many pubs, and Krishna Menon set out to have as many public libraries, especially mobile ones. During the Second World War, he was one of just three members of the Council and 'served as an indefatigable civil defence worker and air-raid warden'.

In 1946, he became the first chairman of the St Pancras Arts and Civic Council, which was inaugurated by Dame Sybil Thorndike, the great Shakespearean actress who, along with her husband, was to remain close to Krishna Menon till his demise. Thirty-six hours before he suffered his first heart attack in London in March 1974, he would call on her. She was the last person in England he was able to visit. This Council organized the St Pancras Arts Festival, the precursor to today's Camden Arts Festival. In January 1955, when he was at the height of his global fame, St Pancras conferred the Freedom of the Borough honour on him in the presence of a number of distinguished men and women from the UK and India. He was only the second recipient of such an accolade after George Bernard Shaw.

Krishna Menon made many friends while he was a councillor. Barbara Betts—who later as Barbara Castle became the youngest woman MP in 1945 and later a member of Harold Wilson's cabinet—was one. Castle's biographer quotes a letter she wrote to her mother after the funeral of her 'significant other':[10]

> . . . Michael [Foot] and Ritchie [Calder] stood round me like a bodyguard sheltering me with understanding, & Krishna took me home. It was a genuine goodbye from genuine mourners, with real comradeship.

Castle would send a message to Krishna Menon on 19 January 1955 on hearing of his being honoured with the Freedom of the Borough award:

> . . . Seldom is such poetic justice done in public life . . .

Another person to serve as a councillor alongside Krishna Menon for some years was J.B.S. Haldane, considered to be among the greatest biologists of the twentieth century. On 14 July 1933, he had written to Haldane's sister Naomi Mitchison, herself a noted author:

> I was glad to hear from Messrs Lane that the contract for your book for the 'Twentieth Century Library' has been arranged . . . I wonder whether you would give me an introduction to Mr. J.B.S. Haldane as I want to approach him for a book on some subject of

his choice. It is no use writing him in the usual formal way and I thought you would perhaps be willing to help me.

Haldane was a brilliant scientist but even then notoriously eccentric, a reputation his sister confirmed in her reply to Krishna Menon a few days later:

> About my brother, I hardly know what to say. He is a very difficult person, and also a very busy one. The only way to approach him is through his wife, Charlotte Haldane, who is also a rather difficult person. I am afraid I'm not persona grata at all!—and the moment he is being quite friendly but I never know how long it will last. The only times I have ever suggested he should write anything, he has always been very cross . . . By the way he is used to getting (and, I believe, does get) much better terms than most of us!

Haldane, an ardent admirer of India and of Nehru, was to spend the last seven and a half years of his life in India, first in Calcutta and later in Bhubaneswar, having obtained Indian citizenship in October 1960. He was also among the strongest supporters of the India League, especially in the 1940s, ever ready to accede to Krishna Menon's requests for speaking and writing in favour of Indian independence.

For a brief while, Evelyn Denington overlapped with Krishna Menon as a councillor in St Pancras and continued later in the London City Council. Marie Seton's notes on the conversation she had with Denington in mid-1958 read:

> K's [Krishna Menon's] efforts for Independence in the years between the wars is his most important contribution. He kept India before the Labour Party who were previously disinterested in India and unaware of it. K's indefatigable efforts kept India in mind. K was all the time keeping the question alive by going to the village to speak to one man and a dog. He went to the smallest ward, to the village halls, to local parties to speak . . . he went to the out-of-the-way places where no one went.

Sometime in 1934 or 1935, Krishna Menon also got to know someone who would later be the vicereine of India during 1947–48. This is what one of her early biographers wrote:[11]

> One of Edwina'a socialist friends in London before the war was Vengalil Krishnan Krishna Menon, a Middle Temple lawyer-cum-politician who described himself as a teacher, journalist and publicist . . . Edwina enjoyed his quick mind, his intellectualism, his ardent socialism and anti-imperialism. It was through Krishna Menon that Edwina learned more about his disciple Jawaharlal Nehru . . .

This 'disciple' description of Nehru vis-à-vis Krishna Menon is definitely an exaggeration. How exactly their first meeting happened is not known but Krishna Menon and Edwina Mountbatten became good friends long before he and her husband got to know each other and long before the Mountbattens became part of Nehru's world. Edwina's relationship with Nehru was undoubtedly very special and unique. But she and Krishna Menon too wrote to each other often and were to be the co-presidents of the India Club when it was launched in London in January 1951. A few months later on 15 July 1952, from the warship *HMS Surprise* at Portishead, she was to send Krishna Menon a cable:

> I am thinking of you and especially today dear Krishna and with real affection, gratitude and admiration.

It has been recently revealed that in November 1955 the US Federal Bureau of Investigation (FBI) opened a file on Edwina Mountbatten, 'most probably because of her association with Krishna Menon and her various political pronouncements on India and Africa . . .'.[12] When she passed away in February 1960, her last rites were performed at sea off the coast of Portsmouth. One of the dozen wreaths of marigolds floating was that from Krishna Menon, apart from the one from Nehru. Nehru has been assailed for sending a ship of the Indian Navy for the funeral. The truth of the matter is that *INS*

Trishul was a frigate then being built by a British company in Belfast. It was delivered to the Indian Navy on 14 January 1960. On its way to India, it stopped off in Portsmouth.

Notes

1. A good discussion of these different groups is in Owen (2007).
2. Many years later, Anand would write a lightly fictionalized memoir in which Krishna Menon figured prominently; Anand (1984).
3. Beers (2016).
4. Pyarelal (1932).
5. Rao (1963).
6. Lewis (2005).
7. Anand (2019).
8. Kramnick and Sheerman (1993).
9. Sahni (2019) has a brief account of Balraj Sahni and his son shooting for this film in the early 1970s.
10. Perkins (2003).
11. Hough (1983).
12. Lownie (2019).

5

Congress Socialist Party Representative in London (1934–39)

After two years of efforts, a group of young Indian political activists launched the All India Congress Socialist Party (CSP) in October 1934. Its leader was Jayaprakash Narayan and some of its leading lights were Minoo Masani, Yusuf Meherally, Asoka Mehta and Rammanohar Lohia. For the next five years Krishna Menon was very much a part of this group. He wrote regularly for its publication, *Congress Socialist,* arranged for articles to be written for it by notable British personalities, managed its distribution and became its publicist in the UK. He carried on an extensive correspondence with some of its members. In fact, during 1935–40, aside from Nehru, Krishna Menon seems to have written most frequently to Masani. Their correspondence was warm, chatty, full of mutual leg-pulling and, of course, also contained serious observations on the prevailing situation in India and elsewhere. On 13 April 1934, he wrote to Masani:

. . . It [the formation of the CSP] is the best piece of news that I have had from India for a long time . . . You must be prepared to be left without any co-operation from Labour people at this end if you are collaborating with the C.P. [Communist Party] or the I.L.P.[Independent Labour Party]. As you probably know the

I.L.P. are now in alliance with the C.P. though they quarrel about everything . . . I do not pretend to tell you what is good for you but if you want effective sympathy from the bulk of the Labour movement it is necessary that the group you are forming at present is not tied up to the 3rd or the two and a half international or to the dozens of auxiliary and little camouflaged organisations of the C.P. My own position is that while I am a left-wing socialist, a believer in the almost immediate establishment of a socialist equalitarian society I have little use for the C.P. here or in India. I have personal friends among them and some good ones but my metaphysics and politics and economics lead me in a different direction.

I am prepared to act in your interests here and when the time comes to work it into the India League if you require it. I think I shall be able to get a little committee or at any rate a contact group with men like Laski and so on . . .

A month later on 15 May 1934, Krishna Menon informed Masani that he 'would like to join the Congress socialist group as an overseas member'. He also told him:

You may be interested to know that I have managed to get a resolution on the agenda of the socialist league conference committing a future socialist government to the calling of a constituent assembly . . . The India League has drafted (Prof Laski and myself) a memorandum on the constituent assembly and it is signed by influential people . . . I think our work on this so far has been useful . . .

By the way I understand that you are editing or have a great deal to do with a new paper in Bombay. Would it be too much to ask if you could arrange to let me have the London work for it? I can promise you a good service but I will not manufacture news. I hate having to ask you for this as I know you will be embarrassed if you have to refuse . . .

. . . It is not necessary to affiliate with the Labour party or be under its thumb, but if you want to be effective at all so far as informing the working class it is necessary that your representative

should have access to the labour movement and not be in opposition
to it . . .

> There is a lot I want to write to you about but unless I have
some evidence that you receive the letters and are prepared to reply
to them it is little use!

This letter reveals how desperate Krishna Menon was throughout the
1930s to pick up writing assignments for Indian newspapers. It was
a way of providing news to a larger audience in India on events in
England but more importantly, it was a means of earning some money
mostly for ploughing back into the India League. His archive is full of
such entreaties to various national and regional publications.

His success rate was pretty good, and at one point of time in the late
1930s, he was writing 'London Letters', some under his name and some
without his byline, in about a dozen Indian newspapers and magazines.
When his name was better known, he would be approached by editors
themselves. On 1 March 1938, for instance, Damodara Menon, editor
of the Malayalam newspaper *Mathrubhumi,* wrote to him:

> I am writing this letter in the hope that you will be persuaded to
be our London correspondent. We wish to publish regularly . . . It
would be best if you could write in Malayalam.
>
> Please respond to a call from Malabar which has a special claim
on you.

Obviously Damodara Menon was unaware of his fellow Menon's
dark secret. Krishna Menon replied nineteen days later:

> I have to disappoint you about writing in Malayalam. I cannot do
it for toffee. It means that if you have me you will have to translate
and do the best you can.

Not only was Krishna Menon unable to write in Malayalam but he
could not also speak the language comfortably. However, he would
write regularly for *Mathrubhumi* for many years as he would for many
other newspapers.

The CSP was taking shape but Gandhi had yet to be convinced. He liked the youngsters but was hesitant of their formal association with the Congress. Against this background, Masani told Krishna Menon on 4 June 1934:

> . . . I accompanied Mahatmaji on his walking tour in Orissa having accepted his invitation to discuss our Socialist Programme . . . He is definitely not a Socialist but on the other hand he feels well inclined towards me . . . He agrees that we have a place within the Congress as an organized left attempting to convert the Congress to our point of view . . .

The CSP formally came into being in late October 1934 in Bombay, and soon thereafter on 11 November 1934, its general secretary, Jayaprakash Narayan, wrote to Krishna Menon:

> I wrote you a letter some days back and sent you a typed copy of our Constitution, Programme and Resolutions.
> . . . Nor do we think there is any point in opening a branch of the Party in England or, for that matter, anywhere outside India. We, however, appreciate your suggestion regarding the advisability of setting up a propaganda committee there . . .
> I do not wish that you should deliberately exclude the communists. If you can ensure the cooperation of some of the better types, I would rather welcome it.

Two days later, Narayan wrote to Krishna Menon and Miss M.R. Masani, a student then in the UK:

> . . . I am glad to be able to appoint you Provisional Secretaries of the [Congress Socialist] Party's Propaganda Committee in Britain . . . The Party's work lies in India alone and all that friends abroad can do is secure support and sympathy for our cause. The proposed Propaganda Committee will, I trust, be able to do so . . .

Miss M.R. Masani was Mehra Masani, Minoo Masani's sister, who would also work closely with Krishna Menon but not without

the inevitable friction. Asoka Mehta was forced to placate Krishna
Menon on 13 March 1936:

> . . . About articles [for *Congress Socialist*] you are in <u>sole </u>charge of
> getting them. I wrote to Miss Masani to get Laski's article. Anyway
> in future you are in sole charge of getting articles and please do so
> urgently . . .

In 1937, Mehra Masani returned to India, which made Krishna
Menon the sole representative of the CSP in London. She would
go on, after India's Independence, to have a noted career in radio
broadcasting. Krishna Menon would recruit India-born Betty
Shields-Collins, secretary of the World Youth Congress Movement
and a well-known figure in leftist circles, to work with him on affairs
relating to the CSP. She would, after 1947, as Elizabeth Katherine
Collard, become very active on issues relating to the Middle East and
continue her association with the India League.

Krishna Menon would maintain intermittent contact with
Jayaprakash Narayan but he was always conscious of the fact that 'JP'
was the leader of the socialist group, who enjoyed a warm rapport
with both Gandhi and Nehru. On 17 April 1939, concerned with
'Gandhiji's failing health and his possible demise in the near future'
and with 'Gandhiji's increasing fear that the Congress has become
ethically rotten' and with the 'changing world situation', Krishna
Menon would make an impassioned plea to Narayan for 'unity of
proletarian forces'. He wanted the progressive forces to strengthen
Nehru's hands unconditionally and called for a radical reorganization
of the Congress structure, which he wanted the socialist stalwart to
put forward as his own idea and champion:

> . . . You are the key person in this situation and if it is put forward
> not as a C.S.P proposal, but as one either by yourself or some
> other suitable person, if there is one such available it should be
> carried . . . I have written on this as the situation is desperately
> serious. War is no longer a remote possibility. It may be that, by
> the processes of Munich again or otherwise by imperialist bargains,

respite may be gained, but there can be no settling down for the fascist governments. By their nature they cannot settle down . . .

Nothing was to come of this somewhat quixotic initiative. In any case, the reports of Gandhi's impending demise turned out to be highly exaggerated.

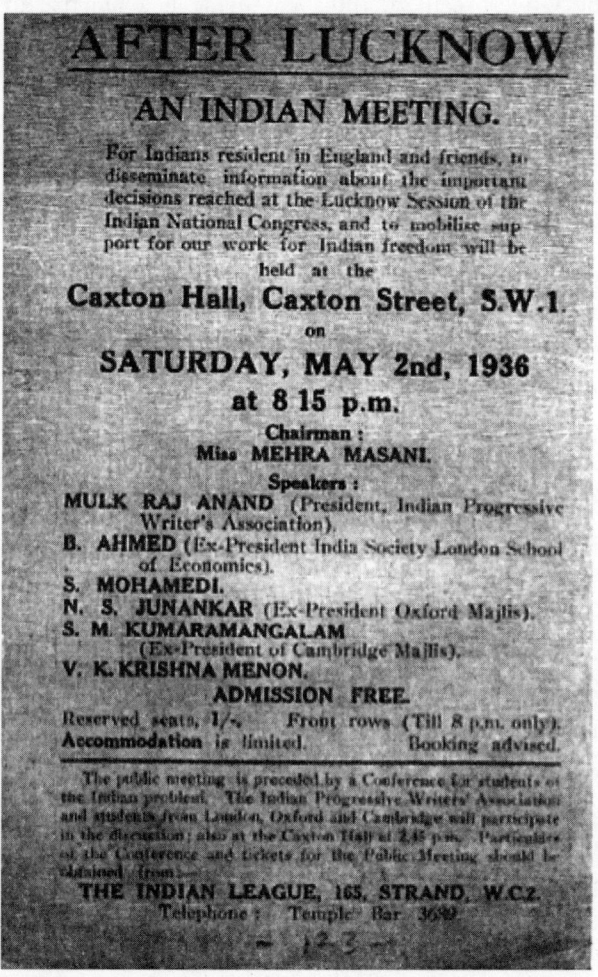

India League poster, London, 1936

Masani spent almost six months, beginning June 1935, travelling in Europe and Russia. But as soon as he landed in London, he ran into problems as his passport was impounded. Krishna Menon was outraged and immediately approached Lansbury:

> Mr. Masani belongs to the Congress Socialist Party and is not a communist or a member of a terrorist or any other illegal organization . . .
>
> The Government of India has made it a practice to refuse passports to socialists who wish to come outside India for any purpose. Also as I explained to you some time ago, legitimate registered trade unions have come under the hostile attentions of the Government.
>
> I am sending you the enclosed correspondence in the hope that you will take this matter up as it is a gross infringement of the movement of individual British citizens, an attempt of the Government of India to direct the policy of the Foreign Office and also prevent the world and even the British Labour Party knowing anything about the socialist advance in India . . .

He also took up Masani's case with Clement Attlee, who would later take over as the leader of the Labour Party and sent out missives to a couple of newspapers, saying:

> [T]o call every liberal radical and every socialist a communist is a trick of the party that rarely does much harm. It is a grave matter, however, when a Government resorts to it . . . . Communist has become in India a name for any opinions that the bureaucracy dislikes . . .

Masani's passport was to be restored but would be impounded yet again a year later, this time in Bombay. Krishna Menon swung into action once more, petitioning British MPs and the media on behalf of his CSP friend.

Krishna Menon, who in the 1950s was to be accused by Masani of being a communist, made his first visit to Moscow only in 1970 or 1971. But Masani was already in Moscow in September 1935 and wrote to Krishna Menon from there:

Hotel Savoy
Moscow
11/9/1935

Dear Krishna:

. . . I am writing to Meherally today direct by air and should write
again on arriving in London on the 15th. In the meantime you
might send the following cable from London in my name

Meherally
Congress House
Bombay

Understand United Press opening office London . . . suggest
Krishna Menon Secretary India League as correspondent. Strongly
recommend him.
I hope you are better and will be really well when I see you next
week.

Although bedridden and in hospital, Krishna Menon put together
Masani's speaking and meeting schedule in the UK. Masani was
extremely gratified at the arrangements that had been made for
him, and on his return to Bombay, thanked Krishna Menon on
29 November 1935:

> . . . I enclose a press cutting of the interview given by me on my
> arrival. I am sure you will agree with me that I have not forgotten
> the India League and its Secretary . . .

The press cutting that Masani was referring to was from the
22 November 1935 issue of the nationalist daily *Bombay Chronicle,*
which carried these headlines on page one:

**Labour Cannot Help
India**

**BUT HEART OF BRITISH
WORKER IS SOUND**

**Mr. Masani On His Tour
Impressions**

Tribute to India League

Among the political groups which have Indian sympathies Mr.
Masani mentions the India League (with its Secretary Mr. Krishna
Menon) which has got the most political contacts and which has
been helping the Indian cause in England with a singleness of
purpose for several years.

Soviet Achievement

Referring to the impressions of his Russian tour, Mr. Masani said
he found tremendous progress there since his last visit in 1927 and
he said he was struck with the marvellous results achieved through
the Soviet policy of dealing with 'National' and 'Communal'
problems.

When questioned by the reporter about the value of foreign
propaganda, Masani replied:

. . . At present there are several organisations such as the India
League of which Lord (Bertrand) Russell is President, D.R.
Grenfell, M.P., is Chairman and Mr. V.K. Krishna Menon is
Secretary, the Friends of India, the India Conciliation Group,
with Agatha Harrison as Secretary and League against Imperialism.
Without making any invidious distinctions, I would like to say
that I found the India League has got the most political contacts
and has been able to do more than any other group. Mr. Krishna

Menon has given the last five years of his life to helping the Indian cause in England with a singleness of purpose in that uphill and discouraging task which has evoked the admiration of many people in that country.

On 2 December 1935, Masani contacted Krishna Menon frantically, reflective of how central the latter had become in the CSP's scheme of things:

> . . . This is a SOS asking you to send the London Letter for the 'Congress Socialist' which resumes publication definitely on 21st December. The date has been put back a week specially so that your letter may be there from the very first issue.
> Now please buck up and don't disappoint me. It need not be very long. But something from you there must be every week.
> Cheerio—Hope you are well.

And a few days later, on 13 December 1935, went yet another message from Masani reflecting the informality of the relationship that had been so quickly established between the two:

> . . . I wish I knew your address. There is no guarantee that any letter addressed to 165 Strand [where India League was located] will reach your hands if the state of your office is the same as when I left! I hope your health is better and you are up doing with your usual energy . . .

Masani also promised that he would speak to his father and another Bombay philanthropist J.B. Petit about securing financial support for the India League. On 10 January 1936, Masani wrote again:

> . . . So sorry to read of your ill-health. You really are having a hard time. But then, 'if winter comes, can spring be far behind?'. So cheer up.

Five months later on 2 May 1936, Masani was to pay another tribute to his friend in London, who was evidently in need of constant reassurance:

> Before dealing with the points in your letters, I would like to say this—we at this end consider ourselves under a debt of gratitude to you for whatever you have been able to do for the Party in London single-handed and without any support from here. Also your London letters for the Congress Socialist are being much appreciated and have been appearing regularly . . .

Just two days afterwards, Yusuf Meherally wrote the first of his several 'Dear Comrade Menon' letters:

> . . . Masani has spoken to me so often about you that I scarcely feel that I am writing to a stranger . . .

Krishna Menon reciprocated Meherally's sentiments on 14 May 1936 saying:

> . . . I was very pleased to receive your letter dated 4th May. I have heard a great deal about you but have never had the opportunity of direct correspondence. I do not feel in any way that I have received a letter from a stranger.

After Nehru had taken over as Congress president, Meherally would write to Krishna Menon on 25 May 1936, conveying the views of his CSP colleagues as well:

> . . . Jawaharlal has been doing exceedingly well after his return to India. At Lucknow he was a pillar of strength to us and during his Bombay visit also he has been of great assistance. In fact, he has taken Bombay by storm; and has electrified the otherwise placid political atmosphere in this City. The most interesting development was that Big Business getting alarmed at his Socialist propaganda denounced his activities in a public statement . . .

The statement of the twenty-one businessmen has aroused great controversy and over a dozen leading merchants' associations have already dissociated themselves from them and voted addresses to Jawaharlal. Such an extraordinary and spontaneous demonstration for Jawaharlal is an eye-opener even to the Right Wing in the Congress.

The CSP was then solidly with Nehru. But within five years, Masani had joined the world of Indian business, which had been very critical of Nehru. Others in the CSP began to feel that Nehru was not 'left' enough for them, while the 'right' in the Congress was firmly convinced that he was leading the party in undesirable leftist directions. Meherally was to come up with the immortal 'Quit India' slogan to describe Gandhi's last mass campaign against the British rule in August 1942.

Asoka Mehta would, three decades later, become a 'right-wing' adviser of Indira Gandhi when she became Prime Minister in January 1966. He was one of the few ministers in her cabinet who aggressively supported the devaluation of the rupee in June 1966, which was to prove politically disastrous for her and the Congress party. But in the 1930s, he was editor of the *Congress Socialist* and in regular touch with Krishna Menon, whose letters would very often be typed 'Dear Metha'. Mehta would badger Krishna Menon for contributions for the *Congress Socialist* from well-known British intellectuals. Krishna Menon almost always delivered but there was a particularly lean period as this letter from him to Mehta of 29 December 1936 shows:

Miss Masani did write and inform me about getting contributions for the *Congress Socialist*. However, as you are probably aware there has been a crisis in this country which has threatened the most cherished traditions of the British people and all our politicians have been thinking about nothing else but the matrimonial affairs of the monarch! How could I get articles or anything else for you when grown-up people give themselves up to kind of mass madness in this way! . . .

I understand that the national convention of Congress representatives to the legislatures will be held. I hope your party will do some thinking and if I may say so strengthen the forces of discipline and insistent advance. This is one of the best things that have happened and the Congress Socialist Party will make a great mistake if it treats this matter like an ordinary conference.

Krishna Menon was referring to the situation created by the abdication of King Edward VIII.

A few weeks earlier he, along with Kamaladevi Chattopadhyay and Mehra Masani, had been nominated to represent the CSP at the International Congress against War, Fascism and Imperialism, which was being held in Glasgow. In the following years, he was to juggle both Nehru and the CSP but by the end of 1939, his break with the CSP and identification with Nehru would be complete. There was an element of ideology involved undoubtedly but we cannot overlook the fact that Nehru by then was being seen as Gandhi's successor and Krishna Menon, more than anybody else, would have been acutely aware of this. Therefore, the element of personal ambition in Krishna Menon hitching his star to Nehru's wagon cannot be discounted at all.

Almost fifty years later, Kamaladevi Chattopadhyay, one of the leading lights of the CSP, was to write in her memoirs:[1]

. . . Though he remained a controversial personality all his life, he [Krishna Menon] was an unforgettable personality. The India League which he headed and ran from the late Twenties, was more than a mini Indian Embassy, for the prestige it enjoyed and the confidence it won. It kept India before the British with clarity, force and insistence reflecting Krishna Menon's own devotion and sincere adherence to the cause of India's freedom. His fearless advocacy often carried the day for India. There was also a soft and kindly side to his nature although he brusquely tried to cover it up.

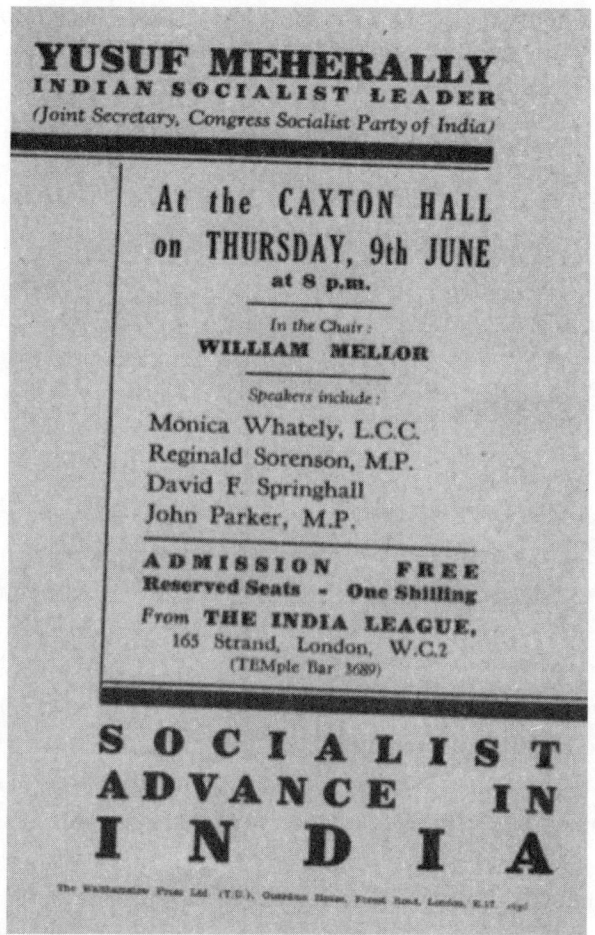

India League poster, 1938

Notes

1. Chattopadhyay (2014).

6

Enter Jawaharlal Nehru (1935)

The year 1935 was to be a watershed year for Krishna Menon. He continued to be an active propagandist for Indian freedom across the UK and organized numerous protest meetings to highlight the oppressive policies of the British administration in India. These were all well attended. As he had been doing for over seven years, he travelled to different towns and cities and spoke to all sorts of groups. He made an impact as this recollection of Reginald Sorensen, who became the India League's parliamentary secretary, reveals:[1]

> I will tell you how I came into the India League. I was once a minister of a Unitarian Church for twenty-five years and every Wednesday during the winter months we had a small literary guild where we discussed all sorts of subjects. An old lady used to distribute leaflets on vaccination, vivisection and other matters. One day she gave me a grubby leaflet about India. I looked at this leaflet of the India League and asked the India League to send us a speaker. The Secretary said, 'Yes I will come myself'. It was Krishna Menon who came, and subsequently he asked, 'Why don't you come and help us in the India League'.

Krishna Menon instigated questions on India in the House of Commons, through MPs such as Sorensen, and bombarded various

dailies with news on India. Two India League posters of those early
months of 1935 tell their own story.

Krishna Menon at a Labour Party meeting, 1935

A PUBLIC MEETING ————

TO PROTEST

AGAINST THE

INDIAN POLICY

OF THE GOVERNMENT

will be held

ON SATURDAY, MARCH 16th, 1935, AT 7 p.m.

At the

MEMORIAL HALL

Farringdon Street, London, E.C.
(Near Ludgate Circus)

Speakers:

MAURICE BROWNE
(the well known theatrical producer who has recently come back after a year's stay in India)

J. F. HORRABIN
(formerly Member of Parliament for Peterborough)

PROFESSOR HAROLD J. LASKI

DR. MAUDE ROYDEN
(recently returned from India)

MISS MONICA WHATELY
(Labour Parliamentary Candidate for Clapham who went to India in 1932 as a member of the India League Delegation)

V. K. KRISHNA MENON,
(Hon. Joint Secretary, The India League)

ADMISSION FREE.

**Reserved Seats, Front Rows, One Shilling
Platform, Two Shillings and Six Pence**
On application.

The India League, 165, Strand, London, W.C.2.

India League protest meeting, 1935

But June 1935 was to be traumatic for Krishna Menon. He lost his father and at about the same time his relationship with the woman he had hoped to marry ended. Barbara Macnamara had been working with Krishna Menon since 1930, first at the Commonwealth of India League and thereafter at the India League. She had studied at the LSE. In August 1932 when Krishna Menon was on his way to India, she had written to him:

> Your letter has just come from Port Said. I want so badly to answer it but daren't. It was so wonderful to get it. It comforts me to be able to talk to you and now and then have the answers before me . . . please let me do this. . . . There is so much I want to say and tell you and talk about. I feel like bursting sometimes and don't know how to wait and face everyone with composure . . . I am trying hard to look after myself for you, so that I may be all that you would like . . . I want to get to know your sister and father— one day I will I know but I want to know . . . It's awful to think that I can't possibly get another letter till September . . . I am going now to see the Registrar at the University College about your re-entry forms . . . I sometimes wish I could enter into that part of your life, but I obviously can't, not yet—one day perhaps.

There seems little doubt that Macnamara was besotted with him. Unfortunately, his letters to her seem not to have survived. For whatever reason, Krishna Menon never got around to asking her to marry him. Tired of waiting, Macnamara decided to part ways and married someone else. The combination of his father's death and her decision had a deep impact on an already over-worked Krishna Menon. He was admitted to the Princess Beatrice Hospital sometime in mid-July 1935 with a combination of illnesses, psychological as well as physical, caused by gnawing arthritis and acute back pain. The drugging would cause a severe loss of appetite. Soon thereafter on 18 July 1935, Macnamara wrote to Krishna Menon's niece Madhavi:

> . . . Yes, Krishna Menon has been ill but I do not think you have need to worry unduly now, as I understand he is very much better.

Unfortunately before he was taken ill, I had to go to hospital with tuberculosis and was unable to see him for some time. However, I was in constant touch with his doctor, who is a first-class man and thoroughly capable & whom Krishna Menon likes: and he told me before I left London that he was then over the worst and in fact he seemed certain of a good recovery.

It appears that he had been overworking and not taking good care of himself and had a good deal of worry of one kind or another, and the combined result of which was a nervous breakdown and a weak general condition . . . I know it is most distressing for you to hear this news but I expect you realize how hard your uncle worked, and in many ways this illness is perhaps a blessing in disguise, as it ensures a rest for some time in bed and he is in excellent hands. Please ask your mother not to worry unduly . . .

The letter makes clear that Krishna Menon's family knew about Macnamara and kept in touch with her. Her final letter to him was on 16 September 1935:

. . . I should naturally have been ready to come if necessary and if I felt any good could be done to either of us. But however much it hurts to hear it I feel I should say honestly that I do not think it is any use going on as we are now. I am afraid it is only prolonging the agony for both; I feel that it is hopeless and I want to end an unhappy and unsatisfactory position. There is no use writing at length or saying much of what one feels, or what a step like this costs me, but I am afraid I should not be happy with you, and consequently could not make you happy. There is a chance of my being happy elsewhere; I am going to take that chance. I have thought and worried over the situation ever since it first arose and particularly since I have had a chance to think while down here. The only possible way I think is to cut off and both try to start afresh. I know what you will say as far as you are concerned but I can only ask you to remember the past and give me a chance to be happy without making it too difficult . . . Please forgive me for not having made a success of what I wanted more than anything else to make a success of, and for all the pain I have caused and am causing you.

Macnamara disappeared from his life completely but resurfaced briefly again fifteen years later in January 1950, happily married and 'glad of the chance to renew old friendships'. While there were a number of young women who would replace her as far as the India League's activities were concerned, none became an integral part of Krishna Menon's personal life on any sustained and meaningful basis. That was to change in 1938 when Anna Pollak joined the India League as a volunteer and soon established a deep emotional relationship with Krishna Menon.

In a letter to one of Krishna Menon's biographers on 7 May 1992, Pollak wistfully recalled the past, capturing the prevailing atmosphere in the India League:[2]

. . . She [Barbara Macnamara] was just a name to me when I first met Krishna but I gathered he had had a special relationship with her but was pipped to the post by a rival. He did, I think, in those days find certain English women attractive and probably longed for a share of distraction and warmth but I also think his temperament (inhibition?), obsessive pilgrimage [addiction to work] and arduous workload would never have allowed him to be tied down in a conventional way . . . I believe my long and rewarding friendship with him persisted because I was not feminine enough to make trivial demands and, in any case, had my own career to build and living to earn! You see, Krishna was totally dependent on so-called voluntary workers. He couldn't afford paid staff and he no doubt sensed at once whom he could or could not trust. We were a mixed bunch of idealistic young women, ready to type, file (K called it pickling), clean and run errands; all had other paid jobs and interests but all were of course fascinated by Krishna's fervor, dynamism, and selfless compulsion despite the long hours and many discomforts (cold, heat, interruptions for tea, tea and tea; journeys home with bombs falling, etc.etc.).

Clearly the India League was a one-man, many-women army. Pollak was not the only one of Krishna Menon's female friends and colleagues to become aware of his special relationship with Barbara Macnamara. Sybil Dickson worked in the Commonwealth of India League in late 1930 and kept a diary. Her entry for 17 October 1930 reads:

> Menon in just before lunch looking very ill and as cross as a bear. I am sure he works so intensely and spends too much mental energy on his work. The poor dear is too willful to listen to reason on so insignificant a subject.

She writes on 4 December 1930:

> I was late. Saw this McNamara girl. How now what is all this. VKK dictated letter to her in longhand.

And the very next day:

> Pretty McNamara, impressive. Things won't be the same again. I am jealous.

It was the visit of Jawaharlal Nehru to London in October–November 1935 at the invitation of Horace Alexander and Agatha Harrison that pulled Krishna Menon out of his sickbed, even though he seemed to have not recovered completely. Nehru wrote to Krishna Menon on 18 October 1935 from Badenweiler in Germany, where his wife, Kamala Nehru, was undergoing treatment for tuberculosis:

> Dear Mr. Menon:

> I hesitate to give you trouble while you are still in hospital but as you were good enough to invite it, I have overcome my hesitation. I have now definitely (subject of course to unforeseen developments in my wife's condition) decided to leave for England

with my daughter on October 28th . . . We shall travel by rail and reach London (Victoria) at 16.20 on the 29th.

I wrote to Masani some time back and asked him to fix up rooms for me, if possible, at Mount Royal near Marble Arch. But he appears to be touring and may not get my letter for a long time. May I therefore request you to get this done? . . .

I propose to spend in all about 8 or 9 days in England. During this period I should like to visit Oxford (perhaps for 2 days if I can manage it) and Birmingham for a day, where I have promised a visit to Horace Alexander. If possible I should like to go to Cambridge also but I am not very keen on this . . .

. . . I should also like to meet Prof Laski and Ellen Wilkinson, and if possible Stafford Cripps. If you want me to meet any worthwhile newspapermen or others I would gladly do so . . .

Could you kindly drop me a line, or better still a telegram, to say that arrangements have been made for our stay and mentioning the place? I could then communicate to others.

Yours sincerely,
Jawaharlal Nehru

This was the handwritten letter that could be said to have transformed the lives of both men. Krishna Menon's original letter to which this was Nehru's response is not available but there is a reference to it in Masani's memoirs:[3]

Sometime during the summer of 1935, on Jawaharlal's invitation I joined him in Badenweiler, a health resort in Germany, where his wife was slowly dying of tuberculosis . . . I remember one morning at breakfast Jawaharlal threw a letter across to me and asked: 'Who is this Krishna Menon? What do you think of him?' In the letter, Krishna said that he could, with the collaboration of Victor Gollancz of the Left Book Club, arrange meetings for Jawaharlal who was to visit England later that year. I told Jawaharlal about Krishna's hunger strike and the low state of his morale and said that it would revive him greatly if Jawaharlal was to extend to him his patronage. Jawaharlal said: 'In that case, I shall do so' . . .

This may well have been an embellished account by Masani four decades after the event and after he and Krishna Menon had fallen out. It is certainly odd that Nehru should express ignorance about Krishna Menon because he had, in fact, written to him two years earlier on 21 December 1933:

> I have been laying stress on calling a constituent assembly elected under adult or near adult franchise. I think this is the only feasible solution of the political problem as well as the communal problem. Gandhiji also accepted this proposal. You ask for a declaration of Congress opinion on the subject but you must remember that under existing circumstances no official declaration on behalf of the Congress can be made as no Congress committee can even meet. I am sure there will be no difficulty on our side in cooperating with any group in England on the basis of self-determination by means of a constituent assembly.

Thereafter, the two had written to each other in 1934 on the repression in Bengal. So, contrary to Masani's recollections, Nehru was certainly not unaware of who Krishna Menon was when he and Masani were having breakfast.

On 29 October 1935, Nehru reached Victoria Station in London to be welcomed by a huge crowd that included Bertrand Russell, Ellen Wilkinson, Horace Alexander, Agatha Harrison and Krishna Menon. He was in London only for about ten days. By the standards of his later visits in 1936 and 1938, this trip was very low-key, relaxed and almost wholly private. Nehru's most authoritative biographer wrote of this visit:[4]

> . . . The most lasting impression on Jawaharlal was made not by any Englishman but by Krishna Menon, whom he then met for the first time . . .

On 15 November 1935, a day after he had turned forty-six, Nehru wrote to Krishna Menon after returning to Badenweiler:

My dear Menon:

. . . My visit to England tired and exhausted me . . . At the same time I found it rather stimulating also. It was my first experience of activity after two years of seclusion and I always find this exhilarating. I met many people who interested me—and, alas, many more who did not. I am not in the habit of hurling complimentary epithets at people, but you will understand me when I tell you it was a delight for me to come in personal touch with you. I would have been very much at sea without you to turn to in London and I am very grateful to you for all the trouble you took over me in spite of your ill health. Do get well soon.

Your wonderful grapes have been greatly appreciated here and my wife took to them immediately. She wants me to thank you for them . . .

Letters from India tell a woeful tale and ask me when I shall return as if I would make much difference. But the call from India grows and I feel it in my bones and some day or other it will be too strong to resist.

Again I must repeat—get well soon.

Yours sincerely,
Jawaharlal.

'My dear Krishna Menon' had become 'My dear Menon'. Four days later, Nehru wrote a long letter to the president of the Indian National Congress, Rajendra Prasad, in which he reported on his visit to London and said:

. . . In London I met with members of various India groups individually and severally. You know about them. There is the [India] Conciliation Group (Carl Heath and Agatha Harrison, etc). They are good people, mostly Quakers, who believe in bringing about contacts between prominent Indians and men in authority . . . I like these people, but I must say that I do not attach much importance to this trend of work . . .

Then there is the Friends of India Group. Also good and doing useful work in publicity, but generally ineffective. There are no outstanding personalities among them . . .

A third group is the 'India League'. This has become connected with the left-wing of Labour and has some prominent men in it, like Harold Laski. Because of this it is definitely socialistic in outlook. Of the three it is the only really political organization. The man who runs it is V.K. Krishna Menon whom you perhaps know. I met him for the first time. He is very able and energetic and is highly thought of in intellectual, journalistic and left-wing Labour circles. He has the virtues and failings of the intellectual. I was very favourably impressed with him. Unfortunately he has been very ill and has spent the last six months in the hospital.

This interaction between the two was to be the beginning of an unusually intimate relationship, with Krishna Menon becoming an integral part of Nehru's family. Krishna Menon must have indeed genuinely impressed Nehru, for the latter was to write again on 20 November 1935. This time it was a 'Dear Krishna' letter:

. . . A young friend and colleague of mine from my native city of Allahabad will soon be in London, if he has not already arrived. His name is Feroze Gandhi. He is not in anyway related to the Mahatma. He is a Parsi. He is a bright lad, about 22 years old, who threw up his studies in 1930 during the civil disobedience movement and has been in prison several times. He did very good work for us and showed unusual enterprise and ability in organizing work . . .

He is now going to England with rather vague ideas about continuing his education in the LSE or the London University.

His old school and college people in India have refused to give him any certificate or commendation because of his political misdeeds . . .

I am greatly interested in this boy not only because he has been very loyal and brave colleague and the one who has helped me in many ways, but also because I think that he has the makings of a worthwhile person in him . . . I would be very grateful to you if you could help him. How could you do so, I do not know. You can decide for yourself after you see him and have a talk with him. I am writing to him to visit you.

I hope you are improving and not rushing about too much.

Krishna Menon did meet Feroze Gandhi as Nehru had wanted him to, and very soon, the young man got involved actively with the India League. He and Krishna Menon were to remain very close for the next twenty-five years, till Feroze Gandhi's untimely death in 1960.

Nehru was spending time in Badenweiler, completing what was to be his autobiography, which was to be called *In and Out of Prison*. He wrote to Krishna Menon on 9 December 1935:

I sent you this morning the remaining part of *In and Out of Prison*. This completes the work. I have hurriedly read through the manuscript and made a number of changes . . . No doubt there are many other errors which require correction, also possible alterations in other ways. I shall be glad if you will point them out to me . . .

. . . I would like the book to appear as early as possible. It has a certain political significance for India at present, but later on it may be a little stale, from this point of view at least.

The feeling has been growing upon me that I must go to India for the Congress—this is quite apart from the question of the presidentship [of the Congress]. I would from many points of view prefer not being president . . .

. . . I can visit England in the last week of January and for not much more than a week . . .

Drop the Pandit if you value my good opinion!

A few days later on 31 December 1935, Nehru wrote again to Krishna Menon on the matter of his autobiography and also spoke about his plans to visit London. He asked Krishna Menon to set up meetings with the groups agitating for India's freedom and with personal friends such as Aldous Huxley, C.F. Andrews, Ellen Wilkinson and others. He ended with another plea:

. . . I am grateful to you for having dropped the 'pandit'. Why not allow 'Mr' to go the same way? This ceremony in personal relations bores me.

Nehru had already published three books but all of them in India. The manuscript that he mentioned in his letter to Krishna Menon was to be his first to appear internationally. Krishna Menon was its editor and arranged for it to be published by John Lane The Bodley Head, finalizing the agreement in all its details with the publisher. He made a number of useful suggestions for improving the manuscript but his most important contribution was to change its title. On 19 February 1936, Lindsay Drummond, one of the directors of John Lane The Bodley Head, wrote to Krishna Menon:

. . . I wonder if you have been able to think more of the title of the book . . . I personally feel that just NEHRU'S AUTOBIOGRAPHY is probably the most suitable title . . .

The next thing we know is that Krishna Menon cabled Nehru, who was then in Montreux in Switzerland on 4 March 1936:

Present title unsuitable. Consensus of opinion in favour of Jawaharlal Nehru An Autobiography . . . Please cable.

The next day came a telegram from Nehru:

HAVE IT YOUR OWN WAY

Nehru's autobiography announcement, 1936

Curiously, Krishna Menon is thanked nowhere in Nehru's autobiography but there is one passing mention of him:

> At the Southport Labour Party Conference in October 1934, a resolution was submitted by Mr. V.K Krishna Menon 'expressing the conviction that it is imperative that the principle of self-determination for the establishment of full self-government for India should be implemented forthwith'.

Actually, Krishna Menon had succeeded in having resolutions on self-determination for India moved in two other similar conferences as well—at Leicester in September 1932, with Harold Laski and Stafford Cripps taking the lead; and at Hastings in October 1933, where George Lansbury himself took up the cudgels on India's behalf.

Life would now never be the same for the thirty-nine-year-old Krishna Menon. So far he had been a student, agitator, pamphleteer, propagandist, public speaker, editor, lawyer, councillor but more or less on his own and without any significant support from Indian political leaders. He had developed excellent contacts in the British Labour Party and in British literary and cultural circles. He was well known as an indefatigable crusader who kept the flag of India flying. The next thirty-nine years of his life would be dramatically different. He would soon become Nehru's closest confidant, publicist and envoy and, thereafter, become a famous world figure. Annie Besant had 'discovered him' sometime in 1917 or 1918. Laski had mentored him in the late 1920s and 1930s. Nehru would now become his patron saint for almost three decades.

Notes

1. Reginald W. Sorensen, Oral History Archives, Nehru Memorial Museum and Library.
2. Chakravarty (2006).
3. Masani (1977).
4. Gopal (1975).

7

Nehru's Man in London (1936–38)

1936

The previous year Nehru had been in touch with two of his good friends, both British, about publishing his autobiography. These were the Anglican missionary C.F. Andrews and the historian Edward Thompson. But after he met Krishna Menon, he realized he had found the man he had been looking for. As he told his sister, Vijaya Lakshmi Pandit, on 5 January 1936:

> . . . I hope you have sent me Father's photographs. John Lane, the publisher, who is likely to bring out my book, is keen on having a number of pictures in it. I do not like this idea and I certainly object to my pictures appearing. I have told them that I can't be bothered with this but I have given your name to V.K. Krishna Menon (whom I have appointed my representative for publications, serialization, etc). Perhaps he may write to you.

Krishna Menon certainly did, and thus began a close friendship with another member of the Nehru family. After India's freedom that friendship became turbulent as both Vijay Lakshmi Pandit and Krishna Menon considered themselves competitors for Nehru's mind space. Nehru, for his part, accommodated both of them easily, even though their diplomatic styles were different—his sister was seen as pro-West and Krishna Menon was considered to be a West-baiter. But that was in the future. In the late 1930s and even in the 1940s, they shared a warm and affectionate relationship. On 8 February 1939 when the Gandhi–Subhas Bose struggle for supremacy in the Congress was at its peak, Mrs Pandit would write to Krishna Menon from Lucknow at midnight:

> I don't know why I am inflicting this letter on you except for the fact that I am terribly upset and disturbed and writing is always an outlet for one's feelings . . . I am sick and tired of the present state of affairs . . . we have reached a state of deadlock . . . I am leaving for Wardha tomorrow to see the old man [Gandhi]. I am going merely for the solace which the old man gives me . . .
>
> And what are you doing? If there is trouble in India you had better set to work harder than ever before to keep us in the English limelight . . .

Seven years later on 27 March 1946, writing from Allahabad when the transfer-of-power negotiations were taking place, she would tell Krishna Menon:

> . . . There is so much I would like to say to you but it must wait. I wish you would write to me once in a while . . . Bhai [Nehru] was due from Malaya this morning . . . He is greater than he has ever been—but entirely wasted and misunderstood in the context of the present political scheme. What a world.

Thereafter, however, their relationship began to sour. For his part, Krishna Menon always felt greater ideological and personal kinship with Nehru's daughter than with the older of Nehru's two sisters. He also could not have been unaware that the aunt–niece relationship itself was not without its tensions.

Nehru went back to London on 28 January 1936. The previous month he had written to Krishna Menon on 23 December 1935:

... I am glad you are occasionally modest. I would welcome even immodesty at times, for I suffer from it myself. I am quite sure that either you or the India League (acting through you) would make excellent and most efficient arrangements—far better than I could do. And hope that you will give me this help. You understand of course that I can have no personal objections to the India League as such taking charge of me. But considering all the circumstances I think it would be undesirable for me to appear under the auspices of a particular organization, however worthy it might be.

Nehru wanted Krishna Menon to help finalize his programme in London but did not want the India League to have anything to do with it officially, at least at the time. Krishna Menon replied first on 8 January 1936:

... Regarding your own programme (please forgive me for writing on India League letterhead on this business!!), the first item will be a Conference of European, American and British Press Representatives (not Reporters) on Friday night. The public reception of which I spoke, will be on Monday night and the programme is filling up.

I am consulting every interest concerned and I would like to feel that in this matter, I have your confidence. The Groups that are being arranged cover a wide variety of interests and I hope that this will meet with your approval . . . I do not think that there is anything further to write about . . .

... With regard to the public functions I have put the facts before you. We cannot afford to make a fiasco of it. I am not out of respect for your desire putting 'India League auspices'. But the notices of it must have some responsible imprints . . . It is impossible to put this function under joint and cooperative auspices as once I start doing that I shall be in difficulty about whom to let in or not . . .

Eleven days later, Krishna Menon asked Nehru for a power of attorney 'with regard to the Autobiography', explaining:

The letter of authorization I hold may not be good enough if things do not go off smoothly. I am sorry to give you this trouble . . .

He then went on to deal with a subject that would preoccupy both him and Nehru for the next two years and bring them even closer:

We have formed a Spain–India Committee here . . . I am acting as chairman and . . . have stated in very general terms that I am echoing your sentiments when I say every effort should be given to assist the Spanish people . . . We are endeavouring to raise enough money for an ambulance. It will of course be impossible unless we get some money from India . . .

As it turned out, Nehru's visit was meticulously put together by Krishna Menon. A young twenty-four-year-old woman, who was secretary to Hugh Dalton, then the Labour spokesman on foreign affairs, helped him in this task. Sheila Grant Duff, later to become a well-known journalist and author, wrote about this brief but impactful period of her life in her memoirs,[1] describing Krishna Menon thus:

A South Indian from Malabar, he looked as if he had stepped out of the tomb of Tutankhamun, saturnine, emaciated and limping heavily with a walking stick. But he had considerable presence and a fiery command over the numerous hangers-on, Indian and English and mostly from the London School of Economics, who thronged the drab and dingy premises of the India League in the Strand.

There was no shortage of suggestions. Horace Alexander wrote to Krishna Menon on 10 January 1936:

I have written to my friend Gerald Shove, an economics don at Kings, Cambridge asking if he could arrange for Jawaharlal Nehru to meet Keynes, Dennis Robertson and perhaps one or two others to talk over urgent problems of Indian economics and finance at Cambridge. Shove is a very good man, with a 'left-wing' mind and he will know just what is needed I think.

Nehru was to meet the greatest scientist of the twentieth century when he visited Einstein in Princeton in October 1949, but the prospect of meeting perhaps the greatest economist of the twentieth century unnerved him a bit, and he told Alexander a week later:

> . . . I have left the programme in Menon's hands—he can consult others. I would gladly meet the Cambridge economists but I must confess that the prospect of talking economics with this very learned crowd rather terrifies me.

The visit to Cambridge, however, never materialized. Krishna Menon spent three weeks drawing up Nehru's itinerary, speaking engagements and private appointments. It was a jam-packed schedule, and Krishna Menon drove himself crazy, along with the others planning it. A few days before Nehru arrived, Wilkinson sent Krishna Menon a note:

> Don't worry yourself into a nervous breakdown. Nehru is big enough and well-known enough to make success of any meeting, and if you have worn yourself into such a state that you are throwing fits all over the place it won't improve matters.

The crème de la crème of British public life was invited to meet Nehru and almost everybody accepted. Aldous Huxley was asked to speak at a public function scheduled for 27 January 1936 and sent this letter to Krishna Menon eight days earlier:

> I enclose a few lines for your welcome to JN. When speaking the other day on the telephone I had forgotten that I had an engagement on the 27th and shall probably not be back till late in the evening which will make it difficult for me to come to the meeting. So please do not count on me . . . In any case I hope to see JN at luncheon on either Tuesday or Thursday (28th & 30th) or at tea on Wednesday 29th.

Huxley's message meant to be read out by Krishna Menon at the public meeting was:

Exactly ten years ago at the beginning of 1926 I was at Cawnpore [Kanpur]. So were the delegates of the All India Congress. Through the kindness of Indian friends, my wife and I were allowed to attend their daily meetings.

One incident stands out in my memory with a special clarity; for it was symbolical, it had a general as well as a particular and local significance. Motilal Nehru had just concluded his principal speech and the applause was dying away, when a middle-aged man rose to his feet, and with agitated gestures, asked for a hearing. He spoke in a broken voice and tears were actually rolling down his cheeks as he explained in English, that he had come from some place far to the south of Madras, had travelled for I forget how many days and nights and spent more than a hundred and fifty rupees only to listen to his revered leader's statement of policy—and the revered leader had made his statement in Hindi, a language, of which he, a speaker of Tamil, did not understand a single word. The nights in the train, the rupees, the energy and enthusiasm—all had been wasted.

The episode, at once pathetic and comical, brought home to me in a most striking way the difficulties which beset the path of Indian nationalism. Diversity of language is only one, and that by no means, the most serious of the problems confronting those whose aim it is to make their country free and united. My respect for the men who have devoted themselves to the cause of Indian liberty and Indian unification is as great as their task is arduous. I am glad to have an opportunity of expressing this respect for one of the most ardent of them, one of the most single-minded, Jawaharlal Nehru.

Linguistic politics would rock India in the 1950s, and even today, language remains a highly emotive issue with zealots trying to make Hindi the single national language. As it turned out, because of the funeral of King George V, Nehru's public meeting was rescheduled and Huxley was, in fact, to speak at it.

With the death of King George V, Edward VIII took over as king on 20 January 1936. It speaks volumes of British intelligence and its sources that twenty-three days later Scotland Yard reported:

It has been gathered from what is considered quite a reliable source that NEHRU intimated a desire, while here, of seeing King Edward, with whom he was at Magdalen College, Oxford, and expressed admiration of His Majesty's personal qualities. Apparently, however, he did not make any endeavour to realize his wish to secure an audience with the King.

It is obvious that Scotland Yard's 'quite reliable source' had taken it for a right royal ride—Nehru had, in fact, studied at Trinity College, Cambridge. So much for Scotland Yard reports.

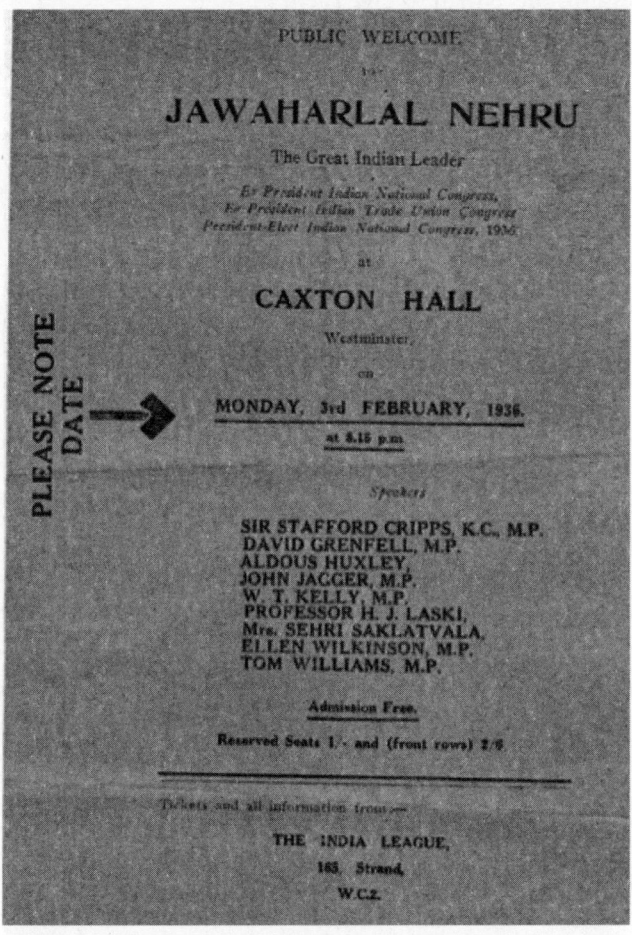

India League poster for Nehru's public meeting, London, 1936

Nehru himself described his hectic visit from Lausanne on
22 February 1936:

> . . . I was twelve days in London—twelve full days spent in
> meeting many people and groups, and much talk and argument
> and the answering of questions. I went with no particular object
> or intention. I sought nothing in particular except to meet people
> I wanted to see and to renew my acquaintance with various
> currents of thought. It was almost an educational visit for me, and
> though circumstances made me talk a great deal, I went to receive
> impressions more than to give them . . .

Nehru addressed the Labour Party and a cross-party group of
parliamentarians. He met with all organizations working for India's
freedom. He addressed four public functions, had numerous one-on-
one meetings with noted personalities from different walks of life and
gave interviews to a few publications. This visit and Krishna Menon's
role in it had been noticed everywhere, including by Masani, who
wrote to him on 3 February 1936:

> . . . I hope Jawaharlal's visit did your health more good . . .

It certainly had and was just the lifesaver Krishna Menon needed.
After returning to Lausanne, Nehru wrote to Krishna Menon on 8
February 1936:

> I have written to you about many matters but this evening I am writing
> just a few lines. I must thank you for the tremendous amount of trouble
> you took over fixing my programme. I feel guilty and unhappy to
> have become such a burden to you in your present state of health. I
> know you had done all this not so much because of me but for the
> sake of bigger things—and perhaps my visit was worthwhile after all.
> But what seems to me all wrong is for you to take such liberties with
> yourself. It does not pay. Look after yourself for a while at least.
>
> Also I want to convey my gratitude to all those bright young
> persons who helped us so much during the last fortnight. I was
> happy to find so much interest in India and her people among
> them. I hope it will endure.

Among other things, Nehru had also found time to sign the agreement with his publisher for the publication of his autobiography, for which Krishna Menon wrote this blurb:

> Jawaharlal Nehru is one of the greatest men of our times; the most dynamic figure of modern India. His influence and reputation extends far beyond the borders of his own country as his life and achievement have attracted the attention of the modern world . . . A great fighter of social justice, he does not compromise on points of principles; but even in the heat of the fight he enjoys the respect of his friends as well as his opponents . . .

Nehru's future son-in-law, Feroze Gandhi, had already become part of Krishna Menon's life in November 1935. Nehru's daughter would now follow suit. Krishna Menon wrote to her again on 23 March 1936:

> Dear Miss Nehru:
>
> A photograph of yours is to be published in your father's autobiography, but I am not sure of the exact form which you would like your name to take. The name on the back of the photograph is Indira Priyadarshina—should it be this, or Indira Nehru, or Indira Priyadarshina Nehru? Would you be so kind so as to let me have a card by return . . .

Indira Nehru was then in Bex in Switzerland, and she replied three days later:

> Dear Mr. Menon:
>
> I am not very particular about my name, although I do have a preference for 'Indira Priyadarshini'. I should like to point out, however, that the last letter of Priyadarshini is an 'i' and not an 'a'.
>
> Sincerely yours,
> Indira Nehru

With his knowledge of Sanskrit, it is perplexing that Krishna Menon didn't catch on that 'Priyadarshina' was obviously a mistake. Anyway, Nehru's daughter pointed it out and thus began a relationship that was to last thirty-eight years, with Indira Gandhi visiting Krishna Menon twice at his residence on the day he passed away, apart from being at his funeral.

On 11 July 1936, Indira wrote to her father from Badminton School at Bristol:

> . . . I had lunch with Krishna at a Chinese restaurant; he seems to be much better & certainly sounded more cheerful . . .

Five days earlier, she had apologized to Krishna Menon:

> Thank you so much for the delightful Chinese lunch. I thoroughly enjoyed myself. I am sorry I left you so abruptly in the middle of the road. I got mixed up with the numbers 11 and 39 and thought number 11 was a very infrequent bus . . .

It was while she was part of Krishna Menon's orbit in London along with Feroze Gandhi that Indira Nehru befriended the man who would become her most powerful aide during the first five and a half years of her prime ministership. P.N. Haksar would remain one of Krishna Menon's unabashed, but not uncritical, admirers for the next four decades.[2] Feroze Gandhi and his future wife too would remain devoted to Krishna Menon although, after India's war with China in October–November 1962, Indira Gandhi would maintain a political distance from him.

While he was in London, Nehru got news that he had been nominated to the post of Congress Party president, taking over from Rajendra Prasad. This was going to be the second time he would be wearing what Gandhi called a 'crown of thorns'. It would also be the tenure during which his relationship with Krishna Menon would deepen—personally and politically.

A few days after he had thanked Krishna Menon for making his London visit such a success, Nehru met with the ideologue of the Communist Party of Great Britain (CPGB), Rajni Palme Dutt, in Lausanne. Nehru's authoritative biographer called this a 'chance meeting' based on what Palme Dutt had told him.[3] But the evidence, as Palme Dutt's biographer later marshalled, leads to a completely different conclusion.[4] Palme Dutt actively sought out the meeting, using as cover the fact that one of his colleagues was a fellow patient at the sanitarium where Nehru's wife was also undergoing treatment. He sent a six-page report to Comintern (Communist International) on 19 February 1936:

> I had 16 hours talk with the Professor [Nehru] over two days . . .
>   . . . For the first few hours he wished to talk and ask questions on the general world situation . . . On this is only worth noting (1) strong interest in People's Front; (2) attitude to SU [Socialist Union] fairly close, in contrast to M [Masani], less affected by ILP [Independent Labour Party] notions, a little more relaxation in a liberal direction would be desirable, but on the whole a strong sense of common interest, and better understanding of foreign policy than M . . . ;(3) definite antagonism to fascism, and hostility to BO's [Subhas Chandra Bose's] fascist leanings; (4) in English questions looks most favourably to Laski and Cripps . . .

Nehru took over as Congress president in April 1936 at the Lucknow session of the Indian National Congress. Dutt's biographer has written that Nehru's presidential address reflected his long conversation with the British communist leader. It is, therefore, not surprising that soon after his speech Nehru was attacked as 'the leader of the Communistic school of thought in India'.

Rajni Palme Dutt was no stranger to Krishna Menon, who had been in frequent touch with him in 1935 so as to get him to write a book or two for John Lane. But their relationship deepened after Palme Dutt's meeting with Nehru. The former returned convinced that even though he was still under the influence of Gandhi and saw himself as essentially a 'centrist', Nehru had promised to 'support the proposal of trade union affiliation, support the inclusion of left elements and take a sympathetic attitude to the role and propaganda of our friends [communists] in the Congress'. Ever since it had been formed in 1925, the British communist party had been committed to Indian independence. But it is fair to say that after the Nehru–Palme Dutt conversations in Lausanne, the CPGB identified itself solidly with the Indian National Congress and saw it as the rallying platform for what it called 'anti-imperialist unity'. This would have profound consequences for Krishna Menon's relations with the CPGB. By 1939, Krishna Menon, who was no friend of the communists at the beginning of the decade, was being seen as a full-blown Red at worst and a 'crypto-communist' at best.

One of the first things Nehru did after becoming president of the Congress was to establish a foreign department of the party and put the CSP firebrand Rammanohar Lohia in charge of it. Lohia would become one of Nehru's (and Krishna Menon's) most vociferous critics in the sixties. But on 25 May 1936, Nehru told Krishna Menon:

> . . . We have formally started this department [foreign department of the Congress] and put it under the charge of Dr. R Lohia, a bright and earnest young man with a Berlin Ph.D. Inevitably we have to go slow to begin with as there is so much to be done. But I think we shall be able to do good work. We propose to develop contacts with all and sundry to begin with . . .
>
> Do you remember our talk about the publication of a series of small books dealing with Indian problems, chiefly economic? Is there any possibility of some such thing being done at your end?

Krishna Menon replied on 10 June 1936 that the India League was heartened by this development and added:

> We hope that it will be effective in the assistance of the work we have endeavoured to do with so little guidance in the past.

He and Lohia would continue to have an animated correspondence for the next three to four years. Nothing in this exchange of letters would indicate that the two would subsequently become politically estranged.

At that point such an outcome looked far-fetched. Excited by Nehru's assumption of the presidency of the Congress Party, Krishna Menon wrote in the June 1936 issue of the Labour Party's monthly, *Labour*:

Socialism Fills the Stage in Indian Politics

By V.K. Krishna Menon

A passage in Jawaharlal Nehru's address to the Indian Congress at Lucknow, in Easter Week, which summarises the very significant change that has come over the Indian scene:-

' . . . I see no way of ending the poverty, the vast unemployment, the degradation and subjugation of the Indian people except through Socialism. That involves vast and revolutionary changes in our political and social structure, the ending of vested interests in land and industry, as well as the feudal and aristocratic Indian States system [princely rule] . . . '

. . . The emancipation of the Indian masses in the terms now envisaged by Nehru with his colleagues is not just an Indian issue but a very decisive factor in the liquidation of imperialism and the establishment of Socialism and Peace. Here is a great opportunity; it is up to the Labour Movement to recognize the very vast and significant changes to which I have referred, to welcome the emergence of Socialism in India and seek to establish in alliance with it a newer relationship towards a more peaceful world order.

Krishna Menon was now riding two horses at the same time: While propagating the message of Nehru, he busied himself in the affairs of the CSP, telling Masani on 19 June 1936:

. . . I am at the moment trying to build up a machine for the socialist party of India [meaning CSP] without forming a branch or a policy committee . . . Things are shaping up well enough . . . It would be a good plan if you asked socialists in different parts of the country to write as it keeps one in touch with the feeling of the movement and personalities and enables one to speak more effectively about it . . .

I must congratulate you on your very good work. I hope you are doing well and earning a living somehow.

Finally, Nehru wrote to Krishna Menon on 23 August 1936, saying that the Indian National Congress had resolved to nominate Krishna Menon to represent it at the World Peace Congress to be held in Geneva from 3 September 1936 to 6 September 1936. Nehru had been asked by two of his distinguished European friends—the French author Romain Rolland and the British diplomat Robert Cecil—to send someone to attend the Congress. After initially telling Krishna Menon that 'it is quite impossible to do so', Nehru changed his mind with a little prodding from Lohia and wrote:

. . . As Congress representative you will naturally endeavour to give expression to the Congress attitude . . . Generally we stand for progressive forces, the anti-Fascist forces, without being committed to socialism . . . In European politics our sympathies are with the anti-Fascist elements. In Spain today our good wishes go out to the Government and we wish them success against the Fascist and other reactionaries who have rebelled.

I do not know what opportunities you will have to put the case for India before the Geneva Congress . . . Stress should be laid on the peaceful technique of mass action that we have been following in India. This is not only as a means, but as indicating our strong attachment to the idea of peace.

The Congress was actually held in Brussels. Krishna Menon's speech must have had an impact, for Rammanohar Lohia was to write to him on 31 October 1936:

. . . We all appreciated the speech so very much and I pray you accept our congratulations on such a creditable performance. I am sure you must have made a very good impression on the Congress . . .

A few days later on 12 November 1936, Krishna Menon sent a twelve-page confidential report to Nehru on what had transpired at Brussels. He started off by saying:

> May I say first of all that I went to Brussels with little enthusiasm and with even less of a sense of purposefulness. I was a little astonished that the Congress had taken the affair so seriously at that time. The restrictions on 'politics' which they laid down made me even more cynical and I did not feel happy in the company of aristocracy and the old women of both sexes whose names appeared everywhere in the printed material.

He told Nehru that he reflected the latter's sentiments:

> We do not look upon Peace as the business of the rest of the world and sit back as a helot nation but that in spite of the difficulties would labour to organize the people of the world for constructive Peace.

Giving himself a pat on the back, he continued:

> The Congress was deeply impressed by our participation and I think it may be said without exaggeration that even the English liberals who were present, (who are the worst of all the imperialists I know) responded to this. The net result of my attendance as your representative at the Congress . . . was to put India on the map so far . . . as the world peace movement is concerned. This is what I hear from several sources.

Krishna Menon also reported some private conversations he had had in Brussels. One was particularly important, for the man he spoke to was to cause India enormous problems at the UN in 1948 on the Kashmir issue. This was Philip Noel-Baker, a Labour MP whom Krishna Menon described as a

> liberal imperialist and not too good on India though here again he is of the 'sympathetic type' . . . Baker is a personal friend of

mine and I am sure would do all sorts of personal things if I were to ask for it but he is one of those who having blossomed into Europeanism from English insularity that limit has been reached.

Very soon after the World Peace Congress, an International Congress against War, Fascism and Imperialism was held again in Brussels, between 29 October 1936 and 2 November 1936. This was organized by the International Bureau for Revolutionary Socialist Unity. Masani sent a message to this Congress on 19 October 1936:

> . . . The [Congress Socialist] Party has nominated Mrs. Kamaladevi Chattopadhya, Mr. V.K. Krishna Menon and Miss Mehra Masani to represent it and it is hoped that one or more of them can be present at the Congress . . . Following as it does close on the heels of the World Peace Congress which met recently, with its misleading call for bolstering up the League of Nations and its side-stepping of such vital issues as Ethiopia, Spain and the destruction of Imperialism as a condition precedent to World Peace, your Congress can perform a signal service to Socialists the world over by voicing fearlessly the will and desire of Revolutionary Socialists against chauvinism, reformism and opportunism.

As it turned out Krishna Menon did not attend this second conference in Brussels. But very soon, he was to get the India League actively involved in issues relating to Ethiopia that had arisen following the Italian invasion the previous year and Spain, where the Civil War had broken out a few months earlier. Nehru had declared 9 May 1936 as the day that would be marked as 'Abyssinia Day' by the Indian National Congress, which would stage protests and demonstration against Mussolini's actions.

In his presidential address to the Indian National Congress at Faizpur on 27 December 1936, Nehru reported on Krishna Menon's performance at Brussels and also explained the logic behind sending him there—one that may not have been clear to Krishna Menon himself according to his own confession in the report to Nehru. Nehru told his colleagues:

[T]he urgent and vital problem for us today is political independence and the establishment of a democratic state. And because of this, the Congress must line up with all the progressive forces of the world and must stand up for world peace . . . The World Peace Congress, held at Brussels held in September last, brought together numerous mass organisations on a common platform and gave an effective lead for peace. Our Congress was ably represented at Brussels by Shri V.K. Krishna Menon and the report he has sent us is being placed before you . . . For us, and we think for the world, the problem of peace cannot be separated from imperialism, and in order to remove the root causes of war, imperialism must go . . .

A few months after he had taken over as Congress president, Nehru wrote to Krishna Menon on 29 October 1936:

. . . And now I come to an important matter which requires your careful consideration because it affects you. I suggest that you might come over to India soon, say, for six months or so, and take charge of the civil liberties organization here as a secretary. Don't be put off by the abruptness of the proposal. There are many reasons why I am making it. I think that if you gave a push to the Civil Liberties Union in India and organize it on a proper basis it would go a long way. Apart from this I think it would be a good thing for you to come to India and have a look round and meet people. You cannot do effective work, even in England, unless you renew contacts in India . . . You need not confine yourself to the civil liberties work later, but, to begin with, that ought to be your principal job. It will provide you a definite place in our public life . . . There are of course so many other things which you can also do . . .

Nehru conceived the Civil Liberties Union in April 1936 for 'the protection of civil and individual liberties against arbitrary action by the State'. It was meant to be a non-party, non-sectarian organization. Nehru persuaded Rabindranath Tagore to be its president and Sarojini Naidu its chairman. Nehru had great plans for it and was looking for someone he could trust to get it going. It is not surprising that he thought of Krishna Menon. He also wanted to place 'socialist-minded' people in key positions, like he had done with Lohia a few months earlier. He had made Jayaprakash Narayan, Narendra Deva and Achyut Patwardhan members of the Congress Working Committee.

Krishna Menon was not at all excited by Nehru's unexpected offer. Others may have jumped at it but not Krishna Menon, who said that the 'doctors are not for it' and that he may be of no use in India. He replied on 14 November 1936:

> . . . First of all I want to say that I am very grateful to you for asking me to come over and be of some use and for the degree of confidence that you are prepared to place in me . . . The position however is that my doctors are not keen on my undertaking any new and strenuous work for 6 months in India . . .
>
> . . . I could not get any support for the view that I should give up and go away. Perhaps this was to be expected as others do not want to take on more work or see what is being done abandoned. I saw Stafford Cripps and he went to the extent of telling me whether I would be good enough to quote to you his words, 'that the Indian position here was not to be abandoned at this time . . .'
>
> But the question is one which I must decide on my own responsibility and I am not passing it on to others . . . it was a question of choosing the easier way out I would come straight away. But it is not possible to give up things here just now . . .

Thus, Krishna Menon politely but firmly rebuffed Nehru. His CSP friends had earnestly hoped he would accept Nehru's offer. On 31 October 1936, Lohia wrote to him:

> The Civil Liberties Union is going rather slow . . . The Union needs an efficient Secretary . . . I understand that President Nehru as written to you on this subject and I am sure you will not fail to allow me an opportunity of meeting you here . . .

Had he accepted Nehru's offer, Krishna Menon's acceptability in the Congress might have improved. After Independence, there was widespread resentment among Nehru's colleagues that while they

had carried on a mass struggle, Krishna Menon had never participated
in protests, agitations and demonstrations in the heat and dust of
India, and had never been arrested or jailed. This was certainly true,
although Krishna Menon would take objection to people describing
his life in London as one of 'comfort'. It was not an easy life with no
steady source of adequate income. He would continue to be ambivalent
about returning to India, confusing even Nehru in the process, who
remonstrated with him on 14 December 1936:

> Your letters are quite remarkably vague on the subject of your
> coming to India. In a previous letter you said you could not come
> for some time. Now you mention casually that you might turn up
> early next year. Of course I understand you cannot be sure . . .

India League protest meeting in which Laski and Cripps took part, London, 1936

With one socialist Menon turning him down, Nehru then appointed another socialist Menon—Konnanathu Balakrishna Menon—as the first secretary of the Indian Civil Liberties Union. Six years later, during the Quit India movement, K.B. Menon was to be the brain behind the Keezhariyur bomb conspiracy case. In that village near Calicut, a number of young radicals had been arrested because they had been experimenting with making bombs to fight British rule. K.B. Menon was convicted, and his case went all the way up to the Privy Council in London. Nehru was to write to Krishna Menon on 3 March 1946:

> I think I wrote to you once about K.B. Menon's case in the Privy
> Council . . . I feel we must proceed with the appeal and do our best
> for K.B. Menon. He is a man whom I like and respect. So I hope
> you will take special interest in the matter.

Some years later, K.B. Menon became a member of the Madras Legislative Assembly in 1952 and of Parliament in 1957, remaining unwaveringly committed to his socialist beliefs till his death in 1967.

The Government of India Act passed in August 1935 in the British Parliament provided for elected governments in the eleven provinces of British India. Elections were to be held in the winter of 1936 and early 1937. But even before the polls, there was momentum gathering in the Congress party that should they win it, they should not hesitate to assume power even though the party was opposed to the 1935 Act. Krishna Menon wrote to Nehru on 19 September 1936:

> [T]he press tells us that you are tired out and are resting in
> Allahabad. I hope you are. This hobnobbing with ministerialism
> is accelerating the Imperialist pace on federation. It is bad politics
> and worse strategy. But who am I to offer advice to the president
> of the congress.

This letter would be typical of how Krishna Menon would often write to Nehru over the next quarter of a century and more. Just a couple of weeks later on 7 November 1936, he would bemoan to Nehru:

. . . I know you attach very little importance to what is done here and as president of the Congress you are entirely right in holding that view . . .

But Nehru would take in his stride the self-inflicted tone of hurt on Krishna Menon's part. On 28 September 1936, he responded to the first of the barbs directed at him:

. . . In your last few letters you have given expression to a certain irritation with 'hobnobbing with ministerialism', a proper subject for irritation. Further you go on to say that it is bad politics and worse strategy. And then 'who am I to offer advice to the President of the Congress'. The President of the Congress is not above receiving advice from anybody. In particular I expect both advice and criticism from you all the time. But I think you might give the President of the Congress a little credit for some glimmering of sense . . .

Try to imagine what the human material is in India—how they think, how they act, what moves them, what does not affect them. It is easy enough to take up a theoretically correct attitude which has little effect on anybody. We have to do something much more important and difficult and that is to move large numbers of people to make them act and do all this without breaking up the Congress . . .

Krishna Menon would no doubt have realized that he had unfairly accused Nehru of trying to grab power and thus replied on 13 October 1936:

. . . My remarks were not intended in the least to suggest that ministerialist politics received any encouragement from you . . . I would be a fool to think that these tactics would be yours·. . . . There is no strain of criticism or righteousness in my remark . . .

The Labour Party had just had its annual conference in Edinburgh, and it had been dominated by the issue of Spain and of war and peace. But Krishna Menon informed Nehru:

There was a resolution on India supporting the Constituent
Assembly, but this was not reached. Grenfell [David Grenfell, MP]
was to speak on it and there was to be no opposition from the
platform . . . [He] asks me to write you to say that he does not
anticipate any difficulty in making the Constituent Assembly part
of the Labour Party programme.

Two years later, Nehru and Krishna Menon would meet Clement
Attlee and other important Labour Party leaders such as Stafford
Cripps and Nye Bevan to further discuss the idea of such a Constituent
Assembly. They were to reach an understanding as well.

1937

The year began with Nehru's gruelling election tour of Bihar, United
Provinces and Punjab. On 4 January 1937, he informed Krishna
Menon:

I am dictating this on a moving train. I wonder what I shall be like
after these seven weeks are over. I am pretty tough but by the end
of February I might have to retire to a nursing home for a while.

After addressing some 200 public meetings and rallies, Nehru
returned to Allahabad on 22 February 1937 and promptly recalled
that experience to Krishna Menon:

. . . During the past few months, I have travelled tens of thousands
of miles and addressed thousands of meetings. All this has been a
wonderful experience for me. The surprising thing is that I have
got through in fairly good condition. The election results have
been good . . .

We have now to decide this ministry business . . . and later the
convention. I gather from your letter that you have written to me
about the convention . . .

You have written to me about the difficulties that arise
occasionally regarding the Congress representation at functions

in England. I do not think it is desirable for any formal action to be taken just yet. I do not like your idea of the Congress President appointing a foreign deputy. I think the present informal arrangement might continue . . .

Krishna Menon was then the London representative of the CSP. Clearly, he was aiming for bigger things and wanted a formal institutional position as Nehru's deputy in London. He had earlier proposed to Nehru on 23 January 1937:

. . . I find myself in the position of having to function on your behalf in an informal way . . . and when formal occasions arise . . . I have to cable you. I believe that these occasions when I shall have to act [on Nehru's behalf] are going to grow and some arrangement should be made about these matters which does not create complications . . . It appears to me that the best way would be for the Congress President (not the Congress unless it wishes to do so) to appoint a foreign deputy or representative or whatever he is . . .

But that proposal went nowhere, with Nehru himself killing it instantly. In a letter to Cripps on 22 February 1937, Nehru congratulated him for bringing about unity among left-wing elements in Britain with the formation of a united front comprising Cripps's own Socialist League, the Independent Labour Party and the communists. Nehru sent a copy of this letter to Krishna Menon who was an ardent supporter of the United Front as will be evident from this report of Scotland Yard of 1 February 1937:

. . . I enclose herewith as of considerable interest, a note on the subject of V.K. MENON's views on the political situation in India, which, it is understood have been communicated by him to the British communist leaders in strict confidence. Two points emerge from this evidence: first, that as a result of United Front tactics employed over a period of some months, an undeniable entente now exists between MENON and the Communist leadership in this country; second, that it is clear that MENON regards the Constituent Assembly proposal merely as a shadow scheme behind which the larger machinery for an ultimate soviet system for India can be built up . . .

Scotland Yard was not wrong. There was growing bonhomie between Krishna Menon and the British Communist Party because of the latter's unequivocal support for Indian freedom. Scotland Yard's report on Krishna Menon's infatuation with the United Front of all left parties is borne out by his letter to Nehru on 23 January 1937, in which he had said:

> . . . Political events here are taking a new turn. I hope for the best. The left has come out to challenge the leadership of the Labour Party . . . I must say that apart from Sir Stafford Cripps there is no personality on the left inside the Labour movement itself. Pollit [Communist leader] however is working very totally and is the biggest draw in the country today. The joint programme is very modest, but everyone knows that the programmes are not the whole of this movement . . .

Nehru's letter of 22 February 1937 to Krishna Menon also mentioned the idea of a convention. This was a proposal to have a meeting of all shades of political opinion that existed then in India to discuss the political situation. Such a convention had been held once in 1924 and 1925 and had resulted in a Commonwealth of India Bill being presented to the House of Commons. Annie Besant had played a key role in the preparation and presentation of the Bill. But the situation was radically different now. The Government of India Act, 1935, had been passed by the House of Commons and this gave India a constitution of sorts. Further, elections had been held in the eleven provinces of British India. The Congress, in whose campaign Nehru played a crucial role had secured an absolute majority in six provinces and was the largest single party in another three. But serious differences existed in the Congress, with a majority wanting to form the provincial governments but a small but powerful group headed by Nehru arguing against any haste.

Krishna Menon had written to Nehru the previous month on 23 January 1937, saying:

> . . . I notice that the Congress decision about a convention has aroused attention. You must hardly have the time to think things out in the course of the strenuous election tour. I hear they take you in an aeroplane everywhere now. Speed does not appear to be a blessing if it is used only to overwork some people and you may be forced Mahatma-like to say that they are inventions of the devil . . . I have been more than once tempted to write a series of articles in the Indian press but have given up the idea. If there is anything worthwhile in the ideas press articles will only kill them. I can take the risk of submitting stray thoughts on it in the shape of memorandum to you . . .

To Krishna Menon, the primary issue before the convention was 'the ways and means to wreck the 1935 Constitution'. He also wanted the convention to debate the idea of a constituent assembly, an idea he had put forward a few years earlier, in collaboration with Laski. The paramount need, he told Nehru, was for the convention to stress on unity and discipline and get the Congress at least to speak in one voice on the issue of forming governments in the provinces. Krishna Menon was very clearly against the Congress forming these governments since he believed this would mean the party accepting the idea of a federation, which he saw as the bedrock of the 1935 Constitution.

That Krishna Menon may well have been the author of the idea of a convention is borne out by a letter Asoka Mehta would write to him on 28 January 1937:

> . . . Please send me an article on 'The National Convention' in good time for our special number [of the *Congress Socialist*] that is likely to be out at the time of the convention. It should be a signed article. I want that article urgently from you because others to trying to take away the credit for the idea that originated with you.

The convention was to be held on 18 March 1937 in Bombay but would be confined only to the newly elected Congress legislators. Nehru shared his speech with Krishna Menon before it was delivered, but it was evident that in spite of Nehru's soaring rhetoric against forming governments, the overwhelming opinion in the Congress was exactly the opposite. Nehru bowed to the inevitable after some concessions were secured from the British following Gandhi's intervention.

Nehru and Krishna Menon would exchange hundreds of letters over the next decade. The personal and the political would be interspersed in many of them. On 25 March 1937, Nehru would make an unusual request:

> . . . One small matter. I am getting rather fed up with my name. It is always being mis-spelt and mis-pronounced. The other day a B.B.C. announcer got hopelessly muddled over it and went on ha-haing. Unfortunately I cannot change my name but I propose to make a slight change in the way it is written. Jawaharlal consists really of two Hindustani words: Jawahar and Lal. In India one usually combines the two but this long word has got a terrifying look about it and foreigners cannot get hold of it. So it would be better in future to separate the two. My name should therefore be given as Jawahar Lal Nehru . . .

Nehru may not have wanted it, but he would continue to be referred to as 'Jawaharlal Nehru' and not as 'Jawahar Lal Nehru'. His books would bear the former name, and he would sign his letters as 'Jawaharlal Nehru'. Most people would refer to him as Jawaharlal. But Gandhi's very last letter to Nehru, twelve days before he was assassinated, ended thus:

> *Bahut Varsh Jiyo aur Hind ke Jawahar Bane Raho* (Live long and continue to be the jewel of India)

On 26 April 1937, Krishna Menon wrote to Nehru asking him to lend his name to an appeal that was being made in the UK and other countries against the trial of Trotsky. Krishna Menon by now had become a close ally of the Communist Party of Great Britain and was in almost daily contact with its leaders. He saw the protests against the trials of Lenin's colleagues by Stalin as part of a 'widespread and overt conspiracy against the USSR', parroting the line being taken by Harry Pollit and the Palme Dutt brothers. On 22 May 1937, on his way from Burma to Malaya, Nehru replied:

> . . . About the Trotsky business, there is no question of my associating with it. It is true I was asked to give my name to an appeal from an enquiry into the Moscow trial. I have no intention of doing so. It is true that when I was in Europe I expressed a measure of sympathy for Trotsky because of what I considered unnecessarily harsh persecution. But recent events have not advanced him in my opinion. I must, confess, however that all these recent trials in Russia still remain a mystery to me . . .

A few months later on 11 November 1937, Nehru returned to this subject and explained to Krishna Menon:

> . . . Perhaps you imagine some kind of Trotskyism is spreading in India. There is no such thing here. But the various trials in Russia this year of highly placed individuals gave a great shock to many people, mostly friends of Russia. Those trials may have been perfectly justified, but the mere fact that they occurred showed an unhealthy background. Why should there be this background more than twenty years after the revolution? Why should there be such complete suppression of civil liberty even so long after the militant period of the revolution and the civil war? These questions trouble one and I must confess I can find no satisfactory answers . . .

Nehru had been to the Soviet Union a decade earlier and was an admirer of the massive industrialization push initiated by Stalin in the late 1920s. But it is clear that the purge of his colleagues masterminded by Stalin bothered Nehru deeply and left him puzzled.

The issue of the Soviet Union would cause serious fissures in the socialist movement in India and finally lead to a break in the Masani–Krishna Menon camaraderie. It all started with a pamphlet that Masani circulated sometime in mid-1937, which he called 'A Foreign Policy for India'. He argued that war among European powers was inevitable, that the Soviet Union was making compromises with the imperialists and that under no circumstances should India support England, even if it was allied with the USSR. 'England's embarrassment is our opportunity,' declared Masani. Krishna Menon wrote to Nehru on 25 September 1937:

> I am much perturbed about a pamphlet I have just received in which my friend Masani outlines what he regards as foreign policy for India. It is bad enough for a great movement like the Congress in its present stage of political development not to have a foreign policy, it is much worse to have such a mistaken and muddled one as the one sort of thing outlined. I am writing to Masani myself and asking for a publication of a reply to it in the Congress Socialist paper. Some parts of it exceed the limits of folly to what must be regarded as a serious disservice to the cause of socialism and Indian independence. The rest of it dangerous amateurishness coming as it does from a responsible leader of the Indian socialist movement.

Krishna Menon's violent reaction to Masani's pamphlet forced Nehru to have a look at it as he informed his London friend on 7 October 1937:

> . . . I had not read Masani's pamphlet but your exceeding annoyance at it made me look into it. Parts of it seem rather exaggerated but the feeling behind that speech of Masani is pretty common in India.

It is hard to imagine now that Masani's polemic created such a stir. In early March 1938, Soli Batlivala, a member of the Communist Party of India, who was also a member of the CSP, sent Krishna Menon a manuscript of his response to Masani's pamphlet. It was called 'A Congress Socialist Looks at World Politics'. Batlivala wrote:

. . . I am sure your Foreword would prove to be invaluable—a beacon light from the man India has trusted to be its sole spokesman at the World Peace Congress and other European Conferences, a man on the spot seeing things happen round him . . .

On receiving this request, Krishna Menon did something that would appear to be a confirmation of the growing view that he was a communist wolf in a socialist sheep's clothing. He asked Harry Pollit for advice, which was offered on 28 March 1938:

I have read the enclosed pamphlet very carefully and I think you should write a preface. It is an excellent survey of the situation from the world point of view, not from the point of view that Masani has been guilty of . . . In your own preface, I think you should stress the importance of taking a world view based on the realities of the situation. You know when Lenin was having a fight with some of those who have recently been summarily dealt with, in 1917, he had to make the point that Marxism consists not in looking at what is possible but looking at what are the actual facts of a given situation, and your preface, driving forward for the vital principle of collective security and the role India can play in this, I am sure would make a substantial contribution towards clearing many misapprehensions which the Masani Group are responsible for . . .

Krishna Menon was to write the preface to Batlivala's counter to Masani. And what were Masani's own reactions to Krishna Menon's anger? On 27 July 1937, he said:

. . . There is one more matter in your letter to which I should refer and that is about what you call a 'Trotskyite drift in the Congress Socialist. I am afraid you have now transferred your old bitter antagonism to the C.P. [Communist Party] to the Trotskyites!! . . . I must make it clear that our Party is not a Stalinite organization and is not prepared to take everything on trust from Moscow. We feel that the real friends of the Soviet Union cannot shut their eyes to the unhappy drift of things there, if socialism is not to be damned by the happenings in the U.S.S.R . . . As regards the Party it has not taken up either a pro-Trotsky or pro-Stalin position . . . So please do not get worried about this matter. If you like, we can discuss it further in our personal correspondence but it is too unimportant to worry about for you and me.

The year 1937 also saw Krishna Menon expand the India League's footprint to cover freedom movements in other countries as well. This was in keeping with Nehru's strongly held view that the Indian independence movement could not be seen in isolation of world developments and was actually part of a larger struggle against imperialism and fascism in Asia and Europe. Ceylon, Spain and China would begin to figure prominently in Krishna Menon's agenda. The involvement with Ceylon was, however, not to be as intense as it was with Spain and China. A joint public meeting was organized by the CSP and the Socialist Party of Ceylon in London in June 1937. Krishna Menon and S.A. Wickremasinghe of the Sama Samaja Party were the prime movers of this two-day initiative. It dealt with concerns of both plantation and industrial labour. The joint statement issued by them before the conference highlighted the activities of the two parties and declared:

Very little is known in this country [UK] of these movements— their significance and their struggles. Their importance to the peoples of the world and their relation to the general world movement for democracy and social justice is hardly recognized. Yet in the world today, the struggle of the people in these countries under imperial domination, against both imperialism and indigenous exploitation is one of the most significant movements of our time . . .

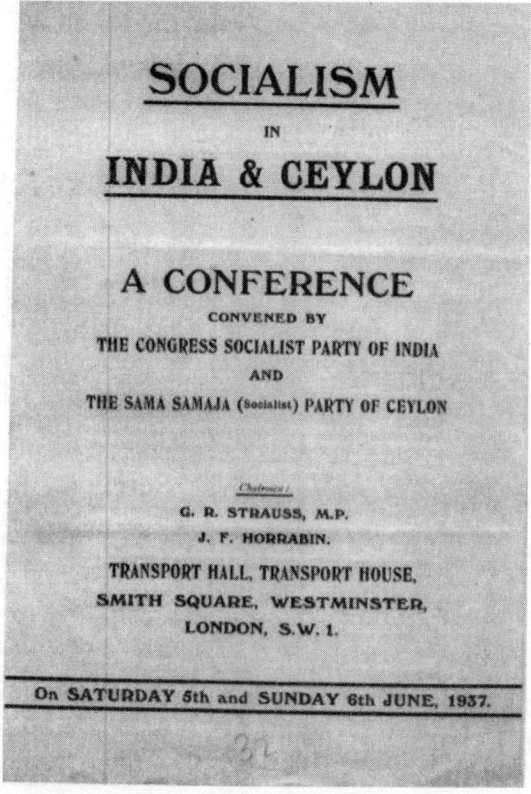

India League–Congress Socialist Party meeting on India and Ceylon, London, 1937

Krishna Menon was pleased with the outcome and told his 'comrades' in the CSP soon thereafter:

. . . A Conference on Socialism in India and Ceylon was held in London in June and lasted two days. It was very successful and stimulated interest in socialism and allied movements in India . . .

Masani replied to him on 7 July 1937, saying:

. . . I shall place your report of the London Conference before the Executive [of the CSP]. I have no doubt they will be delighted at the work you have accomplished.

He followed it up soon thereafter with praise for Krishna Menon:

> The Executive Committee of the Party at its meeting had before it the report of the London Conference on Socialism in India and Ceylon.
>
> The Committee was very grateful at the success of this venture which was due primarily to your initiative and energy and has asked me to convey to you its appreciation of the notable contribution you have made to the fostering of closer relations between British and Indian Socialists and a better understanding in England of conditions here . . . Now that Miss Masani has returned to India you will be the Party's sole representative in England.

This was the high point in the Krishna Menon–CSP relationship.

The previous year, Krishna Menon had formed a Spain–India Committee. The Spanish Civil War, which became a defining issue in world politics, had begun sometime in July 1936. By February 1937, Madrid, which was the Republican stronghold, had been besieged by rebel forces led by General Francisco Franco for almost three months. Nehru and Krishna Menon were to travel to Spain the next year, but for now they collaborated in raising funds for medical supplies. With contributions coming largely from Bombay, coordinated by Nehru's brother-in-law G.P. Hutheesing, Krishna Menon was able to present a Red Cross ambulance for use in Spain in September 1937. The committee also provided an opportunity for Indira Nehru to appear on a public platform for the very first time. Before she did, she reported to her father on 5 March 1937:

> As I wrote to you in my last letter, Menon has persuaded me to speak at an 'Indian Evening' arranged by Mrs. Saklatvala and the India–Spain League. I thought it was going to be a tiny affair but alas! I was sadly mistaken. Strachey is also speaking & public will consist of people like the London School of Economics students! However, one must make the best of a bad job. I propose busying myself for at least two days in pamphlets and books on Spain . . .

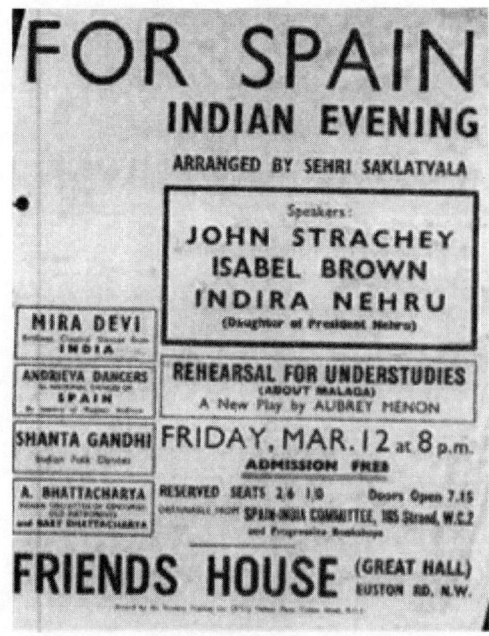

Indira Nehru's first public speech, India League meeting, London, March 1937

The 'India Evening' was held on 12 March 1937 and raised close to eighty pounds. Two days later, Krishna Menon informed Nehru:

> Indira made a nice little speech at our Spanish entertainment with Isabel Brown and John Strachey. I shall be seeing her before she goes back to India.

Indira's presence there led to more invitations to speak to Indian audiences and to write for the ILP's *New Leader*. A few months later, she joined Oxford University where Krishna Menon would continue to meet with her when he went to speak there.

Spain was a passion for Krishna Menon for much of 1937 and 1938 as it was to be for the British left. The India League was very active in organizing public demonstrations. In these years, Nehru and Krishna Menon carried on an extensive correspondence on Spain because the former was very particular that whatever the Indian National Congress did for Spain from India be coordinated closely with whatever

Krishna Menon was planning to do from London. Masani and his colleagues in the CSP too were heavily involved in the fundraising efforts for Spain, taking out appeals in prominent Bombay dailies.

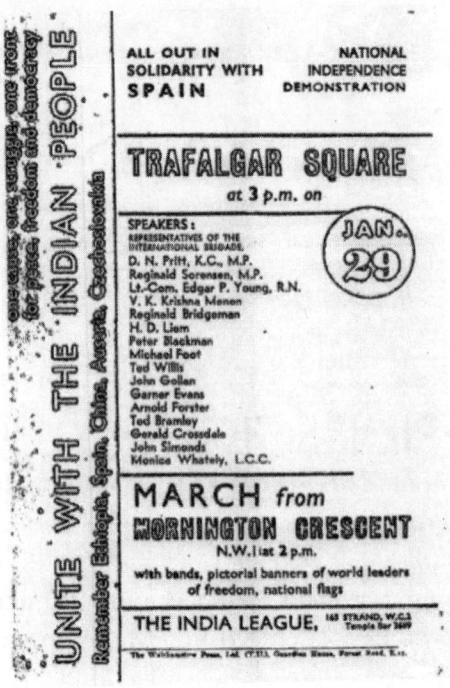

India League public meeting on Spain, London, 1937

One of the young Indian students in the UK who would be intimately associated with the Spanish cause was Rajni Patel, then a student at Cambridge. Patel was a card–carrying communist, like his fellow student Mohan Kumaramangalam. They would become ardent acolytes of Krishna Menon, who was well aware of their communist links. On 18 December 1936, he had written to Patel, who was then leaving for Spain with a delegation:

> . . . You may be aware that I represent the Congress Socialist Party in this country and I should like to authorize you to speak for the socialists in India and express their sympathy and moral support in the cause of the Spanish workers. I should also like to add that Nehru

has written to me that the Congress as a whole is deeply concerned about the issue of Spain and is on the side of the Spanish government.

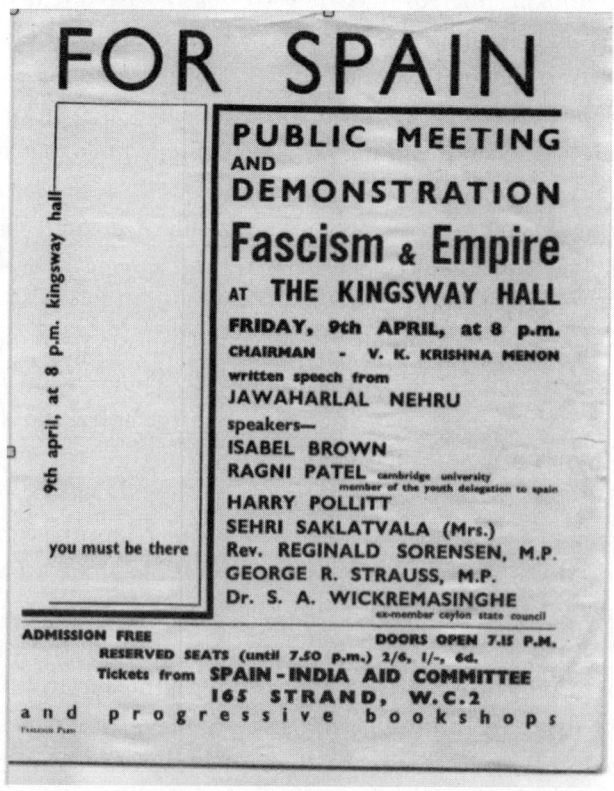

India League public meeting on Spain, London, 1937

Five years later when Patel would be arrested by the British on his return to India and jailed, he would write to Krishna Menon on 14 September 1941 from his detention in Deoli in present-day Rajasthan:

> . . . Before his arrest, Jawaharlalji wrote to me saying (shall I say almost complaining) that there was no news from you except for a brief cable and then the ruthless bombing of London started and I used to read with horror that the vicinity of your office was a favourite target for the Nazi Barbarians. Naturally I became most concerned and anxious about my old cynic friend especially because

I could well imagine him sitting nonchalantly in his office, while the Nazi deathbirds hovered above Strand, swallowing a veganin tablet, drinking the strongest possible tea the twentieth time in the day and dictating a letter or an article to his new secretary! Thank God this breathless anxiety did not last long for soon the newspapers informed me that you were alive and kicking and Reuters have been reassuring me recently quite often that you are more alive than and kicking as hard as ever . . .

Now I want to know about your health. Are you feeling any better? I bet you are still swimming in tea and starving yourself? Oh, I would be so glad if tea were to be strictly rationed in England . . . I see from Gollancz's announcement of forthcoming books that you are writing for their 'A Tract for the Times'. I am mighty pleased that you have shaken off your lethargy at last and decided to do justice to your brilliance . . .

This is as good a description as any of Krishna Menon from someone who worked with him closely in the late 1930s. Later, Patel would be part of the core campaign team that would get him elected from Bombay North in 1957 and 1962. For a few years in the early 1970s, Patel would be known as the 'uncrowned king of Bombay' before his falling out with Indira Gandhi's son Sanjay, sometime in 1975.

Japan invaded China a second time on 7 July 1937. On 2 September 1937, Krishna Menon got the India League fully involved on the side of China. A resolution passed that day by the Executive Committee of the India League read:

The Executive Committee of the India League expressed its deep sympathy with the Chinese people who are the victims of wanton aggression by imperialist Japan and are subject to horrible brutalities, widespread massacre of men, women and children. The Committee appeals to His Majesty's Government to fully respect the obligations under international law, specific treaties, and the Covenant of the League of Nations which guarantee to China the independence of her people and the integrity of its territory.

This resolution was sent to the British government at the highest levels. Another one that was simultaneously passed was sent to the Chinese and Japanese ambassadors in the UK:

> This meeting of the Executive Committee of the India League protests against the wanton aggression by Japan against the people of China and the violation of her territory resulting in great cruelty and suffering now being inflicted on the Chinese people, men, women and children in total disregard of international law and morality.

The British government acknowledged receipt of the India League resolution, the Chinese ambassador welcomed it and the Japanese envoy simply ignored it.

At about the same time, Krishna Menon was invited to be a member of the China Campaign Committee, which had a good number of prominent British personalities on it. Its moving spirit was the well-known publisher Victor Gollancz and its driving force was Dorothy Goodman. Gollancz was promoting Edgar Snow's *Red Star over China,* which had then just appeared and which would prove very influential in moulding world opinion on Mao and the Chinese communists. Krishna Menon was an integral part of the professional lives of both Gollancz and Goodman. His presence in the China Campaign Committee was dutifully reported by Scotland Yard on 6 October 1937:

> V.K. Krishna MENON was present on the platform with several speakers, who included Professor Harold J. LASKI, at a meeting held under the auspices of the 'China Campaign Committee' (c/o The China Institute, 91 Gower Street W.C.) at Whitefield's Tabernacle, Tottenham Court Road, W. on 30th September called in connection with the Sino-Japanese War, presided over by the Rev. A.D. HELDEN.
>
> The full attendance of about 1000 persons (about 100 refused admittance) included about 300 Chinese and 50 other Orientals, most of the latter of student type.

Gollancz was of great help to Krishna Menon in his India League propaganda work. He ran a Left Book Club, which attracted the leading lights of the international left movement. Scotland Yard reported on 17 November 1937:

V.K. KRISHNA MENON

A Lecture on 'India' was given by V.K. Krishna MENON to the Stepney Group of the Left Book Club at Friends Institute, 488A Commercial Road E. on 5th November, which was attended by 35 persons. This was due to commence at 8 p.m. but MENON did not put in an appearance until close to 9 p.m.

In his address MENON declared that the British Press was disinclined to publish news on Indian affairs. He then outlined what he termed the growth of the movement in India against British imperialism up to the present day. He spoke for nearly an hour.

Krishna Menon was expressing his frustration with mainline British dailies, including the liberal Manchester *Guardian*. He would, on the other hand, have greater success in publications of the Communist Party of Great Britain such as the *Daily Worker* and the *Labour Monthly* and of those associated with the Labour Party such as *Labour*, *The Tribune* and the *New Statesman & Nation*.

Abyssinia was also engaging Krishna Menon during this year, again reflecting the concerns being voiced by both Nehru and Masani back in India on behalf of their respective parties. On 1 September 1937, he wrote to Sylvia Pankhurst, the firebrand leader of the suffragist movement:

Thank you for your letter of 31st August asking for representation from the India League at the Conference on Abyssinia to be held on September 9th at the Central Hall. I shall be very glad to speak as you suggest. If you would like us to distribute any literature in connection with the Conference or the demonstration we should be very glad to send them out . . .

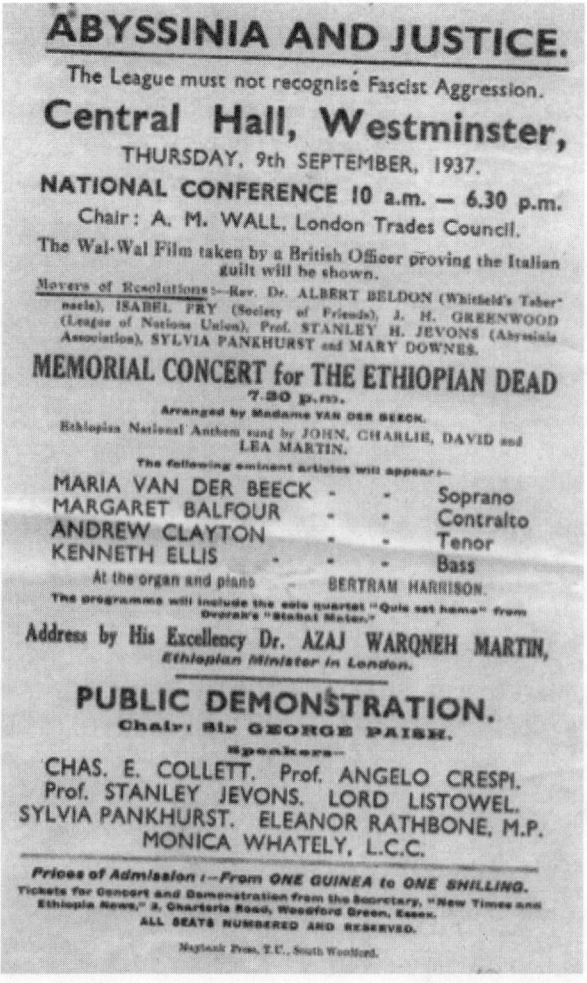

Public meeting on Abyssinia where Krishna Menon spoke, London, 1937

The India League's pan-India activities were to be showcased for the first time in an organized manner on New Year's Eve, at the heart of establishment London—Trafalgar Square. Spain, Abyssinia and China occupied pride of place. The West Indies and Africa were not yet on the India League's radar screen. That was to happen a little later.

India League public meeting on Abyssinia, Spain and China, London, 1937

In the twenty-odd years he was an agitator and protester in London, Krishna Menon must have made a few thousand speeches, both planned and impromptu, in various forums in the UK. Almost invariably, these speeches were extempore. Many of them did get reported but all of them got the attention of the British authorities. Reports prepared by his hosts are few and far between but one that has survived in Scotland Yard files is particularly instructive and worth quoting at some length:

On Thursday June 3rd [1937] the Joint Discussion Group . . .
had the privilege of discussing Indian affairs with KRISHNA
MENON, a distinguished representative of the Indian Congress
Party. Unfortunately, he assumed that because we were civil
servants, we must necessarily be prejudiced against the Indians
(shades of the I.C.S.!), but he gave nevertheless a plain statement
regarding the attitude of the Congress Party to English rule and
caused some uneasiness in the minds of those of us who still believe
in the 'civilising mission' of the British Empire.

The victory of the Congress Party [Menon said] at the recent
elections, despite every possible restriction on freedom of election,
is proof that the mass of the population regard the English as
interlopers rather than as benevolent guardians. The white man
rules India not for its good but for its goods and the Indians have
grown steadily poorer during the century . . .

Mr MENON spoke with humour and without bitterness . . .
During discussion Mr MENON . . . maintained that if left to
govern themselves, the Indians were capable of adjusting their
differences and advancing education (perhaps not in English), and
social progress.

We were extremely grateful to Mr MENON for talking with
us in what must have seemed an uncongenial environment and
we, not being blinded by vested interests, shall endeavour to study
events in India with open-mindedness and insist that justice be
done in our time.

This is quite an extraordinary account, which gives great credit not
only to Krishna Menon but his hosts as well. His archives are replete
with somewhat similar letters of appreciation from all sorts of bodies—
book clubs, trade and industry associations, labour unions, schools,
colleges and universities, local units of the Labour Party, church
organizations and the general public. An overwhelming majority of
such letters would be from women's clubs, where Krishna Menon
was evidently a hit.

Election to provincial assemblies had been held, and the Congress
had done exceedingly well. Nehru had been the star campaigner and

had won these elections for the Congress almost single-handedly. His mass appeal and charisma had carried the day. But he, like Krishna Menon, was not keen on the Congress forming governments in the provinces where it had received a huge mandate. Nehru had some support for his stance but an overwhelming majority of Congressmen favoured the assumption of ministerial office. The crucial Congress Working Committee meeting to decide the issue one way or the other was about to take place when Krishna Menon wrote to Nehru on 23 June 1937:

> . . . The cryptic remark made by the Mahatma that no Congressman should make any statement till the working committee meets alarms me. From a democratic politician speaking and acting in ways that are not unintelligible to ordinary folk one would not fear such a statement. In the present case it looks as though there may be another bombshell . . .
>
> I am not a believer in political heroics or martyrdom and am a realist. Words do not worry me but their contents do. I beg you to consider whether you should now tell the working committee that you have gone all the way to meet every point of view and the time has come when the Congress should not set the pace to itself as demanded by the constitution [of 1935] which it has rejected and its makers . . . Therefore I hope and wish that at the next working committee we will end this chapter and a new lead will be given to the Congress to carry on its work for independence . . .

Clearly, Krishna Menon was opposed to the Congress forming the ministries. But Nehru sensed the mood among his party colleagues, and after some concessions were extracted from the British thanks to the intervention of Gandhi, the Congress came to power in eight of the eleven provinces. They were, however, to last just about two years, resigning on the issue of India's participation in the Second World War.

Towards the end of the year, Nehru would, on more than one occasion, express his feeling of extreme tiredness and exhaustion and tell Krishna Menon that he was feeling jaded and somewhat burnt out. Krishna Menon counselled him on 29 December 1937:

> . . . I am sorry that you are so tired out. I have been wanting to write to you for some time now about the absolute necessity of your taking a little time off in absolute withdrawal from public activity . . . The situation in India appears to me to demand that you should have respite from propaganda for a short while to devote yourself to the serious decisions that you would have to take. The kind of Gandhian retirement without its mystic explanations appears essential in the case of people on whom so much depends . . . I am afraid I have fully used the liberty you usually permit me and I must not say more . . . If I could afford it in some way or another I would like to come to India to inform myself and to discuss with you lots of things . . . As I said to you the socialist movement in India makes feel not very happy often times . . . Mr. Bose is coming here on the 10th . . .

1938

Subhas Chandra Bose took over from Nehru as president of the Indian National Congress at its Haripura session in February 1938. Before that, he paid a brief visit to London. Like he did for Nehru earlier, Krishna Menon helped put together Bose's schedule. On 3 January 1938, he wrote to J.F. Horrabin:

> Mr. Subhas Bose is coming to London next week for a brief visit and we are arranging a public meeting to welcome him . . .
> . . . He is a leading Congressman, a former President of the Indian Trade Union Congress, and in all probability will be elected as the next President of the Congress to succeed Nehru, with whom he is closely associated.
> We feel sure that you will agree that it is desirable that Mr. Bose should have a representative welcome from leaders of British public opinion, and hope that you will join in this welcome and accept our invitation to sit on the platform . . .

Horrabin was a pillar of the India League and a Labour MP. After Bose returned to India, he evidently had a conversation about his London visit with Nehru, who was to write to Krishna Menon on 3 February 1938:

> . . . He [Subhas Bose] told me however that you are far from well and generally worried as well as somewhat depressed. I am sorry to learn this. There is much that depresses us in the present state of the world but after all it does not help one to become a victim of circumstances.

It is highly probable that Krishna Menon's mood swings were a result of not only 'the state of the world' as Nehru put it but also the medication he was on following his prolonged hospitalization in the second half of 1935. He also suffered from arthritis and was a very poor eater, subsisting, as the folklore went, largely on 'tea and buns'. Such dark moods would recur till the very end of his life, and Nehru would put up with it sympathetically with a 'this too shall pass approach'. On 20 February 1940, Nehru wrote to his daughter from Allahabad, psychoanalysing Krishna Menon, having seen him just three times in five years but on the basis of the barrage of letters he had received in that time:

> . . . If you want to know what depression is you should read Krishna's letters to me. He works himself up terribly and, and bad as the world is, imagines all manner of things which are worse. And then, with many apologies he gives me a lot of good advice not knowing how I would take it all. I like him of course to give the good advice. It helps. But he should not get so excited. It is not good for him. His nerves have never been his strong point.

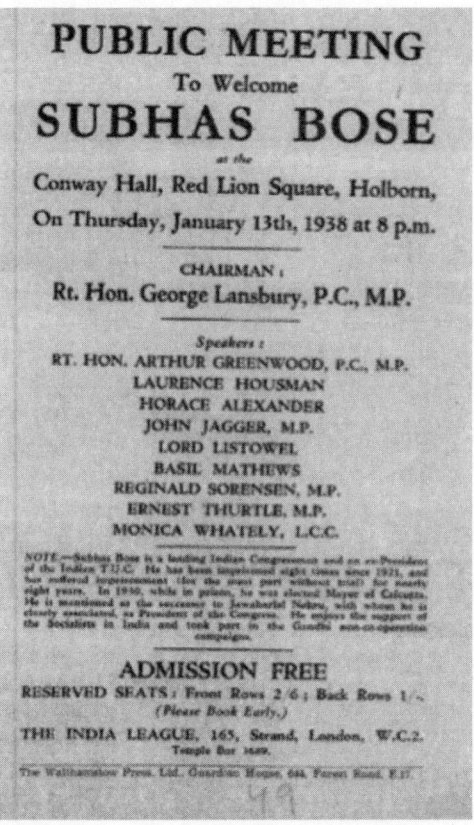

PUBLIC MEETING
To Welcome
SUBHAS BOSE
at the
Conway Hall, Red Lion Square, Holborn,
On Thursday, January 13th, 1938 at 8 p.m.

CHAIRMAN :
Rt. Hon. George Lansbury, P.C., M.P.

Speakers :
RT. HON. ARTHUR GREENWOOD, P.C., M.P.
LAURENCE HOUSMAN
HORACE ALEXANDER
JOHN JAGGER, M.P.
LORD LISTOWEL
BASIL MATHEWS
REGINALD SORENSEN, M.P.
ERNEST THURTLE, M.P.
MONICA WHATELY, L.C.C.

ADMISSION FREE
RESERVED SEATS : Front Rows 2/6 ; Back Rows 1/-.
(Please Book Early.)
THE INDIA LEAGUE, 165, Strand, London, W.C.2.

India League public meeting for Subhas Chandra Bose, London, 1938

After he became president of the Congress, Bose would make use of Krishna Menon to get advice on political issues from people such as Harold Laski and Stafford Cripps. On 12 February 1938, just a few days before he was formally installed as president, Bose wrote to Krishna Menon:

I am writing to you on a very important matter. The Local Self-Government Minister of the Central Provinces, Mr. D.P. Mishra wants to initiate legislation for the radical reform of the local self-government machinery in the province. The Governor of the Central Provinces is raising objections on the grounds that certain provisions of the bill encroach on his preserves—(law & order, special responsibilities). Prof Keith who has been consulted has given his verdict in favour of the Minister. Now, I want you to consult Prof. Ivor Jennings and Prof H. Laski on this matter—and perhaps any others whom you consider necessary. You will find herewith the points on which the Governor is objecting. We want a verdict from some authorities on Constitutional Law as to whether the Governor is right or the Local Self-Government Minister. I may tell you that the Minister and the Cabinet are very keen on the Bill . . . Please treat this as urgent.

But Bose and Krishna Menon were never able to establish a rapport with each other. There would be a brief moment of informality when Bose telegraphed the British Prime Minister on 25 February 1939 against UK's policies in Spain and asked Krishna Menon to take up the matter in the House of Commons. Krishna Menon would reply six days later saying that he would do so and added:

> . . . I notice with some surprise that the letter addressed to the Secretary of the India League signed by you personally starts off 'Dear Sir'. Surely that does not express our relationship . . .

In any case, it was evident to Krishna Menon later in the year that there was a struggle for supremacy in the Congress between Gandhi and Bose, a struggle in which Nehru's heart was perhaps with Bose but his head was with the Mahatma. Moreover, Bose's lieutenants abroad, most notably Pulin Seal in London and A.C.N. Nambiar in Europe, never hit it off with Krishna Menon, with Seal and Nambiar thinking he was not sufficiently critical of British imperialism and was ever willing to strike compromises.

J.B. Kripalani would be Krishna Menon's bête noire after 1957. He would contest against him in February 1962 in an election that was to capture national and international headlines. He would continue his tirade against Krishna Menon right through 1962 and finally demand and secure his resignation after the debacle in the war with China in October–November of that year. The two sparred

again a year later, when Kripalani brought a no-confidence motion
against the Nehru government in August 1963 and the star speaker
in defence of Nehru, apart from the Prime Minister himself, was to
be Krishna Menon. They first clashed in 1938. Kripalani's first letter
to Krishna Menon was harmless and even a bit positive. He wrote on
3 August 1938:

> I am glad you have accepted Jawaharlal's proposal and consented
> to write to us periodically about foreign affairs . . . We should get
> news regularly at least once a fortnight . . .

Six days later, ever ready to imagine a slight, Krishna Menon replied:

> Pandit Jawaharlal Nehru has written to me from Czechoslovakia
> that the Working Committee has passed a resolution in which
> it refers to the International Peace Campaign (IPC) and to me.
> I gather from his letter that the Resolution expresses a lack of
> confidence in relation to the IPC work and my part in it . . .

Kripalani responded within forty-eight hours:

> The Working Committee has passed no resolution expressing lack
> of confidence in you . . . There was only one resolution last year
> authorizing you to attend a meeting of the I.P.C. After that there
> was no resolution. The Working Committee therefore decided
> that you be informed that every time you attend a conference, you
> must refer the matter to us and get our permission.
>
> I did not send this resolution to you. I had an idea that in this
> connection you perhaps consulted the President Shri Jawaharlalji.
> So I informed him what had been done. He has since written that
> you always took your instructions from him. We have therefore
> decided that you should continue to function as before.
>
> Jawaharlalji has written to us that there is to be a conference at
> Glasgow about the end of this month called the Peace and Empire
> Congress. He wants us to authorise you to represent the Congress
> there. You have our authority for the purpose . . .

Nehru then took it upon himself to defend Krishna Menon, which he did to Kripalani on 24 August 1938 from Budapest:

> The present position is that Krishna Menon is a member of the executive committee of the I.P.C. [International Peace Congress] on behalf of the Congress. Thus in so far as the work of the I.P.C. is concerned he represents the Congress. He is not otherwise in any way a representative of the Congress. Roughly speaking the I.P.C. work consists of bringing together all organisations interested in peace . . . They have tried to send food to Spain, to organize hospital work in China . . . Menon, in addition, has naturally laid stress always on the Indian aspect—the bombing of the north west frontier and on real peace being incompatible with imperialism. The peace movement is growing strength and in England largely on account of Menon's efforts, it is becoming anti-imperialist . . .

This pattern would continue till Nehru's death—of Nehru defending Krishna Menon stoutly to his colleagues. The latter, on his part, never made any attempt to make himself acceptable to other Congressmen, knowing very well that he would always have Nehru firmly on his side. Both would end up paying a very heavy price for this. As far as Krishna Menon's presence at the Glasgow Conference was concerned, as usual, Scotland Yard had a report ready on 5 December 1938:

V.K. Krishna MENON

> . . . MENON spoke at a public meeting held at the Ilford Town Hall on 1ˢᵗ October under the auspices of the local Peace Council.
> Dealing with the current European crisis, he emphasized the necessity of the masses of Britain to join forces with the common peoples of India and the Soviet Union in order to overthrow fascism and imperialism. One was apt to forget, he said, that although war had for the present been averted in Europe, bombs were still being dropped on the inhabitants of Palestine and the Northwest Frontier of India.
> MENON attended the Peace and Empire Congress held under the joint auspices of the Scottish Peace Council, the

National Peace Council and the International Peace Council at Glasgow on 24th–26th September as a delegate of the India League. He moved a general resolution expressing antagonism to fascism and denunciation of the British Government's action in betraying peace in Spain, Austria, etc. which was adopted by the Congress.

The high point of the year for Krishna Menon was undoubtedly Nehru's visit. The two were already close and had been writing to each other frequently. Nehru had also appointed Krishna Menon as his literary agent or representative. His daughter and future son-in-law were active India League volunteers. His 1938 visit to London further deepened the friendship between him and Krishna Menon, a friendship that was to withstand Krishna Menon's contretemps and controversies time and again.

Krishna Menon had been active on pan-Indian issues in the first few months of 1938. On 6 April, Scotland Yard reported:

V.K. KRISHNA MENON

MENON spoke at a demonstration held in Marylebone N.W. on 24th March to protest against the action of the local Council in permitting the German Nazi Party in London to hold meetings at Seymour Hall, Marylebone.

A fortnight later, Scotland Yard was at it again:

V.K. KRISHNA MENON

On 9th April Menon was one of the speakers at a demonstration in aid of Republican Spain which was held by the St. Pancras Council of Action at Islip Street, Kentish Town N.W. and which was preceded by a march through the streets of the Borough.

On Easter Sunday (17th April) the Irish republicans in London organized a march from the Paddington Green W. to Trafalgar Square, where a meeting was held to commemorate those killed in the Irish Easter Rebellion of Easter 1916. Some 800 persons participated in the march, among them being Menon and another Indian whose identity is unknown.

From time to time, Krishna Menon would express support for the Irish—a legacy of his association with Annie Besant no doubt. He would speak every once in a while to audiences in the UK, saying that he had always taken a keen interest in the struggle for the complete independence of Ireland because the Irish and the Indians were fighting the same enemy—British imperialism. During the years of the Second World War, he would stress repeatedly that Britain's refusal to 'grant autonomy to India and her attitude towards the Irish problem' were incompatible with her war aims. But he would denounce the Irish Republican Army as a 'motley collection of hooligans'.

However, Nehru's impending visit was Krishna Menon's main preoccupation then. On 28 April 1938, Nehru, writing from Allahabad, gave Krishna Menon full authority to put his visit together:

> . . . About my visit, please make such arrangements as you think desirable. You might consult Indira . . . So far as my programme is concerned you much make yourself responsible for it, acting of course in consultation with various odd groups and individuals.

Knowing Krishna Menon very well by now, Nehru continued,

> Every attempt should be made not to irritate any group . . . Spain I would like to visit. I do not know that will be possible or desirable . . .

A few days later on 9 May 1938, Nehru informed Agatha Harrison, who was working with Krishna Menon, on his visit:

> . . . On the last occasion [1936] I made it more or less a rule not to see people who were officially connected with the British government. I do not propose to do that this time. But I must say that I am not keen on making any advances towards them. If any of them desires to meet me and this meeting can be conveniently

arranged, I shall not object. I am writing on these lines to Krishna
Menon also . . .

Krishna Menon was well aware of the significance of this visit.
The situation both in England and India since Nehru's last trip had
changed substantially. He wrote to Nehru on 24 May 1938, giving
him the schedule that had been drawn up till then. It was jam-packed
as Krishna Menon had filled every hour available:

The present arrangement is as follows:

Travel from Italy to Spain
Return to Paris about 21st.
Broadcast in Paris on the 21st.
Press Conference in London on Thursday 23rd
24–26 Week-end Stafford Cripps
27th Monday Public Welcome in London
30th June meet members of the Indian community
(May have to go to Paris if the great international rally to call for
arms for Spain and to save the republic comes off. Awaiting to hear
from Dolivet)
5th July Tuesday: Royal Institute of International Affairs. Subject
'India Today'
6th July: Lecture on 'India Today' at the Large Queens Hall (Left
Book Club); open to public (Collection for Congress medical
mission to China)
6th or 7th July morning: Dr. Sherwood Eddy's Americans at Toynbee
Hall
8th July Friday: Indian London Majlis (Students) tea time.
9th and 10th July Week-end: Lord Lothian
15th and 16th: Conference on 'PEACE and EMPIRE'.
Presidential Speech, Friday evening.
17th July: National Independence Demonstration in cooperation
with Chinese and Spain organisations at Trafalgar Square, for
Indian, Chinese and Spanish freedom presenting all as part of one
problem.

These items refer only to public engagements. I have not included
interviews or meetings with groups arranged at private invitations
of useful people.

I want to plead not guilty to any effort at trying to make an
'overwhelming programme' . . . Miss [Agatha] Harrison is very
helpful and so have some members of the more responsible
members of the Indian community . . .

After writing thus far I have had a telephone call from the British
National Committee of the I.P.C. and the National Committee of
Civil Liberties wanting to hold receptions officially. I could not
find my way to refusing these and so I with due politeness accepted
them on your behalf. So the programme becomes more and more
overwhelming as the days go by . . .

Nehru and Krishna Menon met in Genoa, and the two then
went to Spain for a five-day visit as guests of the Republican
government there. They were accompanied by Bhicoo 'Bee'
Batlivala, who had come along with Nehru. In fact, Nehru had sent
a detailed letter to his party colleagues from the *S.S. Biancamano* on
11/13 June 1938, when it was somewhere in the Mediterranean.
It ended thus:

Miss B. Batlivala who is a fellow passenger, has kindly acted as
my secretary during the voyage and has helped me greatly. She
accompanied me to Cairo and Alexandria.

Daughter of a prosperous Bombay textile-mill owner and educated
in England, Batlivala was among the youngest to be called to the
Bar from the Inner Temple in 1932. She was to become prominent
in India League activities and toured the US in 1939–40 for around
six months, speaking to various audiences on civil liberties in India
and India's freedom. She was able to garner considerable local media
attention wherever she went. She was a very effective speaker on
behalf of the India League, as this letter to Krishna Menon of 25 May
1939 from a Mary Fox would testify:

The Presbyterian Settlement
56, East India Dock Road
Poplar, UK

Dear Mr. Menon:

This is a rather belated way of saying 'Thank you very much' for sending Miss Batlivala to our women's meeting . . .

She delighted the women themselves, whom I have never seen more interested in what a speaker had to tell them, and she made us feel that with the problems of India there is also a real need to see things in their true perspective.

I know that I have the opinion of the meeting when I send you our best wishes for the success in your enormous task of informing the British public of the situation, and wish personally to add my wish that the campaign for India's freedom, may be successful.

Bhicoo Batlivala, or 'Bats' as Krishna Menon would refer to her, is a completely forgotten figure now. She married an Englishman Guy Mansell sometime in 1938, settled down in London and years later opened an international girls school in Kent, which still exists. She appears to have stayed in touch with the Nehru family and Krishna Menon till at least the mid-1950s.

India League all-women public meeting, London, 1941

Right through rest of the year, Nehru and Krishna Menon would exchange letters on the supply of foodstuffs and medicine to Spain by people Nehru called 'the bourgeoisie of Bombay'. On 21 November 1938, Nehru was to tell Krishna Menon that he was

> fortunate enough, in spite of my leftist views and tendencies to have a measure of popularity with the merchant class in Bombay.

In 1935 and 1936, Nehru was well known. But this time in 1938, he commanded greater stature in the world and was already being seen as Gandhi's successor. His autobiography had sold hugely. The Congress had done very well in the provincial elections. He had been Congress president for two successive terms. This was definitely a new Nehru. He spent a fortnight in the UK, diligently sticking to the back-breaking schedule put together for him by Krishna Menon.

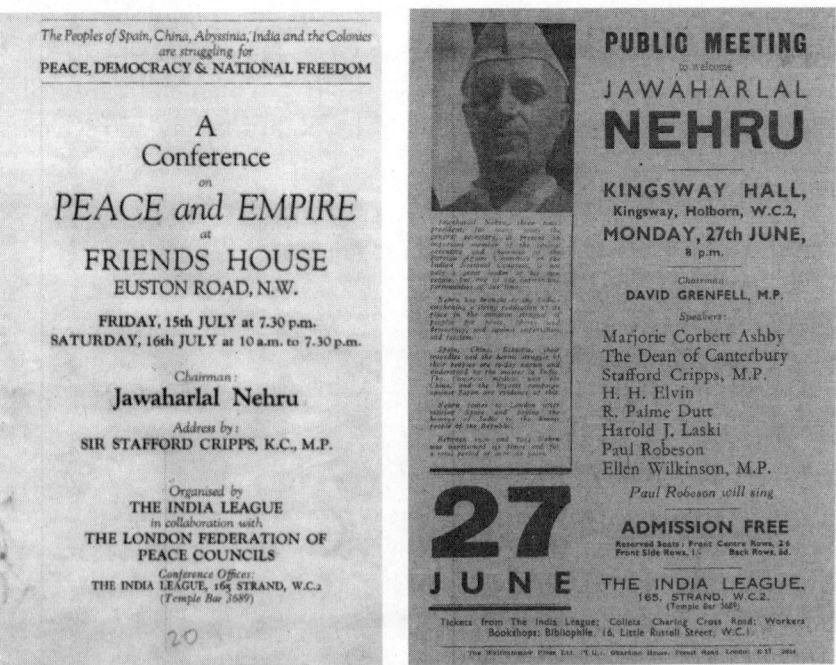

India League public meeting addressed by Nehru and Cripps, London, 1938

While Nehru met with a very large number of people on this visit, including with officials of the British government, perhaps the most significant meeting was the one that took place at Stafford Cripps's farm, which Krishna Menon had carefully planned in collaboration with the host. It was to get Nehru and Clement Attlee to get to know each other well. This meeting was recorded by Attlee himself in an unpublished version of his autobiography. In the typed manuscript, Attlee mentions in his own hand 24 June 1938 as the date of his conversation with Nehru. The idea of the ill-fated Cripps Mission of 1942 emanated from this meeting.

Two leading lights of the Labour Party—Nye Bevan and Richard Crossman—and a noted anti-colonial journalist Leonard Barnes were also present. Barnes was to write about the proposals discussed at this meeting in his book *Empire or Democracy*. On 27 February 1939, Barnes told Krishna Menon:

> I am distressed to find that you are worried and think that the publication of the Indian proposals may create difficulties. I assure you that it didn't occur to me for a moment that there was any danger of this. Our previous correspondence had suggested to me that as long as there was no indication of how the proposals arose, you were content to leave to my discretion the use of the substance of them in my book. At the time when I first wrote to you, I also wrote in a similar sense to Laski, and as I heard nothing further from him I assumed, perhaps with insufficient warrant, there would be no objection to what I had in mind.
>
> . . . As regards my book, it is due to appear in a fortnight and it is therefore too late to alter the text. There is, of course, nothing in the text to indicate the source of the proposals, or to implicate any individual or group or party . . .

Why Krishna Menon was worried is difficult to understand because Nehru had already informed his senior colleagues, in a note sent to them on 1 August 1938 from Houlgate in France, of what had transpired at the meeting with Attlee. Barnes's book[5] described the terms on which a transfer of power would take place when Labour

took office, which were discussed at length between Attlee and
Nehru in their meeting of 24 June 1938. These terms included: a
constituent assembly elected on universal suffrage to decide on a
future constitution; representation of princely states in the constituent
assembly; the lapse of all British treaties with princely states, with the
passage of the constitution; and a settlement, with a bias in favour of
India, of the long-standing problem of India's debt. Most of these
terms were indeed to form the basis of the transfer of power in 1947.

There was one meeting that Krishna Menon was not keen on but
that Nehru wanted included in his schedule. This was with Philip
Kerr, or Lord Lothian as he was known. Lothian was a politician,
diplomat and newspaper editor and had been an admirer of Gandhi
in the early 1930s. Later, he became part of a circle called the
'Cliveden Set', which acquired a reputation, deserved no doubt, of
being in favour of appeasement of Nazi Germany. Krishna Menon
was not in favour of Nehru meeting Lothian and his friends. Nehru's
daughter was even more stoutly opposed to it and had, in fact, said so
to him on 23 April 1938:

> . . . I have been seeing Krishna about your trip. The only thing
> that is worrying me is your intention of staying with Lothian—and
> please don't think that it has anything to do with what Krishna
> thinks of him . . . He is a very prominent member of the 'Cliveden
> Set', the set that forced Eden to resign and the set that is commonly
> known as 'Hitler's friends in Britain'. He is a thorough Fascist and
> makes no bones about it. Your staying with him would amount
> to the same as if you spent a weekend with Hitler himself or with
> Mussolini. It would create a terrifically bad impression on all people
> in this country who are even slightly 'left' & who sympathise with
> India & the Congress . . .

So why did Nehru disregard his daughter's strong advice as also
that of Krishna Menon? He was to studiously avoid meeting any
German leaders when he was in Munich, and Mussolini when he
was in Rome as part of his European trip. But he made an exception
in Lothian's case. Nehru explained his decision to his daughter on

30 April 1938, an explanation that would have undoubtedly been shared with Krishna Menon as well:

> . . . I am not surprised at your feeling strongly about Lothian. I feel more or less the same way . . . But still after careful consideration I decided to accept his invitation . . . It is a long-standing promise and I don't want to break it . . . I happen to be something more than a prominent leader of a group or party. I have a special position in India and a certain international status. I have to function as such whatever my personal likes or dislikes might be. If anybody thinks that by my visiting Lothian I am betraying my cause, or adding to Lothian's prestige, or tarnishing my own reputation, I cannot help it . . . If I am so weak so as to be influenced by him then I am not much good anyway. It may be that I am in a stronger position to counter him later. I feel therefore I should accept. I shall be sorry if you are unable to accompany me . . .

Another meeting of Nehru, this time at the prestigious Royal Institute of International Affairs, created a different type of problem. The institute is located at Chatham House and its meetings are subject to what, even today, are called 'Chatham House Rules'.[6] What these are will be clear from this letter that its acting secretary, Margaret Cleave, wrote to Krishna Menon on 4 August 1938:

> I feel I ought to let you know that we have been informed from two different sources that information regarding remarks made in the discussion following Mr. Nehru's address at Chatham House on July 5th have been received in India. The first was a reference to a statement made by Mr. Bose in connection with the remarks by Sir Frederick Whyte; the second was an article from the 'Bombay Chronicle' which has been sent to me which describes the discussion as a whole.
>
> As you know, it is our definite ruling that meetings of the Institute are private and though information received at such meetings may be used no reference to the source of its receipt or to the names of persons who speak should be made. The Council

very much regrets that its rulings should not have been adhered to on this occasion and as we communicated with you in the first place with regard to Mr. Nehru's address I feel that my only course is to inform you of the position.

I shall be most grateful if you would be good enough to let me know whether you can make any suggestions regarding the name of the person who might have provided this information in contravention of the rules which govern the admission both of members and of their guests.

Krishna Menon replied six days later:

I am in receipt of your letter of August 4th and note its contents. I do not quite know what you expect me to do about it. I really do not know what the second paragraph of your letter means. Surely you do not hold me responsible for everyone who attended your meeting or any leakage which may have taken place. I regret I am unable to make any suggestion as to detecting the source of the leakage of information, as you ask me to do in the final paragraph of your letter.

Stung by this reply, Cleave complained to Agatha Harrison:

I have just received the enclosed letter from Mr. Menon. It has the distinction of being the rudest letter that I have received at Chatham House during the whole of the seventeen years I have been here.

Harrison replied to Krishna Menon's barbs the same day:

I have received your letter of August 10th. I think if you will re-read my letter to you of August 4th you will realize that its only purpose was in common politeness to inform you that a leakage had occurred in contravention of the Institute's rules at a meeting in connection with the arrangements for which we had been indebted for your assistance. Since the rules of the Institute have been contravened enquiries are being made as to the source of the leakage and the help of anyone possible will be solicited in tracing it.

There are no records to indicate what happened thereafter. But this must surely be one of the very few occasions when Chatham House rules were broken and the ever-controversial Krishna Menon would figure in the episode even if he were not guilty of the leak. One of the witticisms attributed to him is this: when asked why he always attracted controversy, he said that if controversy chased him, he would meet it halfway!

Nehru's visit also resulted in Krishna Menon having a rare spat with Masani and his CSP colleagues. The spat presaged their parting a year later. On 30 August 1938, an incensed Krishna Menon wrote to Asoka Mehta:

> . . . I very much regret that the Congress Socialist has published a report of the Conference on Peace and Empire recently held here which is untrue in material particulars and essentially mischievous . . . It appears to be implied in your report that the Conference and the resolution were dictated and engineered by the Communist Party. As Secretary of the India League I take strong exception to this lie. The I.L.P members alone imported the partisan and organizational fight into the Conference . . . It is ridiculous to suggest that there was any attempt to soft pedal the fight against imperialism or for National independence and self-determination.
>
> I am in profound disagreement with a considerable part of what is printed in the Congress Socialist but I have refrained from making a protest as I feel that the Socialist movement in India cannot gain by the emphasis of differences between socialists. In this matter, however, I have an obligation to do so, and I believe I owe it to your readers.

Mehta published the letter without any changes in the *Congress Socialist* but it was becoming increasingly evident that the relationship of Krishna Menon with the CSP was under considerable strain. This, in spite of Masani's request to him a few months earlier on 14 March 1938:

> Dear Comrade:
>
> The Annual Conference of the Congress Socialist Party meets at Lahore on April 12 and 13.
>
> It would hearten the delegates to the Conference to have a message of greetings from your organisation.

This was a standard letter sent to many but Masani added in his own hand:

> Dear Krishna: Please send a few words of personal greetings from yourself also.

Nehru spent fifteen days in the UK and thereafter went to France, Germany, Hungary, Switzerland and Czechoslovakia. He came back to London and, before finally leaving for India, wrote to Krishna Menon on 11 October 1935 from Bexhill, a seaside town in the south-eastern part of England:

> During these past few months I have come into close contact with many young men and women who work for the India League, and a feeling of comradeship has grown between us. I have admired the way they have given their time and services in the cause of Indian freedom, and I shall often think of them when I am far away in India. Soon I shall be going back home. Before I go I should very much like to meet them again and to say goodbye to them. As I am leaving on the 24th morning perhaps the best time for us to meet will be the 23rd afternoon. I suggest therefore that we might all foregather at Ormonde House on the 23rd October (Sunday) at 4 pm . . .

Krishna Menon had a large fan following among students from well-to-do families in India, who went to England to study mid-1930s onwards. These students later went on to have distinguished political careers, some as leftists and others as communists.[7] In addition to Mohan Kumaramangalam and Rajni Patel, Nikhil Chakravarty and his wife-to-be, Renu Roy, were also part of Krishna Menon's orbit, as were Kumaramangalam's sister Parvathi and her husband-to-be, N.K Krishnan. Jyoti Basu and Bhupesh Gupta too were part of this fraternity. On 28 October 1938, Nehru would write to Krishna Menon:

> If you go to Cambridge, get in touch with Homi Bhabha who is a Fellow of Caius College. He is a brilliant physicist and has an intelligent appreciation of political events. I met him today for a few minutes as he was going to England on his way back from India. He has some information about some really good scientists who are at a loose end because of the anti-Jew movement . . .

Krishna Menon did meet with Bhabha but their relations were generally low-key, even though both were to be part of Nehru's innermost circle later. There is some evidence to suggest that Bhabha considered Krishna Menon too leftist for his liking,[8] while Krishna Menon felt Bhabha was too eager to please the Americans. Krishna Menon also abhorred the development of nuclear weapons. There is an unverifiable story that when India carried out its very first nuclear test on 18 May 1974, Krishna Menon, who was then in hospital in Delhi with less than five months to live, literally summoned Indira Gandhi and gave her a dressing down.

In July 1938, the Indian National Congress sent a five-member team of surgeons along with medical supplies to help the Chinese army that was fighting the Japanese. The team was led by Dr Madan Atal, a cousin of Nehru's wife. It was serendipity that both Nehru and Krishna Menon appeared to have thought of Dr Atal almost at the same time. On 31 March 1938, Krishna Menon wrote to Shelley Wang, who was closely associated with the Chinese Ministry of Foreign Affairs at Chungking and with the Chinese Foreign Minister T.V. Soong:

. . . I introduced to you the other day Dr. Atal. He is a brother-in-law of Nehru. He graduated in medicine in London about 20 years ago and was a house surgeon in a hospital in a responsible position. In India he is a well-known doctor . . . Recently he went to Spain and was there for eleven months on different fronts, doing valuable medical work of which I have heard excellent reports from reliable sources.

I discussed with Dr. Atal the idea of going out to assist in the struggles of China against Fascism and he is willing to give his services. If this is acceptable to your people, Dr. Atal will go to India at once and endeavour to raise a small medical mission . . . Once I hear from you that your authorities accept Dr. Atal's services, I will cable Nehru to make an immediate appeal for Chinese medical aid . . .

We will be able to arrange for Dr. Atal's passage, etc., but once he is in Chinese soil he will be fully at the disposal of the Government and as you realize, must be their responsibility while he is in the country . . . There is one final point. If one of the Chinese leaders would take the opportunity of cabling to Nehru their thanks for the offer and the great need of China for medical assistance, it would help to swell the volume of opinion and build solidarity between our peoples . . .

Krishna Menon then got in touch with Nehru, who was independently thinking along similar lines. Krishna Menon was able to raise around 300 pounds during Nehru's talks and lectures in London, which was put in a bank account under the name of 'Congress Medical Aid to China' and operated by him on behalf of the Congress. Nehru would meet with both Shelley Wang and Atal during his visit to London and firm up the Congress medical mission to China.

Dr Atal was to stay in regular touch with Krishna Menon after his team reached China. He would write to him from time to time, asking for medical books and supplies of not only medical items but also of things such as boot laces. Krishna Menon looked after Atal's finances in London. That the Indian medical team, which took with it ambulances, X-ray sets, disinfecting apparatus, cars and many cases of medicine, made a huge impression on the Chinese is evident from a letter dated 24 May 1939, which Krishna Menon received from a top Chinese leader:

Dear Friend:

It has been our pleasure to hear from our common friend Dr. Atal about the splendid work you have done for Spain and India. The Indian medical unit, which you have been instrumental in sending, has arrived with us in Yenan and have begun their work energetically and have been warmly received by all the members of the 8th Route Army. In the name of the members of the 8th Route Army we wish to thank you for your help and hope that you will continue your good work and constantly help us in all ways possible so as to help in driving out the Japanese imperialists from China.

Yours sincerely,
Mao Tse Tung

A similar letter was sent to Nehru as well. Krishna Menon replied on 12 July 1939:

Dear General:

I received your letter of 24th May with grateful appreciation. Our countrymen here and in India are glad to know that the Indian Medical Unit is with the 8th Route Army and that you are pleased with their work.

It is a great privilege for India to be associated even in this humble way with the heroic struggle of the Chinese people against Japanese Imperialism and Fascism.

We have heard from India that Pandit Nehru will soon be visiting China. I very much hope that you will have an opportunity of meeting each other.

Nehru did go to China soon thereafter but could not meet Mao, having had to rush back after Germany's invasion of Poland began. He did, however, have long conversations with Mao in Peking in October 1954. Krishna Menon made his only visit to China in May 1955 but I could not establish conclusively that he had an audience with Mao. In October–November 1962, Mao's decision to wage war on India would destroy Krishna Menon politically and inflict significant damage to Nehru's legacy.

One of the members of the Atal team, Dr Dwarkanath Kotnis, would stay back and marry a Chinese woman. He has become an iconic figure in China and been immortalized on celluloid in India as well. Atal too became very attached to China, went back there in November 1957 and passed away in Peking a month later. When the Second World War broke out, and it appeared that Krishna Menon's interest in China was flagging, he would receive a request from none other than Madame Sun Yat-Sen to continue his work for her country out of London.

Towards the end of 1938, as I had mentioned earlier, Anna Pollak would enter Krishna Menon's life. They would write to each other very often, especially during 1940–46. That he was extremely fond of her and enjoyed her company is obvious from his numerous 'Dear Emily' letters to her that continued till the early 1970s. He encouraged her to develop her musical interests and talents, and in later years, she became a famous mezzo-soprano. Pollak's obituary that appeared on 29 November 1996 in the London *Times* eulogized her as a very gifted musician but strangely made no reference to her very active India League years. Instead, it mentioned that 'in her youth she was reputed to have had a close friendship with Jawaharlal Nehru before he became Prime Minister of India'. She may well have known Nehru although there is no evidence of their friendship. On the contrary, it is without doubt that her one abiding passion, other than opera, was Krishna Menon. Pollak remained unmarried and, in her final years, lived with Erica Marx, a descendant of Karl Marx. She later recollected:[9]

I joined the India League at the end of 1938 having worked (between theatre jobs) for Isobel Brown's anti-fascist group. Started by filing, cleaning (!), making tea, eventually typing (sort of) and printing News India on the Gestetner [cyclostyling machine] . . .

Other voluntary workers:- Feroze Gandhi, Marjorie Nicholson, Rajni Patel, Agatha Harrison, Haksar, Shelvankar . . .

Visitors: EM Forster, Cripps, L. Woolf, Indira Gandhi, Gallacher, Pritt, Paul Robeson, Haldane, Levy, Sorensen, Michael Foot . . .

<u>3rd Sept 1939 War declared</u>

KM and I stood on Waterloo Bridge in a suddenly deserted and deathly still London. KM: How long will the war last? Three months?
KM addressed meetings all over Britain—became an Air Raid Warden in
St. Pancras . . . Worked often all night thru' the Blitz . . .

Her entry in the *New Grove Dictionary of Music and Musicians* says, 'Despite her virtual lack of formal musical or vocal training, Pollak was one of the most musical, versatile and satisfying singers of English opera of the post-war period and an actress of great accomplishment and style.'

Notes

1. Duff (1982).
2. I have chronicled Haksar's life in Ramesh (2018).
3. Gopal (1975).
4. Callaghan (1993).
5. Barnes (1939).
6. A 'rule' according to which information disclosed during a meeting can be used but without attribution—explicit or implicit.

7. Ramesh (2018).
8. Ibid.
9. These handwritten notes of the late 1980s were made available to me by Janaki Ram.

8

The War Years (1939–44)

1939

Nehru wrote over a hundred letters to Krishna Menon between 1935 and 1940 and received as many in return. Over 60 per cent were written during the two years of 1939 and 1940. Nehru's letters dealt mostly with Indian politics, the Congress party, the *National Herald* affairs, his thinking on international issues and the publication of his books. Nehru was the chairman of the board of the *National Herald*, the daily newspaper launched in August 1938. Krishna Menon would be an integral part of it over the next decade. His letters to Nehru were mostly about his assessment of British politics and political personalities; his views on European and other world matters, particularly Russia, Spain and China; his advice to Nehru on what the Congress's stance should be in its negotiations with the British government; and ideas on what Nehru ought to be doing as the country's pre-eminent leader, next in importance only to Gandhi. In 1939 particularly, the letters also dealt with the serious illness of Nehru's daughter, who had to be hospitalized in Switzerland for pleurisy. These letters make fascinating reading even eighty years after they were written. They reveal two lonely individuals who took their political role very seriously and who were comfortable with each other, revelling in their exchange of ideas, and very British in their temperament though intensely committed to the cause of Indian independence.

Of the letters that Nehru wrote to Krishna Menon, none would be as poignant as that of 17 May 1939. The Congress was going through an intense battle of supremacy between Gandhi and Bose. Substantively, on economic policy at least, Nehru was closer to Bose, but Gandhi was Gandhi. Nehru's relationship with him was not just political but also very personal and emotional. In the backdrop of the acrimonious feud raging in the Congress, he wrote to his London confidant:

> I have been sending you letters from time to time dealing with various matters that arose. I shall continue to do so, for the mind keeps on functioning through sheer habit. So also I shall carry on with my usual activities, though I realize more and more how I am losing in efficiency. But I want to tell you briefly the state of my mind. It is bad. I have lost all pep and feel devitalized, and my interest in life seems to be fading away. Don't be alarmed. I can still function fairly effectively and it may be that I shall recover my vitality. For the moment, however, the outlook is not encouraging. Most of the things that I value and for which I have worked seem to be going to pieces . . . Nearly all the conceit I possessed in such ample measure has been knocked out of me . . . What has happened in Spain has affected me greatly as a deep personal sorrow. What has happened and happening in India, being near to me, affects me continuously. The kind of human material that I see about me, the all-pervading pettiness and vulgarity, the mutual suspicion and back-biting and so many other things distress me beyond measure . . .
>
> I am sorry to write to you and to distress you . . . I do so . . . partly to relieve myself. There is hardly anyone here to whom I can speak with frankness about myself here. But please do not worry. It is a phase which will pass perhaps.

The last few lines of this extraordinary letter give a clue to understanding the unusual Nehru–Krishna Menon camaraderie. Nehru saw in him a kindred spirit and wrote to him regularly to unburden himself, sharing thoughts he would not with any other person, including his own daughter or sister.

The events in the Congress in the first few months of 1939 unsettled Nehru immensely. It was clear that he and Bose had not just developed ideological differences but their personalities too had begun to clash. Heated letters were exchanged between the two. This episode, based on their correspondence, was the subject of a dispassionate analysis by an eminent Indian historian.[1] For the purposes of this biography, what is revealing is that the only person Nehru opened up to was Krishna Menon sitting in faraway London. The first of these confessions was on 22 February 1939 and was from Gandhi's ashram in Wardha:

> . . . Subhas has gone off the rails and has been behaving badly in many ways. His principal supporters are very irresponsible and unreliable people and it is quite impossible for me to join this motley group with whose viewpoints on national and international politics I do not agree . . . Apart from principles and politics, Subhas's methods of work are difficult to put up with. He has paralysed the AICC office and passes orders over its head in all manner of election matters and local disputes—these orders are flagrantly partial and against our rules or procedure.

A few weeks later on 31 March 1939, back in Allahabad, Nehru continued to be piqued with Bose and wrote again to Krishna Menon:

> . . . Subhas Bose's attitude is the reverse of helpful and under his direction a virulent propaganda is being carried on all over Bengal . . . He has completely alienated the Congress Socialist Party and many other advanced elements . . .

Four days later, Nehru was at it once more:

> . . . There seems to be an unbridgeable gap between Gandhiji and Subhas. Subhas owing to his illness has become even more difficult

to deal with and he is full of an idea that there is a conspiracy against him . . . I feel very helpless and I see no way out for the moment.

One of Subhas's grievances against me . . . is his objection to the foreign policy I have sponsored. In a recent letter to me he talks about the folly of my espousing lost causes and of always condemning Germany and Italy . . . Subhas has lately come to the conclusion, most unjustifiably that I am pulling the strings against him from behind the scenes. As a matter of fact, I have done my utmost to stand up for him and to tone down the hostility of the old leaders to him . . . But what is more important is the emergence, in Bengal and elsewhere, of communal and semi-communal groups who have become champions of Subhas . . .

Nehru was keen on offering employment to Jewish professionals fleeing Germany and other European countries but he faced opposition from his colleagues, mainly Bose. Krishna Menon too was keen on India offering asylum. On broader political issues, Nehru did not agree with the position taken by either Gandhi or Bose. In the deadlock between the two, Nehru was caught right in the middle. This unsettled him considerably. But undoubtedly there was more to this crisis that had engulfed him as he was about to turn fifty. Not available in his archive for some reason but available in Krishna Menon's is an earlier letter of Nehru's that reveals the troubles he was going through. On 2 March 1939, he had written to Krishna Menon:

Allen Lane of the Penguin Books came to see me yesterday [in Allahabad]. Among other things, he discussed the possibility of bringing out old essays of mine in his series. I told him you were thinking of making some arrangements about them and referred him to you.

I want to tell you that for some little time past I have been mentally very ill and it is with difficulty that I am carrying on. This has nothing to do with the political crisis, but this of course added to this burden. It is just possible that even physically I might have a breakdown, though this is unlikely as I have got a very regular constitution which can stand almost anything. I am not writing this to add to your worries. But I felt I ought to give you a friendly warning about myself.

We can only speculate on the nature of Nehru's personal anguish. There is no clinching evidence for any one explanation. My own guess is that he may have been told by his daughter that she wanted to marry Feroze Gandhi, and that news may well have agitated him. Nehru liked Feroze, encouraged him politically and had helped him out in London but marriage to his daughter was an altogether different proposition.

Meanwhile, Nehru's profile as an author was developing. Early 1939 saw Krishna Menon arranging for the publication of Nehru's second international bestseller, *Glimpses of World History*. The publisher was Lindsay Drummond, for whom Krishna Menon had already edited a number of well-received books in an 'Educational Books' series. One of the earliest books in this series was by K.S. Shelvankar. The book, *Ends Are Means*, was a riposte to Aldous Huxley's *Ends and Means*. Krishna Menon was also to help Shelvankar publish his soon-to-be famous *The Problem of India*, which was Penguin's first book on India. It was promptly banned in the subcontinent but was nevertheless read very widely and made its author a celebrity. Penguin's first book on India may well have been *Glimpses of World History*, for which Krishna Menon had completed negotiations in March 1937. But that deal fell through for a variety of reasons, including the fact that John Lane The Bodely Head had collapsed.

Perhaps in recognition of the crucial role he had played in making it possible, Krishna Menon wrote the foreword to the first UK edition of *Glimpses of World History*:

'GLIMPSES OF WORLD HISTORY' was written in different prisons in India during the three years between October 1930 and August 1933 . . .

Pandit Jawaharlal Nehru took advantage of his enforced rest, his 'leisure and detachment' as he calls it, to write on world history. He wrote it in the form of letters to his young daughter . . .

These letters were gathered together when Pandit Nehru had a brief respite, prior to his last period of two years in gaol after being arrested once again on the 12th February 1934 and sentenced for 'sedition'. His sister . . . Vijayalakshmi Pandit . . . arranged for their publication in book form as 'Glimpses of World History' in 1934 [in India].

Pandit Nehru resumed his active life in public affairs after his release in 1936. The period since then has been one full of activity and responsibility . . . The present volume is in many ways a new book. It has been revised, to a considerable extent re-written, and brought up to date to the end of 1938 by the author himself . . .

'Glimpses of World History' is no mere narrative of events, valuable as the work is in this respect, but also a reflection of the author's personality . . .

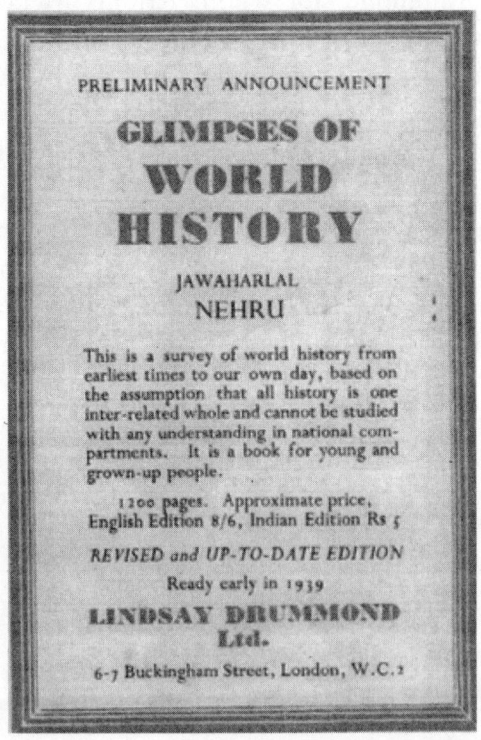

Pre-launch announcement of Nehru's second book with which
Krishna Menon was associated, London, 1939

Two years later, Krishna Menon would arrange for the publication of yet another of Nehru's books, *The Unity of India*, to be published by Lindsay Drummond. It was a collection of Nehru's articles and speeches, and it too had a foreword by Krishna Menon:

The Unity of India is a selection from Jawaharlal Nehru's writings and Press statements on diverse topics during the five-year interval between his last imprisonment [that ended on 3 September 1935] and the present [that began on 31 October 1940.] They were originally mostly written in the crowded compartments of Indian third-class railway carriages, in the intervals between great meetings of important Congress committees, often in the small hours of the morning after a whole day of political campaigning or grave discussions.

Jawaharlal Nehru entrusted me the task of making the necessary selection of his writings and of putting them together for the publishers. I have had no opportunity of consulting him about the form of this book, nor has he seen its proofs. Correspondence between us has been restricted for a number of reasons and my hopes that I should be able to obtain his approval for the final form of this book have proved vain on account of his imprisonment. I hope, however, that he will see a copy of this book sometime—in prison or outside.

I have also added, at the request of the publishers, a number of footnotes, notes and other appendices to make the text easily understood by those whose knowledge of Indian affairs is limited.

To Jawaharlal Nehru I am deeply grateful for his generous confidence . . .

NEHRU

An important announcement

Lindsay Drummond are glad to be able to announce the publication in February of a

NEW BOOK BY NEHRU

It will contain *his very last writings before his imprisonment*, including his *statement at his trial.*

THE UNITY OF INDIA is a collection of Jawaharlal Nehru's writings for the last three years. They cover every subject, and must be read by all who wish to understand the Congress attitude.

The world may not see another book from Nehru for some time. His voice is no longer heard, but his message still lives.

THE UNITY OF INDIA

edited and annotated by Krishna V. Menon
432 pages   Lindsay Drummond,   12s. 6d.
                             6 Buckingham Street, Strand.

Pre-release announcement of Nehru's third book with which Krishna Menon was associated, London, 1939

Between April and September 1939, Krishna Menon wrote over twenty letters, each running into many pages, to Nehru on the political situation in Britain as it faced a threat from Germany. These were based on his conversations with a wide array of people in politics, academia and the media. They provided a running commentary to Nehru on what was happening in Europe, a subject that deeply interested and concerned him. The running thread in these letters is the emergence of a unity of left forces to deal with the threats from Nazism and fascism. Krishna Menon's dilemma is evident in these letters. On the one hand, he was acutely conscious of the need to sustain this left unity and fully backed it; on the other, he was aware that the issue of Indian independence had to remain on Britain's political agenda.

These letters also dealt with personal matters, as did this one of 8 April 1939:

> . . . You may remember some conversations we had about Feroz [Gandhi] when you were here [in 1938]. I told you he was a lad with character whatever his other traits be. I said that with knowledge and what has been going on recently has confirmed me in that view. He has had of course tremendous advantages over some others that he has been with you for long before he came here. About recent political events he had no more knowledge of facts than others but he was one of the few young people here who showed any commonsense. Also I find that even after a row he never tells tales—even when he talks to himself or thinks aloud as he may do frequently!

As soon as war broke out Krishna Menon wrote to the *Manchester Guardian* on 9 September 1939. It would be safe to assume that he was not only articulating his own views but also reflecting Nehru's in some ways:

> I am deeply concerned with the prospect of world war and it depresses me exceedingly to realize how British foreign policy is directly leading to war. It is true that Herr Hitler has the last and determining word in this matter, but Herr Hitler's decision itself will largely depend on the British attitude . . .
>
> In any case we in India want to [end] fascism and imperialism and we are more convinced than ever that both are close akin and dangerous to world peace and freedom . . . Only free and democratic countries can help freedom and democracy elsewhere. If Britain is on the side of democracy then its first task is to eliminate empire from India. That is the sequence of events in Indian eyes and to that sequence people of India will adhere.

The same day he advised Nehru:

There should be a statement [from the Congress Working Committee] of war aims. The statement of war aims should include the liberation of countries taken by Hitler, no truck with fascist powers, Italy or Japan as allies, no secret engagements and the insistence of self-determination. Peace aims should include no reparations, no conquest and recognition of our independence on the basis of self-determination and a Constituent Assembly. During the war our contributions should be free and based on our consent which means recruiting not on a mercenary basis and labour corps but India taking part in her own defense primarily and for the defense of liberty on the basis of liberty, democratization of army, etc.

Almost as soon as he got the message Nehru cabled back his agreement on the suggestions, and five days later, the Congress Working Committee (CWC) passed its historic war resolution at its meeting in Gandhi's ashram at Wardha. A few weeks later on 25 October 1939, Krishna Menon wrote to Nehru about his reading of British thinking on India based on the conversations he had had with various MPs. He also updated Nehru on his daughter's health, which had been a matter of continuing concern for him:

Indira is much better. She will have to stay in hospital for another three weeks. Dr. Bhandari is trying to get her off to Switzerland to which I am told she is agreeable . . .

The situation here is that government will not make any advance now or at any time of a kind that you can accept. They know what we want but they think that they can avoid agreeing to it . . .

The developments of events shows the correctness of the Congress attitude. The demand for clarification of war aims is gaining strength here . . . Parliament is about to debate India but the parliamentary debate is no epoch-making event . . .

. . . The Empire says Congress is not India. There is only one way of answering this question effectively . . . The position is that the Empire must settle with the Congress and agree to India's independence. Congress must settle with the others on the Indian side such differences as can be met and are genuine . . .

The debate in the House of Commons was to take place on 27 October 1939; two days later and twenty-four hours earlier, MPs, mostly from the Labour Party and a few from the Liberal Party, were briefed by Krishna Menon. This time he was joined by another Indian, Maulana Hasrat Mohoni of the Muslim League. Mohoni was a die-hard socialist, and his views and those of Krishna Menon's converged on many matters. Mohoni was one of the founders of the Communist Party of India in 1925 and a firebrand Urdu poet who had coined the revolutionary slogan *Inquilab Zindabad* (Long Live the Revolution). He stayed back in India after 1947, dying in Lucknow four years later. That day, in one of the committee rooms of the House of Commons, Mohoni told the British MPs that the Muslim League had agreed with the Congress's demand for independence. Scotland Yard was to prepare a detailed almost verbatim report on this meeting.

Nehru turned fifty on 14 November 1939, and Krishna Menon gave him the good news that 'Indira is making excellent progress and Dr. Bhandari is well satisfied' and that 'there is no anxiety about her and no fear of a relapse'. He went on to add:

Gandhiji's statements no doubt mean something different from what average people understand from them but they have a confusing effect. I am not suggesting that he should not make them as it would be impertinence on my part to say so . . . At this distance it is difficult to understand things . . . There is no prospect so far as I can see of this or any other government coming to an agreement on the lines Congress seeks except after a victorious resistance . . .

Krishna Menon had numerous friends and well-wishers in England even as he kept accumulating critics and enemies. Harold Laski was undoubtedly his intellectual and political mentor. Next only to Laski in Krishna Menon's ideological world in the 1930s was Stafford Cripps, firmly entrenched on the left in the Labour

Party. Cripps had also been a strong advocate of the unity of all left forces, including the communists, to deal with the threats posed by fascism—a stance supported by Krishna Menon enthusiastically. The two had come to know each other in 1932 or thereabouts. Krishna Menon would write every now and then for Cripps's *The Tribune*, and Cripps would take a regular part in India League demonstrations and meetings. Their friendship deepened once Cripps became aware of the high esteem in which Nehru held Krishna Menon.

India League public meeting, London, 1939

Cripps was planning his first visit to India in the later part of 1939, and on 29 October 1939, Krishna Menon informed Nehru:

I am to let you know that Sir Stafford may be coming to India in early December on his way to China. He has as you know given up his practice altogether.

Two days later he provided further details on Cripps's trip:

> . . . He hopes he may be able to stay for under three weeks . . . He
> is not coming on any mission but as a friend of yours and says he is
> going to put himself in your hands as regards what he may do there. I
> told him that it would be best for him to see every one. The Viceroy,
> Jinnah and others who are against the Congress and Indian aspirations.
> He would like to stay with you for at least part of the time and desires
> the whole matter to be left with you . . . It would be good for him to
> see something of the villages and the Congress organization. But one
> thing I do know he cannot afford to travel. It is surprising with his
> large income at the Bar when he was there he should today be like
> this. I think he is much better for the change . . .

Krishna Menon met with Cripps frequently in November 1939 to
firm up his visit. He informed Nehru of Cripps's tentative schedule
on 20 November 1939 and went on:

> . . . It would be extremely valuable to know what Sir Stafford has
> to say and no one appreciates more than I do his great sincerity and
> his enthusiasm to do right things but I had at no time very great
> and uncritical reliance on his judgment . . . He is going to America
> after China and it is this aspect of the matter that is of the greatest
> importance.
>   . . . Since his expulsion from the Labour Party Sir Stafford is
> mainly functioning as an individual and he appears to have approach
> to the Cabinet and everybody else . . . On India, he has lately been
> in touch with Sir Stanley Reed and Sir George Schuster. [They]
> are obviously not of the [Samuel] Hoare or Winston [Churchill]
> kind. They will go farther and they might even pay lip service to
> the idea of a constituent assembly . . .

Nehru replied on 2 December 1939:

> . . . I wish you had come out with Cripps. I understand Cripps
> fairly well. His visit here will make no difference to us, or very

little but I hope it will help him to understand a little more the Indian problem.

As Nehru had anticipated, Cripps's first visit to India in the first fortnight of December 1939 was not earth-shaking in any way but it did help establish his reputation back home as an 'India hand', having friendships with those who mattered in the subcontinent. It was this reputation that would lead to his going back in 1942 and 1946 as an official representative of the British government to work out a framework for the transfer of power. But on both occasions he failed. This would lead to considerable strain in the relationship between Krishna Menon and Nehru. Many years later in early 1958, Lady Isobel Cripps, Stafford Cripps's widow, would speak to Marie Seton, who would note down their conversation:

> Lady Isobel Cripps says that K.M. [Krishna Menon] was on close terms with Stafford Cripps but he never conducted his relation with him like anybody else. He had an aversion to making any appointment with Cripps through his office or secretary. He would ring up Lady Cripps sometimes as early as 7 a.m. and 'demand to see Stafford' . . .
>
> Lady Cripps now says that she was always fond of Krishna but she has to make an effort to be objective about him today because she has now been told by people in India that 'K dripped poison to Nehru about Cripps throughout the years'. Whether it is true or not, she has been led to believe that K.M. played a vindictive role against Cripps, particularly over the 1946 mission . . .

While Krishna Menon was busy finalizing Cripps's visit to India, he was also making a determined effort to be the fourth Indian to be elected to the House of Commons. After considerable lobbying on his part, his candidature for Dundee was endorsed by the National Executive Committee of the Labour Party on 25 October 1939. Jute trade unions were influential in Dundee and Krishna Menon had local activists campaigning for him.

But in an extraordinary turn of events the Dundee *Courier and Advertiser*, in its issue of 19 April 1940, was to carry this news:

> Mr Krishna Menon was removed from his position as prospective Socialist candidate for Dundee in consequence of alleged activities with bodies opposed to the official policy of the Labour Party . . . Mr Menon is a London barrister and a native of India . . .

The charge was clearly that Krishna Menon was a communist. But this decision to cancel his candidature did not sit well even with the strongly anti-communist Jute and Flax Workers' Union, which passed a resolution in a special meeting held on 12 May 1940:

> This AGM [Annual General Meeting] . . . learns with amazement that the DTC&LP [Dundee Trades Council and Labor Party] has revoked the decision of the Selection Conference which unanimously adopted Mr. Krishna Menon . . .
>
> We most emphatically protest against the undemocratic procedure adopted . . . without any explanation or consultation . . .
>
> We, knowing Mr. Menon's popularity and worth to Dundee and Indian jute workers, the enthusiasm with which he has thrown himself into the fight for workers interests . . . express our profound and complete confidence in him . . .
>
> This meeting demands that the DTC &LP rescinds its decision . . .

Thereafter followed a detailed investigation by the Labour Party and finally on 29 November 1940, G.R. Shepherd, national agent of the Labour Party, wrote to Krishna Menon:

> . . . The National Executive Committee has expressed the view that the procedure followed by the Dundee Trades Council and Labour Party was wrong . . .
>
> At the same time the National Executive Committee came to the conclusion that no useful purpose would be served in maintaining your candidature for Dundee . . .

The National Executive Committee [NEC] . . . recognizes you
as a representative of an important section of Indian public opinion
and it believes that your first loyalty lies in that direction. Whilst
it cannot, even if it had the desire to do so, question your right as
a British subject to seek entrance into the House of Commons, it
does not believe that you ought to seek such entry through the
British Labour Party . . .

Krishna Menon was first announced as a candidate. Then, his
candidature was cancelled ostensibly because of his proximity to the
Communist Party of Great Britain (CPGB). Now he was being told
that he could not agitate for India's independence while seeking
to represent the Labour Party in the House of Commons. It was a
volte-face by the Labour Party because Shapurji Saklatvala, a card-
carrying member of the CPGB, had earlier, in 1922, contested
for the House of Commons as a Labour Party candidate and won.
Saklatvala was a nephew of the founder of the Tata empire—J.N.
Tata—and became the third Indian to become a member of the
British Parliament.

Krishna Menon, who had been a member of the Labour Party
since 1924 and a borough councillor since 1934, was incensed and
did not take this stinging rebuff lying down. He sent Shepherd a long
and emotional reply on 23 December 1940, accusing the Labour
Party of nothing less than racism:

> . . . The National Executive Committee have now introduced a
> national and racial bar into the Labour movement . . . Labour Party
> policy is now declared by its Supreme Executive to be opposed
> to the basic conceptions of self-determination and national
> independence of subject peoples, and at best to be some form of
> benevolent and patronizing imperialism . . .
>
> It has been my good fortune to share the comradeship and
> to receive the friendship and confidence of large numbers of
> men and women in the Labour movement who, I feel sure,
> will not understand or accept your doctrine . . . In relation to
> India, my position remains unchanged. I am unrepentant in my

allegiance . . . The people of India have no quarrel with the people of this country. Their struggle is directed against an exploiting and oppressive system . . .

This extract does not do full justice to the scathing indictment of the leadership of a party with which Krishna Menon had been so intimately associated for so long. Soon thereafter on 16 January 1941, Krishna Menon would write to James Middleton, secretary of the Labour Party:

The recent decision of the NEC makes it impossible for me to remain a member of the Labour Party. The national and racial bar that you have imposed leaves me no option but to terminate my long association with the Labour Party.

As you are probably aware, I am Chief Whip of the Borough Council Labour Party at St. Pancras and hold other posts in the Labour Movement. I will be able to make the necessary arrangements in regard to all this in a week's time, so if it is convenient to you, may this resignation take effect at the end of next week.

By 1939, Scotland Yard was convinced that Krishna Menon was a communist in all but name. Surveillance on him intensified, and on 8 March 1939, the authorities were told:

V.K. KRISHNA MENON

MENON represented India at a meeting of the General Council of the International Peace Campaign held in London on 18th and 19th February and attended by delegates from thirteen countries . . .

In his speech MENON said: I have been instructed by the Indian National Congress to make clear that the resolution recently adopted by the Indian Legislative Assembly on the initiative of the Congress Party, recommending Indian withdrawal from the League of Nations, does not mean abandonment by the Indian people of the policy of collective security. This action is a protest against the British Government's refusal to apply Article 16 and make the League effective.

On 28th February MENON was to have spoken at a meeting held by the China Campaign Committee at Conway Hall, Red Lion Square W.C., in connection with that body's anti-Japanese campaign. The speaker who preceded him, however, took up too much of the time available and MENON was not, in consequence, called upon to address the meeting.

For British police authorities, Krishna Menon not speaking was as much news as his speaking. May Day celebrations evoked the interest of Scotland Yard, which reported on 1 May 1939:

MAY DAY DEMONSTRATIONS

The communist May day demonstration was held on 1st May and took the form of a march from the Thames Embankment to Hyde Park in the afternoon and a march from the Park to Chennies Street W.C. in the evening . . . Some 3000 persons participated in the principal march including a contingent of 60 Indians who were grouped under the banner of the India League and led by V.K. Krishna MENON.

At the Park MENON was one of the speakers. He said: ' . . . As an Indian I am entitled to address thousands of young people in this country, and am going to ask them whether they will cease to be citizens and become part of an imperialist army to engage in oppression . . . It is our business if we believe in the ideals of democracy and peace to bring down this government . . .

The resolution passed at the demonstration included a demand for the extension of full democratic rights for all peoples within the British Empire, and the complete independence of India, and the Irish by the abolition of Partition.

This particular Scotland Yard report engaged the attention of no less a man than Sir Samuel Hoare, who was then the home secretary. He then 'directed' his aides to also bring it to the notice of Lord Zetland, then secretary of state for India. Krishna Menon was referring to the Partition of Ireland in 1922. Little would he have realized that eight years after he had called attention to it, India too would be subject to similar vivisection. This particular May Day speech of his also showed how close he had got to the British Communist Party. Over the next few years, Krishna Menon would be as intimate with Harry Pollit and Rajni Palme Dutt as he had been with Laski and Cripps in the 1930s. This would, of course, mean greater scrutiny of his day-to-day movements and activities by Scotland Yard and other intelligence-gathering agencies.

Spain and China had been Krishna Menon's non-India preoccupations the past two years. Now he would take more interest in pan-African issues. This reflected his association with people such as George Padmore and Paul Robeson, who were even more ideologically inclined to mainstream communism than he was. On 9 June 1939, he wrote a long review article in Cripps's *The Tribune* based on three books that had just been published on the West Indies, one of which was by W. Arthur Lewis, who would win the Nobel Prize in economics exactly forty years later. The full-page piece by Krishna Menon read:

ESCAPE FROM THE PLANTATION BARRACKS

The group of islands in the Caribbean Sea now known as the West Indies, is one of the oldest and most exploited parts of the Empire. They were discovered by Columbus romantically 'by mistake' for India. There the romantic part of history ends. The rest is rather sordid. Settlers swarmed in. Slave labour amassed fortunes in cocoa, coffee, sugar and cotton for them. The very 'prosperity' which has enabled the fortunes to be built during the eighteenth and nineteenth century was based upon the misery and oppression of the toilers. Prosperity has gone. The misery has become intensified and once again West Indies has become news. There have been riots and strikes, firing and oppression. Oil and sugar interests are asserting the rights of civilization over the people who are refusing to sit mute under exploitation and tyranny. A political conscience

has arisen. Labour and Trade Union movements have taken shape
in the islands . . .

His article in *Keys,* the quarterly journal published by the League of
Coloured Peoples that had been started by the Jamaica-born Harold
Moody, attracted the attention of Scotland Yard on 12 July 1939.
Right through the 1950s when he was India's top envoy at the
United Nations, Krishna Menon would be an indefatigable crusader
for the end of colonial rule in countries such as Algeria, Cyprus,
Congo and other African countries and for the ending of apartheid in
South Africa. This would be one reason that he came to be intensely
disliked by the Western powers during that decade.

Germany's invasion of Poland on 1 September 1939 caused
Nehru to cut short his China trip and return home. He was not then
a member of the CWC. When he came back he was persuaded to
become a member and also the chairman of a three-man subcommittee
comprising of two others—Maulana Abul Kalam Azad and Sardar
Vallabhbhai Patel—to deal with the completely altered political
situation. Gandhi and Rajagopalachari came out spontaneously
in support of Britain, while Bose wanted civil disobedience to be
launched immediately. Nehru was somewhere in between, and his
position was: 'If Britain fought for democracy, she should necessarily
end imperialism in her own possessions and establish full democracy
in India.'[2] On 16 September 1939, Nehru sent Krishna Menon a
copy of the statement issued by the CWC on the Congress's
position on the war. Four days later in an editorial in the *National
Herald*, Nehru wrote, 'India can no longer consent to be treated
as part of the Empire. She will not permit herself to be used as a
subject nation ordered about by others. Whether in peace or war,
she must function as a free nation.' Krishna Menon gave the CWC
statement the widest publicity in the UK. That included sending it
to a man who was the Congress's most virulent enemy in England
and who would take over as Prime Minister eight months later. On
2 October 1939, Krishna Menon wrote to Winston Churchill, who
was then just an MP:

I beg to enclose for your information a copy of the statement of policy of the Indian National Congress on the War situation.

Congress has appointed a War Emergency Committee of three of which Pundit Jawaharlal Nehru is the chairman. He, more than any other individual in India, is the guardian of the 'moral conviction' to which you referred in your broadcast speech of Sunday last.

Pandit Nehru wrote to me sometime ago about your greetings and good wishes for the success of his mission in China. That visit has been remarkably successful though it had to be sharply curtained owing to the outbreak of the war and the consequent necessity of Nehru's presence in India.

I thought you would perhaps be interested in seeing the text of this statement, which I learn is Nehru's draft and has the full support of Mr. Gandhi especially in view of recent developments. If I can give you any further information I shall be most happy to do so.

Churchill's reply is not traceable but a little while earlier a flabbergasted Nehru had written to Krishna Menon on 15 August 1939 on the eve of his departure for China:

I had a long cable from the Chinese Ambassador in London relayed to me by the Consul in Calcutta. In this cable he sent me his good wishes and greetings. It ended up by a curious and unexpected sentence as follows:

'Winston Churchill requests me to send his good wishes for success of your mission'.

What is the world coming to?

The very same day that he wrote to Churchill, Krishna Menon also wrote to W.P. Crozier of the *Manchester Guardian*, a leading journalist generally sympathetic of the Indian cause:

. . . You would no doubt have appreciated from the Congress statement which is Nehru's draft, that he is looking at the problem not merely in India's but in the world context . . .

Perhaps I should anticipate the question I so often meet—what do we propose we should do—and answer it . . .

The element of such a solution appear to be (1) a statement of objectives which would recognize India as a free nation on the basis of self-determination; (2) that the full implementing of this objective is not sought to be delayed by a procedure of instalments or by checks and safeguards and other delaying processes . . . (3) immediate steps to enable India to function as a free country, that is, so altering the nature of her central authority as to make it a government of the people . . .

Two days before he had written to Crozier, Krishna Menon had sent a couple of letters in quick succession to Nehru. This was not unusual for him. There were occasions when he would write three to four letters in a day to Nehru. In one of these communications of 30 September 1939, he suggested a five-point scheme for the Congress to adopt:

I.   A declaration of objective, a guarantee that India will take its rightful part in present policies and in the peace terms . . .

II. That there should be a transitional provisional government which is based on the de facto support of legislatures newly elected on franchise already in use in India . . .

III. Congress seeks a government that reflects the will of the people as a whole and have always regarded the guarantee of minority rights as essential in any scheme . . .

IV. If this is agreed at once a further transitional arrangement for the next couple of months till there is an election is necessary and for that purpose it is suggested that a council of three provisional ministers (two Congress) and others . . . be appointed and that in that period the government do not undertake any more ordinances or legislation that is absolutely necessary and which is assented to by this council . . .

V. An emphatic declaration that India is attempting no
blackmail but refusing to be drawn into any adventure of
which she has no control and of the direction of which she
knows little . . .

Krishna Menon was dead opposed to the idea of a federation and
told Nehru so. He categorically preferred an 'autocratic centre' rather
than a dyarchy. He ended his letter with an amusing confession, a
liberty he would often take with Nehru:

Personal

I apologise for the shocking way in which this letter is typed. There
is no one here and I am not well. Most people think I am in bed.
So please do not feel unduly irritated at incomprehensible words.

By now Nehru was used to Krishna Menon's awful typing and
completely illegible handwriting. He was also used to Krishna
Menon's mind working overtime even as he lay ill in bed. But nine
years later Nehru was to tell Krishna Menon that it was 'not an easy
matter to read your handwriting'.[3]

Krishna Menon's five-point scheme must certainly have appealed
to Nehru, who wrote to Krishna Menon on 11 October 1939 from
Wardha, which suggests that Gandhi too would have been aware of
what Krishna Menon was proposing. After giving Krishna Menon
a description of the various forces at work within the Congress and
telling him that 'there is a deep-seated antipathy' of coming to terms
with Britain, Nehru finished by saying:

. . . The proposals you make are generally good . . . It seems to
me that under the present circumstances we cannot formulate any
definite proposals on behalf of the Congress for the transitional
period. In our talks with the Viceroy however we adopted the
general line taken by you and thus made some definite suggestions.
I cannot see how all this is going to lead to a proper compromise.
The forces against it are too strong and the inertia of a century old

Government of India is something terrible. Even the shock of war
does not affect it much . . .

Seven months later Churchill became Prime Minister and what little
opportunity may have existed for Krishna Menon's proposals moving
forward were squashed.

By the end of 1939, Krishna Menon was able to score a victory
of sorts at the highest levels of the Congress. Thus far, while he and
Nehru had been canvassing for the idea of a constituent assembly
to draft a constitution for a free India, Gandhi's response had been
somewhat lukewarm. But on 25 November 1939, Gandhi wrote
an article entitled 'The Only Way' in *Harijan* which started with
a confession:

> Pandit Jawaharlal Nehru has compelled me to study, among other
> things, the implications of a Constituent Assembly. When he
> first introduced it in the Congress Resolutions [on 14 September
> 1939], I reconciled myself to it because of my belief in his superior
> knowledge of the technicalities of democracy. But I was not free
> of skepticism. Hard facts have, however, made me a convert and,
> for that reason perhaps, more enthusiastic than Jawaharlal himself.
> For I seem to see it as a remedy, which Jawaharlal may not, for
> our communal and other distempers, besides being a vehicle for
> mass political and other education. The more criticism I see of the
> scheme, the more enamoured I become of it. It will be [the] surest
> index to the popular feeling. It will bring out the best and the worst
> in us . . .

The same day Nehru wrote to Krishna Menon saying that Gandhi
had become the greatest convert to the idea of a constituent assembly,
something Krishna Menon had been championing for over five years.
It was a vindication of his efforts at keeping this idea in circulation.
His thoughts on a constituent assembly for India had been developed
in the early 1930s with the help of Laski and Labour MP David
Grenfell, and he persisted with it. Of course, in parallel, Nehru too
had been thinking along similar lines.

1940–44

Krishna Menon was a regular contributor to the *National Herald*, and invariably what he wrote was published. But once—and perhaps only once—what he wrote was rejected by Nehru himself. Krishna Menon had sent the article to Nehru on 24 January 1940, who did not send it on to the editor. This was because Nehru believed that the former's judgement of the political situation in India was not correct and that he had overestimated the chances of any agreement between the British government and the Congress. Krishna Menon had also been critical of Nehru for capitulating to Gandhi's position too easily on all matters and for supporting a position that did not take into account the global dimensions of the war. Obviously, Nehru saw the Second World War fundamentally from India's point of view, whereas Krishna Menon started from the position that the conflict was a global war against Hitler and Mussolini, in which India must play a role because 'the victory against fascism is our victory too'. On 26 December 1939, he had told Nehru:

> . . . I do not know whether in view of the personal views I hold about the war it is found inappropriate that I should be occupying the position that I do with you . . .

But to give him full credit, whatever personal views he may have held, Krishna Menon went out of his way to propagate the official Congress stance aggressively. But in private, he accused Nehru of compromising all too often and not giving a firm and clear leadership to socialist forces in India. Implicit in Krishna Menon's criticism was that Nehru did not confront what he considered the 'right-wing old guard' in the Congress, represented by the likes of Patel, Rajendra Prasad and Rajagopalachari. Nehru replied on 2 March 1940:

> . . . You need not apologise when you write in criticism of me. Not only have you a perfect right to do so but I welcome it very much. What is more, this is not a matter of personal likes and dislikes. We are dealing with vital matters of great importance

and personal feelings cannot be allowed to come in the way . . .
You seem to have a grievance against that I remain silent when
I should give a lead or should contradict some wrong statement.
I am not very silent as a rule, but it is true that I dislike publicly
criticizing my colleagues even though I might disagree with them.
Public controversies do not help matters and do not bring about
the desired results . . .

Not only did Nehru ruthlessly self-analyse but he also turned the
spotlight on Gandhi himself:

Gandhiji . . . is not a static factor or person. His language is different
from the language of politicians . . . He is a tower of strength for
Indian freedom and his yeas and nays make a difference. Ever
since war began he has gone through many painful processes
of thought and gradually he has accepted various propositions
and made them his own . . . Previously he accepted them in a
much vaguer way and sometimes interpreted them according to
his own fashion. This applies both to the idea of a constituent
assembly and to independence . . . He is convinced that events
are moving towards a conflict in India which means some form
of civil disobedience. When this takes place he envisages it as
something on a very big mass scale . . . There will be an element
of finality about it.

This being his general outlook, it seems to me essential for all
of us to support him, unless something happens which makes this
almost impossible . . . If you keep all this in mind, you will be able
to understand Indian events better . . .

Krishna Menon would wax eloquent on Gandhi in the 1950s and
1960s, but the fact remains that he was never able to comprehend
Gandhi the way, for instance, Nehru, Patel and others did. He was
also unable to comprehend that to Nehru organizational discipline
was of paramount importance. Nehru was not averse to being
revolutionary in terms of ideas, but he was not prepared to be a rebel
in terms of action if that meant confronting and defying Gandhi.

Krishna Menon had four years earlier tried to get Gandhi to write a book on his philosophy. But that had not succeeded. He had not forgotten the idea, and sometime in February 1940, Krishna Menon suggested to Nehru that he would be the best person to write a book on Gandhi, which he would then get published in the UK speedily. But Nehru was reluctant, and he replied on 8 March 1940:

> . . . As for a biography of Gandhiji, it is quite impossible for me to undertake it for reasons other than those of time. An active politician can never write frankly and freely about his colleagues. I have refused even to write articles on the subject . . .

He went on to acknowledge his differences with Krishna Menon on the prevailing situation in Europe, revealing that Nehru was no blind supporter of the Soviet Union:

> It is true, I think, that in some matters not immediately relating to India, there is a difference in viewpoints between you and me. I entirely agree that the British and French Governments are exploiting some of the small nations for the furtherance of their imperialist designs. It follows from this, as well as from our own national reasons, that we must not be parties to this game in any way whatsoever . . . At the same time it does not follow, to my thinking, that we must plump for the other thesis that Russian action in Finland has been right or justifiable. Personally, I do not even think it is expedient . . .

Nehru ended wistfully by saying:

> . . . But I must stop here. How I wish that I could have long talks with you. But that seems to be beyond our reach for some time at least . . .

During this time both Nehru and Krishna Menon were preoccupied with disseminating the message of India's anti-colonial struggle. Krishna Menon had always wanted to go to America to spread the gospel of India's freedom. He had tried once in 1931 but that attempt had fizzled out, most probably because of lack of funds. Then in 1939, three of his colleagues—Bhicoo Batlivala and Rajni Patel from the UK and Kamaladevi Chattopadhyay from India— spoke to American audiences and evoked much interest. Spurred by this, Krishna Menon made one more effort to cross the Atlantic. Nehru wrote to Maulana Azad, who had become Congress president earlier in the year, on 21 April 1940:

> You will remember your discussing with me the question of someone going on our behalf to America . . . not just as a propaganda tour delivering speeches, etc., but someone with sense who could meet our many friends in America and make arrangements for future work on an efficient basis. America is full of goodwill for us . . . As it is not possible to send anyone from here, I have been thinking of some suitable person going from England to America for this purpose . . . The only such person I can think of is Krishna Menon . . . not as our formal representative but unofficially, though with our goodwill.
>
> I had not mentioned this at all to Krishna Menon, but he has been thinking on the same lines and he has written to me independently that he was considering the prospect of going to America. His chief difficulty is one of funds. I would suggest that at least 100 pounds be sent to him as soon as possible. Apart from this, I shall personally try to contribute something to this end . . .

The previous month, on 14 March 1940, Nehru had written to Krishna Menon saying that Azad had written his presidential speech entirely in Urdu and had then asked Nehru 'to take the responsibility for translating it into English'. Nehru called the speech 'an address essentially of an advanced and liberal Muslim divine'. Saying that Azad reminded him in some ways of the French encyclopaedists of the nineteenth century, Nehru went on to describe the new Congress president at some length and ended by telling Krishna Menon:

I am writing this long and rather unnecessary letter to you to give you some background of our new President. This will help you to understand somewhat . . . The real reason for writing this letter is that suddenly I found I had some time at my disposal.

Azad agreed to Nehru's proposal and Krishna Menon's America trip was being planned. Nehru even wrote out a long letter of introduction full of praise for Krishna Menon. But the trip soon hit a snag. The home department of the Government of India telegrammed London from Simla on 30 April 1940:

> We understand that V.K. Krishna Menon is contemplating a visit to America with view to influencing American and neutral opinion, in connection with which he is seeking support from Nehru and letter from the President of the Congress. Visit is dependent on the provision of funds which may prove obstacle, but we feel strongly that passport facilities for this mission should not be given and trust that you will agree that steps might suitably be taken to ensure that if application is made, visa is withheld.

As it turned out, Krishna Menon had to wait for another six years to make his maiden visit to the US, and he was to do so officially as a member of the Indian delegation to the UN.

By 1940, British authorities were more than convinced that Krishna Menon was openly supporting the Soviet Union. A British government internal note observed on 2 January 1940:

> . . . For some past MENON's views on the subject of Finland have been almost indistinguishable from those advanced by the Communists, but so far as can be ascertained, he has arrived at this standpoint not because he is on the road to becoming a genuine Communist, but because being an opportunist, he argues that to condemn Russian aggression in Finland is to support the present Government, which according to him had always wanted a stick to beat Russia and has found one in the invasion of Finland. He regards that invasion, not as a crime against a small nation, but as

just possibly a diplomatic faux pass . . . He is understood to have
said that from the moral standpoint, the invasion was 'bad manners',
but that on rational and political grounds it was justified . . .

Adding to their suspicions was an article he wrote in the February
1940 issue of *Russia Today*, the organ of the Russia Today Society.
The article was entitled 'Socialism and Empire: Russia's Challenge',
and Krishna Menon was identified as the 'Secretary of the India
League and in close contact with the Indian Congress Socialist Party'.
The India Office record of 7 February 1940 of the article said:

> This article certainly constitutes a very open espousal of the Russian
> cause . . . It is probable that Menon will not be particularly pleased
> at being described as 'in close contact with the Congress Socialist
> Party' as to the best of my knowledge, he has ceased to have any
> liaison with them since the Haripura [1939] Congress . . .

In the article Krishna Menon clearly irked the British government by
comparing the conditions of the citizens of the Soviet Republic of
Tadjikistan favourably with those of Indians:

> Much has been written about Russia, mostly European Russia. An
> Oriental might perhaps be forgiven for allowing himself to think
> that perhaps the greatest achievement of Soviet civilization is in
> the vast revolution in the living conditions of the most backward
> peoples of the former empire of the Tsars. Some of these Asiatic
> peoples live across the Indian border . . . India's industries were
> ruined under the East India Company . . . Her great towns like
> Murshidabad and Mongyr are tragic memories now, her famous
> muslins and even her handicrafts have decayed . . . The Tsars did
> the same thing to Bokhara, but Tadjikistan today has her industries
> and their development is encouraged and assisted by the central
> resources of the U.S.S.R.

Krishna Menon confused the British to no end by his links with
the CPGB. On the one hand, he had exceedingly warm relations

with the top leaders of the CPGB such as Pollit, Bradley, the Palme Dutt brothers and Gallacher. The India League worked very closely with the CPGB and its various affiliates in promoting the cause of India's freedom. More than the Labour Party, it was the CPGB that was categorical and consistent in its support for Indian independence without any caveats. But an internal India Office note of 10 May 1940 noted:

> . . . Menon has no genuine Party loyalties: he is first and foremost anti-British and thereafter only, an extreme Socialist. He is not a Marxian Communist, having neither the brains needed to work out Marxian dialectics for himself, nor the type of character which would enable him to accept spoon-feeding from those who have. He joined the Labour Party with an eye to the main chance (in so far as Indian independence is concerned, not for reasons of personal aggrandizement) but has never subscribed loyally to the Party's views . . . For him . . . the war . . . has been a side issue compared to that of Indian independence. He has taken his stand uncompromisingly for complete freedom for India outside and beyond Dominion Status and for the setting up of a Constituent Assembly to determine India's future Constitution.

The general view of the British authorities in London all of 1940 was that Krishna Menon's views on India and world affairs reflected that of Nehru's and that he was a 'near communist' and worked intimately with the communists to propagate the idea of Indian independence. A certain reluctant admiration for him comes through in many of these reports.

Meanwhile, events in Britain were moving dramatically. Churchill replaced Chamberlain as Prime Minister on 6 May 1940 and Krishna Menon gave his assessment to Nehru twelve days later:

> . . . In the Cabinet the imperial sentiment dominates . . . Amery [secretary of state for India] . . . is a profound believer in the imperial mission. It is inconceivable that either self-determination or independence can be reconciled to his views . . . Amery is

totally ignorant of Indian politics and he will be in the hands of officials and tradition and even more in the hands of Linlithgow [viceroy] . . . Cripps is running round in circles and seeing this great man and that . . . His plan appears to be that some delegation, in which I think he includes himself either as a member or as a mediator with plenipotentiary powers should go out to India and settle with Indians on the spot. He is bold enough to tell the folks that some courageous step like this is essential but he is not able to realize that men who rule us do not behave in that way . . .

I am proposing to see some of my old pals who are now great men with Cabinet jobs. I think it would be bad manners on my part not to inform their minds . . . We have lost our former friends, the one time pacifist Ellen [Wilkinson] is now the loudest warmonger . . . The people are getting familiar to the prospect of the Germans attacking this country itself . . .

On 22 July 1941, about a month after the Second World War had taken a dramatic turn by the German invasion of Russia, the British government announced its long-awaited plan of action for India. Even before reactions came from India, Krishna Menon swung into action and produced a fifteen-page booklet, *India, Britain and Freedom*, denouncing it in no uncertain terms. The booklet was as usual distributed widely and evoked positive comment. He ended the pungent analysis by declaring

A free India is a potent ally. A subject India is a weak spot in Britain's moral armour and a weak link in the chain of the battlements of world freedom. The liberation of India is the strongest and most convincing appeal that Britain can make to the subject peoples of Europe to rise against their oppressors . . . The people of Britain must call upon the Government to . . .

(a) *recognize the National Independence of India;*
(b) *agree to self-determination and a Constituent Assembly;*
(c) *agree to a Provisional Government with full competence and able to command the confidence of the Indian people;*

(d) *establish civil liberty forthwith;*

(e) *release the political prisoners;*

(f) *propose a treaty of mutual friendship and the reference of all outstanding
    disputes to arbitration.*

We have seen in the recent brief but historic weeks, new alignments,
new faith, new enlightenment and new understandings. It gives us
hope and it should give us confidence.

Krishna Menon was obviously referring to the whole new situation
created by Britain's support for Russia following Hitler's Operation
Barbarossa. But Churchill remained unmoved.

Popular India League pamphlet, London, 1941

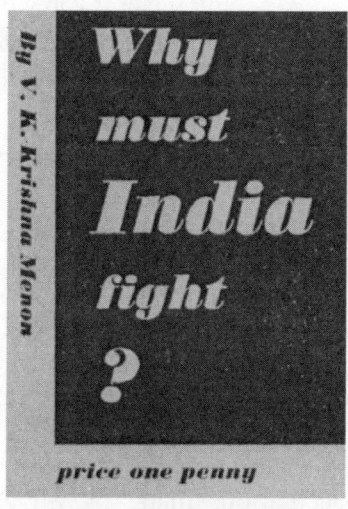

*One of Krishna Menon's best-known
pamphlets, London, 1941*

Nehru's eighth round of imprisonment began on 31 October
1940. His previous term in jail was between 28 October 1934 and 3
September 1935, when Krishna Menon was not part of his personal
or political or literary world. The two had lost contact with each
other, and on 13 July 1941, Nehru bemoaned to his London friend
and literary representative from the District Jail in Dehra Dun:

It is ages since I heard from you or had any real news of you. Indira gave me some scraps of information but they were vague . . .

I learnt from the newspapers that my book 'The Unity of India' had come out . . . I was interested to read, however, in an article by Arthur Moore, the editor of the Calcutta Statesman . . . that he found the book well-displayed in the bookshops of New York, Los Angeles and San Francisco, and many Americans were reading it 'earnestly' . . .

The American edition of my autobiography has reached me at last. On the whole it is satisfactory . . . It appears that the book has had a remarkably fine reception in the US . . .

Do send me news about yourself. The delays and difficulties in the way of letters are obvious. Still it is worthwhile trying to surmount them. If you write, address your letters to Anand Bhavan Allahabad. This is the safest address as I am always liable to be transferred to some other jail.

Two months later Nehru wrote to his daughter:

. . . I have got a copy at last of *The Unity of India* . . . I like the get-up of the book. Krishna has taken a lot of trouble over it. I have not heard from him at all. You must have seen his long letter in *The New Statesman*.

In that letter which was published on 24 May 1941 in *The New Statesman and Nation*, Krishna Menon had defended Nehru from accusations made by Sir Alfred Watson, one-time editor of the Calcutta daily *The Statesman*, that he was being accorded special treatment in jail:

The suggestion that Mr. Nehru is a specially treated prisoner is entirely untrue. According to the law of India he is not even a 'political' prisoner, but just a common criminal undergoing rigorous imprisonment . . . Sir Alfred Watson is also in error about the Congress . . . It subsidises no one and no group outside India. There are occasions when a person is authorized to speak on its behalf. I have had this privilege for some time but the Congress neither directs or controls any propaganda here . . .

Even though they had lost touch, Nehru weighed heavily on Krishna Menon's mind. He launched a high-voltage campaign to have Nehru released and organized a number of public meetings and protests, beginning in London on 23 November 1940. He got many noted British personalities to speak, such as Reginald Sorensen, Rajni Palme Dutt, Julius Silverman and H.N. Brailsford. He organized public messages of support for Nehru from others such as Laski and Haldane. These protests evoked a lot of interest in the public at large, who had thus far not concerned themselves with India. India League suddenly saw subscriptions come pouring in, and men and women from across the UK wrote to Krishna Menon deploring the British government's incarceration of Nehru. But some were hesitant as well. On 19 April 1941, Mabel Ridleigh, treasurer of the Women's Cooperative Guild, wrote to Krishna Menon:

> . . . I am sorry that I cannot allow my name to be used at the moment for your campaign. Mrs. Cook is under the impression that the India League is in close cooperation with the Communist Party and as the Guild as an organization is not working with them, she feels that the National Executive must be careful not to be linked with them.
>
> I want to assure you that Mrs. Cook has every sympathy and so have I with the [India] League and also other members of our Committee. If you could let me have your assurance that the India League is not connected with the Communist Party and let me have the answer at our Guild office address by Thursday morning latest it would add strength to your request when I put up your letter before my committee who are meeting that day.

Clearly, it was not only Scotland Yard that believed that Krishna Menon was in bed with the Reds. He defended himself to Ridleigh five days later:

. . . So far as the India League is concerned its work is quite open . . . with regard to your query whether we are connected with the Communist Party the answer is No.

The India League is non–party organisation and has always been so . . . It is an independent organisation seeking no alliance with any political party or indeed any organization . . . It is a movement to support freedom and self-determination for India . . .

We could not make it a rule that Communists, I.L.P., Labour or any other group should not be associated with our work anywhere but in fact we keep to our business and it has worked quite satisfactorily so far . . .

I have given you the facts at length not to argue a case as I do not feel called upon to do so but I felt quite sure that you are anxious to be of assistance and also because I think these stories are put out by interested parties and most people accept them either because they are indifferent to our purpose or because they are prepared to accept any such stories for reasons of their own . . .

But this high-decibel campaign seemed to have had little impact on the person who really mattered—namely, Churchill. Nehru remained jailed for fourteen months. But 'Britain's Prisoner', Krishna Menon's widely circulated pamphlet on Nehru, did attract the notice of the home department in New Delhi on 21 February 1941:

The attached copy of 'Britain's Prisoner' a pamphlet published by India League, London on 26-1-41 is for information. This pamphlet was specially produced by V.K.K. Menon for distribution at the Independence Day meeting organized by the India League and held at the Conway Hall. This pamphlet is more objectionable than the usual run of India League publications.

The file went up to one R. Tottenham, who noted on the file five days later with some admiration for Krishna Menon's effort:

Pretty quick work. Written on Jan 26th and contains Abul Kalam Azad's sentence at the beginning of the month. I presume action has been taken to prevent its entry into India.

Like much of Krishna Menon's written work in this period, this too was banned in India but was to be available in the UK. Whatever he was doing was certainly attracting the attention of the British authorities. On 15 December 1941, the home department again noted:

> The resolutions passed at the meeting of the India League's National Convention on 10.8.41 which demanded, inter alia, the recognition of India's right to independence, and the immediate release of prisoners and the establishment of full civil liberty, were the outcome of the well-organised efforts of the League which were being carried on for a considerable time, often by exaggerated, and sometimes false, allegations about the treatment of political prisoners in jails, and jail administration in India in general . . . It has become obvious that some sort of counter-propaganda in England and the tightening up of censorship in India of outgoing press and private telegrams, was necessary. It is hoped that the measures which would no doubt be taken in England . . . will prevent the India League from creating further false impressions about India and we may await further developments.

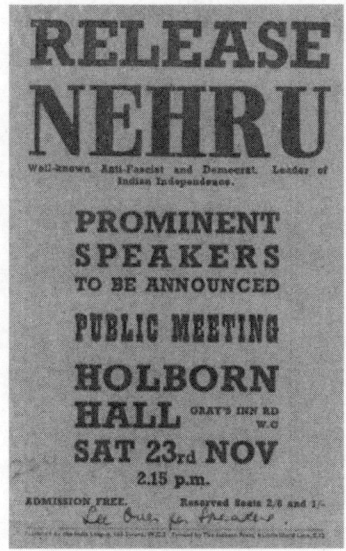
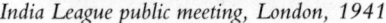

India League public meeting, London, 1941

Another of Krishna Menon's widely read and circulated pamphlets, London, 1941

Scotland Yard had reported on the India League Convention of 19 August 1941 which was a grand success. But some people who Krishna Menon wanted to be present could not attend and sent messages of support instead. Three were from the 'usual suspects'. Laski said:

. . . The delay in fulfilling the unanswerable claim of India to self-government is, in my judgment, not only indefensible in itself, but one of the main sources of suspicion that Great Britain is not fighting for its declared objectives in this war. I think no better aid could be given to our cause than (1) the immediate release of Indian political prisoners, (2) the fixing of a date by which self-government in India will come into operation and (3) the summons of a Constitutional convention to work out a form of government for India . . .

Haldane was characteristically pungent and provocative:

I know only one theory which would justify the continuation of British rule over Indians. This is Hitler's theory of superior races, against which we are supposed to be fighting. Only after we have granted national independence to India can we logically ask the German people to do the same to the conquered nations of Europe . . . The continued suppression of India is not only a disgrace to Britain. It is a danger.

And, of course, no India League assembly could be complete those days without a message from Pollit:

. . . Your conference meets during one of the greatest crises in the history of mankind, one in which India has a role to play second to no other country. It is deplorable that our own Government's attitude towards the Indian people is so inexcusable . . . If the British Government would immediately release Comrade Nehru and other political prisoners, it would in my opinion, be the first practicable step towards assisting the Indian people to take their stand alongside the British and Soviet people and this development would facilitate the achievement of other desirable measures of justice and freedom for India.

But two messages were unusual. The first was from Emmeline Pethick-Lawrence, wife of Lord Pethick-Lawrence, who would, four years later, take over as secretary of state for India in the Attlee government and have much to do with Krishna Menon from a position of authority. She said:

> . . . Democracy is on trial for its life. The greatest of all issues is in question. Can liberty and ordered government be maintained and extended throughout the civilized world? The war has shaken to its roots the old political order, national and international. Now is the time for vision and for the power to seize the opportunity for effecting and constructive change. Nothing is more vital to the peace and welfare of the world than a consummation of free and equal union between the British Commonwealth of Nations and the great community of Indian peoples . . .

Margery Corbett Ashby was a well-known suffragist and Liberal politician. She was quite involved in India League activities, but this time she gave Krishna Menon the cold shoulder:

> My experience of the meeting at the Conway Hall was so unfortunate that I must frankly say that I don't want to come on to the platform on Aug 10th. I had refused because I was expecting to be at another conference which has however been postponed for a week. At the last meeting one of the speakers demanded that Churchill and his government should go, which seems to be silly as if we had an election many MPs would go. Churchill would remain as the national and popular leader. Then when you had consulted me about the Daily Worker and I gave you my opinion Mrs Haldane who had listened to us first announced the *Daily Worker* would be sold. It wasn't well organised and the resolution passed was left for nearly a fortnight before being sent to Amery.

I am really keenly interested in India and I have been twice to see
Amery. I have tried in vain to interest the Liberal Party. I do so
wish I could help you but I find myself involved with people I
can't trust and policies only declared at the last minute.

Krishna Menon's relations with his communist friends changed
subtly following the German invasion of Russia in June 1941. When
this happened, a majority of the British communists were in favour
of Britain, providing maximum support to Russia even if it meant
diminished focus on India's independence. A home department
note of 5 August 1941 on Krishna Menon's activities captured this
shift well:

> Up to the date of the German attack on Russia, Menon's
> partnership with the PEOPLE's CONVENTION and the
> COMMUNIST PARTY OF GREAT BRITAIN was resulting
> in a good deal of help and publicity for the Indian Independence
> Campaign. From the end of June onwards, Menon's position
> has undoubtedly deteriorated . . . There is no evidence of an
> actual rift, but each side of the alliance is finding the other a bit
> of an embarrassment in the changed situation and is compelled
> to exercise more forbearance and tact to avoid creating one. The
> state of affairs is a reflection of the difference of opinion which
> exists within the Communist Party itself . . . The support that can
> be given by the Party to Menon's Campaign is indeterminate,
> half-hearted and may dwindle still more, since Menon adopts
> the attitude that the fight for Indian Independence must go on
> at all costs . . .

Krishna Menon's views were shared by Palme Dutt, who clearly
was badly outnumbered on this issue within his party. But the
show went on regardless, and Krishna Menon addressed numerous
rallies organized by the communists and their various organizations
over the next few years. All of 1941, for example, he spoke
uncompromisingly and unequivocally for India's freedom at
People's Conventions in different places, which included London,

Sheffield, Glasgow and Dundee, and challenged in his own way the shift in the mainstream communist stance on Indian independence. 'Russia first, India later' was the British communist position after the German invasion. 'India first, Russia later' was Krishna Menon's stance, from which he did not budge in spite of his undoubted sympathy for the Soviet Union.

One report by Stanley Baron in the *News Chronicle* of 13 January 1941 gives a flavour of one such People's Convention:

Convention[4]

I went along yesterday to the morning session of the People's Convention which though modestly dissociating itself from any particular party label, has been front page news in the various organs of the Communist Party for some weeks past. About 1500 delegates from workers' organisations in different parts of the country managed to get into the main meeting at the Royal Hotel, Southampton . . . On the platform Miss Beatrix Lehmann, Miss Indira Nehru (daughter of the Pandit) and Messers Haldane, Gallacher and Krishna Menon . . .

There was, however, a particularly sharp and barbed thrust from Krishna Menon who, speaking of the poser put to the Indian people—would they prefer a Nazi Government or a British Imperialist one?—observed, 'People as stupid as that would probably ask a fish if it preferred to be fried in margarine or butter'.

Nehru was finally freed on 3 December 1941 but it was to be only for a few months. On 9 August 1942, when the Quit India movement was launched, Nehru went back to his 'home away from home', as he once called it, and stayed there till 15 June 1945, the longest single stretch that he would spend in jail. This time again Krishna Menon would launch an aggressive protest movement but with hardly any effect except garnering public sympathy for Nehru. It was during this tenure in prison that Nehru would produce his greatest literary work—*The Discovery of India*—which, as in the case of Nehru's previous three books, Krishna Menon would help get published in the UK after it was brought out in India by a Calcutta-based publisher.

Krishna Menon had always been friendly with Ivan Mikhailovich Maisky, the legendary Soviet ambassador in the UK. But unlike Krishna Menon, Maisky had excellent contacts with the Conservatives, including, of all people, Churchill. In fact, Maisky went out of his way to cultivate the Tories, something that Krishna Menon never did. Maisky's style was more polished and suave. Socially too, he was more gregarious than the brooding India League activist. While Krishna Menon invited British communist leaders to the functions of India League, he had been somewhat careful about Maisky, who was known as 'Stalin's Man' in London. All that, of course, changed after the German invasion of Russia. It was therefore no surprise that Krishna Menon invited Maisky for a function on 5 September 1941 in honour of Rabindranath Tagore, who had passed away the previous month. Scotland Yard reported on it twelve days later:

A public meeting in commemoration of the late Rabindranath TAGORE was held under the auspices of the India League at the Conway Hall on 5th September. A great deal of publicity had been given to this function and to the fact that M. MAISKY the Russian Ambassador was to be on the platform with the result that the Conway Hall could not accommodate all the people who desired to attend . . .

About 30 persons were on the platform including Edward THOMPSON (chairman); the speakers M. MAISKY, Dr. Hewlett JOHNSON (Dean of Canterbury), V.K. Krishna MENON, Hsiao CHI'EN, Miss Beatrix LEHMANN (actress), R. SORENSEN . . . E.M. FORSTER . . . The speaker's table was draped with the Indian National Congress flag. The usual India League literature was on sale including V.K. Krishna MENON's pamphlet 'India, Britain and Freedom' . . .

M. MAISKY the first speaker was greeted with a tremendous outburst of cheering and hand-clapping. He said that TAGORE was a personification of the spirit of the Indian people . . . V.K. Krishna

MENON read messages of tribute to TAGORE from a number of
people . . . He stated with much irony that no messages had been
received from India . . .

Maisky was suddenly recalled to Moscow in 1943 after a long
eleven-year stint in London. Krishna Menon kept in close touch
with him after the Tagore Memorial, as he would inform Nehru a
few years later.

However, despite the changed political circumstances
following the Soviet Union's entry into the war, there were still
some deep areas of disagreement between Nehru and Krishna
Menon. The year 1941 ended with Nehru expressing irritation
with Krishna Menon—one of those 'rarest of rare occasions'
but the latter had earned the rebuke. On 30 December 1941,
Krishna Menon once again gave expression to his ambivalence
on the Congress's position on the War. He cabled Nehru that
the Congress should keep its hostility to British rule aside for
the time being; rally the people against fascists as it had in 1936
and 1937 during the time of the Spanish Civil War; and declare
its solidarity with Russia and China, irrespective of Indo-British
relations. Nehru responded a day later:

> You exhibit complete misunderstanding about the situation here.
> The line you suggest is impossible for adoption by the Congress
> where every group strongly opposed it.

To be fair, Nehru and some others like Rajagopalachari were
prepared to consider conditional Indian support to the war but the
overwhelming majority led by Patel and Rajendra Prasad was opposed
to it—both on the grounds that the British should be left to stew
in their own juice and also because of the Congress's commitment
to non-violence. Gandhi too had abandoned his earlier support and
come out strongly in favour of mass civil disobedience because of the
intransigence of Churchill in London and, more so, Linlithgow in
India. Some months earlier Nehru had confessed to Krishna Menon
on 21 September 1941:

. . . The Gandhian technique of action is never very easy to
understand unless one has been in close contact with it . . .
Remember always that the language Congress uses at Gandhiji's
instance, is peculiarly mild and inoffensive when it is thinking of
action . . .

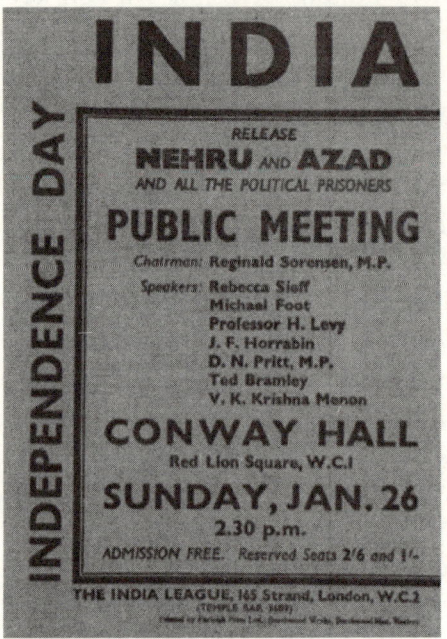

India League public meeting, London, 1941

Cripps, who was then Lord Privy Seal in Churchill's war cabinet,
went out to India a second time during March–April 1942. He
had visited the subcontinent three years earlier when he was just
a Member of Parliament. But this time around, he was going as an
official emissary with 'full power to discuss with the leaders of Indian
opinion the scheme which the War Cabinet has agreed'. The main
points of this scheme were:

[T]he convening of a constituent assembly elected on a system of
proportional representation by freshly elected provincial assemblies,
the recognition of the possibility of Pakistan by conceding the

right of every province that was not prepared to accept the new Dominion constitution to retain its existing constitutional position and the request for collaboration, while the war lasted, of Indian parties with the British Government, who would continue to bear the full responsibility for India's defense.[5]

Cripps spent three weeks in India. Much has been written on his much-hyped but finally ill-fated mission. One early scholar concluded that 'the Cripps mission was crushed by the monolithic millstones of Churchillian Conservatism and Congress nationalism'.[6] I do not propose to go over what happened during Cripps's time in India. Since this is a biography of Krishna Menon, I am more interested in his role. He remained in London and was to be briefed by Nehru twice in the expectation that the Congress point of view would get wide publicity abroad. But even before Nehru's cables arrived the India League had already started its publicity campaign to defend the Congress's rejection of the Cripps package. This was to be memorably described by Gandhi as a 'post-dated cheque drawn on a falling bank'. Actually, the talks had broken down on one issue: the Congress insisted on having an Indian as a member of the all-powerful viceroy's Executive Council—the cabinet of the government of British India—responsible exclusively for the country's defence. This was not acceptable to Linlithgow. On July 1942, an Indian ICS officer Sir Malik Feroz Khan Noon was indeed appointed as the defence member but not with the powers that the Congress had been demanding. Noon was later to become Prime Minister of Pakistan in December 1957 but would last just ten months.

The first cable from Nehru to Krishna Menon was on 13 April 1942, a day after he had written to US President Franklin Roosevelt explaining why the Cripps mission had failed. He followed it up with another cable forty-eight hours later. Scotland Yard reported on 28 April 1942:

Having learnt that Sir STAFFORD CRIPPS would make a statement on India in the House of Commons on Tuesday [28 April 1942], MENON was forced to reorientate his plans for

publicizing the contents of the two cables he received from
NEHRU, dated April 13th and 15th respectively. A meeting to be
held in a Committee room of the House of Commons on Tuesday
was called off as being in the circumstances useless and instead a
Press Conference was held on Monday at 3.30 p.m. at the Waldorf
Hotel . . . In addition to Press representatives, leading members
of the Communist Party of Great Britain and various members of
Parliament were invited, the main purpose of the meeting being to
place copies of the Nehru cables in their hands before Sir Stafford
could make his statement.

MENON made a long statement based on Nehru's cable and in
addition made the following points:

(1) Although British Press reports have said that while the Cripps
mission had failed, it had nevertheless improved British–Indian
relations. This was untrue. Far from creating better relations it had
created an 'enormous amount of bitterness' . . .
(2) There was not one Party in India which supported the British
proposals . . .
(3) He was asked if India would prefer British or Japanese rule
and replied that India was not seeking a change of masters: Indians
wished to be masters in their own house.
(4) He said that Eastern Bengal was very anti-British and the
situation would be 'ticklish' if the Japanese marched on . . .
(5) The British Government he said, was not capable of organizing
Guerilla warfare in India.
(6) It was not easy to believe that the British Army was an Army of
liberation when 1700 to 1800 Communists, Socialists, and Trade
Unionists were in prison, treated as criminals . . .
(7) He said there was a great desire in India to reach a settlement but
that the first move would now have to be made by a mediator and
that agreement must be on the basis of a National Government . . .
(8) Cripps had said in effect that (i) legislation could not be
embarked on during war; and (ii) unless power is handed over
by legislation, there can be no transfer of power in India. Such an
objection did not arise when Churchill offered union with France.

(9) The concession of the transference of power offered by Cripps had been withdrawn at the last interview when he insisted that the Viceroy would function as Prime Minister . . .

If evidence was ever needed that Scotland Yard had penetrated Krishna Menon's establishment completely, the next few lines in its report would clinch the issue:

V.K. KRISHNA MENON is himself engaged in drafting a pamphlet based on Nehru's cables. This will be on sale at the 1st of May Rally as well as copies of 'India—What Next?' only just completed by MENON (of which 40,000 copies have been ordered from the printers) . . .

This was not all. Scotland Yard continued:

CRIPPS–MENON INTERVIEW

Very confidential information has been received to the effect that V.K. Krishna MENON saw Sir Stafford CRIPPS at the latter's invitation on 24.4.42. He informed a friend subsequently that he (Sir Stafford) had admitted to having seen the two NEHRU Cables before they were released for delivery to him—and that he had only had them many days late—thanks to Government permission. MENON formed the impression that CRIPPS did not understand the Indian problem at all but thought (a) India was moving in the past, (b) British attitude to India had completely changed, and (c) the British conception of a Government was one in which the Muslim League should form half the Executive, the other half being constituted by the Congress, the Hindu Mahasabha and all other categories together. MENON was understood to have said that such a Government would be impossible and, in any event, that was not the issue. The issue was between the British Government and the National Government. He left the interview still convinced that Nehru's version of what had transpired between him and Cripps was the correct one and that in his statement Cripps would do nothing but maintain his point of view, which was contradicted by the Nehru cables.

Nehru and Cripps had been on extremely good terms and shared deep mutual regard all through the 1930s. Both shared the same year of birth and came from similar well-to-do backgrounds. Their political ideologies were the same and, in fact, Cripps had once been called 'the Nehru of England'.[7] Krishna Menon too had known Cripps for over a decade. They moved in the same circles. They had done legal cases together. Cripps was one of the strongest supporters of the India League. But 1942 was to change all that and both Nehru and Krishna Menon became disenchanted with Cripps. In fact, the break was so bitter that on 18 April 1942, Scotland Yard reported Krishna Menon as having said:

> Cripps is 'a knave as well as naïve' . . . He went to India as a lawyer, as an advocate of the British Cabinet; He is a Yes-man of the Prime Minister and has lent himself as the instrument of denial of power to India.

The original mistake may well have been a sense of exaggerated expectation of what Cripps could do on the part of Nehru and Krishna Menon, but the Cripps of 1942 was not the Cripps of the 1930s, when he was not in positions of power and authority. Cripps's actions rankled in Nehru's memory for long, and three years after the debacle over the Cripps Mission, Nehru would, on 3 September 1945, still be ruminating on this episode to Krishna Menon:

> There is one thing I want you to know. I have not yet got over Stafford Cripps's behavior just after his visit to Delhi in 1942. Even during the negotiations he behaved badly and I was surprised. As soon as the negotiations broke down he made various statements in Delhi, Karachi and later in London which were full of attacks on the Congress. Some of the so-called facts he stated were absolute distortions and there were complete inventions. Probably he was not responsible for all this and spoke from the Government of India's brief. But when these statements were categorically denied by various responsible persons—including me—he might have had the decency to withdraw what he had said. Instead of this, he repeated his previous

statements, which meant of course that either he or I was a liar . . . All this was doubly unfortunate because much was expected of Cripps. I think the person most responsible for what happened in Delhi in 1942 was Churchill, but I must say that Cripps proved that he was not capable of handling a difficult situation satisfactorily . . . I do not doubt his sincerity and I have always stood up for him whenever he has been criticized in India. But something more than self-righteousness is necessary to understand and deal with a difficult problem . . .

A few months after the failure of the Cripps mission, Gandhi launched the Quit India movement in August 1942. There was a mass upsurge all over the country, and the British government responded by putting all the top Congress leaders in jail. On the military front, the Allies were suffering reverses in South East Asia. The combination of these factors led President Roosevelt to decide to send a special envoy to India. This decision was taken sometime in October 1942 and the man chosen for the assignment was William Phillips, who had been US ambassador to Italy. Roosevelt neither met with Phillips nor gave him any clear instructions on what was expected from his mission. Phillips obviously thought he had a broad enough mandate to sort out the problem in regard to India.

A well-attended India League conference, London, 1942

Phillips spent time in London talking with top British government functionaries and with some academics and others interested in India. On 17 December 1942, he met with Krishna Menon. It is inconceivable that the British were unaware of this meeting. In any case, they seemed to have done nothing to prevent Phillips from seeing Krishna Menon. Phillips recorded in his diary the same day:[8]

> . . . Mr. M [Krishna Menon] was clearly out of sympathy with the attitude of the British government towards India. He believed that the Government here has really no desire to change the situation in its relation to the Indian Government, and that many proposals put forth, such as the Cripps Mission were [not] meant as real solutions . . .
>
> . . . He recommended the creation of an Allied Command in an Indian theatre which would include China, Russia, the Anglo-American interests, etc. It would thus be Indian territory plus other territories from which there may be bases of operation and supplies against the enemy. There should be a generalissimo created. There would be no objection to an Englishman . . . There should also be an Indian commander-in-chief . . . This office would also presumably be filled by a British general.
>
> Mr. M talked at length of the Indian Government. We must give up the Cripps idea, he said, and try and form a provisional government under the hegemony of the British government. In this regard he thought the Viceroy would remain, not because he would be wanted by Indians but because it would be necessary from the point of view of the British Government . . .

This conversation seems to have impressed Phillips because two days later he wrote to the US secretary of state, Cordell Hull:

> There are two little trial balloons which I passed on to John Winant [US ambassador in the UK] and which he is carrying back with him to Washington today. One is a suggestion emanating from Cripps, another from a highly intelligent Indian, a friend of Nehru

[Krishna Menon] and I have asked John, if possible, to let me know to Delhi, in a cryptic message, how they are regarded by you and the President.

Three years later on 29 July 1945, Krishna Menon was to tell Nehru of his meeting with Phillips:

> . . . I was impressed by his genuineness though I did not think he had any extraordinary gifts. His main concern at first was to learn, and so at different sessions I outlined the Indian problem to him before he left for India. He was anxious to find the answer to the question whether there was an interim way out in India and asked me for a memorandum, which I prepared, and which he took to India and also, I understand transmitted it to his principals. At that time the creation of the S.E. Asia Command had not taken place, and he was particularly impressed by that part of the scheme, seeing in it presumably the advantages from a war point of view. However, when the S.E. Asia Command was set up after Churchill's meeting with Roosevelt at Ottawa, one saw the essential political content, which was in the suggestion that was made, was not there. Later when Mountbatten was about to leave, it was further whittled down to the exclusion of India from the Command. Mountbatten himself was not prepared to see this later development, as I gathered from him . . .

So it appears that Phillips's meeting with Krishna Menon did have some effect on American military thinking in Asia, although the core of Krishna Menon's idea was shot down by Churchill. But in 1943 India did become the main Allied base for operations in South East Asia. What this letter also shows is that Krishna Menon had had direct contacts with Mountbatten during 1943–45, sometime before Nehru had met Mountbatten.

Interestingly, Scotland Yard had informants deep inside Krishna Menon's inner circle. On 9 September 1942, the authorities were informed of his forthcoming programme well in advance:

13ᵗʰ Sept. Brighton, Kettering

20ᵗʰ Perth (This is a big meeting staged by the local Communist Party)

23ʳᵈ Letchworth (Communist Party auspices)

25ᵗʰ Fabian Society Conference

26ᵗʰ Birmingham

30ᵗʰ London (some kind of Women's Conference)

Scotland Yard was not the only source of information for the India Office. On 10 November 1942, David Robertson, a Tory Member of Parliament, wrote to Leo Amery, the secretary of state for India:

> I enclose herewith an original letter I have received from Mr. Krishna Menon, of the India League dated 30ᵗʰ ultimo . . .
>
> Surely it is time that this League was suppressed, and Menon and his associates interred . . .
>
> I have met Menon twice . . . there is no doubt in my mind that Menon is an extremist of the worst possible kind, and I feel he should not be allowed to retain his liberty.

Menon had sent Robertson a copy of a resolution passed by the India League on 29 October 1942, appealing to Roosevelt, Chiang Kai Shek and Stalin to 'initiate speedily such action as will bring about negotiations and a settlement' as far as India was concerned. The negotiations were to be between the British government and India's national leaders, most of whom were then imprisoned or detained. The resolution said that the 'deplorable situation in India' was doing grave harm to the cause of world peace and that Allied Nations should use their good offices to end Churchill's intransigence reflected in the abject failure of the Cripps Mission.

Amery replied to Robertson on 19 November 1942 and it must rank as a classic of sorts:

> Krishna Menon is indefatigable as a mischief-maker and I only wish it were possible to deal with him as you suggest. But he is also

very clever and takes good care, at any rate in anything he says in English, to keep sufficiently within the law to make it difficult to intern him. I believe his Hindustani speeches are much worse, but it is difficult to get direct evidence about those.

Anyway, between ourselves, we are watching him carefully.

The top British government official on India was badly misinformed about Krishna Menon's linguistic skills. He could speak no Hindustani, and English was the only language he could give a public speech in. That was to be the case all the way up to his death. Obviously, Amery was mistaking him for someone else.

In early 1943, the British government presented to Parliament a White Paper on the prevailing political situation in India. The White Paper sought to demonstrate that negotiations with the Congress would be catastrophic and injurious to both the Allied cause and India. It justified Churchill's policy of 'no talks' with Gandhi, Nehru and their colleagues. The White Paper was clearly triggered by growing American concern with British policy in India and the appeal being made to Allied leaders by people like Sorensen and Krishna Menon to force Churchill to abandon his imperialist policy vis-à-vis India, both from a political and military point of view. Roosevelt and Churchill had jointly issued the Atlantic Charter in August 1941, and ever since then the India League had been demanding its applicability to India as well.

In March 1943, Krishna Menon rebutted the White Paper forcefully. He called the various documents purported to be Congress policy that were adduced by the White Paper in support of British policy 'either fabrications or having emanated from irresponsible, anarchic or adventurist sources who have exploited the name of the Congress'. He termed their use as dishonest and unscrupulous. He ended by saying that the 'allegations made are against men and women who cannot answer—they are in the Government's prisons and concentration camps'. It was perhaps the most elaborate defence he was to ever mount of Gandhi and Gandhian methods, which had in the past often flummoxed and frustrated him.

India League public meeting on Atlantic Charter, London, 1943

Krishna Menon's attack on the White Paper earned plaudits, and his archives contain a large number of congratulatory messages received from a wide cross-section of people. One such appreciation came from Ivor Montagu, who had founded the International Table Tennis Federation; the Swaythling Cup given to the men's team winner is named after his father. His uncle was Samuel Montagu who, a quarter of a century earlier, had been secretary of state for India and responsible for the Montagu–Chelmsford Reforms of 1919 which ushered in an era of elected representatives in India. Ivor Montagu, a die-hard communist, wrote:

> I can only express the shame which every Britisher must feel at the fact that such a policy as that being pursued by our Government, such a document as the White Paper, such deeds as the monstrous murder of the heroes of Kayyur can be pursued, published and precipitated by our Government.

Kayyur is a village some 100 kilometres north of Krishna Menon's birthplace, where the first communist uprising against local landlords had taken place in 1940 in what was to later become Kerala. Several people had been killed, and four communist workers were found guilty and hanged just as the White Paper was hitting the headlines.

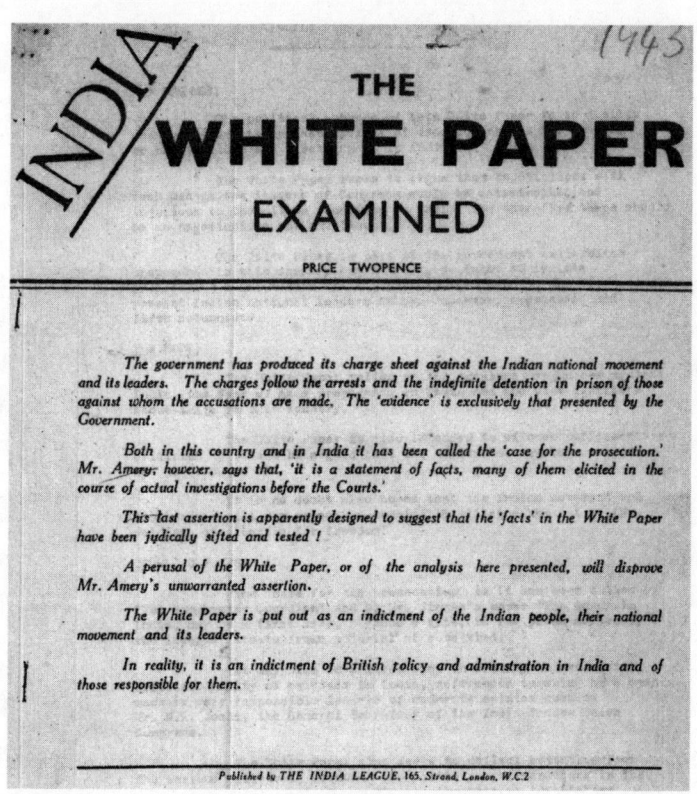

Krishna Menon's monograph on British White Paper on India, London, 1943

Nehru's ninth and final round of imprisonment had begun on 9 August 1942, the day the Quit India movement was launched. It was to last almost three years, and he would be released on 15 June 1945. During these three years, there was virtually no correspondence between him and Krishna Menon—a most unusual happenstance for both of them. On 3 July 1943, Nehru wrote to his daughter who, by now, had become Indira Gandhi after her marriage to Feroze Gandhi the previous year:

> I cannot give you any new address for Krishna. I do not think I have had a letter from him during the last three years nearly. You can try his old address in Strand.

Nehru did not forget his London comrade, for on 22 April 1944, he wrote to his daughter. The last line of that letter reads:

> Have you heard from Krishna Menon?

A little over a fortnight later on 6 May 1944, he was at it once again asking Indira Gandhi:

> Do you ever hear from Krishna Menon?

And what was Krishna Menon doing when Nehru was longing to hear from him? For one, he was doing what he did best—producing hard-hitting pamphlets meant for wide distribution. In the early days of 1943 he brought out a booklet titled 'Independence', and after giving a capsule history of the freedom movement thus far, ended by proclaiming:

> 1943 this sees India in turmoil. An unhappy land where its true leaders are imprisoned, its urge not merely for India's freedom, but for participation in, and sacrifice, for, the larger world freedom thwarted by imperialism . . .
>
> Meanwhile . . . India faces a terrible food shortage and in many areas famine. It is the worst period in the last fifty years—the Secretary of State for India the 'great Moughal of Whitehall' whose power to deny is immense, has little to offer . . .

But the greatest of all India's handicaps is the lack of freedom to determine her destiny, to allay the hunger of her people, to take her rightful place among the peoples of the world in pursuit of the common purpose of human freedom.

The 'great Moughal (sic) of Whitehall' was a reference to the India-born Leo Amery, while in reality, Krishna Menon's real target should have been the 'great Moughal of 10 Downing Street'. Churchill's attitude is now widely acknowledged to have exacerbated the horrific famine in Bengal and other places. For most of 1943 and part of 1944 as well, the India League went into overdrive on famine relief campaigns across the UK. An India Relief Committee was set up with Clement Davies, a Labour MP, as president and Krishna Menon as its chairman. It opened over twenty branches in different towns and cities of England and Scotland, and mobilized the supply of medical aid and essential drugs for supply to famine-stricken areas. Public meetings were held from time to time, not only to call for immediate measures of relief but also to keep alive the India League demand for steps to end the political deadlock.

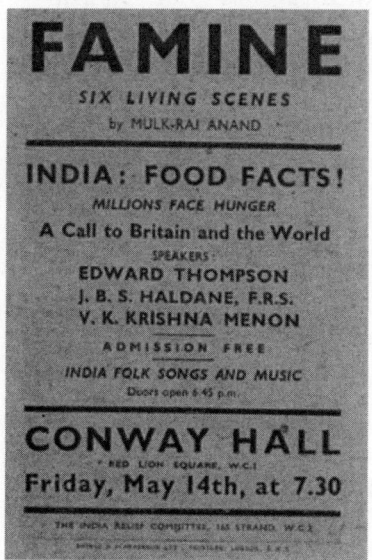

India League public meeting on the Great Bengal Famine, London, 1943

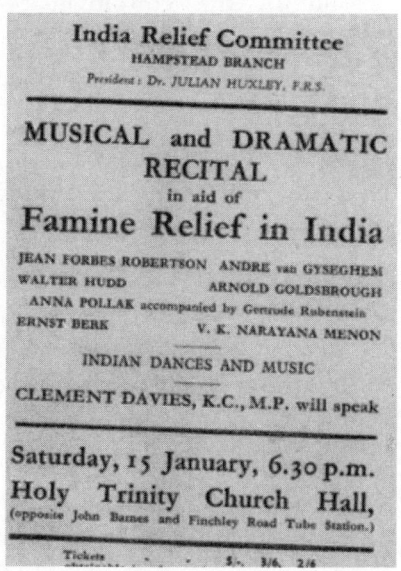

India League famine-relief musical evening, London, 1943

While he was engaged in these relief campaigns, Krishna Menon was doing his best to avoid being called up by the British government to undergo training in engineering trades, so that he could be deployed in the armaments industry. He had first received a notice from the Ministry of Labour and National Service in August 1942, directing him to 'enter into and receive training for inspection and viewing at a Government Training Centre'. This was to be 'the lightest type of employment which would require the least possible energy'.

Krishna Menon was clearly flustered by the notice, which may well have been the British government's move to silence him politically. Evidence for this comes from the correspondence of the previous year between the then viceroy, Lord Linlithgow, and Leo Amery, the secretary of state for India in London. On 31 March 1942, Linlithgow would tell Amery:

> . . . Krishna Menon and his organization have constantly misrepresented the Indian problem before the Press and public at home, and have consistently intrigued to create in Parliament and in the constituencies prejudice against our Indian policy . . . I do hope you will seriously consider the expediency of seizing some favourable occasion to get him put out of the U.K. . . .

That was not to be all. A few months later on 23 June 1942, Linlithgow was to again tell Amery:

> . . . I would ask again (I have often bothered you about him) whether it is not possible to do something to impede his freedom of action. You have a good deal of material about him, and if there were any way in which we could bring him under a little closer control of whatever type, I do think there would be a great deal to be said for it. He, and this little group of somewhat malcontent people in the Commons like Sorensen, give rise to a disproportionate amount of difficulty out here . . .

Clearly, Linlithgow and Amery could not get Krishna Menon out of their exchanges. On 30 November 1942, the viceroy told the secretary of state for India a third time:

> . . . I could not help regretting again that it has not been found possible to a suggestion which I have I think made once or twice that should take pains to break up Menon and break up the India League with him. I am certain that as long as he is there he will be a focus of discontent and difficulty and I should myself have thought that he was really worth taking a little of a chance. Perhaps you would think this worth turning over in your mind . . .

The viceroy sounded like a mafia don out to eliminate a nuisance. Amery replied on 16 December 1942:

> My impression is that interest in the India League is really dying down here in spite of the efforts of Krishna Menon and his league to maintain some sort of activity. We are watching that gentleman closely but up to date have not found sufficient justification for taking action against him . . .

It was not just Amery who would be reassuring the viceroy about Krishna Menon's growing 'irrelevance'. Sir A. Ramaswamy Muduliar had been a member of the viceroy's Executive Council and, in July 1942, became one of two Indians to be appointed to Churchill's war cabinet. After India's Independence, he had a distinguished career in the Indian private enterprise. But on March 1943, he would write to Linlithgow:

> The threatened fast of Mr. Gandhi, which we anticipated in August and which he delayed for six months, has now come and gone. The threat fell flat in America where I was in the earlier stages of the fast and in this country [the UK] also. Mr. Krishna Menon and the India League tried to whip up some agitation but without success. In fact through their posters they overdid it and covered themselves with ridicule. 'Gandhi suffers for India and the World'

was one of the posters. At a time particularly when young men of
all creeds and stations of life, the flower of humanity, were every
day making the supreme sacrifice for the sake of the future, a slogan
like that would hardly be appreciated, especially when it concerns
a man past the biblical period . . .

But Linlithgow and Amery had underestimated Krishna Menon
and his resourcefulness when pushed to the wall. He immediately
got in touch with two Indian doctors who had been associated with
the India League—Dr P.C. Bhandari and Dr C.L. Katial. He got
certificates from them and replied on 9 February 1943 to the summons
he had received six months earlier. Bhandari was a radiologist, and his
medical report dated 27 January 1943 read:

This is to certify that Mr. Krishna Menon has been under my
professional care for some years. He is suffering from:

(1) Severe angioneurotic odoema
(2) Recurrent attacks of lumbago and sciatica
(3) Insomnia
(4) Dyspepsia

He was some years ago in hospital for observation for tuberculosis
[of the] kidney but no definite diagnosis was made. His physical
condition is very poor. He has to get along with a stick because
of the condition of his back and sciatica and his angio–neurotic
oedema makes appearance at any and all parts of his anatomy at any
and all times seriously incapacitating him and his chronic insomnia
adds to his other troubles.

  As long as he can plan his own life according to how he finds
himself from day to day he can put in quite useful brain work but
it is always unpredictable as to how he will be the next day. He is
quite unfit for any manual work and he cannot be depended upon
to undertake any regular duties in any capacity whatsoever . . .

Katial was a noted public figure, having become the first Asian mayor
in the UK in 1938. Krishna Menon got him to give him a 'political

certificate'—how valuable he had been as a borough councillor for almost a decade, how the Indian community was proud of him for waging a sustained campaign for India's freedom, and how he had served as a very active civil defence warden when London was being mercilessly bombed by the Luftwaffe.

With both these testimonials Krishna Menon confronted the Ministry of Labour and National Service, which was nevertheless not entirely convinced. Protracted correspondence followed but at the end of it all, Krishna Menon won the day and was spared the ordeal of undergoing training to equip him to work in some factory involved with Britain's war effort. Bhandari would later be in charge of India League affairs when Krishna Menon would be away in India June–September 1946. After India's Independence, Katial would be in charge of an employee insurance programme for a while before he returned to the UK.

All of 1944, as he had done the previous four years, Krishna Menon addressed gatherings—both small and large—of the British Communist Party. The previous year on 19 January 1943, the British Communist Party had passed a resolution on which he had worked with Pollit and Rajni Palme Dutt:

. . . Immediate steps need to be taken to end the present impasse in India by the establishment of an Indian National Government which can tackle the grave internal economic crisis and mobilise the people and resources of India for joint struggle and victory.

His friendship with Pollit had deepened and extended to his family. On 22 July 1943, Pollit had written to him:

Dear Krishna:

Many thanks for the gift. My children say you look after them better than their father does.

And much earlier, he had mourned the passing away of a leading communist and written to Pollit on 13 March 1941:

I read with regret in the press this evening of the death of Tom
Mann. I have read and heard from Mrs Besant of his participation in
the struggle for the freedom of the Indian people. His conception
of and fight for freedom extended to the whole world and all
peoples and give those of us who are left to carry on the struggle,
in one way and another, an example of persistence, courage and
devotion for which we are all grateful.

Till the end of his life, Krishna Menon was fascinated with toys,
and after his death, when an inventory of his belongings was taken
at his residence, some 10,000 books would be catalogued plus toys
of all kinds. Khushwant Singh, who worked with Krishna Menon
during 1947–49, would write in his memoirs that the latter liked
pretty faces, fancy suits and toys![9]

But to return to 1944, the British Communist Party resolution
was a victory for Krishna Menon because just two years ago, while it
supported full independence for India, the party had placed Russia's
interests higher than that of India's. Assemblies were held in different
parts of the UK, and Krishna Menon's presence was eagerly solicited.
He would take pains to point out that he was not a member of any
communist organization but 'he represents people who desired the
freedom of their own country'. A special branch report of a conference
organized by the *Daily Worker,* a publication of the CPGB, on 2
April 1944, had this to say in grudging admiration:

> A rather remarkable demonstration took place when V.K. Krishna
> MENON rose to speak. The whole audience stood up, and led
> by ACLAND, greeted him with prolonged applause. MENON
> said that the Government's Indian policy was suicidal; that Indian
> leaders must be set free; Mr. Amery must be dismissed; and that the
> principles of the Atlantic Charter, Cairo and Teheran be applied
> to India.

The officer concerned read this report and passed it forward on 23
April 1944 with the comment:

I was interested to see that MENON had an unusually warm
reception at the Conference.

Nehru was to turn fifty-five on 14 November 1944 but he was
still in prison with no immediate prospect of release. Krishna Menon
organized an India League function to mark the occasion. The
highlight of this gathering was undoubtedly the cable sent by Gandhi
two days earlier that was read out:

JAWAHARLAL IS A JEWEL AMONG MEN. HAPPY IS THE
LAND THAT OWNS HIM. SOMETHING IS RADICALLY
WRONG WITH THE SYSTEM THAT HAS NO BETTER
USE OF PERSONS LIKE HIM THAN AS PRISONERS.

Two months later Gandhi was to send another message to the India
League as it celebrated Indian Independence Day on 26 January 1945:

INDEPENDENCE ESSENTIAL FOR WORLD PEACE AS
ALSO FOR INDIA'S. IT MUST COME BUT EARLIER IF
ENGLAND AND OTHER POWERS SEE THE OBVIOUS.

Krishna Menon had met Gandhi only twice—first in London in 1931
and a year later in Poona. He had confessed to Nehru that very often
he simply could not understand Gandhi and the positions he took.
But he was well aware that, for all of Nehru's charisma and mass
appeal, the last word in the Congress party was that of Gandhi's, with
even Nehru deferring to him even when they disagreed.

Notes

1. Mukherjee (2014).
2. Gopal (1975).
3. When one of his juniors in his law practice of the 1960s, N.M. Ghatate,
   told him that Nehru's handwriting was clear while his was unreadable

Krishna Menon was supposed to have remarked: 'That is because, Ghatate, my mind moves faster!'

4. Clearly a play on the word 'convention' to indicate heavy communist involvement in it.
5. Gopal (1975).
6. Moore (1979).
7. Ibid.
8. Manuscript Division, Houghton Library, Harvard University.
9. Singh (2002).

Resuming Contact with Nehru (1945)

By the beginning of 1945 it was clear that the Allies would finally triumph in the war. Krishna Menon, a supporter of both unconditional Indian independence and also of Britain in its war against the Nazis and the fascists, organized the Indian Independence Day celebrations on 26 January 1945 in a better frame of mind than in the previous years.[1] This time he reached out to Gandhi as well as to a number of prominent British personalities for their messages of support.

Laski responded readily saying:

> As long as I can remember, my whole heart and mind have been with Jawaharlal Nehru on the issue of Indian freedom, and at a time when our own independence is at stake, I naturally feel even more strongly that I am proud to share his outlook.

Pethick-Lawrence was soon to take over as secretary of state for India and would have to deal with Krishna Menon as a member of His Majesty's government. But for now he sent a message as a long-time well-wisher of the India League:

> As the war approaches its end and I, in common with lovers of freedom all over the world, anxiously desire to see a settlement

on liberal lines of the complex problems of India. Is it too much
to hope that a solution, to which all sections in Britain and India
must make a contribution, can be found, which will redound to
the honour and credit of all concerned.

By 1945, public opinion had begun to shift, and over fifteen years
of lobbying, pamphleteering and propagandizing by Krishna Menon
was beginning to have some impact.

Krishna Menon had resigned from the Labour Party in January 1941.
But four years later on 12 February 1945, he would write to his old
mentor Laski who had, by then, become chairman of the Labour Party:

> I enclose for your information a copy of a letter that I have sent
> to the Secretary of the Labour Party. As you will see it is my
> application for readmission into the Party. I resigned in December
> 1940.
>
> I am in agreement with the resolution on India accepted by
> the Annual Conference [of the Labour Party] and also with the
> general policy of the Party so that there is no longer any reason,
> as far as I am concerned, why I should remain outside. As the
> correspondence enclosed explains why I was forced, with regret, to
> resign, I do not wish to write to you at greater length. I am quite
> certain that you would not have expected me to act differently at
> that time.

Krishna Menon would soon be readmitted into the Labour Party,
and fate ensured that the same G.R. Shepherd who had written to
him five years earlier with the 'bad' news would now write to him
on 27 April 1945 and convey some 'good' news:

> I am very glad to say that the National Executive Committee at its
> meeting on the 25th instant agreed to raise no objection to '[your]
> membership of the Labour Party.

Not only would he be readmitted but for a brief while would even
be considered as a possible candidate for the parliamentary elections

in July 1945, which would sweep the Labour Party into power. However, Russell Talbot would write to him on 15 June 1945:

> With reference to the proposed nomination of yourself as candidate for Combined Universities at the forthcoming General Election, I and my friends who were responsible for writing to you to accept this nomination, have to say that on close consideration it has now become apparent that since a number of candidates will be contesting the Election, we are of the opinion that in view of the many important considerations which attach to your position, we do not feel justified in advising you to proceed further in this matter . . .

With the German surrender, Britain was in a state of exultation. But Krishna Menon, while celebrating, was also deeply ambivalent as his public statement of 8 May 1945 revealed:

> We rejoice that the overwhelming defeat of German imperialism offers the hope of liberation to millions of European people, not least of them the German people themselves. It makes the ending of the war in the East by the early defeat of Japan more urgent and possible.

He went on to bemoan:

> In the hour of victory the Indian people see their leaders in prison, their liberty denied in their homeland and their role misrepresented in the comity of nations . . .

Nehru was finally released on 15 June 1945 after almost three years of imprisonment. Two days later Krishna Menon and Sorensen cabled Nehru:

> India League Executive and Parliamentary Committees and our entire Indian organization in the country desire us to send you our heartfelt greetings and our great sense of joy and relief at your

release and our general belief and confidence in your guidance and
look forward to immediate resumption of vigorous political life
at the same time hoping that you will spare yourself unnecessary
personal exertion . . . While news from India is conflicting and
confused, workers for and friends of India are confident that your
courage, vision and determination will serve the cause of India
there and in the world.

Nehru's release from jail meant that he and Krishna Menon could
resume their correspondence. Krishna Menon wrote to Nehru on
29 July 1945, giving him an update on what he had been doing in
London since the two had last met six years earlier:

1939–41: The position as taken up in the October resolutions
[of the CWC] of 1939 was fully publicized . . . The contacts
established in the pre-war years was maintained . . . In spite of the
Government's propaganda here and abroad and in spite of the later
action of Subhas Bose, I believe progressive people everywhere
accepted our genuine anti-fascist and democratic convictions . . .
1941–42: During this period I had frequent contacts with the U.S.
side. Mr. Winant was good enough to receive me as one of his
early callers, and I know that in the early part of his career he did
everything possible to help in posing the Indian problem from the
point of justice and necessity . . .
Post-1942: Since the August resolution and the development
of the war to its final phases, we have been very largely on the
defensive. Amery's propaganda at that time was very strong, and
it was to paint us as being pro-Japanese, authoritarian, pacifist and
reactionary.
China: I have tried my best to keep up contacts with our Chinese
friends . . . Contacts with unofficial Chinese have been good
though the general attitude of the Chinese towards Indians, and
vice versa, is not as good as it used to be.
Spain: There are remnants of the Republicans, with whom contact
has been maintained . . . We may still look forward to a happier day
for our Spanish friends . . .

I have up to the period of 1942 called on leading British
politicians of all parties, except Conservative on your behalf . . .
Once I called on Attlee after he was in the War Cabinet. Courteous
but not helpful. Cripps after he returned [from India] was very hurt
and immersed in the past but more helpful now . . .

A new government has come in. It is too early to say how it
will grapple with the problem. The signs are hopeful, though in
relation to India I dare not entertain any illusions.

While Krishna Menon was giving him a report on his activities,
Nehru, with his daughter, went trekking to Kashmir in the second
fortnight of July 1945 and wrote to him twice from there. On 31 July
1945, he gave Krishna Menon a tutorial in subcontinental politics:

. . . Both Indira and I have enjoyed this twelve-day trip and profited
by it. I feel physically fitter and mentally much refreshed . . .

Sheikh Muhammed Abdullah, the President of the Kashmir
National Conference, is a remarkable man in his own way and he
has proved himself to be an effective mass leader . . .

. . . Pakistan, when analysed, leads to two principal conclusions:
(1) It is inconceivable that Pakistan can be imposed on the southern
districts of the Punjab (which are predominantly Hindu and Sikh)
or the western districts of Bengal (which are predominantly
Hindu). Thus if ever Pakistan comes into existence it must lead
to the partition of Punjab and Bengal . . . (2) Both in Punjab and
Bengal there is a strong feeling, among Hindus and Muslims alike,
against partition of the province . . . So there is the riddle: the
Pakistanis, if they are keen enough and strong enough, can have
Pakistan only after the division of Bengal and the Punjab, and
this they do not want because they get economically backward
areas . . . and also because of the sentiment among Punjabis and
Bengalis against division of their provinces. This is the rub and
because of this Jinnah refuses to define what he wants.

Pakistan would probably have been a much feebler affair today
but for the encouragement given to it by British officialdom and
some diehards in Britain. But the final impetus to it was given

by the Cripps proposals [in 1942] . . . The Communist Party of India has been doing raging and tearing propaganda in favour of Pakistan . . . I think they have acted very foolishly indeed . . .

It was because of the CPI's position on Pakistan that Russia became suspect in Congress circles. This suspicion was to last till the early 1950s and, in turn, affected perceptions of Krishna Menon as his reputation was that of being a Sovietphile.

Krishna Menon had evidently sent Nehru some papers on an improved spinning wheel that some friends of his in England had suggested, but Nehru had not received them. He continued:

> . . . It seems obvious to me that however rapid the pace of industrialization (by the big machine) in India a vast field will remain for small-scale and cottage industries both of the whole-time and auxiliary variety. The supposed conflict between the big machine and the small or cottage machine is thus largely imaginary . . . The conflict can be reduced to very small proportions, especially if it is agreed that large-scale industry should be socialized or state-owned.
>
> The answers to your queries [on the spinning wheel] will, I hope be answered by someone on Gandhiji's staff . . . With my very limited layman's knowledge I might, however, inform you that most village and cottage spinning is done between 15 and 20 counts . . . When I spin I usually produce counts 25 to 30. At my fastest, and when I am in the right mood, I have spun 400 yards of 30 counts yarn an hour. I have spun up to 43 counts. My usual speed is 350 yards of 27 counts yarn an hour. My yarn is good and strong. Experts spin much faster . . .

Why this detailed description by Nehru of his spinning skills? This was because Krishna Menon had been fixated on some ideas for developing an improved spinning wheel. He had told Nehru first on 12 July 1945:

> . . . It is hoped an improved wheel, scientifically constructed, would increase output and improve quality considerably. I have

borne in mind that wheel would have to be cheap, simple and, at any rate in due course, capable of being made in India . . . I do not think Gandhiji would regard it as not conforming to his ideas if the wheel was improved scientifically . . .

He then went on to provide Nehru with technical details of the improvements being proposed and told him,

If the basic idea is acceptable and Gandhiji will give his general blessing, I can see in it an immediate prospect of dealing both with famine and also with the basis of a scheme for diffused industrialization which will bring relief to the countryside . . .

Krishna Menon had some friends in Sheffield working with him on the improved design. He wanted Nehru to send his proposals to Gandhi because he thought Gandhi would take them more seriously if they came from Nehru. Krishna Menon ended the last of his three letters to Nehru on this subject on 2 August 1945 by saying, 'I have given the spinning wheel a great deal of thought in the last few years.'

Nehru complied with Krishna Menon's request and sent all his letters on the improved spinning wheel to Gandhi. The master spinner was himself to take this somewhat unusual conversation forward, and Gandhi wrote to Krishna Menon on 8 August 1945:

Panditji has sent me your letter to him.

I am not frightened of the word 'machine'. Therefore, if a life-giving machine can be made in India and will do the work of the spinning wheel more quickly and better, I would have it and pay a tempting prize to the inventor . . .

Your experts do not seem to know their work . . . Now I give you my opinion. I fear the labours of your experts will be fruitless. Let them go to Manchester and study the spinning machines in Manchester. They will soon discover that what they can give will be an indifferent copy of the old type spinning jenny which may be used in villages but to no purpose. We do not want to go from the town factory to the village factory.

You will be wrong if you suspect that I wish to discourage you . . . For if anybody can produce a machine analogous to the Singer sewing machine I should dance with joy. It is said that his love for his wife was so great that he would spare her the drudgery of working her needle with the hands. He presented her with his humane machine. I would like to welcome another such Singer, only not for one woman but for the starving millions of India.

But this exchange on improved spinning wheels was only a temporary diversion from what Krishna Menon considered more pressing business. A new Labour government had taken over, and a number of his India League friends now held important ministerial positions. He wrote to Nehru on 2 August 1945:

> . . . Cripps believes, I think, that his ideas on India will become Party policy. Attlee, however, has shown himself to be a greater man than he hitherto appeared to be . . . I saw Cripps for about an hour, and also had one or two telephone conversations. He is personally charming as usual and inquired about you most tenderly . . . He thought the Cripps proposals the only way to solution and could not think of any other way . . . The present India policy appears to be to ask the Viceroy to come over to discuss matters . . . I am going to press here privately that Wavell should see 'Indian leaders' before he comes over.

As Krishna Menon had informed Nehru, Wavell was indeed asked to come over to London for consultations with Attlee and his colleagues. Krishna Menon was in regular touch with Cripps, who briefed him in detail of the talks with the viceroy. Other sources of information included Nye Bevin, Ernest Bevin and Herbert Morrison. On 31 August 1945, he sent a long letter to Nehru regarding the British government's opinions on India policy, saying that Wavell would soon announce some new proposals for breaking the deadlock. He added:

. . . There is no desire in the Government to play up Jinnah but I
have personally little doubt that they will use him if it suits them . . .

Soon thereafter, he got back to his pet idea, which he had been
canvassing for since the early 1930s and wrote about to Nehru on 4
September 1945:

. . . From 1932 onwards we have spoken of a Constituent Assembly.
History is full of instances of C.A.'s [Constituent Assembly's]
having met, and ended in fiascos. We ought to make an attempt
at planning it . . . My suggestion is that the [Congress] Working
Committee should set up a PREPARATORY COMMISSION
now in respect of the Constituent Assembly . . .

I would like to take my courage in both hands and ask that I
may be included on the Preparatory Commission, if it was decided
to be set up . . . This has been on my mind for some time but I
have only [now] gathered enough 'nerve' to do it. In any event, if
there is any work I can do, I would like you to ask me to do it . . .

In his long years of association with Nehru, this must have been one
of the very few occasions when Krishna Menon actually lobbied for
anything for himself. Nehru replied a few days later saying that he had
placed the proposal for a small commission to go into the question
of a constituent assembly before his colleagues who, however, felt it
was premature. Nehru added that his colleagues were 'much too busy
with the elections and with Congress organisations'. In this same letter
Nehru also wrote that he wanted Krishna Menon to come to India:

. . . for it is necessary to have personal contacts here and view the
situation at close quarters. It is ages since I saw you and I would
love to have nice long talks.

The Constituent Assembly would start functioning from 9
December 1946. A few months earlier, in July 1946, the Congress
would set up a non-party 'panel of experts' under the chairmanship of

Nehru to plan for the Constituent Assembly. Krishna Menon would be a special invitee to this group where he would, for a brief while, collaborate with K.M. Munshi to not only suggest procedures for the Assembly's functioning but also produce a draft constitution of sorts. He would also become a global envoy for Nehru.

Elections to the House of Commons were scheduled for July 1945. The campaign had been very bitter with Churchill using language that observers later felt cost him the election and won sympathy for Labour. Krishna Menon almost became a candidate but that was not to be. A few weeks before the polls he wrote to all Labour Party candidates on 6 June 1945:

> . . . The speedier end of the war with Japan and stable conditions in the East also require the unity and strength of an independent India under a democratic government. We request you to ask your electorate to declare that it wants for India the same national freedom, social security and internal stability and friendship that it should rightly desire and demand for this country. It is our fervent hope and our earnest request that you will give this policy in relation to India . . . place in your election address and campaign . . .

There is no evidence that Krishna Menon's appeal was taken seriously by his Labour Party colleagues. Six days later, he wrote to Laski:

> . . . The outlines of these proposals are pretty well known . . . I need not tell you that this Churchill gift of self-government (!) was produced after the break-up of the coalition, and by the present Election Government. It is no use disguising my strong feeling that the whole business is part of an Election manoeuvre, because it is realized that India is not an election issue, there is a fairly large volume of feeling in the country, realized even by Mr. Churchill's crowd, which must be satisfied that something is being done, and people must be made to believe that it is now up to the Indians themselves . . . It appears that the whole question of any popular control and power is to be put off and as I see it, the set-up proposed will effectively prevent any advance towards independence . . .

The viceroy had been in London for nine weeks and these proposals, which virtually brought about parity between the Congress and the Muslim League, had been firmed up by him and Amery with Churchill giving the finishing touches. Krishna Menon bluntly told Laski, 'Labour support for Churchill's India policy side by side with Beaverbrook's empire crusade would be a tragedy.' He wanted the Labour Party to express itself unequivocally on Indian matters prior to the general elections.

Amery too was contesting from Springbrook, and of those opposing him was Krishna Menon's old friend and comrade-in-arms Rajni Palme Dutt. Both Gandhi and Nehru wished him success. Nehru said:

> I have known him for many years and admired his ability. Apart from the personal factor, his success has obviously also, a symbolic value in the circumstances.

Krishna Menon wrote to Laski regarding Palme Dutt on 16 June 1945:

> . . . Quite obviously as a member of the Labour Party I can't go to the constituency and join the campaign and give him any support. The Labour candidate there is a good man, but has far less support. In any event there is no chance of his winning the seat for Labour . . .

Not for the first time would Krishna Menon's political judgement be found faulty. Percy Shurmer, the Labour candidate, won by a landslide, winning about 58 per cent of the vote, as compared to Amery's 35 per cent and Palme Dutt's paltry 8 per cent.

The Second World War had lasted almost six years. The subcontinent had emerged as the largest Allied creditor after the US. Britain owed her £1.335 billion ($5.23 billion, which is about $59 billion today). At a conservative estimate, the debt to India amounted to about a fifth of the UK gross national product. The famous Bombay Plan prepared by a group of Indian industrialists for the post-war economic development of India was published in 1944. Naturally, one of the main anchors of this plan was the availability of these sterling surpluses to India. On 15 September 1945, Krishna Menon wrote a five-page mini treatise on this subject to Nehru:

> The industrialists demand the return of debt in goods—capital goods . . . [Britain] is interested in the export of consumption goods, and priority for capital goods for India will be very low in the scale. The industrialists have no claim on this debt. It is not their money. It is the Government's money, which means it is the people's money for which the peasantry of India have paid dearly. That is how the debt is made up. The Bombay Plan is fundamentally wrong in its methods of financing, though of course the articulate industrialists in India will argue to the contrary.

Krishna Menon went into considerable detail to explain to Nehru how the immediate return of the sterling balance may benefit a few industrialists such as the Tatas and Birlas but it would not benefit the country. He also suggested that India demand the constitution of a National Planning Commission, something that was also close to Nehru's heart and would come into being five years later. Kannan Srinivasan, author of a forthcoming new book on the complex sterling balance issue, had this to say to me about this letter:[2]

> This is a brilliant note, especially given that he was kept out of the negotiations. He was entirely prescient about the fact that Britain would dump goods and supplies in India, especially obsolete military supplies including navy and Air Force supplies, as well as goods that it was pointless to take back to the UK, and facilities they had created for the war, and Indian goods supplied to the Middle East. He also shrewdly realised that Britain would try and conclude arrangements before Independence, but may have been unaware of how many measures had already been secretly carried out without any consultation beginning 1941.

India and the UK would enter into an initial agreement on sterling balances on 15 August 1947. But just five days later, the UK would suspend the convertibility of the pound, which meant that dollars would no longer be available to India to purchase rice, wheat and industrial goods from the US, which it wanted to do. It was stuck with British currency. To make matters worse for India, Britain devalued the pound in 1949 making the value of India's legitimate claims diminish by 30 per cent. Krishna Menon's letter of 15 September 1945 was prescient, as Srinivasan puts it, because he had warned Nehru of British machinations that would adversely affect India's interests. He would continue to complain to Nehru right till 1949 that the Indian finance ministry and Reserve Bank officials were keeping him out of the negotiations even though he was India's high commissioner in the UK.

The Labour Party scored a stunning victory in the 1945 UK elections, and Attlee became Prime Minister. Krishna Menon now had friends at the highest levels of the British government. He continued to badger them. He wrote a stiff letter to Attlee on 27 September 1945, protesting the use of Indian troops in the areas liberated from Japanese rule:

> Reports appear in the press that Indian troops are being used against the people of Indo-China, Malaya and other Asiatic territories recently liberated from Japanese rule and in the suppression of the endeavours for national independence by these peoples . . .
>
> The Indian people, as you are aware, have no quarrel with the peoples of Indo-China or Indonesia but on the other hand have every sympathy and a feeling of solidarity with these peoples, striving to liberate themselves from imperialism as we ourselves are and strive to do . . .
>
> The India of the future, as an independent country, must live on terms of amity and good neighbourliness with the peoples of Indonesia and Indo-China, with whom we have a great deal in common . . .

A day later Pethick-Lawrence's private secretary, Francis Turnball, sent a note to his boss:

> Since you spoke to me some days ago about your interview with
> Mr. Krishna Menon, I have been wondering what could be done
> to reduce his influence in political circles. I should like to suggest
> the possibility of sending a small party of Members of Parliament
> to India this autumn, perhaps about November or December . . .

Pethick-Lawrence acted on Turnball's suggestion and, after getting
Attlee's nod, wrote to the viceroy, Field Marshall Wavell, on
26 October 1945:

> . . . I was approached by [William] Dobbie [MP] who is
> Chairman of the India League, with the suggestion that a party
> of Labour members, who are members of the India League, and
> Krishna Menon should be given facilities to go to India. I had
> rather expected to receive a request of this sort . . . I do not feel
> that there would be any justification for giving Krishna Menon
> facilities though some people tell me that it might be beneficial to
> let him have contact with people in India. I have known Menon
> for some time and I gave him an interview a few weeks ago. I
> do not feel that he is at all likely under any conditions to be a
> helpful factor. Perhaps you could let me know whether you agree
> with this assessment or whether you have any reason to think that
> there would be advantage in giving him the opportunity to make
> contacts in India. He is, I believe, primarily Nehru's man though
> he purports to purvey the views of Congress as a whole.

Pethick-Lawrence had one attitude towards Krishna Menon
outside the government but in power, he looked at him differently.
A ten-member all-party delegation of British MPs left for India on 2
January 1946 and spent slightly over a month in the country. Krishna
Menon did not accompany the team but Reginald Sorensen, a die-
hard India Leaguer, was in it. A few days earlier on 31 December
1945, Krishna Menon had cabled Nehru:

SORENSEN PROFESSOR RICHARDS MRS NICHOL
BOTTOMLEY AND LORD CHORLEY OF THE BRITISH

DELEGATION ARE GOOD FRIENDS OF OUR WORK
HERE WE HAVE NO RELATIONS WITH REMAINING
FIVE STOP HAVE MET FIRST FIVE AND DISCUSSED
THEIR ATTITUDE STOP REQUEST AND HOPE THAT
THEY WILL BE TREATED AS FRIENDS WITHOUT
PREJUDICE TO THE POLITICAL ATTITUDE TO
THE DELEGATION EXPRESSED BY YOU WHICH I
RESPECTFULLY CONCUR

Sorensen would write a book *My Impressions of India*, which was published in June 1946. In the preface, Sorensen had this to say:[3]

> . . . For many years I have acted as Parliamentary Secretary of the India League. It is an unusual organization, in that although its activities have been extensive it has no paid officials and depends entirely on the voluntary service of its friends in this country [the UK]. Mr. V.K. Krishna Menon, M.A., B.Sc., Barrister-at-Law, its Honorary Secretary, is equally unusual. He seems to live on nothing but tea and bun, and this dynamic ascetic, apart from his work as a Borough Councillor, literally lives day and most of the night for India. I dissent from him in many respects, but I deeply honour his exceptional knowledge of Indian affairs, the explosive zest of his mind, his fine integrity and his friendship.

After the parliamentary delegation had returned to London, Attlee's government announced that a Cabinet Mission comprising Stafford Cripps, Pethick-Lawrence and another MP, A.V. Alexander, would proceed to India on 19 March 1946. Krishna Menon was not impressed and was to tell Nehru on 20 February 1946:

> . . . It is Cripps No. 2. It would be a mistake to think that because Churchill is not the P.M., Cripps will be our ally as we thought in 1939 . . . He is an asset to the Government as a purveyor of goodwill! If the mission succeeds, it will be Cripps. If it fails, it will be us. Alexander is an imperialist. He believes in the Churchill

cult . . . Pethick is the most honest of the lot. But he is very old and doddering. Even Pethick-Lawrence is not thinking of independence . . . We mean by independence, freedom to rule our lives and to choose our friends. Britain does not want us to have friends, but to be a satellite.

Notes

1. At its Lahore session held in end–December 1929, the Congress had declared 26 January 1930 as Purna Swaraj Day. This tradition continued till India actually became independent on 15 August 1947. Thereafter, India became a republic on 26 January 1950. Thus, 26 January is doubly significant in Indian political history.
2. Email correspondence with me, 8 September 2019.
3. Sorensen (1946).

10

Nehru's Sounding Board and Global Envoy (1946)

Krishna Menon had left India in 1924 at the age of twenty-eight and had come back only once in 1932. He made his second visit to the country of his birth in 1946. This time he spent around ninety days in Delhi, Allahabad and Bombay, and visited Calicut as well. He was seeing Nehru after a gap of eight years. In the next two years he would play an important role in the transfer of power negotiations, acting as a sounding board for Nehru.

Maulana Azad had been president of the Congress since 1940. Normally, the term of a president was for a year but in extraordinary circumstances, the incumbent could get a second term as well—this had been the case with Nehru in 1936 and 1937 and with Bose in 1938 and 1939, although Bose did not complete his second term. But Azad was unique in that he had occupied the top position five years in a row. Krishna Menon wrote to Nehru on 28 January 1946:

Here are two matters which I thought I should mention to you.

(1) There is talk here that Maulana Azad will not be re-elected president. If this should turn out to be true it will do us a great deal of harm in the present circumstances. No more unpropitious moment for a change has occurred in our history.

No doubt you are conscious of this but I hope you will not take my mentioning it amiss.

(2) There is reason to think that the imperial side has a plan of 'settlement' when after the elections 'Indians refuse to come terms'. As you will appreciate it, these will be terms that deny the substance of independence and prolong tutelage, but it will be dressed up well . . . It is hoped here that Gandhiji can be won over on the tag of goodwill and also it is believed that the fear of violence will assist in this line . . .

Nehru was well aware of the situation, and his personal preference was to have Maulana Azad re-elected. He wrote to Krishna Menon on 5 February 1946:

. . . About Maulana Azad and the presidentship of the Congress, I should like him to be re-elected but I think it is unlikely . . . The real difficulty is the Maulana himself who is not inclined to stand for election. He is keeping bad health and feels very tired. He is terribly sensitive and agrees to stand only if there is practically a unanimous demand for it and no counter proposal . . .

So far we have not discussed this matter in the Working Committee or even elsewhere though there is some speculation in the press. The names usually mentioned are: Maulana's, Vallabhbhai Patel's and mine. I am clear in my own mind that I should not stand . . .

About your second point, I generally agree . . . What I wrote to Cripps—I sent you a copy of the letter—is the minimum. Once independence is admitted and a freely elected constituent assembly with unfettered powers, then other matters can be discussed . . . The real difficulty on our side has been of course the communal situation.

As Nehru had anticipated Maulana Azad did not continue as Congress president. And as he had hinted, he himself was catapulted to that position once again, even though by his own admission to Krishna Menon, he was not keen on that happening. But he had little choice in the matter, and Krishna Menon cabled Nehru in early March 1946:

> GLAD TO LEARN MAULANA AZAD IS ASKING YOU
> TO ACCEPT NOMINATION PRESIDENCY IN VIEW OF
> HIS OWN DECISION NOT TO STAND STOP VENTURE
> EXPRESS VERY EARNEST AND PROFOUND HOPES
> YOU WILL ACCEPT DESPITE YOUR PERSONAL DISLIKE
> STOP I MAY NOT SAY MORE

In April 1946, Nehru took over as Congress president for the fourth time in seventeen years.

Nehru had been wanting Krishna Menon to visit India and had written to him the previous year on this. He would repeat his request on 17 January 1946:

> I think I have asked you once whether there was any truth in the press report that you were coming to India. I hope there is. I should very much like to meet you and I am sure it will do you good to renew your acquaintance with the Indian scene.

But Krishna Menon kept putting it off on one pretext or the other. Finally on 24 March 1946, at the end of another ten-page letter advising Nehru what to do and what not to do in his discussions with Wavell, he had written:

> . . . It appears to me, therefore, that our strategy in the coming negotiations is to decline to be drawn into any questions of the composition of the so-called Central Government, the discussion of Indo-British relations or a Constituent Assembly unless and until the British hand over sovereign authority to a provisional government . . .
>
> There is one other point to which I want specifically to refer. That is, the mad idea that Cripps is going on about a 'Confederation'. What he means is not a confederation at all, but a confederacy . . . The idea which Cripps is toying with as

usual undigested and unconsidered, and quite unpolitical, is that
India should consist of small states which for certain purposes
would agree to come together as in the European confederacies
of old . . . I submit that even to the whisper of this confederacy
idea, by whatever name Cripps may call it, we must offer initial,
total and unbending opposition and denounce it in the most
scathing terms . . .

    I want to come back to India, if nothing else to see you . . . I
want to be there at the next Congress session if I can, and though I
have no place in the public life of India, it will help me understand
the more dynamic side of our national movement.

Krishna Menon never let go of any opportunity to appear
wounded, even if those injuries were mostly self-inflicted. He would
play this 'I am a nobody' role before Nehru time and again. On 29
April 1946, he informed Nehru:

    . . . I am trying to make arrangements to come to India in the latter
    part of June. Do you think this is all right? Perhaps you will be
    good enough to let me know what you think of it? . . .

This was what Nehru had been hoping for, and on 5 May 1946, he
replied:

    . . . I should like you to come here in June or whenever you can. I
    have long been of opinion that you should visit India and gain first
    hand acquaintance with conditions here. By June we should know
    where we stand. Perhaps there may be a meeting of the new All
    India Congress Committee in June.

Earlier, on 27 April 1946, Krishna Menon had given Nehru
numerous suggestions for Congress's negotiations with the
viceroy, the most important of which was that they should insist
on a completely Indian national government at the Centre in the
interim. Nehru told Krishna Menon and this would have pleased
him no doubt:

. . . I read out your letter to Gandhiji, Maulana and Patel. Gandhiji said it was a good letter by which I suppose, he meant that he agreed with your analysis generally. But he added, much as he would like to follow your suggestions about the interim period, the facts here did not permit him or others to go quite so far.

Clearly, Nehru had plans for Krishna Menon that went beyond being a propagandist in London. The latter finally complied with the former's plea and landed in Delhi on 20 June 1946. Two days later he wrote back to his colleagues in the India League, who were holding the fort in London in his absence:

Dear Everyone:

It is far too hot to think or write . . . I am going to Allahabad tomorrow and from there to Bombay for the A.I.C.C. by the 4th or 5th of July. I shall send you a letter on the political situation . . . A bulletin giving interpretation should be circulated to members and contacts and Indians. The Muslim League and the Government are in league. You all will be able to appreciate the Congress's attitude if you know that the Congress on the one hand no longer regards the pushing out of the British a formidable job, and on the other hand it is desperately anxious for a peaceful transition and prepared to be conciliatory for this purpose . . . [Cabinet] Mission will put a sunshine face on it, but things will erupt by autumn. Jawaharlal is very kind and most embarrassingly attentive to personal comforts, etc. . . .

The very next day he cabled the India League, almost certainly on the basis of his conversations with Nehru:

CONGRESS DECISION MEANS WILLINGNESS PARTICIPATE CONSTITUENT ASSEMBLY FOR ATTAINING OBJECTIVE COMPLETE INDEPEDENCE UNITED INDIA TREATING ASSEMBLY SOVEREIGN BODY BOUND BY ITS DECISIONS ALONE

On 2 July 1946, based on his communication, the India League
sent out the first of its bulletins on the evolving political situation in
India to its network in the UK:

> It is intended to keep our friends and contacts posted with all the
> information at our disposal on the situation in India . . .
>
> The correspondence now published by Mr. Jinnah has revealed
> that Lord Wavell had, it appears, secretly made pro-Muslim League
> commitments which forced the British mission to refuse Congress
> the right to determine its own personnel within its own quota
> of representation in the interim Government, a right which had
> been previously conceded by the Mission, accepted by the Moslem
> League and believed to be inviolable by the Congress . . .
>
> The imperative necessity of an interim national government,
> rejection of the veto of the Moslem League and the sovereign
> character of the Constituent Assembly form the only basis on
> which a satisfactory settlement can be reached . . .

On 16 July 1946, the India League sent out a note to its Parliamentary
Committee:

> Krishna Menon goes on to add the following suggestions for the
> special attention of the Parliamentary Committee of the India
> League. He considers it important that these points should be made
> in the course of the debate on Thursday:
>
> (1) An unequivocal demand that a time limit should be fixed for
>   the Caretaker regime.
> (2) The prompt establishment of the best possible provisional
>   government terminating de facto imperial authority at Delhi . . .
> (3) The recognition of the sovereign character of the Constituent
>   Assembly in conformity with Labour's pledge of self-
>   determination.
> (4) . . . an unequivocal declaration that no assistance or
>   encouragement will be given to princely autocracy in the
>   States.

On 20, 21 and 22 July 1946, a committee of independent experts was set up by the Congress party to do the background work for the Constituent Assembly. This committee was chaired by Nehru and had among its members noted administrators like N. Gopalaswami Ayyangar, lawyers like K.M. Munshi, economists like K.T. Shah and D.R. Gadgil and other public figures like K. Santhanam. Krishna Menon 'was present by invitation of the chairman'. The first day was important because it drafted a resolution to be adopted by the Constituent Assembly. Krishna Menon's hand was very much in evidence in it:

> This Constituent Assembly declares its firm and solemn resolve to proclaim India as an Independent Sovereign Republic, and to draw up for its future governance a constitution wherein . . .
>
> The territories that now comprise British India, the territories that now form the Indian states, and such other territories and parts of India that are outside British India and the States and are willing to be constituted into the Independent Sovereign India, shall be a Union of them all . . .
>
> And wherein
>
> All power and authority of the Sovereign Independent India, its constituent parts, and organs of government are derived from the people;
>
> And wherein
>
> Shall be guaranteed to all the people of India by law, and secured to them by declared social objectives and purposes, economic organization and administrative machinery
>
> (a) justice, social, economic and political,
> (b) equality of status, of opportunity, and before the law,
> (c) freedom of thought, belief, vocation, association and action
>
> subject to law and public morality;

And wherein

Adequate safeguards shall be provided for minorities, backward
areas and backward classes . . .

This draft drew upon over fifteen years of conversations that Krishna
Menon had been having in London with various people, most notably
with Laski. Very large portions of it were to be incorporated into the
final Constitution, which was to come into effect from 26 January
1950. The phrase 'Independent Sovereign Republic' was, by his own
admission, Krishna Menon's. He attended the second meeting of the
experts' committee held in mid–August 1946 at Sardar Vallabhbhai
Patel's residence in Bombay, where the rules of procedure for the
functioning of the Constituent Assembly were finalized. He left for
London a month later, missing the final meeting of the group in
Delhi on 4 December 1946, just five days before the Constituent
Assembly had it first sitting.

On 2 September 1946, the Congress formed the interim
government and Nehru became member-in-charge of external affairs
and Commonwealth relations. He was also vice president of the
Executive Council, which had the viceroy as president. J.B. Kripalani
took over from Nehru as Congress president. Krishna Menon cabled
the India League about the interim government saying that this was
virtually 'Nehru's Cabinet'. He added:

NEXT IN STATURE IN NEHRU'S CABINET IS SARDAR
VALLABHBHAI PATEL HOLDING PORTFOLIO HOME
AFFAIRS AND INFORMATION BROADCASTING. PATEL
AN ORGANISER AND PARTYMAN HAS FEW RIVALS IN
COUNTRY. SEVENTYONE YEARS OLD COMPARED TO
NEHRU'S FIFTYSEVEN. PATEL IN EXCELLENT HEALTH.
IS REPORTED TO BE STRONGMAN OF CABINET . . .
    C RAJAGOPALACHARIAR HAS BEEN ASSIGNED
PORTFOLIO INDUSTRIES CIVIL SUPPLIES. WAS
FORMERLY PREMIER IN MADRAS IN FIRST CONGRESS
MINISTRY IN THAT PROVINCE. SUBTLE INTELLECTUAL

FIRM ADMINISTRATOR HE MAKES EXCELLENT EXPONENT OF ANY CAUSE HE CHAMPIONS. RAJAGOPALACHARIAR COUNSEL WHICH GANDHI HAS ALWAYS FOUND INVALUABLE WILL BE OF EQUAL BENEFIT TO PRESENT CABINET.

Krishna Menon never struck a rapport with Patel, who would have another Menon—V.P. Menon—as his key adviser for the next four years. On the other hand, Rajagopalachari, whom Krishna Menon had first met in September 1932, would be largely responsible for the latter becoming an MP for the first time in May 1953. They would retain a warm personal relationship in spite of their ideological differences, and on his death in 1972, Krishna Menon was to pay handsome tributes saying, 'Rajaji legitimized dissent in Indian democracy.'

Krishna Menon went back to London in the last week of September 1946. As soon as he landed on 24 September 1946, he found a cable from Nehru that had been sent the previous day waiting for him:

> Should like you to contact Molotov, Soviet Minister for Foreign Affairs in Paris immediately regarding supply of foodgrains to India.

Nehru was deeply concerned with the 'grave food situation in India and impending famine in many parts of the country'. He wanted Krishna Menon to press for the supply of food grains, mainly wheat, from 'a friendly people who are our neighbours'.

At the same time that Nehru was cabling Krishna Menon, Wavell was sending a telegram to Pethick-Lawrence:

> Nehru will probably telegraph you today a proposal that Krishna Menon, the Congress propagandist, should visit certain European countries as 'personal representative of Vice-President of the Interim Government' to make contacts and report on possibilities of development of India's relations. The Government of India are to pay the bill and H.M.G. [His Majesty's Government] will be

asked to provide the facilities. I think this is a most ill-advised and ill-timed proposal. I have told Nehru I dislike it . . . I am advised that I cannot constitutionally over-rule my Cabinet on this issue.

Krishna Menon met Molotov in Paris on 28 September 1946 for two hours. Two days later the *Daily Express* in the UK had this report:

TEA-AND-BUNS MAN FROM N.W. GOES TO PLEAD WITH MOLOTOV
SEND FOOD TO INDIA TO AVERT FAMINE

Express Staff Reporter

Back in London after a two-hour talk in Paris with Mr. Molotov Russia's Foreign Minister, was Krishna Menon Indian-born borough councilor for St. Pancras, N.W.

Menon, who his friends say, lives on tea and buns, went to see Mr. Molotov to ask for food for India. He told him, in effect, that India needed 2,000,000 tons of cereals to avert famine. 'It was a successful trip', he said last night at his room in Camden-square, N.W. 'Now I report to Pandit Nehru'. Nehru is the vice-president of the interim Government. Menon is his special diplomatic envoy. Menon, too, is the unpaid secretary of the India League . . .

It is clear from the Soviet archives, however, that Krishna Menon actually discussed more than food supply with Molotov. This is what an American historian who has delved into these records has written about this conversation:[1]

His [Molotov's] notes on a conversation with emissary V.K. Krishna Menon mentioned that closer bilateral ties would 'meet the interests of both countries and would advance world peace and progress'; he then struck the latter phrase from the record. The Soviet Foreign Minister had thus envisioned pursuing mutual interests with a nascent Indian government—but did not see India within the Soviet framework of progress aimed at world revolution.

Krishna Menon's record of his ninety-five-minute conversation with Molotov, sent to Nehru a few hours after it had taken place, admitted that it would be unrealistic to expect food aid from the Soviet Union in any meaningful quantity in view of the problems that Molotov had mentioned about food supply in that country. The food question did not appear to have been discussed at any great length. What Krishna Menon had spent time on was the opening up of relations between India and the Soviet Union in all respects, including diplomatic, economic and even military. India was not yet an independent country, and hence it was natural that Molotov questioned Krishna Menon on the freedom that Nehru had to pursue a foreign policy that was not, in the main, dictated by Great Britain. Krishna Menon was at pains to reassure him that Nehru desired to establish friendly relations with all countries, including the UK, and had high hopes of building a partnership with the USSR.

Molotov's reply to Nehru, handed over to Krishna Menon later in London for onward transmission, read:

> . . . The Soviet Government express their readiness to develop friendly relations with India and to exchange diplomatic and other representatives with your country . . .

But giving the reason that 'there was drought in important agricultural districts of the USSR', Molotov politely refused Nehru's plea for the supply of cereals.

Nehru wanted to move quickly to establish diplomatic ties with different countries. After many twists and turns, he proposed K.P.S. Menon as special envoy to Moscow and Krishna Menon as special roving envoy to some European countries. Wavell objected to Krishna Menon's appointment on the grounds that he was a 'noted Congress propagandist' and that 'he had hardly spent any time in India at all for many years'. For over a month Wavell resisted, but finally after an exchange of letters between him and Nehru, the Government of India made the appointments of the two Menons official on 28 November 1946. K.P.S. Menon was to continue, on an official level, the conversations begun by Krishna Menon with Molotov, while Krishna Menon himself was to be a special representative to conduct informal conversations with west European countries on the subject of exchange of diplomatic representatives. Simultaneously, Krishna Menon was also appointed as an alternate member of India's delegation to the UN, which was headed by Nehru's sister, Vijaya Lakshmi Pandit.

But before Krishna Menon left for New York, he met with both Attlee and Cripps. On the British Prime Minister, he informed Nehru on 18 October 1946:

> . . . The reception was extremely frigid and the whole conversation did not last for more than a few minutes. I would not like you to gain the impression that this was an angry interview or anything like that, but only that the atmosphere was one of complete frigidity . . .

On the Cripps meeting, Krishna Menon wrote separately the same day:

> . . . He was personally most friendly and courteous, but politically he had nothing to say by way of appreciation of the Congress side . . . He then took it upon himself to tell me that I ought to get my position cleared up, and other various other pieces of advice about having an office and all the rest of it. Also he said that I must now represent not only the Congress but the League point of view . . .

The day before, Krishna Menon had also written to Nehru suggesting that he should be allowed to take over as high commissioner of India in London in early 1947, unless 'you can find someone who fits the bill better'. Many years ago, Krishna Menon had told his sister Janaki Amma that 'modesty is a good virtue but it has its place'. He certainly never underestimated himself in any way. He went on to tell Nehru:

> It has so happened that since I began to know you in 1934 I have always had to ask for the work I have done on your behalf,

whether it was arranging your programmes, or latterly, work on the International Peace Council, or the [National] Herald, or Congress publicity, or even the present semi-diplomatic jobs that you have entrusted to me. In one sense I am greatly privileged in that I can say to you that I feel drawn to it, and probably do it better than anyone else who is immediately available. I well remember that you wrote to me that you had no one you could think of whom you could send to Brussels, and with great hesitation I ventured to suggest that perhaps I could do it. It is not an easy task for me to do these things but as I said at the beginning of the letter, it would be bad for me if I were permanently inhibited where you are concerned . . .

Krishna Menon's assignment to the UN led the US State Department to make frantic inquiries from its British counterpart as to who he was. Long after he had reached New York, the British government responded in a straightforward factual manner:

V.K. KRISHNA MENON who was born in Calicut, Madras on 3.5.1897 belongs to a respectable Nair family. He came to London in 1924 and studied at the London School of Economics where he took his B.Sc. He was also called to the Bar and has lived in London since, combining a little legal work with occasional jobs of a literary character. His principal activity, however, has been on behalf of the INDIA LEAGUE, a propaganda organization originally started by the well-known Theosophist Miss Annie BESANT, but which for the last fifteen years has been the unofficial mouthpiece in London of the INDIAN NATIONAL CONGRESS. More recently still MENON has come to be regarded as the personal representative of J.L. NEHRU now Vice President of the Interim Govt., with whom he is on intimate terms. He recently saw M. Molotov, on NEHRU's instructions with a view to paving the way for diplomatic relations between India and the U.S.S.R., but the final negotiations are to be handled by someone else. He has, however, been charged with the duty of visiting various capitals of Western Europe with similar objects in view. MENON is a Municipal Councillor under Labour Party

auspices for the Borough of St. Pancras. He was at one time Labour
Party parliamentary candidate for one of the Dundee divisions, but
his nomination was rescinded by the Labour Party in 1940 because
of his association with the COMMUNIST PARTY. Although this
association still continues (possibly not so openly) he was readmitted
to membership of the Party in 1945.

Krishna Menon's assignment to the UN caused a storm in India
too. On 12 November 1946, in the Central Legislative Assembly,
Ahmed Jaffer, a Muslim League member, grilled Nehru on it and
expressed his serious reservations on Krishna Menon. Nehru replied:

> The question of appointing Mr. V.K. Krishna Menon to explore
> possibilities of establishing diplomatic relations with certain
> countries in Europe has been under consideration. It was considered
> desirable to make an informal and semi-official approach at first
> before a formal approach was made. Meanwhile he was asked to
> meet various representatives of foreign governments in London
> and elsewhere on behalf of the Vice President [Nehru] to convey
> the greetings of the Interim Government and to state that we
> desired to develop friendly relations with those countries . . . Mr.
> Krishna Menon has been working in an honorary capacity and has
> been paid only his travelling expenses . . .

Jaffer questioned the wisdom of the appointment of Krishna Menon
as an emissary to Molotov 'in view of then known pro-communist
views of Mr. Menon and his close association with the Communist
Party in Great Britain'. Nehru defended his choice:

> Mr. Menon was chosen obviously because he was considered
> an excellent person for this kind of work. I will not go into the
> Honourable Member's insinuation about his communist views
> etc; I also hold communist views on many matters. As a matter of
> fact the result of Mr. Menon's visit to Paris to meet Mr. Molotov
> has been very fortunate for us, as Honourable Members might see
> what is happening in the United Nations Assembly where a large

number of countries are supporting us in our stand in South Africa, and in other matters . . .

Jaffer was not satisfied and continued to needle Nehru, who declared that the decision to appoint Krishna Menon was taken in consultation with all the members of the cabinet, which included, of course, the viceroy, Patel and Rajagopalachari.

Krishna Menon, true to his nature, continued to be insecure about himself, especially vis-à-vis Nehru who had to reassure him on 13 October 1946:

> I want to make it clear that I have complete faith on you and I am quite sure whatever step you will take will be taken after full consideration and with a view not to create any difficulties. So far as I am concerned that is alright. But other people, who do not know you well have also to be taken into consideration and hence I have suggested to you might bear these people also in mind. Yesterday Amrit Kaur forwarded a letter to me from some English woman in England, whom I do not know but who apparently is well-known to Gandhiji. She had written to him that she and others were a little concerned at your appointment as a Personal Representative of mine to tour about various European countries. She said that there could be no doubt about your ability and sincerity but you had not got on well with many people and sometimes irritated them. This, of course, has no particular significance. I mention it so that you may know the various influences that are at work.

Krishna Menon was having problems getting along with his colleagues in the UN delegation, particularly K.P.S. Menon. He lamented to Nehru on 23 November 1946:

> You ask me and even more imply that I am to tell K.P.S. Menon everything and also that what I tell you is seen by him. You have no doubt your reasons for this . . . You must do what you please. I would like to assure you, however, that I am not led into this view by his personal attitude which came to me as a rude shock. If you

had not written to me that I have not forfeited your confidence I would be far more unhappy than I am as the only inference that one could make would be that the servant reflects the will of the masters.

Krishna Menon then proceeded to write some ten pages, giving Nehru a blow-by-blow account of all the contacts he had established with different countries and of the conversations he had had with their senior diplomats. As he was concluding this letter, his insecurities revealed themselves yet again:

There is one matter which I have reserved to the last . . . In your letter sent with Mrs. Pandit you have very kindly told me that you have confidence in me. I am very grateful for your taking care to tell me this. It has helped me a great deal during the weeks I have been here. Without it I may have been far more unhappy than I am . . . I have seen and heard things which have hurt me very much and had made me wonder. I would like to say very earnestly that I have confidence in you. I say this with all respect and add that without it I would find it hard to function at all in the present situation both in India and what I have experienced here.

There are too many 'I's in this letter. It is largely due to the personal nature of the work entrusted to me . . .

As for K.P.S. Menon, years later in his autobiography, he recalled his association with Krishna Menon in 1946:[2]

. . . I must confess my first reaction to V.K. Krishna Menon was one of vague irritation. Even when he said nothing—and he did not say much the first few days—he looked so superior . . .

Once I had a head-on collision with him. In one of the rooms at Lake Success, we were discussing a resolution on the admission of new members . . . to the United Nations. Mrs Pandit was to speak on this subject. I had prepared a speech for her and Krishna Menon started picking holes in it . . . Mrs Pandit would not or could not choose between Krishna and myself. Perhaps she even found a little feminine pleasure in the spectacle of two men—and two Menons—squabbling as did Weightman, then Foreign

Secretary who said it was a good idea to set a Menon to catch a Menon. I wrote describing this incident to Anujee [his wife] and in her reply she said, 'if you could have a row with him he must be a peculiar man'. That letter, instead of being delivered to me at Room 801 in the Gotham Hotel, was delivered to Krishna Menon in Room 901 in the same hotel. He opened the letter, scribbled on the envelope: 'Regret, opened in error', and sent it to me . . .

. . . On my return to Delhi Nehru greeted me with the words, 'So the two Menons couldn't get on with each other!'. I explained . . . that I found Krishna Menon insufferable. Nehru listened patiently, and after a few minutes silence said in a philosophical vein that the world consisted of all manner of people, that there were some men of great ability who suffered from a sense of frustration, that this frustration showed itself in various ways, and that if such men were entrusted with responsibility, they could be of great use to the country . . .

The clash of the Menons had repercussions for Krishna Menon's reputation. His old friend from Theosophical Society days B. Shiva Rao was to write to the distinguished jurist Tej Bahadur Sapru on 9 January 1947:

. . . I have had long talks with K.P.S. Menon who has just come back. While the work of the Indian delegation was first-rate and but for Mrs. Pandit's admirable advocacy we might not have won against South Africa, other aspects of the work are not, I am afraid, to our credit. Mainly because of Mr. Krishna Menon's imbalanced activities the impression has been created that India is virtually a satellite of Soviet Russia. I believe Jawaharlal's plain instructions to the delegation were that while we should stand up for our rights and those of other colonial and independent peoples, we should not give the impression that we are anyone's satellite. This impression, I have been told by more than one person who is competent to pass judgment, has created a great deal of hostile opinion against us in the United States.

This would be the refrain in the years to come—that while he was ready to sting the US and the UK, he would make apologies for the Soviet Union. Krishna Menon's argument was simply that the Soviet Union was not a colonial power and that India should deepen its friendship with it. Nehru too was aware of the carping and wrote to Krishna Menon on 29 January 1947:

> . . . One of the most distressing features of the situation is the backstairs gossip on a wide scale about internal Congress divisions even in the Interim Government. Some press people and others have gone rather out of their way to criticise me and point out my many failings. Other press men have defended me. Among my many sins are following a policy in the U.N. which has irritated the United States authorities as this policy was supposed to be pro-Soviet. My association with you is also brought into the picture as you are supposed to be inclined towards the Soviet [Union]. It is stated that our attitude at the U.N. has resulted in a lack of cooperation between India and the U.S.A. in regard to obtaining machinery etc. for development.
>
> I want to tell you that I am convinced you have acted perfectly correctly and I have no complaint on that score. But it is no easy matter to go about explaining all this to various people. It was because of this that I asked you to go a little slow in your approaches to European countries. Naturally behind all this is a certain personal factor, but I cannot go into that right now . . .

Nehru was no starry-eyed romantic as far as Krishna Menon was concerned. He did not say so in so many words but what he was implying was very clear—that Krishna Menon was a proxy target with the real target both within and outside the Congress being Nehru himself. This would continue to be the story for the next decade and a half. People who did not want to criticize Nehru openly and directly because of his unique personality, position, record of sacrifice and stature trained their guns on Krishna Menon instead.

The Congress and the Muslim League continued to be at loggerheads almost on a daily basis. Matters dragged on for all of November 1946, and finally, the British government called Jinnah, Nehru and a few others for talks in London to break the deadlock.

Jinnah was accompanied by his sister Fatima, who would contest for the presidency of Pakistan nineteen years later, while Nehru had Krishna Menon on his side for most of the time. These talks proved futile. Immediately on Nehru's return, the Constituent Assembly had its very first meeting in Delhi on 9 December 1946. This is what Krishna Menon had been wanting and writing about for almost a decade and a half. Two weeks earlier he had sent Nehru 'for his private use' a draft constitution that he had put together while in New York. Unfortunately, that draft has survived only in parts but whatever has certainly reflects concerns then uppermost in Krishna Menon's mind. For instance, the right to education was proposed, making it 'legally incumbent of every State of the Union to introduce free and compulsory primary education up to the age of 14 years'. Such a right was to be introduced in the Constitution only in the year 2001. He also proposed a separate section on 'rights of workers', and of course, had elaborate provisions to guarantee religious and cultural freedom. It also contained some idiosyncratic ideas as admitted a decade later by K.M. Munshi, Krishna Menon's collaborator on the draft:[3]

> . . . V.K. Krishna Menon and I devised an organ of Government called the President in Council which was to be sort of a 'King in Council' such as known in the older days of British Constitutional history. It was also given some of the powers of the American Senate. So ingenious a device makes interesting or rather absurd reading at this distance of time. This attempt at solving an insoluble situation by a constitutional device, even if it had been accepted by the Muslim League, would have been unworkable. It was a fanciful attempt and a forlorn hope . . .

Notes

1. Engerman (2018).
2. Menon (1965).
3. K.M. Munshi, 'Constituent Assembly's "Three Musketeers"', *The Times of India*, 15 August 1956.

11

Assisting Nehru and Mountbatten (1947)

There was a flurry of letters from Krishna Menon to Nehru on his visits to Hague, Paris, Rome and other European countries. On just one day—1 February 1947—he wrote five letters on what India's foreign policy should be. Nehru was having huge problems dealing with the Muslim League and, in the midst of his preoccupations, somehow found time to address Krishna Menon's anxieties on 9 February 1947:

> . . . I want to assure you that your distress is unjustified except insofar as many things that happen distress us all. Our judgments and actions are conditioned and limited by a variety of circumstances so that apart from our initial inclination we are affected by many other factors. I have repeatedly hinted to you that I cannot function as I would like to because of things happening here. In some matters my judgment may not be the same as yours because of these other factors. I do not think they have made any difference to my affection or to my confidence in you, and you need not worry about that. What I [am] sorry about is that I am not in a position at present fully to utilize your great experience and ability as I would like to . . .

But Krishna Menon's communications to Nehru were not always cries of distress or laments at how the world was treating him and not being sufficiently appreciative of his genius. And it was not as if he was negative about others. He could be generous in his praise of unlikely people. On 15 February 1947, he wrote to Nehru:

You had asked me about my impressions of Sir Girija Shankar Bajpai . . . As you know much has been said against him, and he has been spoken of as anti-Indian . . . I cannot say that I was entirely free from a certain degree of 'pre-judgment' . . .

My later meetings, however, confirmed the impression that I formed of him when I first met him with Mrs. Pandit. He is one of the ablest men I have met. He is mentally very alert, and in spite of the Civil Service context, he has a resilient mind. I found he had a grasp of what was going on in the international field . . . As a diplomat he has made an excellent impression . . .

I also discovered that he kept pretty alive to changes in India, and adjusted himself . . .

Finally, the Government and the country would stand to lose by not making use of his talents, which are considerable. In my opinion, for what it is worth, he is not the kind of man, with his past, whom I would like sent off to a capital, but he would be of immense use to you in Delhi at hand . . . He has immense capacity for organization . . .

This letter does Krishna Menon enormous credit. Bajpai was one of the pillars of the British establishment and someone who would instinctively not appeal to Krishna Menon. Yet Krishna Menon recommended him in glowing terms, paying him unusual encomiums. It is possible that Nehru had already made up his mind but soon after Krishna Menon's testimonial, Bajpai was appointed as head of India's foreign service, the first secretary-general of the Ministry of External Affairs. He would, along with Krishna Menon and some others, play a crucial role in persuading Nehru to get India to join the Commonwealth in 1949, when Nehru was deeply ambivalent and large sections of the Constituent Assembly were hostile to the idea. Bajpai would ideologically, especially in relation to Tibet and China, be closer to Patel, but he enjoyed a very warm personal relationship with Nehru, who dissuaded him from resigning on more than one occasion.

Freedom at Midnight by Larry Collins and Dominique Lapierre was published in 1975. An account of the very last year of the British Raj in India, it has perhaps sold more copies than any other book in the history of Indian publishing.[1] It is quite evident that the book is based on extensive interviews with the last viceroy, Lord Mountbatten, and access to his papers, which are now mostly in the public domain. There is a nondescript-looking footnote in the first few pages of *Freedom at Midnight* that has escaped public attention, perhaps because it was just that—a footnote. But it tells an important story:

> Although Mountbatten didn't know it, the idea of sending him to India had been suggested to Attlee by the man at the Prime Minister's side, his Chancellor of the Exchequer Sir Stafford Cripps. It had come up at a secret conversation in London in December [1946], between Cripps and Krishna Menon, an outspoken Indian left-winger and intimate of the Congress leader Jawaharlal Nehru. Menon had suggested to Cripps and Nehru that Congress saw little hope of progress in India so long as Wavell was Viceroy. In response to a query from the British leader, he had advanced the name of a man Nehru held in the highest regard, Louis Mountbatten. Aware that Mountbatten's usefulness would be destroyed if India's Moslem leaders learned of the genesis of his appointment the two men agreed to reveal the details of their talk to no one. Menon revealed the details of this conversation with Cripps in a series of conversations with one of the authors in New Delhi in February 1973, a year before his death.

There is no written evidence anywhere to substantiate what Collins and Lapierre wrote regarding Krishna Menon's central role in Mountbatten's appointment. Peter Clarke, the distinguished British historian and Cripps's definitive biographer, told me:[2]

By putting together other parts of the jigsaw of surviving evidence, I came to the conclusion that Cripps was indeed the source of the idea that Wavell should be replaced by Mountbatten. Whether Menon had a part in instigating this idea remains unclear on this evidence.

A recent biography of the Mountbatten couple has a similar story to tell:[3]

> In January 1946 Mountbatten was again suggested [as viceroy] by a former Vicereine Lady Willingdon, and also Stafford Cripps, probably at the suggestion of the Secretary of the Indian League in London Krishna Menon.

Actually, Mountbatten had been considered for the viceroy's position both in 1942 and 1943 but that proposal had not gone ahead.[4] *Freedom at Midnight* came out when Mountbatten was alive, and it was not contradicted by him in any way. Krishna Menon was distraught with Wavell and knew that Nehru had met Mountbatten for the first time in Singapore in January 1946, where the Englishman was stationed as the supreme allied commander. Wavell had tried to impose restrictions on Nehru's visit to Malaya, fearful of his popularity with the Indian community there, but Mountbatten had intervened to ensure that Nehru's visit went ahead as planned. Mountbatten had also earned quiet plaudits among Indian leaders in the famine year of 1943. Nehru's authoritative biographer S. Gopal has written:[5]

> Lord Mountbatten in command in South-East Asia diverted 10 per cent of the shipping at his disposal for import of foodgrains into India but Churchill, who seemed to regard famine relief as 'appeasement' of the Congress, vetoed this and reduced his shipping by 10 per cent. Mountbatten on his own transferred 10 per cent of his reduced shipping to food imports.

Krishna Menon was also well aware of Mountbatten's impeccable royal connections and his exalted position in the British ruling class.

It helped that he had known Edwina Mountbatten well for over a decade.

On 22 February 1947, the Associated Press had put out a report datelined London quoting a source close to Nehru as saying that the viceroy was being changed and that it was 'a move to placate Nehru who has long been known to regard Wavell as an obstruction to a settlement with the Muslim League'. The report also said that 'Mountbatten and Nehru had become personal friends during the latter's visit to Singapore in March 1946'. Nehru was aghast at the report, promptly dissociated himself from it in the strongest possible terms and sent a note of apology to Wavell, expressing both personal distress about the report and high regard for the outgoing viceroy. While the identity of the source was never established, it seems reasonable to conclude on the basis of all that is known now of that period that it may well have been Krishna Menon himself.

Attlee had offered the job of viceroy to Mountbatten on 16 December 1946. Thereafter, Mountbatten negotiated the terms of his appointment, and it was on 29 January 1947 that King George VI formally approved it. A month later on 23 February 1947, Nehru wrote to Krishna Menon:

> As the tempo of events is moving much faster, most of us are thinking of finishing the work of the Constituent Assembly by September next [it would be done a year behind schedule]. In this work I shall require your help and I hope you will be able to stay some time with us here. Please, therefore, come prepared for a stay and don't try to rush back. Not only for the Constituent Assembly, but for so many other matters your presence here will be extraordinarily helpful to me . . .
>
> The two men that Mountbatten is bringing out with him, Mieville and General Ismay, are not the type which inspire confidence regarding Mountbatten's outlook. As you have met Mountbatten before, it might perhaps be worthwhile for you to see him in London before he comes. Indeed I am told you have met him already. Although personal factors do not ultimately make much difference, still in the short run they do affect events . . .

Nehru scribbled on the top of it: 'This letter is badly drafted and badly typed—still I am sending it—JN)'. Krishna Menon would make such an apology very often but this was the first and last time. Four days later, Nehru gave a run-down to Krishna Menon on what was happening politically at home particularly in regard to the Muslim League's approach to the interim government and the Constituent Assembly. Nehru appeared to have been reconciled to the prospect of the Muslim League being obstructionist and spoke of a possible 'division of Punjab and Bengal'. He also spoke of the attitude of the princely states towards the Constituent Assembly, reserving his harshest comments for the stance adopted by the Nawab of Bhopal and the Dewan of Travancore, C.P. Ramaswamy Aiyar.

On 27 February 1947, Krishna Menon would re-establish contact with Mountbatten after a gap of four years. He wrote to the viceroy-designate:

> You will perhaps remember that just before you left for South East Asia as Commander-in-Chief we met at your house and also that arrangements we made for further talks the following day had to be cancelled as you had to leave rather earlier than expected. I did try to meet you more than once on your brief visit here [London] during the war but was not successful. If it is convenient and causes no embarrassment I shall be glad to come and see you . . .

The two met soon after, and Krishna Menon wrote again to Mountbatten on 4 March 1947:

> I have given considerable thought to what you said to me when I came to see you last week . . . I have tried to make what I have to say as concrete and direct as possible but it requires explanation and possible 'adjustment'. I will come and see you on the morning of Thursday, 13th March . . .

Mountbatten took over as viceroy in Delhi on 24 March 1947. But before he had done so, he had met Krishna Menon twice in London—on 25 February 1947 and on 13 March 1947—after which

Krishna Menon sent the viceroy-designate notes he had prepared
of their conversations. The notes covered the crisis in the interim
government, the machinery for taking over, the Princes (that is
the princely states in India) and Indo-British relations. Krishna
Menon faulted Wavell for not accepting that the entire onus of
administration should be in the hands of the interim government.
He argued that 'it was both logical and incumbent on the British side
that its power (as distinct from influence) should rapidly diminish
and vanish altogether by 1948'. He laid stress on the importance
of the Constituent Assembly that had started its deliberations four
months earlier. He suggested the partition of Punjab and Bengal,
giving Karachi to Pakistan and Calcutta to India, and proposed that
India build a port at Chittagong.

Krishna Menon followed Mountbatten soon to New Delhi and
would spend about a month and a half there. These forty days or so
were to set the ball rolling for India and Pakistan to emerge as two
separate countries in mid-August 1947. On 31 March 1947, Nehru
hosted an informal breakfast meeting at his residence for Mountbatten.
Krishna Menon, who was staying with Nehru, was also present and
was described later by Mountbatten's aide Alan Campbell-Johnson as
'aquiline and intense'.[6]

Krishna Menon had his first formal meeting with the new viceroy
on 5 April 1947. Mountbatten recorded:

> Mr. Menon, whom I saw twice in London before coming out,
> came to see me at 12.15 and stayed to lunch at 1.15. I asked
> him categorically whether Mr. Gandhi's scheme of turning over
> the Central Government to Mr. Jinnah could be made to work.
> Mr. Menon replied emphatically, but with due consideration for
> Mr. Gandhi, that he was afraid that not even Mr. Gandhi could put
> this particular scheme through even if Mr. Jinnah could be made
> to accept it.

The very same day Nehru wrote the first of his numerous letters to
Mountbatten, commending to him the report Krishna Menon had
prepared earlier on the establishment of diplomatic relations by India

with various European countries and Russia. The Prime Minister of Nepal had also just then made a similar suggestion, and Nehru wanted Mountbatten to take action on them.

It was evident that Nehru was using Krishna Menon as an informal backchannel to Mountbatten and his aides, especially Campbell-Johnson. Krishna Menon met Campbell-Johnson on 8 April 1947 and spoke to him about how the Muslim League had come into being and expanded, largely as a response to the Congress becoming a mass movement. A month later the two would have a conversation on the boy scouts movement in India, a particular passion as far as Krishna Menon was concerned.

Krishna Menon called on the viceroy a second time on 17 April 1947. Mountbatten recorded of the hour-long meeting:

> Mr. Krishna Menon reminded me that he was staying out here specially in the hope of being of use to me personally as a friend (or acquaintance) of some four years standing, to help give me the background of what was going on in Congress circles, and to help me put over any points that I found too delicate to handle directly myself. He offered to stay as long as he was of use, and I have asked him to stay at all events till next week . . .
>
> He asked me how I had got on with Jinnah and I told him that I might have to yield to a truncated Pakistan. Krishna Menon said that although Congress would regret this, he did not think they would resist it any longer if I made a point of it; and he offered to help me put this idea over with Nehru if required . . .
>
> After some discussion about the origin of India wishing to shake the dust of the British Empire off her feet, he admitted that he himself had been responsible for inventing the term 'Independent Sovereign Republic' for the Resolution in the Constituent Assembly; and he said that he now regretted choosing such drastic terminology so early on in the final stage . . .

When Mountbatten said that on no account should the Constituent Assembly renounce the link with the Crown since even Ireland had that link, Krishna retorted:

The Congress difficulty would be to retain a link with the Crown because for purely political warfare motives Congress had been attacking the Crown as a symbol of oppression, and it would be difficult to explain to the people such a fundamental change in political outlook.

to which the viceroy's counter-retort was:

That is your headache. You cannot have your cake and eat it too. Unless the Congress could find some way of accepting the link with the Crown and putting it over to the people, I am not prepared to play.

Krishna Menon then suggested a scheme of dual nationality but Mountbatten found problems with it. Then followed an exchange regarding which side should take the first step to keep India within the Commonwealth. Mountbatten told Krishna Menon that the first step had to come from the Congress leadership, while Krishna Menon insisted that it had to come from the viceroy. Finally, Mountbatten asked Krishna Menon what he proposed, and this is what the viceroy went on to record:

I then asked him what he proposed. He said: If the British were voluntarily to give us now Dominion Status well ahead of June 1948, we should be so gratified that not a voice would be heard in June 1948 suggesting any change except possibly to the word dominion if that had been actually used up to that date.

I said that I was in favour of taking steps if it was a feasible proposition. If the Muslims were to stay in a Union of India, I would certainly recommend Dominion Status next month; but since I knew they were not, I could not possibly recommend the present Interim Government be given dominion powers; the Muslim League would violently object to being placed in a position of permanent minority in the Cabinet.

He asked me whether I could not propose equal dominion status to Hindustan and Pakistan, and the States that joined these two confederations. I said: 'Certainly provided I could retain full powers over defence, since I would have to coordinate the use of a single army for both Indian dominions'.

He said that Dominion Status without control over the Army would be laughable and would never be accepted by the Indians.

I told him to go away and think of any solution by which dual dominion status could be granted; with a machinery that would satisfy the Muslim League that the army was being fairly administered and operated. He said he would think over the problem. I told he had no authority to quote me, that he could discuss the tenor of the discussions with Nehru as long as he made it clear that I would never take the first step . . .

This conversation between Mountbatten and Krishna Menon is, given all that we now know of the events of those fateful weeks leading up to 15 August 1947, truly a turning point. It was a 'Eureka' moment of sorts for Mountbatten. The record of the viceroy's staff meeting held the very next day began thus:

HIS EXCELLENCY THE VICEROY said that a germ of a new plan has come into his mind as a result of a conversation which he had had the previous day [with Krishna Menon]. This concerns the question of India remaining, in some way, within the British Commonwealth. The main points of the plan, which he wished senior members of his staff to think over, were as follows:-

1. There was difficulty or who should take, or who should appear to take, the first step . . .
2. This difficulty could be overcome by taking advantage of the resolution which had already been passed by Congress asking for immediate Dominion Status and granting it . . .
3. The grant would have to take place this year . . .
4. Some workable solution must be found to prevent the grant of Dominion Status resulting in the complete control of the Congress of the Muslim League . . .

5.   The control of the Indian Armed Forces would have to remain
      in the hands of the Viceroy . . .

Krishna Menon then met Mountbatten on 22 April 1947. The
latter had discussed the contents of their earlier conversation with his
close aides, and Krishna Menon would certainly have briefed Nehru
at least. This time around, Mountbatten and Krishna Menon spent
two hours with each other, and the viceroy recorded:

> I had a long and friendly talk with Mr. Menon over a cup of tea
> [cups in Mr Menon's case]. We properly let down our hair together
> and discussed every aspect of the plan being worked on, and in
> particular of its relation to the world situation. I found that he had
> very shrewd views on the trends of governments in the U.K. and
> America and on world-wide politics . . .

Mountbatten wrote to Krishna Menon that very night:

> . . . I was tremendously interested and encouraged by the talk we
> had this evening and hope that you will come and see me as soon
> as I get back from Madras . . .

It was at this meeting that Mountbatten unveiled his plan for the first
time, based on the conversation that he had had with Krishna Menon
five days earlier. In his own words:

> . . . I suggested to him a solution along the lines he himself had
> raised the last time, namely Dominion Status before June 1948 so
> as to avoid the necessity of having to make any declaration when
> we left, and thus leave India within the Commonwealth. My
> proposal was that if we could possibly get the scheme working
> in time, Pakistan and Hindustan should be declared independent
> dominions, with a Central Defence Council, a single army
> (pending partition) and with myself at the head of the Central
> Defence Council and as Governor-General of both Dominions
> on a constitutional basis . . .

He seemed rather smitten with this idea, but said immediately that it would be far better to declare India a single dominion which would consist of two parts—Pakistan and Hindustan, since he still harped on the fact that to give each side dominion status was advertising the complete separation of Pakistan . . .

Finally he told me that Pandit Nehru was over-working to the point of a breakdown; that he had a relay of shorthand typists in and out all during the day and night . . . He wished me to take Nehru away for two-three days, anywhere restful, so that we could get to know each other—'For', he said, 'between you two, you can solve all the problems of India'. He told me that Nehru was becoming unpopular with the Hindus through his international and unbiased outlook . . .

Krishna Menon kept meeting Mountbatten informally over the next few days, but sadly, records of these informal conversations do not exist. On the morning of 8 May 1947, Nehru arrived in Simla in response to an invitation from Mountbatten, and two days later, Krishna Menon also showed up at the viceroy's instance. There were no other leaders invited. The record of the viceroy's staff meeting held there on 10 May 1946 began thus:

THE RETENTION OF INDIA WITHIN THE COMMONWEALTH

HIS EXCELLENCY THE VICEROY said that he had had a talk that morning with Mr. Krishna Menon on this subject. Mr. Krishna Menon had pointed out that it was he who had first suggested early transfer of power to India on a Dominion status basis. Mr. Krishna Menon had also stated that one of the advantages in such a plan which most attracted Pandit Nehru was the latter's belief that he (His Excellency) would be able greatly to influence the [princely] States. Mr. Krishna Menon had said that the main difficulty was that, even if Pandit Nehru and Sardar Patel agreed to the scheme, the rest of the Congress Party would have to be persuaded accordingly . . .

RAO BAHADUR MENON . . . went on to say that Sardar
Patel had already put out a statement requesting an early grant of
Dominion status . . .

Rao Bahadur Menon was none other than V.P. Menon, then
Mountbatten's adviser (officially known as reforms commissioner)
and soon to become Patel's adviser formally, although he was
already in daily touch with him, as was Krishna Menon with
Nehru. On the night of 10 May 1947, much against the wishes
of his staff, Mountbatten shared the details of his plan, as revised
and approved by London, for the quick transfer of power with
Nehru and asked him to sleep over it and let him know early next
morning what he thought of it. Mountbatten had perhaps been
led to believe by Krishna Menon that Nehru would go along.
But Krishna Menon was unaware that London had made some
crucial changes. The next morning saw, in Mountbatten's words,
'Nehru's bombshell'.

Twenty-three years later, while presiding over the third Nehru
Memorial Lecture being delivered by Krishna Menon in London on
12 November 1970, Mountbatten recalled that after going through
his plan Nehru was so upset that 'he burst into Krishna Menon's
room at 2 a.m. [of 11 May 1947] speechless with indignation'.[7]
Nehru, no doubt after a discussion with Krishna Menon, wrote
to Mountbatten on the morning of 11 May 1947 that while he
could go along with what he had originally proposed, the changes
inserted by Attlee's government amounted to connivance at the
Balkanisation of India because it envisaged giving Dominion Status
to 600-odd princely states as well. This plan that has come to be
known as 'Plan Balkan' died after the receipt of Nehru's angry but
politely worded letter and was to be replaced by a plan prepared
by V.P. Menon, which would ultimately become the basis of
independence.

An interesting non-political vignette into the happenings at the
Viceregal Lodge at that time is provided by Mountbatten's daughter
Pamela in the diary she maintained:[8]

Sunday 11th May

Yesterday evening Panditji [Nehru] gave us a demonstration of standing on his head, a performance he goes through for about ten minutes every morning and during which the major problems of India are solved! . . . I had a long talk with Krishna Menon, about the most cynical person I've met so far but very interesting.

A month earlier, in fact, she had recorded her first impressions of Krishna Menon, which caught the man perfectly:[9]

Saturday 5th April

We had a big lunch party [in New Delhi] . . . I sat next to Mr. Krishna Menon, Nehru's representative in Europe and in manner far more English than any Englishman . . .

Following Nehru's epistolary outburst on 11 May 1947, both Mountbatten and Krishna Menon went back to London— Mountbatten to consult the British government on his plan and Krishna Menon ostensibly to brief the British government of Nehru's plans for establishing diplomatic relations with different countries. The latter left on 17 May 1947 and the former a day later. That there was more to it than met the eye in their presence in London at the same time is revealed by a letter Krishna Menon wrote to Mountbatten on 21 May 1947 when both of them were in that city:

I have now (since I saw you this morning) a letter from Panditji . . . [It] deals with the question of immediate Dominion Status and his talks with you on this subject . . . I should point out that the transfer of power as under Dominion Status is integral to finding a solution. Congress will not find it possible to agree to any arrangement which leaves this matter unsettled and prevents the Central front from functioning even moderately well . . .

I rather think that it is felt that you have not quite appreciated the strength of opinion held on this matter. As I am anxious that there should be no misunderstanding, I am writing to you even though I have seen you this morning! If Mr. Jinnah wants a total separation, and that straight away, and if we agree to it for the sake of peace and dismember our country, we want to be rid of him, so far as the affairs of what is left to us of our country are concerned. I am sure you will appreciate this, and also that it is not a matter of detail but is fundamental . . .

The British cabinet met on the evening of 22 May 1947 under the chairmanship of Attlee. Mountbatten was also present. The matter under discussion was the 'transfer of power to India and the grant of Dominion status to the resulting successor states'. Mountbatten made a detailed presentation of his proposals. At the end the cabinet decided that Cripps would 'discuss with Mr. Krishna Menon what arrangements could be made for the conduct of the interim government during the period between the decision to partition India and the actual transfer of power'. The next day, Arthur Henderson, the junior minister in the India Office, met Krishna Menon and recorded the conversation the same day:

In the course of a conversation here this morning Mr. Krishna Menon made the following points:

1. The Congress Party leaders were prepared to accept a modified scheme of partition as the basis of peaceful settlement of the Indian constitutional problem. He . . . indicated that an attempt would be made to secure from Mr. Jinnah a statement that he would not continue to make claims in respect of Muslim populations in other parts of India . . .

2. He was most emphatic in expressing the view that even so the basis of any settlement must be that the partition would take the form of certain areas 'splitting off' from the Indian Union and should not be the division of India as such into two separate entities, Hindustan and Pakistan . . .

3. He expressed the view that in the event of agreement being reached as to partition, the present Interim Government should

be replaced by two Cabinets, one for what he called the Indian Union and the other for Pakistan. He stressed the view that the Congress Government of the Indian Union would seek to be regarded as the direct successor of the present Government of India in the international sphere . . .

4. He indicated that for the time being Dominion status would certainly be acceptable to Congress India; but it was doubtful whether they would wish to remain a Dominion indefinitely . . . His view was . . . the Union of India should be a sovereign country with its officers owing allegiance to it and not to The King direct . . .

The same day that the British cabinet met—22 May 1947—the London *Times* and other newspapers had carried statements of Jinnah on his idea of Pakistan. Krishna Menon was quick on the draw and wrote immediately to Mountbatten. Among other things, he took serious objection to Jinnah's demand for a corridor linking West and East Pakistan, saying:

The corridor demand, which at one time was as 'futuristic' as Pakistan, is now definitely made. Not only will it not be agreed to, but the guarantee against such demand is vital to the rest of India.

Krishna Menon went on to accuse Jinnah of breach of faith in regard to the agreement on princely states and told Mountbatten:

. . . I would beg of you to consider that there must be a limit to appeasement, both by India and you, and that the final result is not a parallel to the surrender of Sudetenland. It is India's frontiers that are being made alien States! I am sorry that now again, when it comes to something final, you are faced with repudiation, for that is what the Press statement amounts to. It must warn us to be prepared with alternatives, which would have to be forcibly presented.

The Labour Party's annual conference was being held at Margate. Krishna Menon wrote to Cripps on 27 May 1947, telling him that he was coming there to have further conversations on various aspects of the transfer of power and that it was important for him to see Bevin as well. He also sent Cripps notes of these previous discussions on the steps to be taken by the British government once Partition had been agreed upon. He described to Cripps the broad contours of the parliamentary legislation that needed to be passed in the House of Commons to enable the Indian and the Pakistani government to start functioning.

That the two Menons did not exactly like each other is evident from the minutes of the viceroy's staff meeting held on 4 June 1947, where V.P. Menon was recorded as having said:

> RAO BAHADUR MENON stated that Sardar Patel had told him that he thought Mr. Krishna Menon was becoming a busybody. He pointed out that Sardar Patel and Pandit Nehru were invariably in complete agreement on fundamental issues . . .

Krishna Menon's ubiquitous presence was not appreciated by Lord Ismay, Mountbatten's military adviser, either. Two days after V.P. Menon had put down Krishna Menon, Lord Ismay suggested, in another of the frequent viceroy's staff meetings, that while Krishna Menon had been 'extremely useful in London where Pandit Nehru was not available', now that the discussions were in Delhi and on administrative matters, Mountbatten should suggest to Nehru that Krishna Menon's 'services as a link were no longer of such value as they had been'. Mountbatten was in a dilemma, bemoaning that 'Pandit Nehru was continually asking him to see Krishna Menon' but accepting the fact that 'whatever the merits of using him as a "contact man" might be, it was clear that Mr. Krishna Menon was Pandit Nehru's right-hand man'.

The very day V.P. Menon had characterized Krishna Menon as a 'busybody', the latter wrote to the viceroy saying that Gandhi had had a 'long talk with me yesterday' and was very disturbed. He urged Mountbatten to be more than mindful of Gandhi's concerns and assure him that what was distressing him was also on the viceroy's mind. On receiving Krishna Menon's message, Mountbatten asked to see Gandhi, and this meeting took place on 4 June 1947 at 6 p.m., just before Gandhi's prayer meeting. It was Mountbatten at his Machiavellian best, after having been primed by Krishna Menon. His record of the meeting states:

> . . . He was indeed in a very upset mood and began by saying how unhappy he was. I replied immediately that whilst I could understand and indeed shared his upset feelings at seeing the united India he had worked for all his life apparently destroyed by the new plan, I hoped to convince him that this plan was nevertheless the only possible course.
>
> I told him although many newspapers had christened it 'The Mountbatten Plan', they should have really christened it 'The Gandhi Plan', since all the salient ingredients were suggested to me by him . . .

Mountbatten then explained to Gandhi how all his precepts and principles had been scrupulously followed in arriving at a compromise that would involve no coercion or violence—both of which Gandhi wanted to be avoided at all costs. He also told Gandhi that as he had been demanding, the British would quit soon and transfer power on the basis of Dominion Status. Gandhi would later tell Mountbatten of 'you and your magic tricks', referring to this meeting triggered by Krishna Menon's letter.

Whatever the murmurings about his role, Krishna Menon kept chugging along unfazed by what was being said about him. He was staying with Nehru and that strengthened his position even further. A referendum had just been held in the North West Frontier Province (NWFP). It had been a victory for Pakistan. Krishna Menon wrote to Mountbatten on 14 June 1947:

> . . . Mr. Bevin said at Margate that the withdrawal from India meant the consolidation of Britain in the middle east. Is our frontier still the hinterland of this imperial strategy? Does Britain still think in terms of being able to use this territory and all that follows from it? There is considerable amount of talking in this way and if Kashmir for one reason or another chooses to be in Pakistan

there is a further development in that direction—I do not know
what British policy is in this matter. I do not know that you would
know it either. But if this be British intent it is tragic. It will be a
grave miscalculation . . . If Kashmir and N.W.F.P. go to Pakistan,
all hopes of the plan being a settlement will prove fanciful . . . We
may be menaced by many years of conflict . . .

Krishna Menon added a line at the end: 'Please don't keep this letter.'
But Mountbatten kept it, and it is now very much a part of the official
records showing how prescient Krishna Menon was on Kashmir.

A few weeks later Krishna Menon was appointed India's first
high commissioner in London. Mountbatten congratulated him on
10 July 1947:

. . . I cannot let you leave India without giving you my warmest
personal thanks for the way you have helped me in all these difficult
negotiations. I feel that history will show that you have helped the
future of India very much by the advice you gave me.

I am glad to think that I shall have a personal friend as the first
High Commissioner in London . . .

The next day, the vicereine followed in her husband's footsteps and
wrote to Krishna Menon:

My dear Krishna:

Before you leave I feel I must send you a line to tell you how
much your friendship and wise counsel as well as your confidence
has meant to us both in these last months—the patch has not been
an easy one and I can never be sufficiently grateful for all you have
done to smooth it for all concerned and for your invaluable advice
and real vision as well as sound judgment.

You will be very much missed here but we are so happy with
your new high appointment and there is no one more fitted to
carry out this vital task. Both India and our country are indeed
fortunate that you are to undertake it.

You have all my heartfelt good wishes and I know that if we ever send you an SOS you will fly back to answer it.

Edwina Mountbatten of Burma

Krishna Menon arrived in London on 13 July 1947, carrying letters for Attlee from both Mountbatten and Nehru. No official announcement was made of his new assignment. That was to happen a little less than a month later. But old impressions of him remained. On 18 July 1947, Listowel, the new secretary of state for India, wrote to Mountbatten:

> . . . Krishna Menon came to see me . . . It has to be admitted that in the past the impression he has created in home circles has by no means been favourable but, in view of his selection as High Commissioner in the United Kingdom for the Dominion of India, it is encouraging to know that his services have been of such assistance to you in the difficult negotiations in Delhi in recent weeks. I am arranging for him to meet with some Opposition leaders to whom at the moment he is, by no means, *persona grata*. The great need at Indian House at the moment is, of course, for someone at the top with real organizing and administrative capacity. I rather doubt whether Krishna Menon will supply this need . . .

Listowel knew his man well. Krishna Menon would notch up some great successes as high commissioner over the next five years but his lack of 'real organizing and administrative capacity', as Listowel feared, would forever tar his reputation as well as that of his protector—Nehru.

Back in London, Krishna Menon was busy lobbying with members of both the House of Commons and the House of Lords on the legislation that would create the two new Dominions. His main worry was about the princely states and the view in some influential circles in London that Dominion Status could be granted to them as well. He was fiercely opposed to this, reflecting the view of the Congress leaders back in India. In this Cripps supported Krishna Menon's position to the hilt, and Attlee saw the merit of the argument

that he was making. On 18 July 1947, Krishna Menon congratulated
Mountbatten on the passage of the Bill saying:

[T]he Bill has become law and your efforts have been successful . . .
The Lords were particularly tame and cooperative. The undercurrent
of opposition in the Commons did not come to much . . . It is all
over, even though there is little enthusiasm anywhere. Partition
and strife casts its shadows dark and long.

Your letter and a personal note from Jawaharlal which I
brought here were sent to Downing Street on Sunday last when
I arrived here. It was at once sent on to Chequers [country home
of the British Prime Minister], where the P.M. was. His secretary
telephoned me before six and the P.M. saw me at 10 the next
morning. You have educated them all in hustling . . . There is no
lack of desire on the part of P.M. to be of assistance . . .

I have also seen Listowel, Henderson and Cripps, all of whom
promised to do what they could in speeches to indicate that
H.M.G. would not welcome Balkanisation or Dominion Status for
Princes. All of these were very cooperative . . .

Everyone here is deeply appreciative of the strenuous and
unique part that you and Lady Mountbatten have played. The
Congress has risen in the estimation of the people, not least by their
refusal to be fooled into asking for an Indian Governor General
following Mr. Jinnah and the taunts of some people . . .

After the Bill had become law, Mountbatten replied to Listowel
on 25 July 1947:

I fully appreciate all that you say about Krishna Menon. I was aware
that he is 'persona non grata' in many circles at home and I would
not say that he was popular or entirely trusted here. But he has
been the very greatest help to me in the past difficult four months.
Fortunately I made his acquaintance some years ago in England
when he was very much an outcast because of his left-wing views
and activities. He has never forgotten this and I have found him a
valuable contact between Nehru (whose complete confidence he

has) and myself, and through him I have been able to be particularly well informed about the trend of Congress thought and opinion. In fact, with V.P. Menon and his close contact with Vallabhbhai Patel I have been able to know all that has been going on in both 'camps' in the Congress Party.

Krishna Menon's appointment was still causing considerable controversy, and even as late as 9 August 1947, Listowel told Mountbatten:

A certain amount of opposition to Menon's appointment is showing itself here, more particularly in Indian circles in London. Menon certainly has a past to live down, but we will do all we possibly can to help him establish his position.

The foundation of Indian independence was the partition of Punjab and Bengal to create Pakistan. Two boundary commissions were set up, and a noted jurist, Cyril Radcliffe, who had no connection whatsoever with the subcontinent, was appointed its independent chairman. It appears that initially 'Sir Patrick Spens, the reigning Chief Justice of India had been a unanimous choice by all parties but for some reason he was never called upon'.[10] Listowel, who delivered the Nehru Memorial Lecture in London on 24 June 1980, recalled:

As he [the chairman of the boundary commissions] was to have a casting vote, he would in fact decide the boundaries between the two new Dominions, and this obviously required the judicial mind of someone outside politics. I was advised that the best choice would be a High Court judge, with a brilliant record at the Bar Sir Cyril Radcliffe. He was a man of singular artistic taste . . .

Radcliffe came to India on 8 July. His 'award' was submitted on schedule on 15 August 1947 and published two days later. He went back to England, destroyed all his India-related papers and never ever spoke or wrote of this particular assignment of his. Many years later, W.H. Auden was to immortalize him in his famous poem called *Partition*. Jinnah, who had practised in London between 1930 and 1934, was well aware of Radcliffe and approved of the choice instantly but the Congress took some days to agree. Finally, Nehru came around. Kuldip Nayar, the well-known Indian journalist, wrote in his autobiography published in 2012:[11]

> . . . Nehru approved his [Radcliffe's] name after consulting that sneaky fellow Krishna Menon, as Radcliffe put it, when I met him in London on 5 October 1971.

All of July 1947, cables flew back and forth between Nehru and Krishna Menon on the situation in Indonesia, caused by the hostilities started by the Dutch government. Quite apart from his personal friendship with Indonesian leaders such as Soekarno, Nehru was very worried that the 'prolongation of conflict would threaten the peace of the whole of South East Asia'. For at least two weeks, Krishna Menon was meeting British cabinet ministers with messages from Nehru on this issue. In between, he found time on 20 July 1947 to send Nehru a four-page note called 'NATIONAL GOVERNMENT ETC', in which he said:

> A National Government of India under a democratic parliamentary system must be a team representing as much homogencity as possible, and in my view could not be an elected committee . . . The essential quality of the next Government must be strength and stability, and capacity for team work. It should therefore be a 'Ministry of all talents' and should not exclude men of administrative competence whose patriotism is beyond question but who may not have been Congress workers. We cannot afford to sacrifice efficiency this stage . . .
>
> There are reports in the papers here today that the Congress Working Committee are meeting to select the next Government. I hope this is not true . . .

Krishna Menon need not have worried. Thanks to Gandhi, who had the full backing of Nehru and Patel, some of the Congress's bitterest critics such as Dr B.R. Ambedkar and Shyama Prasad Mukherjee were included in free India's very first cabinet that was sworn in on 15 August 1947 and given important portfolios.

On 9 August 1947, the viceroy wrote to Krishna Menon in a language that reflected the camaraderie that had developed between them:

> I am writing to offer the congratulations of the Governor General of the Dominion of India to the High Commissioner of the Dominion of India in London since both appointments take effect together on the 15th of August. As you know, I am very pleased that you have got this appointment . . .

And the vicereine followed with her own letter a day later:

> . . . You are of course very much missed here and it was always so nice to feel that we could turn to you for advice and consultation and ask you to straighten out some of the more complex crises and complications . . .
>
> Gandhiji's visit to Kashmir has gone off extraordinarily well . . . I have seen Panditji a great deal at his house and here [Viceroy's House] and we had the most friendly and interesting talks on all kinds of subjects . . .
>
> I fear you will not have a particularly easy time in England but I am sure you will be able to cope . . . I know my husband has sent you a good deal of news in his last letter and I expect you hear most things from Panditji so I won't give you any more highlights from here . . .

Even before he formally took over as India's high commissioner in the UK on 15 August 1947, Krishna Menon's new assignment was making waves. On 1 August 1947, M.O. 'Mac' Mathai, the all-powerful aide to Nehru, wrote to him:

> . . . Even without formally taking charge, you seem to be as busy as a beehive about all manner of our problems. You, who never

take rest, advised Panditji to get away for a few days. Physician heal thyself!

Krishna, I am giving you the following information in strict confidence. Bhandari [an Indian doctor in London active in the India League and close to both Nehru and Krishna Menon] sent Panditji a few days ago the following telegram: 'Have learnt from reliable British sources name of the new High Commissioner, London. Pleased from reasons of personal regards and friendship only. Will loyally back what you command, but consider it important to acquaint you that this choice will be widely and heartily unpopular equally in Indian and British circles . . .' Panditji hasn't taken any action on this cable—I mean he hasn't sent a reply. I would like to urge on you that you should continue to have cordial relations with Bhandari and others. I have no doubt that in your hour of 'triumph' you will display enough statesmanship. Stretch your hand of cooperation to all—even to your enemies . . .

Take good care of yourself. Rest well and don't rely too much on tea and your nerves . . .

Those were the days when Mathai and Krishna Menon were buddies. Thirty years later in his memoirs, the former would skewer his fellow Malayali, but in the late 1940s and 1950s they were thick as thieves, with their correspondence reflecting their close relationship. Bhandari was not wrong. Krishna Menon's appointment had indeed angered many but some welcomed it as well. Kinglsey Martin wrote on 6 August 1947 in the *New Statesman & Nation*:

There is a kind of poetic justice in the appointment of Krishna Menon as Indian High Commissioner to England. It is proof of the reality of Indian freedom. Krishna Menon might have been a highly successful barrister. He has all the gifts, including brilliant forensic ability. But during the twenty-five years I have known him in this country, he has never allowed any ambition to compete with his absorbing passion for Indian freedom. I am not saying that he has always been wise as a propagandist, but no one could help admiring his devotion, shown in a severely ascetic life, dogged by poverty and ill-health. Now he comes to the country, against which he has fought, to represent his own free nation. And, after a year's close work with Jawaharlal Nehru, to whom he is personally devoted, he brings with him a new and responsible consciousness of the problems that face Britain and India.

There is one other somewhat unusual event of 15 August 1947 that merits recall. Krishna Menon had earlier, on 30 July 1947, sent a message to Nehru:

> I would like to make the following suggestion about the hoisting of the flag in this country. It is a matter of courtesy to let the Union Jack fly on the building at the same time. This would be appropriate even if India were not a Dominion, as it would be only showing fraternity. I would not suggest that the Union Jack should be hauled up at the ceremony. It should be let to fly before in a normal way, and our flag should be hauled up on its own mast. This will not be a derogation of our own status or dignity, and meets all points of view and will be welcomed as a good gesture. It does not commit us to the future . . . I feel sure that it would be looked upon as the behaviour of a politically mature people . . . It would also perhaps please Gandhiji.

Nehru replied three days later:

> About the Flag, we shall send you instructions later. But my present inclination is that you might fly the Union Jack also on August 15th. Subsequently, only the National Flag should be flown, except on special occasions . . .

Both flags did fly together that historic day outside India House—the office of the Indian High Commission—in London. Nehru had been in British jails in various spells for a period of almost ten years. Krishna Menon had protested and agitated in the UK for two decades. Yet, when freedom came, both were ready to make such gestures to their erstwhile colonial masters.

But that red–letter day was not without drama—how could it not be when Krishna Menon was involved? The function began at exactly 11 a.m. on 15 August 1947 outside India House, Aldwych, in London. The British government was represented by Herbert Morrison, Pethick-Lawrence and A.V. Alexander. Krishna Menon was silent through the hour-long ceremony, which was begun by the acting high commissioner, M.K. Vellodi, an old friend and a fellow Malayali. Vellodi had been cut up that Krishna Menon had been appointed his successor without him being given prior intimation; he had made his extreme displeasure known to Krishna Menon. Nehru had asked Krishna Menon to keep the news of his appointment to himself. But it had leaked, and Vellodi had been rightly incensed. Nehru had to intervene to assuage Vellodi. At the end of the ceremony, around fifteen minutes to noon, Vellodi formally handed over charge to Krishna Menon. The man who attended the flag-hoisting ceremony of his country as acting high commissioner would half an hour later attend the flag-hoisting ceremony of Pakistan at Lancaster House as the full-fledged high commissioner of his country. Vellodi would go on to have a distinguished civil service career in India.

Two days later Peter York wrote a fulsome tribute to the newly appointed high commissioner of India in *Reynolds News* and ended it by saying:

> . . . Perhaps Krishna Menon is no longer a Theosophist. A pity if he
> is not. Modern Theosophy's dictum that 'Whatsoever a man reaps
> so he must have sown' fits him like a nice, new glove.

Annie Besant would have been proud of at least this Krishna, even as she had been somewhat disappointed with the other.

Independence had come to India largely because of upheavals and mass movements crafted and led by Gandhi at home. Krishna Menon had no role whatsoever in this. Independence also came because since the mid-1930s, public opinion in Britain itself became more sympathetic to and supportive of the Indian cause. In creating this 'climate of opinion' Krishna Menon had made significant contributions, perhaps second to none. In addition, Indian independence was the outcome of negotiations between the British government and the Congress party, particularly between 1945 and 1947, in which Nehru was absolutely pivotal. And Krishna Menon was his confidant during this process. His role in the partition of India was known to people of that time.

One person, in particular, was to hold him responsible for it. Maulana Azad, who was at the centre of things at that time—along with Gandhi, Nehru and Patel—wrote his memoirs of that period which was published in 1959, a year after his death. But that book had some passages that were not, in keeping with Azad's wishes, included in the book and were to be made public three decades later.[12] In these passages he was extremely critical of Patel and more admiring and warm towards Nehru. He believed that Nehru was in the beginning firmly opposed to Partition but later changed his mind. Azad wrote:

> . . . Krishna Menon had communist tendencies but when he saw that Lord Mountbatten was friendly to him and might help him to get a position [as high commissioner to London], he became pro-British overnight. He impressed Lord Mountbatten with his friendly feelings for the British. Lord Mountbatten felt that Krishna Menon would be useful in persuading Jawaharlal to accept his scheme for the partition of India. It is my belief that Krishna Menon did influence Jawaharlal's mind on this question.

Notes

1. Collins and Lapierre (1975).
2. Clarke (2002) and also in email conversation, 8 April 2019.
3. Lownie (2019).
4. Ziegler (1985).
5. Gopal (1975).
6. Campbell-Johnson (1951).
7. Quoted in Gopal (1975).

8. Mountbatten (2007).
9. Ibid.
10. Lownie (2019).
11. Nayar (2012).
12. Azad (1988).

The Post–1947 Years

12

High Commissioner in London (1947–51)

15 August 1947–31 December 1947

K rishna Menon took over as Indian high commissioner in London on 15 August 1947 and was immediately in the thick of a huge controversy that was to cause yet another rift between Nehru and Patel. The trigger was a young thirty-year-old man called Sudhir Ghosh, a self-styled 'emissary' of Gandhi who had persuaded Patel to appoint him a public relations officer in the Indian High Commission some six months before Independence.

It all began when Nehru wrote to Krishna Menon on 27 February 1947:

> I suppose you have met Sudhir Ghosh. Vallabhbhai Patel is sending him to London to act as Publicity Officer. It is a difficult job, and, so far as I know, India House [the High Commission] has not done this kind of work previously. I hope you will help and advise Sudhir Ghosh in his work . . .

The Cambridge-educated Ghosh then launched a new group called 'Friends of India' which was promptly seen by Krishna Menon as a rival organization and as an encroachment on his natural territory. Ghosh wrote a long letter to Patel on 28 May 1947, complaining bitterly against Krishna Menon, accusing him of being a communist and having communist lieutenants. The mildest language Ghosh used in the letter was that 'Mr. Menon . . . is a difficult proposition in spite of his undoubtedly exceptional abilities'. Patel passed Ghosh's letter to him to Nehru three days later, saying, 'I feel that something should be done to put matters right without undue delay.' On 31 May 1947, Nehru wrote to Ghosh saying that it was 'perhaps natural that the India League people should look with apprehensions at the formation of a new Group about which they had heard nothing' and went on to advise him that the 'best thing is to explain this clearly to the India League people as well as to others that it is in no sense a rival organisation'.

Nehru and Patel were having their differences over much bigger issues. Ghosh had played on this and complained to Patel that Krishna Menon was spreading the story that 'Ghosh had been sent by Patel in spite of opposition from Pandit Nehru and much against his will'. It is impossible to verify the veracity of Ghosh's claim but Nehru dealt with it in his letter to him on 20 June 1947:

> . . . [O]ne thing should be clear to everybody that for anyone to say that you represent Sardar Patel in London and somebody else represents me in fantastic nonsense; further that Sardar Patel and I are carrying on different policies of the Government is equally silly. We differ in some matters, as intelligent people differ, but we work in the closest cooperation, not only because of our long association and regard for each other, but also because the situation demands it . . .

Nehru then went on to advise Ghosh on how to function in London and said:

> . . . I happen to know a good deal about both Krishna Menon and his work in London as well as about the India League. Personally, I have a huge regard for Krishna Menon and his work and consider him one of our ablest men. He has been doing very good work and we expect him in future to do even more responsible work . . .

You should keep in touch with him and if you have any grievance you should tell him about it . . .

I find from your letters such as I have seen in the past and recently that you have not developed enough restraint yet and restraint is a very necessary quality in a person dealing with matters of the moment . . . I am writing to you frankly, because I like you and I want you to get on . . . But I want you to discipline yourself a little more and develop some restraint . . .

Things were relatively quiet thereafter, and two days after he had taken over as high commissioner, Krishna Menon told M.O. Mathai:

. . . Sudhir Ghosh is going to be a handful, but I am going to do my best to keep him, make a P.R.O. out of him. I may fail, but it will not be for want of trying. The man is so incompetent that it is difficult, and his being unreliable and conceited makes it worse.

The problem was simple: Ghosh saw himself as answerable only to Patel, as minister of information and broadcasting, while Krishna Menon believed that all employees in the High Commission reported to him, first and foremost. On 26 September 1947, Krishna Menon sent the first of his two long telegrams to Patel, essentially telling him that Ghosh had to be reined in. He followed it up with another message ten days later, saying that the public relations department in the High Commission had now been brought under the direct control of the high commissioner and his deputy (Vellodi). Patel replied by telegram to Krishna Menon on 6 October 1947, virtually asking him to put the reorganization plans on hold and politely demanding specific instances of the problems Ghosh was creating.

Ghosh was to unwittingly provide the ammunition for his self-destruction in London soon thereafter. It all started with a telegram Ghosh sent Patel on 14 October 1947:

IN VIEW OF THE GROSSLY EXAGGERATED PROPAGANDA IN THE BRITISH PRESS AND THE DIFFICULTIES OF COMBATING IT IT WOULD BE A

GREAT HELP FROM THE POINT OF VIEW OF MY
WORK HERE IF I COULD PAY BRIEF VISIT TO DELHI
AND PUNJAB. ISMAY CAN GIVE ME LIFT IN HIS PLANE
TO DELHI END OF THIS WEEK. IF YOU APPROVE I
WOULD LIKE TO COME. I WILL OF COURSE SECURE
APPROVAL AND SANCTION OF MY SUPERIORS.

Three days later Patel replied by telegram:

NO OBJECTION YOUR COMING WITH ISMAY

This exchange makes it clear that Patel merely acquiesced with what
Ghosh wanted to do. Yet, in his memoirs, Ghosh embellishes the
story. According to him:[1]

> In the first week of October I received a cable from Vallabhbhai
> Patel telling me that Lord Ismay, Chief of Staff to Lord Mountbatten
> was coming to London for consultations and that I was to return to
> New Delhi in Ismay's special plane for a short visit.

Krishna Menon complained to Nehru that Ghosh had acted on his
own and that he had got information on his visit to Delhi from Ismay.
Obviously, the high commissioner was livid and appealed to the Prime
Minister. Nehru, realizing that Ghosh had a direct line to the deputy
prime minister, wrote to Patel on 24 October 1947 saying:

> I am sorry that there has been this continuous friction between
> Krishna Menon and Sudhir Ghosh. It is clear that work can only
> be done if a certain discipline is maintained in a large establishment.
> Krishna Menon has complained that there has been no discipline at
> all and hence work has suffered greatly at a very critical time.

Patel replied a day later, defending Ghosh to the hilt, saying:

> . . . At the time Krishna Menon was appointed, I had grave
> misgivings as to whether he would allow Sudhir Ghosh to function

at all. I know he cannot tolerate the presence of anyone who has as high contacts as Sudhir had . . .

Patel's deep suspicion of Krishna Menon was evident in that letter to Nehru. Ghosh came to India and met Nehru, who then wrote to Patel on 8 November 1947:

> Sudhir Ghosh came to see me two or three days ago and we had a talk . . . It seems clear from various accounts . . . that Krishna Menon and Sudhir Ghosh do not fit in with each other and it is unfair to both to be yoked together in one place . . .
>
> From all accounts that I have received from various sources, Krishna Menon has done very good work . . . There is general appreciation of his work from different quarters, including many that were previously unfriendly . . . The consequence of this is that Sudhir Ghosh should not be stationed in London . . .

Krishna Menon was badgering Nehru that Ghosh should not continue and that it was either him or Ghosh in London. Nehru, for his part, had made up his mind that Krishna Menon had to stay and Ghosh had to go. But Patel continued to defend the latter and was critical of the former. On 14 November 1947, he wrote to Nehru, giving full expression to his feelings. But he must have realized that Nehru had made up his mind for he ended by saying:

> . . . Nevertheless, I had it in mind even before—and I stick to it even now—that if Krishna Menon is prepared to force the issue to this extent as to say that if Sudhir returns he would leave or that Sudhir could not fit in with him, then Sudhir must come back . . .
>
> Both in this letter and the previous one, you have referred to the good work done by Krishna Menon. I should not like to make any comments on this matter.

Six days later Nehru wrote to Krishna Menon and gave him the news he had wanted to hear for the past two months:

I am sorry there has been so much trouble over Sudhir's work in the India House. As he could not function there to your satisfaction it was obviously not desirable for him to continue there. But now that this episode is closing, I trust you will see to it that it ends properly and with as little ill-will as possible. I should not like Sudhir to leave with some kind of a blackmark against his name. He has to work elsewhere and should be able to do so under favourable auspices.

Nehru was large-hearted and magnanimous but he had expected too much from his highly strung high commissioner, who had meanwhile prepared a 'charge sheet' against Sudhir Ghosh. Nehru upbraided Krishna Menon on 25 November 1947:

. . . [T]he Sudhir Ghosh episode is bad enough but I do wish that you would not take it quite as seriously as you have done. It was totally unnecessary and unwise of you to send a list of charges. It was far easier to ask for his recall . . . You know the situation here and Sardar Patel is very sensitive about his own nominees . . .

The Sudhir Ghosh saga saw a few more letters between Nehru and Krishna Menon and between Nehru and Patel before coming to a close finally by mid-December 1947. But a year later Krishna Menon would again be in confrontation with Patel, and this time over a matter far more serious. Ghosh was to be elected to the Rajya Sabha in 1960 with the support of the Congress and the Praja Socialist Party. He enjoyed the backing of B.C. Roy, the West Bengal chief minister. Two years later he applied for and got admission into the Congress party as a full-fledged member. On 8 August 1962, he would write to Nehru:

I venture to enclose another letter I have received from Senator Hubert Humphrey; he makes some comments on difficulties of India–America relations . . . [They] seem to be more obsessed about a person than about policy; they do not get on with Mr. Menon but they fail to state clearly what is their quarrel with the policy he advocates (and they know he does it with exceptional ability) in the U.N. I wish it were possible to bring about a little better understanding between Mr. Menon and leading Americans in human sort of way . . .

I went to see Mr. Menon a few weeks ago, after the lapse of many years; I found him much more generous and mellow than I had anticipated. He even expressed his willingness to help me to make some better use of my time; it meant a lot to me.

Nehru replied the very same day:

Krishna Menon knows a large number of Americans and gets on very well with them. Oddly enough, he got on very well with [Henry] Cabot Lodge. Unfortunately, he has not been able to hit it off with others.

Krishna Menon did not have too many friends, well–wishers and admirers in India at that time but M.O. Mathai was certainly one of them. He had started work as an assistant of sorts to Nehru in 1946 and had quickly established himself as his key and powerful aide. Krishna Menon wrote to him two days after taking over:

. . . Have you begun to work at the office, or at any rate go down there? I hope you don't let things drift. Panditji appreciates you very much, and you have the strength of character and honesty to be useful and make things worthwhile. I hope you will use your mind a little and think things out. Did Panditji ever have a long talk with you? He is very odd about talking. I think it is very trying for all, but it is only part of his shy nature. He seems to be getting on better with the Mountbattens . . .

I have resigned from the secretaryship of the India League from last week. The work will go on, perhaps better than before.

The same day Mathai had also written to Krishna Menon that the Prime Minister's Secretariat was being formed and that he was planning everything as Krishna Menon had suggested. He replied to Krishna Menon six days later and was full of praise for him:

. . . I am proud of you for the magnanimous attitude you have taken in the face of petty provocations. That is the way of a true diplomat. That is also the attribute of greatness which some interested people refuse to recognize in you . . . Occasionally read the 5th, 6th, 7th and 8th chapters of the Gospel according to St. Mathew. I am myself an atheist, but I read these chapters and draw inspiration therefrom . . .

Yes, I have decided to join the Government. Panditji had a long talk with me . . .

All right-thinking men and women in India feel that India's case in London is safe in your hands. History, if it is fair, will record your valuable services to your mother country . . .

1948

Over the past few months Krishna Menon had developed friendly relations with his Pakistani counterpart in London, Habib Rahimtoola. Just two days following India's Independence, he had written to Nehru:

I called on the Pakistan High Commissioner yesterday, at his hotel, taking the view that it was more courteous and generous to do so rather than wait for him to come t0 see me. He seems quite a nice fellow personally.

That had raised many eyebrows in some sections of the Indian community, who were just waiting for Krishna Menon to trip up. On 19 January 1948, he went across to Rahimtoola's house as a gesture of goodwill. This created a storm back home because by then India and Pakistan had locked horns over Kashmir. Patel was information and broadcasting minister and had excellent relations with publishers and editors. It is not inconceivable, as Krishna Menon suspected, that he added fuel to the fire. Nehru had to intervene and, three days later, cautioned Krishna Menon:

I saw in the papers that you specially went to the Pakistan High Commissioner's house as a gesture of goodwill. There is nothing much in that. But I feel it would be better if we did not indulge in too many gestures which are not reciprocated. They produce a bad effect here, where, as you know, there is great tension.

In August 1947, Mountbatten had fully and enthusiastically backed the appointment of Krishna Menon as India's high commissioner to the UK. But Patel had been against it and never reconciled himself to that appointment. He met Mountbatten on 14 February 1948, who has left behind a record of that fifty-minute conversation, a portion of which reads thus:

> . . . Sardar Patel told me that we are now reaping the fruits of three cardinal blunders which had been made in connection with our relations with the U.K. and the UNO [United Nations Organisation] . . . The first was the appointment of Mr. Krishna Menon as High Commissioner since he was known to be a communist sympathizer. Secondly, there was the appointment of Mr. Asaf Ali as our Ambassador in America (since his wife, Aruna, was practically a communist) . . . Thirdly there was the line which Mrs. Pandit had taken when she attended the extended general meeting of UNO . . . The tragedy was that. Pandit Nehru was neither a communist nor pro-Russian; but he had succeeded in giving the impression to the rest of the Commonwealth and America that India was going to run against them. This, Sardar Patel felt, was the basic reason of the hostility to India and friendliness to Pakistan at UNO . . .

Patel was clearly chafing over how the Americans and the British were dealing with the Kashmir issue. On 20 January 1948, the UN Security Council had passed its first resolution on Kashmir, and it had deeply disappointed India. Patel was attributing US and UK support for this resolution to the fact that India was seen to be in the Soviet camp. The mischief, from India's point of view, had actually been caused by Philip Noel-Baker, head of the British delegation to the UN and, ironically, a man who had known Krishna Menon very well for almost two decades. On 20 February 1948, Nehru would tell Krishna Menon:

... Noel Baker ... is your old Professor and friend. I think he has
behaved very badly in the Security Council and he ought to be
made to realize how we feel about it ...

Krishna Menon had taken Baker's classes on international relations
at the LSE in the late 1920s. In 1959, Baker would win the Nobel
Peace Prize for his advocacy on nuclear disarmament—a cause that
Krishna Menon would champion no less vigorously. But Baker's
position on Kashmir in 1948 was something of an enigma because
it went against the positions held by Attlee, Cripps, Morrison and
Mountbatten. On 23 January 1948, at the UN, Baker 'endorsed the
Pakistan stand on the Kashmir issue and stated that fighting could be
stopped only by assuring the tribesman [who had invaded Kashmir
with Pakistani support] of a fair and speedy settlement. This argument
was in opposition to the Indian contention that hostilities should stop
first before further steps were undertaken.' He continued to harp on
the need for the UN to maintain a balance between India and Pakistan,
a position that infuriated Nehru and his colleagues to no end. Later in
the year, Krishna Menon would write to Nehru on 3 October 1948:

... My own view (not prejudice or eccentricity) is that Noel Baker
is up to some mischief. He is playing a lone hand but as before may
face H.M.G. with a fait accompli. He has forgotten nothing and
learned nothing. He is bitter against us on Kashmir, though he is
not pro-Pakistani in general.

It would take the combined might of both Mountbatten and Krishna
Menon to get Attlee to moderate and modulate Baker's stance but
the initial damage had been done.

On 24 June 1948, a twenty-five-year-old highly qualified
Indian woman with a law degree joined the staff of the Indian
high commissioner in London. She had earlier worked with S.K.
Kirpalani, an ICS officer who had, following Partition, been given
the top administrative job in the Ministry of Rehabilitation in New
Delhi. She was enterprising and efficient, as Kirpalani was to recall
many years later in his memoirs.[2] Her name was Kamala Jaspal.

Kamala Jaspal soon took complete charge of the high commissioner's office, of the high commissioner himself, and of his life with its many ups and numerous downs. On 7 October 1948, Krishna Menon sent a telegram to K.P.S. Menon, now the number two man in the foreign service next to Bajpai:

> Rukmini Menon and Kamla Jaspal employed in this office as Executive Officers have applied for recruitment to Foreign Service. I consider both qualified academically and in capabilities.
>
> Grateful for your directions whether selection board which will be sitting shortly can entertain their applications.

Both the women Krishna Menon recommended were very soon selected by an interview board in London headed by Laski for the fledgeling Indian Foreign Service. Jaspal was officially 'Private Secretary to the High Commissioner' but British intelligence reports referred to her as the 'Queen of India House'. Some of Krishna Menon's close friends alerted him to the widespread gossip that his relationship with his private secretary had generated. Rajkumari Amrit Kaur, health minister in Nehru's cabinet and a prominent member of the minuscule minority that genuinely cared for and was fond of Krishna Menon, knew Jaspal well. On 25 July 1950, she would write to Krishna Menon:

> . . . Kamala tells me you have not been well again. The 'again' is superfluous for you are in a chronically unwell condition which is very distressing. Do something about it. How is the numb feeling in your hand and what about the attacks of giddiness? Rest is the only cure and strict regime while you take the rest in a nursing home. Why do you not do that much for your friends . . .

Thereafter she would keep writing to Krishna Menon to take rest and good care of his health. On 8 July 1951, she would share her anguish with him:

> . . . I had a chat with P.M. last night. He is worried about your health. He said you were in no condition to work when you

came here and should have gone into a nursing home at once on your return . . . He is very anxious that you should be restored to complete health . . . So do listen to the P.M. He needs stalwarts like you. He is so good and if you are fit you will cope with everything. You cannot live on your treatment for long nor on drugs. Complete rest will alone do [the] trick we all want . . . I hated leaving you in your present condition but pray constantly for your speedy recovery and for your cooperation towards it . . . One of the joys of coming to London is to see you and work with you . . .

But Krishna Menon was unmoved by all this concern and would write to Amrit Kaur on 3 August 1951 from Dublin:

I am grateful to you for all your friendship and affection but sorry that your judgment of me has been so wrong . . . I would like to say that I am sorry you jump to conclusions without knowledge of all facts and also that I shall be leaving here on my return for good. If the inferences drawn, not only by you but in other quarters apply only to personal problems and the equation arising therefrom, I would not have minded. I mean the facts about this office and work which responsible people have in their minds is based on gossip . . .

Eight days later Amrit Kaur would decide to be more direct and blunt and write to Krishna Menon:

. . . I won't say more of the personal factor than what I have said to you in person. But I am convinced that all of us are not in the wrong. There is discontent in your entourage and it would be a healthy thing to have a transfer of the lady concerned. She is not doing a job of work where she is for reasons beyond her control. Her career may be nixed if she continues there. It is worthwhile giving her a chance away from India House to find her feet. . .

She was to write to the high commissioner again a year later, on 12 September 1951:

. . . I had more than one frank talk with you in which I begged of you to consider Kamla Jaspal's future career and release her from her duties as your Secretary. You refused to listen to me and I pleaded with you to the end. Her presence in my opinion was having an adverse effect on you and herself and on India House in general. As a true friend I had to tell you the truth as I saw it . . . Even if everything is a lie or a misrepresentation, even then the good name of yourself and India House must be maintained and more than anything else the girl's career must be saved. I have told you again and again while I know you are not capable of a mean act, Kamla is being badly affected and she has to be saved. Why should you encourage her to wreck her career? Do act sensibly and get yourself restored to health . . . You have many good friends . . .

Krishna Menon's grandniece Janaki Ram, who spent time with Kamala Jaspal in the early 1990s, is convinced that he was smitten by her. Khushwant Singh, the noted journalist, had a ringside view for a year and provided a salacious account of their relationship in his reminiscences,[3] which upset Jaspal and her family no end. Singh also skewered Krishna Menon quite a bit, making it clear that he didn't like him. But on 14 September 1951, his feelings were different. Singh would write to Krishna Menon that day:

It was kind of you to invite me to the programme in connection with Bihar relief tonight . . .

I am grateful for the sentiments you have expressed in your letter. I must have been mistaken in presuming that you did not want to see me—an assumption I made from the fact that you did not see me for about three weeks prior to my officially leaving India House—and therefore I thought it best to spare you the embarrassment of a conventional goodbye. I am much relieved to learn that I was perhaps wrong. I have another few weeks before I sail home—and as things are there is little likelihood of our roads meeting again. I would like to repeat once more that I considered it a privilege to have worked under you and although the parting could have been otherwise prevailing sentiment remains one of affection.

Janaki Ram described the Krishna Menon–Kamala Jaspal relationship like a 'sort of Professor Higgins–Eliza Doolittle relationship', immortalized in George Bernard Shaw's book *Pygmalion* and in the blockbuster film of the 1960s *My Fair Lady*.[4] The letters of Krishna Menon to Jaspal that have survived certainly point in this direction. He left India House in mid-July 1952, and she would leave for New Delhi in end-November 1952. On 18 November 1952, as she was about to fly back, he would write to her from New York:

> . . . I have known you for about five years and perhaps know you better than a great many people and more than most people I have had the occasion to know. I have seen you at work and in other contexts and both in and out of office. For your intelligence, capacity and talent I have the greatest admiration . . .
>
> I have some kind of personal satisfaction in that a lovely young woman of mine did so well . . . I know that you have suffered in your career owing to the jealousies of other people and on account of the reflection of jealousies to you . . .
>
> I may be writing like an old man, if it is only that you have looked after me a great deal in office and in illness. I am very grateful. Although official relations always did create certain barriers you have given me the affection of a daughter and the loyalty of a friend . . .
>
> You are going back to India where affection from your parents, jealousy from most and tongues of malicious gossip will await you . . .
>
> I wish you all good fortune and happiness and the wisdom of your spirit—I am glad to have known you.

Jaspal was appointed to the Indian Foreign Service on 22 December 1952—the third woman to accomplish this feat, a year after Rukmini Menon was appointed. She would later get married, become Kamala Shastri and have a son. It does not appear that she and Krishna Menon maintained any contact after 1953.

Just about seven months into the job Krishna Menon was already telling Mathai that he was about to depart. On 29 March 1948, he wrote:

I shall not be here long. It is impossible to hold this baby when you are constantly sniped at and do not have the confidence of the Government as a whole. There are few difficulties at this end and we get more than what most people do out of H.M.G. . . .

Strangely, he told Mathai that the two people spreading 'mischief' against him were 'K' and 'B'. K was Dr C.L. Katial and B was Dr P.C. Bhandari, the very same doctors who had certified him 'unfit' for emergency war service just four years earlier. All through his life Krishna Menon demonstrated an uncanny knack of turning even friends and well-wishers into critics and enemies. Katial was about to return to India to be the first director of the Employees State Insurance Scheme and Krishna Menon couldn't resist telling Mathai, 'I am sorry for India's health insurance scheme. However, it is none of my business.' Mathai, on the other hand, had sound advice for the high commissioner in London: 'Please take care of your health; do not work too hard and drink less tea.'

That Krishna Menon could have violent mood swings, even on the same day, is evident from the fact that while he was writing to Mathai that he was destined not to stay long at India House, he was also writing to Nehru on the matter of his salary. He had not drawn any salary since he had taken over and now told the Prime Minister:

. . . I do not know what the scheduled salary of the H.C. [high commissioner] is. It is somewhere about 3000 pounds a year. I have no intention of drawing this high salary . . . I want to draw what can be reasonably regarded as a living wage . . . which in my view should be between 350 pounds and 650 pounds . . . The salary matter is something I want you personally to decide on. I would also ask that no publicity is attached to this.

For my own personal use I don't need a car and don't propose to get into the habit of using one. It is a question of what should be done from the Government's point of view. There would be

adverse comment either way; on the one hand that I have let down
India's prestige, or on the other that there is extravagance. Neither
would be true. Looking at it objectively, the right course is to order
a car of the Daimler type which will last and would be regarded as
conforming to normal practice.

As if the Prime Minister didn't have enough headaches to deal with, he
was being saddled with the responsibility of deciding this particular high
commissioner's salary and the car to be purchased for his official use. To
be fair Krishna Menon did apologize for raising these matters 'to the level
of a reference to you' and justified it by adding 'but I know what people
will make of these things'. But one thing that can certainly be said in his
favour was that he didn't want any publicity given to the fact that he was
settling not for the usual comfortable salary but opting for a 'living wage'.
Nehru replied to Krishna Menon on 14 April 1948:

> . . . About the High Commissioner's salary, I entirely understand
> and appreciate what you say; at the same time, I think it would not
> be advisable for you to live completely like a hermit . . . As High
> Commissioner you can hardly live in a garret. It would not be
> proper at this stage to reduce the salary of the High Commissioner
> but it is open to you to draw any amount you like . . .

But the bureaucracy ensured that the matter dragged on, and it would
only be on Christmas Day two years later that Krishna Menon would
finally tell the Prime Minister:

> . . . I would like to have this matter out of the way before you
> visit . . . No constitutional difficulty about having an unpaid High
> Commissioner does arise. I have no time to have this proclaimed and
> I do not advertise it. All that I have said—and I feel I ought to insist
> now more than ever—is that I ought not to take this money . . .

On 3 May 1948, Krishna Menon suggested to Nehru that
Mountbatten should remain as India's governor-general till the end
of the year:

It is not that India would stand still without Mountbatten, but with Hyderabad and Kashmir on our hands, it is a wise and necessary step. If I can be of any small service in the matter, I should be glad to be . . .

The arrests [of communists] in India are making a bad impression . . . I hope that Dange will be released. His position in the world of international trade unionism makes him a world figure . . . We should know that repression would not solve anything, and make these people heroes and martyrs. I am well aware of your own distress in the matter . . .

Contrary to Krishna Menon's expectation and advice, Mountbatten demitted office a month later to be replaced by C. Rajagopalachari. As for his views on the arrests of communists that were taking place because of armed rebellions in parts of India, Krishna Menon would, in a matter of a few months, find himself in serious trouble with the 'Iron Man of India', Sardar Patel.

As the end of the first year of his tenure was approaching, Krishna Menon evidently slipped into one of those dark moods that overwhelmed him periodically and wrote to Nehru on 28 July 1948:

It will be a year on the 15ᵗʰ August since I have been here. Although no time limit or period of tenure was mentioned to me when I was asked to take over, I am aware that you have as a rule regarded appointments to headships of missions as for twelve months. I feel that I should therefore offer to be relieved and replaced and I do so . . . Keeping me in this post has also been a personal battle for you, and for that reason also I should place myself at your disposal in this way . . . I have not done well here as I wished and indeed had hoped . . . I should like you to feel free to terminate the arrangement of my being here and not have any personal feelings about it . . .

But these dark moods did not prevent him from sending long telegrams to Nehru on Kashmir, as he did on 13 August 1948:

. . . We give Pakistan greater opportunities of illegalities and breaches of decency if we don't have diplomatic relations . . . We would also probably cause greater threats to Hindus in Pakistan . . . It is either an index of despair or anger unless this is the prelude to declaring war, it is an ill-considered step by which we will gain nothing.

Now with regard to war, I hope that you will set yourself against any declaration of war by us taking the initiative . . . We should not put ourselves in a position of our having been the big bully invading little Pakistan. We will become the aggressive party . . . The declaration of war may force UK's hand in withdrawing officers. We can well do without British officers in the Army but what about the air force? It also cripples the navy which is vital to us though hardly so recognized. Our defence procurement will come to a standstill . . . and our fuel position will be desperate . . . So I plead with you to give up this line of thought at present. It is bad strategy . . . This is not a place for being soft on Pakistan, or run away from battle. If there is going to be any war let Pakistan declare it, and not we . . .

Three days later, he sent a 'Top Secret and Personal' telegram to Nehru:

I would most respectfully submit that if [the UN] Commission proposes cease-fire we could not reject or resist the proposal without outing ourselves completely in the wrong with UNO [United Nations Organisation] and world opinion. We would be entitled to ask for assurances as part of our acceptance of proposal . . . We would also have to say that the position held by Pakistan forces should not in any way be taken as having our recognition or acceptance . . . Once there is cease-fire or even as soon after we have accepted in principle cease-fire proposal we could ask for withdrawal of Pakistan army as implied in UN Resolution. On the other hand any appearance of the flouting of the proposal for cease-fire would do us infinite harm and put us in the position of being the guilty party . . . I would also submit that a cease-fire would not from a military point of view do us any harm . . .

Krishna Menon had actually been sharing his views with Nehru for quite some time on larger Western strategy in regard to Kashmir.[5] On 20 February 1946, he had written to Nehru saying:

I do not know to what extent you have been able to get a picture of the realities behind the recent U.N.O. Conference . . . The British Government under Bevin, Noel Baker and the rest are playing the game of a western bloc on the one hand and retaining imperialism on the other. The conflict with Russia was and is serious. The U.S.A. is playing one off against the other . . . Oil is the one thing that was everywhere at the U.N.O. . . .

On 17 April 1946, he had warned Nehru that India 'must at all costs keep out of being in the British and American machinations' and that Anglo-American policy towards the subcontinent 'could not be seen in isolation from its policy in regard to Persia [Iran]'. He kept telling Nehru—and this was in 1946—that oil would dictate Anglo-American strategy in the extended region and that 'Anglo-American interest in Kashmir was primarily and basically tied up with the question of [military] bases'.

Krishna Menon was in very frequent touch with Attlee, Morrison, Bevin, Cripps and Mountbatten, not only on Kashmir but also on Hyderabad. India was getting a bad press on both issues, and while India had taken Pakistan to the UN, the Nizam of Hyderabad had taken India to the world body. Krishna Menon met Attlee for an hour on 24 August 1948 and 'presented all aspects of the Kashmir and Hyderabad situation'. He informed Nehru:

While he was very appreciative of the way we had approached the Kashmir issue, HMG do not have any intention of supporting Hyderabad though it is firmly held that our entry into Hyderabad would weaken our position and put us on a level with Pakistan on Kashmir. I did not argue the point . . . In my respectful submission

the course to adopt at this end, repeat at this end, appears to be
press firmly our point of view and not to lose patience.

Some months later, on 5 November 1948, Walter Monckton
would approach Krishna Menon for his help to enable him to be
appointed as the Nizam of Hyderabad's legal adviser. Krishna Menon
then told Nehru that Monckton should, in fact, be retained by the
Government of India on the Nizam's instructions but have nothing to
do with political or constitutional matters. He wanted the Monckton
appointment to go through not only because they had known each
other for over a decade but more importantly because Monckton was
a well-known figure in the Conservative Party circles. He felt the
appointment would be a 'good P.R.' for India, especially since there
had been criticism in the UK media about India's 'police action' in
Hyderabad, which had deposed the Nizam in September 1948. As
it turned out, Monckton was allowed to be retained by the Nizam
but only for his private and personal affairs. He would certainly have
been paid handsomely but ten years later, when he was approached
by Marie Seton for his recollections of Krishna Menon, he replied
that he had nothing much to say. Krishna Menon's role in trying
to defuse the Suez Crisis in December 1956 and shortly thereafter
would also have rankled with Monckton since he had been defence
minister in the UK cabinet then.

As he was pleading Monckton's case with Nehru, Krishna
Menon was also reporting to him a long conversation he had had
on 5 November 1948 with Cripps at the latter's request. Cripps had
suggested that General Eisenhower be appointed as a mediator under
the UN auspices on the Kashmir dispute. He explained to Krishna
Menon the merits of his proposal, and Krishna Menon, in turn, told
Nehru two days later:

> My own impression is that Stafford is quite sincere . . . and, as usual,
> thinks he has found a formula . . . If the U.K. puts forward the
> whole of Stafford's proposal, it creates embarrassment for us, and
> if we accepted it, it would create difficulties for the Government
> of India and lead to greater conflict and disorder, if not a betrayal

among our people in Kashmir . . . We should say 'yes' to the mediator proposal provided that the Security Council at the same time calls upon both sides to accept the cease-fire proposals . . . With respect it appears to me to be most desirable that we do not get involved in some U.N.O. machinery which would result in our being faced with an award or in the Kashmir Government being displaced . . .

Nehru was not enamoured of Cripps's proposals. Nothing came of them immediately although in December 1949 the UN Security Council asked the Canadian General, MacNaughton, to mediate and then appointed Owen Dixon as a 'UN Representative' in March 1950 and Frank Graham in April 1951.

Krishna Menon was never close to Attlee as he was to, say, Cripps or Laski. But as high commissioner he had had many opportunities to meet the British Prime Minister. Consequently, Krishna Menon's respect for him increased appreciably. Their relationship must have deepened further in the year because on 1 September 1948 Krishna Menon was to write Attlee a letter that was unusual by any standard:

. . . In the last twelve months I have come to know you better than I did in the past and if I may say so with respect, have developed a genuine affection and regard for you . . .

We have, during the last month or two, been up against polite refusals all round, particularly in defence matters, and while I appreciate all the difficulties, I have the uncomfortable feeling that I am letting my side down by not recognizing that we are very much on the outside and will perhaps remain so. The Kashmir business in New York was a great shock to us, perhaps far more than I have been able to convey to you. Thanks to your intervention, it has somewhat improved but it is a running sore which has affected the good relations between our two peoples . . .

For your own and personal information (as the whole of this letter also is), I would tell you that I have at last told my Prime Minister that I feel I am not doing much good here . . . He trusts me completely and I have the discomforting fear that he often

relies on my judgment and capacity. It is far better to tell him that
these are no longer as potent as they might be.

Krishna Menon's letter, with the envelope marked 'Personal and
Secret', is preserved in Attlee's archives at Churchill College,
Cambridge University. On the envelope is written in hand 'PM
replied in his own hand. File with personal papers' and dated '3.9.48'.
Unfortunately, the reply is not traceable but soon thereafter, on 14
October 1948, Attlee wrote a 'Dear Krishna' letter to the Indian high
commissioner:

> I am so sorry to hear that you have been ill: how tiresome for you
> particularly at this time.
>   My best wishes for a speedy recovery.

Krishna Menon had indeed been quite ill and bedridden for a
number of days in early October 1948, so much so that he was not
present at the India League reception for Nehru at Kingsway Hall
in London on 12 October 1948. Nehru was making his first visit
to the UK as Prime Minister and the high commissioner was absent
in various celebrations organized for him by his friends and well-
wishers. Nehru was handed over a message from Fenner Brockway,
Krishna Menon's old friend and sparring partner:

> Welcome dear Prime Minister to London. I hesitate to intervene
> in Indian affairs. There may be reasons for the absence of Krishna
> Menon from the Nehru celebrations of which we are unaware. I
> am one of those with whom Krishna has quarrelled over a long
> period, but there is no doubt that during the critical days of struggle
> he did more for India in Britain than any other man. It is for this
> reason that many of us would like to see Krishna here. Forgive our
> urging.

Over 2000 people were present at the function, which was presided
over by Pethick-Lawrence. Laski and Edwina Mountbatten were

among those present. Nehru must certainly have had Brockway in mind when he addressed the gathering:

> I am very sorry to miss our friend and colleague the High Commissioner Krishna Menon. I am sorry, although I have to tell you I am largely responsible for his not coming here. I insisted on his remaining in bed. In fact, I was so afraid he might come, in spite of his high fever, that just before coming here I went to his room and saw to it that he was almost forcibly kept in bed.

Nehru's public statement in his support would surely have been the tonic Krishna Menon needed to be up and about. He resumed work soon after Nehru left and sent him an idea that has now become part of Indian public life. He wrote to the Prime Minister on 12 November 1948:

> I have been wondering whether the idea of a scroll underneath the Crest in the Seal of India was ever considered. If it has not been thought of and requested, perhaps you might think it worthy of consideration. I mean no disrespect to those who decided on the design as we have it now, in putting forward this idea. Such a scroll could be in Sanskrit characters (in place of Latin in European countries) and could be designed. Perhaps three words for Truth, Service and Honour may be suitable. It would be hypocritical to include non-violence . . . A scroll I think will make the design more complete and symmetrical and also make it the Seal of India and not of Asoka.

Four days later, the Prime Minister replied:

> I have received your letter of the 12th November about having a scroll underneath the Crest in the Seal of India. Some thought was given to this at one time, but it did not lead to any result. The difficulty was we did not know how to describe India in Sanskrit or Hindi. There is a great argument about it. But it might be

worthwhile to consider your new suggestion. I am sending it on to the Constituent Assembly people.

The motto for the State Crest that would be selected and unveiled on 26 January 1950 would be '*Satyameva Jayate*' (Truth alone Triumphs). But there would be no scroll as Krishna Menon had suggested.

Even though he was giving ideas after ideas to the Prime Minister, he would get into a dark and morose mood every now and then. On 16 December 1948, he wrote one of his frequent 'Very Personal' letters of distress to Nehru:

> As you know, rumours are persistently circulated about my being removed or replaced. I am not personally very concerned about them . . . As I had requested you to relieve me of this office and you told me I should not do so and was perhaps being rather irresponsible for making that suggestion, two things are clear: (1) that I am quite prepared to leave, and (2) that you do not wish me to do so and therefore these rumours have no substance.
>
> At the same time this has an unsettling and disturbing effect on a number of people and circles. It is not healthy in the present situation that the U.K. circles should think of me as 'marked for removal' or as going to Russia . . . The rumour is linked up with Mrs. Pandit taking my place here . . . Coupling her name is only part of the general mischief . . .
>
> If you agree that allowing these statements to hold the field is prejudicial to India's interests . . . you will no doubt consider whether, in some form, it should not be denied—especially as your sister's name is brought into it. If, on the other hand, you gauge the situation differently, please let me know as I would like to instruct myself with that knowledge.
>
> While I am writing on this nauseating subject, may I also mention I have no desire or interest to be found another post, as Diplomacy or whatever this work comes under, is not for me a career. I propose to go out of things altogether and for good. Needless to add that I am, in present circumstances, the least

suitable person to go to Russia and that I have no desire to add to your embarrassments or mine . . .

He need not have worried but would have been reassured by Nehru's reply five days later:

> . . . The rumours you refer to about your being recalled or replaced have of course not the least bit of justification or substance. There is a spate of rumours of this kind here from time to time relating not only to you but to many others in the Foreign Service. There are two or three Press correspondents in Delhi who have made it their special job in life to have a dig at me in regard to the Foreign Service and they continually spread various kinds of rumours. It is difficult to go about contradicting everything that is said . . . The rumours specially cluster around Vijaya Lakshmi. I am supposed to be guilty of nepotism in pushing my own family. As a matter of fact there has been no question at all of your leaving India House or Vijaya Lakshmi going there . . .

In one of his letters to Mathai, Krishna Menon speculated on the source of these rumours and told the Prime Minister's aide that he thought they emanated from 'across the road'. This was an allusion to Vallabhbhai Patel, whose office was in North Block, diagonally opposite Nehru's in South Block.

The third regular session of the UN General Assembly was to meet in Paris from 21 September 1948 to 12 December 1948. Krishna Menon desperately wanted to be a member of the delegation that was being headed by Vijaya Lakshmi Pandit. He wrote to Nehru on 1 August 1948 saying that 'the session is likely to be ticklish especially behind the scenes' and that 'there would be a large collection of diplomatic representatives from London'. He could not help adding, 'I hope I could be of some use, perhaps, but you are the best judge of that.' Nehru did not agree and informed his sister two days later:

> He [Krishna Menon] had hinted on more than one occasion that he might be added to our UN Delegation . . . Although I have

great admiration for his ability and understanding of problems, I
do not think he will fit in with the Delegation. But I have always
found a talk with him on any subject has thrown light and helped
me to understand a problem better, even though I disagreed with
him . . . Treat him gently and understandingly. He is a frightfully
sensitive and rather emotional person. The Mountbattens are his
great admirers. I must say he has done a very good job of work in
London. There are some Indians . . . who criticize him very much.
But the great majority of Indians there have appreciated his work,
and as for the U.K. Government, from Attlee downwards they all
praise his work. He has grown considerably during the last year.
But of course he continues to be a little difficult to get on with at
times . . .

Decades later Vijaya Lakshmi Pandit would write in her autobiography
about her tenure as high commissioner in London, which lasted six
years from 1955 to 1961:[6]

I had known from the beginning that London would present me
with many difficulties. Our first High Commissioner there had
been Krishna Menon, whose appointment had been supported
by the Mountbattens but had caused discontent among a part of
the large Indian community. There were a number of Indian
nationalists settled in Britain who had risen to eminence as
doctors and barristers and among them were some who felt they
were entitled to this prize . . . A brilliant and versatile man,
he [Krishna Menon] had overpowering ambition, which he
sometimes tried to hide under a cloak of pseudo humility. He
was like a Victorian woman, a person of moods and periods of
depression.

Krishna Menon was perhaps one of the very few persons
advocating India's continuance in the Commonwealth. Even Nehru
had initially not been in favour of it. On 27 December 1948, the high
commissioner wrote to his Prime Minister:

With regard to the Commonwealth talks, I would respectfully ask you to extend your infinite patience a little longer. I was also beginning to be sceptical whether these people really wanted us in. And I shot it at both of them [Attlee and Cripps] bluntly (and separately) but was taken aback a little. Apparently they were not aware they were giving that impression and were most anxious that we should not gain it . . .

I have made it clear that (a) we had always proceeded on the basis of <u>no</u> allegiance to the King . . . ; (b) we did not want to remain in an outer circle with the present Dominions (and or Pakistan) in an inner one; (c) the Irish position was unsatisfactory to us . . . The difficulty on their side is real. It relates to the position of the King.

For all his admiration of Eamon de Valera and the Irish, Krishna Menon did not support the move of the Republic of Ireland to walk out of the Commonwealth and certainly did not want India to follow that path. He did not underestimate the problems in arriving at a mutually acceptable solution and would devote considerable time and effort over the next few months to finding such a compromise.

1949

At Nehru's instance, T.G. Sanjeevi Pillai (yet another Malayali!), director of the Intelligence Bureau, went to London in December 1948 to explore cooperation with the British security service on 'questions of common interest'. He met Krishna Menon on 5 December 1948 and, according to the note recorded by India's top sleuth, a month later on 4 January 1949:

. . . Mr. Krishna Menon then asked me if I was in England representing the Home Ministry. I told him that I was deputed by the Home Ministry, that the Prime Minister was consulted before the deputation was sanctioned, and that I was there on behalf of the

Government of India. He then led the conversation taken by the Government of India against the Communists. He expressed the opinion that the action of the Indian Government was altogether unsupportable. He strongly criticized detention without trial. He said that the Government of India was now acting exactly as the British Government in India had acted against the Congress previously. He was uncompromising in his criticism of the action taken against the Communists in India. He thought it was barbarous and inhuman. He then told me that the Government of India could with greater advantage use the Intelligence Bureau for rounding up black-marketers and agents of corruption instead of hounding and harassing the Communists . . .

Patel was incensed with Sanjeevi Pillai's account of his meeting with Krishna Menon. He wrote to Nehru on 6 January 1949:

. . . I need hardly say that I feel very distressed about it and am deeply pained to find Krishna Menon adopting the attitude and views which he expressed in his interviews with Sanjeevi. I am thinking how I should formulate my own attitude on this question, but I thought I should let you know that I was passing through a period of mental distress and anxiety on this issue.

Nehru had already read Sanjeevi Pillai's note and now came this missile from Patel. He responded almost immediately on the very same day:

. . . I was myself greatly distressed at the information given by Sanjeevi in his note and I can well appreciate how you must have felt about this matter. It amazes me how and why Krishna Menon should have talked in this way. I can only explain and excuse it to some extent by imagining that he was under some deep mental strain and consequently upset. He is often rather ill and sometimes his nerves give way when he is unwell. In any event what he is reported to have said is totally inexcusable . . .

At the same time Nehru wrote to Krishna Menon expressing surprise at what he had told Sanjeevi Pillai and asked for his version of the conversation that had taken place. Meanwhile, Patel had met with the governor-general, C. Rajagopalachari, and evidently had shared his extreme anguish at Krishna Menon's harsh comments on how the home ministry was dealing with the communists. Rajaji then informed Nehru on 11 January 1949 of his conversation with Patel and suggested that Krishna Menon could be asked to express regret for his remarks about Patel to Sanjeevi Pillai. Nehru replied once again the very same day:

> . . . I quite agree with you that Vallabhbhai's grievance in this matter is legitimate . . . I am afraid that Krishna Menon, for some reason or the other, has lost complete control of himself and said things he should never have said. He acted imprudently and without regard to proprieties and conventions and normal restraint which he should exercise. He is an extraordinarily nervous individual and sometimes gets completely upset by rather trivial happenings. His ill-health adds to this.
>
> When I was in London last [October 1948], as I was leaving, he mentioned to me that he would like to resign. I asked him not to be silly. From a variety of reports and from my personal knowledge, I have come to the conclusion that his work at the India House has been first-rate . . . At the present moment it would put us in difficulty if he resigns . . .

Nehru then reprimanded Krishna Menon on 11 January 1949:

> . . . In this report much is said which has surprised me exceedingly. I know your feelings about certain matters in India. While I understand them, I do not agree with your appraisal of the situation here. We have had to deal with a particularly virulent and violent attack and I just cannot see how any government can tolerate this kind of thing. The type of violence we have had to deal with has been of the worst kind involving numerous murders, arson and looting. However, quite apart from the merits of the problem or

one's opinion in regard to it, it does seem rather extraordinary for
you to address an officer of the Home Ministry and express your
opinion strongly against the Home Ministry and the Government
of India . . .

Acting on the governor-general's suggestion, Nehru ended the letter
by making a plea:

> . . . If in a moment of excitement you said something which
> was against propriety and convention, I have no doubt you will
> acknowledge this error and express your regret for it. This would
> be fair to all concerned.

It was natural for Nehru and Patel to be concerned with communist
activities in different parts of the country, particularly in what was
then Hyderabad state and the provinces of Madras and Bengal.
The communists, taking a cue from Moscow, had rejected the
independence of India as being a sham and denounced Gandhi and
Nehru vituperatively. The new country racked by the horrors of
Partition was now confronted by the threat of communist-led
insurrections of the type that were being witnessed in large parts of
South East Asia, including neighbouring Burma.

In a matter of four days between 16 January 1949 and 20 January
1949, Krishna Menon wrote thrice to Nehru. He defended himself,
stoutly calling Pillai's report 'an action of an agent provocateur' which
was 'not even fair game in Intelligence work, unless it is intelligence
as applied to enemy nationals when at war'. He categorically denied
having made any reference to 'the Home Ministry or to Sardar
Patel'. On the issue of his criticizing the Indian government's policy
regarding communists, he told Nehru on 16 January 1949:

> I do, however, distinctly remember that he brought up the
> Communists again, and I told him that I was not concerned with
> Communists and did not hold with what they were doing in
> India but the view held by those who felt about these matters was
> about the imprisonment of people on the basis of secret service

information. I did say that police reports on political opinions made, as they must be, by policemen who knew little about these affairs, placed people at the mercy of the police and the State would become a police state . . .

He expressed his readiness to confront Pillai in Nehru's presence in Delhi to 'have this matter thrashed out'. He then went on:

Sanjeevi, in fact, did tell me things about the Government and even broad hints about the Sardar, no doubt as part of the technique of gaining confidence but I did not rise to this and I have no intention of repeating it!! For your information, I know a little about Sanjeevi's antecedents and what he has done and his general contribution to our life does not surprise me . . .

Sanjeevi's report must have distressed you as much as it has done me. I am worried about this. You will be aware that I have offered to resign or to be relieved in such way as you wish. I hesitate to say this again for the reason that it might be misunderstood and regarded as a vulgar and indecent form of protest . . .

In the last of this flurry of letters Krishna Menon indicated his willingness to express regret and left the matter entirely up to Nehru to be dealt with in the manner he deemed best, implying clearly that Nehru was free to demand and get his resignation. The curtain was rung on this episode by a long letter from Nehru to his high commissioner on 26 January 1949, after he had had consultations with Rajaji, who was also shown the three of Krishna Menon's letters that he had sent in self-defence. Nehru once again took full responsibility for Sanjeevi Pillai's mission, saying Patel had nothing to do with it and telling Krishna Menon in no uncertain terms that the mission did not involve spying on the high commissioner and his staff in any way. He went on to add:

. . . Sardar Patel may not like you, but he has, on several occasions, expressed his appreciation of the work you have done . . . In this particular matter . . . I do not think Sardar Patel is at all to blame . . .

Thank you for sending me your note of regret. So far as I am concerned that was unnecessary and in some respects it goes beyond what is needed. I am not making any use of it. Rajaji suggests that instead of any such form of regret, you might write a personal letter to Sardar Patel. Something to the following effect:

> I have heard with deep regret that a report made by Mr. Sanjeevi of his conversations with me has caused some annoyance to you. I have not seen this report and I have no notes of the conversation . . . Our conversations were entirely informal . . . I did not either protest or argue policy with Mr. Sanjeevi. I did not refer to the Home Ministry or you. It is possible that Mr. Sanjeevi did not quite follow what I was talking about . . . But irrespective of the accuracy of Mr. Sanjeevi's report to you, I should like to express my deep regret for any annoyance caused to you.

Perhaps you could write something more or less on the above lines to Sardar Patel.

Krishna Menon did express his regret to Patel 'if his remarks to Sanjeevi had caused any distress to the Home Minister or had cast any bad reflection on the policies of the Government of India'. Nehru told Krishna Menon on 5 February 1949 that 'this matter may be considered as ended'. But the fact remains that this was one occasion when Krishna Menon was not at fault and indeed had been unfairly set up and 'fixed' by India's top intelligence operative. Patel believed his spymaster instantly and believed the worst of Krishna Menon without getting his side of the story. On Patel's death a year later Krishna Menon would write to Rajkumari Amrit Kaur on Christmas Day:

> . . . He was a great man often with small weaknesses and I fear sometimes though not often a small man with great weaknesses— but no one would doubt that he was a patriot. I think India will miss him . . .

Three years before he passed away Krishna Menon would get into a controversy in Parliament in July 1971 for allegedly putting pressure on the government to favour, of all companies, Coca Cola. The fact that he would even speak on behalf of the American multinational would, on the strength of all that he had stood for all his life, appears most puzzling. Perhaps the reason he even asked the minister concerned to 'look into their grievances and do the needful' was because Bipin Patel—the Sardar's grandson, who was then heading Coca Cola in India—had approached him.[7] But there was also the fact that his friend since college days, K. Palani, a businessman, was a bottler for Coca Cola in south India.

While all these letters and telegrams were flying back and forth between London and New Delhi on what Krishna Menon had said or not said to malign Patel, Krishna Menon took care to inform Nehru of something else that was on his plate. He wrote on 16 January 1949:

> You are aware that for a number of years I have been connected with publishing in an editorial capacity . . . From such work I derived editorial fees and royalties . . . It was one of the few things I could do without tying myself up to an office. In this capacity I dealt with your books also. I continue to do this in such spare time as I may find, and it is necessary for me (a) to do something which prevents me from going to seed mentally and to keep up some semi-intellectual interest, (b) to be able to go back to something which I am capable of doing.
>
> I am not a civil servant, and so far as I know I do not have to take Government permission for doing this, as it is like writing a book, unless I commit myself politically so as to embarrass my Government. At present, I am not having my name printed except on series which I have created. I am, however, mentioning this to you so that no suggestion of non-disclosure is made by interested parties at some time in the future.

For a few years Krishna Menon had had an interest in Meridian Books, a London publishing house that had brought out Nehru's *Discovery of India* in 1946. The venture would fold up by 1952.

Krishna Menon would certainly appear paranoid from the Sanjeevi Pillai episode. But in reality his fears were not entirely unjustified. Guy Lidell, a top British intelligence official, recorded in his diary on 22 July 1949: 'We are doing what we could to get rid of Krishna Menon.' British intelligence had the entire staff of the Indian High Commission under surveillance and prepared periodic reports of so-called 'Communist infiltration of India House' containing descriptions of important staff members. That some of these staff members were sympathetic to the communist cause was indubitable. P.N. Haksar had been a member of the Communist Party of India. Anila Graham was married to a British communist leader and Patsy Pillay to a South African one. They were unrepentant Marxists but by no stretch of the imagination could they even remotely be seen as Soviet or Chinese 'moles'. These reports that only reflected British paranoia continued till the time Krishna Menon was high commissioner. Over five decades later a British scholar, after carefully analysing the MI5 files on Krishna Menon during the period he was high commissioner in London, would conclude:[8]

> In hindsight it is clear that MI5 misjudged the nature of the threat that Krishna Menon posed to Britain's national security between 1947 and 1952 . . . Prior to 1947, MI5 was overly influenced by Menon's readiness to collaborate with the CPGB in pursuit of Indian self-government. Following India's independence, it proved unduly dismissive of evidence that Menon had broken with King Street [location of CPGB's headquarters] . . . In over-egging the security case against Menon, MI5 encouraged the Attlee government to run excessive risks with Anglo–Indian relations . . . Moreover . . . [it] adversely effected Britain's relations with India well into the Cold War.

Ever since September 1948 the British and Indian governments had been in talks and correspondence with each other on how India could reconcile its self-declared status as a 'sovereign independent republic', with the British view that the King should be recognized as the 'head' or the 'fountainhead' of the Commonwealth. There was opposition in the Constituent Assembly to India remaining in the Commonwealth itself in the first place. Even Nehru was none too enthusiastic about the idea. Mountbatten, Krishna Menon and Bajpai were the three people trying to convince Nehru and Patel that the balance of advantage lay in India becoming a full-fledged member of the Commonwealth but without in any way appearing to be subservient in any form to the British monarchy.

As mentioned earlier, Krishna Menon had written to Nehru on 27 December 1948, asking Nehru to extend his 'infinite patience' a little longer and informing him about his talks with Attlee and Cripps. After reassuring Nehru that he had stuck to India's non-negotiables relating to the position of the King, Krishna Menon had added:

> . . . They all accept that we would not accept the Crown as they do, or declare our allegiance . . . I have had an hour with Cripps and Attlee . . . and the whole discussion was to find a way out. We have let it stand adjourned until both sides think it out further . . .

A month before Nehru was to depart for London for the Prime Ministers' conference convened by Attlee, the British premier wrote him a 'long screed' on 20 March 1949, making an impassioned plea for retaining the King in the Indian Constitution and saying:

> . . . As you know we have found it very difficult to find a satisfactory alternative to the Crown as the legal basis of the special Commonwealth relationship . . . But it is not the legal importance of the Crown I am anxious to stress now, so much as the psychological importance of the position of King George and his family.
>
> How does this apply in the case of India? Does a republic really appeal to the masses of India? . . . I should have said that the general tradition in Asia is in favour of a monarchy . . .

You in India were very fortunate in that the man who caught the imagination of the people was Gandhi . . . Had your national movement been led by a man of a different sort, you might well have had a dictatorship . . . At the present time, with statesman such as yourself, Sardar Patel and Rajagopalachari in the leading positions, the danger of dictatorship may seem remote, but it might arise in a great sub-continent like India.

You may object that The King is an Englishman, a man of alien race, representing a domination now past and over. I wonder whether this objection is valid. I am an Englishman, but for centuries the English have had Kings who have been Angevin, Welsh, Scottish, Dutch and German, and we have not worried about it . . .

I think there are, therefore, solid advantages in retaining The King in the Indian constitution. Of course, his representative [governor-general] would be recommended by the Indian Prime Minister . . . I wonder whether it would not be possible to draw from Indian history distinctive titles for The King and for the King's representative . . .

This was a last-ditch effort by Attlee to retain India in the Commonwealth but on British terms. India, on the other hand, insisted on becoming a member as a 'sovereign independent republic'. The impasse was complete and total. It is generally believed in all accounts of Krishna Menon's life that he broke the impasse and made India's membership in the Commonwealth a reality. Bajpai's son, Shankar Bajpai, himself a distinguished diplomat, mentioned to me that the solution was provided by his father. Archival evidence points to a third man as having provided the formula to break the logjam. N. Gopalaswami Ayyangar was minister of railways and transport in Nehru's cabinet but, more importantly, a person Nehru trusted greatly for his legal acumen, political judgement and administrative capacity. He also enjoyed the full confidence of Patel. He wrote to Nehru on 13 April 1949, a few days before Nehru's departure:

... With reference to your observations at this morning's Cabinet meeting on my suggestion that India should not recognize the King as HEAD of the Commonwealth but should recognize him only as the symbol of unity of the Commonwealth, I have, since coming home, looked into the Statute of Westminster . . . I would suggest . . . for your consideration our declaration being limited to the recognition of the position of the King as 'the symbol of the free association of the members of the Commonwealth of the future' . . .

Nehru liked Ayyangar's formulation, and it became part of his negotiating brief. In the room with Nehru in London to finalize the compromise solution were Krishna Menon and Bajpai. On 27 April 1949, a historic declaration incorporating it was issued in London:

The Governments of the UK, Canada, Australia, New Zealand, South Africa, India, Pakistan and Ceylon, whose countries are united as Members of the British Commonwealth of Nations and owe a common allegiance to the Crown, which is also the symbol of their free association, have considered the impending constitutional changes in India.

The Government of India have informed the other Governments of the Commonwealth of the intention of the Indian people that under the new constitution which is about to be adopted India will become a sovereign independent Republic. The Government of India have however declared and affirmed India's desire to continue her full membership of the Commonwealth of Nations and her acceptance of the King as the symbol of the free association of its independent member nations and as such as the Head of the Commonwealth . . .

The Governments of the other countries of the Commonwealth the basis of whose membership of the Commonwealth is not hereby changed, accept and recognize India's continued membership in accordance with the terms of this declaration . . .

After this declaration was made public, Cripps wrote to Krishna Menon:

> This is to congratulate you upon the successful outcome of the meeting of Prime Ministers which you did so much to secure. Without you and your unflagging efforts I am sure we could never have arrived at so happy a conclusion. It is a great work for all of us and will be regarded as a fine piece of constructive statesmanship in a world where there is too little of that commodity.

This was high praise indeed. Krishna Menon was undoubtedly the earliest and most ardent champion of India remaining in the Commonwealth and contributed most heavily to Nehru's change of stance on the matter. It was no surprise, therefore, that Attlee's statement on 19 June 1952 at the impending departure of Krishna Menon as high commissioner drew attention to it:

> There will be widespread regret at the retirement of Mr. Krishna Menon from the position of High Commissioner for India in the U.K. He had served India well and faithfully during a most eventful period. His wise counsel was available when the difficult question of the position of India in the Commonwealth was under discussion and he did a great service to all in helping find a solution . . .

In response to the criticism that India was spending far too much on foreign missions, and in particular in the High Commission in London, in May 1949, Nehru had sent Subimal Dutt, the number three man in the Ministry of External Affairs, to London to conduct an on-the-spot inspection. Dutt spent five weeks in London carrying out his assessment. He riled Krishna Menon with his scathing thirty-one-page report. The high commissioner complained to the Prime Minister on 16 June 1949:

> . . . On the general question I have tried to convince you that my usefulness to you or India is over. You would not accept it. I am

able to make no contribution either to policy or administration . . .
In fact, as time passes, the sense of futility grows. I have also
become somewhat of a nuisance and am giving the impression
of touchiness and petulance . . . I am forced to the conclusion
that neither hard work, nor devotion to a cause, integrity or even
results count in this work. Dutt's report, which I have glanced
at, contains a number of pinpricks, some fundamental proposals
which do not take into account the realities of the situation, and
in fact are based on ignorance of facts and circumstances. If Dutt's
recommendations are carried out, India House will revert to the
pre-1947 position . . .

Thirteen days later he was more critical of Dutt's report and wrote
again to Nehru:

. . . I have given the most careful thought to all that has been
developing and I am forced to the conclusion that I am ill-adapted
to the situation. My continuing here will cause you more worry
and distress more than anything else . . . I had asked that at least 2
paras in the report which reflect on my character and integrity be
suspended from consideration. I regret that it has not been possible
to do this . . . I would like you to believe that I am not suffering
from any persecution complex . . . There is no room for a person
like me in the context of the report . . . I hope you will forgive
me if I express my regret that such a report, which is contrary to
instructions given, should have been entertained at all . . . I think I
should say in fairness that my capacity to work and think is impaired
and while I will do the best until you make other arrangements,
I am distressed to think that you are not well enough served . . .

Replying to Krishna Menon on 1 July 1949, Nehru defended
Dutt as a 'very conscientious and quiet officer' and that there was
'no desire to discredit or find fault'. For the next three months there
would be extended correspondence between Nehru and Krishna
Menon on this issue, with the high commissioner donning the
mantle of the grievously wounded party who had been most unfairly

wronged by the bureaucracy. Nehru would patiently put up with these epistolary tantrums before throwing up his hands in despair on 29 September 1949 and telling Krishna Menon that 'after reading your letter however, I have rather lost interest in all this business'. Much later in the letter he told the high commissioner that he did not quite see how Krishna Menon's personal integrity came into the picture. He ended by saying:

> . . . It is of course open to you to come to any decision you like. But to write to me in the way you have done just a few days before I am likely to meet you, seems to me to be rather extraordinary. Indeed you have not left any room for a personal talk on this or connected subjects. I have written this letter to you with a feeling that it is rather futile to write all this in view of what you have said. I have written often to you about this and other matters. There is not much point in repeating myself.

From time to time Krishna Menon would lament to Nehru about the prevailing state of affairs in India as he saw it and also express disappointment that his advice on various matters—big and small—did not appear to count for much with the Prime Minister. After receiving a bundle of such letters of self-pity, Nehru replied on 24 August 1949:

> . . . I am inclined to agree with you about the services [military] playing a far more important part here in the formation of policy etc., than they should. In the final analysis this is due to our own Ministers [a reference to Baldev Singh, the defence minister] and not so much to the services, who merely try to carry on their old tradition . . .
>
> You should know me well enough to know what value I attach to your advice on any matter. You do not have to tell me that that advice is not only far more helpful to me because of your greater understanding but also because it comes from an independent mind which has not lost its resilience in routine activities. I sometime fear that my own mind is losing such resilience or such it possesses . . .

Your presence somewhere within reach is a great comfort to me. I really have few persons with whom I can discuss any matter with any confidence. If I ask you to stay on in India House, it is not so much for any personal reasons but for larger public reasons and for reasons apart from even India House . . .

During the seventeen years he was Prime Minister, the only person with whom Nehru shared uninhibited intellectual camaraderie was Krishna Menon. This letter was a very early acknowledgement of that kinship. Even so, there were many issues on which Nehru and Krishna Menon disagreed. Closer relations with the US was certainly one of them, with the latter being sceptical of its prospects and its value. On 31 August 1949, Nehru wrote to his high commissioner in the UK:

. . . The American Ambassador told me today that President Truman is sending his personal aircraft to take me from London to Washington. We have not had any direct message about this yet . . .

Krishna Menon reacted violently to this idea, for eight days later Nehru wrote to him again showing the difference in their thinking in spite of their closeness to each other:

Your advice to me not to accept President Truman's invitation to travel by his plane from England to America, is difficult to follow. I do not myself see how, in any event, I can refuse such an offer without grave and uncalled for discourtesy. I am going to the U.S. not on any private business, but purely because of President Truman's invitation . . . Nor do I understand why this should make people think my visit is a command performance . . . For a year or so I have been receiving invitations from the President of the U.S. to visit him. I have avoided going to the U.S. At last I agreed. Whether my visit there is supposed to bolster up American policy or not, is a matter to be judged by events. As a matter of fact, our refusal to accept President Truman's advice in regard to

the Kashmir matter is sufficient indication of how far we carry out
the wishes of the U.S. Government . . .

His position with Nehru notwithstanding, some Indian groups in
London, such as the Overseas Indian Association and the Federation
of Indian Associations in Great Britain, who had been hostile to
the India League, never reconciled themselves to Krishna Menon's
appointment as high commissioner. On 9 November 1949, J.K.
Ram, secretary of Swaraj House, another such group, wrote on all of
their behalf to Nehru:

Dear Panditji:

It is exactly two weeks since various organisations in London
sent you a pre-paid cable requesting you to receive a deputation
from us, and now for a year we have been writing to you to
contact us. From all these attempts we have not even received an
acknowledgement from you. We are not sure whether you have
received them or have any knowledge of them.

   What are we to do? . . . As a Prime Minister you cannot be
partial and openly take sides to one particular organisation [India
League] . . . As a result of either your or your staff's negligence
we are forced to come out in the open with our complaints and
grievances. We intend demonstrating regularly and periodically . . .
This is not an ultimatum, but a well-considered and well-conceived
decision . . . The India House [where the Indian High Commission
was located] must be cleansed at any cost and put in order and we
will see that this is done. It is up to you, Panditji, to act promptly and
satisfy the popular demand of the Indian community in London, and
this will incidentally save washing our dirty linen before the public.

P.S. A copy of this letter will be sent to the Indian and English
Press.

This was, by any standard, a most impertinent letter addressed to the
Prime Minister of India. Almost every letter that Nehru received

in his long public career of almost four and a half decades was acknowledged and replied to promptly. Unfortunately, I was unable to locate the reply to this particular letter denouncing Krishna Menon and virtually blackmailing Nehru. But going by his track record Nehru may well have replied to it defending the former stoutly.

1950

On 20 March 1950, Nehru wrote a truly extraordinary letter to Krishna Menon, reflecting the politics of the country at that time:

> I want to tell you that for a variety of reasons, in which I need not go now, I have decided to give up the Prime Ministership fairly soon. This thought has long hovered in my mind and indeed I had mentioned it to two or three persons here, including the President. Events in East Bengal and their reactions have made me think furiously and I feel I am not of much use in my present capacity. There is far too much friction and a pulling in different directions and intrigues. It is my intention to wait for the passing of the Budget and then to present my resignation and the resignation of the Cabinet to the President . . .
>
> What the future holds, I do not know. But I am clear in my mind that I should adhere to this resolution. Of course, all kinds of pressure will be brought to bear upon me to change my mind. But I must have a period free from office and I want others to shoulder the burden . . .
>
> I would not like you to leave your post because I have retired from the scene. You should keep going and wait for developments, such as they may be.
>
> Please do not mention this to anybody.

There were only a small handful of people in whom Nehru confided about his decision to resign. He wrote to Rajendra Prasad, the President of India, and to his sister Vijaya Lakshmi Pandit the same day as he broke the news to Krishna Menon. A day later he took Girija Shankar

Bajpai also into confidence, telling him that he should continue to be the head of India's diplomatic establishment. He added for good measure:

> You will appreciate that Krishna Menon's position in London might be even more difficult than anyone else, after I go away. Nevertheless I thought he should not make my retirement as an excuse for resigning.

Krishna Menon was stunned by Nehru's contemplated move. It was a wholly unexpected bolt from the blue, and he replied a week later:

> Your letter has come as a great shock to me. I cannot (and I should neither hope nor desire to) influence your mind in a decision of this nature and gravity. Having regard to the grave consequences of your decision which are obvious to me, I venture to presume on the bonds of my affection to lay my thoughts before you, feeling confident in myself that you will not misunderstand my reason for doing so.
>
> A decision of this kind at some earlier period of the last three years would have had different consequences. It might even have had good results. But not now. In the present extremely serious situation, an action of the kind you contemplate will plunge the country headlong into anarchy and bloodshed . . .
>
> In my humble opinion the present situation calls for assertion from you, but in a contrary direction, regardless of consequences. I feel sure that such an assertion will be accepted and the country will benefit. Any other action would only stimulate the evils to which you refer . . .
>
> Events will have moved so fast in the next few days that the decision you are contemplating and even what I write now will have become out of date. Whether for that reason or otherwise, I beg of you in all earnestness, and fervently hope, that you will not adhere to your present decision.
>
> If unhappily you decide to persist, it would hardly be right or useful for me to stay. What good could I do? How would I

function? What would I represent? I am sure you must know that
this would be an impossible situation . . .

    I fondly hope this will become unnecessary by a revision on
your part of the course you contemplate. I have no right to say or
ask this, but equally I do not feel I have the right not to do so . . .

Undoubtedly, the situation in East Bengal and the attacks on Hindus
in that part of Pakistan, which had created war-like conditions on the
eastern border, caused Nehru great pain and anguish. But there were
other factors that must have weighed heavily on Nehru's mind. He
had wanted Rajaji to be the President of India but Rajendra Prasad
enjoyed vastly greater support in the Congress party. Most crucially,
Patel backed him strongly. Moreover, he sensed an irreparable rift
between himself and Patel on many domestic and international issues.

    But this 'mood of abdication' did not last long, and soon thereafter,
the Prime Ministers of India and Pakistan entered into an agreement
called the Nehru–Liaquat Pact in New Delhi on 8 April 1950 to bring
peace between the two countries on their eastern borders. Krishna
Menon's role in the run-up to the pact was somewhat curious. He
sent Nehru two telegrams in quick succession on 27 March 1950.
The first went thus:

    I saw Attlee today at 6 o'clock and was with him for an hour . . .
    The discussion was entirely informal and on a personal basis.
    Mr. Attlee displayed unusual friendliness and concern . . . What
    is communicated to you in the immediately succeeding telegram
    was discussed at my initiative at the first instance . . . I give this
    background to the proposal in the immediately following telegram
    which I feel will enable you better to appreciate it . . .

The 'immediately following telegram' clearly revealed all of Krishna
Menon's unabashed Anglophone sympathies:

    The Prime Minister asked Rahimtulla [Pakistan high commissioner
    in the UK] and me to meet him this evening at 9 p.m. . . . Attlee said
    he felt sure that all of us were concerned about the grave situation in

Bengal and would desire to see every possible step taken to resolve the difficulties . . . He asked whether an elder statesman from this country, say Lord Addison could usefully be present in India and Pakistan at this juncture to be available for any assistance required. It was made clear that they were not offering mediation or sending a mediator but only offering good offices . . . I would like to assure you that it [the offer] was made in the friendliest spirit and the fact of calling both of us together was not meant to be anything but having it all in the open so that the proposal would not be charged with suspicion . . . I would with the greatest respect submit that this is a suggestion which we should entertain . . . Grateful for [the] most immediate reply.

It was no surprise that Nehru turned down Attlee's suggestion made at Krishna Menon's instance.

On 24 April 1950, Krishna Menon lost the second of his mentors when Laski passed away—in some ways more important to him intellectually than his first, Annie Besant. Although older by just three years, Laski was almost a father figure to Krishna Menon. Their relationship had spanned a quarter of a century and there is no doubt that Krishna Menon was indebted to the LSE professor and one-time Labour Party chairman in very many ways. Thirteen years later on 23 February 1963, Krishna Menon would recall Laski in an article he would write for the *Sunday Times* magazine on 'My Years in England':

I spent ten years at the London University, at the London School of Economics and the University College. I was also called to the Bar. At the former place one became almost part of the stones and mortar as it used to be said. I read under Professor Laski, a very great teacher and a wonderful human man. Smaller minds than his have projected their own diminutiveness and sometimes said that he was just merely amusing or clever or well read. He was, however, a profound scholar, thinker, a sincere friend and guide. He was also a great patriot who rebelled against injustice of any kind. It will be generations before he is fully understood.

He made history and political science [come] alive and made us realize that social sciences cannot be understood in a vacuum. His place can never be filled except by the understanding of his work . . . I was deeply moved and impressed by his approach to his students. He appeared to leave one alone to work and yet one learned a great deal.

War had broken out in the Korean peninsula in mid-July 1950. A few weeks later on 4 August 1950, a British intelligence official posted in New Delhi would send a report to his superiors in London:

You may be interested to know that the High Commission have completely reliable information to the effect that Pandit Nehru's recent approaches to Marshal Stalin and Mr. Acheson [US secretary of state] were suggested to him by Krishna Menon. The High Commission are tempted to draw the inference that the suggestion was not born in Krishna Menon's brain (still less in his heart), but that it may have emanated from Russian sources. I should be interested to know if you have any information to corroborate this . . .

Back came the reply ten days later:

I am afraid it is impossible for us to say whence V.K. MENON derived the idea of an Indian approach to Stalin. He is in touch with the Russian Ambassador here and he may still be in touch with R.P. DUTT and Harry POLLIT of the British Communist Party whom he knows intimately. On the other hand, Menon's views on world politics have for many years been pro-Russian and there is every reason to believe that they continue to be so. He is known to be bitterly opposed to Mr. Bevin's Foreign Policy and to be very anti-American. It would, indeed, be surprising if, at heart at all events, he did not support Russia's attitude to Korea. With this mental background he may well have derived the notion that an approach to Stalin would lift India [away] of the British American camp into which he may thought that she was drifting . . .

This would be Krishna Menon's first foray into the Korean issue. Thereafter, it would be Nehru and K.M. Panikkar, India's ambassador to China, who would orchestrate India's mediation efforts till Krishna Menon catapulted himself on to the scene at the UN in October 1952 and gained international recognition.

Later in 1950, another serious crisis engulfed Nehru. Krishna Menon would, from time to time, urge the Prime Minister to assert himself more and be less democratic and more ruthless in the affairs of both the government and the party. Krishna Menon's point was that Nehru was not leveraging his unique position in Indian public life to maximum advantage. On 25 August 1950, Nehru replied:

> . . . You have to accept me as I am and not try to improve me too much. I am not a political boss and I cannot function as such. I have a considerable influence over masses of people. I can make a difference to an election campaign and so on and so forth. But I cannot run a political machine . . .
>
> The Congress Presidential election which is taking place in the course of the next few days has brought matters to a head. Three candidates are Purushottam Das Tandon, Kripalani and Shankarrao Deo. Not one of them is suitable . . . I suggested Rajaji at one time. He would not agree. Tandon is being supported fully by Vallabhbhai Patel. This, in spite of the fact that I informed him and others that if Tandon is elected, I could not be in the Congress Working Committee and very probably I would resign from the Prime Ministership . . .
>
> There is one thing about which I would like to warn you. Do not be hasty in any action that you might take. Wait a while and see what happens here. It would be unbecoming of you to take a leap if you learn that I have indulged in a jump. There will be plenty of time for you to decide . . .

Krishna Menon replied a week later, as political events in India were reaching their climax:

> By the time this letter reaches you things would perhaps have moved and taken the course of further deterioration . . . With

great respect I agree that in the eventuality to which you refer
and may well result, there is no course open but to dissociate
yourself from Congress. Gandhiji did the same on relevant
occasions . . . To accept a situation of this kind in quiescence
would be a violence to the masses who believe in you. But
again with respect I would submit that the leadership of the
government is a very different question. That office is now based
on the confidence of the people and it is for those others who
have other views to challenge your position or to get themselves
out . . . The relinquishment of leadership of government in
the present state of affairs, internal and external, is fraught with
'risks'. . . but this thing is not a 'risk'. It is the way to certain
disaster. Not a risk!

The Mountbattens left for Germany yesterday. Dickie returns
on Monday, Edwina and Pamela will be away for ten days or so.
They saw me just before they left and as they know the position
they were very concerned and were most anxious that I should
write to you . . .

The crisis had indeed come. Tandon had been elected Congress
president with Patel's backing at the Congress session in Nasik in
end-September 1950. Initially Nehru kept himself away from the
Congress Working Committee but held back from resigning as
Prime Minister for the time being. A few weeks later, he agreed
to be a member of the Congress Working Committee but made
clear his disapproval of Tandon and his other nominees. On 15
December 1950, Patel passed away, paving the way for Nehru's
total supremacy over the Congress. He would succeed Tandon a
year later.

As the year was drawing to a close, Nehru was soon to make his
fourth visit to London as Prime Minister. The Commonwealth Prime
Minister's Conference was being held in early 1951. As usual, Nehru
took some time off official engagements to catch up with friends.
And as always, a visit to the country home of the Mountbattens was
part of his schedule. He had been there on all the previous visits to
London and had been accompanied by Krishna Menon. But this time

around, the high commissioner politely declined the invitation and wrote to Edwina Mountbatten on 24 December 1950:

> You kindly asked me to come to Broadlands with the Prime Minister. As you probably are aware, I spend most of my time in bed nowadays, that is, except when I am active on a job. Also, I rather feel that the P.M. would appreciate his being free from my presence and company to enable him to rest and relax! It is very kind of you to have asked me. I am sure you know how much I appreciate the thought, but on this occasion I feel my presence would be an intrusion—not on you, but on the P.M.'s very necessary quiet. Also, he would have his sister with him whom I have no doubt you will be asking. It must seem inappropriate to intrude into what is a family circle.
>
> However, if during his stay in Broadlands should it be convenient to him and you, I will call, if I may.

It is possible that Krishna Menon was being tactful and wanted to stay away from the Mountbatten's family estate to allow Nehru and Edwina to spend time together without him hovering around. Edwina certainly wanted him to come along with Nehru, and Nehru too gave no indication that he wanted his high commissioner to stay back in London. Or this may have been just one of those moments in Krishna Menon's life when he felt that even his closest friends didn't care for him enough and when he would try and appear to be a martyr.

1951

India faced acute food shortages in the early months of 1951 and famine stalked some parts of the country. The only option available to Nehru was to approach the Americans for wheat. But the political conditions that the US stipulated were unacceptable to him, so he instructed his ambassador in Moscow, S. Radhakrishnan, to start negotiations with the Soviets. Radhakrishnan was successful, and as soon as news of this became available, the US changed its stance and offered wheat to India unconditionally. This is what India's Food and Agriculture Minister K.M. Munshi, Finance Minister C.D. Deshmukh and the senior bureaucracy wanted in the first place.

The only person to support Radhakrishnan's efforts was Krishna Menon, who himself had negotiated five years earlier with the Soviet Union for the supply of wheat. At that time the Soviets were reluctant. Now, however, the geopolitical situation was different, and the Cold War was gathering steam. The Soviets had become more forthcoming. In a series of telegrams to Nehru in April and May 1951, Krishna Menon pleaded for the strengthening of Radhakrishnan's hands. On 8 April 1951, he told Nehru that 'our Ambassador in Moscow should be given the necessary confidence and encouragement'. Krishna Menon wanted Nehru to give Radhakrishnan the flexibility to reassure the Soviets that India would not be wedded blindly to free-market principles in food policy and would take 'every legitimate step', including procurement by the government.

In May 1951, a hundred thousand tonnes of wheat from the Soviet Union arrived in India. Soon thereafter, the Americans, fearful of the Soviets getting a strong foothold in India, spurred into action and became more liberal in their approach to wheat supply to India.[9] This episode is important on two counts.[10] First, it was perhaps the only occasion 'in a long acquaintance of over fifty years' when Krishna Menon and Radhakrishnan saw eye to eye. Eleven years later, the latter would play a pivotal role in the former's exit from Nehru's cabinet. Second, it is clear that Krishna Menon saw an active role for the government in food policy, which was not exactly shared by Nehru's senior colleagues. Procurement of foodgrains such as rice and wheat came to be introduced in a structured and systematic way only in January 1965.

Despite all his accomplishments as high commissioner, Krishna Menon's tenure is remembered mostly for what has come to be known as the 'jeeps scandal'. It has remained a permanent blot on his name and legacy. But the truth is much more complicated than what his critics and detractors propagated and what has since become conventional wisdom. The scandal had broken in early 1951, with the submission of the government's audit report for 'Defence Services' for the year 1950. In a section entitled 'Certain Contracts entered into by the High Commissioner of India in the United Kingdom during 1948–49', it reported:

> In the latter half of 1948 [when military operations were being planned or on in Kashmir and Hyderabad], the High Commissioner for India entered into four contracts for the supply of Jeeps and other military equipment with a group of associated private companies. No recorded information is available to audit how the group of associated companies were selected . . . All the contracts were signed by the same individual on behalf of the different companies concerned.

The report pointed out that of these four contracts, three were terminated by mutual agreement as no supplies materialized. It is the fourth—for the supply of jeeps—that was problematic. It reported 'the loss of 143,162 pounds or Rs 19 lakhs roundly which had been incurred by the State in respect of the contract for the purchase of 2000 second hand jeeps'. Krishna Menon had entered into a contract in late 1948 with a British company floated, it would be later revealed, by one of his British friends, for the procurement of such jeeps from Europe since they could not be purchased from either the US or the UK, which had banned their sale in view of the hostilities that had taken place between India and Pakistan. One hundred and fifty-five jeeps arrived in India in March 1949, after inspection by a reputed British company. But these jeeps were rejected by the Indian Army. This meant that the advance that had been paid for the supply of 849 jeeps in the first round had to be forfeited.

In March 1951, Krishna Menon arranged for a second contract for the supply of 1007 jeeps, which had a provision for the recovery of losses incurred under the first contract. While acknowledging this, the audit report concluded in a stinging manner:

> It is difficult to resist the conclusion that the entire management of the first transaction has been unbusiness-like and has proved detrimental to the interests of Government.

Nehru wrote to Krishna Menon on 27 February 1951:

> . . . This whole business makes one feel uncomfortable and it is
> no easy matter to explain it to enquirers. What troubles me is
> the way some things were done which landed us into difficulty.
> Of course, our need was great and we had to go through
> abnormal channels. Nevertheless we were rather badly caught
> and it is not easy to justify all this to the public, if occasion arises
> for that . . .

That occasion would soon arise in Parliament, and on 10 April 1951,
Nehru would make the first of his several defences of Krishna Menon
over the next nine years on this issue:

> In this matter a great deal has been said in the country and
> something was said in this House also and a certain word which
> was used has been used very often. That word is 'scandal'. Now,
> I can say more especially about one matter into which I have
> personally enquired as well as in regard to this jeep matter, having
> gone into it thoroughly I should like to state with such personal
> authority as I possess that the only scandal about this matter is the
> use of the word 'scandal' all the time. The House will remember
> that this transacti0n took place two and a half years ago at a critical
> moment in the country's history. Those circumstances have to be
> remembered . . .

Nehru assured the House that 'close examination reveals nothing to
which Government can take serious exception, except that we learnt
from certain errors certainly'. He spoke too soon for the issue would
blow up once again a year later.

Meanwhile Krishna Menon was running into problems with no
less a person than the British Prime Minister himself. On 7 May 1951,
a top British intelligence official Percy Sillitoe recorded this note:

> I saw the Prime Minister on Friday evening, May 4ᵗʰ when I
> mentioned to him the recent conversation I have had with the

Commonwealth Relations Office about Krishna MENON . . . I warned the Prime Minister of our views on MENON, since the Indian High Commissioner sees the Prime Minister from time to time. The Prime Minister was very interested in what I had t0 say, especially with regard to the Communists and Fellow Travellers on MENON's staff.

Sillitoe had prepared a five-page note on Krishna Menon earlier in which he had also mentioned the 'suspicion that has attached to Menon in regard to the placing of Government of India's contracts for arms, ammunition, etc with dealers in London' and that 'his close associate in such matters has been a black market operator called Cleminson, who also has a history connected with arms deals, etc'. But what bothered Sillitoe more was this:

> Irrespective of Menon himself, there is a security risk in the Indian High Commission due to the continued employment of several communists, fellow-travellers and sympathisers there . . . Menon is an intriguer. His own wants are few. He is pro-Russian but not a communist; he is no lover of the British, but he did all he could to keep India in the Commonwealth . . . Taking everything into account, Menon and the office of the Indian High Commission represent a security risk.

The intelligence agencies of the two countries had established direct contact with each other, and Krishna Menon had objected to this vehemently. Now Sillitoe was telling Attlee that 'Top Secret' government-to-government communications too should bypass the Indian High Commission. This was communicated on Attlee's behalf to Nehru. Nehru, in turn, wrote to Krishna Menon on 14 June 1951, bringing to his attention that at least six members of the staff of the Indian High Commission in London were, in the opinion of British security agencies, communists. Four of them happened to be women. Nehru explained to his high commissioner the background, based on the developments that had taken place in New Delhi that very morning:

. . . The U.K. High Commissioner conveyed a message to us from Mr. Attlee. This message was to the effect that, according to their information, there were some persons in India House of whose reliability they were not assured. They had arrived at this conclusion as a result of information received by them and investigations carried out by their intelligence. H.M.G. in the United Kingdom, it was added, did not presume to suggest, either that we should accept this information as correct, or, on the strength of this information, to take action against the said persons. H.M.G. were, however, under an obligation to ensure the secrecy of information on international and other issues of common concern to India that they might make to the Government of India. H.M.G. were, therefore, constrained to inform us that, hereafter, such information will be communicated to us through the U.K. High Commissioner here and not through our High Commissioner in London. This decision, it was added, had been taken by Mr. Attlee after full investigation and consultation with his highest officials.

To say that Krishna Menon was outraged at receiving this letter from Nehru would be an understatement. He replied five days later and began by defending the six persons named by the British government as security risks:

I received your letter of the 14th of June about certain members of the staff of this mission. I am very distressed and surprised. I shall first deal with each of the names as far as I know:

(1) Pamela Violet Cullen: Miss Cullen was in this office before Independence and came to us from the Foreign Office. She is exclusively concerned with the work of film publicity . . . She does her best, with our limited resources, to get our government films shown in schools, etc., and otherwise made known. I say this for your information, as what the British Government gathers about people, as I have known in the past to my cost, is often inaccurate.

(2) Anila Graham nee Bonnerji: This is a case well-known to you
[She was the granddaughter of W.C. Bonnerjee, first president of
the Indian National Congress in 1885]. She was associated with
the Communists when she was a student . . . She was personally
recommended here by Professor Laski. I have a very high
knowledge of her knowledge and ability.

(3) Patricia Patsy Pillay nee O'Leary. Mrs Pillay is a South African
married to an Indian. Her husband is employed in a shipping
company in the city and, I believe, is a Communist although he
is not known to be engaged in any activity. It is not difficult to
understand that a white woman married to an Indian in South
Africa should have Left sympathizers or convictions, or even be a
Communist! . . . She has done nothing against us.

(4) James Patrick Haley.

(5) Walter Sanger. I have no information about these two and I
have no strong views on them, but there have been no complaints
that either of these persons are unreliable . . .

(6) Mrs Phoebe Ahmed nee Corbett . . . Mrs Ahmed is employed
in the Education Department as a clerk. She is an Australian and
her husband is an Indian employed in the Stores Department. She
does not handle or have access to confidential papers of the kind
under mention.

. . . The UK Government cannot properly tell us that they will
not communicate information to us through appropriate channels.
They cannot tell us that they will treat your High Commission here
differently because the Mission is not staffed according to their likes.
Carried a little further, this means that we would all have to make
sure that we make ourselves agreeable to the UK! . . . If it is not
possible for us to tell Attlee that his attitude and communications
to us are improper and that you are not prepared to treat your
High Commissioner in the way he suggests, the next best thing we
can do is to act on the principle of reciprocity . . . Secondly, we
should . . . ask for the removal from British Missions in India of
people who are plotting against us and have been employed by the
British police in the past . . .

The Amritsar Session of the Indian National Congress, December 1919. Seated on the chair fourth from the left is Motilal Nehru, followed by Swami Shraddhanand, Annie Besant and Madan Mohan Malaviya. Jawaharlal Nehru is seated on the ground, extreme left.

Krishna Menon and Ellen Wilkinson meeting villagers in Punjab as part of the India League delegation, October 1932.

Executive Committee of the Congress Socialist Party, Bombay, 1934. From left: Yusuf Meherally, Achyut Patwardhan, Ram Manohar Lohia, Sajjed Zaheer, Asoka Mehta, Dinakar Mehta, Narendra Deva, S.M. Joshi, Kamaladevi Chattopadhyay, Mubarak Sagar, Jayaprakash Narayan, Minoo Masani and S.S. Batlivala.

Krishna Menon, Bertrand Russell, Ellen Wilkinson, Leonard Matters, Horace Alexander and Agatha Harrison waiting to welcome Nehru at Victoria Station, London, October 1935.

Krishna Menon and Feroze Gandhi at a demonstration in London, probably late 1936.

Krishna Menon, Indira Nehru and Jawaharlal Nehru, London, 1938.

Bhicoo Batlivala, Nehru, Dolores Ibarruri and Krishna Menon, Barcelona, 1938.

The historic 24 June 1938 meeting at Stafford Cripps's country home. From left: Harold Laski, Cripps, Nehru (only left arm visible), Krishna Menon, Clement Attlee, Leonard Barnes, Nye Bevan and Richard Crossman.

Liaquat Ali Khan, Mohammad Ali Jinnah, Baldev Singh, Lord Pethick-Lawrence, Nehru, Krishna Menon and Fatima Jinnah, London airport, December 1946.

Prince Philip, Mountbatten, R.K. Shanmukham Chetty (India's first finance minister), Attlee, Edwina Mountbatten and Krishna Menon, London airport, June 1948.

From right: Nehru, Krishna Menon, M.O. Mathai and presumably two security officers, Srinagar, September 1948.

Vallabhbhai Patel and Krishna Menon, probably New Delhi, 1948.

Krishna Menon, C. Rajagopalachari and K.M. Panikkar, New Delhi, early 1949.

Nehru, Edwina Mountbatten and Krishna Menon at a Greek restaurant in Soho, London, most probably end–April 1949.

Krishna Menon with sculptress Frida Brilliant, London end–1948/early 1949.

Krishna Menon reading a message from the Government of India ending Privy Council jurisdiction over India, 8 February 1950. Seated are the Lord Privy Council and Philip Noel-Baker, secretary of state for Commonwealth Relations, who almost single-handedly spoilt India's case on Kashmir at the UN in 1948.

Harold Laski, Krishna Menon, Frida Laski and Nye Bevan at the Indian High Commission, London, most probably 15 August 1949.

Krishna Menon and Vijaya Lakshmi Pandit at the UN, November 1952.

Krishna Menon with his Soviet counterpart, Andrei Vyshinsky, at the UN,
November 1952. Andrei Gromyko is next to Vyshinsky.

Krishna Menon with Pakistan's Muhammad Zafrulla Khan at the UN,
most probably late 1954.

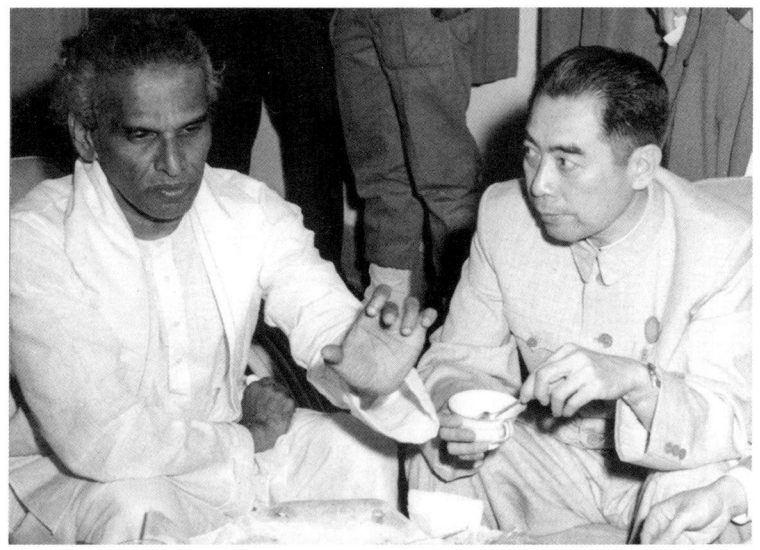

Krishna Menon and Chou En-Lai meeting for the first time at Bandung,
Indonesia, April 1955.

Krishna Menon with President Gamal Abdel Nasser of Egypt, Bandung,
Indonesia, April 1955.

Krishna Menon with Indira Gandhi and Rajiv Gandhi, New Delhi, probably mid-1955.

Krishna Menon at the height of his popularity in the US, New York hotel welcome, mid-1955.

Krishna Menon with Anthony Eden either in London or New York, early 1950s.

Eisenhower, John Foster Dulles, Krishna Menon and G.L. Mehta (Indian ambassador in the US) at the White House, Washington DC, June 1995.

Krishna Menon with actress Julie Adams at a Hollywood studio during the making of *Away All Boats*, June 1955.

Homi Bhabha and Krishna Menon at the UN, probably late 1955.

Krishna Menon, Ho Chi Minh and Nehru, New Delhi, February 1958.

Krishna Menon with Dag Hammarskjold at the UN, late 1950s.

Film actress Nutan flanked by Krishna Menon and Dr A.V. Baliga, Bombay, late 1950s.

Edwina Mountbatten, Krishna Menon and Pamela Mountbatten, New Delhi, late 1950s.

Nehru, Chen Yi, Krishna Menon, Chou En-lai, S. Radhakrishnan and Govind Ballabh Pant,
New Delhi, April 1960.

Nehru with the two ideological opposites in his cabinet: Krishna Menon and
Govind Ballabh Pant, New Delhi, probably early 1960.

Fidel Castro flanked by Krishna Menon and Nehru after their visit to his hotel in Harlem, New York, September 1960.

Krishna Menon, K.C. Reddy, Morarji Desai and Nehru at a cabinet meeting, New Delhi, early 1960s.

Ideological rivals but personal friends. Krishna Menon with S.K. Patil, early 1960s.

President John F. Kennedy and Krishna Menon at the UN, November 1961.

Lt General B.M. Kaul, Krishna Menon and Nehru, New Delhi, probably 1962.

Handing over of site for Mahatma Gandhi Memorial at Tavistock Square, London. Second from the left: Krishna Menon, Indian High Commissioner M.C. Chagla, Indira Gandhi, Nehru and Mayor of St Pancras, 19 September 1962.

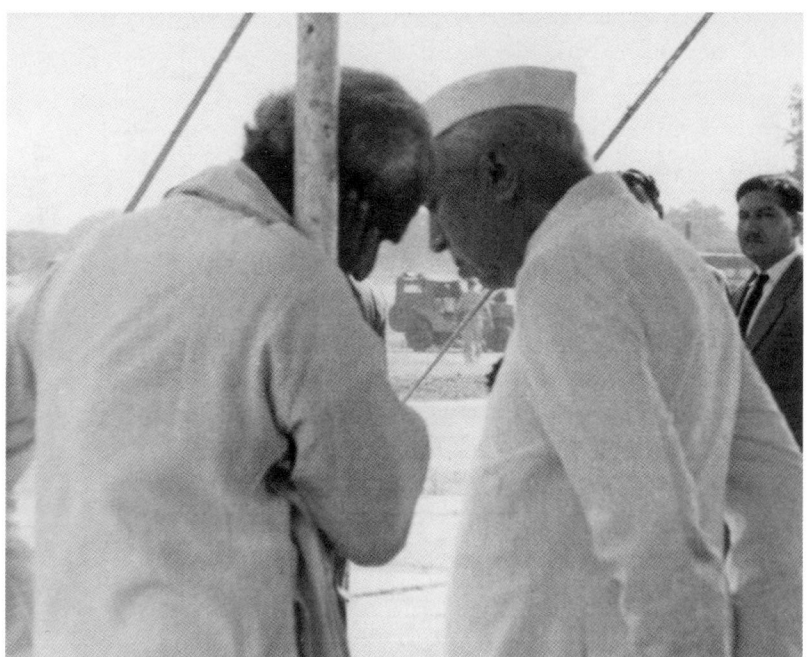

Krishna Menon and Nehru confabulate before the latter's departure for Colombo, New Delhi airport, 12 October 1962.

Krishna Menon on the night of the Chinese invasion at a public meeting, New Delhi, 20 October 1962.

The last photo of Krishna Menon as defence minister with Nehru at a UN Day function, New Delhi, 25 October 1962. A few days later he resigned.

Nehru, Krishna Menon and Lal Bahadur Shastri in conversation, New Delhi, possibly early 1963.

Krishna Menon with Indira Gandhi a few hours following Nehru's death, New Delhi, 27 May 1964.

Krishna Menon at Nehru's funeral, New Delhi, 28 May 1964. 'When the pyre was lit he collapsed. Someone brought some water and sprinkled it on his face. Very soon he revived and stood there with a vacant look in a state of deep shock.'

Krishna Menon with President Nasser, one of his closest international friends, Cairo, mid-1960s.

A defiant Krishna Menon giving an election speech contesting as an independent candidate, Bombay, January 1967.

Senior advocate Krishna Menon with fellow lawyers outside the
Supreme Court, mid–1960s.

Madhu Bhandari, Kumudesh Bhandari, Krishna Menon and Siddharth
Bhandari, Moscow, most probably mid–1970.

Among the last-known photos of Krishna Menon. With Siddharth Bhandari on his residence lawns, mid–1974.

President Fakhruddin Ali Ahmed paying his last respects to Krishna Menon, New Delhi, 6 October 1974.

Krishna Menon and his collection of walking sticks.

Krishna Menon and his Indian-wear wardrobe.

The school where Krishna Menon studied in Calicut that still runs.

The school named after Krishna Menon's earliest mentors that still runs in Chennai.

Nehru had taken care to tell Krishna Menon that the Indian government was under no obligation to accept the 'U.K. Government's judgment or advice about any member of our staff'. But he had ended his letter by saying:

> At the same time we can hardly insist upon their adopting a procedure which they are not willing to adopt.

Krishna Menon took great umbrage at this and remonstrated to his Prime Minister:

> It is also a little difficult for me to understand how it would be proper for me to continue to be the head of this mission on the basis of limited confidence and as belonging to a low caste among High Commissioners. There are a number of people in the service of HMG who are very hostile to us, who are working for Pakistan against us and who have had a long record of anti-Indian sentiment. Are we entitled to ask for their removal or that our papers should not be shown to them? . . .
>
> With very great respect I submit that the last sentence in your letter causes me the greatest surprise of all, but since you have numerous worries I do not desire to add to them by arguing about it. The British Government still appear to think that they can order us about . . .

In this matter, Krishna Menon was entirely in the right. Paranoid officials of the British establishment, aided and abetted by Krishna Menon's enemies at the top echelons of the bureaucracy in New Delhi, caused a first-rate crisis which would cast a long shadow on Indo-British relations. It certainly hastened Krishna Menon's departure. It was not just communist influence, however, that bothered Sillitoe and his colleagues. Right from 1947, Sillitoe had been warning the British government that 'the India League provides a useful platform for the development of anti-South African government propaganda which could not with propriety be conducted from India House'.

While the British were bothered about the alleged communists around him, in India, Krishna Menon was now being talked about not so much for his diplomatic achievements but more for his role in the jeep saga. Sensitive to the growing criticism of the high commissioner, Nehru had informally asked some senior officers to get at the truth. Krishna Menon was very upset by this and sent Nehru a telegram on 31 May 1951, drawing his attention to the fact that the chairman of the company with which the defence contracts had been signed was 'General Sir James Marshall Cornwall, KCB, CBE, DSO, MC', who was also a 'Military Adviser to the Foreign Office'. He went on:

> I submit with great respect that it would be against public interest and highly embarrassing for the Mission if anyone who does business with us is to be subject to inquisitorial proceedings or as happened to statements unwarranted by facts by auditors.

But the investigations continued with Nehru's knowledge and approval. Compounding Krishna Menon's travails was the state of his health, always precarious in any case. Nehru wrote to him on 2 June 1951:

> I am very much worried about your repeated relapses and illness. I feel more and more that you should take long rest in order to become fit. I would undoubtedly do so if I was unwell.

He followed it up three days later after giving expression to his own state of mind:

> I returned from Kashmir at midday today after two days leave. These two days were exceedingly strenuous and I have returned tired instead of refreshed. For sometime past, I have become nervy, which is a bad thing. If I cannot stop myself from further deterioration in this respect, I shall think of leaving off all work for sometime . . .

. . . All the news I have received about you from a variety
of sources, including your own letters, goes to show that you
continue to be very ill and sometimes are completely bed-ridden.
You may of course carry on by sheer will power but it is clear
to me that you must not continue any work till your health is in
better condition . . . There is no chance, as far as I can see, of your
recovering health so long as you go on at this pace . . . I would
suggest that you should take three months' leave . . . and forget
about India House . . . To go on working, in your present state of
health, seems to me to be completely wrong . . . I would therefore
suggest that you might take three months leave or you can make it
two months and see how you feel like later . . . Crises will continue
to pursue us and it is better that you should come back after a spell
and deal with them.

A few days later on 15 June 1951, Nehru was at it again and pleaded
with Krishna Menon:

I wrote to you some days ago suggesting that you should take three
months' leave and take rest and treatment. I am quite sure that it
is not right for you, in your present state of health, to continue
working hard. I know well that your absence from India House
for a while will create difficulties for us. But there are certain rules
about health which must be followed . . .

Thereafter on 19 July 1951, with Krishna Menon and his doings
preying on his mind, Nehru wrote to his finance minister, C.D.
Deshmukh, and provided a candid assessment of his high commissioner
in London:

. . . In some ways Krishna Menon is a person of remarkable ability
and capacity. From a purely intellectual point of view, I cannot
remember having met any person with a keener intellect. He is a
man of high integrity and his whole life has been one of simplicity
and sacrifice.

So much for his good points. At the same time he has a number of serious failings. He is not an easy person to get on with; he is highly sensitive, somewhat self-opinionated and tries to do everything himself which no head of mission should do. His capacity for work is remarkable, but even so he overshoots the mark. His physical ill-health is continually coming in his way and he lives on tonics and the like.

A man like this is a problem and difficulties continually crop up. One has to balance his extraordinary capacity for good work with failings . . .

That Nehru was having enormous difficulties dealing with his high commissioner became more than obvious six days later when he wrote to Krishna Menon, who was to describe reading it as a 'shattering experience'. Nehru was devastatingly honest and direct:

. . . You complain of being harassed by petty and big things. Of course you are harassed and I am harassed and all of us are harassed. But I feel that a good part of the harassment is perhaps due to your own reactions which are sudden and sometimes strong.

You advise me on various matters and I consider your advice very valuable. But you seem to think that I function here as an autocrat and that you should also function there in London in a similar capacity . . . I cannot and should not take major decisions without reference to my colleagues. The impression . . . is that you hold them and most people here in utter contempt . . .

You refer in one of your letters to my trust and confidence. Of course you have got that as well as my affection. But that does not necessarily mean that your judgment of what is happening in India or what can be done here is right. After all we have to carry people here and the mere rightness of an opinion is not enough. Sometimes your approach makes it difficult for me to carry people here . . . I think that often you do injustice to yourself and needlessly add to your difficulties and others' difficulties.

I have written to you repeatedly that you should take leave and cut yourself off from work completely for some months . . . It will be good for you to get away. I said in a letter to you that your staying on is neither fair to you nor to your work and you asked me what I mean by this. I meant first of all that a person who is in ill-health and often in a highly nervous condition cannot give his best to the work and his nervousness comes to others . . .

Krishna Menon was astonished by this letter, to say the least, even though it was from a caring and concerned Nehru. He wrote to Nehru on 3 August 1951, saying that he had not expected to live to see the day that Nehru would write such a letter. Two days later he appealed in a mood of extreme self-pity to his friend M.O. Mathai:

I do not think that even you know my mental and emotional relation to Panditji which is now getting on to twenty years although most of it is a one-way traffic as it would be when one party is such a great figure . . . He has also made it clear that he resents my submitting advice . . . My devotion to him will last as long as I live. That devotion now calls for my disappearance . . .

Nehru followed it up with yet another long and equally forbearing communication on 25 August 1951. He was trying his utmost to reassure and calm down his volatile high commissioner:

. . . I had hoped that you would not misunderstand me and that you would realize that I could only send that letter to a person for whom I had great affection and respect and to whom I was closely attached. I know that parts of my letter might perhaps hurt you a little. But I had to take that risk, because I wanted you to know what I had in mind . . .

You know my attachment to you and you ought to know how I value your judgment. But surely you do not expect me not to exercise my judgment occasionally even though it may not fall in line with yours. I would not expect you to do anything of that kind to me. You have been, for a long time past, physically unwell and your ill-health increased . . . I realized well enough that your trouble was not so much of the body . . . as of the mind . . .

Perhaps you think and indeed you have said so sometimes, that I hear tales about you . . . All the information I had about you during these past few months was from persons who are our mutual friends and who have great affection for you and wish you well . . .

You have a feeling perhaps, and you have hinted at it, that I do not trust your judgment sufficiently. May I say that you show sometimes a great lack of trust in my judgment. I have to deal with the situation here and have to function according to my lights . . .

I am writing to you today with some hesitation, because I do not know what reaction a letter of mine might produce on you. That feeling itself is not good because that comes in the way of my free writing and talking. Besides, these letters and arguments do not help very much . . .

Nehru's aide Mathai too was very concerned with Krishna Menon's general condition and, on his own volition, asked the Prime Minister for permission to go to London to see things for himself and cheer the high commissioner up. So Mathai went to England for a few weeks and briefed Nehru at some length about what he had seen and observed. He had met with Mountbatten as well, which was duly reported by the former viceroy to Nehru on 21 September 1951:

Edwina and I have had long and valuable talks with Mac. I understand that Krishna's doctors are recommending very strongly that he should be relieved, at least temporarily, from his appointment if his health is to be saved. Sorry as I shall be to see him leave the appointment, even for a short time, I am too attached to him to wish him to continue when his health is at stake . . .

Mountbatten then went on to make an extraordinary suggestion for a replacement for Krishna Menon in London:

. . . I have absolutely no doubt who the right man would be and I have a feeling you will agree with me that it must be Rajaji . . . The British could not fail to be really flattered if India sent her former

Governor General to represent her in London. The personal prestige attached to Rajaji quote apart from his having been Governor General is very great . . . I hear that Rajaji is anxious to retire from active political life, but I think he would find London quite restful. . .

Rajaji was then India's home minister, having succeeded Sardar Patel. He would indeed retire from active public life in November 1951 but that retirement was to last just five months since he became chief minister of Madras state in April 1952. There is no evidence, however, to suggest that Nehru did, in fact, talk about Mountbatten's suggestion with Rajaji himself.

Meanwhile, Krishna Menon protested vehemently to Nehru on 24 September 1951—that he was not sick in any way and that he would continue to be loyal to the Prime Minister personally in spite of what he called Nehru's 'cruel letters'. If any proof was needed of how ill Krishna Menon was, it was demonstrated by the use of these words for Nehru's well-intentioned letters. Five days later Nehru told Mathai:

> . . . I decided some months ago that Krishna must leave the High Commission. But I was not in a hurry and I wanted him to suggest . . . I saw a progressive deterioration . . . That is the only real tragedy in life and the tragedy is all the greater when it comes to a man of Krishna's brilliance and integrity and self-sacrifice. Death or suicide are bad and painful but they do not wipe out the past. They just put a full stop to it. But inner degradation and disintegration are far worse . . .

Nehru admitted to Mathai that he had 'temporised' for too long and that something drastic had to be done right away. But before he could decide, Krishna Menon took umbrage at Nehru's letters and, on 1 October 1951, gave him a rundown on his medication, which had caused great concern to Nehru:

> . . . I just wanted to say that from your letter you have some mistaken notion or been told some wrong things about what I have

been taking as sedative or sleeping tablets, as you refer many times to 'powerful tonics'. Mathai also talked about 'drugs' and asked me whether 'Is it not a fact you take drugs'!!! I am not offended at this! But quite obviously the impression is that I have been or am a drug taker! It is all very silly and spread by busybodies and old maids of both sexes. I do not and have not taken drugs, even nicotine which smokers take in. Sedatives and hypnotics are not habit forming and are properly prescribed . . . They are barbiturates which are eliminated through the kidneys. They create no craving and such toxic effects as they may have are neutralized by adequate dose of other tablets, even when required. Lots of healthy people in our day have periodical or occasional sedatives. I had none of them, Anyway I do not take them any more and I slept for over a month now without medicines.

But Nehru was not to be swayed, and on 14 October 1951, he laid down the line for Krishna Menon:

. . . You must apply for leave for six months . . . You must give a full chance to the doctors and to yourself to get well. It is no good playing about at this. I want you to take this leave immediately and go off to Switzerland or wherever the doctors send you. Do not trouble yourself about your expenses on treatment or travel. That will be our responsibility . . . I have taken a long time to come to this decision and there is no need now to argue about it. It should be treated as a firm decision and acted upon without further delay. After your treatment in Switzerland, or wherever it might be, and when you are declared fit, I should like you to come to India for a month or so. There is a great deal I want to talk to you about . . .

This letter of mine might again give you a shock, but you know me well enough, I hope, to realize that I have written to you because of my great affection and regard for you and because of my strong wish that you should get well and continue for many years the service of India to which you have devoted your life.

Nehru's 'orders' would not have reached Krishna Menon because the very next day he told the Prime Minister that his health had improved 'out of all recognition', that he was back to normal and had pulled himself out of the 'self-pity and the fussiness of friends and well-wishers'. He also informed Nehru that he had consulted a leading psychiatrist Dr Edwin Armstrong Bennet, who had pronounced him to be normal. Bennet was a well-known author as well, having written a book on the famous psychoanalyst Carl Jung. On 15 October 1951, Krishna Menon sent Nehru Bennet's report, which read:

> . . . In my opinion, it is not necessary for him to have any medical treatment at the present time . . . He could well be described as a highly-strung person . . . However, now that he is becoming older he cannot do everything he has done in the past. It will be necessary, therefore, for him to be in touch with his medical advisers, and if there are signs of strain, then he must take a certain amount of sedatives . . . I recommend he be given only small quantitates of the well known barbiturates such as secconal and sodium amytal. We have got to save him and protect him for his over-enthusiasm. With wise handling and taking a long view, I am of the opinion that there is no reason why he should not continue to do full and responsible work for many years.

But the letter contained more than a summary of Bennet's assessment of Krishna Menon. It was full of melodramatic breast-beating that showed how self-obsessed Krishna Menon was or, at least, had become in that phase of his life:

> . . . I do not want to be a victim of pity or self-pity any more and prefer to regard all this as an episode . . . I hope you will not misunderstand it, but an illness (which I could have handled better) has taught me that, in essence, one stands alone . . .
>
> I have looked through your letters of the last few months again. They are hard and more admonitory than ever before . . . I have realized—and accepted—that you no longer have the same proximity of mental and spiritual relation to me as before . . .

I am prepared to go if you wish me to do so . . . But please let not an illness which no longer weighs me down be held to be the cause of it . . . You are the only person left, after Laski died, for whom I could feel an unequalled degree of devotion and attachment. It was reciprocal perhaps but I was slipping and taking the reciprocity for granted! My loyalty and devotion is mine and will endure . . . You may discover this some time in the future . . .

Nehru was sympathetic yet firm. He cabled Krishna Menon on 26 October 1951 to express happiness at his turnaround recovery but also added, '[Y]our sudden recovery is good but then there can also be sudden relapses.' Nehru reiterated his instructions of twelve days earlier, which had so unsettled Krishna Menon, but praised his 'strength of will' that 'is a great asset which keeps you going'. Krishna Menon had asked Nehru whether he could come back and see him early in November 1951. Nehru poured some cold water on this proposal, saying that he was terribly busy for some time but that Krishna Menon was welcome to come to India later, provided he stayed for some good length of time.

The Prime Minister, immersed in India's first elections, would have been entitled to think that this was the end of this sorry episode involving his self-delusional friend and colleague in London. But he had not bargained for the high commissioner's obduracy and capacity for emotional blackmail. This blackmail was evident in yet another of his self-recriminatory letters to Nehru on 30 October 1951:

. . . I confess that your telegram of October 26 came somewhat as a shock . . . it affected me both emotionally and intellectually, but I have not allowed it to affect my objective approach or judgment much less knock me out . . .

I however felt quite clear in my mind that: (1) I should accept your decision with grace and without argument and leave as soon as possible; (2) that I should take every possible step to ensure that the minimum harm and dislocation should occur and the change should appear to be done with smoothness and dignity; (3) that any immediate steps would be premature, and even letting it be

known or appear that I was leaving or was likely to leave was most
ill-timed at present; and (4) that illness as a cause would appear
now as the most unconvincing—it would even raise a laugh for
the most part . . .

Then Krishna Menon revealed something extraordinary he had done
to bolster his position vis-à-vis Nehru. The only thing that can be
said in defence of what he did is that at least he brought it to Nehru's
attention—of course with selfish motives. He went on:

> . . . I felt, having regard to my being a concerned party, that I
> ought to obtain what advice was reasonable and safe to take and
> would not be open to objection in your mind. I therefore had
> talks with Agatha Harrison and the Mountbattens which I thought
> you would not disapprove. Agatha Harrison thought and said so
> that the matter should be considered 'after four or six months'.
> She urged me to place before you a reasoned statement . . . The
> Mountbattens also said this independently and thought that the
> course you have directed, while it was imperative some time ago,
> was not required, or at any rate, urgently required now . . .

Krishna Menon suggested that he be allowed to leave as high
commissioner in early February 1952, which meant a three-month
relaxation of Nehru's ultimatum. He then launched into another
set of 'I am the hurt party here', 'I am well and you have been
misinformed', 'You have been unduly harsh on me' arguments. He
made it out that Nehru had betrayed twenty years of their friendship
and had not stood up for him strongly. In this, however, Krishna
Menon was comprehensively wrong and self-serving. He ended by
telling Nehru that he would not take leave for rest or medical care
as he was 'remarkably well and fit' and would not take treatment
as 'my doctors do not advice it'. In other words, Nehru's orders
would be disobeyed, and in return for that, he was asking for three
months grace. From his point of view, dragging Agatha Harrison
and the Mountbattens into the picture had saved his departure in
November 1951 and also earned for him a longer rope with Nehru. As

things turned out, Krishna Menon remained high commissioner till mid-July 1952.

But even with all the private traumas he had been going through for the past few months, Krishna Menon did not forget his 'baby', which had now become a full-blown adult. On 9 November 1951, he reached out to all his India League colleagues:

> I think it is most desirable for a few of us who have, in our own ways, participated in the work of the India League—some over the years and others more recently—to come together for a review, and also to look forward. We can, without false pride, say to ourselves that we had faith in dark days to strive for a cause which seemed then remote from fulfillment. Today, although it may not so easily be evident, the cause is essentially the same . . . Writing to you now, I am reminded of the early 1930s, when, to those who afterwards became stalwarts, knowledge and conviction had to be gained . . . We may feel that we are groping, and yet that we are groping after something. Only adventure can find it. Therefore I ask you (purely on a personal basis) to come for a private and informal meeting at the India League, 47 Strand, W.C.2., on Thursday 22nd November at 6 p.m.

It would be an evening of recollections and reminiscences, an evening during which many British women (and a few men) who had worked voluntarily and selflessly for India's freedom mesmerized by Krishna Menon's personality would revisit the old times nostalgically.

Notes

1. Ghosh (1967).
2. Kirpalani (1993).
3. Singh (2002).
4. Ram (1997).
5. Ankit (2016).
6. Pandit (1979).

7. This was told to me by N.M. Ghatate, who worked with Krishna Menon in his legal practice during 1967–74.
8. McGarr (2010).
9. Engerman (2018).
10. I draw upon Gopal (1989) for details of this episode.

13

Exit as High Commissioner (1952) and UN Envoy (1952–57)

1952

Right through the last few months of 1951 Krishna Menon did his best to resist Nehru's pleas to take leave and receive medical treatment. Claiming to be a devotee of Nehru, he did everything in his power to stonewall him, even if Nehru's image took a beating in the process. It was a behaviour that was both self-obsessed and self-delusional. Not even yet another missive from Nehru on 4 January 1952 moved him:

> You are a very sensitive person and I am always afraid of saying or doing anything which would hurt you or upset you. And yet not to say it or do it leads to subsequent hurt and, what is worse, misunderstanding. Life is difficult enough. It does little good for us to make it more difficult. I hope that you will consider what I have written calmly and think of the wider context in which I have had to function . . .

On 4 January 1952, Mountbatten wrote to Nehru:

> The other day Krishna came to see me at the Admiralty in connection with the three frigates which are being released for India.

He has handled this question, as he has handled all the armaments questions of which I have knowledge, with very great skill . . . He surprised me by saying that he would be leaving India House as the three months extension which you gave him would be up [in February] . . . He went further and said he hoped I would not 'interfere' in this matter, but I refrained from giving any promise. I am sure he has no idea that I am writing to you . . . In the last two or three months since the Conservative Government came to power, Krishna has done a superb job . . . Remembering how very friendly he was with all the Ministers of the Labour Government, I must express my astonished admiration at the way he has handled the Conservative Government . . . I am not, however, advising you to ask him to stay on, because I think he sincerely feels that you really do want to make a change, and he is a big enough man not to want to stand in the way.

Nehru replied ten days later:

. . . More than two months ago I wrote to Krishna Menon that it will be advisable for him to have a change. He was getting tied up in all kinds of ways and I wanted him to come to India. My own idea was that he should remain in India and even be a Minister here for some time. But I said that it was impossible to decide anything till the elections are over . . . That is the present position and he should stay on at least till sometime in March. After that I should like him to come here on leave . . .

India's first general election campaign was in full swing, and Nehru had a crushing and punishing schedule. Even so, he wrote to Krishna Menon on 14 January 1952 that he should wait till the election results were in before coming to India. Krishna Menon replied six days later:

. . . I would like you to feel that you do not have to worry about me anymore, even though others seek to use you against me and succeed . . . I am less and less distressed by the treachery and intrigue in high places and by disloyalty!

Every cry of distress and self-pity from Krishna Menon would evoke a response from Nehru as he went from public meeting to public meeting. He replied on 27 January 1952:

> . . . I suppose you are annoyed with me and imagine that I do not give you enough protection against attacks, or even that I encourage them. You should know, without my telling you repeatedly, what my feelings are about you. I have been deeply pained and upset at many things that have happened here, but I must confess that you have made it exceedingly difficult for me or anyone to deal with the situation as that arises. Part of the attacks on you are really meant to be attacks on me . . . So far as I am concerned, there has been no question of my doubting your integrity and it has pained me to refer these matters to you. It may be that there are occasional errors of judgment which any person can make. I have written to you fairly frankly on previous occasions and told you I had come to the conclusion for a large variety of reasons that it was neither good for you or for me for you to continue as High Commissioner in London . . .

A day earlier, Nehru had shared his extreme anguish on Krishna Menon a second time with C.D. Deshmukh:

> . . . I have been greatly troubled over developments there [Indian High Commission in London] during the last few months and more. They have become so complicated that I can hardly follow them or understand them . . . Krishna Menon did an amazingly fine job of work . . . during the first two years of his High Commissionership. Later continued ill-health and other reasons lowered the quality of that work and produced many other problems, some of which have been troubling you and me for a long time past. I was greatly worried of these matters. On the one hand, he was a man possessing some very rare qualities . . . I have hardly come across a keener intelligence and brain . . . Stafford Cripps, Harold Laski and others had the highest respect for him . . . His integrity appeared to me to be unquestionable . . . With all this he was self-willed,

self-opinionated, highly sensitive and difficult to get on with . . .
He had a tendency to rely on people sometimes when he should
have been more careful. All this got him to entanglements.

I still think that the best course would be for Krishna Menon
to leave India House. I have asked him to take leave about the
middle of March and to come to India then.

Krishna Menon had by now realized that his time as high
commissioner was up. Nehru had dealt with him very patiently and
given him a long rope. But worse was to follow. By early March 1952,
the findings of the government's audit for defence services for the year
1951 had been finalized. It reported new facts on the jeeps matter.
In the first jeeps contract, the advance that India had paid had been
forfeited. Krishna Menon had then entered into a second jeeps contract
in March 1951, in which the advance lost in the first jeeps contract
would be adjusted. The second contract too was placed on pretty
much the same friends of Krishna Menon and was for the supply of
1007 new jeeps by September 1952. However, up until March 1952,
only forty-nine jeeps had arrived in India, as a result of which the
Indian government had decided to sue the British company arranging
for these jeeps from Belgium for breach of contract. The audit report
then went on to say that the Indian high commissioner had entered
into contracts for the supply of arms and ammunition from a 'European
continental country [France]' through London-based intermediaries,
thereby paying a higher price that, however, was not quantified.

It was this audit report that led Nehru to write a four-page 'Top
Secret and Personal Letter' on defence contracts to Krishna Menon
on 14 March 1952:

. . . I became interested in these contracts when the first jeep
contract came up for criticism in Parliament last year . . . I was
myself satisfied that in view of the urgency of the situation, when
the order was sent from India, some unusual and abnormal steps
were necessitated. I think there were some lapses in the drawing
up of the contract and greater care should have been exercised in
regard to some matters.

The first jeep contract was then converted into the second jeep contract and apparently any losses that we might have suffered were covered by this contract. We explained this to Parliament. That explanation involved an assurance that all would be well in the future. As a matter of fact, all has not been well and we have not obtained deliveries of the jeeps according to contract . . .

I have got the impression that most of our armament business somehow goes through the hands of a single firm or rather a group of associated firms which are connected with each other in a variety of ways. Now they are known as Sir James Marshal Cornwall and partners. Previously they were the S.C.K. Agencies. In some way or other, Potter and Cleminson were also associated with one of the partners in the firm previously. It seems to be unwise in principle to get tied up with one firm or group. In practice this has led us into all kinds of difficulties . . .

Our invariable rule should be that we must avoid intermediaries except when there is no possible course open to us. We deal with foreign Governments or foreign manufacturers . . .

It seems to me that our effort to concentrate procurement in London has led to this concentration being in the hands of Sir James Marshal Cornwall and their associates. In other words, this firm has almost developed a monopoly in supply to us . . .

Krishna Menon replied first on 25 March 1952:

. . . I fear that your impressions and conclusions rest on what has been said to you, and perhaps all around, and even more on what had not been conveyed to you . . . For myself, I am much less disturbed now by these continual misrepresentations and calumnies than I used to be . . . I have let these slanders go unchallenged for too long, believing they were for the most part founded on somebody's lurid and deceased imagination but since it appears that this persistent campaign had had some effect upon you . . . I have determined to run all this to earth, so far as I can. In setting out the facts I assure you I will have no reservations in regard to myself—

none whatsoever . . . Whatever they disclose, I will accept the full responsibility for them . . .

Nine days later Nehru denied Krishna Menon's insinuation that he had been misled and repeated what he had said earlier:

I am very clear in my mind that intermediaries should be avoided wherever possible in such dealings. Also we have dealt far too much with the same set of people in regard to most of our needs . . . In this matter your personal integrity is not questioned . . . It is not much good talking about lurid and deceased imaginations. We have to deal with facts and we have to convince the public and Parliament.

Then followed from Krishna Menon on 11 April 1952 an eighteen-page, seventy-one-point defence to Nehru of his actions on all the accusations that had been made on the procurement of jeeps and arms and ammunition. It was, as Krishna Menon called it, a 'thesis'. There were no caveats whatsoever in that defence, no hint even in between the lines that something had gone wrong somehow somewhere. There was not even an implicit admission that the decisions he had taken were liable to be misinterpreted, that the complete dependence on one supplier (and that too not a manufacturer) could give rise to legitimate questions and suspicions. He went to the extent of defending his using 'middlemen', which Nehru had so vehemently objected to. At one stage he described 'middlemen' as those who 'render service which is part of manufacture' and provided evidence that the 'middlemen' had been appointed by the manufacturers themselves as 'agents'.

Two of Krishna Menon's British friends who were used as intermediaries were E.H. Potter and Robert Cleminson. Potter was ubiquitous and was involved in one way or another with all the companies with which Krishna Menon had signed defence contracts. But the opinions about Potter and Cleminson was divided among Nehru's senior colleagues to whom the Prime Minister had sent all the papers and asked for their opinion. N. Gopalaswami Ayyangar, the defence minister, told Nehru on 4 July 1952:

> Potter is a shady character and probably a crook. Whether Cleminson was in league with him for some time and has since broken away from him on account of possible disclosures is a matter on which it is not possible for us to form a firm opinion. On the material I have seen my conclusion is that the story that Potter paid Cleminson something like 40000 pounds either for securing the contract for the jeeps and for ensuring smoothness between him and the High Commissioner in his carrying out of that contract is in all probability a myth for which Potter alone is responsible. There is enough to justify in refusing to believe Potter.

Two days later C.D. Deshmukh wrote to the Prime Minister:

> I am satisfied Cleminson is lying and that he received the money in respect of the jeep contract.

Nehru sent Deshmukh's letter to Ayyangar and asked for a second opinion. Ayyangar reiterated his view that Potter was lying, although he did point out that Potter had direct access to Krishna Menon. After agreeing with Ayyangar and telling him that 'there were undoubtedly unsatisfactory features in this whole business' and that 'no one seems to have come out with particular credit', Nehru informed Krishna Menon on 13 July 1952 that 'there was nothing to substantiate the charge against Cleminson'.

It is reflective of the Nehru–Krishna Menon relationship that, while all this correspondence on defence contracts was taking place, Nehru was thinking of the next assignment for his high commissioner. On 25 March 1952, he had written to Krishna Menon:

> Moscow is a difficult and important place and it is not easy for us to [find a] suitable person. If you would agree to go there, as I hope you will, my mind will be lightened. It is not necessary for you to

go there for any long period. I would suggest a year to begin with but the period may be lengthened.

Three days later Krishna Menon declined the offer, saying he would be most unsuitable to represent India and that, in any case, by his own reckoning he had fallen out with the Prime Minister. On 29 March 1952, he wrote to Nehru again saying:

> . . . I am very unsuitable person to represent India in Moscow . . . I would have been of the same view even if I were not out of favour. All I now seek is to leave and fade out quietly and with dignity . . . I am sorry you have come to rate my sense of values as that of a careerist! I must have laid myself open to this estimation. Perhaps I am wrong. Perhaps you may yet find this estimate wrong. I have little doubt that this will be so when I have seen you.

Even though he was at pains to stress that he was declining the Moscow offer not out of sullenness, much less resentment or petulance, Krishna Menon certainly knew how to make Nehru feel guilty. Nehru repeated the offer on 3 April 1952, saying that 'it would be a good thing if you went there [Moscow]' but also added, 'Naturally if you are unwilling to go there, I cannot compel you to do so. But I do think your going there would be a good thing from every point of view.' But Krishna Menon was adamant, and instead of him, Nehru would send K.P.S. Menon.

Krishna Menon lost one of his closest British friends on 21 April 1952. Stafford Cripps and he had known each other intimately for two decades. The next day Agatha Harrison wrote to him:

> My thoughts turned to you when the wireless news said that Stafford had passed away. For I know how much he meant to you even if, in earlier days, you did not agree with him. Both from them [Cripps and his wife] and from you—there glimpsed the steady friendship between you. His going is a blow even though just recently it was rather expected.

The same day Krishna Menon sent a message to Isobel Cripps:

> Indians all over the UK and all others associated with India are deeply grieved to learn of Sir Stafford's death. Their sincere sympathy abides with you in your bereavement and loss which they share. Sir Stafford has a memorable place in the history of our two countries and his unique role in the destiny that is shaping us has earned gratitude eternal of both our peoples. Sir Stafford set for us an example of service and fraternity which combined courage with purpose and passion with wisdom and the steadfastness and simplicity he lived has inspired us all. We think of you with affection and gratitude and always will.

He would make an extra effort to keep in touch with Isobel Cripps over the next few months and also arrange for her and Frida Laski to go to India later in the year as Nehru's guests. Krishna Menon would reach out to Isobel Cripps, who wrote to him on 29 September 1952:

> Thank you for a happy lunch and for the lovely book. I have thought things over and ask for your understanding. When we are both back again I shall be delighted to come and meet people but at the moment I just feel I don't want to see others than my personal friends. I am finding this coming back to life without Stafford rather hard.

A year later Krishna Menon was at the marriage of Peggy Cripps and his Ghanian friend Joe Appaiah. This was an interracial wedding that invited much comment. She would write to him on 18 June 1953:

> My mother has passed on to me your messages and I am afraid I am rather late in thanking you but as you may imagine getting ready to be married is a full-time occupation. I think you know my fiancé quite well. We are getting married on July 18th.

Immediately following Cripps's death, Krishna Menon became almost unhinged since it became abundantly clear that Nehru was not going to budge and he would have to leave the post of high commissioner. At the same time he was also under a heavy cloud for the manner in which he had entered into defence contracts. He continued to feel persecuted and wallowed in self-pity. Finally, 14 May 1952 may well have been the darkest day in Krishna Menon's life, for he wrote a number of letters on the theme of death—verging on the suicidal—to some of his close family and friends. To Nehru, he wrote that his being asked to leave was the result of a deep-rooted conspiracy and that the Prime Minister had not done enough to protect him. He went on:

> . . . It could not be plainer that there is no useful function I can perform and it is best to go for good. I die with even less of the sense of purpose that I had in the evening. There is nothing more I can do. Kindly do not put this down to excitement. What is the alternative? . . . There is only life that one can offer you . . . I think if I stop here, at least a few people will believe that I have not abandoned self-respect and all sense of values . . . I would like to say that my affection and loyalty remain unchanged and my hopes . . . that I shall yet evoke some response remains. It is a long 20 years. It ends I hope for <u>you</u> to make a <u>new</u> beginning.

To Indira Gandhi, he was more morbid:

> I saw you first as a timid child some 20 years ago in Poona. Then for many years in England we got to know each other and became friends. In recent years, I have known you more and with deep affection my respect and regard has grown . . .
>
> I leave you all to function in the way that is open to me . . . Panditji has the fullness of my affection and loyalty. I don't always agree with him but I never ceased to love and respect him . . . However my departure is not a protest and less an escape or the result of fear or petulance . . . I have lost the access to his mind although he loves me as he always did . . . He may feel grieved, I am afraid he will. I have no option. I yield to you in my affection and loyalty to him but to no one else. I have admired him and said so. So Indu, you are all that is left of a true relationship.

This is not conceit or flattery. It is my considered feeling and my knowledge . . . Tomorrow is another day. I would be dead but Jawaharlal will be a new man. It will be a shock for him but he will accept it as my token of loyalty and service . . .

Then he wrote two letters to his sister Janaki Amma. In the first, he told her:

From you I must hope for forgiveness—forgiveness for what I am about to do . . . Hold the family together. That is what I ask of them one and all . . .

And the second went thus:

. . . I sent you my last will some years ago. I have not changed it . . . My last will and testament is I leave to my sister Janaki Amma as I die possessions of property, rights, chattels or money . . .

To Bridget Tunnard, his fiercely devoted associate at the India League for well over a decade and who would be the mainstay of the League till her death in 1971, he wrote:

. . . The time has come when you may not have me around. I have come to this position when I can serve the cause I believe only in death and not in life. This sometimes happens . . . When I am gone, please if it helps think of the years behind . . . Please do not grieve for me. It will be the wrong thing. I am gone on a job! I am quite happy doing so.

Kamala Jaspal was told:

. . . I am going for good. You are one of the people who will understand and when the personal shock has passed view it as not a 'tragic end' but part of the services one is called upon to render . . . There is no other way of drawing attention and bringing about the necessary sense of fundamental changes of purpose except of the readiness to take this step—which in the case of others, could be a sacrifice. I am happy doing this than sit idle while Rome burns.

. . . I am quite aware that I have not demonstrated adequate recognition of your earnestness and appreciation of your quite exceptional courage and sense of honour . . . I have been upset and shocked by evil tongues and slander, but you appear to have been enough fortified by your knowledge of yourself and your sense of honour . . . I suppose you will take the line that evil speakers and doers can do what they like. I refer to this at this time, because I do not want you to think that I have been oblivious to the pain that slander at one time must have caused till people found out it was not having any effect or provoking anyone . . .

. . . Our personal relations have been healthy and your devotion and real affection would cause you to grieve . . . I want you to feel assured of my great affection and respect for you . . . I owe you much, especially in the care you have taken of me . . .

I am now old . . . You have been very much like a close relative, a son or a daughter though I am shy of saying so. Let that remain if you so wish it.

There were two other letters, one to someone called Hari, whom I have been unable to identify, and another to Cleminson. Writing these letters giving notice of his impending suicide may have been a catharsis of sorts at that perilous moment. It is impossible to establish conclusively that Krishna Menon was actually going to kill himself because Nehru had finally got him out of India House. A more likely explanation for these letters could be that they were an anguished cry for help, that he was calling attention to his extreme agony in the most dramatic way he knew. The originals of these handwritten letters are in his archives, so we must assume they were never sent. The possibility of their being typed and sent is very remote.

But that suicidal mood seems to have passed quickly. Three days later he informed Mountbatten in a perfectly normal way:

My dear Dickie:

The papers say that you are at Naval exercises. I presume you come ashore sometimes, even though the tradition appears to be that Admirals, unlike Generals, are in the place of operations.

As you probably know already, I leave here and everything else for good at the end of next month . . . I do not know (as I said to you when I saw you last) whether and when I shall meet you again. I would like to say that it was a privilege to have known you and I am grateful for all your kindness and for your friendship. It was an important epoch, when I knew you most, and you were good enough to give me your confidence. It is by my choice denied to the historian to know much about it . . .

My regards to Edwina and Pamela.

Krishna Menon need not have worried. He would stay in close touch with the Mountbatten family for the next decade at least. Just before he relinquished that position, Mountbatten would write to Krishna Menon on 5 July 1952, and Edwina would add a postscript:

As you know I myself feel that you should continue to serve your country in some high capacity when you have a long rest. I know that Panditji feels the same way, and I am quite sure that his affection for you has not changed.

I am sure you realize what a vital part you played in the whole history of the transfer of power in India. If I had not had the good fortune to meet you long before there was any question of my going as a Viceroy I should have been deprived of the most invaluable advice and assistance.

As I told you before, I think it is a great tragedy that you are depriving history of your own stories in these matters. I agree that the stories should not be published but I do think that it should be written down for posterity and perhaps out in the India House archives or put among your personal papers . . .

Dickie

PS

My special love to you, Krishna dear.

Edwina

Ten days later Krishna Menon would reply to his friend 'Dickie':

> . . . I left yesterday evening. I think of your friendship with warm
> gratitude and the memory of great things which we alone know.
> My love to Edwina, Patricia and Pamela.

Krishna Menon had especially been fond of Pamela, the younger
of the Mountbatten daughters, and three years earlier there had
been some talk of her taking up a job in the High Commission.
Nehru, on Rajaji's advice, had dissuaded Krishna Menon, saying
that Mountbatten's daughter working at India House would inflame
the press in Pakistan and add to Mountbatten's notoriety in that
country.

Coincidentally, on the very day Krishna Menon left the
High Commission formally for good, that is 15 July 1952, British
intelligence services filed a report on Robert Cleminson. Cleminson
was described as a son of a Methodist preacher, who had come
into contact with Krishna Menon early in the war (late 1939 or
early 1940) in St Pancras when both were engaged in civil defence
work. Cleminson is supposed to have helped Krishna Menon with
'the bare necessities of life' and since then they had remained close
friends. In 1949, he was reported as having 'started to put his Indian
connections to more profitable purpose'. The intelligence report
noted a conversation between a 'source' and Cleminson one evening:

> Cleminson has never been to India and says he dislikes most
> Indians . . . Cleminson sees Krishna Menon at least once daily.

Cleminson has the businessman's interest in India . . . He is fond of Krishna Menon and respects his honesty . . . Krishna Menon seems to have few secrets from Cleminson, if any . . . He has done a lot for Krishna Menon and was even present whilst he was being given 'shock treatment' for hysteria. He has always stood by him when he has been in need.

A few days after he left as high commissioner, Krishna Menon received a letter from someone which, in light of what was to happen a few years hence, appears ironical. On 23 July 1952, General K.M. Cariappa, the outgoing army chief, wrote to him:

I thank you very much indeed for all you did for me during my recent visit to England . . . If ever you come to Delhi before the end of this year, please do come and stay with me. If you are not able to come till sometime next year, then there will always be room for you in my home in Mercara.

I thank you for all the help you gave me and my officers during your office. As I said in my short talk on the occasion of our farewell party for you on the evening of 11th July at the Indian Services Club, we know what a good deal of hard work you have put in to get us whatever we wanted for our Army. I thank you for it all.

Yet, just seven years later, Krishna Menon would stand accused of destroying the Indian Army.

On leaving India House, Krishna Menon had called on British Prime Minister Winston Churchill, who was back at 10 Downing Street and had mellowed considerably and even become an admirer of Nehru. This admiration would only grow over the next two or three years. According to Krishna Menon's account of the 1 August 1952 meeting, which he sent to Nehru, Churchill had asked him whether he left as high commissioner on good terms with his Prime Minister. Krishna Menon had replied that 'he had known Nehru for many years and he and Nehru had a close relationship before there were any questions of an official relationship'. Krishna Menon had assured Churchill that his personal relationship with Nehru continued to be the same but told Nehru that he did not feel that Churchill had agreed with him. The subtext in this was a gentle accusation that Nehru had told Churchill something about the background to his high commissioner's exit. Nehru was in bed with a rare knee injury but mollified Krishna Menon on 6 August 1952 by telling him that there had been no communication regarding him between the two Prime Ministers.

Nehru had already made him one job offer which Krishna Menon had refused rather contemptuously—that of ambassador to Moscow. Then Nehru made him a second offer as this letter from his sister Vijaya Lakshmi Pandit to Krishna Menon on 24 September 1952 revealed:

> I am so happy that you have consented to join the Delegation to the United Nations. I have been away from the U.N. for two years and this Session is specially a delicate one. I cannot imagine what I would have done if you had refused. I hope you are prepared to take the major burden of all the work and responsibility . . .

Krishna Menon did not sound very enthusiastic when he replied to her six days later:

> . . . the Prime Minister very kindly asked me if I would join the delegation and although I do think I will be of much use, as you probably know I agreed to go as he wished me to do so . . . I am fully aware that you have taken on a heavy task and that you have every right to expect all of us to relieve you of as much of it as we can. So far as I am concerned I would like you to feel assured that I shall be at your disposal . . .

Meanwhile on 27 September 1952, Krishna Menon resumed his practice at the Bar in London after a gap of almost seven years. A few days later, as he was preparing to leave for New York, Krishna Menon was knocked down by a taxi while walking down a London street. Given his belief in conspiracy theories, with him as the victim, he would have probably thought that it was a deliberate attempt by his enemies to finish him off once and for all, but the truth is that it was just an accident. On 12 October 1952, Nehru wrote to his sister, who was by then in New York:

> I saw in today's paper that Krishna Menon was knocked down by a taxicab in London. I presume he was not hurt much . . . I hope you will keep in close touch with him . . . because he can be of great help . . .

Vijaya Lakshmi Pandit thought she had the measure of her deputy and, three days later, reassured her brother:

> Krishna has been very helpful and friendly and I am sure he will give the delegation the full benefit of his experience and ability. One has occasionally to humour him a little and I think I know him well enough to keep him happy. At the moment he is very grateful to me for the 'mothering' that I have given him; so all is likely to be well.

Pandit had spoken too soon. This was the first and the last time she would have anything positive to say about Krishna Menon to Nehru. In a few days she was to change her tune completely and complained to her brother on 4 November 1952:

> . . . Krishna has sole charge of Korea because he will not take anyone into confidence and also because he has a persecution mania. He causes me anxious days and sleepless nights. It is like dealing with a temperamental teenager whose greatest need is to be loved but who won't let anyone love him! . . .

A day later, she was at it again, reporting to Nehru:

> . . . I have been very disturbed by Krishna's handling of the Korean issue. Right from the beginning he has adopted an attitude of extreme secrecy about the whole matter . . . I do not mean to

belittle Krishna's efforts which have been on the highest plane, but I feel time is of the essence and I wished we had shared with friendly Delegations some of our thoughts which so far have been confined to members of the Commonwealth alone . . .

But while he appeared to be giving his own delegation members a troubled time, Krishna Menon's impact at the UN on the efforts to resolve the Korean issue would be almost instantaneous and hugely positive. On 25 June 1950, North Korean forces had crossed the 38th Parallel into South Korea, and the Korean War had begun. Right from the beginning Nehru had been very concerned with the conflict and its broader impacts. Till early 1952, he had involved four people in his efforts at brokering a peace agreement at the UN: Pandit, then Indian's ambassador in the US; Krishna Menon; K.M. Panikkar, India's ambassador in China; and B.N. Rau, India's Permanent Representative at the UN. On his arrival in New York in early October 1952, Krishna Menon plunged into diplomacy— mainly with the UK, Canada and other Commonwealth countries. In a matter of a few days, by 25 October 1952, he had prepared a draft resolution on the most vexing issue then—namely, the treatment of the prisoners of war.

The core of his solution was fairly straightforward—that the UN would, after the Armistice, set up an independent commission to take custody of all prisoners who did not want to be repatriated to their respective countries and thereafter decide upon their final status. This suggestion was backed by the British and Canadians, and even China (which was then not a member of the UN), indicated its support. But it was rejected in strong language by Dean Acheson, the outgoing US secretary of state, on the grounds that it did not settle permanently the fate of the non-repatriate prisoners. It gave, he believed, 'the Communists a ready made pretext for breaching the Armistice'.

Not deterred by Acheson's firm rejection, Krishna Menon worked on his proposals closely with the British and Canadian delegations. Support for his draft resolution gained ground but Acheson was unmoved. Then all of a sudden, what had till then been only under informal discussion became a formal resolution, with

India tabling it on 19 November 1952. The Americans were furious and spread the story that Krishna Menon was a Trojan Horse for the communists.

Four days later it was the turn of the Soviet Union to denounce Krishna Menon. The Soviet foreign minister, Andrei Vyshinsky, accused him of playing the American game. First, he was labelled a communist agent. Now he was being called a stalking horse for the US. Only Krishna Menon could manage to accomplish such a feat in a matter of five days. With Vyshinsky's attack, Acheson changed his stance, praised the statesmanship of Krishna Menon and initiated moves to have his resolution amended to make it acceptable to the Americans. However, Krishna Menon was in a state of shock at Vyshinsky's attack, which was wholly unexpected. He received this letter from Panikkar, now Indian ambassador in Cairo, on 22 November 1952. It would have probably cheered him up—if indeed anything could:

> I have been following with the greatest admiration your valiant efforts to get an agreed formula on the Korean peace talks. Though the proposals are on the same lines as we discussed when you came to Delhi, only your personal influence could have secured for them the support, which has automatically changed the whole posture of affairs. That Eden should have supported it, I could understand, for much of the original proposals were formulated as a result of your discussions with him. That Casey [Australian foreign minister] and the French Delegation should have supported it is indeed an achievement.
>
> From the meagre news one gets from the papers it is not possible to judge what the prospects are of the resolution getting through the political committee. But whether it succeeds or not, you have done something which is of lasting value, because you have really organized world opinion in favour of a constructive proposal.

But thereafter Krishna Menon would be in a foul mood. Nehru sensed this and wrote to Vijaya Lakshmi Pandit on 25 November 1952:

. . . I know Krishna has been difficult . . . What can one do with him? I suppose, now that his resolution is more or less over, he will sulk even more and blame others for it . . .

But Nehru was mistaken. Krishna Menon's resolution got a new lease of life by, of all people, Acheson. Recognizing that the resolution enjoyed wide support, he initiated moves to have it amended to make it more acceptable to the Americans. The amended resolution was adopted by a huge majority on 3 December 1952 but not unexpectedly, the Soviet bloc rejected it and a few days later China followed suit. Krishna Menon took on the role of the martyr and sent a telegram to Nehru on 4 December 1952 saying, ' . . . since there is reason to think I have not given satisfaction I shall be grateful if you will consider what you wish me to do and instruct accordingly.' Three days later Nehru reassured him as only he could by telling Krishna Menon that he had done his utmost and that there was no question of any lack of appreciation for his efforts. Nehru blamed the USSR and its influence on China for stymieing Krishna Menon's efforts. The only thing to do now, Nehru advised Krishna Menon, was 'await developments'.

Years later Acheson would give a detailed account of what happened at the UN in November 1953 in his memoirs.[1] He would refer to 'The Menon Cabal' that comprised of Krishna Menon; Lester Pearson, the Canadian foreign minister; and Selwyn Lloyd, the junior minister in the British foreign office, which had made life difficult for him. He called both Krishna Menon and Pearson 'adroit political operators'. According to Acheson, Anthony Eden, who came on the scene later, also was co-opted into the 'Menon Cabal', which had the support of the Australian foreign minister, R.G. Casey. It was quite an achievement—Krishna Menon had split the Western world and the Americans were naturally furious. But to give Acheson credit, he acknowledged that 'the Menon resolution had become the accepted vehicle of action'.

Pearson, the foreign minister of Canada, was then the president of the UN General Assembly. He maintained a daily diary of events that took place on Korea at the UN in the months of November and

December 1952. It is the most detailed eyewitness account we have from one of the key players. The central character in the diary is Krishna Menon, and Pearson recorded from 27 October 1952 when he first met him:[2]

> The first delegate to approach me . . . was Krishna Menon of India . . . [He] wanted to discuss with me how the Assembly could assist in bringing about an armistice . . . Menon put forward at length ideas which he had previously advanced at a Commonwealth meeting . . . I tried to persuade Menon to put his ideas on paper . . . [and] also encouraged him to keep the lines open to Peking . . .
>
> . . . The Menon draft, as it stands right now, is all right in principle but will need a good deal of careful consideration in detail. There are two points which will particularly worry the Americans . . .
>
> Early Saturday morning (November 8) Krishna Menon phoned me. He was very downcast . . . and feels that the Americans are being obstructive and difficult . . . I did my best to put him in a better frame of mind . . . He reacts warmly to a little praise and encouragement . . . Sunday, November 9. I saw Dean Acheson this morning and went over the Indian proposal, point by point. He was not unsympathetic . . . but would certainly wish to have some changes made to the draft. On Thursday November 13, in the afternoon I met with Selwyn Lloyd and Krishna Menon . . . and we went over Menon's draft with a view to making changes in it which would help meet the American objections. Menon was very reasonable and accepted most of the changes . . .
>
> On Tuesday, November 18, our friend Krishna once again came to see me. He is to speak tomorrow . . . We are worried . . . that he may be too provocative against the Americans. Krishna made his speech this afternoon (November 19) . . . he was objective, unprovocative and, at times, moving.
>
> This afternoon [23 November] . . . Vishinsky, to our great surprise and even before Acheson spoke, damned the Indian resolution all over the lot and was almost as hard on its author . . . Everyone wondered why . . . Possibly because the Indian initiative

is making too much of an impression on Peking . . . Acheson [then] went ahead with his prepared speech . . . Both its praise of Menon himself and its use of Menon's own speeches to prove the necessity for further 'clarifications' to the Indian draft, were bound to make our Indian friend uneasy . . .

Tuesday, November 25 . . . at midnight . . . Lloyd phoned to say that, after a Homeric struggle, he had persuaded Menon to accept amendments . . . Menon, though he may be a difficult person, does not break his word . . . On Monday [1 December], he made his speech . . . Vishinsky then made a vicious assault on what he called the rotten 'Indian compromise'. Afterwards the vote was taken and was unanimous in favour of the Indian resolution . . . the Plenary [session of the General Assembly] (December 3) went through smoothly and the resolution, after a good enough speech by Menon, was adopted by 54 in favour, 1 abstention and 5 against.

But four and half years later Pearson became a critic of Krishna Menon and would write to his high commissioner in India, Escott Reid, on 8 March 1957:[3]

His [Krishna Menon's] usefulness to the cause of good international relations has, as far as I am concerned, disappeared. I recognize at times he can be most helpful and conciliatory, as he was, for instance over Cyprus but on the whole he is a bad person to have at the United Nations as the spokesman, not only of India but on many occasions of Asia. The contrast between his moral lectures to us about the Middle East, his wavering on Hungary, and his tough realistic approach to Kashmir was too glaring to do anything but detract from India's reputation.

Casey, who had been governor of Bengal during 1944–46, also maintained a diary when he was foreign minister of Australia. There are many references to Krishna Menon in it showing the friendship that had been struck between two ideological opposites.[4] Casey's observations are worth quoting at some length since they reveal much of Krishna Menon:

2 November [1952]

I wanted to talk to Krishna Menon for the purpose of (1) trying to get to know more about him politically, and (2) discovering what his mind was on the Korean problem. I had to listen to twenty minutes mixture of law and philosophy which sounded as if it was pretty clever if I'd had the slightest inkling as to what it was all about, which I hadn't. However, from some past talks with him, I realised that he usually rolled the pitch like that and then got down to something that you could understand . . . His idea . . . is that the prisoners of war (on *both* sides) should be taken to a neutral place and be taken over by four 'neutrals' (say Poland, Czechoslovakia, Switzerland and Sweden) who would try to induce them to return to their own countries . . .

6 November [1952]

Krishna Menon is turning out to be, on occasion, a very useful fellow. He's a strange individual, lots of brains, and with enough of a foot in the other camp [the Soviet side] to be useful . . .

12 November [1952]

In the course of a half-hour talk . . . he [Krishna Menon] went on to say that he had drafted the resolution for India to become a Republic.

18 September [1953]

I hear that in his heart of hearts Krishna Menon is a great supporter of the Commonwealth.

12 June (Geneva) [1954]

Krishna Menon came to see me at 9 p.m. I asked him if India would fight if *she* were the subject of Communist aggression. He said (with a little heat) that India *would* resist . . .

In the course of this talk with Krishna, he threw into the ring his belief that Australia would be wise, in her own interests, to adopt a quota system of immigration for Asian peoples, as Canada has done . . . I said that it had not achieved much in Canada, as very few Indians applied for places in the quota. Krishna said that the fact that very few Indians wanted to go to Canada permanently was not the point . . . The important thing was that the Canadian quota system of immigration had greatly improved the Indian attitude towards Canada which was much better than the Indian attitude towards Australia.

2 July [1954]

Krishna Menon and I sat on a sofa for half an hour and had one of our usual talks. Stimulated by a pint of orange juice, he said that his belief was that the United States was out to dominate the world, which I said was more completely unreal than anything I had yet heard him say. He added that he was convinced that Britain was the only country at all adequately equipped for world leadership . . .

Krishna Menon would turn out to be right about the US but hopelessly wrong about Britain, whose decline as a global power would begin a few years hence with its misadventure on the Suez Canal. Krishna Menon would come to be intensely disliked by much of the British establishment for his role in resolving the Suez crisis.

1953

Mountbatten had just been promoted, and Krishna Menon was among the first to congratulate him warmly. The former viceroy replied on 3 February 1953:

Thank you very much for your very nice letter congratulating me on my promotion to Admiral. I have been wearing this uniform on and off in an acting capacity ever since 1943 and am glad that their Lordships at the Admiralty have at last made an honest man of me after ten years! . . .

I read the accounts in the *Times* of your doings with the UNO
with great interest. You seem to have done a very fine job there
and I am so glad that you took it . . .

Korea had raised Krishna Menon's global profile. But even when
he ought to have been happy with what he had accomplished on
Korea in a matter of two to three months, he donned the role of
a grievously wounded soldier and berated Nehru on 12 February
1953:

> . . . [I]t is a fact that often times and far oftener than I like I feel
> almost at the end of my emotional and mental tether in regard to
> what I feel has, and in fact appears to have, come between us . . .
> Ours was not a relationship which is very usual and was sustained
> by ourselves alone . . . I have written to you because I know great
> realities subsist . . .

Vijaya Lakshmi Pandit had been telling her brother about the
problems Krishna Menon was causing her and the delegation by his
secretive, whimsical and conspiratorial style of functioning. Five
days later, Nehru reassured him as he always did, patiently and
sensitively:

> . . . I tried to read [your letter] more than once trying to understand
> what ails you. I realize of course that you wrote in some distress
> of mind and that you feel unhappy. You ask me what has come
> between us. I am not aware of anything having come between us in
> any real sense. I have the same affection and regard for you as I have
> ever had. Sometimes I do not understand or like what you might
> say or do. That happens with everyone. With our most intimate
> friends we have moments of distance or lack of understanding.
> That moment passes and the basic feeling remains. Does anyone
> know or understand another fully? It does not matter very much if
> one dislikes or distrusts. The real thing is basic affection and respect
> and a belief in the integrity of each other. Nothing has happened
> to shake that as far as I am concerned.

I was happy to have you here and loved the talks we had. I was glad to know that there was a possibility of your coming to India for good, for I wanted you not to be far from me.

So, please do not imagine that [which] is not there and do not distress yourself about it.

He was being reassured not just by Nehru but also by Indira Gandhi, who wrote to her father on 11 May 1953 from London:

. . . I have seen Krishna Menon several times; he comes to all my functions and I have had lunch & dinner with him. He seems to be remarkably fit and cheerful.

Indira Gandhi was visiting the UK then and wrote again to Nehru six days later:

. . . To go back to Krishna, I know he is quite moody & extremely irksome but he does have a brain and a keen awareness of the world situation. Agatha [Harrison] is quite dazzled by the way he handled the U.N. She says everyone was full of admiration and it was a truly wonderful bit of work. She says she knows that Krishna had a great deal to do with the tone of Attlee's speech [on Korea in the House of Commons] and even indirectly of Churchill's . . . If Krishna leaves London, we will lose touch with the centre of things and will sink to our former position of running behind & trying to catch on . . .

Krishna Menon was indeed about to leave London for good after twenty-nine years of residence there. He had been thinking of a political career back home. On 18 February 1953, he quite brazenly asked Nehru to make him a minister without portfolio in his cabinet. Nehru was not keen and offered him the vice-chancellorship of Delhi University, a prestigious post that Krishna Menon turned down 'huffily'. Then when a vacancy in the Rajya Sabha opened up with the death of N. Gopalaswami Ayyangar in early February 1953, Krishna Menon put forward his own name

to Nehru as a replacement on 1 March 1953. The Prime Minister
replied nine days later:

> . . . You refer to Rajaji being able to find a seat for you in the
> Council of States. Rajaji was here the other day and I mentioned
> this to him. If it is possible, he will probably do so . . .

Then sometime in mid-May 1953, when he was back in London
after spending time at the UN, Krishna Menon received a cable from
M.O. Mathai:

> Rajaji desires to know whether you would like to be elected to the
> Council of States in an existing vacancy in Madras. Apparently he
> discussed the matter with you when you visited Madras. Please let
> me know what reply I should send Rajaji on your behalf.

Rajaji was quite taken up with Krishna Menon, even though
ideologically they were poles apart. On 30 November 1950, when
he was still governor-general, Rajaji had written to Krishna Menon:

> Would you forgive my impertinence if I express my very deep
> appreciation of the manner in which you have worked at the
> Nepal problem. My admiration was expressed to Jawaharlalji but I
> felt I must write to you also . . .

Krishna Menon accepted Rajaji's offer to fill the Rajya Sabha
vacancy, and immediately, speculation started that he was going to
join Nehru's cabinet. But his nomination also came under severe
attack from several people. H.V. Kamath, who had been a member
the Constituent Assembly and a follower of Subhas Bose, issued a
stinging statement on 10 May 1953 saying that Krishna Menon's five-
year tenure as the high commissioner in London was a 'sorry tale of
incompetence, extravagance and criminal waste of national resources'
and that his record was 'an unredeemed and ignominious failure'. He
feared that Krishna Menon would soon 'not only become an MP but
also a full-fledged minister' and when that happened Nehru would

have 'cocked a snook at Parliament and contemptuously driven another nail in the coffin of Parliamentary democracy'. Kamath was right only on one count. Nehru did, in fact, want to bring him into the cabinet. On 30 May 1953, Krishna Menon's niece Madhavi wrote to him:

> . . . You know you have been elected to the Council of States. They say Pandit Nehru is very eager to get you into the Cabinet. But I do not feel you will be happy there. C.D. Deshmukh and others are not very fond of you and there will be a lot of jealousies. Why do people dislike those who are not even remotely interested in them, I wonder? Everyone dislikes everyone out here . . .

In fact it was not the finance minister, C.D. Deshmukh, who would oppose Krishna Menon's entry into the cabinet. Only one man really put his foot down, and this was Maulana Azad, the education minister who held Krishna Menon substantially responsible for changing Nehru's mind on the Partition in 1947.

In the meantime, things had begun to change dramatically on the Korean situation. The death of Stalin on 5 March 1953 led to a complete rethink on the part of the Soviets and the Chinese, and it now appeared that the core of Krishna Menon's proposals was acceptable to them. The US had a new administration too, with Eisenhower having become President earlier in January 1953. Krishna Menon came up with a fresh draft while the Americans prepared their version that was not radically different from the Indian draft, marking a distinct departure from the Truman–Acheson line. The two drafts got merged and thereafter, Brazil sponsored the Indian–American draft resolution, a smart move that led to the Soviet bloc giving up its objections and agreeing to it. The resolution passed unanimously on 16 April 1953, the first time in three years that the UN had achieved unanimity on the Korean issue. Events moved quickly thereafter, with the new Eisenhower administration as well as the Soviet bloc demonstrating flexibility. The Korean Armistice Agreement was finally signed on 27 July 1953.

Much has been written on the Korean war, and it continues to evoke considerable academic interest. The most recent scholarly analysis comes to the following conclusion:[5]

> During the first half of 1953, the necessary conditions to end the Korean War were established with Eisenhower's election and Stalin's death. But these developments alone were not sufficient to end the fighting, since the solution to the outstanding prisoners of war question still had to be agreed. For that reason the Indian resolution provided the essential means to end the Korean War since its terms eventually proved acceptable to both sides. India's most important role in bringing the conflict to an end had thus taken place back in the autumn of 1952. Even so, India did further facilitate the signing of the Armistice Agreement in the spring of 1953. Nehru, acting through Menon, showed great patience and foresight resisting the temptation to push for further UN action and instead placed his trust in the negotiators at Panmunjom. New Delhi then pressed both sides to move ever-closer to the Indian resolution . . . India must be given the credit for nudging along the process toward peace.

Following the Armistice Agreement, in October 1953, a Neutral Nations Repatriation Commission (NNRC) was set up—with Poland and Czechoslovakia representing the Soviet bloc, and Sweden and Switzerland representing the Western bloc. India was appointed its chairman. The NNRC had been Krishna Menon's original idea. It was mandated to decide on the fate of some 2000 prisoners of war. A custodian force was also established, and this was to be provided by India. Nehru appointed Lt General K.S. Thimayya as the NNRC chairman, and Thimayya, in turn, selected Major General S.S.P. Thorat as the head of the custodian force. Thimayya was to gain huge encomiums for his role as chairman, although he was seen by one of his political advisers as too ready to please the Americans.[6] Four years later, Krishna Menon, as defence minister, would have much to do with General Thimayya and Lt General Thorat—the two top men in the Indian Army—and his confrontation with this duo would have disastrous consequences—not only for himself and them but also for Nehru and India.

While he was running around at the UN trying to work out a lasting solution to the Korean issue, Krishna Menon received a telegram marked 'Important' from Nehru on 6 April 1953. It read:

> French Ambassador here has protested about a report of an interview appearing in the French magazine called Information dated April 1 in which you are alleged to have criticised France for many of its policies in Europe and elsewhere which were inspired by a spirit of war. Further, that Catholicism is leading a crusade against communism and that France must withdraw its troops from Indo-China. Could you please let us have the particulars about alleged interview so that we can reply to French Ambassador.

Krishna Menon's reply was almost instantaneous:

> I have given NO interview to French magazine 'Information' and have heard of its name only from your telegram. Have made NO statements about Catholicism and Communism . . . The only reference that could possibly be construed as my having referred to Indo-China could be that in answer to question at Wisconsin University, Madison [in the US] about India's view and relation to Indo-China, I said that . . . India hoped for peaceful settlements of armed conflicts and the withdrawal of foreign troops . . .

Dr M.S. Swaminathan, one of the key architects of India's Green Revolution in the sixties and seventies, was then a student at the University of Wisconsin. He was in the audience when Krishna Menon spoke there. He recalled to me that he still remembered an exchange between a woman, who was critical of India's position on Korea, and Krishna Menon. As she sat down after her comments, Krishna Menon replied, 'Madam, you have one great gift that I do not have on this subject and that is the gift of ignorance!'

Later in the year Krishna Menon got a leg up when Vijaya Lakshmi Pandit became the president of the UN General Assembly.

This was a prestigious post that rotated among countries annually. She became the first woman president and was just the eighth person to occupy this position. Her appointment was a reflection of Nehru's huge personal standing in the world community. Krishna Menon took over from her as head of the Indian delegation to the UN. He had first spoken at the UN on 12 December 1946, and it was on Franco's Spain. He had drawn from his involvement with the issue of Spain from the mid-1930s. Thereafter, he had spoken on Tibet on 21 October 1951 and on Korea on four occasions between 19 November 1952 and 28 August 1953. He debuted as a speaker on 28 September 1953, as leader of the Indian delegation. He started off with words of praise for someone who had confessed to being tormented by him:

> It is my happy privilege to offer Mrs. Pandit the felicitations of our delegation and our country on this happy occasion when she is presiding over the deliberations of this Assembly during this year. While we are sad that we should be deprived of her wise guidance and counsel from within the ranks of our delegation, we are happy that she has been offered this greater opportunity of service to the world community. It is a tribute that this Assembly has paid to her person, to our country and to the womanhood of India and of the world in general. The Assembly stands to profit by her wise guidance and by her genial personality.

Then he went on to tackle issues that were to resonate at the UN over the years; calling for summits between the US and the USSR, China's entry into the global body, expanding UN membership to include countries like Japan, accelerating decolonization in Africa and elsewhere, ending apartheid in South and South-West Africa, permanent peace in Korea and Indo-China, complete nuclear disarmament and development assistance for the poorer countries. After this tour d' horizon, he ended thus:

> Therefore, under the President's guidance we shall go forward with faith and determination, relying upon the collective wisdom of us

all to achieve solutions, or the beginning of such solutions, which we can render possible in the context in which we help to shape events, so that, as Dante said, 'On this little plot of earth belonging to man, life may pass in freedom and with peace'.

Of his UN speeches, it was to be later said by R. Venkataraman, who was part of India's delegation to the UN along with Krishna Menon for many years and who later became the President of India:[7]

> Krishna Menon was like a seismograph in the United Nations, vibrating to every fluctuation in world affairs and registering India's reactions to each one of them. There was such a thing as a Menon Scale which, like Richter's, recorded vibrations of different intensity depending on the gravity of the tremor. And so Krishna Menon at the U.N. was capable of cautioning, warning and exposing every specious move on the part of the Big Powers . . . His speeches were blunt. But, not surprisingly in a student of Harold Laski, they possessed an extraordinary sophistication. Totally free from all clichés and from the polemical jargon that characterises such statements, Krishna Menon's speeches were an intellectual repast. Studded with quotations from the early classicists such as Dante and Voltaire, they also refreshed his audience's memories of statements made by Lincoln, Jefferson and William James.

Fortunately for posterity, five volumes of these approximately hundred speeches delivered over a period of a decade were to be published in the mid-1990s. The speeches were 'a prodigious exercise in prepared extemporisation'.[8] They reveal much not only of the man but also of India's approach to regional and global issues of peace, security and development. They show how, ahead of his times, Krishna Menon was and also to provide a partial explanation of why Krishna Menon came to be detested so much in the West. His personality quirks apart, what he was saying was an anathema to the ruling establishments in the Western world at that time. Here was a man from a newly independent country telling the major powers of the world what they should be doing and how the world should be structured.

Krishna Menon believed that with Vijaya Lakshmi Pandit's appointment as president of the UN General Assembly, she should maintain an 'arm's length' relationship with the Indian delegation to maintain her impartiality. But she had other ideas and insisted on being involved in every detail of the delegation's functioning. She wrote to Nehru on 26 October 1953 complaining about Krishna Menon:

> . . . You have not seen Krishna Menon in action so it is a little difficult to describe how he invests the simplest matter with an aura of mystery. He works tensely and at a high emotional pitch and the popular picture of him is of a man driven by a sense of overpowering urgency rushing between delegations and trying to unravel all knots at the same time. This combined with his constant reiteration about being the Prime Minister's personal representative acting only on orders has given the impression that he speaks for you personally and what he says is what he has been instructed to say. I am being asked why he does not have the permission to act on his own discretion like other leaders and if he is actually relaying Nehru's personal views. All these things give those who wish to distort our actions a good enough opening—and they use it.

Vijaya Lakshmi Pandit felt that Krishna Menon did not think much of her intellectually. She went on to write:

> . . . I believe he quite honestly does not think me capable of handling matters of high policy etc . . . I do not now speak to Krishna on any important matter. I see him very seldom . . .

A hassled Nehru replied on 4 November 1953:

> It seems to me, whether in Delhi or elsewhere, that by far the best part of my time is taken up reconciling people or in soothing them when they get baffled with each other . . . I do not know if in other countries people are continually faced with these difficulties of individuals behaving too individualistically. In the Soviet Union,

I suppose, when this happens they are liquidated . . . Krishna, as you well know, is a person who function in a highly individualistic way and wants to keep all the strings in his own hand . . . All I can do is bring these matters gently to Krishna's notice . . . Oddly enough, Casey [Australian foreign minister], who was here some days ago, spoke to me about Krishna and said that Krishna had greatly toned down and improved in this session of the UN and was doing a good job of work. It may be that this was just meant to please me . . .

Vijaya Lakshmi Pandit was to become high commissioner to the UK in March 1955. Even after that, she just could not shake off the long shadow of Krishna Menon and complained to her brother that his friends in London were trying to discredit her. Nehru would write to her on 10 February 1957, providing a very candid appraisal of his friend:

> . . . I have known Krishna Menon now for a long time and have a fairly good appreciation of his abilities, virtues and failings. All these are considerable. I do not know if it is possible by straight approach to lessen these failings. I have tried to do and shall continue to try. This is a psychological problem of some difficulty and has to be dealt with, if at all successfully, by indirect methods. I propose to deal with it both directly and indirectly.
>
> I hope I have the capacity to judge people and events more or less objectively. I am not swept away by Krishna . . . Krishna has often embarrassed me and put me in considerable difficulties. If I speak to him, he has an emotional break-down. He is always on the verge of some such nervous collapse. The only thing that keeps him going is hard work. There is hardly a person of any importance against whom he has not complained to me at some time or other. Later, he has found out that his opinion was wrong and he has changed it . . .

The year 1953 was not all about Korea and seeking a political role at home. Krishna Menon also waded into economic policy. Conscious perhaps of his educational qualifications in economics from the LSE, Krishna Menon would, from time to time, send his ideas on the subject to Nehru. On 12 April 1953, he sent the Prime Minister an analysis of what he felt was going wrong with India's economic policy. He was very critical of the increasing reliance on foreign aid and of the finance minister's statement that the Indian economy depended crucially on assistance from the US. He feared that this would erode India's independence, and in a scathing indictment he wrote:

> . . . In 1947 India had considerable assets; the position is different today . . . we have now placed ourselves in the position where dependence (and all that follows) is now part of our long-term plan. Therefore, the basic approach and policy must change if we are to retain our independence . . . The present (having to look to United States aid, and other similar positions) is no sudden development: it is the inevitable consequence of a policy that does not base itself on the people, the internal resources of the country and thinks of fiscal and economic matters in terms that are not sufficiently related to the vast expectations of the people and the conditions of a politically enfranchised and liberated people.

Krishna Menon did not offer any specific suggestions for change, and not surprisingly, Nehru chided him gently on 24 April 1953:

> . . . You repeatedly warn me of danger and suggest a complete reversal of what we do. I do not quite know how you expect me to reverse everything . . . I cannot function in isolation. I can, I believe, give a trend to events in a particular direction and even carry people with me. The advice you have often given me is not precise and you seem to indicate that the only worthwhile thing to do is to reverse engines completely. It is not even clear to me how this is to be done.

By the latter half of 1953, Krishna Menon had become somewhat of a sensation across the world, including in the US, particularly for his performance at the UN. Two letters he received from people he did not even know remotely reflected his newfound popularity. A young woman Marilyn Mascara wrote on 25 August 1953 from Long Island, New York:

> I listened to your fine speech today and would like you to know (unimportant though my opinion may be) I have the utmost respect and admiration for you and your people . . . I've never been abroad. I only know what I've read about India as a country . . . Though our nationalities differ; our religions are unlike; our social and educational backgrounds are uncomparable; yet your combined (humble but proud and courageous) love of peace . . . seems synonymous with my own . . .

And a few months later on 1 November 1953, a student at the Harvard Law School who later became a noted legal personality— Lawrence Albert Spector—wrote to him very sheepishly from Cambridge, Massachusetts:

> A combination of your modesty and my naiveté prevented me from knowing just who the Indian gentleman was on the plane trip from New York to Boston today whom I talked to. I even asked him to spell out his name for me! For this I have paid the utmost farthing. Most of my dormitory roommates were in my room this evening as I came home. I asked one the question, 'Who is Krishna Menon?'. My roommates are still laughing at me. I do beg your pardon for my ignorance and possible impertinence during our conversation. I can only say that at the law school one has time only for studies and seldom time for the newspapers. But this is no escape hatch for me . . . The only possible positive result from this is that I have resolved to become the world's foremost authority on the Indian Delegation to the United Nations in one month, and to particularly review all available information on one Mr. Krishna Menon, a very modest and kind gentleman . . .

Spector had been so embarrassed by his gaffe that he soon went to New York to meet with Krishna Menon and other members of the Indian

delegation to the UN. On 10 December 1953, another unknown
American called Sylvia Hollander wrote to him from the Bronx in
New York:

> It is with great humility and a sense of gratitude that I write to
> express how deeply moved both my husband and myself were by
> your appearance last week on Ed Murrow's television programme.
> Not only were we stirred by your eloquence, but the sentiments
> which you expressed echoed our own feelings . . . It is rare indeed,
> in these perplexing times, to hear an individual whose profound
> thoughts ring with the clarity of honesty and heartfelt emotion.
> Just as you do, we most firmly believe that in the ultimate success
> of the United Nations . . . Thank you again for the very interesting
> respite you're appearance offered to us and countless others who
> were fortunate enough to see you.

Ed Murrow would soon make a key contribution to ending the McCarthy
era in the US and would always retain the admiration of Krishna Menon.

1954

On 24 April 1954, Nehru made a statement in Parliament on the
situation prevailing in Indo-China. He suggested a six-point formula
for peace in Vietnam, Laos and Cambodia. Nehru's statement was
somewhat unique in the sense that it was one of the very few he read
from that he had not drafted himself. This was Krishna Menon's draft
as the American ambassador in India. George V. Allen noted in his
cable back home on 25 April 1954:

> Krishna Menon, who drafted Nehru's statement on Indo-China,
> says first half is for domestic and South Asian consumption and that
> Western Powers need concern themselves only with the second
> half . . . Only difference between Indian proposal and American,
> he says, is that under Nehru concept, China and Russia should
> join with US and UK in guaranteeing non-intervention. This
> would result, he believes, in more or less neutralizing Indo-China

and create [a] buffer zone to prevent any further Chinese expansion towards South Asia and India.

Two days later an international conference began in Geneva to discuss the Korean issue. Nineteen countries were represented at the conference to which India was not invited. A second phase of the conference was to deal with Indo-China, for which the participants had yet to be finalized. On 28 April 1954, Nehru, accompanied by Krishna Menon, went to Colombo for a 'mini summit' of Asian premiers involving those of Burma, Ceylon, India, Indonesia and Pakistan. The conference was able to pass a resolution unanimously, based almost wholly on Nehru's six-point formula that called for an end to the intervention of foreign powers in Indo-China.

At Geneva, the US secretary of state, John Foster Dulles, met with the British foreign secretary, Antony Eden, and the French foreign minister, George Bidault, on 1 May 1954. Part of the discussion was on who should chair the Indo-China phase of the conference and who should be invited. According to the American record of this meeting:

> . . . Regarding chairmanship, Mr. Bidault hazarded that Molotov might propose an Indian chairman, and would probably have in mind Krishna Menon . . . After some discussion, it was agreed that India would be very unsuitable under any circumstances, although Mr. Bidault said that Madame Pandit would not make a bad chairman, if it was to be an Indian. However, he reiterated that India would be unsuitable . . .
>
> . . . The Secretary [Dulles] said that while we recognized that France had primary responsibility in connection with the Indo-China discussions, the US would find it very difficult to accept an Indian chairman such as Krishna Menon.

These three then decided to have nine participants—US, USSR, UK, France, China, Vietnam, Laos, Cambodia and the Viet Minh. After further conversations, Eden and Molotov were designated co-chairs. This Indo-China phase of the Geneva conference began on 8 May 1954.

As the Geneva talks meandered along, Krishna Menon left for New York to attend some meetings at the UN on 11 May 1952. He stopped off at Cairo for talks with President Nasser and the Egyptian Prime Minister. While he was in Cairo he got a message from Eden to see him in Paris. The two spent some three hours together the next day and the discussion was exclusively on the ongoing Geneva conference. Eden and Nehru had been in touch about the progress being made at the talks, which had not amounted to anything so far. Eden believed that the Colombo declaration offered a useful framework for breaking the deadlock at Geneva. Eden must have sounded out Nehru about Krishna Menon, or Nehru may have mentioned Krishna Menon. Whatever the precise detail, it is clear that Eden was happy to have Krishna Menon's presence at the conference but only for the part that was concerned with Indo-China.

On 23 May 1954, Krishna Menon landed in Geneva and was welcomed by Horace Alexander and Agatha Harrison, his old Quaker friends from England, who were in Geneva as peace activists and campaigners. Also present was his colleague from the India League years of the 1930s—K.S. Shelvankar. Shelvankar was then the London correspondent of *The Hindu* and was covering the Geneva conference for the newspaper. He would report on every detail of what Krishna Menon did over the next six weeks as he flew in and out of Geneva. Shelvankar's reports were obviously based on briefings by Krishna Menon, and through him, Shelvankar was also able to get access to other political personalities who were attending. More than anything else, Shelvankar's dispatches provide a clear picture of whom Krishna Menon was meeting. These dispatches are important because, as was his wont, Krishna Menon kept no records of his conversations at Geneva.

As soon as he landed, Krishna Menon got into a three-hour tête-à-tête with the Chinese Prime Minister, Chou En-lai. This was the very first time the two were meeting. They would meet frequently in Geneva over the next few weeks, and a year later Chou would host Krishna Menon in China for ten days. Thereafter, they would meet a couple of times in New Delhi in April 1960. We don't know what the Chinese premier thought of Krishna Menon other than his 'my good friend' description to Nehru in one of their conversations.

After his first extended conversation with Chou, Krishna Menon met with Molotov and Bidault the same day. Forty-eight hours later he spoke with the head of the American delegation, Dulles's deputy Bedell Smith, who prepared this summary of their talk:

(a) The conference should reach agreement on Korea, if only agreement in principle that Korea should be united and an agreement to disagree . . .

(b) Agreement could be reached on Indo-China. He estimated Chou En-lai as a man 'with whom one could do business' and Molotov as 'quite different and much improved'.

(c) There should not be a partition in Indo-China [meaning Vietnam] . . .

(d) It is unrealistic that all military problems can be settled without some corresponding political settlements . . .

(e) I asked (because I knew) what his ideas were about a supervisory authority. He said that to be effective it would have to be accepted by all five major participants. India, if agreed by all and requested to do so, would probably accept the responsibility along with some European nation . . .

There were reports that by early June 1954 the French were particularly optimistic about a ceasefire in China. On 2 June 1954, the French cabinet met, and the deputy foreign minister, Maurice Schumann, briefed it on what was taking place in Geneva. He 'stressed the mediating role of India's Mr. V.K. Krishna Menon and commended his efforts to conciliate the conflicting views of the Western and Eastern delegations'.[9] Jean Rubattel wrote in the *La Nouvelle Revue*, Lausanne, on 5 June 1954:

This diplomat [Krishna Menon] . . . has had a series of interviews with the Chiefs of all delegations. His mission can be described as a quest for information . . . Mr. Menon has done more. His arrival coincided with a certain slowing down in the Geneva discussions. Within a single week he met Mr. Chou En-lai four times, Mr. Bedell Smith twice, Mr. Eden several times and Mr. Molotov. He lunched with Mr. Bidault, talked to the Vietminh leaders and met the Vietnamese. By the very force of things, he has acted as a sort of courier, a means of transmitting suggestions. Whatever the delegates did not want to say openly or whatever they wanted to keep beyond the limits of a definite proposal was passed on to Mr. Menon. It is indeed a remarkable task that is being carried out by this Indian statesman whom every Minister listened to with the gravest attention.

By mid-June 1954, the conference on Korea had collapsed and the one on Indo-China had to be adjourned because of the fall of the French government. On 14 June 1954, Shelvankar sent this dispatch:

. . . Mr. Krishna Menon is leaving today after nearly three weeks of intensive diplomatic activity. While he has met and had talks with leaders of all the delegations at the Indo-China conference, no two of the principal personalities at Geneva have perhaps had such prolonged talks together as he has had with Chou En-lai. He saw the Chinese Prime Minister no less than nine times and on an average each talk lasted nearly three hours. His contacts with Mr. Eden have also been particularly close and continuous. One positive gain from all this activity might well be a clearer appreciation by all Governments concerned of the importance of India and India's role in the settlement of Asian problems . . .

The conference adjourned on 20 June 1954. Soon thereafter Chou decided to break his journey in New Delhi on his way back home from Geneva. He was in New Delhi on 25 and 26 June for talks with Nehru on mostly the progress made at Geneva. Before leaving for New Delhi on a special aircraft sent by Nehru, Chou spoke exclusively to Shelvankar, the only interview he would grant during his entire time in Geneva. The Chinese leader admitted that the progress of the conference on the Indo-China question had been 'rather slow' but hoped that, over the next three weeks, a breakthrough would be effected. For his part, Krishna Menon became a frequent flier and went off to

London and New York, finding time to be in Glasgow in between to collect an honorary doctorate from the university there. The citation referred to him as 'an honest broker between East and West'.

Krishna Menon was back in Geneva on 11 July 1954 to resume his 'behind the scene' talks. Bidault, meanwhile, had been replaced by Pierre Mendes France. France and Krishna Menon quickly established a rapport with him. The delegations of Vietnam, Laos and Cambodia were lukewarm about Krishna Menon but he and Pham Van Dong, who was representing the Viet Minh, hit it off well. Shelvankar too got to know him, and this stood him in good stead when he was appointed India's consul general in Hanoi fifteen years later. On 13 July 1954, Alexis Johnson recorded his conversation with Nehru's special representative:

> . . . He [Krishna Menon] talked at some length on Viet Minh, who while undoubtedly Communist, were also nationalists and seriously desired to maintain [a] relationship with [the] French. He said that they would not be puppets of Moscow or the Chinese and that in normal course of events they would constitute a more or less 'neutral' group such as India, although they would be oriented towards Communists while India is oriented toward West.

On 20 July 1954, it was officially announced from Geneva that the Indo–China peace agreement was to be signed that night, bringing to a successful end the conference that had begun seventy-three days earlier. The Press Trust of India put out this report from Geneva:

> Mr. V.K. Krishna Menon's efforts as much as the anxiety of both sides laid the foundations for an Indo–China peace, said conference circles here tonight. But Mr. Menon, Mr. Nehru's personal envoy, asked of his role in the talks told a correspondent, 'I am an old fool. I am here only as a tourist; just a bystander. If people ask to see me or come and see me, well that's very nice'. It was acknowledged by both sides that it was Mr. Menon who brought them face to face in private conversations in the first phase of the conference and again now in the final phase of the talks he helped clear up

misunderstandings and impressed on each side to take into account the difficulties of the other. It is regarded here as significant that Mr. Bedell-Smith, US Under-Secretary of State lunched with Mr. Menon yesterday, shortly before Mr. Smith clarified the US attitude to the secret plenary session of the conference.

The final agreements arrived at in Geneva were based substantially on both the Colombo resolution and Nehru's six-point formula drafted by Krishna Menon. In that sense, he could be considered one of the architects of the agreements. One scholar[10] has described the final hours at Geneva thus:

Pierre Mendes France and Pham Van Dong occupied the starring roles, with Zhou, Eden and Molotov also seizing the spotlight. India's foreign minister Krishna Menon was a Zelig-like figure in these final hours always there in the background, ready to supply a supportive nod of the head or word of encouragement.

A Manchester Guardian *cartoon on the race to have an accord on Indo-China at Geneva. Mendes France is in the lead, followed by Krishna Menon and Pham Van Dong, July 1954.*

A critical outcome of this conference was the establishment of three 'International Commissions in each of the three countries [Cambodia, Laos and Vietnam] for control and supervision of the applications of the provisions of the agreement on the cessation of hostilities in Indo-China'. It was a measure of Nehru's personal prestige and Krishna Menon's indefatigable diplomacy in Geneva that India was unanimously nominated to be its chairman, with Poland and Canada to be its other two members.

Pierre Mendes France would pay tribute to Krishna Menon while speaking in the French National Assembly on 23 July 1954, in which he described the Geneva conference as 'this ten-power conference— the nine at the table—and India'. Three years later, however, Krishna Menon would antagonize the French by his fiery speeches at the UN on 22 February 1957 and 4 December 1957, calling for the complete independence of Algeria. On one of these occasions, he would have an argument with the French delegate who said Algeria was the domestic question of France since it was a part of Metropolitan France and Algerians were Frenchmen. Krishna Menon's retort would be: 'British colonized us, discriminated against us and humiliated us but they spared us the indignity of calling us Englishmen!'

Krishna Menon and Eden had worked constructively together to help substantially resolve the crisis in the Korean peninsula in late 1952 and early 1953. Now they had collaborated to bring about a peace agreement in Indo-China. It was an unlikely pairing because Eden was an arch-Tory, an acolyte of Churchill. But the two had partnered very well. However, two years later, they would have a bitter disagreement over Britain's role in the Suez Canal crisis, which would lead to Eden's resignation in early January 1957. On 9 January 1957, Krishna Menon would issue a statement from New York:

> I am sorry to hear that Sir Anthony Eden has had to resign on account of ill-health. I have had the privilege of his friendship and I can never forget the great contribution and initiative he had shown in avoiding what would have become a world war in Indo-China and the part he took in the settlement . . .

It was also during the conference that Agatha Harrison passed away in Geneva on 10 May 1954. She was there as an independent observer. Krishna Menon had known her for over two decades, and although their friendship had its rocky moments, there is no doubt that she was not only fond of him but also very proud of his accomplishments post-1947. He broke journey in London on his way from Geneva to New York to speak at a public function in her honour, where he hailed her as 'a great and good person who sought no office or title for herself'.

As he was basking in the glory of Geneva, the issue of the defence contracts for which Krishna Menon had been pilloried so much resurfaced. Nehru wrote to him on 19 June 1954:

> . . . The subject of my letter is an unpleasant one which somehow pursues us in spite of our efforts to be done with it.
>
> This is the jeep contract and the various disputes in connection with it between the Government of India and Sir James Marshall Cornwall & Partners. The present position apparently is that there are claims and counter-claims . . . We have been advised that we should take out a writ against the company in respect of damages for non-delivery of jeeps . . . It is the contention of Sir James Marshall Cornwall & Partners that at the time they agreed to enter into the contract for the supply of jeeps, 'there were other agreements not therein incorporated but which formed part of the consideration of the contract . . .' The reference is particularly to an alleged assurance to give a contract to the company for the supply of jeep spares.
>
> To meet this case . . . our lawyer has stated as follows:
>
> A statement from him (i.e. Mr. Krishna Menon) must be available and it is not really possible to decide whether the proceedings can be prosecuted with any hope of success until such a statement has been obtained . . .
>
> Will you please let me know what you advise us we should do in this matter . . .

The dispute was not on one but three contracts, as Krishna Menon was informed a day later by Nehru:

1. The first contract was for the supply of 1007 jeeps . . . Only 50 jeeps have been supplied [this is what Nehru had referred to].

2. The second contract was for the supply of ammunition. The ammunition has been supplied and payments made. The Company has, however made a further claim for 9000 pounds for certain extras which it claims is due to it under the terms of the contract.

3. The third contract was for the supply of grenades. Here also the goods have been supplied and the payments made but, as in the second case, the Company is claiming an additional sum of 5000 pounds.

Krishna Menon, who was by then in New York, replied to Nehru twice on the same day—4 July 1954. The first of these letters was a 'My dear Jawaharlal', 'For Himself' one in which he supported the issue of a writ against the British company and told Nehru:

The lawyers in London may, therefore, be informed that Krishna Menon has given no assurances as alleged, and that he could not have given any such, and further that we stand by the written agreements.

The issue for you to consider is also whether the Head of a Mission either during office or subsequently is to be subjected to the legal proceedings in the Court of another government. Further what is the position of the person concerned in regard to diplomatic proprieties and his status as a citizen of India?

The purpose of these proceedings is not to reimburse the Government or to see that Government's rights are vindicated but to pursue me with one thing or another in the hope that it will destroy me. I have no objection. I would like a little notice of this as I should perhaps see if any lawyer friends of mine will help me out in the protection of my own interests in Court.

I am most anxious that this matter does not cause you any embarrassment. I do not seek any special treatment . . .

The second of the letters was a 'My dear Prime Minister' one and more official-sounding, in which he told Nehru that he had no authority to make oral agreements. He added:

> All agreements entered into by the Government of India with parties are governed by the conditions set out in respect of such agreements, which are made available to intending suppliers, and parties are precluded, so far as I am aware, from entertaining or being bound by other terms. Therefore, no question of undisclosed considerations can arise.

This matter would drag on for the next six years but soon thereafter Krishna Menon got some very good news most unexpectedly. On 24 August 1954, R.P. Sarathy, the director of audit, defence services, sent a 'Most Secret' eighteen-page note to Nehru, which gave a whole new twist to the jeeps saga for which Krishna Menon was being pilloried. On the basis of the new facts that had come to light, Sarathy concluded:

1. The Army Inspector's report on the condition of the 155 jeeps that they were all class IV (unusable) was not wholly correct. The condition of the vehicles must have been actually better than class IV considering that no heavy repairs were needed to bring them to class I (usable) . . .

2. According to the terms of the contract the inspection in India was limited to the extent of ensuring that the vehicles were in a running condition and no damage had been incurred in transit. It did not cover the mechanical inspection of the vehicles which had already been carried out by M/s Lloyds' inspectors under the contract . . . The cancellation of the contract on the basis of the Army Inspector's report was hasty and ill considered . . .

3. It would have been wiser and in the best interests of Government to have accepted at least the 849 vehicles passed by M/s Lloyds' Inspectorate for which the advance payment of 137690 pounds had been made. If the vehicles needed

further repairs in India to bring them to class I condition they could have been done . . . Government could even have attempted to get some compensation from the contractor to recoup at least part of the repair charges . . . If Government had adopted this course they would not only have saved the loss of 18 lakhs but they would have saved in addition Rs 16 lakhs and odd of being the extra expenditure incurred by them in buying the equal number of Willy's Overland jeeps in lieu of the Anti Mistants jeeps which were rejected . . .

4.   The entire blame for the loss of Rs 18 lakhs which Government have suffered on this jeeps deal would seem to lie on the Army Authorities in India who on a dubious inspection report rejected the jeeps which were received in India and pressed for the cancellation of the whole contract, even after they were warned by the High Commissioner that such cancellation will be considered a breach of contract on the part of Government and Government thereby stood to lose considerable money. Subsequent events have proved that the contract by itself was a sound one . . .

This certainly exonerated Krishna Menon of any wrongdoing on the first of the two jeeps contracts. Since the 'Defence Ministry refused to send their Inspectors to Italy to have the jeeps inspected before shipment', it had led Sarathy to conclude that 'the entire transaction at the Indian end was handled ineptly by officials and the only explanation for their strange behaviour seems to be that they might have got panicky on account of public criticism both in Parliament and the Press . . . ' What was interesting was that the same Sarathy had signed the 1951 audit report that had damned Krishna Menon. Evidently, with new facts surfacing, Sarathy had changed his stance.

Geneva was indeed a fine achievement for Krishna Menon, and it may well have influenced Nehru to overcome his initial reluctance and attempt to get Krishna Menon into his cabinet. Krishna Menon was being hailed as a statesman both in India and abroad, and Nehru may have thought his political acceptability would have been enhanced. He raised the issue once again with Azad who, on 1 August 1954, threatened to resign if Nehru inducted Krishna Menon. Nehru would plead with Azad eleven days later:

> I shall be grateful if you will let me have your decision about the matter we have discussed so often recently regarding Krishna Menon. I have been working under great strain for some months. To this has been added mental anguish during the past two weeks. The issues before me are far-reaching and involve my future life. It is becoming difficult for me to concentrate on my work till I know clearly what I shall have to do.
>
> Should you so wish it I can come over to see you again.

Azad was unrelenting, and Nehru had to wait another two years before he could bring Krishna Menon into his cabinet as a minister without portfolio on 14 February 1956. But Azad's obduracy on the man the Prime Minister had the closest 'intellectual affinity' with played a part in another resignation episode as far as Nehru was concerned—his second in four years. On the eve of his visit to China, Nehru wrote to the chief ministers on 10 October 1954 saying that he was quite clear in his mind about giving up the presidentship of the Congress and that he was contemplating resignation as Prime Minister as well. A day later Mathai sent a copy of that letter to Krishna Menon:

> The enclosed will interest and disturb you. How I wish you were here. I miss you always, but more so now. I doubt if in the final analysis PM will take the step for, after all, he is not a completely free man. But you can never tell . . .

Nehru stayed on as Prime Minister but succeeded in giving up the post of the president of the Congress. However, on 24 October 1954, he suffered a severe blow when Rafi Ahmed Kidwai, his senior colleague and closest friend in the cabinet, passed away. A day later Krishna Menon cabled Nehru, who was then in Peking:

Deeply grieved about RAFI Sahib. I am very concerned about its effect on you emotionally and about the greater weight of worries and burdens that it creates for you. Hope you are well. Regards to INDU and MATHAI.

Immediately, speculation started over whether Krishna Menon would be inducted as Kidwai's replacement. The British diplomatic and intelligence establishment went into a frenzy, fed with anti-Menon information by many, particularly by N.R. Pillai, the head of India's foreign service, and by A.D. Gorwala, an ex-ICS-officer-turned-crusader-against-communism. Three days before Kidwai's death, British High Commissioner Alexander Clutterbuck had told his colleagues in London:

> I do not attach much importance myself to the notion that he [Krishna Menon] has Communist leanings, nor have I heard this seriously advanced here by anyone who knows him at all well . . . The trouble with him is really two-fold:
>
> 1. His fierce anti-Americanism which comes out in almost everything he says and does and causes him at times to lose all balance and perspective . . .
> 2. His tortuous mind, which makes even the simplest issue complicated and a matter for intrigue and manoeuvre . . . and his inordinate ambition and self-conceit . . .
>
> I fear . . . that things are working up for the appointment of Krishna either as Minister of External Affairs, or as a 'Minister of State' under Nehru, or at the lowest Special Adviser to the Prime Minister with Cabinet rank. From our point of view any one of these possibilities will be just as bad as the other . . . The prospect is not too cheerful but there is still some months in hand and one can only hope that— perhaps through the combined hostility of everyone who has had anything to do with him—Krishna may yet slip up in his calculations. I fear, however, that this is wishful thinking.

It would take another fifteen months, Kidwai's death notwithstanding, for Krishna Menon to enter Nehru's cabinet. But before that he would make a huge splash internationally and become a celebrity—and an unusual one at that as this news item in the *Times of India* of 1 February 1955 would show:

Red Indians Call on Mr. Menon

NEW YORK, January 31:

Four Red Indian chieftains and a squaw in their colourful head-dress and beaded leather dress came to the UN Security Council meeting yesterday to meet the 'big Indian chief' of whom they had heard a lot. Mr. V.K. Krishna Menon, the chief Indian delegate, later met them and shook hands with them. A spokesman for the chieftains said that they admired Mr. Menon's fight for world peace—P.T.I.

As the year drew to a close, Esther Bright, a leading light of the Theosophical Society of England, who had been part of his life in the late 1920s, wrote to him on animal welfare. Krishna Menon replied on 9 December 1954:

I was very happy to hear from you and to see your handwriting after so many years . . . The Government of India have appointed a Committee to consider legislation on [Prevention of] Cruelty to Animals. Although I am Chairman of the Committee, I have been unable to give any time to it owing to my frequent absences from India . . . I saw Rukmini Arundale for a short while here [New York] . . . She is now a Member of Parliament and is active in promoting this legislation . . .

The legislation was to become a reality in 1960. Earlier, when he was high commissioner, he had written to Rajkumari Amrit Kaur, health minister in Nehru's cabinet, drawing her attention to reports in the British media about the export of monkeys from India for research purposes. She had replied on 9 December 1948:

Your letter about the monkeys being exported from here for research purposes interested me. I hate vivisection but how can we get away from it so long as allopathic progress depends on research on animals and then why should we be extra sensitive about monkeys, why not about rabbits, rats, weasels, guinea pigs, etc. We are often illogical and I cannot ban this export of monkeys much as I personally dislike the idea of giving suffering for anyone—animal or human.

The year 1954 was also to see the beginning of the American media's love-hate (mostly hate) relationship with Krishna Menon. First off the block was *Life* magazine, which carried an eleven-page hatchet job on him in its 25 October 1954 issue by its correspondent in India, Alexander Campbell. The headline said it all:

MOUTHPIECE EXTRAORDINARY AND TROUBLEMAKER PLENIPOTENTIARY

As India's UN delegate and Nehru's intimate, Krishna Menon plagues the West, comforts the Reds

Campbell had done extensive background work on Krishna Menon, going back to his days in England. He had spoken to many of Krishna Menon's critics, including Vijaya Lakshmi Pandit. The evidence suggests that he also spent time with Krishna Menon. But the article, factually correct to a very large extent, had a simple message—that Krishna Menon was not only an apologist for, but also a champion of, the communists in Russia and China. One of the examples given by Campbell right at the beginning of his article for its subject's ideological proclivities was Krishna Menon's intervention at the UN a few days earlier, in which he had suggested that the two Germanys should get together and talk things out as a first step to reunification. This reunification was to take place thirty-six years later. The article had some good lines though. One passage described Krishna Menon as a Boris Karloff lookalike playing John the Baptist.

The CIA also got interested in Krishna Menon now. On 7 December 1954, Allen Dulles, its director, requested his British counterpart for 'background information which you may be prepared

to disclose on KRISHNA MENON'. He and his brother, US
Secretary of State John Foster Dulles, were 'interested in particular
whether anything is known of MENON being involved in some
scandal in connection with the purchase of vehicles'. Two days later
the Dulles brothers got their reply:

> MENON had connections with the B.C.P. [British Communist
> Party] and with other political groups which supported the Indian
> Independence movement. This association with the B.C.P. came
> to an end after the granting of independence to India in 1947 when
> he had no further need of their support in this issue.
>
> Financial scandals not being a security responsibility would
> not be pursued in detail by us. Our records however suggest that
> there was never any substantiation of allegations of irregularity
> in the matter of purchase of jeeps and other military equipment
> for the Government of India with which MENON, as High
> Commissioner here was concerned.

In a few months Krishna Menon would meet with John Foster
Dulles and have six extended conversations with him over the year—
in New York, San Francisco and Washington DC. Way back on
23 November 1946, Krishna Menon had written to Nehru from
New York, where he had been attending the very first UN General
Assembly session:

> In the United States, if there is change in the administration,
> the power behind Vandenberg who will be in charge of foreign
> affairs is a man called Dulles. Apparently he is the only man in
> the Republican party who knows anything about world affairs.
> He is a 'backroom boy' well informed and serious . . . He is a
> wise bird, republican, but very realistic. He has gone out of his
> way in the last few days to come and discuss in corridors and
> seek opinions.

Dulles himself, not Vandenberg, was given charge of foreign affairs
when the Eisenhower administration took over in January 1953. The

popular jibe 'dull, duller, dullest' was coined by his critics to describe him. He and Krishna Menon would get on each other's nerves.

1955

Krishna Menon's dream run had started in November 1952 with Korea and continued in 1953 with his being elected as an MP, and in 1954, with his success at the Geneva Indo-China Conference. To be sure, he had had his dark moments as well, reflected in his letters of self-pity to Nehru. But he was now a juggernaut in the public imagination. He would scale new heights of global popularity in 1955. This was the year he would meet the US President twice in the space of three months and the US secretary of state six times in as many months. He would also make his maiden visit to China which would create an international splash. But as was to be the case all his life, the highs were also accompanied by pathetic lows, all of which were self-inflicted.

The year started with a mostly flattering profile of his in an article entitled 'Camden Town to New Delhi' that appeared in the *New Statesman and Nation* on 29 January 1955. The previous year, Chou En-lai, Ho Chi Minh, Pierre Mendes-France, Konrad Adenauer and Nehru, among others, had been featured in the magazine. Kingsley Martin, its editor, had known Krishna Menon very well for over two decades, and barring Kashmir, the two thought alike on almost all other issues. Martin blamed Nehru's excessively sentimental attachment to his ancestral land for the imbroglio in Kashmir, a view that would always be hotly contested by Krishna Menon. The profile captured him well:

> In spite of tremendous personal magnetism and an almost unique ability to persuade people to devote their lives to his causes, friendship is difficult for him . . . Where some people have chips on their shoulders, Menon has scars. Thus he attracts private affection rather than popularity. He never stays unnoticed. His voice, his appearance, his views all conspire to make him the centre of attention . . .

Krishna Menon's first meeting with Eisenhower on 15 March 1955 was by itself not particularly remarkable. No full record of it exists although the US archives say that the 'talk had been confined to internal developments in India, including the recent elections in Andhra and the reasons why Menon felt for its development India needed a socialist economic approach'. Nine days later Krishna Menon had the first of his six meetings of 1955 with John Foster Dulles. He told the US secretary of state that 'the Peking regime had no expansionist ambitions', that 'direct and informal contact would have to be established between the Americans and the Chinese Reds' and that 'a third party might be useful in this connection'. At the end of the meeting the records mention that he told the American ambassador to India as they came out of the secretary's chamber that he was considerably satisfied with the talk with Dulles and that he 'felt confident that tensions in the Far East would be relaxed if people could be brought together and start talking'. The whole problem then was that the Americans did not want to talk to the Chinese and vice versa.

A David Low Cartoon in the Manchester Guardian *on Krishna Menon's efforts to defuse tensions between the US and China, January 1954*

A month later Nehru and Krishna Menon were at Bandung in Indonesia for the first-ever summit of twenty-nine Afro-Asian countries. In light of what was to happen many years later, it is worthwhile recalling that Pakistan opposed China's participation at Bandung but both Nehru and Krishna Menon were very strongly in its favour. Finally, Pakistan was overruled. Krishna Menon was also in favour of Israel's participation but that did not materialize because of firm Arab opposition. Ten years later Krishna Menon was to speak about Bandung to a Canadian political scientist, Michael Brecher, who wrote his intellectual biography of sorts:[11]

> . . . [T]he day before the Conference our Prime Minister and the Indonesian Prime Minister got together with those persons who had earlier prepared the Agenda for the Conference. Pakistan was not there at that time. I said to the Prime Minister privately, 'this won't do'. Then Pakistan arrived and smashed up the whole thing. So we had to begin all over again . . .
>
> Chou's role at Bandung . . . was that of a good liberal who wanted a settlement . . . [He] wanted to be an Asian—and to be accepted as such—and to play the role of a statesman . . . [He] was . . . introduced to everyone by me . . . He played a useful role except in very few instance, for example with the Pakistanis. When the latter became very difficult in a key meeting presided by Nasser, then he said, 'we cannot go any further' . . . I would not have believed at that time that he would be the Prime Minister of a country that would invade India. We had little difficulties and so on, but I would still have anticipated that he would have opposed large-scale fighting.

On 28 April 1955 Nehru, in his fortnightly letters to chief ministers, praised Krishna Menon's role at Bandung and added:

> . . . As I was saying goodbye to Premier Chou En-lai he mentioned to me that he would like to have further talks with Krishna Menon and had invited him to go to Peking for this purpose as soon as

possible. I welcomed this proposal and told him that Krishna Menon would go there within the next two weeks or so. He will go there quietly and with as little fuss as possible. Publicity cannot be avoided altogether but, so far as we are concerned, we should play it down . . .

A few days later, while addressing Congress MPs, Nehru expanded on Krishna Menon's contributions at Bandung and noted:

Krishna Menon has an amazingly fertile intellect for dealing with such situations. I do not know of anyone else who has that. That is, if one thing is not agreed to, he will find a dozen alternatives for it, trying to meet each person's viewpoints and so going on expressing. I may say, instead of what might well have happened in case like me; I would have got irritated and walk out or do something . . .

Chou and Krishna Menon had sat next to each other for a long time in Bandung. The former invited the latter to visit China to discuss further the release of the American pilots who had been shot down and imprisoned, and also the issue of Formosa. Krishna Menon made his first-ever trip to China, arriving in Beijing on 12 May 1955 and staying there for ten days. But just when his talks with Chou were about to hit their stride, he sent Nehru a 'For Himself' letter a day later:

I have been endeavouring to compose a letter to you and had even hoped to do so before I left India. This did not happen because in the nature of things the letter and what it ought to say was not easy. I have availed myself of odd moments while travelling and sought to write it. I am still at it. It has grown long and, I fear, argumentative . . . I have begun to doubt whether I will complete writing it in time for it to reach you before I return there. Hence this briefer letter, in which I shall seek to set out the essentials of not only the conclusion, but the realization that I must give in and give up.

The reasons, if reasoning is the approach to such matters, are many and it is also the cumulative effect of thinking on my party as well as of events. I have come to this, and cannot escape the realization, even if I tried that:

(a) I have ceased to have a sense of function.

(b) I do not have the qualities that render me useful or 'functionable'.

(c) Such qualities and capacities as I have are not in keeping with postures and developments in our country.

(d) Such personality and capacity I possess excite jealousy and opposition to an inordinate extent, irrespective of any and all endeavour I make to efface myself and be submissive.

(e) That far from being a help to you, or relieving you of your burdens, I am an embarrassment and add to your worries.

(f) I find my sense of self-respect and integrity severely taxed . . . I am an expendable factor, and one that should offer to be expended.

(g) To be functioning and to overcome all the adverse factors, I have to endeavour and achieve far more, many times more than any other person . . .

(h) The effortless ease with which I am made to feel (not by you) that I am an alien element, and an adverse influence and an interloper, has now been so well developed that it has its effect on all including you and me . . .

. . . I have had the privilege of the relationship with you which is best known to you and me. It would be disloyalty not to say all this to you, but fade out instead. This is why I write. It is not protest, pose or to create or seek any effects and least of all to complain. It is the expression of a realization of an end having come to one's functionality and at the same time of the persistence of the awareness not only of things, ideas and events, but of values as well . . .

. . . I have no sense of bitterness or hostility to anyone, but I have no longer any part to play that can be useful. I do not want to be anywhere when it adds to your burdens . . . No single person in the world carries more burdens than you do. No single national or international leader has the devotion of the masses inside and outside their countries that you have. And no statesman, no leader finds his greatness so ill-used by others and made the convenient instrument for hindering the very purpose which he seeks to promote and preserve.

. . . I have said enough to convey to you my thought. It will not come as a surprise but you may wonder why now; what is the occasion. There is no special occasion . . . This visit to China comes at an awkward time and I do not want it or the nature of its results one way or another to be connected with this. Hence I decided to write before I embarked on it. That is all . . .

This letter, which may well have been a catharsis for a man continually haunted by demons—real and imaginary, had more, much more angst and expressions of disillusionment. Krishna Menon was frustrated that he was not yet in Nehru's cabinet. He was clearly not satisfied with Nehru handing him special assignments on the world stage and at home. He was also unhappy that nobody in the Congress party other than Nehru stood up for him. That there was jealously was indubitable. The previous year, the inaugural year for the national awards, Krishna Menon had been conferred the nation's second-highest civilian honour, the Padma Vibhushan (Pahela Varg), only one of five to receive the award in that category. The news of that award had prompted this letter from the Prime Minister's daughter on 15 August 1954:

I just want to say how happy I am to see your name on our first 'honours' list. As you know, you have always had a very high place in the hearts of all those who have had the privilege of really knowing you. It is high time that the state gave official recognition to your great talent and service to India.

Love.

Indu

That this honour had gone to someone who had only partially 'relocated' to India only in 1953, and even then spent his time mostly abroad, would have rankled many. That he had an extra-special relationship with Nehru and would stay with him while in New Delhi would have caused resentment to many. Nehru had gone out of his way to make Krishna Menon feel wanted. He had involved him in the drafting of the famous Avadi Resolution of the Indian National Congress adopted in January 1955 and that committed India to a 'socialistic pattern of society'. Nehru had involved him fully, both in the formulation and execution of foreign policy.

Yet Krishna Menon felt he was entitled to something more. That he had been very, very reluctant to come back to India was evident from a letter he had written to Nehru way back on 20 January 1952 and to M.O. Mathai a day later. Bizarrely, he had even threatened to kill himself rather than return to India.[12] He was actually mortified by the prospect of making India his home after having lived in London for almost three decades, but that deed had been done and there was no prospect of a permanent return to London.

Krishna Menon went off to China on 11 May 1955. He was there for ten days and had six rounds of talks with Chou on the release of the US pilots and also on the continued bombardment of offshore islands Quemoy and Matsu, which had alarmed the US. He also had an audience with Chairman Mao, who had written to him sixteen years earlier thanking him for organizing medical relief for the beleaguered Chinese army. He stopped over in Hong Kong on his way back but kept mum in his interactions with journalists. He became animated only when asked about Chairman Mao's health, which was then the subject of much speculation, and responded by saying that 'he thought Mao appeared in far better health than he (Menon) himself'.[13] He landed in New Delhi on 26 May 1955, and the very next day, Nehru informed Eisenhower that Krishna Menon's talks with Chou had been very successful and that the Chinese had decided to release the four airmen. Eisenhower thanked Nehru a day later and 'expressed willingness to have Menon to come to Washington for informal and private talks'.

On 28 May 1955, Krishna Menon sent Nehru a record of the conversations he had had with Chou but couldn't resist saying:

I have already reported to you very briefly (perhaps too briefly) the net results obtained in Peking. I fear, however, that the impression I left on you is that although my visit there served some purpose, it has not achieved anything substantial to enable further progress to be helpful . . . It is natural that I should regret that the results achieved have not given you satisfaction. I have, myself, as you will see from the notes had the awareness of my poor powers of negotiation and advocacy which must account, from the impression I gained from your reactions, for the failure to obtain the release of all prisoners. I mention this item because except for this, all the advance that is possible and indeed required has been obtained. Further that these advances correspond to the American hopes as I understood from the impressions I gathered . . . The partial failure in regard to the prisoners, in my estimate, with no doubt the unconscious desire to justify oneself, appertains to the continued detention of the remainder, and not to a determination that there shall be no progress in this matter. I myself believe that if there is any response from the other side all the prisoners will be released. Further, while the prisoner issue is of great importance from the point of view of public feeling in the United States and to enable a better approach to negotiation itself, this could not be presented to the Chinese as a basic purpose of the talks.

. . . My notes on the prisoner issue, which cover many pages, will I hope indicate to you that I have both pleaded and pressed this matter as best as I could. I would also recall the fact that before I left I mentioned to you that I had neither hopes nor indeed any reasons to think that I would make much progress. I expressed to you my diffidence myself and can therefore justifiably say that I did not engender any optimism. This note is written not for the purpose of self-justification, but so that it should be taken into account in regard to my handling of the future of this endeavour.

Krishna Menon sent Nehru a complete record of the six meetings he had had with Chou between 12 May 1955 and 20 May 1955, running into a total of some eighteen hours. The record ran into a hundred and fifty pages. They had spoken about almost all regional and global issues, barring India–China relations. The only time bilateral ties figured was when the Chinese premier mentioned the need to increase air services between the two countries and when Krishna Menon made a brief reference to Tibet saying that he disagreed with the argument that India had capitulated on it because Tibet had never belonged to India anyway. The focus was, of course, on Sino-US relations and how they could be normalized. At one stage the conversation went thus:

> Chou: . . . If negotiations between China and the US are to take place we have to do a lot of work. There are many things we have to do. It would not be a question of merely ten days you spend here, but you may have to spend many ten days here . . .
>
> Krishna Menon: I am not a skillful negotiator. I just come here and say what I think can be done. I am not here to negotiate a settlement. I am here to seek methods of finding ways to a peaceful approach and do such things as yourself may not do because you are one of the parties . . .
>
> Chou: You are too nervous. We have invited you as a friend of ours and as a man in whom Prime Minister has full confidence. I know you as one of the people who are very close to us.
>
> Krishna Menon: I want the PM to accept from me that I have not come here to negotiate the release of prisoners . . . We are discussing methods to lower tensions, contributions from this side and contributions from that side. It so happens that the question of these American prisoners is a matter which has a great part to play in lowering tensions . . .

Towards the end of their conversations Chou would tell Krishna Menon:

. . . In the first stage contacts between China and the US can take
place in Moscow, New Delhi and London through their respective
representatives in these three places. Even with those contacts you
yourself will have to remain the go-between because although you
have said you were not a negotiator you cannot as well shake off
the responsibility of a go-between and you understand the situation
of different parties and that facilitates the solution of the question.

Seventeen years later Chou would have a similar discussion with
Henry Kissinger. Any normal human being would have been satisfied
with what had been achieved. But Krishna Menon being Krishna
Menon imagined ghosts where none existed. Nehru reassured him a
few hours later:

I am surprised to read your note. How did you manage to get
the idea that I considered your visit to Peking a partial failure? I
think you have done an extraordinarily fine piece of work with
far-reaching consequences.

Dulles wrote to the Prime Minister on 29 May 1955:

I am happy to receive your message of 27 May and to know that
in your opinion the talks between Mr. Krishna Menon and Mr.
Chou En-lai indicate that it is possible to put the relations between
Communist China and the USA on a basis which will be free from
the threat of the use of force . . . I am glad that you feel that my
talk with Mr. Menon in Washington last March helped in making
progress. I am always anxious to know of all relevant facts and
since you feel that Mr. Menon's talks at Peiping do not easily lend
themselves to report by telegram I should be happy to talk to Mr.
Menon again . . .

On 30 May 1955, in a jam-packed press conference in New Delhi
which created international headlines, Krishna Menon announced the
imminent release of the four pilots. But he was uncharacteristically
coy and reticent, demonstrating that he could play by the rules of

game when the situation so demanded. *The Hindu* of 31 May 1955 had the most extensive report:

CHINA TO RELEASE FOUR U.S. AIRMEN
MENON'S DISCLOSURE: MAJOR STEP IN EASING TENSION

Mr. V.K. Krishna Menon announced here today that the Chinese Government had decided to release four of the 11 American airmen detained by them . . . To Pressmen who have been pressing hard during the last few days to meet him, Mr. Menon said that his visit, as was summed up by Mr. Chou En-lai himself, 'has been extremely useful and we can look forward with hope'. Mr. Menon explained that one of the obstacles in the way of proper understanding between the United States and China was the lack of contact . . . If critics who had always alleged that Mr. Krishna Menon was unfriendly to the United States had heard him today there was no doubt they would begin to revise their opinion . . . There is a vast volume of friendly feeling and a desire for peace and goodwill in China. It is exactly the same in the U.S.A. . . . Mr. Menon said that while in China he had several conversations with the Chinese Prime Minister and other leaders. 'The bulk of these conversations are private and will remain private' . . . Mr. Menon referred to Mr. Chou En-Lai's statement that China was willing to see a settlement of the Formosa question by peaceful measures, if that were possible. 'So, by and large, I think, there exists today a set of conditions that can make progress possible'. Mr. Menon added: 'If I have not told you much, do not jump to the conclusion that there is not much to tell. One must choose the time and place'.

Within a few hours of Krishna Menon's press conference, the Chinese government officially corroborated what he had said, and the next day the four pilots were released in Hong Kong. This was another feather in his cap. He had accomplished something the UN secretary-general, Dag Hammarskjold, had tried to get done for the past five months without success. It was, therefore, not a surprise that when he was informed of Krishna Menon's feat, the first reaction of Henry Cabot Lodge Jr, the US ambassador to the UN, was: 'Mr. Hammarskjold would be quite burnt up at Mr. Menon for having moved into his act and taken over his role as mediator.' He was to expand on this theme to Dulles on 9 June 1955:

Herewith some thoughts on Menon's relationship with Chou.

1.   There is first the theory that you mentioned that Chou is using him in preference to Hammarskjold (a) because he does not like the United Nations and (b) because he wants to build up Menon, who is anti-American and pro-communist for future use as a mediator.

2.   There is a second theory, which is that Menon meddlesomely intruded himself on Chou, that Chou gave him the information for him to release to the papers and at the same time gave the information to Wistrand the Swedish Ambassador in Peking. He is understood to have given it to Wistrand in such a way . . . that the news came from New Delhi before it was put out in New York.

3.   I think what Chou really wants is direct talks with the United States without any go-between . . .

This all seems to add up to the conclusion that while Chou will use Menon for nuisance value, he is not building up Menon as a go-between . . . To this conclusion I would simply add the thought that direct talks between Communist China and the United States would probably make the Soviet Union extremely nervous and would provide us an opportunity to maneuver a lessening of solidarity between the two big Communist powers . . .

What Lodge had to say about direct talks between the US and China would become a reality sixteen years later. Lodge and Krishna Menon would strike up an unusual friendship, which would last till the latter's death. On 20 February 1961, Lodge would reminisce to an Indian academic:

> For almost eight years I saw a great deal of Mr. Krishna Menon . . .
> During that period of time there were occasions when the policy
> of India and the policy of the United States were not the same and
> when we both naturally carried out the policies of our respective
> countries to the best of our ability. It seemed that these were the
> occasions which are always well published.
>
> There were also occasions—which were not so well
> publicized—when the policies of our two governments were
> similar, and on these we worked together in what I think was a
> constructive way. I think particularly of the resolution of February
> 2, 1957 which authorized the stationing of the United Nations
> Emergency Force at the entrance to the Gulf of Aqaba, on which
> Mr. Krishna Menon and I worked together. Our joint efforts
> resulted in a text which obtained a two-thirds vote of the General
> Assembly. This resolution played a decisive part in converting that
> particular part of the Palestine area into a peaceful place, where
> before it had been explosive and dangerous.
>
> These, and many other, experiences showed me that Mr.
> Krishna Menon is not only a man of ability, but also a man of
> his word . . . Work at the United Nations entails more than the
> conduct of official business, and I am glad to be able to say that our
> personal relations are friendly and cordial. I know my wife and I
> both enjoyed getting to know Mr. Menon, and I hope and believe
> that he would say the same about us . . . When my wife and I
> visited India in 1958, he was a wonderful host to us . . .

Krishna Menon went to Washington to meet with Eisenhower, Dulles and others, just as Nehru was in Moscow on his first trip to the USSR in twenty-eight years. This was non-alignment being demonstrated visibly. Nehru met Molotov on 8 June 1955, and during their conversation Krishna Menon's visit to China came up. With Nehru was K.P.S. Menon, then Indian ambassador in the USSR, whose record of the meeting said:

> . . . Mr. Molotov . . . appreciated the skill of Shri Krishna
> Menon, whom he described as an old friend and an experienced
> diplomat . . . Mr. Molotov remarked that he knew that the American
> reactionaries did not very much like Shri Krishna Menon . . .

We don't know what K.P.S. Menon thought of this praise from
Molotov for the other Menon, whom he did not particularly
care for.

As Krishna Menon landed in the US, the *New York Times* carried
a prominent article by its India correspondent, A.M. Rosenthal, in its
issue dated 5 June 1955. Titled 'India Softens its Tone to the U.S.',
it dwelt at length on Nehru and ended up talking of Krishna Menon:

> . . . As a trusted spokesman of the world's most important men,
> Mr. Krishna Menon becomes, himself, one of world's most
> important men. The job he is doing now is Mr. Krishna Menon's
> most important job. Naturally enough he wants to succeed.
> Entirely aside from power and politics in the Far East, there are
> some obstacles in the way. Chief among them is the fact that he has
> made a reputation for himself as being antagonistic to the United
> States. Although he bristles at the suggestion, he is doing some of
> the work of a mediator. A mediator antagonistic to one side is a
> contradiction in terms and in recent months Mr. Krishna Menon
> has seemed to become aware of that. In the past couple of months,
> Mr. Krishna Menon has made speeches urging his Indian listeners
> not to forget the importance of American public opinion on Far
> Eastern issues . . . Mr. Krishna Menon has not become soft and
> bland and he never will. When he gets to the United States, his
> adeptness at the sharp retort may get the better of him and he will
> be back where he started. But as of now, Mr. Krishna Menon is no
> longer using that cane of his to crack American knuckles.

Krishna Menon met Eisenhower a second time on 14 June 1955
along with Dulles. But before that, he made quite an amazing
request to his friend Norman Cousins, editor of the *Saturday Review
of Literature*. This was recorded by an aide of Richard Nixon, the

Vice President of the US, who received a call from Cousins a day earlier, conveying Krishna Menon's desire to meet Nixon:

> Cousins . . . indicated that, in his opinion, Menon was suffering from 'rejectionist neurosis' and he felt that if the Vice President would see Krishna Menon, it would help greatly. Cousins suggested that the manner in which this might be handled would be for the Vice President's office to contact the Indian Embassy and indicate an interest on the Vice President's part in talking with Menon when he was in town . . .

Krishna Menon's approach to Nixon was most unusual but so was the fact that Nixon's office acceded the manner of his request and actually set up the meeting which, as it turned out, was no more than a photo opportunity. There is no record of the meeting but there is one of Krishna Menon's meeting with Nixon's boss:

> . . . Mr. Menon made clear that he was not acting as the authorized representative of either Communist China or the United States. He was merely trying in a friendly way to prevent a tense situation from becoming worse and developing into war. He reported his talks with Chou En-lai and the attitude toward the Formosa area. He felt that if direct negotiations should begin then what he referred to as 'lesser problems' as the prisoners could be resolved . . . The President [said that] there were some things that we could not negotiate about and still stand upright in the world. Mr. Menon pleaded for 'magnanimity'. Mr. Menon said he hoped to be able to see the President again. The President said that if this would serve a useful purpose, he was agreeable in principle.

The verbatim transcript of Krishna Menon's meeting with the US President ends with Eisenhower saying, 'By the way would you mind having your picture taken with us?' The photograph shows them in a very civil and pleasant mood. But Eisenhower's diary entry of that day was devastating:

Krishna Menon is a menace and a boor. He is a boor because
he conceives himself to be intellectually superior and rather coyly
presents to cover this under a cloud of excessive humility and
modesty. He is a menace because he is a master of twisting words
and meanings of others and is governed by an ambition to prove
himself the master international manipulator and politician of the
age. He has visited me twice in company with Secretary Dulles
to talk about establishing some basis of mediation between Red
China and ourselves . . .

Eisenhower was not entirely inaccurate in his description of Nehru's
roving envoy. But whatever the American President may have
thought of him, Dulles would continue to meet with Krishna Menon
to discuss all manner of issues but most particularly Sino–US relations.
Nehru's envoy continued to hammer away the point that there was
no substitute to direct contact—either formal or informal—between
the US and China to resolve the issues that agitated both of them.
Their meetings combined seriousness with moments of humour,
banter and quick repartee from either side. On 6 July 1955, when
Dulles said that the 'renunciation of the use of force was a high moral
principle that civilized nations should adopt', Krishna Menon asked
'whether reconciliation was not also a high principle'. The record of
the meeting then went on:

> The Secretary said it was, and that if India could help remove the
> concept of force from the minds of the Chinese Communists, steps
> towards reconciliation would be possible. Mr. Menon said that
> India had already used its strong endeavours in this direction. 'If
> you could let us impress Peking' he added, 'that we had access to
> your mind, we could be more effective'. The Secretary said he had
> opened every possible recess of his mind to Mr. Menon during
> their several long conversations . . .
>
> He [Dulles] remarked that he had spent more time talking to
> Mr. Krishna Menon during the last three weeks than he had with
> any other foreign diplomat during a similar period since he had
> been Secretary of State. Mr. Menon protested that he was not a

diplomat. The Secretary said, smiling, 'Well, whatever you call yourself'.

When Mr. Allen [US ambassador to India] was accompanying Mr. Menon to the elevator, Mr. Menon remarked in a tone of hopelessness, 'Your Secretary has said to me in so many words: "Go away, you are not serving any useful purpose"'. Mr. Allen said that the Secretary had given him a very direct and simple task, which should be easy and agreeable for any Indian to carry out. His task was to persuade the Red Chinese to renounce the use of force. Mr. Menon said he could not go back to Peking without something more in his hand.

In the historiography of Indo–US relations, Dulles and Krishna Menon are the villains on either side. But for a few months in 1955 both got on famously with each other and India almost pulled off a rapprochement of sorts between America and China, something Pakistan would finally achieve in 1971. For all his fulminations against 'neutrality' and suspicions of India's foreign policy, Dulles actually fought for US aid to India at a time when such aid was crucial.

If ever there was a time when Krishna Menon enjoyed a good press in the US, it was in June–July 1955. The front page of the *New York Times* on 5 June 1955 had three prominent photographs: those of the four freed American airmen, Chou and Krishna Menon. The *New York Herald Tribune* of 12 June 1955 had a full-page interview with him. The *Washington Post* of 17 June 1955 had an editorial on him called 'Way of the Peacemaker'. The *Whittier News* had a front-page banner headline 'Over 2200 Hear Menon Speak' and carried a photograph of him with his old British friend from the early 1930s, Horace Alexander. On 16 June 1955, the *Christian Science Monitor* had a long opinion piece on him called 'Envoy Extraordinary—Menon'. Influential columnists featured him: Malvina Lindsay's 'Getting Along with Krishna Menon' in the *Washington Post* of 9 June 1955, Chalmers Roberts's 'Menon's Mission: Contact, not Conflict' in the *Washington Post* of 2 July 1955, and Joe Alsop's 'The Menon Mission' in the *Herald-Tribune* on 19 June 1955.

Krishna Menon made two other notable contributions on the world stage in 1955. The UN had been considering the admission of eighteen new members for almost five years. But the entry of two was holding up the entire process. The Soviet Union was objecting to Japan becoming a member because of the dispute over the Kurile Islands. China (i.e. Taiwan) was objecting to Outer Mongolia. Khrushchev and Bulganin were visiting India and Krishna Menon got Nehru to speak to them about changing the Soviet stance. The net result was that a 'sixteen-state' resolution was introduced jointly by Canada and India, which paved the way for sixteen of the eighteen countries becoming UN members in December 1955. Japan would become a member a year later but Mongolia would have to wait for another six years to be admitted.

On 24 November 1955, Krishna Menon received a letter from Herve Alphand, the head of the French delegation to the UN. He was pleased no end and promptly sent it across to Nehru:

> In the name of and instructions from Prime Minister Antoine Pinay, I have the honour to convey to you the thanks of the French Government for the leading part you have taken in bringing about the decision arrived at yesterday in the General Assembly on the subject of the 'Algerian question'.
>
> I am happy to transmit this message of my Government and to have the opportunity of telling you again how much I have appreciated the exceptionally effective action which you have kindly taken to ensure the success of the efforts of all those who desired to bring about the conditions which would permit France to take her place again in the Assembly of the United Nations.
>
> Your personal intervention has been decisive: the high position of the Government which you represent, your unquestioned moral authority, your talent for persuasion and your unequalled ability for negotiation have alone brought about this unanimous agreement on the formula which was proposed through your initiative and which could secure the approbation of all. My Government has full knowledge of the role which you have played and is grateful to you for it.

On 11 October 1955, Krishna Menon had sent a telegram to Nehru saying that the French government had recalled its delegation to the UN and that there was talk of France withdrawing from the UN. This was because the Arab Group led by President Nasser of Egypt had proposed the inscription of Algeria on the agenda of the General Assembly. A day later, Nehru instructed Krishna Menon to support this move but also told him that his speech could be a mild one that stressed the 'imperative need of a solution acceptable to Algerian nationalist opinion'. Thereafter, negotiations commenced to break the deadlock, and Krishna Menon produced a formulation by 25 November 1955, which had everybody's acceptance including the Arab Group and France, albeit somewhat tardily. The formulation was brief and did not convey the complexity of the negotiations that led to it:

The General Assembly

Decides not to consider further the item entitled 'The question of Algeria' and is therefore no longer seized of this item on the agenda of its tenth session.

548th plenary meeting,
25 November 1955.

A year later the French would revise their opinion about Krishna Menon over the Suez Canal issue.

As the year drew to a close, it was not a surprise that in his customary fortnightly letter to chief ministers on 30 December 1955 Nehru wrote:

India's delegation has received praise for its work from a variety of countries. Everyone recognized the outstanding part of India during this session [of the UN General Assembly] and the extraordinary resourcefulness that our delegation showed in finding solutions to difficult problems. The Algerian issue was one such problem which threatened to come in the way of all other work. Our delegation

managed to deal with this matter with remarkable ability. Not only
did they succeed in removing the deadlock but in doing so, they
gained the goodwill of all parties. The leader of our delegation,
Shri V.K. Krishna Menon was largely responsible for the great
success of our delegation's work. Indeed he was the outstanding
figure during this session of the UN General Assembly. Apart from
many appreciations of our work I have received personal messages
commending the work of our delegation and its leader from the
Governments of France and Canada. India played a notable part
also in the admission of sixteen new member states.

But the year had not been about foreign affairs alone. Krishna Menon
had also waded into the emotive issue of those years—that of linguistic
states. The States Reorganisation Commission set up in December
1953 was about to submit its final report when he sent Nehru a
lengthy note on 28 September 1955 arguing passionately against the
creation of a new state of Kerala on the grounds that it could well end
up becoming a communist citadel. He told Nehru:

> There is no emotional fervor for linguism in the Malayalam
> speaking area as there was in Andhra. It is a recent and artificial
> agitation of which the main exponents are a few fanatical people.
> The best and greatest support comes almost entirely from the
> elements that are against the Congress and the Government,
> namely the Socialists, Communists and such others. The reason for
> their support has nothing to do with the merits of the issue, but are
> solely determined by the hope of conquest of power . . .

He went on:

> In the Tamil country in contradistinction there will develop an
> indigenous type of fascist orientation which is the racial Tamil
> outlook. A separate Tamil province will be very anti-Indian, anti-
> national . . .
>   Therefore the only hope and right procedure in my view is to
> create a Southern State, a Dakshin Pradesh, as a corollary to Uttar

Pradesh, which could include the present Tamil Nad, Travancore, Cochin, Malabar and possibly Kanara upto Kasargode . . .

We will Balkanise India if we further dismember the States instead of creating larger units. It would be quite a different question if these areas were merely local government areas like the counties of England, dividing a unitary India into 30 or 40 administrative divisions. But this is not practical politics, for one thing, the U.P. . . . will not allow it.

After the Commission's recommendations had been made public formally, Krishna Menon again bombarded Nehru on 3 November 1955:

. . . I want to once again raise my voice for what it is worth against implementing the proposals in regard to Madras and to put forwards the creation of a Southern State of present-day Madras and Travancore-Cochin . . .

May I now refer to some other aspects?

(1) More powers to the Centre and making the States less able to be much more than administrative divisions . . .
(2) Some equity in size and importance in regard to the various units.

As for Kerala I have no doubt that the whole of the issue is artificially created and has no political or sociological basis . . .

Nehru must have read these long (and long-winded) notes patiently. He replied six days later:

. . . When you wrote to me previously and sent me a long note on Kerala etc., I circulated your note to a number of my colleagues in the Cabinet and in the Congress Working Committee. Many of them agreed with you. But I am afraid you do not quite appreciate the kind of forces we have to contend with in India at the present moment. When you suggest that States should become merely administrative divisions and far greater power should be concentrated in the Centre, you say something which is utterly beyond anyone's capacity to do at the present moment . . . It is almost impossible to have a Southern Province, much as we would like it. We have tried our best and failed. We have decided, therefore, not to bewail our lot but to face the situation as best as we can.

Krishna Menon is a demigod in Kerala and an untarnished legend to most Malayalis. It is, therefore, somewhat ironic that he opposed the formation of Kerala, something no Malayali would oppose. Judged in today's context Krishna Menon's views on linguism appear hopelessly quixotic. India did not Balkanize as he had feared; in fact, Indian unity was strengthened immeasurably by the creation of linguistic states. But on one issue he and another member of the Commission, whom Krishna Menon had held responsible for pushing the idea of Kerala, were united: K.M. Panikkar had given a dissent note arguing for the splitting of UP on the grounds of not having one state exercising disproportionate influence on the nation's polity—this is a point that Krishna Menon too had made to Nehru.

On 27 October 1955, the Political Committee of the UN General Assembly passed a resolution after inviting all members of the UN to a conference to finalize the establishment of an International Atomic Energy Agency (IAEA). This was a significant victory for Krishna Menon personally against heavy pressure from the US and the UK. The original resolution moved by the Americans in February 1954 called for the setting up of the IAEA only by countries possessing nuclear resources and technology. It came up for discussion eight months later. India had not been consulted even though it had supplied thorium nitrate and beryl to the US in the early 1950s. From the beginning Krishna Menon took the view that the new agency should be under UN auspices, a position backed fully by Nehru and Homi Bhabha, the czar of India's fledgeling nuclear programme. Krishna Menon's position was also that countries such as France, Portugal and Belgium, which had colonies in Africa rich in atomic minerals, would enjoy 'undue advantageous positions'. On 12 November 1954, Nehru had, after consulting Bhabha, agreed with Krishna Menon's stance. The IAEA would start functioning as part of the UN family from July 1957.

1956

The year started promisingly for Krishna Menon. After almost three years of opposition, Maulana Azad finally yielded to Nehru's entreaties and allowed Krishna Menon to enter the Union cabinet. But this was only a partial victory as Krishna Menon found himself being sworn in on 14 February 1956 as just a minister without portfolio, but with the responsibility to assist the Prime Minister in foreign affairs.

He had expected something more meaty and substantive. He was, of course, going to continue as head of India's delegation to the UN and Nehru's main adviser on foreign policy. In September 1956, Nehru appointed him a member of the Planning Commission as well. Finally, Krishna Menon appeared to be getting somewhere politically at home. Perhaps most important, he asked for and secured an official bungalow right opposite the Prime Minister's residence. This was to be his home for the next eighteen years, right up to his death.

The membership of the Planning Commission would open up avenues for Krishna Menon to get involved in economic policy as well. For the next couple of months this is what he did in addition to global diplomacy. On 7 May 1957, he would send Nehru a fourteen-page note with his views on various economic matters. It was clear that he was not in full agreement with the approach of Finance Minister T.T. Krishnamachari, popularly known as TTK. He would be critical of TTK, forcing the resignation of the governor of the Reserve Bank India, B. Rama Rau, in January 1957. He would caution Nehru against TTK's policy on taxation saying that he felt 'India had reached the point of diminishing returns long ago so far as the higher level of income is concerned'. Eight days after Krishna Menon's note, TTK would unveil his Budget that would earn him the sobriquet of 'Tax, Tax and Kill'. For a hard-core socialist Krishna Menon would display unusual pragmatism and tell the Prime Minister that the export capacity of India was still far from exploited, whether of goods or services, and that while 'it is an error to fight shy of control, it is equally an error to introduce blanket control'. And he couldn't resist warning against the growing dependence on wheat imports from the US.

However, 1956 would be most noteworthy for the Suez Canal crisis that led to the Anglo-French-Israeli invasion and the revolution in Hungary. These were almost contemporaneous, much like what was to happen six years later when the Cuban Missile and the Sino-Indian crises happened almost in parallel. Krishna Menon would play a pivotal role in resolving the Suez Canal crisis, with active diplomacy in Cairo, London and New York, but his role at the UN during the Hungarian revolution would lead to severe criticism both in India and the West.

In June 1956, Nehru went to the US at the invitation of Eisenhower, who took great pains to ensure that they spent a lot of time together, both formally and informally. Krishna Menon tried to muscle his way in as part of Nehru's delegation but the Prime Minister, aware of American antipathy to Krishna Menon and genuinely wanting to build a new relationship with Eisenhower, put paid to his hopes. A month later Nehru was in Brioni in Yugoslavia to meet with President Tito and President Gamel Abdul Nasser of Egypt. There was absolutely no hint in Brioni about the tremors Nasser would soon cause. Nehru accompanied Nasser on the way back and spent a day in Cairo on 20 July 1956. Krishna Menon joined him in his talks with Nasser, which were on Algeria, Cyprus and the Middle East. There too, Nehru and Krishna Menon never sensed what was soon to come. They left Cairo on 21 July 1956, and five days later, in a speech in Alexandria, Nasser announced the nationalization of the Suez Canal. Krishna Menon would later say that he supported what Nasser had done but Nehru was more ambivalent in saying, 'I would have done it differently.'[14]

Both Nehru and Krishna Menon had developed a warm personal equation with Nasser but Eden was allergic to him. In Krishna Menon's later recollection:[15]

> Eden always thought Nasser was a kind of junior Mussolini or Hitler; he always talked to me like that. Nasser was a blind spot with Eden . . .

Eden, for his part, would be less than complimentary about Krishna Menon for his role during the Suez crisis, referring to him in his memoirs[16] as the 'aviatory Mr. Krishna Menon'—not inaccurate in itself but certainly conveying a deeper negative meaning. To give Eden his due, right from the beginning he recognized that Nehru would play an important role in resolving the crisis. It was at his initiative that India was invited for a conference in London, which Eden had convened to discuss the possible international control of the Suez Canal. Even though Nasser flatly refused to participate, Nehru went ahead and deputed Krishna Menon to attend the conclave. He asked him to meet Nasser on his way to London. Krishna Menon's stopover in Cairo did not change Nasser's resolve.

The London conference began on 16 August 1956 under the chairmanship of British Foreign Secretary Selwyn Lloyd, who was to later provide a hilarious account[17] of how his chairmanship had come about. Krishna Menon had met Lloyd the previous day, and the latter wrote:

Krishna Menon and I were still on friendly terms. We had worked together at the United Nations on Korea with what I thought were satisfactory results. He was a strange man, universally disliked and distrusted. But when he wanted, he had a certain charm, and his mind was acute. We never discussed any problem without my feeling in my own mind at the end of our talk that some new point had been ventilated or some light thrown upon what was up to then obscure. In spite of this, Krishna Menon afterwards made everything quite complicated . . . Then I told Menon that the Americans thought I should not be chairman of the conference. He professed indignation . . . Menon then, with typical ingenuity produced an alternative suggestion which he knew the United States delegation would dislike intensely. If Britain did not provide the chairman, it must be by rotation in alphabetical order . . .

Later that morning I saw Dulles and he repeated his view that it was undesirable for me to take the chair. I did not advance my claims. I said perhaps he was right, but I hoped he knew what the alternative would be, rotation day by day by alphabetical order. That was Menon's idea, and I suspected he would carry a majority of the members with him. I hope I suppressed what I think would have been a very legitimate chuckle when I said this. Sure enough, Dulles was horrified, as I knew he would be, and that was the end of that.

At the conference Krishna Menon suggested a compromise formula that provided for 'minority representation of International user interests, without ownership rights, on the Egyptian corporation for the Canal, a consultative body of user interest, and transmission by Egypt to the United Nations of the annual reports of the Canal Corporation [to be set up by Egypt]'. He made one other suggestion that 'if the Egyptian Government claimed to bar Israeli ships from the Canal as a legitimate act of war, they should abide by any decision of the International Court of Justice at The Hague on this subject'. Once again, Krishna Menon got flak from both sides. At the UN, in November 1952, both the US and the USSR had attacked his resolution on Korea. Now he was being attacked by the British and the French on one side for being an apologist for Nasser, while the Egyptians too rejected his compromise formula. Under the circumstances it was no surprise that Dulles's suggestion for an international board of control over the Suez Canal prevailed, leading Krishna Menon to consider a walkout of the conference, a step Nehru dissuaded him from taking.

The stalemate continued till early September 1956 when Nasser asked Nehru to get negotiations started largely on the basis of what Krishna Menon had originally proposed and what he (Nasser) had, in fact, originally opposed. The key point in the Krishna Menon formula, which Nasser latched on to, was unfettered control over the Suez Canal and that was indeed to be the starting point of the next round of negotiations that now took place under the UN auspices in New York. Hammarskjold, already smarting from how Krishna Menon had stolen a march over him the previous year in China, kept him out of the negotiations, which involved mostly Britain, France and Egypt. According to an account of the Suez crisis written by Mohammed Heikal, the most influential Egyptian journalist of that era:[18]

The following day, Saturday, 13 October [1956], Krishna Menon's anger reached boiling point. He met Ali Sabri in the Waldorf Astoria and complained that he was being deliberately excluded from the meetings in the Secretary-General's office and said he held Fawzi and Hammarskjold responsible for this outrage . . . He then rushed off to the Security Council where he installed himself in the Indian delegate's seat. He scribbled something on a piece of paper and passed it on to Fawzi saying, 'Kindly send this to your President in cipher'. The message was that he asked Nasser's permission to leave New York because negotiations were now confined to three-four people meeting in the Secretary-General's office. 'Everybody tells me that Dr. Fawzi is behind my exclusion', the message ended.

On 11 October 1956, the US recorded a conversation between a high US official and 'Ambassador Hussein of the Egyptian delegation to the UN':

He [Ambassador Hussein] believed strongly that it would not be helpful in the present situation to have representatives of various other countries trying to become 'heroes' by pressing their own plans for a solution. He mentioned particularly Spaak [Belgian] and Krishna Menon in this connection and gave me the impression that he and his Egyptian colleagues were not at all enthusiastic over the Menon proposal or his efforts to inject himself into the situation.

Krishna Menon had only two allies in his Suez adventure—Nehru and Nasser. He and Nasser had developed close bonds and had, in fact, met earlier in the year for wide-ranging talks on regional and global issues. On 2 October 1956, Krishna Menon would tell Lloyd that 'one of his difficulties was that Nasser was easier to deal with than Fawzi. Fawzi would complicate any negotiation or agreement.' The record of the Krishna Menon–Lloyd conversation of that day continued:

Menon came to see Foreign Secretary again at 1030 pm the same evening and went through the matter again. He rang Foreign Secretary

up at 945 am on the following day to say goodbye. He reproached
Foreign Secretary for not wishing him luck and asked him to arrange
for Prime Minister [Eden] to send a telegram to Nehru emphasizing
the importance that he [Eden] attached to the Menon mission. He
said that Foreign Secretary must not let him down.

Hammarskjold's talks with the British, French and Egyptians concluded
on 14 October 1956, with an agreement to meet again in Geneva for
a second round in a fortnight's time. He had come up with a six-
point peace plan that was, in reality, the Krishna Menon five-point
plan increased by one. But exactly a fortnight later Israel launched the
first phase of the Anglo-French-Israeli military campaign in the Sinai
and the Suez Canal crisis took a whole new turn.

Hammarskjold's antipathy to Krishna Menon is borne out by
a letter he wrote to Alva Myrdal, then the Swedish ambassador to
India, on 15 August 1956. The English translation of this letter reads:

> . . . On a personal level Mr. Menon dislikes me tremendously . . .
> He has never managed to have any success when it has come to
> exploiting me as part of his games . . . I have in all my innocence
> got in the way of his attempts to expand his position in Washington
> regarding the Chinese prisoner of war issue . . . I have chosen to
> appoint a man from Pakistan Mr. Bokhari as successor to one of the
> Asian posts in the Secretariat . . . Mr. Menon has already begun this
> manoeuvre for an Asian—preferably an Indian of course—Secretary
> General when my term of office comes to an end in 1958.
>
> If Mr. Menon's feelings toward me are lukewarm, his reaction
> to Mr. Bokhari is as cold as ice . . . Mr. Menon has pushed
> Mr. Nehru's antipathy to Pakistan to the brink. Further as far
> as Mr. Menon is concerned, Mr. Bokhari comes across as [a]
> successful spokesperson for Pakistan in the Kashmir conflict . . .
> Mr. Menon's reaction is also that of a Southern Indian belonging to
> the untouchable caste to a Northern Indian prince, and the Hyde
> Park's autodidact reaction to a Cambridge Don . . .

This letter shows Krishna Menon had got under Hammarskjold's skin.
But the Swede's caste-based sociological analysis of Krishna Menon's

reaction to Bokhari was not only mistaken but also juvenile. Krishna Menon, on his part, while felicitating Hammarskjold handsomely on his appointment to a second term, also took some gentle digs at him in the UN General Assembly on 26 September 1957. Krishna Menon was the last speaker and had the audience in splits like he used to:

> . . . I have something in common with the Secretary General. I do not always understand him, and he does not always understand me. But both of us go back afterwards and try to understand each other . . . During the last year, with the developments in the Middle East—and, earlier with the developments in the Far East—opportunities have presented themselves to the Government of India to be in close touch with the Secretary General on many administrative matters. We also had the privilege of welcoming him to our country and informing him—not through pamphlets but through our ordinary people in the villages—that India had heard about the United Nations; in fact, he was asked what his salary was . . . The Secretary General now faces another five years of strenuous and useful work. Speaking quite privately, however, I should like to tell Mr. Hammarskjold what I have said does not mean we shall make no criticisms during the five years to come. In other words, we should not be told, 'For ever keep your peace'.

The two would continue to spar over the next four years, with Krishna Menon holding on to the view that not only did Hammarskjold typify Scandinavian sanctimoniousness but he was also not prepared to confront the US and other Western powers adequately.

Eventually, the epitaph to Krishna Menon's role in defusing the Suez crisis would be provided in his obituary in the London *Times* of 7 October 1974:

> When in July [1956] President Nasser nationalized the Suez Canal, he took a leading part in the negotiations that followed. In retrospect it is clear that India had as great an interest as Britain in reaching a settlement and the plan presented by Menon in August

[1956] would have salvaged more for British interests than was eventually gained (or lost) by force . . .

In fact, the now-declassified account of Eden's 'interview with Krishna Menon' of 18 October 1956 reads:

> Krishna Menon complained that we had not studied his proposals very thoroughly. Mr. Menon claimed that they were better than what we had got at the Security Council. He said that time would not improve our position; the Prime Minister disagreed. Mr. Menon went on to say that his only desire was to be helpful. The Prime Minister fears that Mr. Menon, although not apparently in a hostile frame of mind, may encourage the Egyptians to feel that they have nothing more to fear from us.

THE MANCHESTER GUARDIAN TUESDAY MARCH 5 1957

"SORRY, FOLKS, THE BOSS HASN'T GOT HIM WIRED FOR SOUND YET"

David Low on Krishna Menon's Suez diplomacy, late 1956–early 1957

Just as the UN was grappling with the Suez crisis, another flashpoint emerged. On 24 October 1956, the Soviet Union moved troops into Budapest to quell the revolt that had started the day before. A much larger Soviet intervention took place eleven days later. There was violence and bloodshed. While on the Suez Krishna Menon was, on the whole, constructive, deriving his authority from both Nehru and Nasser, on Hungary he blotted his copybook and came in for severe criticism both at home and abroad for being a Soviet apologist. But like everything connected with him, the truth is more multilayered, and there is a gap between how his actions were perceived and what he actually did. Krishna Menon had only himself to blame since he never explained his behaviour until almost a decade later, and that too to an academic whose reach was necessarily limited.

The background to this is that India did not have a full-fledged ambassador in Budapest. India's diplomat in the city was M.A. Rahman. He would, many years later, be feted in Hungary after the collapse of the communist regime in 1989 for his role in assisting some of the key revolutionaries of 1956.[19] K.P.S. Menon, India's ambassador in Moscow, was holding dual charge, and therefore, it was natural that he gave importance to the Soviet version of events. Krishna Menon too was inclined to give the Soviets the benefit of the doubt, initially calling the happenings in Budapest a domestic affair to be sorted by the Hungarian government in the manner it deemed most appropriate. On 4 November 1956, he abstained from voting on a resolution that condemned the Soviet military intervention passed by a huge majority in the UN General Assembly. It was predictably opposed by the Soviet Union and its allies, but it was Krishna Menon's action that raised many eyebrows and seemed to confirm what his critics were saying—that when push came to shove he would bat for the Soviet Union.

Krishna Menon's abstention and his speeches that gave the impression that India was 'soft' on the USSR evoked an outcry in Parliament. He was criticized bitterly by Asoka Mehta, his erstwhile Congress Socialist Party colleague of the 1930s. Another socialist leader who would attack Krishna Menon in strong language was J.B. Kripalani, who would in the years to come become his most prominent baiter. Nehru was spared in these attacks because he had, unlike Krishna Menon, been speaking out in very clear language against the Soviet action as an attack on freedom and dignity.

Then Krishna Menon started his diplomatic efforts with the Hungarians and was able to convince them that they should allow UN Secretary General Hammarskjold to visit Hungary, make inquiries and submit a report to the General Assembly. That he was able to do so without going through the Soviets was a tribute to his persuasive skills when he decided to use them in a non-offensive manner. But the Hungarians could not guarantee a date for Hammarskjold's visit instantly, which is what the Americans wanted. Instead, Lodge supported a resolution moved by Pakistan and Cuba, which contained a provision for conducting 'free elections' in Hungary under UN auspices. This was a red rag to a bull as far as Krishna Menon was concerned, and he voted against the resolution, which was passed on 9 November 1956. He explained the logic of his action the next day after being accused by the Cuban delegate Emilio-Nunez-Portuondo of being a valiant defender of the Soviet Union:

. . . The Soviet Union is strong and does not need my support. The Cuban representative has asked if I am obeying another Government's whim. Perhaps, the Cuban delegate is speaking from experience . . . India belonged to no military alliance nor was it under the domination of any other country . . . India did not need to be told about the fundamentals of liberty . . . I hope that the same passion for fundamental liberty that was now being shown [by the US, Netherlands and Cuba which had preceded him] would be forthcoming when the question of colonial territories and conditions in Africa were discussed in the United Nations . . . India wants the trouble in Hungary ended and supports the view that Hungary must have its own Government. But this is not the same thing as demanding that elections should be held in Hungary under UN auspices. India cannot subscribe to any phraseology or proposals which disregard the sovereign rights of States represented in the [UN] Assembly. We cannot subscribe to the idea that any sovereign state can agree to elections under the United Nations . . . On the question of medical supplies I am in agreement with the humanitarian purposes of the U.S. resolution.

It was a highly nuanced position, but the nuance was lost not only in Western capitals but also among the community of his critics in the Indian Parliament and media. Then a curious event took place that month, which has not got its proper place in the history of the UN's decisions on Hungary. Twelve days later, Krishna Menon introduced a resolution along with Ceylon and Indonesia, which too got passed in the General Assembly. It called upon the Hungarian government to agree to the UN secretary general's request for 'direct observation of the situation by his nominees without prejudice to its sovereignty'. This was definitely not to the liking of the Soviet Union and its allies. Krishna Menon may well have wanted to dispel the impression that India was blindly following Moscow's line.

On 12 December 1956, he made a speech that could be read as a volte-face on his part in response to Nehru's instructions. He said:

> India did not demand the withdrawal of Soviet forces from Hungary in view of their context. India's objection was to the use of the Soviet forces in Hungarian internal affairs. It might have been justified if there had been a *coup d'etat* but what had happened in Hungary was a national uprising and the use of Soviet forces to suppress it was not appropriate.[20]

But this explanation came a month too late, and by that time Krishna Menon's reputation had taken a severe beating.

Why did Krishna Menon abstain from voting on the 4 November 1956 resolution for which he was to be pilloried so much? The obvious explanation would be Kashmir—that Krishna Menon was willing to wound but not strike against the USSR, knowing full well that India was crucially dependent on it for the cast of its veto power if India was pushed to the wall on the Kashmir issue in the UN Security Council. Much later, Krishna Menon was to categorically reject that there was such a link.[21] The fact that the Soviet Union abstained on the resolution on Kashmir in the UN Security Council in early 1957 certainly lends credence to the view that far from being happy with

Krishna Menon's role on the Hungarian matter, it was irked and showed its displeasure by abstaining. A few days later, however, the Soviets changed their stance and vetoed another resolution in the Security Council on Kashmir.

In the midst of the Suez and Hungarian crises at the UN, on 14 November 1956, Krishna Menon surprised Western powers by withdrawing a proposal made by India nine months earlier to include the question of Antarctica in the agenda of the UN General Assembly. A leading scholar of Antarctic politics has written that the original Indian proposal 'suggested that claims to national sovereignty in Antarctica represented outdated vestiges of European colonialism and believed that the UN offered the best means of administration for the southern continent'.[22] However, the proposal had irritated Chile and Argentina, both of whom made their displeasure known to Nehru, who got India to back off. But the pot had been stirred, and by mid-1958, India had once again begun to speak on the subject forcefully. Krishna Menon can certainly claim some credit for the twelve-nation Antarctic Treaty that was signed in Washington DC on 1 December 1959 for which India was not invited. A few weeks earlier, he had rubbed it in by saying in one of his speeches in New York:

. . . . My delegation had the temerity to bring it [the subject of Antarctica] up two or three years ago and upset the whole Latin American continent. But I am glad to hear by rumour—for nobody has told us—that in Washington on 15th October the twelve nations active in Antarctica pledged their determination to keep that continent free of war . . .

Ultimately, India was to become its member twenty-three years later[23] and now has a major presence in Antarctica.

Krishna Menon's activities in 1956 had both pleased and displeased many. But one person remained steadfast in his appreciation. Mountbatten wrote to him eight days before the eventful year came to a close:

You really are the kindest and the most thoughtful person for on the day of my last and final promotion your charming gift of a cigar holder arrived. The more I see of your work, the more I admire what you are doing. You will certainly have a great place in history when it comes to be finally written . . .

Notes

1. Acheson (1970).
2. Munro and Inglis (2015).
3. Reid (1981).
4. Millar (1972).
5. Barnes (2013).
6. Ramesh (2018).
7. Foreword in Reddy and Damodaran (1997).
8. This phrase is used in Ignatieff's biography of Isaiah Berlin. Ignatieff (2000).
9. *The Times of India*, 3 June 1954.
10. Logevall (2012).
11. Brecher (1968).
12. Gopal (1979).
13. *The Hindu*, 24 May 1955.
14. Brecher (1968).
15. Ibid.
16. Eden (1960).
17. Lloyd (1978).
18. Heikal (1986).
19. Rahman (2016).
20. Rajan (1963).
21. Brecher (1968).
22. Howkins (2016).
23. I have discussed this in Ramesh (2017).

14

Defence Minister and UN Envoy (1957–61)

1957

This would be the year when Krishna Menon would emerge as a hero all over India for his performance on Kashmir at the UN. It would also see him getting elected to Parliament with a huge majority without much campaigning. It was almost entirely on the strength of his performance at the UN and because the Prime Minister invested his personal charisma and authority to ensure that he won. It would also see him finally get a weighty portfolio in Nehru's cabinet.

For a few weeks Krishna Menon had been telling Nehru that he wanted to contest the Lok Sabha elections that were to be held in February–March 1957. This, he felt, would give him greater political acceptability and respectability. He had sent a telegram to Nehru from New York on 11 December 1956:

> I would like you to know that in the event of my continuing in public life I would like to do so as a member of the popular House of Parliament. I have always felt subjectively that my being in the second Chamber was incongruous.
>
> I shall be grateful if effective consideration can be given of my standing for election from a seat in metropolitan Bombay

or Madras. In Madras I do not want in any way to come in the way of Krishnamachari who sits for South Madras which is the only constituency in the State where I have the prospect of being in contact with the people. In Bombay there is a constituency which has a large South Indian population and also the City is cosmopolitan. I also venture to believe that it is a good thing for persons who are not local politicians to seek a suffrage on an All-India basis cutting across lingual and State affiliations. I believe that my standing there would also have a good impact on international opinion in proclaiming that international work and policies are highly thought of in India. I would prefer this [Bombay] to Madras . . .

    If there is any political impropriety or personal embarrassment in my mentioning this please do not hesitate to tell me . . .

Nehru replied by telegram a day later:

. . . I would myself prefer you to be in the Lok Sabha though it does not matter much if you continue in the Rajya Sabha. I am speaking to the persons concerned in Madras and Bombay. It may be difficult to make changes now because of certain decisions taken. However I shall try.

While this exchange was taking place Krishna Menon went off the rails and wrote to Nehru on 26 December 1956:

You have no escape in the scheme of things and you do not seek it. I am the wrong kind and create more conflicts and difficulties—so it is best for me to go . . . I have realized for a long time that I was being kept on and am quite a stranger . . .

My own sense is that this letter may have been provoked by the intense criticism of Krishna Menon's stand on Hungary and the widespread impression that he had wilfully ignored Nehru's instructions not to appear supportive of the Soviet stance. But Nehru ignored this latest outburst and wrote to him on 4 January 1957:

. . . The question of your election has been discussed here and we do not quite know what to decide . . . As I informed you, S.K. Patil has told me that he will be glad to have you stand from North Bombay . . . He thinks this should not be a difficult seat for you to win . . . Kamaraj Nadar is also prepared to give you what he calls a 'safe' seat but not in Madras city. Some Kerala people have also offered to put you up as a candidate. If you have to stand for the Lok Sabha, I imagine that the north Bombay seat would be the best of these three . . . Some of my colleagues feel, however, that it is not worthwhile for you to stand, especially at this stage for the Lok Sabha. Even Indu feels that way and thinks that you should continue in the Rajya Sabha. Indeed she says that she talked about this to you and you had then agreed to her suggestion . . .

Three days later Krishna Menon made up his mind and informed Nehru:

. . . I would like to accept Bombay North as recommended . . . I am much moved by the personal interest and consideration you have given to this matter. I have given you my reason for the position I have taken which I feel sure you will accept as my conviction. I also much appreciate the desire for retaining me in the Rajya Sabha as an indication that they value my services . . .

But what Indira Gandhi had told her father bothered him, and on 8 January 1957, Krishna Menon sent yet another telegram to Nehru:

. . . I respect INDU's advice very much and the reasons for it and her concern about my getting hurt . . . I do not want to run away from a contest . . . have also thought about the consequences of a defeat and I feel I ought to be prepared to accept them . . .

Two days later Krishna Menon told the Prime Minister that 'the course I have decided on is the right one irrespective of whatever may happen in the future'. He added:

... I hope that at least until the Kashmir debate is out of the way and in the interests of the nation and its causes those concerned will refrain from arranging leaks to the press and statements by so-called spokesman (of the ministry of external affairs) to indicate that I am on the way out and am nearly persona non grata, as a result of many reasons, including your visit to the United States, apart from general incompetence and unsuitability and that you have come to certain adverse conclusions and have even mentioned them to others . . .

Nehru was in Rajgir near Nalanda with the Dalai Lama, who was visiting India in connection with the 2500th birth anniversary celebrations of the Buddha that had commenced in May 1956. He replied to Krishna Menon from there on 12 January 1957, telling him that he would be the Congress's candidate for the North Bombay seat and added:

Your presence at nomination is not necessary but usually considered desirable. Please do not worry about odd statements in the press by irresponsible writers. They have no importance. I had one such statement contradicted. We quite realize, great pressure on you on Kashmir, disarmament and generally deteriorating world situation. We are happy that you are dealing with these matters . . . I understand privately that Peter Alvares of the PSP [Praja Socialist Party] is standing against you and that Democratic Research Service and other organisations sponsored by Masani and others as well as the organized Catholic Church will work against you. Foreign agencies will also be indirectly involved. Though personally I would have liked you to contest a by-election somewhat later to the Lok Sabha, I should now like to ask you to hold your chin up. Your contest will have great significance . . .

In view of the persistent propaganda that Krishna Menon was fronting for the communists, M.O. Mathai sent him a cable on 13 February 1957:

Your chance of getting elected from Bombay North constituency is very good and there is no cause for anxiety. Prominent persons like Rajni Patel, A.V. Baliga, Mulk Raj Anand and others who have close association with the Communist Party of India openly working and campaigning for you. They have proclaimed they have formed a committee and are collecting funds for your election. This has created an unfavorable impression in Bombay and elsewhere and is proving embarrassing for you and the Congress organisation. Several important friends have pointed this out to PM. When you return to Bombay PM would like you to be careful and not let the impression gain ground that there is some sort of alliance between you and the communists. You should not stay with Rajni Patel or anyone who is known to be associated with the communists.

A day later Krishna Menon replied to Mathai:

I heard something about the matter you have mentioned and I agree with you . . . The question is what I can do from here. I do not intend to associate myself with the Committee.

To dispel any lingering doubts, Ajoy Ghosh, the general secretary of the Communist Party of India, issued a public statement on 18 February 1957 that the communists would not support Krishna Menon and would work to defeat him.

But it was not the elections that kept Krishna Menon busy and pre-occupied. On 17 November 1956, the Jammu and Kashmir Constituent Assembly had adopted a constitution for the state that was to come into effect from 26 January 1957. In early January 1957, Pakistan complained to the UN Security Council that this decision of the J&K constituent assembly subverted the six resolutions passed by it during 1948–50 on the Kashmir issue. The Security Council commenced debate on Pakistan's representation on 16 January 1957. A few days later Krishna Menon would create history. He would first take the floor on 23 January 1955 for five hours and five minutes and continue the next day for another two hours and thirty minutes. This marathon speech has entered the

Guinness Book of World Records as the longest ever by a wide margin at the UN. It was a bravura performance, and it was for the first time in seven years that India's case on Kashmir was made with passion, eloquence, historical facts and political realities. The impact in India was electric and made Krishna Menon a hero. It was a different matter that the Security Council was unmoved by Krishna Menon's oratory and passed a resolution unanimously on the night of 24 January 1955, calling for the maintenance of the status quo in Kashmir and reminding India of its earlier commitment to conduct a plebiscite in the Valley. The USSR abstained, still sulking from Nehru's and Krishna Menon's stance on the Hungarian crisis the previous month.

A month later the Security Council resumed the debate, and Krishna Menon made four more long speeches—on 8, 15, 20 and 21 February 1957. This debate ended with the USSR changing its position on Kashmir dramatically and vetoing a resolution introduced by the US, the UK and others, but abstaining on another, which called upon the Swedish diplomat Gunnar Jarring to visit India and Pakistan and hold talks on the Kashmir issue. At end of a month of verbal duels and pyrotechnics, Krishna Menon had denied Pakistan a victory—if anything, the outcome was not entirely unacceptable to India. Both Nehru and Krishna Menon welcomed the Jarring mission but said it should take place after the elections had been completed.

Carlos Romulo of the Philippines was the president of the Security Council when Krishna Menon made his marathon speech. He was to recall that experience twenty-six years later:[1]

> . . . And he [Krishna Menon] was quite an arrogant fellow, a good friend of mine but quite arrogant. And the first time I presided over the Security Council to take up the Kashmir question, this fellow Krishna Menon said, 'Since our President has just come to this podium as the President of this Council, I suggest we adjourn for one week so that he can study this question of Kashmir.' I said, 'May I inform the distinguished delegate from India that the President is now ready to discuss this question because I have

studied it carefully for several months'. Well, we discussed it. Then he took the floor for 8 hours after which he fainted. Well, we took him to the room next to the Security Council, gave him smelling salts. He revived but of course that was a ploy. He was a candidate for Parliament in Bombay and he wanted this. So, they took pictures of him and all that so when he came to, I said, 'Krishna, you know you won the Oscar award?'

What hit the international headlines was Krishna Menon's collapse on the night of 17 February 1957. He had appeared on a television programme recorded in Washington and returned to New York with a high temperature and a very low blood pressure. His doctor, William Hitzig, attended to him continuously. Two days later Hitzig explained what had happened:

> Mr. Menon has been undergoing a great deal of physical and mental strain. He has taken an awful load on his shoulders. This strain led to gradual exhaustion and finally this morning when he awoke he manifested an acute circulatory collapse, with a blood pressure that dropped down to a very low level. His blood pressure later went up. His condition is called postural hypotension. When he stands up his blood pressure drops. He has to lie down to maintain his blood pressure. This is sometimes an acute condition which comes from fatigue, exhaustion and strain. His illness insidiously began on Friday [February 15] when he was talking in the Security Council. Mr. Menon developed acute drenching sweats. Despite this he was able to go to Washington.

The same day Krishna Menon informed a worried Nehru:

> I am better now and will be able to function on Wednesday in the Security Council unless there is a relapse which is not expected.

The Kashmir debate over, Krishna Menon headed home. But the glutton for self-punishment that he was, he first stopped over in

London to meet the new British Prime Minister, Harold Macmillan, and discuss issues related to the Suez with him and Selwyn Lloyd. Then he flew to Cairo to confabulate with his good friend Nasser and not-so-good a friend Fawzi, again on what was happening on the Suez issue and the UN Emergency Force. He arrived in Bombay only on 6 March 1957 to a rousing reception. Numerous messages of congratulations and good wishes awaited him, including one from G.M. Sadiq, president of the J&K Constituent Assembly, who said, '[The] people of Kashmir are grateful to Mr. Menon for espousing their cause in the Security Council at great risk to his health.'

Krishna Menon had barely three days to campaign. But he need not have worried. His campaign had already drawn a galaxy of personalities—film stars, lawyers, doctors, teachers and students. It was also being managed by S.K. Patil, the strongman of Bombay, and another person who was to be the uncrowned political king of Bombay two decades later—Rajni Patel, Krishna Menon's acolyte in the India League years of the late 1930s. Patel had written to Krishna Menon on 18 January 1957:

> I appreciate how difficult it is for you to come until the problem of Kashmir is over. However, as soon as that problem is over, you should make an airdash to Bombay. It will be a keen contest but at the same time people who are in touch with your constituency feel confident that you are bound to be elected. K.K. Shah [local Congress leader] has suggested to you that it is not necessary for you to be in Bombay except for a short time. I am afraid I take a different view of the matter and after consulting friends, I am of the firm opinion that it will be a very good thing if you can spend at least two to three weeks in Bombay even if you cannot spare a longer time.

On 6 February 1957, Nehru had also done something unusual to help Krishna Menon's election. He issued a long public appeal which, as he admitted, was uncharacteristic of him. The *Times of India* carried it in full the next day:

DO VOTE FOR MR. MENON
Premier's Call to Bombay Public

... Although I am not issuing any appeals for individual candidates, many of whom are my old colleagues and comrades, I am issuing this particular appeal to the voters of Bombay, that great city that has played such a memorable part not only in our struggle for freedom, but also in the growth of our industry . . . My principal reason for issuing this appeal is to mention especially the name of my old and valued colleague Mr. V.K. Krishna Menon . . . We have asked Mr. Krishna Menon to stand from Bombay city so that the citizens of Bombay may have an opportunity to give their verdict on the major international policies of the Congress and the Government of India. With these policies Mr. Krishna Menon has been intimately connected for many years. We felt that it was right that the voters of Bombay which in many ways is the political nerve-centre of India, should pronounce on them and give their verdict generally on the policy of non-alignment which India has followed . . . Mr. Krishna Menon being engaged in the Security Council, cannot easily undertake an election campaign which otherwise he should have done. It is for this reason that I have issued this appeal . . .

Nehru had made Krishna Menon's election a referendum on his foreign policy. But there was another issue agitating many sections of society in Bombay, including some communist and socialist leaders who otherwise would have flocked to Krishna Menon. There was a popular demand for a single Marathi-speaking state of Maharashtra with Bombay as capital which, after many twists and turns, had not been agreed to by Parliament the previous year. Parliament had supported the continuation of a composite multilingual state of Bombay.[2] This position would change three years later but for now, Nehru, Krishna Menon and the Congress were not seen to be supportive of the Marathi cause. This explains why Krishna Menon did not win by a thumping majority—his margin was about 48,000 votes as opposed to Patil's, which was almost 60,000.

But a win is a win, and Krishna Menon had won without campaigning in any meaningful manner and speaking to audiences only in the few public meetings he addressed in chaste English which went over the heads of almost everybody. As soon as the results were announced he thanked the people of North Bombay for their support and promptly took off for Cairo for yet another round of discussions with Nasser and Fawzi on Suez. On his arrival back in Bombay on 21 March 1957, he announced that the Suez Canal would be reopened for traffic in about a month's time and that the UN Emergency Force was supervising the withdrawal of Israeli forces from the Sinai and would guard the armistice line to prevent any further trouble.

Nehru was putting together his new cabinet, and on 16 April 1957, he wrote to Krishna Menon:

I am including your name in the list of Cabinet Ministers. I trust you will agree to this and take charge of the Ministry of Defence.

Nehru also sent a note to the top officials of the Ministry of External Affairs the same day:

Tomorrow the new Council of Ministers is going to be appointed and sworn-in. In this Council, Shri V.K. Krishna Menon will be the Defence Minister. I should like him, however, to continue his close association with External Affairs and, more specially, to deal with matters relating to Kashmir, Indo-China, Goa and the United Nations in so far as the Ministry of External Affairs deals with them. He should, therefore, get necessary papers, relating to these matters as well as any others dealing with important developments.

After being sworn in as a member of Nehru's thirteen-man cabinet, Krishna Menon took over as India's fourth defence minister on 17 April 1957. There was hardly any murmur because he had, for the moment, silenced his critics and his enemies by his stellar performance on Kashmir at the UN. But that performance was only the Act I Scene I of the Kashmir drama in New York in 1957. Act I Scene II was later in the year when he would make nine more

thundering speeches on the subject between 9 October 1957 and
2 December 1957. This was after Jarring had come and gone and
thereafter submitted his report to the Security Council. Although he
had not been able to sway the Security Council in January–February
1957 by the intellectual brilliance of his speeches that demonstrated
his knowledge of law, politics and history, he could take some
satisfaction from the fact that Jarring's report vindicated the stand
Krishna Menon had taken.

Was Krishna Menon's appointment as defence minister totally
unexpected? Evidence suggests otherwise. Nehru had wanted
a livewire as defence minister after three somewhat indifferent
performers in that portfolio—Baldev Singh, Gopalaswami Ayyangar
and K.N. Katju. An already overburdened Nehru had himself held the
defence portfolio first between February 1953 and January 1955 and
later between January 1957 and April 1957. Krishna Menon certainly
fit the bill. More than that, he had been thinking of defence matters
for quite some time. On 27 February 1954, Krishna Menon had
suggested to Nehru 'qualitative changes in the army and the air force
and an increase in the size of the navy'. He had laid considerable stress
on making use of modern science and technology, such as radars,
for improving India's defences. Then on 8 April 1955, he had sent
Nehru a well-reasoned eight-page note on 'Defence Expenditure and
Economic Development', among the earliest writings on this subject
in India by a political personality. He wrote this in the background of
the two regional military alliances that had been signed—the South
East Asian Treaty Organization (SEATO) in September 1954 and the
Central Treaty Organization (CENTO) in February 1955. He was
actually quite prescient:

> Increased expenditure on defence from now right through the
> next Five-Year Plan period [that is till 1962] has or will become
> inevitable . . . The imbalance in relative military strength and
> Pakistan's adoption of Western view of the doctrine of negotiating
> from strength renders the situation very unhealthy, and it is not one
> that public opinion will or Government can condone. The question
> that immediately arises is how we are to provide the additional

resources for increased expenditure and whether we can have economic development and arms at the same time . . . The defence position as it is developing may well force us a reconsideration of the Plan [development spending] and its resources . . .

At that time the dominant economic view was one of 'export pessimism'. Remarkably and quite unusually for a socialist of his type, Krishna Menon went against this view and advocated for greater focus on exports to augment external resources to buy defence equipment. He also went on to suggest that 'restrictions on freer enterprise is today unnecessary' and if these restrictions are removed, more resources could be made available for government investment in defence. To raise additional resources within the country, Krishna Menon recommended the use of India's private gold holdings 'more rationally and fruitfully' in the public interest. He ended by telling Nehru that the main purpose of the note is:

> to indicate my line of thinking in regard to consideration or reconsideration of economic and development problems in the light of inevitable advance in defence expenditures . . .

and that

> there are several important matters of an organizational and administrative nature which are not merely of detail but are basic to any implementation of the ideas that appear in this note.

Krishna Menon would be pilloried later for neglecting defence spending. His note of April 1955 shows that he was, contrary to conventional wisdom, a very early advocate of increased defence expenditure. He championed that idea when it was unfashionable and when his later critics said that increased defence spending would be detrimental from an economic point of view, in addition to being morally repugnant in a country that had Gandhi as the Father of the Nation. Krishna Menon would make many mistakes as defence minister but he could not be held solely responsible for less-than-

adequate defence spending. The finance ministry of those times
would have a heavier cross to bear on this account.

Just twenty days after Krishna Menon took over as defence
minister, General K.S. Thimayya was appointed the chief of the
Indian Army. Thimayya was close to Nehru and the two shared
a warm, easy relationship. In 1954, when Thimayya's sister was
widowed at a young age with four small children, Nehru put her
to work in his secretariat, and thereafter, she worked with Indira
Gandhi for almost two decades. When Nehru decided to take a few
days off at the Kaziranga wildlife sanctuary in Assam in October 1956,
he asked Thimayya to join him. Earlier in October 1953, he had
sent Thimayya to the Korean Peninsula as chairman of the Neutral
Nations Repatriation Commission, a body invented by Krishna
Menon and set up by the UN. In early 1954, Thimayya had been
awarded the Padma Bhushan, just a notch lower than the Padma
Vibhushan conferred on Krishna Menon.

Thimayya was third in order of seniority. Yet, given his track
record, his public persona both within the army and outside and
his equation with Nehru, he was appointed the army chief. Krishna
Menon would undoubtedly have been consulted but having known
Thimayya earlier, he would have registered no objections to the
seniority principle being overlooked. Four years later he would
invoke this very principle while selecting Thimayya's successor.
The combination of Krishna Menon and Thimayya was expected to
infuse new life and dynamism into the Ministry of Defence, which till
then had had a somnolent reputation. Nobody could have expected
or guessed that within two years the two would be at each other's
throats.

A few days after Thimayya had taken over, the Municipal
Council of Srinagar feted him and Krishna Menon together. On 19
May 1957, the president and members of the Council presented a
public address, extolling Krishna Menon's performance at the UN
Security Council earlier in the year:

> . . . while you have earned the tribute of the country as a whole,
> you have gained the abiding gratitude of the people of our State.

Even though your health was gravely impaired, you spared no efforts to defend a righteous cause.

The same address recalled fondly the role of Thimayya in Kashmir in 1947, saying that 'the people of Kashmir gratefully cherish his friendship and the sympathy and understanding he showed while defending the State against the invaders'. This address reflected the widespread expectation that the Krishna Menon–Thimayya duo would transform the country's defence preparedness.

Krishna Menon's star was now shining brighter than ever before. But he was still very much in the grip of his demons and wrote 'one of his characteristic letters of masochistic bitterness' to Nehru on 10 June 1957, after having met with the Prime Minister:

> . . . You do not need me . . . I must therefore bring things to an end . . . I can make no impact on your mind . . . I have tried hard and endured much, but it is all to no purpose. I do not mind or grudge the effort or the pain, but there comes a time when one cannot live with oneself any more, deprived or purposeful function . . . I have always loved you and will not stop doing so wherever I may be.

This was truly inexplicable. Krishna Menon was defence minister. He was also head of India's delegation to the UN. He had won an election handsomely. He had earned huge kudos for his defence of India's position on Kashmir at the UN. Yet here he was, lamenting his plight and imagining that he was not wanted by Nehru and his colleagues.

The world could not guess that Krishna Menon was writing these agonized letters to Nehru. He dominated the headlines both in India and abroad. Two pieces were particularly significant, and both speculated on his being a successor to Nehru. They were by no means 'puff' pieces and were quite surprisingly understanding of the man, his strengths and weaknesses, his fancies and foibles, his achievements and failures. In both instances, the authors had spoken with Krishna Menon, and it was clear that while they were not starry-eyed about him, they recognized his value and worth. The first article titled 'Krishna Menon—A Clue to Nehru' appeared in the *New York Times* on 7 April 1957 and was written by its India correspondent, A.M. Rosenthal, who was to later become the editor of that newspaper. The second by Serrell Hillman appeared in *Esquire* magazine on 1 August 1957 with a provocative title, 'The World's Most Hated Diplomat'. But the article was actually very positive and carried praise for him from American diplomats who had worked both with and against him at the UN and from some others who admired him. One of them would later become Vice President of the US in 1964—Hubert Humphrey.

Domestically too, Nehru was clearly planning a larger role for Krishna Menon. He must have seen him as the natural leader of the 'left' in the Congress after he himself had left the scene. For a few years, Krishna Menon had been playing a more active role in the annual sessions of the Congress, not only on foreign policy resolutions but also on matters related to economic policy. In late 1957, Nehru expanded Krishna Menon's canvas and got him to take more interest in the politics of his home state, Kerala, which now had a communist government in power. The Congress organization in the state was extremely perturbed, and Krishna Menon became a natural channel for bringing their grievances to the notice of the Prime Minister—though the channel knew little about the state and did not even speak the local language. A year later Nehru would get Krishna Menon to chair an important party committee on public-sector enterprises, with which Feroze Gandhi would also be closely associated. In June 1959, Krishna Menon was to be one of the main speakers at a seminar held by Congress Party at Ooty on economic planning and policy.

It had been almost a decade since Krishna Menon had anything to do with the India League officially. But he was still its honorary chairman. The League was being run by Reginald Sorensen, Julius Silverman and Bridget Tunnard. Its mandate had been changed after India's Independence to work for greater cooperation between India and Britain. So it was on 5 May 1957, less than three weeks after he had become defence minister, that Krishna Menon, concerned with the UK's stand on Kashmir at the UN, wrote to his India League colleagues:

> . . . We are all aware that in Britain there is much antagonism towards us—the Prime Minister and myself particularly—for the position we took in regard to the British attack on Egypt along with France and co-terminous with Israel . . . The Prime Minister [Nehru] said in Parliament for the first time that he felt disturbed and that the Commonwealth relationship should be examined . . .

Then he went on to describe, for the first time, his own role in the Suez issue:

> . . . [I]n regard to Egypt I was listened to with utmost courtesy and patience and often I took them near a settlement which but for Eden's unfortunate personal view of Nasser and Selwyn Lloyd's bungling, ambitious and miscalculated approach and the inordinate amount of jealously all round, might have been called off. Today they would welcome . . . if the Indian plan of last October were accepted by Egypt in full. The conditions for it, however, no longer exist. We, therefore, began in last December to persuade Egypt to offer to the world its own basis for settlement . . . which would satisfy international concerns and interests . . . Nasser pressed the Prime Minister to ask me to visit Cairo for talks with him in the middle of March. The present settlement was hammered out and drafted during the two days I was there and finally agreed to by Egypt an hour before I left Cairo. The Egyptians showed the plan to others . . . not for negotiations but as a matter of courtesy. It leaked out although both Egypt and we had kept it very quiet. Americans say that the French leaked it in order to kill it, but it appeared in full text in the New York Times two or three days after a copy was given to the American Ambassador in Cairo! The Americans sought to amend it . . . the Egyptians were in constant touch with us and the amendments since incorporated in the final plan were also worked out in association with us . . .

The purpose of this letter is for us to consider in London what in the present circumstances can be done to popularize Indian policy in regard to world affairs, peace and world cooperation and on Kashmir and on her own internal developments as well as the important purpose of promoting Indo–British relations. I want to say to you that the time has come to take a fresh wind and chart a course towards the same goals with which we started nearly 30 years ago. More particularly, I would like to know what can be done in these matters specially for informing the Labour Members of Parliament, the Labour movement, Women's and other movements and also the religious groups as before. We have to get back into stride . . . Some of us cannot forget that all this trouble about Kashmir was started by Noel Baker in the Security Council when a Labour Government was in office . . .

Clearly, while Krishna Menon had left the India League, the India League had not left him; old wounds caused by the party to which he had once belonged still rankled. But he remained an Anglophile. On 23 July 1957, he told Nehru about the negotiations he had started for the purchase of fighter aircraft from the UK:

I have kept you informed about the progress in regard to the procurement of essential aircraft from the United Kingdom. The arrangements I have been able to make in regard to the supply of these are reasonably satisfactory to the Air Force. Two squadrons would be in position this year. These arrangements were finally reached with the U.K. Government by continued negotiations.

A little while earlier Krishna Menon had embarked on a somewhat unusual initiative. In the seven years that he and Chou En-lai were friends, this was perhaps the only occasion on which they had exchanged letters. Chou had written to Krishna Menon on 15 June 1957:

I have received with great pleasure your message . . . I wish to thank you and Prime Minister Nehru for introducing us to

Mr. and Mrs. Patnaik. Prior to and following the visit of the Dalai
Lama to India [in 1956], several round flights between Lhasa and
Bagdogra were successfully made by aircrafts of our two countries.
This affords new possibilities for strengthening the communication
links between India and the Tibet region of China. But, so far as
the existing economic and technical conditions of the Tibet region
of China are concerned, there will be difficulties on our side, if the
airline as planned by Mr. Patnaik is to be opened between Calcutta
and Lhasa.

Biju Patnaik, a Congress colleague of Nehru, was a daredevil pilot
who had shot to fame in July 1947. When the Dutch had resorted
to armed action to retain their control over Indonesia, Patnaik had
defied them and flown the Indonesian Prime Minister, Sutan Sjahrir
, out of Djakarta to attend an Asian conference convened by Nehru
in New Delhi. He owned a company called Kalinga Airlines and
had met Nehru sometime in May 1957 to start a freighter-cum-
passenger-airline service to Tibet. Nehru had encouraged Patnaik but
expressed doubts on whether the Chinese would agree. Thereafter,
Patnaik met Krishna Menon, who was more excited by the idea than
Nehru was. Krishna Menon had then established informal contact
with the Chinese premier. But the idea did not go very far, and in
any case the entire situation would change in March 1959 with the
Dalai Lama fleeing to India.

Even though he was defence minister now, Krishna Menon
continued to assist the Prime Minister on matters related to foreign
policy and, of course, remained the head of India's delegation to
the UN. This would have deleterious consequences, especially after
1959, because it meant that he would be out of India for around
three months every year. Initially, it did not matter much, and
Krishna Menon transacted much official business through letters
and telegrams from New York. On 2 October 1957, he wrote to
O. Pulla Reddy, the defence secretary:

I hope you are well. I know you must be heavily over-worked. I,
however, expect to hear from you about yourself and other officers

and how the work is going on. I had no news of the Ministry at all
except a brief telegram in reply to mine . . .

He then proceeded to give detailed instructions to Reddy on
various matters relating to the ministry and the armed force. He
continued:

> . . . I have not heard from the Chiefs of Staff or my Scientific Adviser.
> You might mention this to them and give them my regards. I hope
> you and Mrs Pulla Reddy are well and that my absence has assisted
> you in settling down as you do not have the trouble of looking
> after me and seeking to educate an untutored Minister. Also I have
> little doubt that my absence will cut down the number of meetings.
> With regard to meetings I think the permanent Committees of
> the Defence minister should meet regularly whether I am there or
> not . . .

Pulla Reddy replied to his minister nine days later. Krishna Menon's
letter of instructions was three pages long. Reddy's letter of compliance
was twice that length:

> Many thanks for your letters of 2nd October 1957, received by me
> yesterday evening. I was all the time thinking of writing to you,
> but there was nothing sensational round here and again I did not
> wish to distract your time and attention from the much bigger
> questions you have on hand at the moment. I give below a few
> items which may be some interest to you . . .

Reddy then gave Krishna Menon a long rundown of things that were
happening back home which the defence minister ought to know.
They included the following:

> As soon as I got your letter, I called up the Additional Secretary
> and all the Joint Secretaries, and acquainted them with all the
> points made in your letter and asked them to progress vigorously
> the items that are still pending. The CNS [chief of naval staff] is

out somewhere in Punjab on a brief leave. General Thimayya has
gone out on tour . . . The Air Marshal returned from his trip to
England . . . and is now more or less in daily touch . . . I have
informed him that you will be glad to hear points of interest. The
Scientific Adviser is on a brief leave . . .

As regards the Naval Expansion Paper, Finance have not agreed
to purchase immediately the new Destroyers because of difficulties
of foreign exchange . . .

The question of allocation of foreign exchange for the next
half year was considered by the Cabinet. Finance, in the first
instance, allocated only Rs 20 crores against our demand for Rs
66 crores . . . but I had represented to the Prime Minister that
the allocation was very inadequate, and at his intervention, the
allotment has now been raised by Rs 20 crores. The Chiefs of
Staff, particularly the COAS [chief of army staff] feel that even the
increased amount allocated to the Services is very inadequate . . .

The tempo of work continues to be as heavy as ever and we
are doing the best in your absence . . . We are following with close
interest your remarkable speeches in the United Nations Security
Council, and I observed universal admiration for the way you
presented our case . . .

What Pulla Reddy told Krishna Menon about the prevailing foreign
exchange position had been communicated to the defence minister
by T.T. Krishnamachari himself the previous month. The message
was that the 'foreign exchange situation is extremely serious and will
affect not only the execution of the Plan [development spending] but
also the maintenance of the economy and defence. Defence would
not be able to get even half of what it had asked for.' This position
would not improve over the next three or four years and would
have a damaging impact on defence preparedness. History has blamed
Krishna Menon for neglecting defence without taking into account
this broader picture of the availability of foreign exchange (and even
rupee) resources for vital defence imports.

The year 1957 was undoubtedly when Krishna Menon finally
established himself in Indian politics. In some ways he had reached

the very top with speculation swirling that he could, at some future date, even take over from Nehru. If Pant was seen as the high priest of the 'right-wing', Krishna Menon was seen as the archangel of the left. But even at this moment of personal triumph something was seriously wrong. Marie Seton, who was then visiting India, wrote to her friend Ronald Moody, the noted sculptor, and his wife, Helene, from New Delhi on 15 May 1957. She was staying with the Prime Minister and his daughter, and wrote:

> K [Krishna Menon] took me out to dinner with some friends of his. I cannot remember when I ever felt as I do at this moment. I feel a witness to the most pitiful thing I have seen and I do not know what on earth I can do to make things one scrap better. If K has been haunted before by insecurity fears, it is nothing to compared to what he is today. My dears, I am living in the bosom of those who have an inner security but it does not help them that they have because somehow he does not even feel he belongs with them or to them. He is in a more desperate state than he has ever been—the man who feels he is surrounded by enmity and rejection. I think he will die unless there is some conceivable way to make him feel he is not hated and I do not want him to die in this agonized state of mind . . . It would have been better if he had never come back, never become anything at all. I have never believed in 'success' or 'power'; but for him it has been worse than anything else in his life—agony—now it has reached a frantic pitch. I am glad I got here even if it is extremely painful . . .I realize I have the deepest affection and nothing else is going to alter that . . .

Seton went on to describe Krishna Menon as 'one haunted by a phantasmagoria of hostility made worse by a long exile. He has lived without belief that anyone really wanted him, was ever really fond of him'. It is quite bizarre, if Seton is to be believed, that when he actually should have been more than gratified at what had come to him thus far, courtesy Nehru and his own talents, he was in the abyss of self-doubt.

1958

Krishna Menon's growing political profile at home coincided with the third resignation episode involving Nehru. Within a space of five days in February 1958, Nehru's political and personal world received two shocks. On 18 February 1958, his finance minister, T.T. Krishnamachari, was forced to submit his resignation because of a spirited campaign carried on in Parliament against some dubious investments made by the government-owned Life Insurance Corporation of India (LIC) in companies owned by a businessman Haridas Mundhra, whose reputation was blemished to begin with. That this campaign was led by none other than the Prime Minister's son-in-law, Feroze Gandhi, would have added to Nehru's extreme embarrassment and discomfiture. Krishnamachari and Nehru had formed a mutual admiration society for decades, and the finance minister was known for his drive and dynamism. Then Maulana Azad, who had fought by Nehru's side for decades, passed away on 12 February 1958. Azad had stoutly opposed the induction of Krishna Menon into Nehru's cabinet for two years before yielding reluctantly in 1956.

These two departures apart, Nehru had been feeling despondent over other events in the country, and while speaking to the Congress Parliamentary Party on 1 and 3 May 1958, he announced that he wanted to take a 'short break', a 'temporary retirement' as it were. The UK high commissioner in India, Malcolm Macdonald, reported to London on 21 June 1958:

> . . . With the death of Maulana Azad and the resignation of Mr. T.T. Krishnamachari, Mr. Nehru has lost two important political supporters, and his position is weaker than it was in relation to a right-wing Hindu section in the Cabinet led by the formidable trio, Pandit Pant, Mr. Morarji Desai and Mr. S.K. Patil. In spite of their over-riding loyalty to him they, and some others have recently made little secret of their irritation at certain of his policies . . . they disagree with some aspects of his Socialistic notions . . . Mr. Krishna Menon now seems to regard himself as a

candidate for the Premiership, if and when Mr. Nehru withdraws;
but although he has acquired a certain national popularity by his
vigourous advocacy of India's Kashmir case in the United Nations
Security Council, he has, so far at least, little widespread support.
He is opposed to (and opposed by) the right-wing in the Congress,
and probably sees his destiny as the rallier and leader of the Congress
left-wing when his patron Mr. Nehru, disappears . . .

It is still not too late for a split in the Congress to occur;
and provided it were a neat split into two parties, it would be a
refreshing development. The Government of India would cease to
be a discordant and overwieldly entity that it has become; Pandit
Pant, Morarji Desai or S.K. Patil would lead a vigorous conservative
party whilst Mr. Nehru, supported by Krishna Menon, would lead
a concentrated socialist party . . . Yet in my opinion a split in the
Congress ranks is unlikely whilst Mr. Nehru is their captain.

The split in the Congress party that Macdonald found desirable was
to take place a decade later. But by that time, both Nehru and Pant
would have been gone from the scene and Krishna Menon would
be in the political wilderness, having resigned from the Congress in
1967. The split would be led on one side by Nehru's daughter and
on the other by the Congress old guard that included Desai and Patil.
A pivotal figure in forcing this split on ideological grounds would
be Indira Gandhi's alter ego, who had worked with Krishna Menon
both at the India League and the High Commission—P.N. Haksar.[3]
Krishna Menon would, since the mid-1930s, refer to him as 'Pandit
Haksar'.

While Nehru was contemplating his sabbatical from politics,
Krishna Menon was taking steps to build his bridges with the
Americans. He invited his American counterpart, Henry Cabot Lodge,
a 'Boston Brahmin' and pillar of the Republican establishment, to
make a visit to India. The invitation had been extended in May 1957,
as soon as he had taken over as defence minister and a conversation
had taken place in Washington DC on 4 June 1957 between US
Secretary of State John Foster Dulles and US Ambassador to India
Ellsworth Bunker.

The secretary said that he had received a letter from Ambassador Lodge stating that the ambassador had been urged by Krishna Menon to make a visit to India. The secretary asked whether such a visit would embarrass Ambassador Bunker:

> Ambassador Bunker replied that a visit by Ambassador Lodge would not be embarrassing for him. He thought such a visit might be helpful. Mr. Krishna Menon was a strange person. He had done a beautiful job of briefing the War College Group which had recently visited India. He had answered all the questions of the group in a reasonable and friendly manner. The War College group had been pleased with its trip to India and that India should be included in all future itineraries of the War College.

Lodge and his wife came to India in February 1958 and then went on to Pakistan, Afghanistan and Iran. Krishna Menon played the gracious host in both New Delhi and Bombay, and by all accounts, the Lodges were delighted by their trip.

A year later on 29 June 1959, a conversation would take place at the US State Department in Washington between very senior officials and the US Ambassador in India Ellsworth Bunker. Bunker was asked about India's defence minister, and his response was recorded thus:

> . . . Ambassador Bunker stated that Krishna Menon had seemed much more friendly to the U.S. and to Ambassador Bunker personally since the visit to India of Ambassador Lodge. As an example, Ambassador Bunker cited his recent conversation with Krishna Menon in regard to the shooting down of an Indian Canberra [aircraft] by the Pakistani Air Force. The Ambassador said that Krishna Menon had been much more restrained in discussing this incident than he would have been two years previously. As an example of Krishna Menon's changing attitude, the Ambassador referred to a remark which Krishna Menon made to him to the effect that the moral stature of the U.S. has increased during the last two years . . .

Mr. Wilcox asked if the reports that Krishna Menon had used Ambassador Lodge during the latter's visit were true. Ambassador Bunker replied that Krishna Menon had indeed used the Lodge visit for his own personal purposes. Nevertheless, Ambassador Bunker added he believed the trip had been on balance worthwhile. The Ambassador said that friends of the U.S. at the highest levels of the Government of India do not like Krishna Menon, and thus dislike to see Krishna Menon in a position to use something like the Lodge visit to increase his stature and to disprove statements that 'the Americans do not like me'. He said that the Prime Minister had driven Krishna Menon with a very tight rein during the last year or so. Two examples of this control occurred during the crisis over Lebanon and the Taiwan Straits. In both cases, the Ambassador said, Krishna Menon had been practically silent, presumably under instructions from the Prime Minister . . .

Bunker drew attention to the uncharacteristic silence on the part of Krishna Menon on Western actions in the Middle East in mid-1958. This was in keeping with Nehru's overall policy of not antagonizing the Americans too much, given the foreign exchange crisis India was then going through. The silence had immediately been noticed by British High Commissioner Malcolm Macdonald, whose main informants always seem to have been Vice President S. Radhakrishnan, India's head of the foreign service, N.R. Pillai, and Nehru's aide M.O. Mathai. Macdonald reported back on 21 July 1958:

As I have reported in recent telegrams, the Indian Government are under very strong pressure in India to recognize the new Iraqi Government. Mr. Nehru is being quite severely criticized, not only by many of his followers but by also some of his colleagues, for not according this recognition forthwith—though he is being supported by other of his colleagues in his refusal to do so.

It will not surprise you to learn that amongst Mr. Nehru's principal critics is Krishna Menon. From the beginning of the crisis he has been in favour of strong public denunciations of the American and British landings in the Lebanon and Jordan respectively, and also in favour of recognition of the new Iraqi Government. The fact that Mr. Nehru has so far accepted neither of these policies is a mark of the decline of Krishna Menon's influence with him on important questions of foreign policy. I have been told by a reliable Indian informant who knows what is happening, that Mr. Nehru has 'kept Menon at arms length' throughout these critical days. He has relied much more on consultation with Pant (the home minister) and with his principal officials . . .

This is all to the good, but we cannot necessarily count on Krishna Menon's influence being anything like eliminated . . . Anyway Menon is no longer ascendant . . .

Macdonald was wrong. Nehru may have, for tactical reasons, given Krishna Menon short shrift on one or two issues involving the US but he would very much continue to lead India's delegation to the UN. One reason for this was the fact that Krishna Menon had come to be accepted as India's inevitable spokesman on Kashmir if and when that issue came up in New York—and the possibility of that happening could never be discounted. But for the first time Nehru asked Krishna Menon to make no public speeches on the Middle East. He also told Krishna Menon not to stay in New York for more than a fortnight unless, of course, Kashmir was on the agenda of the Security Council. That there was some coolness between the Prime Minister and the defence minister for a few months in 1958 was evident.

One reason for this, as Macdonald noted in his report of 24 August 1958, may have been 'the recrudescence of the "jeep scandal"' and Nehru's realization that 'Krishna's part in that jeep business was far from creditable to him'. Macdonald was right, but what he and all others were unaware of was that on 15 May 1958 Krishna Menon had actually sent in his resignation to Nehru:

The Secretary General [N.R. Pillai] told me that the Jeep Case is to be considered at a meeting of the Cabinet Ministers, etc. this afternoon. He also sent me the papers. I informed him that I did not consider it proper or appropriate for me to attend, much less

participate in the meeting. I understand that he conveyed this and
the reasons to you.

After serious thought, I consider it appropriate that I should
place my office at your disposal and your discretion. This, I regard
as necessary, for healthy practice and precedent. Since Secretary
General appears to be dealing with this matter with you, I
mentioned my thoughts also to him this morning.

I have not come to this view in a mood of protest or haste
nor to face your consideration of this matter with a <u>fait accompli</u>
in this respect. I feel I ought to enable you to feel free from any
embarrassment which might exist when a colleague is a party
concerned.

Nehru replied that very day:

> . . . I need not tell you that I do not propose to treat it seriously
> even though you may have meant it as such. You are only remotely
> concerned with this matter. If it is anybody's fault most of us are
> involved . . .

This was a curious reply because it contradicted whatever Nehru
had told Krishna Menon six years earlier on the problems that he
had created as high commissioner by his decisions on certain defence
contracts. It is true that subsequently new facts had come to light
but the fact that certain buddies of Krishna Menon had acted as
intermediaries had never been controverted.

V.R. Krishna Iyer, a noted jurist, would play a catalytic role in
forming the Krishna Menon Memorial Society in April 1975 and,
for two decades, keep Krishna Menon alive in public memory.
Ironically, in 1958, when he was minister in the communist
government in Kerala, he would write to Nehru accusing Krishna
Menon of hobnobbing with people who were intent on destabilizing
and throwing out that government. Nehru replied to his complaints
on 5 September 1958:

> I received your letter of the 1st September two days ago. I was a
> little surprised to get it. If you had wished to find out why my

colleague V.K. Krishna Menon had gone to Kerala and what he was doing there, you could have seen him yourself while he was in Kerala, or written to him. I am told you were in the neighbourhood at the time he was there, and you know him well enough to go to see him. You are aware that he is a Minister of the Union Government and his field of activity is, therefore, the whole of India . . . I am told that among the people who came to see him, was your father. You refer to memoranda being prepared for him and being given to him . . . It is quite possible that some of them might be complaints against the Kerala Government . . . You refer to conducted tours . . . When a Union Minister visits any place, it is the duty of the people there, including the Congress Party, to help in that tour. You might have noticed that Krishna Menon has said nothing in public before or after his tour, about what he thought of certain events in Kerala or what he saw there . . .

It is a historical fact, however, that the communist ministry in Kerala, of which Krishna Iyer was a prominent minister, was dismissed on 31 July 1959 by Nehru, acting reluctantly under pressure from his Congress colleagues, including Indira Gandhi, who was then president of the Congress. Krishna Menon had sided with her on the dismissal issue. Nevertheless, in 1993, Krishna Iyer would author a book eulogizing both Nehru and Krishna Menon.[4]

Every so frequently Krishna Menon would send to Nehru not only letters but also telegrams from wherever he was at the moment. At times, these were on substantive issues but often they meandered all over the place, giving expression to his feeling of despondency and his wanting to leave. Worried by the growing influence of what he believed to be right-wing forces represented by Morarji Desai and T.T. Krishnamachari in the Union cabinet, on 24 November 1958, Krishna Menon sent a telegram to Nehru from New York, saying that there was a sense of drift in the Indian government and that 'we are on a slippery slope and slipping fast'. He was not specific but talked about an impending nuclear catastrophe and the dangers to India from depending too much on American assistance. He also hinted, like he would often do, that Nehru was far too consensual in

his approach and did not assert himself firmly. Two days later the
Prime Minister replied:

> . . . Having been influenced a great deal by Gandhiji, I have got
> into a certain way of working and I think that the means and the
> method of doing something is at least as important as the thing
> itself . . . I would not like to press you to do something which you
> dislike, just as I am sure you would feel the same way about me. But
> we should certainly try to understand each other's viewpoint and
> try to explain one's own and thus influence the other's thinking . . .
>
> As for the cold war, I am afraid I am inclined to lose interest in
> it . . . What I mean is that I do not think we can play any decisive
> role in it and the tremendous forces that are at play will continue
> to go their own way . . .

1959

Krishna Menon had started out well as defence minister, giving the
highest priority to the manufacture of defence equipment in India.
A number of defence production companies were established, and
the Defence Research and Development Organization (DRDO) was
created. His performance in the first eighteen months of tenure could
not be faulted in any significant way. But by mid-1959, Krishna
Menon's relationship with the military top brass had begun to fray.
The service chiefs were beginning to get frustrated on two counts
at least: first, Krishna Menon's style of functioning, which respected
no generally accepted rules of organizational behaviour, and second,
his inability to get key proposals through with his senior ministerial
colleagues. He faced a particular problem with Finance Minister
Morarji Desai, with whom he was always at loggerheads. India had
suffered a huge foreign exchange crisis in 1958 and the financial
position of the government was quite precarious. Over and above that
was Desai's natural instinct to view enhanced defence expenditure
as an assault on Gandhian principles and quite unnecessary, given
other pressing developmental challenges. Krishna Menon just
could not get on with or convince Desai, and Nehru too was

unwilling to intervene, preferring to go by Desai's advice on financial priorities. Once, when Nehru had intervened on proposals made by Thimayya, with the approval of Krishna Menon on upgradations and new appointments in the Indian Army, Desai had, on 14 June 1958, expressed disagreement saying that the 'wholesale creation of high appointments and new ranks would give the impression that India is going in for considerable rearming'.

On 16 January 1959, Nehru was in Ambala to applaud the Indian Army for having successfully completed Operation Amar— the construction of about 1500 housing quarters for various ranks in some 1400 working hours. The star of the function was Major General B.M. Kaul, who had led the project. Handsome tributes were paid to Kaul not only by Nehru but also by Krishna Menon and by the army chief, General K.S. Thimayya. Thimayya and Kaul went back a long way. Both served on a committee that had been set up in late 1946 to suggest a roadmap for the Indianization of the officer ranks of the Indian Army after Independence. Then, Kaul had served as defence attaché in the Indian embassy in Washington and had also been part of India's delegation to the UN in 1948. Thereafter, Thimayya and he had worked together in Korea when the former was chairman of the Neutral Nations Repatriation Commission. In 1958, Krishna Menon had appointed Kaul as quartermaster general of the Indian Army—the top post in charge of managing all logistics. Kaul was an ambitious, politically savvy, 'military bureaucrat' who enjoyed the confidence of Nehru. It has been suggested that this was the reason Krishna Menon became so enamoured of Kaul but that is not entirely true—after all, Nehru and Thimayya too were very close personally, yet Krishna Menon and the army chief would fall out. The explanation may well lie in Kaul's personality, which was to do the bidding of his political bosses enthusiastically. In fairness to Kaul, it needs to be said that he had an enormous drive. And, contrary to what has been written about him, he was in no way related to Nehru.

After the success of Operation Amar, there would be no stopping Kaul. He would emerge as Krishna Menon's closest military adviser and move up the army hierarchy speedily, evidently much against

Thimayya's wishes. By May 1961, he would be positioned so as to take over as army chief two years later. Krishna Menon's confidence in Kaul, and indeed that of Nehru as well, would have disastrous consequences for India in the war with China in October–November 1962. But before that was to happen, Kaul would figure in a shortlist of eight prepared by an American journalist of people who could succeed Nehru.[5] Krishna Menon too would be in this group, although the view of him would be most unflattering and at times border on calumny. But Krishna Menon chose to remain silent while the book became a bestseller.

Tension had been building up between Krishna Menon and the three service chiefs who had a direct personal line to the Prime Minister, which added to the defence minister's discomfiture. Krishna Menon knew well that a British journalist was working on a biography of Thimayya. Thimayya was also drawing American encomiums just as Krishna Menon was the target of US ire. The Americans were convinced that Krishna Menon was the head of the communist cabal around Nehru. On 29 August 1959, the *New York Times* carried a long and prominent profile of India's army chief, with the headline:

India's Trouble Shooter
Kodendera Subayya Thimayya

It was a paean of praise to Thimayya and, after reviewing his career the profile, ended up by saying: 'It has been said of General Thimayya that he likes polo, shooting, ballroom dancing, military history and Prime Minister Nehru.' But just two days later Thimayya sent in his resignation to Nehru:

> You will remember a few days ago I mentioned to you how impossible it was for me and the other two Chiefs of Staff to carry out our responsibilities under the present Defence Minister and that we sought your advice. Since then you have conveyed our feelings to the Minister of Defence and he quite rightly feels that

my talking to you directly is an act of disloyalty to him. Under these circumstances you will understand how impossible it is for me to carry out my duties as Chief of the Army Staff under Mr. Krishna Menon.

I, therefore, have no alternative but to submit my resignation from my present appointment and that you will permit me to proceed on long leave pending retirement. The interest of the Army and my loyalty to the country forces me to take this step after 33 years of service to the Indian Army both in war and peace.

This was meant to be privileged communication between the army chief and the Prime Minister. But the next morning the *Statesman* carried a long exclusive 'scoop' by its political correspondent, saying that Thimayya had resigned and that his naval and air force counterparts may do the same. The headlines were big-banner and spread across the front page with the general's photograph:

GEN. THIMAYYA DECIDES TO RESIGN

OTHER SERVICE CHIEFS MAY FOLLOW SUIT

SERIOUS DIFFERENCES WITH MENON

The article went on to say that while differences had been simmering for quite some time, the immediate provocation for the general's resignation was interference by Krishna Menon in a spate of top army appointments, which Thimayya resented. This was a sensational development, and with Parliament in session, it was but natural that MPs became highly agitated and demanded an explanation from Nehru. That coincidentally also happened to be the day when Nehru went to the airport to meet Ayub Khan, the President of Pakistan, who had decided to break journey at New Delhi airport while flying from Karachi to Dacca. Opposition MPs demanded an immediate statement from the Prime Minister, who somehow was able to buy time for a day on the grounds that he was tied up with the President of Pakistan.

As Krishna Menon's opponents were sharpening their knives, Nehru received another letter from Thimayya on the morning of 1 September 1959:

> Since I sent my letter of resignation to you I have had two talks with you and I have decided to take your advice and withdraw my resignation.

But the damage had been done, and from then on, Krishna Menon was a marked man. Two questions arise: Why did Thimayya write his letter of resignation? And how did its contents find their way into the columns of the *Statesman* in a matter of a few hours?

The second question about the source of the leak is more easily answered. For over five years, the *Statesman* had a military correspondent who wrote on defence matters from time to time. This correspondent was no journalist really. He was none other than J.N. Chaudhuri, a top army officer whose articles would appear occasionally under the byline 'By Our Military Correspondent'. He would become chief of the Indian Army in November 1962. My conclusion is that Chaudhuri was in the loop on Thimayya's resignation and instead of writing the story himself, passed it on to the paper's political correspondent. But there was to be no inquiry on how the leak had taken place. Chaudhuri would later admit in his autobiography[6] to being the military correspondent of the *Statesman* from 1951 for a decade and confess that his 'anonymity was very well kept'. But he was silent on whether he had official permission for this unusual arrangement and, of course, he said nothing on the Thimayya resignation episode.

What appears to have triggered Thimayya's extreme reaction was this: In one of his frequent meetings with the Prime Minister, Nehru seems to have asked Thimayya how things were at the Ministry of Defence. Thimayya expressed his frustration at the way the minister was functioning. Nehru then promised Thimayya that he would speak to Krishna Menon about it, which he did. Thereafter, an infuriated Krishna Menon sent for Thimayya and accused him of going to the Prime Minister directly, bypassing the minister.

Thimayya's defence that he had just responded to Nehru's query did not cut much ice with Krishna Menon, who told him that the minister is the supreme authority. Stung by this, the proud and sensitive Thimayya decided to put in his papers.

That the defence minister's style of functioning created problems for a hierarchy-conscious armed-forces establishment was evident. That the defence minister's strong leftist credentials often came into conflict with the way top members of this establishment, all educated in the UK, functioned was obvious. That Thimayya had a larger-than-life image with direct access to the Prime Minister, which was not liked by his minister who believed in establishing the supremacy of the political class over the military top brass, was also clear. A coup had taken place the previous year in October 1958 in neighbouring Pakistan, and there was loose talk in the cocktail party circuit of whether India's turn would be next. A naturally paranoid defence minister would have found all this sinister, even though the *Times of India* of 4 January 1959 carried this report:

No Possibility of Military 'Coup' in India

Ruling out the possibility of a military 'coup' in India, Mr. V.K. Krishna Menon, Defence Minister, said here today that 'whosoever attempted such a thing would come to grief . . .' Mr. Menon said: 'We have a strong parliamentary system of Government. Our soldiers are well educated and disciplined. They do not meddle in politics.' 'In fact', Mr. Menon added, 'it is silly to think in terms of a military dictatorship'. 'The people', he said, 'were conscious of their democratic rights and the prevailing social conditions widely varied from what led to military regime in other countries' . . .

In addition, Mountbatten had been pressing both Nehru and Krishna Menon to appoint a chief of defence staff (CDS) who would have overarching authority over the army, navy and air force, and had been suggesting Thimayya's name for this post. Krishna Menon resented this lobbying and, in any case, was dead set against the idea of a CDS, thinking that it would give too much importance in policy to a single military man. A month after the Thimayya resignation episode, the UK high commissioner in India, Malcolm Macdonald, met General Thimayya on 6 October 1959 and sent back a report of their long conversation, which was largely on the India–China border question. Towards the end, the topic of the minister of defence came up and Macdonald wrote:

> General Thimayya said one of the great difficulties in all this business had been Mr. Krishna Menon's zeal in representing the Pakistanis as the true enemies of India. Mr. Menon played up and often publicized as extremely unfriendly every small frontier trouble between the Pakistanis and Indians, invariably blaming the Pakistanis. The General did not know why the Minister did this. Perhaps it was because Mr. Menon wished to strengthen the case he had made (with popular effect for himself in India) against Pakistan over the Kashmir issue. Anyway, whatever the reason, the Minister of Defence insisted that India's armed forces should be disposed on the assumption that an attack on India would be launched from Pakistan. General Thimayya had often argued with him on this question, but never with success.
>
> Stimulated by one or two questions from me, the General said that Mr. Menon had no idea of how to deal with people, including officers and men in the armed forces. He tried to steamroller them into agreement with him on all matters; he was unscrupulous in his unfriendliness towards those who stood up to him; and he was cunning in the exploitation of those who were prepared to give way to him. He sometimes ordered posting, promotions and removal of officers according to his own whims . . . He observed that Mr. Menon must know how unpopular he is in India, and that he was perhaps trying deliberately to make himself the master of the armed forces so that he might one day have their support in the achievement of his political ambition to take Mr. Nehru's place either after, or even before, Mr. Nehru's withdrawal from public life.

This was quite an extraordinary charge made by Thimayya to Macdonald—that Krishna Menon entertained dreams of staging a coup against Nehru. Had either Nehru or Krishna Menon known that Thimayya was talking like this, albeit privately, the general would have been asked to go. Macdonald continued:

> The General told me that he had 'bent over backwards' to work successfully with Mr. Menon . . . But the Minister had been obstinate . . . and the situation had become more and more impossible. In the end he had felt it necessary to tell the Prime Minister, and to send in his resignation. The Prime Minister had pleaded with him to withdraw the resignation . . . In response to the very strong pleas by the Prime Minister and out of great respect for Mr. Nehru, the General had agreed to withdraw his resignation.
>
> The General told me that after the news of his intended resignation was published he had received all sorts of messages of support. The Armed Forces were unitedly with him, and so were innumerable politicians . . . Some of Mr. Menon's own colleagues in the Cabinet had privately expressed their support for the General . . .

That Thimayya opened up to Macdonald was highly unusual as, after all, the latter was the UK high commissioner, and the top army man was telling him every detail of what he had said to his Prime Minister and defence minister. Macdonald's record of this conversation with Thimayya, buried in his archive at Durham University in the UK, does call into question the general's judgement, even allowing for the fact that he felt he had been treated badly. He had gone to the extent of telling Macdonald that Nehru's statement in Parliament on 2 September 1959 in his (Thimayya's) defence had been amended by Krishna Menon to make it less strong and that some of Nehru's comments in Parliament, after the statement had been made, were 'typical of the unpremeditated, impulsive statements sometimes made by the Prime Minister in the heat of a moment'. Thimayya had, however, qualified that criticism by adding that 'this was one of his well-known weaknesses and allowances should be made for that'.

To be fair, neither Thimayya nor Krishna Menon ever said anything in public about this episode. But in the Thimayya papers, which has his resignation, is also this:

The 'trivial' subjects discussed with the Prime Minister, were, of the many:-

1.   THE WAR-psuchosis (sic) with PAKISTAN
2.   The APATHETIC attitude of the Minister for DEFENCE regarding CHINESE moves
3.   How the DEFENCE MINISTER did not want the PRIME MINISTER OF INDIA to meet the President of PAKISTAN-AYUB

It is clear that Krishna Menon saw Pakistan as a greater threat to India than China. Perhaps he overestimated the scope for negotiations with the Chinese. But it is also true that Thimayya, while arguing for enhancing India's defence capabilities along the border with China, would, in July 1962, when he was in retirement and just five months before the Chinese invasion, write:

I cannot even as a soldier envisage India taking on China in an open conflict on its own . . . It must be left to our politicians and diplomats to ensure our security . . .

India's leading military historian has argued that 'the Thimayya affair is not so much of civilian interference in professional matters as about military intrusion in realm of policy'.[7] An uneasy truce would prevail but two years later, on the eve of Thimayya's retirement, there would be another flare-up.

But there were some sequels to this involving Rajendra Prasad, the President of India. He would write regularly to Gyanwati Darbar, his aide in his office, whom he treated like his daughter.[8] In these letters Prasad would unburden himself on men and matters. On 20 October 1959, he told her:

Air Marshall S. Mukherjee came to see me this morning . . . He said he wanted to speak to me without reserve . . . There is much discontentment against the Defence Minister . . . All three chiefs felt much disturbed and distressed by his attitude. I asked what is it they resented so much. He said it is difficult to point out any particular act or incident; but his general behaviour and in particular his dealings with individual senior officers in the presence of their subordinates rendered it difficult for them to maintain their self-respect . . . I asked him if he had spoken to PM about the matter . . . He said he had spoken . . .

Two days later Prasad had even more 'juicy' news to convey to Darbar:

[Major] General Himmatsinghji [deputy minister of defence during 1950–52] saw me yesterday. He said he would communicate to me what he had heard . . . There was much discontentment in the armed forces in all ranks . . . There is a small group which considers itself the favourite of the Defence Minister and this is creating not only bad blood but also indiscipline. A situation is developing in which a coup becomes a possibility. I asked him definitely if he, according to his information, apprehended a coup by a minister with the help of the Defence forces . . . He said that there was a strong suspicion that Krishna Menon was working with a view to getting the support of the armed forces in case something happened to the PM. But that has become impossible now as he himself by his own action lost all chances of support of that kind.

Three events took place in 1959 that would cast a long and dark shadow on Sino-Indian relations, culminating in an armed conflict three years later. First, the Dalai Lama fled Tibet and reached India on 31 March 1959. Nehru then announced that the Buddhist monk had been granted political asylum in India and thereafter met him in New Delhi on 24 April 1959. Second, four months later the Chinese entered Indian territory in the North-East Frontier Agency (NEFA), and this has come to be known as the Longju incident. Third, in early

October 1959, there was another Chinese incursion, and this time it was in Ladakh. There was naturally an uproar in India. Krishna Menon was in New York attending the UN General Assembly session and sent a telegram to Nehru on 23 October 1959:

> Have just seen news item that Chinese launched fresh attack, penetrating 40 miles of our territory killing a number of our people and that troops are engaged on both sides . . . Have no information either from External Affairs to Delegation or Defence Ministry to me as might have been expected . . .
>
> Shall be grateful for information about present position . . . Unless there are directions to the contrary should not at least Defence Ministry and Army Headquarters keep me informed about these developments? . . . Is situation becoming bad and deteriorating the armed conflict? . . . I should have thought that Chinese now know that we will not take things lying down and will change their attitude . . .

This was a strange telegram, to say the least. The defence minister was complaining to the Prime Minister from New York that his own officials were not keeping him informed about the crisis that had developed. It had not occurred to him that his place was in New Delhi at this time and not in New York. But he was Krishna Menon. That very day he told journalists in New York that 'the latest clash was in a more sensitive inhabited area' and that 'China will have to go from our territory'. But he continued to plead for China's entry into the UN which, he said, was 'necessary for world purposes' and gave disarmament as an example.

Nehru replied to Krishna Menon briefly a day later:

> There has been a clash between an Indian police party and Chinese troops on the eastern Ladakh border . . . While we are waiting for fuller particulars, we received yesterday protest from Chinese Govt about intrusion into their territory . . . We had a discussion on this incident with the Chiefs of the Army and Air Staff and others this morning . . .

Then on 24 October 1959, Nehru sent Krishna Menon a longer telegram, giving fuller details of what had happened in Ladakh. He again wrote to him three days later, giving him the latest information and adding:

> I am, however, writing to you now more particularly to suggest that you should return here as soon as possible . . . I do not suppose anything extraordinary is going to happen in the next few days or weeks on our border, but the fact is that the temperature of the people is very high. In this state of affairs, I do not think it is right for you to remain in New York. This kind of thing has very irritating effect on people generally and they say that whatever danger threatens India we are casual about it and do not care. I suggest to you, therefore, to come back as soon as possible. In such circumstances the Minister of Defence should be here even though the situation may not be a war-like one. Parliament is meeting on the 16th of November but I think you should come here sooner than that and not wait till the last day before it begins . . .

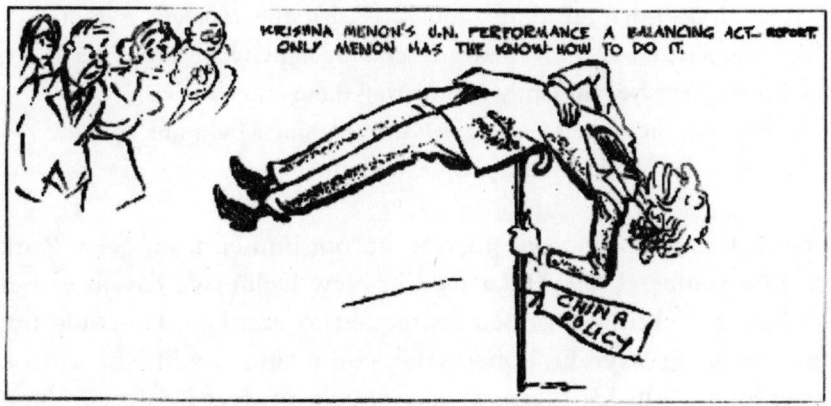

Cartoon in Shankar's Weekly, *25 October 1959*

Krishna Menon, however, was not particularly sensitive to what Nehru was saying and replied on 1 November 1959:

> . . . Have been fully aware of importance of return as early as possible, but events and time-tables here have been extremely

uncertain . . . Latest date arrival in Delhi 10th November . . . I
would have to return here for ten days about 26th or 27th.

Nehru was frantic and clearly irritated, for he sent yet another
telegram a day later:

> . . . Your absence from India, during these crucial days, especially
> affecting defence, has been unfortunate and no one can understand
> it. For Defence Minister to be continuously away when questions
> of defence are coming up daily is difficult to explain. Your going
> back to New York again will not be right in circumstances in
> India. You can have no idea of the anger and passion in the Indian
> mind at present . . .

Krishna Menon continued to stay in New York and told Nehru that
he wanted to brief Afro-Asian countries about the border clashes.
Nehru had to chide him again on 4 November 1959:

> . . . I do not think you should say that the problem is more
> political than military. There are certainly military aspects to it and
> people here are constantly considering these other aspects. To say,
> therefore, the military aspect is not important would not be quite
> correct and would irritate people here . . .

Finally, Krishna Menon decided to uproot himself from New York
on 9 November 1959. He arrived in New Delhi two days later but
not before Nehru had vetoed his request to visit Leh. He could not
resist stopping over in London for consultations with the British
government. On his return after a couple of days Krishna Menon
expressed his wish to go back to New York, which elicited this quite
extraordinary response from Nehru on 25 November 1959:

> In your letter you point out the necessity of your returning to the
> UN after a few days. I have no doubt that your presence there will
> make a difference. But I am quite clear in my mind that in the
> present state of affairs your leaving India would not be helpful and

might have unforeseen consequences. The situation here is bad—
worse even than what appears on the surface. I am not for a moment
referring to the border although this requires careful watching. It is
this internal situation that worries me. I think therefore you should
rule out the possibility of your returning to New York. The first
business is to prevent a collapse in India.

What could have been on Nehru's mind? No biographer of his
has thus far mentioned this letter to Krishna Menon, which is very
revealing. My own view is that the formation of the Swatantra
Party earlier in the year and the increasing attacks on him not only
politically but also personally by its founder, C. Rajagopalachari, may
have unsettled Nehru, and like had been the case since the mid-
1930s, he unburdened himself to Krishna Menon.

The Longju incident galvanized military spending. Some proposals
of an urgent nature for the Indian Army were indeed sanctioned by
December 1959, but thereafter, the Ministry of Finance suggested an
expenditure plan spread over a period of three years. It also suggested
that a combined plan for armed forces should be prepared. This plan
would be finalized and considered only by June–July 1961. It was
to cost some Rs 87 crore with a foreign exchange component of
Rs 14 crore. But by March 1962, only about Rs 42 crore had actually
been released and only about Rs 45 lakh in foreign exchange would
be allocated by the Ministry of Finance. In the post-mortem of
India's military debacle in October–November 1962, these facts are
rarely mentioned. Krishna Menon could not be held culpable on this
count at least as Finance Minister Morarji Desai was also responsible
for consistently denying demands of the armed forces for increased
expenditure.

1960

In March 1960, Krishna Menon created a first-rate constitutional
crisis that took months for the Supreme Court to untangle. This was
to do with the Nanavati case that had been rocking the country at
that time.

On 27 April 1959, Commander Kawas Nanavati had shot dead his wife's lover in Bombay. He was arrested, and soon thereafter, the case riveted much of India. Nanavati was a highly regarded naval officer, much admired by his colleagues. Two members of Krishna Menon's innermost circle—lawyer Rajni Patel and doctor A.V. Baliga—had been an integral part of Nanavati's defence team. Krishna Menon's buddy Russy Karanjia, editor of the Bombay tabloid *Blitz*, was the crusading leader of the 'Save Nanavati' brigade. The entire naval establishment was with him. Six months after the crime a jury on 21 October 1959 found Nanavati not guilty by an 8:1 majority. The judge of the sessions court, believing that this decision was scandalous, referred the case to the Bombay High Court. A two-judge bench heard the case and by noon on 11 March 1960, the verdict of both the judges were in: Nanavati was pronounced guilty of murder and sentenced to life imprisonment.

Then something truly extraordinary happened. Barely a few hours after the high court's judgment, the governor of Bombay State (Maharashtra and Gujarat had yet to come into being), Sri Prakasa, invoked his constitutional powers—powers that had never ever been invoked before in this manner—to suspend Nanavati's sentence till his appeal in the Supreme Court was disposed of and to confine him to the custody of only the naval authorities. There was an uproar in Parliament, and Nehru took the responsibility for having advised the governor. But a few days later on 29 March 1960, the cat was let out of the bag in a widely read column of Max Lerner in the *New York Post*. Lerner wrote after an extended conversation with Krishna Menon, whom he knew well:

> When I asked him about the Nanavati case, he spoke feelingly of Nanavati as an able young officer who had been his deputy adviser when he was high commissioner in London. While he didn't condone killing, he stressed that overwhelming opinion in the Navy, where Nanavati is popular, saw nothing basically wrong in what he had done in shooting his wife's lover. He did not conceal from me that the intervention of the central government through the Bombay governor had been at his request so that the

stain of turpitude should not destroy the career of a promising young officer.

The full bench of the Bombay High Court would uphold the governor's decision but the Supreme Court would, on 24 November 1961, uphold the original judgment, holding Nanavati guilty of murder. He was imprisoned again but would finally be pardoned in March 1964 and emigrate to Canada thereafter. Credit would be given to Krishna Menon for both the pardon and the emigration but his role was most probably zero because by then he was in the political wilderness.

Krishna Menon and the Mountbattens had kept up their relationship for years. On 21 February 1960, Edwina passed away in her sleep while on an inspection visit to British North Borneo. Mountbatten would, of course, use his special equation with both Krishna Menon and Nehru to push, every now and then, for India purchasing defence equipment from the UK and for exchange of defence personnel between the two countries. At times, Krishna Menon may well have found Mountbatten's entreaties a bit unwelcome, for on 8 April 1960, Mountbatten wrote to him saying that he had written four letters and not received any response:

> . . . I have had neither acknowledgment nor reply to any of these four letters and can only hope that this does not mean that you have now decided to end the friendship between us which has existed for so many years. From my own point of view I must say how very sorry I would be if something had caused you to change your feelings about me . . .

Four days later Krishna Menon finally sent Mountbatten a telegram:

YOUR LETTER RECEIVED YESTERDAY. REGRET NOT REPLYING PREVIOUS LETTERS. REQUEST ACCEPT MY APOLOGY. NO DISCOURTESY MEANT.

A very relieved Mountbatten immediately replied:

> I am off for a fortnight's holiday in Ireland in the morning and was
> much relieved to get your nice telegram before departure. I felt
> that there must be some misunderstanding and am glad it is being
> cleared up.

But Mountbatten's lobbying continued, and he would write to
Krishna Menon on 25 July 1960:

> You remember when you last passed through London, you and I
> spoke about the Blackburn NA-39 and I said I would arrange for
> you to have details of this remarkable aircraft. This has been done
> and you will be receiving shortly a brochure from the firm through
> your High Commissioner's bag here in London.
>
> I could perhaps to strike one note of warning. You will see that
> you receive the brochure, that its classification is 'Secret', whereas I
> believe that your people, in dealing with the Ministry of Aviation,
> are only cleared for 'Confidential'! I do not think, however, that
> this need necessarily worry as I had the impression from our
> conversation that your intention was to keep this pamphlet to
> yourself . . .

And a year later Mountbatten would write again to India's defence
minister:

> I paid a visit to your new aircraft carrier the VIKRANT last
> week and attach a copy of a letter I have just written to the Prime
> Minister. I felt I must write to him as well as to you as it was
> with him that I had so many conversations in past years about how
> desirable it was for the Indian Navy to have an aircraft carrier of
> their own . . . The VIKRANT will be a wonderful ambassador for
> India wherever she goes.

Very soon thereafter, Mountbatten would help Krishna Menon
procure tanks from the British firm Vickers.

In April 1960, the Chinese premier, Chou En-lai, came to New Delhi for one last-ditch effort to arrive at some resolution on the border issue, which had taken on a whole new dimension the previous year. He landed in New Delhi on 19 April 1960 with a high-powered delegation that included the foreign minister, Chen Yi. Fifteen days earlier Rajendra Prasad had written down his thoughts about the visit, which he had shared with Gyanwati Darbar:

> Mr. Chou En-lai is coming to Delhi for talks on the border question . . . Krishna Menon in a statement is reported to have said in Hyderabad: 'We shall not be so weak as to say that we will not talk to the Chinese Premier. We shall negotiate with him but not bargain'. While so much talk is going on, expressions like these are liable to be misquoted or misinterpreted out of context . . . In their communication leaders of Parliamentary Opposition parties have expressed the hope that 'there will be no dilution of the India Govt's stand in regard to the border' . . .

Chou had meetings with Nehru of course, but what was unusual was that Nehru got him to meet officially with some of his senior-most colleagues as well—Pant; Morarji Desai, the finance minister; Swaran Singh, the minister of steel; and Krishna Menon. Chou and Chen Yi also called on Vice President S. Radhakrishnan. Krishna Menon had first met Chou in Geneva in May–June 1954. Then they had been together in Bandung in April 1955 and in Beijing a month later. Among all Indians, he had had the maximum interactions with Chou.

Krishna Menon was at the airport along with the Prime Minister and other senior ministers to receive Chou and his team. The Nehru–Chou talks began the next day at 11 a.m. The record of that first conversation says:

> It was agreed that initially the two Prime Ministers will talk only between themselves, but that, later on the advisers on both sides, not exceeding a total number of 6, should also participate. Prime Minister suggested that Premier Chou might meet the Minister of

Home Affairs as well as the Minister of Defence. Premier Chou had
said that he would like to call on the Home Minister. At the end of
the morning talk, Premier Chou said that he would like to meet the
Defence Minister before coming to the Prime Minister's residence
for further talks in the afternoon. It was, therefore, decided that the
Defence Minister would call on the Chinese Prime Minister at 3
pm in Rashtrapati Bhavan . . .

Krishna Menon's only official meeting with Chou lasted two
hours. Till now no record of that conversation had been available,
unlike those of all other meetings of Chou. In the Krishna Menon
archive there is a fourteen-page 'Top Secret' note prepared by him
after his first discussion with Chou on 20 April 1960. This note,
which he had sent to Nehru, said:

Chou En-lai greeted me warmly. Present at the meeting were also
Chen-Yi and Chang Han Fu . . .

    Chou En-lai said he was very glad to see me again . . . [He]
then said that the Prime Minister (JN) had said that I wished to
meet him . . . I did not contradict this although this was not a
fact . . . At a later stage in the conversation he also mentioned that
he had said to our Prime Minister (JN) that he would like to see
me. To this again, as on the previous occasion I merely made a
smiling response . . .

    I took the line which the Prime Minister (JN) had taken
and conveyed to him the deep sense of shock that India had
suffered [from Chinese incursions into Ladakh in October 1959],
making it clear that it was not a shock of fear but of friendship
outraged . . .

    Chou En-lai then replied, I think, for about 20–30 minutes . . .
His first point was to express appreciation for our position in
relation to them and mentioned the United Nations and so on . . .

    He mentioned about Tibet, about Chinese total sovereignty
and Tibetan autonomy. He referred to the Dalai Lama and while
they did not object to political asylum, and could not do so,
and had nothing to say against him, they were shocked with the

reception and the treatment given to the Dalai Lama and that the Dalai Lama was using India as his base of operations and maligning China . . . He seemed to have exaggerated notions of a great Tibetan movement here . . .

. . . He said that China had made no territorial claims . . . and he suggested that we had said that they had made these claims . . . The purpose of this may have been to convey the impression that in the East their position is more or less to let things be and to obtain some definition of frontiers . . .

He said they had come with a very sincere desire to settle matters and we must find a settlement . . .

With regard to the Northern area . . . I did not get into the question of our knowing or not knowing about the roads, but merely said it was an incursion into our areas which he later repudiated. He gave the indication that things should be allowed to freeze . . . I was extremely careful not to say anything in view of our internal position. I also said that neither this Government nor any Government could make compromise in regard to Indian sovereignty and Indian territory . . .

This extract is a highly abbreviated account of a conversation that lasted for over two hours. But even this conveys two things: first, how strongly Tibet and the Dalai Lama played on Chou's mind and how it changed China's policy towards India after the Dalai Lama's flight to India in March 1959; second, how much Krishna Menon was going out of the way to give the impression that he was a team player and did not want to stray from the official line, whatever he felt about it privately. That very night he met Chou over an official dinner and sent Nehru a brief note saying that his second conversation was for about seven to eight minutes and was 'informal and old style'. He told Nehru that Chou recalled their interactions at Geneva in 1954 and in Peking in 1955 and had asked him whether he had any suggestions to make. Krishna Menon had played coy and said that the suggestions would undoubtedly come up with the meetings between the two Prime Ministers. Krishna Menon briefed K. Rangaswami of *The Hindu*, who reported on 21 April 1960:

NEHRU AND CHOU CONFER

FIRST ROUND OF PARLEYS ON BORDER DISPUTE

CHINESE PREMIER'S TWO–HOUR TALKS WITH V.K.K. MENON

NEW DELHI, April 20

Prime Minister Nehru and the Chinese Premier Mr. Chou En-lai talked for four hours today in two sessions . . . In between the two sessions, the Defence Minister, V.K. Krishna Menon, called on the Chinese Premier and was with him for two hours. Mr. Krishna Menon's talks were so prolonged that Mr. Nehru's meeting with Mr. Chou En-lai had to be postponed by half an hour. . . . What has attracted special notice is the Defence Minister's talks with Mr. Chou En-lai and it has come as a complete surprise to those who were indulging in wishful thinking that he had been kept out of the talks altogether . . . Mr. Menon is again expected to meet the Chinese Premier probably tomorrow . . .

There was a bit of self-promotion on the part of Krishna Menon here. In truth, it was Swaran Singh and not he who was assisting Nehru in the talks with Chou. Swaran Singh had been given this position in large measure on account of the pressure mounted by Pant on Nehru to keep out Krishna Menon. But this meeting caused some ripples, for on 22 April 1960, six MPs wrote to the Prime Minister:

. . . You have been good enough to assure us, in regard to the talks between you and the Chinese Prime Minister, you would keep the House informed . . . In this connection we may be permitted to draw your attention to an unusual event reported in the newspapers to the effect that Shri V.K. Krishna Menon, the Minister of Defence, had at the invitation of the Premier of China, an exclusive interview with the latter and none except the Chinese interpreter was allowed to be present. Such reports, you would agree, tend to create misunderstandings all round. May we also have an elucidation whether Shri Menon was also made a delegate on behalf of India to conduct talks with the Chinese Premier.

The MPs who wrote to the Prime Minister included a noted socialist leader N.G. Goray and a first-term MP who was to later become Prime Minister himself, Atal Bihari Vajpayee. Nehru replied to Goray the very next day:

> . . . It is obvious that I cannot make a statement in the Lok Sabha about my talks with Premier Chou En-lai till they are over . . . In your letter you refer to what you call an unusual event, that is, the Defence Minister meeting the Chinese Prime Minister. The only unusual thing about this is the extraordinary headlines and reports in the Press which seems to have lost all sense of responsibility. The Defence Minister called on the Chinese Prime Minister at my suggestion. We have been arranging meetings of the Chinese Prime Minister with a number of our Ministers.
>
> Among our Ministers, the only two persons who have come into contact with Premier Chou En-lai previously are myself and the Defence Minister. The Defence Minister had been for some weeks in Geneva at the time of the conference on Indo-China about five years ago or so and played an important part in the talks there. Even as a matter of courtesy he had to call on him because of his previous acquaintance. But apart from this, I wanted the Chinese Prime Minister to meet some of senior Ministers separately.

Krishna Menon's second meeting with Chou took place two days later, and inevitably, *The Hindu* had this report by Rangaswami on 23 April 1960:

SINO-INDIAN TALKS IN DELHI

OFFICIALS ASKED TO DISCUSS SPECIFIC BORDER DISPUTES

CHOU'S SECOND MEETING WITH KRISHNA MENON

On the third day of India–China negotiations, officials on both sides have been asked to go into specific disputes on the border with maps and documents . . . While informed circles would regard this as a hopeful development they would not venture to predict what the final outcome of the present negotiations will be . . . But the second significant development today was the private dinner which the Defence Minister Mr. V.K. Krishna Menon gave at his residence to the Chinese Premier and his two senior colleagues . . . Mr. Krishna Menon the Chinese Premier is examining the practical solutions to the problems in dispute . . .

Thus far, Krishna Menon had met Chou twice in three days. On 23 April, he met with Chen Yi for almost two and a half hours between 10 p.m. and 12.30 a.m. The two conferred again for some ninety minutes on the evening of 24 April 1960. Chou and his colleagues left India on 26 April 1960, his talks with Nehru having failed to produce any breakthrough on the volatile border dispute.

The only person on the Indian side who had always believed that India must negotiate with the Chinese on a give-and-take basis was Krishna Menon. There is, however, no written evidence that the so-called Krishna Menon formula—that India would accept China's claims in Ladakh, and in return China would accept India's claims on the strategically vital Chumbi Valley— came up in his conversations with Chou. He refused to confirm or categorically deny that such a package deal had, in fact, been discussed between him and the Chinese premier. He would be asked a few weeks later in Bombay about these conversations, and his reply was:

Whatever I do these days makes news. If I drink tea it is news. If I ask for coffee for a change that too is news.

Some years later he was again asked about the mutual-lease idea, and his reply was non-committal:[9]

> There may have been all sorts of ideas . . . Actually the Prime Minister and I had talks on what could be done but other people, some of them senior men, although they did not veto it said: 'Why all this now; we will see when it comes'. It was not understood that in diplomacy if you take the initiative your action has far greater effect. Perhaps they thought it was not necessary. I believe that in 1960 China had made it very difficult for those of us who wanted to do anything. That is what I told Chou En-lai when he came here. I said, 'You may hurt us, but you hurt yourselves more; you have strengthened every reactionary element in this country . . . you have made it impossible for reasonable people to talk and seek ways of settlement'. I don't think Chou En-lai had much freedom [of action] on this.

But from all that we know about his approach to diplomacy it would not be wrong to assume that such a discussion on a long-term lease basis had taken place. Malcolm Macdonald reported to the British home secretary on 13 July 1960:

> . . . There is in fact some reason to believe that not only the Chinese Prime Minister but also the Indian Prime Minister would personally have been ready for a compromise . . . Mr. Krishna Menon informed me with characteristic brutal frankness that the problem could only be settled 'by horse trading' and the Vice President (Dr. Radhakrishnan) confided to me in more diplomatic if feebler language that if the Chinese would yield India 'the shadow' of sovereignty in Ladakh, the Indian should yield to the Chinese 'the substance' of administrative and military control there. Mr. Menon indicated to me that Mr. Nehru agrees with this view, but that he was forced to deny it by the strength of his compatriots' present opposition to any deal. I believe that is a correct description of the Prime Minister's frame of mind.

Srinath Raghavan called his monograph on the April 1960 Nehru–Chou talks[10] 'A Missed Opportunity?' and concluded that 'a solution such as long term lease of territory could have been worked out'. But he also admitted that a bargain, while theoretically possible, was simply not feasible in 1960 because of the pressure on Nehru from his senior cabinet colleagues and parliamentary and public opinion. Krishna Menon was in a splendid minority of one, and Nehru was a politically beleaguered Prime Minister by 1960. Krishna Menon himself recalled this visit later:[11]

> The 1960 visit was spoiled by the fact that we had too many people involved in it. It was not known to what extent the Chinese came here to sort out our differences. I believe Chen Yi was a bad influence and that there were great changes taking place inside China at that time. On our side, inside the Congress and in the country, public opinion had become aroused so that it was no longer possible to talk in terms of negotiations. And the Home Minister [Govind Ballabh Pant] who had by then acquired a powerful influence over the Prime Minister, was not in favour of negotiation.

After Chou had departed, there would be an uproar in both Houses of Parliament. Nehru would be attacked for what was dubbed his weak-kneed policy towards Chinese expansionism on the Indian border. But the main target would be Krishna Menon, who was criticized not only for being too friendly with the Chinese but also for making 'virulent statements against Pakistan'. Nehru was under fire from not only members of the opposition but, for the first time, openly from Congress MPs as well, for putting up with Krishna Menon for too long. On 27 April 1960, Krishna Menon wrote out a letter to Nehru but we don't know for sure whether it was actually sent. It reflected the agony that he had been going through that was accentuated on account of his being sidelined during Chou's visit:

> I shall be grateful if you will kindly agree to my retirement after your return from abroad [mid–May 1960]. I thought I could avoid writing and to come to see you but you were too busy to respond to what I had to say and brushed me away. I had informed you earlier that I wish to go away in August but it is difficult for me to last that long. Normally just when you go out is not the right time to make such a communication. Since you would not speak to me

I have to write this note. I shall be grateful if you will agree to my retirement with effect on an early date after you return.

But Krishna Menon may have been, as usual, unfair to Nehru. In what was truly unprecedented, on 28 April 1960, at a particularly raucous annual general meeting of the Congress Parliamentary Party, Nehru was irked by what one of his old colleagues Mahavir Tyagi had been saying and suddenly lost his cool. He shouted at Tyagi, saying:

> . . . Let us be frank about it. I have had enough of this. I do not want to be leader of this party or any other party because I am slack, advantage is taken of that. Because I am slack, everybody attacks the Government, my colleagues are attacked. Congressmen are attacked. Defence Minister is. Is this how a party should behave I want to know?

Tyagi would be a thorn in Krishna Menon's side and would play a leading part in having him quit the cabinet two years later. A day later another very close friend of Nehru and someone he respected enormously, H.N. Kunzru, an independent member, wound up his speech in the Rajya Sabha with a historical analogy that perhaps only Nehru and Krishna Menon would have grasped instantly:

> During the First World War, Mr. Asquith asked Lord Haldane who had made a very successful Minister of Defence to leave the Cabinet, notwithstanding his friendship with Lord Haldane, simply because England had no confidence in Lord Haldane. Surely we are not doing the Prime Minister any injustice, or Shri Krishna Menon any injustice, if we ask the Prime Minister to follow the same policy . . .

In his reply Nehru could not resist responding to Kunzru's excursion into British history:

> . . . Dr. Kunzru referred to his opinion that the Defence Minister should be changed because the country generally speaking has no confidence in him. Well, if the country has no confidence

in him, presumably it has no confidence in me and the Prime
Minister should change because in the kind of Government
that we have, it is the Prime Minister's responsibility to choose
his colleague and nobody else's . . . He quoted the example of
Lord Haldane. . . It is an unfortunate example because. . . it was
recognized subsequently that it was a most unfortunate step that
the British Government took.

Krishna Menon had met with Chou first on 20 April 1960 and
then again two days later. In between, on 21 April 1960, for the
last time, the jeeps case came up for discussion in the Lok Sabha.
As if Chou was not enough, this was another headache that Nehru
had to once again confront. For nine years the case had been under
scrutiny by one committee of Parliament or the other. For nine years,
Nehru and his senior colleagues—political and bureaucratic—had
been grappling with the consequences of Krishna Menon's decisions
taken as high commissioner in London in 1949 and 1950. Finally,
after almost five years of wrangling, Nehru's government had agreed
to an out-of-court settlement waiving the claim for damages of some
2,50,000 pounds. Parliament naturally wanted to know why, after
having taken the British supplier of jeeps to court, the government
was now withdrawing its claim.

Nehru had to once again go over the facts of the controversial
case and admit that it had been decided to have Krishna Menon
present evidence in the British court on the Indian government's
claim and the supplier's counterclaim. Just the previous month on 16
March 1960, Nehru had informed Law Minister Ashoke Sen, who
was then in Geneva:

. . . We realize that unless Defence Minister gives evidence our case
will be weak. If however he give evidence, even though that will
necessarily be general and from memory of past events, it will have
considerable weight. In view of all these circumstances, Defence
Minister has agreed to give evidence and has offered himself as
a witness unreservedly. It is perhaps unusual for a Minister of

a Government to give evidence in a foreign court. Still we are prepared for it . . .

Krishna Menon was ready to leave for London when word came from there that the jeep supplier would drop its counterclaim. In any case the supplier had become almost bankrupt and hence the final decision for an out-of-court settlement.

[Jeep Scandal]

Cartoon on Nehru and Krishna Menon in the Times of India, *24 April 1960*

That intermediaries were involved in the purchase of jeeps when there was an urgent requirement for them cannot be denied. That these intermediaries were very well known to Krishna Menon from his India League days is incontrovertible. It is also clear that commissions were paid but what is not is whether Krishna Menon knew what was happening as far as the intermediaries were concerned. Was it a case of personal corruption? The evidence that exists—and by the reckoning of British intelligence sources, which had every motive to discredit Krishna Menon completely—leads to the answer 'no'. But to the question of was it a case of cavalier decision-making where public funds were involved when public funds were scarce, the answer must decidedly be 'yes'.

In May 1960, the Border Roads Organization was established. It owed much to Krishna Menon's leadership and Lt General B.M. Kaul's drive. The organization was started perhaps ten years too late but in a short period it created infrastructure without which India would have been even more handicapped than it was in the war with China in 1962. Soon thereafter Krishna Menon prevailed upon Nehru to send delegations to the USSR, Japan and Germany to procure equipment. He was willing even to purchase equipment from the US as Nehru noted to one of his senior officials later. But Krishna Menon's main focus was the USSR. He had already spoken to Khrushchev and other Soviet leaders about the purchase of heavy aircraft, helicopters and earth-moving and road-making equipment.

On 17 August 1960, there was an extensive discussion in the US State Department, which noted 'Krishna Menon's desire to purchase Soviet helicopters in spite of the opposition of the service chiefs'. Krishna Menon insisted on buying helicopters and transport aircraft from the USSR. He would be criticized by his own colleagues for taking India into the Soviet camp. However, what swayed him was not ideology but two hard facts: first, the payment would not be in scarce dollars but in rupees, and second, the assurance of local manufacture, particularly of the helicopters. The discussion in the US State Department acknowledged that in relation to US-supplied helicopters 'both manufacture and the arrangement of licensing agreements with Government of India would be . . . difficult'. Thus, India's very first acquisition of military equipment from the USSR was under the garb of its requirement for constructing roads in border areas, which was true, but their use for other purposes was not precluded.

The 1960 session of the UN General Assembly has gone down in history for the histrionics of Soviet Prime Minister Nikita Khrushchev, who banged the table with his shoe. Nehru's contributions, however, were more substantive, apart from the formal speech he made. On 30 September 1960, he moved a resolution in the UN General Assembly on behalf of India, Indonesia, Ghana, Yugoslavia and the United Arab Republic. While Dr Fawzi, the Egyptian foreign minister, had prepared the initial draft, the final version moved by Nehru was prepared by Krishna Menon. It called for a reduction in East–West tensions, the consolidation of peace in different parts of the world and disarmament. Despite impassioned speeches by its sponsors, the resolution could not muster the required two-thirds majority and was withdrawn by Nehru himself. But the resolution evoked much interest in the US media.

Nehru met with various world leaders at New York. But clearly the one meeting that aroused the maximum attention was the one he had on 28 September 1960 with a young and charismatic revolutionary leader who had captured power in his country just the previous year. Accompanied by Krishna Menon, Nehru met Fidel Castro. Their conversation took place in the heart of Harlem, where Castro was staying. They were together for about fifty minutes. After Nehru left, Krishna Menon stayed back to spend more time with Castro, who had clearly captured his imagination in a way few people had.

1961

On 20 January 1961, John F. Kennedy would take the oath as the thirty-fifth President of the US. Five days earlier a biography of Kennedy written by Ramesh Sanghvi, a well-known Indian journalist of those times, was published in Bombay.[12] It carried a 5000-word foreword by Krishna Menon. After a long and thoughtful discourse on American political traditions and on the functioning of the American political system, Krishna Menon returned to his favourite theme of a 'warless world' and of comprehensive disarmament, on which he had been speaking passionately at the UN for the past few years, often to the irritation of both the US and the USSR. He ended the foreword by saying:

> Wisdom must inform the subject of this story and his advisers and inspire them as it must those whom he has the opportunity to persuade and assure that between war and peace there is a yawning chasm, a 'ditch which cannot be jumped in two leaps'. It cannot be bridged by fear, or sustained by weapons, nuclear or otherwise, miscalled security.

Hence general and complete disarmament, to which as a total project and not merely as a 'goal' or 'objective' or as a 'principle' the nations of the world, principally the United States and the Soviet Union, must stand committed without 'mental reservations'. The rest of the world will comply with enthusiasm and relief. The approach and solution call for courage and faith. We may not think that these would be wanting. The expectations of the world, is the expression of its hope, and the assurance of its truth.

The President-elect has earned and garnered a great fund of world goodwill. It is rare treasure, which does not diminish, but grows with use. It is rare treasure.

Krishna Menon would meet Kennedy ten months later in the White House, and in October 1962, Kennedy would gently but firmly pass the message to Nehru that American military assistance to India during the Sino–Indian war would be conditional on Krishna Menon's being eased out as defence minister.

Thimayya would recommend Lt General S.S.P. Thorat as his successor but that would be turned down by Krishna Menon and thereafter by the Prime Minister as well. Instead, Lt General P.N. Thapar was selected as the fifth army chief invoking the seniority criteria which had been ignored while appointing Thimayya. This, by itself, was nothing unusual and could be defended easily. But what Thimayya and Thorat were to be subjected to was bewildering.

Thapar would write a 'Personal and Top Secret' bombshell of a letter to Thimayya on 23 April 1961, a fortnight before the latter's retirement, making thirteen specific allegations against the man he was to succeed. These allegations included passing on classified information to members of the opposition in Parliament, making very disparaging remarks about the Prime Minister and the defence minister to Indians and foreigners, hobnobbing with arms dealers, and some financial irregularities. On the same day Thapar wrote a similar letter to Thorat as well making five charges of telling diplomats posted in New Delhi that there was far too much political interference in appointments in the Indian Army, of making indiscreet comments against the defence minister, of spending far too much money on farewell parties for Thimayya, and of telling the Americans and South Koreans way back in 1954 that India would not have survived after Independence without American support.

Thapar would not have written these letters without Krishna Menon bamboozling him. This was the defence minister at his pettiest and meanest. He must have kept the Prime Minister informed and got his approval because Thapar began both the letters by saying, 'I am directed by the Prime Minister to request you for your comments on the following allegations,' and ended by saying, 'The Prime Minister is, however, anxious that every opportunity should be given to you to clear up your position in the matter before Government decided what further action should be taken.'

Krishna Menon had a co-conspirator in this sordid episode. That was Lt General B.M. Kaul, who had been in Korea with Thimayya and Thorat and was then the quartermaster general at army headquarters. References to what Thimayya and Thorat had said in Korea could only have come from him, and this is the smoking gun of Kaul's involvement in putting Thimayya and Thorat in the dock. Kaul had many things going for him: at a time when most officers in the Indian Army in the 1940s were seen to be too 'British' in their worldview, Kaul identified himself openly with the nationalist movement. He moved easily in political circles and had come to Nehru's attention soon after Independence. He was made part of India's delegation to the UN in 1948 and thereafter held a series of assignments that, however, were never operational in nature. Along with Krishna Menon and Thapar, he had to quit the army after India's debacle in the October–November 1962 war with China but there was a time when he was even considered one of the eight possible successors to Nehru.[13]

The question naturally arises: why were Thimayya and Thorat the targets of the Krishna Menon–Kaul attack? The truth will never be known but Thorat's son, Yashwant Thorat, recalled:[14]

Thimayya sent Thorat's name as his successor directly to the President of India in his capacity as Commander-in-Chief of the Armed Forces. The President [Rajendra Prasad] approved it and forwarded it to the Government. The Government [Prime Minister and defence minister] sent the file back to the President with a request 'Please reconsider'. The President did not take long to send the file back reiterating his approval to Thorat. The Government stuck to its guns and went ahead and appointed Thapar who was a notch above Thorat in seniority . . . Please remember that this was also the time when the President was publicly speaking of the need to better define his role.

Rajendra Prasad had, in fact, set the cat among the pigeons on 28 November 1960 while laying the foundation stone of the Indian Law Institute, and called for a 'study and investigation in a scientific manner so that we may know what exactly the scope of the powers and functions of the President is'.

Some years later, S.S. Khera, who was principal defence secretary and thereafter cabinet secretary between 1962 and 1964, was to write:[15]

Krishna Menon's actions in respect of top army command during the last few months that Thimayya was Chief of the Army Staff increased the suspicions generally held by many senior military commanders, that he was bent upon creating around him a circle of his own confidants and favourites on whose loyalty he could create . . . These misgivings seemed to find confirmation when Krishna Menon designated General P.N. Thapar to succeed Thimayya and brought in . . . Kaul as Chief of General Staff . . .

In January 1961, one of those rumours which seem to spring out of nowhere began to go round. Thimayya was to attempt a military takeover. Rumour even fixed a date, 30 January the anniversary of Gandhiji's assassination . . . Wherever the truth may lie, there appears to have been in January 1961 some inkling on the part of Jawaharlal Nehru and Pandit Govind Ballabh Pant, the Home Minister of the existence of some sort of danger. Significance appears to have been attached to an order given by Thimayya moving a Division from Ambala to Delhi. At the same time an Armoured Brigade was located at Mathura, 90 miles from Delhi on the Agra Road, a Brigade which was part of the Armoured Division at Jhansi under the command of Gen. Thorat. Kaul who was then Quarter-Master General was asked to ascertain from Thimayya about the purpose of the move; it appears that the order had been sent from Army Headquarters direct to the Divisional Commander . . . In any event, the order was countermanded.

Within a month or two, at the reunion of the Kumaon regiment at Ranikhet in the Almora Hills and almost the last function Thimayya attended before leaving the army, speeches were made, a report of one of which attributed to Thorat a somewhat remarkable statement to be made by a serving officer, criticizing the Government and appealing to the troops for their loyalty to the Army Chief, with no word about loyalty to the Government or to the Constitution of India. The reports said that the general theme of Gen. Thorat's statement was 'Do not let Thimayya go away'.

Questions were raised in Parliament when Khera's book was released and the government denied what he had written. To be fair, Khera never claimed to be writing authoritatively; on the contrary, he stressed that his account was based on 'what was in the air' those days. It does provide some explanation for Krishna Menon's bizarre conduct in having two of the most outstanding army officers India has produced charge-sheeted in the manner they were by Thapar. As it turned out, Thimayya and Thorat sent in their replies to the charges and the matter was allowed to die down. Both retired from the army on 8 May 1961 but a year later, after the first wave of Chinese attacks in October 1962, which led to Krishna Menon's resignation, Nehru personally got Thimayya and Thorat as members of the National Defence Council that had been formed in early November 1962. Thimayya was to later serve as head of the UN forces in Cyprus but died suddenly there in 1965. Thorat served as chairman of the Maharashtra Public Service Commission but continued to advise Krishna Menon's successor, Y.B. Chavan.

Thimayya and Thorat were not the only two top army officers the Krishna Menon–Kaul duo went after with Thapar's connivance. Two other lieutenant generals—Sam Manekshaw and

S.D. Verma—were also harassed. Manekshaw was then commandant
of the Defence Services Staff College at Wellington in south
India. H was accused of 'loose talk' and of putting up portraits of
Robert Clive and Warren Hastings—the founders of the British
Empire in India in the late-eighteenth century—in his office. A
court of inquiry had been ordered which, however, exonerated
Manekshaw. Krishna Menon had to be prodded by Nehru himself
in July 1962 to close the case once and for all. A few years later in
June 1969, Manekshaw would become army chief and carve out
an iconic status for himself in the war with Pakistan in 1971. As far
as Verma was concerned the charges against him were of financial
misdemeanours. It was only after he had met Nehru on 12 March
1962 that he would get an official letter saying, '[The] allegations
made against you have not been proved on the facts available to
the government. The enquiry, therefore, on the basis of these facts
stands terminated.'[16]

But on Verma, in all fairness, it should be mentioned that tucked
away in Krishna Menon's archive is a 'Top Secret' note he had sent
to Nehru on 3 February 1961 when the question of appointing
army commanders had been discussed by the defence minister with
Thimayya and his successor-designate Thapar:

> . . . General Thimayya said that he had nothing against Verma,
> but he said that his wife was not very much liked and in an Army
> Commander this was a consideration. Gen. Thimayya said that
> while he had no personal knowledge of it there was some talk
> about tanks and some 'smell'. In answer to what smell, he said
> that as a matter of confidential conversation that there had been
> talk about him in connection with tank and Army stores. I asked
> whether there was anything done about it. Gen. Thapar said I
> should be told everything. Gen. Thimayya said he knew there was
> this smell and he did not think it was a good idea to keep him
> at Headquarters . . . and when an opportunity arose last year he
> posted him out . . . It was recalled that I had queried this posting
> as Verma was not anxious to go . . . but I had accepted the view of
> the COAS [chief of army staff] . . .

This afternoon, Gen. Thimayya . . . said he wanted to speak to me about Gen. Verma and the view he had communicated to me last Sunday . . . Gen. Thimayya went on to say that he was mistaken about Gen. Verma, that he had made subsequent enquiries and there was nothing in the 'smell'. I told him I note his views, as I do always, but he had spent a long time with me last Sunday and told me quite differently . . .

NOTE: It appeared to me odd that a Chief should make a penal transfer and entertain doubts about a senior officer . . . on information, and tell me 2–3 days thereafter, during which no enquiry had been held or any new step taken, he was all sorry about the man about whom he was willing to accept rumours and transfer. Gen. Thimayya said what he had to say to me as though he had rehearsed it. It did not carry any conviction . . .

Krishna Menon was defence minister. He was also the head of India's delegation to the UN. But the Prime Minister consulted him on matters that had nothing to do with defence or diplomacy. India was about to embark on its Third Five-Year Plan, and Nehru spoke to him about how best to utilize the expertise of economists in the planning process. Krishna Menon gave him some ideas on 11 May 1961. He told Nehru that economists should not be taken away from their academic pursuits but at the same time they should be given adequate opportunities of 'delving into current problems' without becoming 'cogs in the administrative machine and finding themselves having to tilt with it'. Then he went on to discuss three young economists who were to later become three of the greatest names in their profession globally:

. . . My submission is that Dr. Raj . . . will be of little use to himself, to the science of economics and or to our developments if he were pulled out of University research and lecturing, but he would be useful as an overall coordinator of such advisers. He deals with problems in detail and from a practical point of view, and takes care of his data and is not rigid. While a good theoretician, he is a very practical economist and a socialist.

Mr. A.K. [Amartya] Sen . . . is considered by far the ablest
economist . . . and is looked up to by his seniors, but he is only
29. It is difficult to believe, much as I would like to do so, that
he would have a chance to do anything effective in our country
merely as an Economic Adviser to Government, except in the
context that he matters to thinking and action . . . Raj had become
a good economist at 23, therefore was able to use the minor post to
which he was consigned, in research at the Reserve Bank, to profit.

Dr. Bhagwati is much more of a theoretician . . . but is a
very well thought of and profound student . . . His approach is
mathematical, very modern . . .

My suggestion is that we should establish immediately an
Institute of Economics (theoretical and applied) . . .

K.N. Raj had been known to Krishna Menon from the late 1940s
when he had been a student at the London School of Economics. The
two were to become intimate friends. He became a great institution
builder. Amartya Sen would win the Nobel Prize in economics, and
Jagdish Bhagwati would emerge as an authority on international
trade. Raj, Sen and Bhagwati did not really need Krishna Menon's
recommendation to Nehru. Raj, for instance, had worked closely
on India's First Five-Year Plan, and Sen and Bhagwati had other
mentors who would speak to Nehru about them. Krishna Menon
developed his thoughts on how the institute he was proposing would
function and ended up by telling Nehru:

> . . . These are my preliminary thoughts which I have set down in
> the hope that you think about them. I may contribute in a small
> way to developing these ideas. Further, if there is any way I can be
> of assistance in its organisation, I shall be very happy to do so. It
> does sound egotistic, but I believe I have some contact with these
> matter and given some thought to them.

Nehru, and indeed the country, may well have been better off if he
had made Krishna Menon minister of planning rather than defence
minister.

Mountbatten and Krishna Menon had been the closest of friends for almost a quarter of a century. They would see each other at least three or four times a year and write to each other every now and then. Mountbatten would often also lobby with Krishna Menon to get India to buy defence equipment from the UK. But sometime in mid-1961, the two had a bitter disagreement and Mountbatten would appeal to Vijaya Lakshmi Pandit, India's high commissioner in the UK, and to Nehru to bring 'Krishna around'. Mountbatten had conceived of an 'Exercise Unison' in which an imaginary island in the Indian Ocean would be selected, where an imaginary intervention would take place by a task force comprising military from the Commonwealth countries at the request of the UN. Mountbatten had got most Commonwealth countries on board. But Krishna Menon proved obstinate and objected saying that while he did not mind India taking part in the imaginary exercise, the request for the task force must come from 'an imaginary world authority' and not from the UN. Mountbatten also wanted each Commonwealth country to present a general idea of the 'shape, size and disposition' of its armed forces and of its defence policy. Krishna Menon objected once again, ostensibly on the grounds that Pakistan, also a Commonwealth country, would get to know information on India's defence capability.

Vijaya Lakshmi Pandit wrote to Nehru on 10 July 1961, asking him to step in and 'tell Krishna to comply with Dickie's wishes . . . and to rely on Dickie's love of India'. Three days later Nehru sent a telegram to Krishna Menon, who was then in Geneva for a conference on Laos. Nehru told him that he found nothing greatly objectionable in going along with Mountbatten, while making India's position against a permanent UN military force clear. But he left the matter to Krishna Menon to deal directly with Mountbatten. Finally, Mountbatten wrote to Krishna Menon on 12 July 1961:

Thank you so much for ringing me this morning from Geneva. I am most grateful to you for having agreed on behalf of India to the use of the phrase 'a collective task force brought into being by an ad hoc decision of the United Nations' in the context of the Commonwealth exercise at UNISON.

You say that the implications of the matter, especially at present, creates difficulties for India. This puzzles me very much. When the Prime Minister was staying with me in March he made it clear that he was not only backing the U.N.O. as India did at Korea, but in fact was going to send an Indian brigade to the United Nations forces in the Congo. How could I guess that the policy of the Government in India is now completely reversed and that references to 'an ad hoc decision of the United Nations' would be embarrassing . . .

Next time I see you I'll explain in detail about all the trouble I've had with India over this exercise—the only country to give me any trouble at all. However, the main thing now is that all is well and I won't let India down.

Later in the year General Thapar, Lt General Kaul and others attended UNISON. A highly pleased Mountbatten reported to the Commonwealth Relations Office on 31 October 1961:

. . . He [Kaul] went out of his way to repeat again and again how highly he valued the British connection, how wonderful UNISON had been, how glad he was that I had refused to take no for an answer from Krishna Menon about the Indians coming to UNISON.

Mountbatten's ultimate dream, it appears, was to set up a world peacekeeping force. As far as Kaul and Krishna Menon were concerned, they were undoubtedly close but had their differences. A few months later, these differences would take a more serious turn, with Krishna Menon pushing for the acquisition of fighter aircraft from the Soviet Union and Kaul favouring getting them from the US.

A month later Krishna Menon wrote to Nehru about a conversation he had had with Mountbatten in London but on a different subject:

. . . I cannot help feeling that latterly we have been permitting both the British and the Americans to think they can kick us around.

They count everything in terms of money as some of our people
always unfortunately do. I think the time has come to put a halt to
all this . . .

For almost three years, Krishna Menon had been drawing Nehru's
attention to the growing influence of the US in Indian public life.
This bonhomie was with the full knowledge of Nehru, of course, but
that did not deter Krishna Menon. In some ways, this was perhaps the
price India had to pay for its growing dependence on foreign aid and
the establishment of the Aid India Consortium comprising thirteen
countries and coordinated by the World Bank. India had also begun
to depend heavily on American wheat offered at attractive terms. US
economists, mobilized by the Massachusetts Institute of Technology
(MIT), had begun to take great interest in Indian planning. The Ford
Foundation was firming up plans to support Indian educational and
research institutions. There was even some talk of trying to build
a partnership in defence. Later commentators would write that
American influence began after the death of Nehru. However, as
Krishna Menon's laments bear out, it had begun a few years before
his death.

On a proposal from the Asia Foundation, for instance, to open
an office in India, Krishna Menon told Nehru on 27 August 1961:

. . . We may permit them to have an office, if they can find one,
of small dimensions of only one foreigner perhaps and review their
activities either continually or at the end of 2 years as appropriate.
Our attitude and theirs [that of the US] is different from that in
1955. If a more vigourous policy would be pursued against all of
them, I would welcome it for many reasons. But that apparently
is not to be.

Nehru went along with Krishna Menon, whose fears were to be
proved right, for in a few years' time the Asia Foundation's links to the
CIA were revealed. Subsequently, however, it was to reinvent itself.

Krishna Menon's health was never good for any prolonged length
of time. He had suffered from a variety of ailments for decades—

arthritis, insomnia, low blood pressure, to name just a few. He was on constant medication. Despite being a strict teetotaller and a vegetarian, his eating habits were awful and could only have added to his chronic ill health. What happened in the last quarter of 1961, however, was quite serious, and his behaviour must have perplexed many, as this letter from Nehru to one Narendra of the Arya Samaj in Hyderabad reveals. Narendra had written to Nehru on 16 September 1961, and the Prime Minister replied four days later:

> . . . While the facts that you mention must be true, the inference you draw from them is hopelessly wrong. Shri V.K. Krishna Menon has been a strict teetotaler all his life and he is a vegetarian. There is no question, therefore, of his having taken alcoholic drinks.
>
> The fact is that he has been rather ill for some time. About three weeks ago he had a bad fall in his bathroom, hitting his head. He has suffered from acute headache since then. He has had no time to rest because he went with me to Yugoslavia immediately after where he had to work hard. It was soon after his return that he went to Hyderabad. It is because of these severe headaches that he has had to take strong injections and sometimes drugs to tone down his headaches which make him feel giddy.

Krishna Menon, not in the best of health, had accompanied Nehru to the first summit of twenty-five non-aligned nations at Belgrade during 1–6 September 1961. He had played an important part in drafting the final resolution that was issued on the last day. This is when the term 'non alignment' became part of the international political discourse. In reality, however, this term that was to become the staple of Indian foreign policy may well have been used by Krishna Menon at the UN eight years earlier, as he was to later recall:[17]

> . . . We were being ridiculed about being 'neutral'. I said then, 'We are not neutral; we are non-aligned'. We are not aligned to either side, we are non-aligned'. In fact the Prime Minister [Nehru] didn't approve very much of the word at the beginning, but it quickly gained currency.

Neither Krishna Menon nor Nehru particularly cared for or were fond of the term 'non alignment' much less of the idea of a 'non-aligned movement' or a 'non-aligned grouping'. Soon after the Belgrade summit, Krishna Menon spoke at the UN for well over an hour, without even making a mention of the conference. He sent Nehru a message from New York that the 'functioning of the Belgrade group at the UN is not desirable'. He felt, and Nehru agreed, that it limited freedom of action. Two years after Nehru's death, while speaking in New Delhi on 28 September 1966, Krishna Menon raised many eyebrows when he said at an international roundtable that 'there was no question of Nehru toying with the idea of a third bloc since his non-alignment policy was opposed to the idea of blocs'.

Krishna Menon's operation in New York had been fixed for early October 1961. On the way to the UN, he stopped off in London as always and met with, among others, Mountbatten, who has left behind a record of their conversation of 29 September 1961:

> Krishna Menon came to luncheon with me today on his way from India to New York. He had tripped and fallen on his head recently and given his skull a nasty crack. He said he was suffering from periodical numbness in his arm and from time to time was finding difficulty with his speech . . .
>
> I have never known him in such a depressed state about relations between India and the U.K. Krishna Menon has always been the strongest protagonist of Anglo-Indian friendship and no one helped me more than him in keeping India within the Commonwealth. He said he was finding it more and more difficult to stand up for the U.K. among her increasingly large number of critics in India.

Krishna Menon placed on record his strong objections to the BBC's coverage of the Indian Army's activities in the Congo, the grant of British nationality to A.Z. Phizo, the Naga rebel leader, and to the British government's lack of support to the Indian-led peace-keeping operations under the aegis of the UN in the Congo. Mountbatten took these complaints seriously and pursued them

with the British government. He also sent a copy of his record of
the conversation with Krishna Menon to Paul Gore-Booth, the
UK high commissioner to India, who replied on 2 November
1961:

> . . . The occasion seems to have been typically Krishna Menon.
> After a year here one has become used to a pattern which is
> uniform in general though full of surprises in detail. In the field of
> arms purchases, for instances, there is no doubt that he likes to do
> business with us rather than with most people—I doubt whether
> we could have ever got the tank contract [Vickers] without his
> practical sympathy. There is also a streak of sentimental friendship
> at least for a Britain represented by a number of elements in which
> one will have to include (with apologies) the New Statesman and
> yourself!
>
> On the other hand, he seems to take an almost sadistic delight
> not only in criticizing our policies especially when they are
> associated with American policies, but also in quite grotesquely
> distorting information that must be available to him about our
> actions and motives . . .
>
> Delhi goes on discussing this fascinating and infuriating
> character from day to day but I have not yet met anybody who
> claimed to have a nicely blue-printed explanation on what he does
> and why he does it.

Two months earlier, on 25 September 1961, Gore-Booth had
sent to Alexander Clutterbuck at the Commonwealth Relations
Office an explosive 'TOP SECRET' note called 'THE INDIAN
ARMY GENERALS' on the state of affairs at the highest levels
of the Indian Army. The note was based on a 'heart-to-heart talk'
between the military adviser in the UK High Commission in New
Delhi and a 'personal close friend of his, a reliable witness, and in a
very good position to know what is going on'. It presented a negative
picture of the state of morale among officers following the retirement
of Thimayya, discussed a number of these officers by name and ended
by observing:

. . . Three main facts emerge from the above report. One, there is no question that General KAUL is an ambitious man, but it is not clear how far he wishes these ambitions to take him. Two, in order to further his career he has appointed officers around and in key positions elsewhere who subscribe to his ideas. Three, his favouritism has undoubtedly caused dis-satisfaction among the more senior ranks and officers are now gathering into cliques for their own protection because they have little faith in the integrity of their superiors.

The outcome of General KAUL's machinations leads one to suppose that, in due course, he intends a 'take over'. Exactly what he intends to 'take over' is none too clear. Maybe as head of a Military Junta, <u>after</u> Mr. Nehru retires, or simply to be the next COAS [chief of army staff]. At the moment neither of these two possibilities can be said to be definite, for a third and less likely one could come about; i.e., that General KAUL is only acting on behalf of Mr. [Krishna] MENON who himself wishes to replace Mr. NEHRU after his retirement. Whatever General KAUL's intentions are, they are not healthy and they are doing untold harm to the Indian Army today; for dis-satisfaction and nepotism is becoming rife in what was once a stable and respected concern.

This was a damning indictment of Kaul and of Krishna Menon as well. By extension, it could also be considered an indictment of Nehru himself because Kaul was considered 'his man'. Nehru had known Kaul since at least 1946 and, without doubt, had been impressed by him—and Kaul had much to be impressed by. Kaul was a favourite of Krishna Menon too. He was seen to be less of the typical British-trained army officer by both Nehru and Krishna Menon, although he too had been Sandhurst-educated.

Who could have been the British military adviser's informant in the army that led to this explosive note? It may well have been J.N. Chaudhuri, the same senior officer who had leaked the news of Thimmaya's resignation to the *Statesman* two years earlier. He could have had an axe to grind but later events were to vindicate his assessment when China invaded India in October 1962.

Krishna Menon was operated upon in New York on 7 October 1961 for the removal of a clot 'just below the dural membrane outside the brain proper'. He was treated by a team of neurosurgeons led by Dr Leo Davidoff at the Albert Einstein College of Medicine at New York's Yeshiva University. Davidoff wrote to Nehru five days after the operation, and on 15 October 1961, the Prime Minister thanked him for 'the care and trouble you took in this matter' and added:

> We have been anxious about Mr. Krishna Menon's health. Anything that might possibly affect his brain was naturally a matter of the greatest concern to us. After the news of your operation came to us, we felt greatly relieved.

Three weeks later Nehru was in Washington and met with President Kennedy at the White House on 7 November 1961. One consequence of that meeting was that Krishna Menon himself would be at the White House to have a conversation with Kennedy on 21 November 1961. This greatly agitated Kennedy's aides. A briefing memorandum prepared for the US President said:

> It may have been at Krishna Menon's own instigation that Prime Minister Nehru suggested you see him. The Prime Minister may simply have been doing a favour for an old friend, or his willingness to request the appointment may have been calculated to enhance Krishna Menon's prestige in view of the General Election next February when he will be challenged by a highly-respected opponent . . .
>
> Despite Krishna Menon's pose as Nehru's alter ego—which posture is given substantial evidence by Nehru's own behaviour towards him—Menon has little prestige or respect at home in his own right. He has many enemies in India, including several members of the Cabinet and senior Congress party leaders who will undoubtedly take control of the party when Nehru is gone. Nevertheless he has managed by the alternate use of great charm and ruthlessness to retain the Prime Minister's benediction and to confound his foes in a number of situations where another man might have been removed from office for cause . . .

> . . . Our UN Mission's experience has led to the conclusion
> that Krishna Menon is untrustworthy, emotionally biased against
> the United States and inclined at every turn to influence Indian
> policy towards positions at odds with or obstructive to our own.

The meeting lasted just about half an hour. What is significant is
that the American record of that conversation contradicts the briefing
document that Kennedy's aides had prepared for him. The brief
mentioned that Krishna Menon's meeting with Kennedy had been
sought by Nehru whereas the record of the conversation begins thus:

> The President received the Indian Defense Minister to fulfill
> informal commitments that had arisen in a brief encounter
> between them at the United Nations last fall and in the course of
> the President's recent meetings with Prime Minister Nehru . . .

After going over the conversation that covered the state of Krishna
Menon's health, disarmament, Vietnam and Laos, the record ended
by noting:

> With the allotted half-hour over-run, the President saw the India
> Defense Minister out of his office with the comment that if time
> allowed they could obviously go on discussing these matters for a
> good deal longer.

As he came out of the White House Krishna Menon was mobbed
by reporters. All he said was, 'By the time we got talking about issues,
it was time to go.' History would soon prove Krishna Menon right
in what he told Kennedy about Vietnam and Laos. But right after he
returned to India, he became the target of a high-pitched campaign
designed to deny him a ticket for the forthcoming parliamentary
elections. Unlike in 1957, this time, the opposition was vocal and quite
widespread, showing the declining hold of Nehru in the Congress
party. Ramakrishna Bajaj—a leading industrialist of Bombay whose
father, Jamnalal Bajaj, had been fondly referred to as Gandhi's fifth
son—was at the forefront of this campaign. He first wrote to Nehru
on 20 November 1961:

I am writing this letter of mental conflict and anguish. A large number of young men like me have great regard for your inspiring leadership and also fully believe in your foreign policy. I, however, find that many young Congressmen like myself are faced with a dilemma created by Shri Krishna Menon being given a Congress ticket for Parliament.

I hope you are aware of a widespread impression among a large number of Congressmen and youth workers that Shri Krishna Menon is pro-Communist and his interpretation of your foreign policy, his general approach, emphasis and manner of presentation have created wrong and distorted impressions in the minds of people . . . Now that he seems likely to get the Congress ticket, our loyalty will be put to a severe strain . . . the Bombay Pradesh Youth Congress has already taken a stand against Shri Menon. I personally agree with their views . . . I shall be grateful for your guidance in the matter.

The Bombay Pradesh Youth Congress had passed an unprecedented resolution on 18 November 1961 that said:

. . . In the case of Shri Krishna Menon, many of us feel that his behaviour on several questions about the Communist countries and specially the Chinese aggression and his association with Communists, ex-Communists and fellow travellers in India had made him suspect in the eyes of the youth and other citizens of India.

Some years ago, while appearing on American television, Krishna Menon had been asked whether he was a fellow traveller to which he had retorted: 'I travel my own way. If anyone wants to travel with me he is welcome!'

Nehru was facing a virtual revolt in Bombay against Krishna Menon's candidature. The revolt was being orchestrated by none other than a member of Nehru's cabinet, S.K. Patil, who, five years earlier, had welcomed Krishna Menon enthusiastically into his bailiwick. Nehru replied to Bajaj on 22 November 1961:

I have received your letter of the 20th November and am rather surprised to read it. A person who thinks along those lines must think me either a fool or a knave. I am responsible for formulating and expressing the foreign policy of India and know how best to deal with it. To say that Shri Krishna Menon gives a wrong twist to it is to doubt my judgment of that policy and him . . . There are some people who constantly carry on a campaign against our policy in devious ways and try to make Krishna Menon the target of their denunciation, often making statements which have little truth. I value intelligent criticism, but I do not accept this running down of a colleague whose ability and patriotism are not only unquestioned, but far above many of those who adopt these devious methods . . .

But Bajaj would not relent, and a month later on 26 December 1961, again wrote to Nehru. This time he sent a ten-point charge-sheet against Krishna Menon. He called into serious doubt Krishna Menon's role in the freedom movement, highlighted his pro-China stance in 1952 and 1953 on the Korean prisoner-of-war issue, pointed to his pro-Soviet position in 1956 on Hungary, his soft approach to China's actions in Tibet and Ladakh, his mollycoddling of pro-communist trade unions and his continued hobnobbing with prominent personalities of Bombay who were associated with communist front organizations. Bajaj ended his diatribe thus: 'If Shri Menon is not pro-Communist, one wonders why the Communists of India are pro-Menon.' Obviously there were many other forces at work behind Bajaj's letters to Nehru. One such force was, without doubt, Menon's socialist pal of the 1930s, Minoo Masani, who was now a leading light of the right-wing Swatantra Party.

Nehru took Bajaj's second assault in his stride and replied on 29 December 1961:

I have already written to you rather fully . . . I can hardly enter into a controversy with you, and any way it is for you to decide what you wish to do. Evidently, you have so decided, and I have nothing further to write, you can of course see me when you like . . .

Krishna Menon's opponent was to be J.B. Kripalani, who was standing as an independent but was supported by the Swatantra, Jan Sangh and some other parties. Bajaj would join this group very soon.

While this Nehru–Bajaj exchange was taking place on Krishna Menon and the controversy over his candidature raged, the man in dispute was doing something else—masterminding a military operation that he had, ironically, been ruling out for well over five years at least at the UN. This was Operation Vijay, the liberation of Goa, Daman and Diu from over 450 years of Portuguese rule. Portugal surrendered within a matter of hours on 18 December 1961. Krishna Menon's critics were to link Operation Vijay to his need for a 'big bang' success a few weeks prior to the elections, especially in view of the perception that a considerable number of Goans were part of the North Bombay electorate. The US establishment too considered Goa's liberation a result of pressure from Krishna Menon. Nehru's own sister, Vijaya Lakshmi Pandit, would tell Gore-Booth that Krishna Menon had pushed the Prime Minister to give his approval to Operation Vijay. The truth, as always, is substantially more complex than this.

Right through the 1950s Nehru's frequently articulated position was that Goa was unmistakably an integral part of India and that its accession should happen through diplomacy and negotiations. But since June 1956, when John Foster Dulles, the US secretary of state, publicly started declaring that Goa was very much a part of Portugal, the US's vital NATO ally, Nehru's patience began to wear thin. In June 1960, the International Court of Justice ruled in favour of India's right of passage to the Portuguese enclave of Dadra and Nagar Haveli near Goa but the core issue of Goa (and Diu) remained. By mid-1961, Nehru did not categorically rule out the use of force in his speeches in Parliament and outside. On 18 August 1961, he told Krishna Menon that he 'welcomed the Portuguese threat to reach Dadra and Nagar Haveli by land, across Indian territory, or by sea, because this would then [give] India a free hand to deal with Goa'. On 4 September 1961, Lt General J.N. Chaudhuri, who was then officiating chief of army staff, recorded a note:[18]

On the afternoon of 30 Aug '61, while travelling back from the [National Defence College, New Delhi] in a car with the

Defence Minister, the DM [defence minister] mentioned GOA. He said that the PM had now agreed to a plan for the use of troops in or against Portuguese possessions in India might be committed to paper. Later that afternoon in his office . . . the DM again said that a plan as above could be prepared but it should be kept at a very high and top secret level. He was categorical in stating that the number of people to be informed of the existence of this plan was to be limited, while at this stage other Service Chiefs were not to be consulted. In the preparation of a plan, however, reasonable assumptions of air and naval co-operation could be made . . .

On 21 October 1961, while inaugurating a seminar of Portuguese colonies that had drawn delegates from Africa as well, Nehru declared that at no time had India 'renounced recourse to a military solution'. Clearly, he had instructed his defence minister to start making contingency plans, something that his finance minister, Morarji Desai, was to confirm many years later in his memoirs:

> . . . I heard at the end of November [1961] . . . that our troops were concentrating on the border of Goa at Belgaum . . . It was, therefore, strongly rumoured that Goa would be taken possession of by military action . . . Jawaharlalji informed the Defence Committee [of the cabinet] about this in its meeting held in the end of November and said that the meeting of the Committee was called in order to fix a date for marching into Goa. I opposed the proposed step but as I was alone in my opposition, my opposition had no effect . . .

Incidentally, Desai was also to write that Krishna Menon forced the military action in December 1961 to bolster his electoral prospects two months later.

On 28 November 1961, Nehru received a letter from R.B. Kakodkar, who had just completed a 'study tour' of Goa and found the situation ripe for 'police action against Goa'. Nehru replied that very day saying, 'We are taking such action in this matter as we think is required.' He sent a copy of Kakodkar's appraisal and his own reply to Krishna Menon. The next day, Krishna Menon convened a high-level meeting and the three service chiefs jointly recorded this 'Top Secret' note:

> In a meeting held this morning in your office in which the Chiefs of Staff along with the CGS [Chief of General Staff, the number-two man in the army], DCNS [Deputy Chief of Naval Staff, the number-two man in the navy] and DCAS [Deputy Chief of Air Staff, the number two man in the air force] were present, you stated that as a result of recent Portuguese hostile actions against our nationals, Government propose taking certain steps in area ANJADEV Island and that, as the Portuguese were likely to take certain retaliatory measures, we may be compelled to take armed action against their territories in India.
>
> For this purpose you directed us to concentrate forces as soon as possible with a view to operating in the areas ANJADEV ISLAND and the Portuguese territories of GOA and, if necessary, DIU and DAMAN. You have accepted the time of 14 days which we will take to concentrate our forces in various areas for our operational tasks. Necessary orders have been issued to all concerned accordingly.
>
> Your formal approval to these measures is requested.
>
> Vice Admiral R.D. Katari
> 29 Nov 1961
>
> Air Marshall A.M. Engineer
> 29 Nov 1961
>
> Gen. P.N. Thapar
> 29 Nov 1961
>
> <u>Minister of Defence</u>

Their intelligence in New Delhi being what it was then, the Americans quickly sensed that something major was afoot in Goa. An internal US State Department memorandum of 6 December 1961 stated:

1. There has been mounting pressure on the Government of India to take steps to incorporate the remaining Portuguese Overseas Territories on the Indian sub-continent . . .
2. The pressure on the Government of India stem principally from (a) Goan 'nationalists' . . . ; (b) African 'nationalists'; ((c) the opposition parties in India who are attacking the Government of India for a weak foreign policy in relation to Chinese Communist occupation of Indian-claimed territory in Ladakh and the do-nothing policy in Goa.

Calling for US pressure on Nehru to abandon military action, it went on to add:

It is likely that the Indian Defense Minister, Krishna Menon, now running for Parliament, personally feels all the above pressures keenly, but the pressures exist and would be felt by the Indian Government quite apart from his personal involvement.

Six days later another such internal memorandum noted that the US ambassador in India, John Kenneth Galbraith, had just met with Nehru, urging him not to use force in Goa. However, he admitted:

As of this morning it appears that there is a real possibility that pressures on Prime Minister Nehru from various sources (including communist-influenced 'Goan Nationalists' and Krishna Menon, who is running for Parliament) will prevail and that an armed attack will take place . . .

On 15 December 1961, Galbraith sent a message back home after meeting Nehru again and impressing on him the fact that the US was firmly opposed to the use of force in Goa:

. . . It is my feeling that I may have moved him a bit, that he was even looking for arguments [to put off the military action]. Would also note he was very sensitive to the reactions of the President [Kennedy]. It is still my feeling that the decision is to act on Goa or conceivably other enclaves probably tomorrow but possibly we may have produced one more pause for reflection and pressure from Krishna Menon . . .

Operation Vijay, under the leadership of Major General K.P. Candeth—son of Krishna Menon's teacher at Presidency College some forty-five years earlier and hailing from Ottapalam, some 100 kilometres away from Krishna Menon's place of birth—was launched on the night of 17 December. The very next day the Portuguese surrendered, bringing to an end, in less than twenty-four hours, 451 years of colonial rule. Candeth would continue to be an admirer of Krishna Menon. Many years later he would tell his grandniece Janaki Ram:[19]

> He [Krishna Menon] was undoubtedly the ablest Defence Minister the army ever had—we owe him a tremendous debt, because but for him we would not have had a defence industry. He had vision and enormous drive. He could get things done. But his manner of doing things was what antagonized the army. Because we are an organisation where respect, honour and tradition holds a great deal of importance. And we have to command people and we can't do it if someone denigrates you.

The West was livid with Krishna Menon, and to a lesser extent with Nehru, on Goa—they had consciously or unconsciously played the good cop–bad cop routine very well. The US State Department cabled the embassy in New Delhi on 26 December 1961 that the Indian ambassador in the US, B.K. Nehru, had been told that Krishna Menon's visit to New York just as the Portuguese were surrendering was being seen by the Americans as India 'flaunting its action in Goa'.

In his conversations with Michael Brecher some years later Krishna Menon opened up to an unusual extent and spoke extensively of how the Goa operation was planned and its consequences. He was extremely critical of the role of the Americans, and of Galbraith in particular. He did not deny that he had presented a virtual fait accompli to the Prime Minister on the exact time of the operation informing him after it had begun. He would deny that his activism over Goa had anything to do with the elections since there were only a handful of Goans in North Bombay. He would compliment the army, navy and air force for working very well together. Two individuals would be mentioned: Lt General B.M. Kaul was praised for planning the entire operation, and Lt General J.N. Chaudhuri for muscling in and claiming credit for doing nothing. A year later, Kaul would be forced to resign after the military debacle in the war with China, and Chaudhuri would take over as army chief from Thapar, who would also be made to quit. Goa may well have given Krishna Menon and Kaul a swollen head and a false sense of India's military prowess.

Krishna Menon's role in the liberation of Goa earned him huge praise at home even as his critics at home and abroad were spreading the story that it had everything to do with his election. One person within Nehru's closest circle who was extremely critical of Krishna Menon's actions was the Prime Minister's sister; the UK high commissioner, Gore-Booth, would send London a quite extraordinary letter on 3 February 1962 based on a conversation he had had with Vijaya Lakshmi Pandit a few days earlier. It was a thirteen-page letter with two appendices. The first detailed the talk with Pandit, which the high commissioner summarized in the main letter thus:

> . . . On the subject of Krishna Menon Mrs. Pandit gave a hair-raising description of some of the appalling mendacities and disloyalties practiced by him when he was supposed to be a member of the delegation at the U.N., or elsewhere, led by her [for a few months in 1946, 1952 and 1953]. She said that she had the impression

that her brother knew a great deal more about all this than was generally supposed, but for some reason, which even she was not able to fathom he still remained under Krishna Menon's powerful influence . . .

[She said] that 'our friend' (Krishna Menon) was working to a deliberate plan. This was to continue to overwhelm Mr. Nehru with knowledge and argument, to make every effort at impressing Mrs. Gandhi with his brilliance and rightness and to work towards a future Government in which, if he were not the head, he would wield power, using Mrs. Gandhi and Jagjivan Ram, the present Minister of Railways as his constitutional front; one supposes K.D. Malaviya would also have a role to play . . .

I have left out all Mrs. Pandit's purple passages on Krishna Menon and tried to give her interpretation of the central facts and influences.. I think we can accept much of this as I have given it . . . He [Krishna Menon] said to me once that India must go either much further right or much further left, and he was, and is, evidently determined to run the leftward movement . . .

We are giving much thought to the question whether the British can in any way be more than mere spectators in this business. If one feels a desire to reverse the trend, this is not because of objection either ideological or on the grounds of British interest, to 'leftism' as Mr. Nehru has hitherto interpreted it. Nor is it because Krishna Menon is consistently anti-British, since he is not, and one's personal relations with him are, in odd dimensions, by no means bad. It is because his methods and standards are far too close to those of Communist dictatorship . . . I have at present a feeling that we cannot do very much . . .

It is the second appendix in Gore-Booth's letter that was more explosive. It was called 'A Military Coup by Krishna Menon' and contained the British High Commission's assessment of the political situation in India after Gore-Booth's conversation with Vijaya Lakshmi Pandit. In retrospect, it is a bizarre document and clearly reflects what was being spoken of in the cocktail party circuit in New Delhi, of which Indian civil servants and military officers were an important part. This was when the Indian Civil Service (ICS) still ruled the roost and Sandhurst mattered.

> The suggestion is that Mr. Menon now has sufficient power and influence in the Army to be able to engineer a military coup now if he wished. It has also been alleged that a threat of such action was made to Mr. Nehru when the latter hesitated over Goa.
>
> Mr. Menon has been building up his popularity with the Armed Services since he became Defence Minister, and particularly his reputation as a Minister who gets things done. He has given considerable attention to improving terms of pay and conditions of service . . . But this process of building up personal control over the Armed Forces is nowhere near complete and is not wholly assured of success . . . In the present circumstances therefore, if Mr. Menon were to attempt a naked seizure of power, it is highly unlikely that the armed forces as a whole would obey him without question . . . Mr. Menon is too clever to run this kind of risk . . . As regards Goa . . . Mr. Menon was in no position to threaten Mr. Nehru with a coup if he failed to give the necessary orders . . . He may even have said that he would himself give the orders and challenge Mr. Nehru to countermand them.
>
> There are therefore good grounds for doubting whether Mr. Menon would be prepared under any circumstances to stage a military coup. This is not because he would in principle stick at anything in his pursuit of power (here Mrs. Pandit is probably right) but because he must be aware of his own unpopularity (at any rate for the moment) with a considerable proportion of the Army, and in political circles . . . For this reason it seems much more likely that he would use his control of the armed forces to strengthen his political power behind the scenes, retaining the public façade of constitutionality.
>
> There is little doubt that Mr. Menon has money to spend and his position gives him plenty of opportunities to line his pockets at the expense of e.g., foreign defence contractors. There is little doubt either that he buys press support. The weekly 'Blitz' of Bombay, a cleverly produced and sensational Left-wing production

which circulates very widely throughout India is Menon's loudest
and most persistent supporter; Karanjia, its Editor, is known to us
to be at the disposal of the highest bidder . . . Apart from 'Blitz',
the Communist paper 'Link'—though more sophisticated and
less blatant—often supports Menon and could be a recipient of
financial encouragement from him.

Blitz was indeed Krishna Menon's greatest champion. As for
Link, one of its greatest benefactors was A.V. Baliga, the doctor–
philanthropist of Bombay and founder of the Indo-Soviet
Friendship Society in the mid-1950s. He was undoubtedly part
of Krishna Menon's innermost personal and ideological circle.
Also a significant supporter of the magazine was Biju Patnaik, the
industrialist–politician who would later become a legendary figure
in Orissa. Baliga, Patnaik, Aruna Asif Ali and Krishna Menon had
together launched *Link*.

In the latter half of November 1961, Isaiah Berlin, the famed
British philosopher, was in New Delhi to participate in a seminar
organized in connection with the birth centenary of Rabindranath
Tagore. Berlin met Nehru for the first time and spoke with a number
of other Indian public figures. On 30 November 1961, he gave his
impressions of his only visit to the country to Gore-Booth, which
were probably based on what he had been told by his interlocutors:[20]

> . . . Nehru's relation to Krishna Menon is T.S. Eliot's to Ezra Pound,
> the same beliefs at a much lower tension, milder, more compatible
> with respectable life but deriving from the same constellation of
> values, gently, firmly, tolerant, decently anti-Western . . .

And a month later, with India still on his mind, he wrote to another
philosopher, the Canadian Charles Taylor, on 28 December 1961.
Here, he likened Nehru to Franklin Roosevelt—'a man who has
betrayed his class and has become a popular idol'—and added:[21]

> He [Nehru] delights in his own virtuosity and has before his eyes
> constantly the fate of Kuomintang, an ossified nationalist party

which rotted away until it fell before communism. Hence the extraordinary position of [Krishna] Menon whom he keeps by his side not only because he is tied to him by sentimental bonds but also in order to prevent himself from selling out to comfort, appeasement, respectability, a cozy semi-capitalist regime which, he perfectly realizes, means stagnation and ultimately collapse and defeat.

Berlin also told Taylor that 'Nehru greatly enjoys his encounters with the West', saying:

. . . [H]e likes them individually, he is intrigued by them, adores flirting with handsome Western ladies like a Samson who practises brinkmanship with a number of formidable Delilahs, and he loves Western company.

Berlin was meeting Nehru for the first time, and on what basis he formed this opinion is not known. But it was a perfect description of Krishna Menon.

November 1961 was important for another reason. Three of Krishna Menon's pet projects came to fruition. On 4 November 1961, Nehru launched the Indian Navy's first aircraft carrier, *INS Vikrant.* Originally put down as *HMS Hercules,* Krishna Menon, with the full backing of Mountbatten, had masterminded its purchase in 1957. For a political leader of that era, he showed unusual understanding of the importance of building naval strength. He also pushed for, and ensured the acquisition of, two shipyards in Bombay and Calcutta from a British firm that had owned them. These shipyards—Mazagon Docks and Garden Reach—then became essential pillars of the naval establishment. The second obsession of Krishna Menon that became a reality in November 1961 was the successful flight of the indigenously manufactured Avro 748, which would see considerable military and civilian use. Third, he announced the establishment of a factory at Avadi near Madras to manufacture battle tanks. The first of these tanks would roll out two years later but only after he had quit as defence minister. The British Prime Minister, Harold Macmillan, had been very pleased by Krishna Menon's decision on the Avro and had said as much to Nehru two years earlier in August 1959:

> It is sometime since we exchanged messages . . . I was so glad that Krishna Menon was able to arrange things with our people about the Avro aeroplane . . .

However, in mid–1961, Macmillan would not be too happy with Krishna Menon's insistence and persistence in acquiring supersonic military aircraft from the USSR.

Notes

1. UN Oral History Project, 30 October 1962.
2. I have discussed these twists and turns in Ramesh (2019).
3. Ramesh (2018).
4. Iyer (1993).
5. Hangen (1963).
6. Chaudhuri (1978).
7. Raghavan (2010).
8. Darbar (1976).
9. Brecher (1968).
10. Raghavan (2015).
11. Brecher (1968).
12. Sanghvi (1961).
13. Hangen (1963).
14. Email correspondence, 11 November 2018.
15. Khera (1968).
16. Verma (1988).
17. Brecher (1968).
18. Palit (2004).
19. Ram (1997).
20. Hardy and Pottle (2013).
21. Ibid.

15

The Glory and the Fall (1962)

This was the year that started off with a bang and ended up with an even bigger bang as far as Krishna Menon was concerned. But before the bang came two conversations with an American professor at Harvard University, who was visiting India as a consultant to the US National Security Council. What Krishna Menon had attempted to do for the Sino–US relationship in 1955, this professor would accomplish in 1971 and become a legend. On 8 and 10 January 1962, Krishna Menon met with Henry Kissinger. Unlike Krishna Menon, Kissinger maintained records of all his meetings and noted:

> I began the conversation by saying it was very kind of the Defence Minister to spare me the time for the appointment . . . Menon replied that I was undoubtedly one of the Americans who wished him defeated in the next election . . . the American press, American officials and the President [Kennedy] he said were either reporting about him invidiously or had treated him in a high-handed fashion . . . This was particularly true of the President. He said that he was aware of the President's rude behaviour to him had not been directed against him personally but against the Prime Minister. People who were afraid to tackle Nehru tackled him.
>
> I said that it seemed to be inconceivable that his interpretation was correct. After all, the President had been committed to a

strong and developing India long before he became the Chief Executive . . . Krishna Menon replied, 'You are always trying to embrace us. Don't embrace us. We are a proud people' . . .

We then turned briefly to Goa. Menon said that the American objection to the Indian action was a vestige of Western imperialism . . . The attack on Goa was simply a continuation of India's struggle for independence . . .

He then explained India's views with respect to nuclear testing. He said that they had been malicious[ly] misrepresented. India has opposed the resumption by the Soviets of nuclear testing just as much as the American resumption of testing . . . This led him into a long and highly detailed disquisition of the sequence of nuclear test negotiation, the essence of which was that the United States had never really been prepared to have a nuclear test treaty [The Partial Test Ban Treaty would be signed in August 1963 in Moscow] . . .

I met Krishna Menon again on Wednesday, January 10th . . . He was much calmer than the first time. This did not keep him from launching an attack on the Ambassador [John Kenneth Galbraith], who he said was too pro-Indian . . . He said he wanted somebody as Ambassador who represents America, that Indians themselves were capable of representing India . . .

About Indo-China he said that India was perfectly relaxed about the situation there. The United States had caused most of the trouble in Laos . . .

I asked Menon about the difficulties with China on India's northern frontier. He replied that the territory occupied by the Chinese was absolutely worthless, a fact well known to all foreigners eager to launch India into a conflict with China. The worst result of the Chinese moves on India's northern frontier was its weakening of the progressive elements in India . . .

About the Congo, he said that the United States had recently behaved better, but that it bore a heavy responsibility for the murder of Lumumba and the situation in Rhodesia . . .

It is . . . impossible to do justice to the conversation with Krishna Menon because of his method of presenting an enormous mass of detail, all of which is slightly distorted, to create a picture of American inequity, Indian forbearance, and Communist wisdom. It is a frightening thought that Nehru received a great deal of his information on foreign policy and about the United States from this man. On almost every particular, moreover, Krishna Menon's presentation disagrees with those of other senior Indian officials with whom I talked.

In nine months, the war that Krishna Menon thought would not happen did, in fact, take place. India would face severe military reverses, and Krishna Menon would be forced to resign with the US ambassador, Galbraith, playing a crucial role in his ouster. Krishna Menon never really took to Galbraith. He may have resented Galbraith's easy access to Nehru but more than that he found Galbraith's behaviour to be imperial and viceregal, without the sophistication and grace of a Mountbatten.

A few days later on 13 January 1962, Gore-Booth called on Krishna Menon and sent back a detailed report of their conversation which was freewheeling. Gore-Booth wrote that Krishna Menon was not well and reclining muffled-up in a blanket. He was 'reading, for the moment, a book about Portugal from a sternly left-wing point of view'. He went on:

He [Krishna Menon] spoke a little about the Army and said that 'General Thimayya was a fool and not a very nice fool either'. His resignation should have been accepted at once in 1959 by the Prime Minister and there would have been no more trouble. The present trouble was that there was too much whisky in the American embassy. The British knew better than to overdo pressure and propaganda.

On aviation, Krishna Menon said that the British helicopter industry was clearly no use at all and that we ought to get some technical assistance from the French who were far in advance. The Indians would be betting a few more Russian helicopters . . .

Krishna Menon said that Pakistan had nothing to fear from India. He himself was not the fire-eater he was supposed to be on Pakistan and, in fact, he was unorthodox in wanting friendship with Pakistan through economic cooperation. The China business was much exaggerated in Parliament . . . India was not going to throw away lives useless by being bellicose, though there might be further incidents.

On Goa Krishna Menon implied that situation was clear from
Mr. Nehru's speeches and said that while it would have been
difficult to do anything after December 8th, there had been two
postponements and a really worthwhile offer from the Portuguese
could have prevented the use of force . . .

COMMENT

I think that what Krishna Menon says is usually the truth, but not
the whole truth. He retains all his mercurial activity, but he still
has not quite recovered the self-possession which he had before his
injury a few months ago, but he clearly wields and enjoys wielding
power, and nothing is going to stop this machine from roaring
along, except some complete collapse or some, at the moment,
totally unlikely change in the balance of power.

'This machine', as Gore-Booth called Krishna Menon, kept going for
another eleven months before it broke down completely or, more
accurately, was forced to stop functioning. That comment about
American whisky may have been in jest but it reflected the truth
of the fifties—that is how information was obtained from Indian
politicians and civil servants.[1]
    The 1962 election in the Bombay constituency drew national
and international attention. It was, of course, a Krishna Menon versus
Kripalani contest—a contest between a Congressman and an ex-
Congressman. But more fundamentally Nehru was the issue, and he,
like in 1957, did not hesitate to make himself that. On 23 February
1962, he issued an appeal but not as elaborate and elongated as the
one from five years earlier:

I trust that the voters of North Bombay will vote for the Congress
candidate, Shri V.K. Krishna Menon. Unfortunately, this election
has been conducted largely on personal issues. The issues at
stake are those of the Congress policy and programme. Every
Congressman, and indeed others also, should vote therefore on
these policies and programmes, and not be confused by personal
questions. Shri Krishna Menon is a Congress candidate and stands

for those policies and programmes and, therefore, all those who believe in those policies should vote for him.

Nehru was the only big name of Indian politics batting for Krishna Menon. Two other 'heavyweights' had come out openly against him. On 8 February 1962, Rajagopalachari had said, 'If Mr. Menon succeeds, it would be one point to Indian Communists and two points to world Communists.' A day later Jayaprakash Narayan said, '[E]ven though Shri Krishna Menon happens to be a Congress candidate, and has the Prime Minister's support, his victory would in effect be a victory of the Communist Party.' Kripalani dramatically announced on 12 February 1962 that he would withdraw from the contest if Krishna Menon openly condemned the Communist Party and declared that he was not a communist.

There was a surprising degree of American interest in the Krishna Menon–Kripalani contest. On 5 January 1962, *Time* magazine had John Kennedy on its cover, and on 16 February 1962, it would be the turn of his brother, Robert Kennedy. In between, on 2 February 1962, Krishna Menon became only the third Indian after Gandhi and Nehru to appear on *Time*'s cover.

Time *magazine cover, 2 February 1962*

The leading stars of Bollywood had all lined up for Krishna Menon and added much glamour and glitz to his campaign. There was an official campaign run by the Congress party, and there was an unofficial campaign being masterminded by four of Krishna Menon's closest friends, all of whom made no secret of their leftist credentials and sympathy for the communist ideology. They were active in 1957 but became even more active in 1962 because of the opposition to Krishna Menon within his own party. These were Rajni Patel, a noted lawyer; A.V. Baliga, the famous surgeon–philanthropist; Mulk Raj Anand, a well-known author; and Balraj Sahni, a widely admired film star. Thanks to this quartet, almost all the leading personalities of the film world—Raj Kapoor, Dilip Kumar, Dev Anand, Rajendra Kumar, B.R. Chopra, Sahir Ludhianvi, Naushad, S.D. Burman, K.A. Abbas and many others—signed a public appeal in favour of Krishna Menon:

Fellow Citizens and Friends:

We are not political people and normally take no more than a casual interest in elections, etc. But the *Time* article has revealed to us clearly that the attacks on Krishna Menon, from various quarters are only cover to attack our beloved Prime Minister, to weaken and undermine his basic national policies and to overthrow his inspiring leadership.

We do not normally interfere in elections or party politics. But on this particular occasion, we feel it our duty to appeal to our fellow citizens of Bombay to demonstrate that in both the issues under attack from foreign quarters, the issues which are really the foundation of our country's national fabric—an independent foreign policy and a socialist pattern of development—we all stand solidly, overwhelmingly behind our Prime Minister.

We appeal to the citizens of North Bombay to

SUPPORT KRISHNA MENON

KRISHNA MENON'S VOICE IS INDIA'S VOICE

SUPPORT KRISHNA MENON
in order to
SUPPORT OUR BELOVED PRIME MINISTER

While Nehru spoke in Bombay only once during the entire campaign—on 15 January 1962—he referred to the North Bombay contest in many of his election speeches across the country. In Bombay, of course, he spoke at length on Krishna Menon, trying to enthuse his own party colleagues to come out and aggressively work to ensure that the defence minister was re-elected.

The result was not a surprise when it was announced on 1 March 1962. Krishna Menon had triumphed comfortably, more than tripling his margin of victory five years earlier. Almost immediately thereafter, accompanied by Baliga, he called on his defeated opponent at the latter's home. Normally books are written on the entire elections. The 1962 electoral contest in North Bombay was unusual in that it resulted in an academic study all by itself by a professor in Bombay University.[2] This was the first and remains the only such detailed analysis of a campaign in a specific constituency. It captured the colour and controversy of that campaign very well.

After his victory over Kripalani, Krishna Menon was now on top of the world. He had won handsomely. He was now a two-term Lok Sabha MP. He was seen as a possible successor to Nehru—in some polls, third in national popularity after Nehru and Jayaprakash Narayan. To be sure, he derived much of his halo from his proximity to Nehru, but his independent standing in the domestic political arena could not be denied. He returned as defence minister but one man, who had known him since the 1930s in London and who had just become an Indian citizen, wished otherwise. J.B.S. Haldane wrote to him on 5 March 1962:

> Please allow me to congratulate you on your re-election. I do not share all your political views, but I know that your continuation in the cabinet will ensure the efficiency of one or more of the public services. I should like to think that you had done your work for the Armed Forces, and could tidy up some other departments, particularly Education, and Scientific Research and Cultural Affairs, which concern us particularly. But I fear that there is still a lot to do beyond our northern frontier.

If only Nehru had followed Haldane's advice! Krishna Menon genuinely cared about education and would have likely done a first-rate job of being the minister. And after he had resigned in November 1962, Nehru had toyed with the idea of putting him in charge of science and technology.

So it was back to defence and the UN after that. However, at this very moment, his health became a matter of considerable speculation. The deputy high commissioner of the UK in Madras, W.J.M. Paterson, reported to the High Commission in New Delhi on 26 April 1962:

> As you know Krishna Menon was in Madras for a few days last week. He left an impression in many minds here that he is far from well. The ostensible reason for his visit was the fulfillment of a number of official engagements on April 19 . . . Later on the same evening he was the guest of honour at a dinner party given by G. Narasimhan of 'The Hindu' . . . At the end of the meal Narasimhan welcomed the guest and invited him to say the customary 'few words'. There was then some applause but nothing happened. Menon sat gazing at his plate in a sort of reverie until his silence became quite oppressive. Finally he seemed to come to his senses and he rose laboriously and looked around in a puzzled way. His opening sentences were quite normal and he paid a tribute to 'The Hindu' as a paper run by professional journalists and not, like some others, by confectioners and jute merchants. After that he paused, leant forward heavily on the table and with the head bowed mumbled the rest of his remarks in the direction of his plate . . . I was sitting about four places to his right . . . At one point he raised his tone and asked 'Can you hear me?'. On being greeted with a chorus of 'No' from the bulk of his audience he merely remarked 'That's good' and relapsed into his mumble. It was all quite odd . . .
>
> On the following day he had an electro-encephalogram and angiogram, at the General Hospital, where he spent the night. He left for Delhi the next day . . . I think that we can be fairly sure that

another operation will be necessary and that it will be performed
either in New York after the Security Council meetings or later
in Madras . . .

But even before Paterson had informed his superiors, the London
Times had already carried a dispatch on 23 April 1962 to the effect that
Krishna Menon would soon have to have another operation. Such
was the global interest in the man and his doings. But medical opinion
differed. Dr B. Ramamurthy, India's pre-eminent neurosurgeon,
who had examined him in Madras, recommended a second operation
in view of Krishna Menon's persistent headaches and drowsiness.
Another opinion was of Dr Morris Bender of Mount Sinai Hospital in
New York, given after examining Krishna Menon on 30 April 1962.
Dr Bender concluded that 'while there are a few findings indicative
of neurological dysfunction, I do not believe there is sufficient clinical
or laboratory abnormality to warrant intracranial surgery'. As it turned
out, the second brain operation was not performed.

In May and June 1962, Krishna Menon was back in the UN,
making four thundering speeches on Kashmir, which won him further
plaudits at home. That he had taken on Muhammad Zafrulla Khan, the
foreign minister of Pakistan who had got the better of Gopalaswami
Ayyangar in 1948, added to his lustre. After his first two speeches in
the Security Council on 3 and 4 May 1962, the British delegation sent
this report to the Foreign Office in London on 8 May 1962:

Menon arrived in New York at the beginning of last week and
on his first public appearance did look a bit tired, although he did
not behave at all oddly. However, when, after a few days delay, he
eventually spoke in the Security Council debate, he showed no sign
whatever of diminished powers. In fact, the performance which
he gave by way of reply to the Pakistani case was exceptionally
brilliant, and it was widely remarked that he appeared to be in his
best form as advocate in a case of which he is a complete master.
Outside the Council too he behaved with normal—or perhaps I
should say in his case abnormal—courtesy and charm . . .

A little while earlier Indira Gandhi was in the US on a lecture tour, speaking mostly in colleges and universities. She wrote to Nehru on 28 March 1962 from Spokane:

> . . . Krishna Menon, neutralism and Goa—that is all anybody is interested in . . .

And a month later she was in New York, and a debate on Kashmir was soon to start in the UN Security Council. She wrote again to her father on 29 April 1962:

> . . . This whole country & I believe many U.N. people of other countries too, are suffering from a K.M. [Krishna Menon] phobia . . .

It was not just the Americans who were suffering from 'KM phobia', as Indira Gandhi informed her father. Even the Indian ambassador in Washington, B.K. Nehru, appeared to be one of its victims. On 23 May 1962, in the course of a long television interview on the NBC Network, he was asked whether the cut in US aid to India announced by the Senate had anything to do with the 'uncooperative attitude of Krishna Menon at the UN and with what was seen to be his instinctive "anti-Americanism"'. The ambassador replied:

> You know that is a very difficult question to answer. You ask me as Indian Ambassador—I know very well that Krishna Menon is not popular in this country and the manner in which he often speaks at the United Nations irritates the American people. Yes we are aware of that . . .

Ambassador Nehru's remarks caused an enormous furore in the Indian Parliament. Members belonging to different political parties made it a huge issue, of course, for different reasons. For the next few months, this interview would become a matter of acrimonious debate. Krishna Menon kept quiet and did not jump into the fray.

The year 1962 would also see Krishna Menon clash with Homi Bhabha, father of India's nuclear programme, who was then taking steps to build India's capability in space technology. In March 1962, Bhabha had supported an American proposal that involved the launching of satellites by the US and the establishment of tracking stations in India, in addition to Brazil, Australia, Canada, the Philippines and the UK. Bhabha, however, wanted the tracking stations to be operated by Indian scientists. Krishna Menon, on the other hand, held the view that the US proposal was tantamount to having an American military base in India because the entire project was being administered by the US Department of Defence. Nehru, expectedly, sided with both Bhabha and Krishna Menon. On 10 March 1962, he approved the project, subject to the conditions that it would not be used for military purposes, would be operated by Indian scientists and would be temporary with a fixed time limit.

But the two close friends of Nehru would be at each other's throats again very soon. In July 1962, Bhabha made a proposal to Nehru to set up an International Equatorial Sounding Rocket Launching Facility in India. Krishna Menon took the view that this facility should come up under the UN auspices, with both the US and the USSR cooperating in equal measure. He told the Prime Minister in early-July 1962:

> I cannot agree in any circumstances to the US setting up or participating in launching sites in India on their own initiative and without the UN and the USSR. I think this is a dangerous step and contrary to our professed view and should not be pursued.

Nehru was perplexed by Krishna Menon's objections and told him on 13 July 1962 that 'this is a UN project and it is stated that the US, USSR, UK and France are cooperating in it'. Nehru approved Bhabha's proposal but with a rider to please Krishna Menon: a bilateral agreement with the US was not to be concluded before India had had negotiations with the USSR, France and the UK. In a few years, the facility would come up at Thumba in Kerala and would lay the foundations for India's successful space programme.

On 15 July 1962, Krishna Menon wrote to Nehru that he was planning to leave for Geneva. The Prime Minister replied the next day:

> . . . I suppose you have to go to Geneva for the Laos Conference, although the Ladakh situation would indicate your staying on here. I see that the Chinese Foreign Minister is also going to Geneva . . . The sooner you come back the better . . .

Krishna Menon met with the Chinese foreign minister in Geneva on 22 and 23 July 1962. They had met the previous year in May in Geneva during a similar conference. The two were now attending a fourteen-nation conference on Laos. A peace agreement was to be finally signed, bringing to an end Krishna Menon's own unflagging efforts that had begun eight years earlier in this very city. *The Hindu* used an AP dispatch on its front page on 25 July 1962:

CHINA FIRED FIRST

V.K.K. MENON'S ACCUSATION

CHEN YI RULES OUT WAR

MR. V.K. Krishna Menon India's Defence Minister, who this morning had breakfast talks with Marshal Chen-yi, Chinese Foreign Minister later in the evening said: 'These disputed areas in Ladakh are largely unoccupied areas. They have posts and we have posts. Sometimes they say we shoot first: sometimes we say they shoot first—actually they shot first' Answering reporters questions he rejected a suggestion for a wire barrier along the disputed border. 'We are sensible people—we do not put up wire fences', he said. Marshall Chen-yi said tonight he considered the border dispute with India as a localized problem which would not lead to war.

Krishna Menon came back to India on 25 July 1962 but maintained a silence on what had transpired at Geneva. He briefed the cabinet six days later. Meanwhile on 25 July 1962, a future Prime Minister had written to Nehru saying that the frequent absence of the defence minister during a time when India faced a crisis on its borders with China in Ladakh was totally unjustifiable. That very day Nehru replied to Atal Bihari Vajpayee, then a member of the Rajya Sabha, saying that he saw nothing wrong in Krishna Menon going abroad for five days, particularly to attend the last stages of the Laos conference 'in which we have been engaged and have played an important part'. He assured Vajpayee that the Ladakh matter was now under the defence chiefs. Nehru and Vajpayee had extended exchanges when Parliament reconvened the next month, with Nehru saying on 22 August 1962 that he had spoken with Krishna Menon about the latter meeting Chen Yi in Geneva if the opportunity arose and raising the Ladakh issue. Nehru clarified that the initiative for the conversation at Geneva came from Chen Yi himself.

Krishna Menon would never speak of his talks with Chen Yi. When pressed by Michael Brecher some years later, this is all he would say:[3]

> . . . [T]hey were not negotiations of any kind; they were just informal talks . . . It was not organized formal conversation or anything like that . . . Chen Yi was most anxious to see me, so I invited him to breakfast. I called on him too. He called on me three or four times. At that time we had not reached the stage when one could have said we were in conflict, though the Chinese were pushing into what they choose now to call 'the line of actual control'.

In 1981, Arthur Lall, the Indian diplomat who was with Krishna Menon in Geneva during the Laos conference, would write about the Krishna Menon–Chen Yi conversations.[4] He was particularly close to Krishna Menon for over a decade.

> . . . In Geneva a series of three very important meetings took place between Chen Yi, Chang Han-fu and Ch'iao Kuan-hua (until recently foreign minister of China) and, on the other side, Krishna

Menon and me. At these meetings there was both cordiality and a serious exploration of the border dispute . . . At the end of the final meeting Chen Yi surprised us with his proposal that a communiqué be issued to the press. He suggested the following language: 'Two senior Ministers of the Governments of the People's Republic of China and the Republic of India have met and disused the border situation between the two countries. These discussions have been constructive and fruitful, and it is the intention of the two governments that they should lead t0 further talks in the near future'.

Lall went on to recall that Krishna Menon and he had sought approval from Nehru for the communiqué, but because the Prime Minister was busy in election meetings the go-ahead came only after both Krishna Menon and Chen Yi had left Geneva, by which time it was too late. Lall was confident that if there had been another round of discussions as agreed to by Krishna Menon and Chen Yi, 'armed conflict between India and China could have been averted'.

An account of the Krishna Menon–Chen Yi conversations is available in the Chinese archives that were opened for a brief while seven or eight years ago. An enterprising Indian journalist made notes of that account,[5] which he made available to me:

At 8 a.m. on July 23 [1962], Menon treated Mr. Chen Yi for breakfast. During their talk, Menon repeated opinions that were put forward on the 22nd and outlined his suggestion for solving conflicts which happened on the Sino-Indian western borders. Menon suggested that both sides each make clear their western borderlines and the disputed area between the two lines. In this area, both sides could establish posts, but not attack each other. There should be a distance between the posts of each side. Personnel in each post should be roughly equal, and patrols of each side should not cross their border line.

Mr. Chen instantly opposed the suggestion. He said it was in fact with the intention to encircle an area on Chinese territory as an area where Indian border guards could walk freely. China could not agree to this. Mr. Chen suggested that he and Menon issue a communiqué in Geneva that India and China would continue to negotiate to avoid border conflict.

Three months later China would attack India, and India would suffer a humiliating defeat in the war. The price that Nehru had to pay to pacify his own party colleagues and to get immediate military assistance from the US, the UK and Canada would be to accept Krishna Menon's resignation as defence minister.

But before the war commenced, Krishna Menon masterminded a military purchase decision that was to have a positive long-term impact on India's defence capability in the years to come. For some years, India had been contemplating acquiring fighter aircraft to counter the Sabre jets that the Americans had supplied to Pakistan. Negotiations were taking place with France, Sweden, the UK and the US. The Swedes and the French lost out on financing terms and the British on technical grounds. The choice was ultimately between the US and the USSR, with the Indian Air Force as well as the officials in the ministry of external affairs preferring the former. Krishna Menon's closest military adviser, General B.M. Kaul, also favoured the US option. But the US was unwilling to supply the aircraft because it would antagonize Pakistan. On 13 May 1962, the US ambassador in India, John Kenneth Galbraith, sent a telegram back to the US State Department:

Yesterday, in the course of another conversation, FonSec [foreign secretary] [M.J.] Desai told me that following my reps [representations] PriMin [Prime Minister] had told Krishna Menon that MIG deal must come before the cabinet and case would be reviewed with full consideration of our points.

I have been worried in this matter lest Menon think I have been fighting him indirectly and by proxy so today I made an appointment and had [a] long talk. M.J. Desai was present. At times discussion was rough. He once accused me of addressing him as subordinate official of his Min [ministry]; I said I was refraining from apology because I had not done so. In the end we parted fairly amicably and I had feeling that I had made all the necessary points and, as usual, very little impression. Following were the principal interchanges:

1. . . . I said we could give no explanation for provision of $ 850 in civilian aid while leaving to the Russians the task of giving mil [military] assistance . . .
2. Menon said that as DefMin [defence minister] his task was to ensure Indian pilots flew planes equal [to] those of Chinese . . . India was not looking for war or conflict but her borders everywhere [were] subject to almost daily violation or air penetration . . . In a passage strongly reminiscent of some unidentified warmonger he said only strength could ensure peace . . .
3. He said our security arrangements were too difficult . . .

I then made my principal pitch. As a senior member of the cabinet with special knowledge of the US he was surely aware of the effect of this purchase on American public opinion and on pending legislation . . . He said he was conscious of this . . .

There was a lot of pressure on Nehru from both the US and the UK to give up the Soviet option. Thus, not only were they competing at one level but they were also cooperating at another. President Kennedy had written to British Prime Minister Harold Macmillan on 9 June 1962:

. . . I also share your feeling that we must at the very least try to forestall Indian manufacture of MIGs. However, from the standpoint of US public and congressional reaction and its impact on our aid legislation, an initial MIG purchase will be fully as bad. It may compromise the long-range policy of massive aid to India on which we are embarked. Equally worrisome, we see Krishna Menon embarked on a vital test of strength over this issue and reportedly on the verge of success. Therefore we still regard it as of the highest importance to get in with at least a spoiling offer of aircraft as well as engines by mid-June . . . Let me assure you that

I would not tackle you again on this issue, if I did not feel strongly
that the Indian MIG deal will have the most adverse effects on the
interests of us both.

Kennedy told Macmillan that since the Americans were finding it
difficult to offer their aircraft, the British should improve their offer,
for which they would be compensated by the US. Mountbatten and
Duncan Sandys came to Delhi to lobby for Britain. On 24 June 1962,
Krishna Menon sent Nehru a telegram from New York:

> . . . Also seen some reference, as quoted, of your having stated in
> Parliament that we will not adopt the MIGs [Soviet aircraft] or
> other planes if Sabre jets are withdrawn. Respectfully request that
> we make no further statements of this kind because we will walk
> into a trap. The other side [Pakistan] has now been trained on these
> machines and even if withdrawn as a ruse they and even more
> numbers can be delivered any time. Furthermore, the making, not
> the buying, of the MIGs has considerable and crucial advantages
> and consequences to us in the basic production of aeroplanes,
> not only military craft, alloy material, design and technology of
> a character which would change fundamentals of production . . .
> The DCC [Defence Committee of the Cabinet] may kindly be
> called on my return and our team should go [to Moscow].

By mid–July 1962 it had been decided that India would go
ahead with the Soviet offer. But Nehru continued to be worried
about its fallout in the West. He wrote to Krishna Menon on 18
July 1962 that while negotiations with the Soviet Union should
proceed, he did not want to lose the goodwill of any country—
meaning that of the US and the UK. He told Krishna Menon that
the 'whole essence of non-alignment is watered down if you lose
goodwill', adding that it was not a matter of jeopardizing Western
aid but of 'our taking a firm decision in a manner which avoids, as
far as possible, reactions of ill-will'. But a good deal of such ill-will
was inevitable, and luckily for Nehru, Krishna Menon was there as
a shock absorber.

Krishna Menon's views prevailed, and a team was sent to Moscow under the leadership of S. Bhagavantam, the scientific adviser to the defence minister, to finalize the agreement. Krishna Menon and Bhagavantam had been close friends since they had met in London in 1948. They would remain in touch till Krishna Menon's death. In mid-August 1962, Bhagavantam had prepared a 'Top Secret' seven-page note, evidently for the Defence Committee of the Cabinet, in which he highlighted the details of the MIG deal:

The MIG-21 is being offered complete with air-to-air guided missiles of the infra-red variety. Along with the supply of these missiles the Soviets have agreed to offer full manufacturing rights to India . . .

The MIG-21 is a compact aircraft and has, according to our test pilots, the latest power control system . . . The manufacture of the MIG-21 appears to be a relatively straightforward and simple process . . .

. . . Technically the manufacture of this aircraft would be the most expedient way of achieving self-sufficiency in India in the shortest possible time . . .

While it may be possible to make an alternative choice and purchase the first lot of 12 aircraft from another source, probably at a much higher price, and satisfy our immediate operational requirements more adequately; such a course will involve much greater difficulties in manufacture and consequently impede achieving self-sufficiency in any foreseeable future. Such a course will also create problems regarding the missile for this aircraft and the projected version of the HF-24 [aircraft designed by Indian engineers themselves].

Finally, on 22 August 1962, India and the USSR signed an agreement not only for the purchase of the MIG-21 aircraft but more importantly also for their manufacture in India. The MIG-21 agreement was to pave the way for subsequent Soviet supplies of missiles, tanks, guns, submarines patrol vessels and other military equipment that was to serve India well in its wars with Pakistan in 1965 and 1971. India's foremost strategic affairs expert, K. Subrahmanyam, wrote a quarter-century after the deal that Krishna Menon had 'forced the choice of MIG-21 on the Indian Air Force. In retrospect it is clear that Mr. Menon was right in doing so.'[6]

Even though there was continuing tension on the India–China border, there appears to have been some bonhomie between the troops of the two countries as late as August 1962. On 21 August 1962, a worried M.J. Desai, the foreign secretary, sent a note to the Prime Minister:

> Please see the sitrep [situation report] today placed below.
>
>   I have told General Thapar and later Defence Minister that this meeting should not have been held, that this fraternizing prejudiced our position and there can be no question of our accepting the Chinese posts in these areas and co-existing with them. Nor should we do anything which gives them a position of dictating to us what facilities they will permit to our posts.
>
>   No further meetings of this kind will be held—Defence Minister did not, however, feel that there had been anything seriously wrong in this meeting.

Nehru noted the same day, 'I agree that we should not encourage fraternising.' Desai had been suspicious that the Chinese may have been lulling troops into a false sense of complacency. Future events would prove him right. Chinese intentions became clear in early September 1962. On 8 September 1962, Chinese troops first intruded into what was then called NEFA (Northeast Frontier Agency) that was to later become Arunachal Pradesh. But for much of September 1962, both Nehru and Krishna Menon, while giving strong statements against the Chinese, went about their business as usual. Nehru went to France, Nigeria and Ghana, and Krishna Menon was off to New York. As late as 21 September 1962, Krishna Menon was in New York, making his last speech at the UN on West Irian, later to be known as Papua New Guinea.

Over a ten-year period he had made over a hundred speeches at different UN forums. He sent his very last of hundreds of telegrams to Nehru from the UN on 25 September 1962. Nehru was then in Nigeria.

> Leaving here Friday night reaching Delhi Sunday. Border situation has not yet undergone great change. Informed that instructions and programmes as laid down when I left are adhered to . . .
>
> The Secretary General [of the UN], our own delegation and a great many others press me not to leave but this is impossible. I have said I will come back for participation in the General Debate and for the main issues—Congo and Disarmament . . .
>
> I may have to return in ten or twelve days according to progress of business here . . .

As things turned out, Krishna Menon was never to return to the UN.

He came back to India in the first week of October 1962. On 5 October 1962, Nehru wrote to the army chief, General P.N. Thapar:

> I have just received a letter from the President which runs as follows:
>
> > 'I am surprised and pained to see this morning a press report [in the *Times of India*] that a special task force was being sent to NEFA charged with pushing the Chinese out. Such secret military information is not given out. It will give previous warning to the other and endanger the lives of men. I do know why our press men do not exercise more restraint and responsibility. I thought I should convey to you my feelings in the matter. The Defence Minister who is with me feels as I do'.
>
> I was myself greatly surprised and distressed to see the report in the press this morning . . . I am having an investigation made as to how this leakage in the press took place . . .

We don't know what that investigation revealed but what we do know is that the same day Krishna Menon got a press note issued officially. The note denied that a special task force had been created to deal with the Chinese intrusion in NEFA but acknowledged that 'reorganisation of the defence arrangements in the area had been under consideration for some time . . .', which had led the Indian Army corps in north-east India to be split into two units: one to be led by Lt General B.M. Kaul, to be responsible for the border facing China, and the other to be led by Lt General Umrao Singh, to be responsible for Nagaland and the border with East Pakistan. It did not escape attention and comment that it would be the 'first time that Lt General Kaul will be holding a senior command in an operation theatre'. Many years later Major General D.K. Palit, who was then director of military operations, would reveal that Kaul himself had been the source of the leak of his assignment that had so infuriated the President, Prime Minister and defence minister.[7]

History will always judge Nehru, Krishna Menon and Thapar most unkindly for Kaul's NEFA appointment. One view is that Krishna Menon and Thapar had orchestrated it[8] but Nehru had supported them fully. As things turned out, Kaul had to be evacuated to New Delhi on medical grounds from the battlefront on 18 October 1962. His replacement, Major General Harbaksh Singh, later to be the hero of the 1965 war with Pakistan, would be in position a week later only to find Kaul back in Tezpur on 27 October 1962. Slightly over a month later he would finally be relieved and replaced by Manekshaw, then an acting Lt General. Kaul would take premature retirement on 11 December 1962.

Nehru left for Colombo on 12 October 1962, even as Indian and Chinese troops confronted each other in NEFA with casualties on both sides. When Nehru was in Colombo, Krishna Menon made a thundering speech at a Congress party workers' meeting in Bangalore after visiting various defence establishments in the city on 14 October 1962, which was widely reported the next day. The *Times of India* had the most extensive coverage of the Churchillian speech the next day:

WE WILL FIGHT THE CHINESE TO THE LAST GUN
Internal Squabbles Must End—Menon

BANGALORE, October 14

The Defence Minister Mr. Krishna Menon forcefully reiterated here tonight India's determination to push the invading Chinese out of the NEFA areas—'whether it takes one day, one hundred days or a thousand days'—and fight 'to the last man, to the last gun', in the Ladakh region, if attacked. Mr Menon asserted that India's independent foreign policy had paid dividends. Had India aligned itself with one Power bloc or the other, the present situation along the northern frontiers would have sucked her into an international war . . . Whether it was Pakistan or China, India would never let go an opportunity for real negotiation. 'But we cannot be led into a trap by hypocrisy'. Mr Menon recalled that India was entirely aware of China's occupation of a certain area in Ladakh. Four or five years later, China started its intrusion into the Aksaichin area. India had told China that it was doing a wrong thing against a country that had befriended it. India was the second country—the first being Burma—to recognize new China. India would continue to recognize new China because it was ethically and politically correct and 'we will tell the United Nations so'. Even today, India had no quarrels with China. But our differences are with the administration (in China) which maligns and misrepresents us and is menace to our national security. Quite recently, Indian forces had pushed forward in our own area. But Peking misrepresented facts and said that India had entered Chinese territory. He wanted to affirm that India had not violated Chinese territory. He said this in all sincerity because 'even in troubled times, we must stick to certain principles'.

These were brave and indeed, in some ways, even remarkable words, but the die was cast. The full-scale Chinese invasion began on 20 October 1962. This would begin the first round of the war that would last eight days. On the very first day of the Chinese onslaught Krishna Menon spoke forcefully while addressing a huge public gathering organized by the Congress party in New Delhi. He, of course, spoke in English to an audience that knew little of that language. *The Hindu* reported the next day:

WE WILL FIGHT TO THE LAST

MENON ASKS PEOPLE TO GET READY TO FACE 'GRIM DAYS' AHEAD

BIGGEST ENGAGEMENT SINCE KASHMIR WAR

The Defence Minister, Mr. V.K. Krishna Menon told a mammoth public meeting here this evening that 'We are fighting and will continue to fight to hold our territOry in the border', although some of our posts have fallen. The huge gathering cheered the Defence Minister, when he declared: 'We will resist to the best of our ability and we shall not negotiate with the Chinese on the basis of surrender'. Mr Menon stated that 'an aggressive war' was going on since this morning till he came to the meeting. He added 'We had to abandon some territories because we were overwhelmed. In spite of difficulties our troops are not giving in' he added. Mr. Menon pointed out that the present situation was forced upon India by the Chinese and appealed to the people not to give way to anger or fear . . .

The situation, from India's point of view, worsened by the day with territory and men being lost—the latter in substantial numbers. India's defence preparedness and lack of military equipment stood woefully exposed. On 25 October 1962, the man who had first made Krishna Menon an MP nine years earlier spoke out and echoed the sentiments of a very large number of Congressmen themselves. Rajagopalachari suggested that the 'present Defence Minister should be relieved and the Prime Minister should take up the responsibility of the country's defence himself by calling on a suitable General or ex-General to assist him as Minister of State'. A state of national emergency was

declared on 26 October 1962, and urgent requests were made to
the US, the UK and Canada for urgent military supplies. A day later
Nehru, along with Krishna Menon, met with some forty-five agitated
Congress MPs and informed them that 'India had made arrangements
with some countries for securing armaments and equipment'. On
29 October 1962, Krishna Menon made a flying visit to Leh and
Srinagar to boost the morale of the troops while in New Delhi his
ministry put out an official denial that he was resigning. That very
day after his return he, along with Nehru, met over thirty Congress
MPs and reassured them that while 'as the aggressor China had some
initial advantage of surprise moves, India had recovered'.

But on 30 October 1962, Krishna Menon would send in the first
of his three resignations to Nehru:

> In the situation that faces the country as a result of the unprovoked
> invasion of our territory by China I submit it is appropriate and
> necessary that the portfolio of Defence should be taken over by
> you . . . I conveyed this sentiment to you some days or weeks ago
> and much earlier in this crisis. I feel, however, that your assumption
> of the charge should not be delayed. I had offered to serve and assist
> you in the tasks that [you] face in any capacity you wished. I need
> hardly say that such abilities or energies I possess are unreservedly
> and entirely at your disposal now as always.

Just as Krishna Menon was resigning his senior colleague and minister
without portfolio T.T. Krishnamachari also wrote to Nehru:

> I have decided not to trouble you in person frequently hereafter. I
> am doubtful whether it is much use my writing to you either . . .
> Every meeting I attend deepens my disappointment with the
> existing state of affairs. At my age, I am incapable of getting angry,
> which I would like to if I can . . .
>
> Whatever your views might be, and ultimately they count,
> your colleague, the Defence Minister, has demonstrably showed
> his utter incapacity to act. I am told you think that he is the most

intelligent man inside and outside the Cabinet. It might even be true. But intelligence in the abstract is of no use to anybody, least of all the possessor . . . The Defence Minister's methods of going about things will not yield results. You cannot forget the fact that the Defence Minister is persona non grata in most quarters, or at least in quarters that count for us at the moment . . .

Krishnamachari then went on to speak of 'Krishna Menon and his minions' and their incompetence, and gave Nehru some suggestions for improving defence management. He ended the letter with great anguish:

Please do something: something to prevent this atmosphere of a Greek tragedy deepening.

Nehru, with everything blowing up around him, still found time to reply to Krishnamachari within a few hours on the same day:

Thank you for your letter of today's date. Much of what you said . . . I agree with. Part of it I do not agree with. But that does not matter. Anyhow whatever you said and repeat in your letter is very much in my mind. I think that we have set things moving and I hope they will bring quick results.

There is no need for you to feel despondent. I have no such feeling although I have received a number of shocks during the last few days. You can see me when you like or write to me.

A day later Nehru informed the President, Dr S. Radhakrishnan:

At the request of Shri Krishna Menon I am taking charge of Defence. Shri Krishna Menon will be Minister of Defence Production. He will continue to be a member of the Cabinet. As Minister of Defence Production, Shri Krishna Menon will be in charge of the ordnance factories and other manufacturing and industrial establishments in the Ministry of Defence, including also the establishments such as

Hindustan Aircraft, Bharat Electronics and Mazagaon and Garden Reach Docks. He will also be responsible for Defence Research and Development, the Border Roads Organisation and any other matter that may be allotted to him from time to time. These arrangements will take effect from tomorrow, 1st November 1962. I hope you approve of these arrangements.

On the evening of 31 October 1962, an official announcement was made that Nehru was taking over as defence minister and that Krishna Menon would continue as minister of defence production. That morning, Krishnamachari had met Nehru and complained that his phone was being tapped. Nehru was taken aback by this news and promptly asked the home minister and the director of the Intelligence Bureau, B.N. Mullik, to conduct an inquiry. Krishnamachari would write to Nehru on 2 November 1962:

It was just like you to write so promptly regard to my complaint about the tapping of my telephone. The DIB [Mullik] saw me in this connection today. The subsequent information that I got is that the tapping was done at the instance of the military authorities and the persons doing the tapping were withdrawn at 8 o'clock on the night of the 31st October, presumably because of the change in the direction of the Defence Ministry—though it is asserted that no real change has taken place.

Krishnamachari was alluding to an assertion reported to have been made by Krishna Menon. As soon as he took over as minister of defence production he flew to Tezpur in Assam, which was the headquarters of the north-east army corps. He addressed a public meeting there which, by all accounts, was 'mammoth'. If he had done just that he would not have got into further controversy, but then he would not have been Krishna Menon. *The Hindu* carried this news on 2 November 1962 from Tezpur:

Mr. V.K. Krishna Menon said in Tezpur today that Prime Minister Nehru's taking over the Defence portfolio from him was 'merely a move to bring more strength into the administration'. He said the decision had not come to him as a surprise . . . Replying to a question whether the changes that had come into effect today [1 November 1962] had been under consideration for some time, Mr. Menon said 'yes'. He added, however, 'Nothing has changed. I am still a member of the Cabinet and I am still sitting in the Defence Ministry'.

That very morning Radhakrishnan conveyed his displeasure to Nehru, sending him a clipping from another newspaper. The Prime Minister shot back at once:

> The *Statesman* cutting is not quite correct. Probably Krishna Menon said something casually which does not give the right impression. I am in charge of Defence and am dealing with it myself directly and am going to the Defence Ministry daily. Krishna Menon has got a limited responsibility in regard to production matters which are under the Defence Ministry . . .

Technically, Krishna Menon was right but it was hardly the thing to say under such tense circumstances, especially when his exit as defence minister had been widely welcomed. On his return to the capital he denied having made any such statement but the damage had been done. His critics, both within the Congress and outside, now bayed for more blood. Surjit Singh Majithia, who had been his deputy in the defence ministry, was sufficiently emboldened to write to Nehru on 3 November 1962, criticizing the government's strategy in NEFA. Nehru replied to him the same day, saying that the army commanders on the spot had been given full freedom to take whatever action they deemed fit. In response to Majithia's castigation of Krishna Menon, he added:

> . . . You will remember the difficulties of the American forces in Korea and the severe set-backs they suffered there in spite of the latest equipment they had. Also the wiping out of the British Army by the Nazis in spite of good equipment and every effort made. It

is easy to find scapegoats, but it does not show much wisdom to forget surrounding circumstances.

On 3 November 1962, Nehru also wrote to the Nawab of Malerkotla and defended the man who had become the object of hate in the country:

> Thank you for your letter of the 2nd November. I think you are wrong in your judgment of V.K. Krishna Menon. Like all of us, he has his failings, but unlike most of us, he has some remarkable virtues also. It is wholly wrong to say that he is a 'violent Communist'.

On 6 November 1962, Nehru met with all chief ministers who, with just two exceptions, wanted him to sack Krishna Menon forthwith. Of the two exceptions, the chief minister of Jammu and Kashmir, Bakshi Ghulam Mohammed, supported Krishna Menon because of his performance on Kashmir at the UN, and the chief minister of Punjab, Pratap Singh Kairon, expressed no opinion. A year later Krishna Menon would repay Kairon's gesture by supporting him to the hilt when he would come under a huge cloud of corruption charges.

The next day, 7 November 1962, Krishna Menon sent not one but two letters of resignation. This may have been prompted by Nehru. The first letter was long and self-defensive:

> In the crisis that faces our country, the nation as well as our Party should be enabled in every possible way to face it in unity and zeal. The people have responded energetically . . . and spontaneously . . . in support of your and our national policies . . . and done it with understanding and with the knowledge of the military reverses and hard tasks ahead . . .
>
> Nevertheless I am painfully aware of the fact that not only the opponents of our policy and Party but even perhaps an appreciable number of our Party members, some leaders among them, have proclaimed or implied their lack of faith in me and in the Defence Organisation under my stewardship . . . I have no adverse feelings

towards those who have in their anxiety or concern about the country as a result of their reactions to the shock of the invasion been led to misstatements or distortion of facts or of character and role of persons. Public statements by me even within the Party must be necessarily conditioned by (a) considerations of security; (b) the view that I may not involve my colleagues or the Service except by way of factually relevant statements; (c) the knowledge that they may help the enemy; and (d) affect the morale of the troops.

The immediate concern and task of every Indian today is the defence and then the counter-offensives against the invaders . . . All these will be adversely affected by the present tensions and arguments and controversies [that] centre round my person and my being in the Government . . . In the last several months and even more frequently in recent weeks and days I have repeatedly placed my office and personal services completely at your disposal to be used or dispensed with . . .

I request and hope that the length of this letter does not result in the deflection of your attention from its main purpose . . . I once again submit, my resignation from Government in the belief that it may be a small contribution to the war effort . . .

The second letter, sent a little while later, was brief and more pointed:

I have written to you at length separately the reasons that prompt me to request you once again to accept my resignation from Government . . . I have in the last few months, and even frequently in recent months and weeks, placed the office which you have entrusted to me and myself at your disposal . . . You have continued to place your confidence in me for which I am grateful . . .

I submit, however, that it may be in the interests of the Party that I should be relieved of office . . . If my resignation serves in a small measure to forge the strength and unity of the country, the party and the Government, I am amply rewarded. I need hardly say that this letter and the longer one I have sent are at your disposal for whatever use you wish to make use of them.

That morning, Nehru had met with the executive of the Congress parliamentary party. Just the previous evening, sixteen of the thirty-five members of the executive had written to Nehru demanding Krishna Menon's exclusion from his cabinet. The signatories included H.K. Mahatab, S.M. Ghose, Raghunath Singh, C.R. Basappa and Kamalnayan Bajaj, who had, a year earlier, protested to Nehru against Krishna Menon getting a Congress ticket a second time to contest from North Bombay. Thereafter, the 'remove Krishna Menon group' had sent one of its members, R.K. Khadilkar, who was close to him ideologically, to plead with him to quit gracefully on his own. But the defence minister would not oblige and told Khadilkar that his resignation was a matter for the Prime Minister to decide.

At the meeting with MPs on 7 November 1962, the Prime Minister spoke at length on the Chinese invasion and, during the course of that speech, referred to Krishna Menon:

> . . . There has been a great deal of talk and criticism of our Defence Ministry, of Mr. Krishna Menon who was Defence Minister and partly of me too. I do not mind criticism myself but the way it has been carried on has been most unfortunate and it hurts me greatly. Because, shall I say, all these setbacks we have suffered, have been cast on the Defence Minister . . . that would be cruel because all the major decisions and the minor decisions have been jointly undertaken by us . . . I am at least as much to blame as anybody else . . . We have our failings, our faults and so has Mr. Krishna Menon . . . But I can say with confidence that no Defence Minister has worked harder or more efficiently than Mr. Krishna Menon . . . Now I might tell you that during . . . the last many weeks, Mr. Krishna Menon has several times offered his resignation to me . . . It was on the 1st of November . . . that I took over Defence and asked Mr. Krishna Menon to look after Defence Production in which he was greatly interested and which has been largely built up under his guidance . . . But when later I began to feel that his work will be impeded by this controversy and criticism, I thought of the resignation he sent me and which he kept on repeating and I

have had his resignation letter in my pocket all the time. So finally
I decided to accept it . . .

But what the official records don't talk about is the drama that took
place in the meeting. Evidently, Nehru had taken serious objection
to the letter sent by the Congress MPs demanding Krishna Menon's
exit. One account published nine years later, based clearly on
a conversation with the man who would take over from Krishna
Menon, Y.B. Chavan, went thus:[9]

> Nehru defended Menon and offered to resign if the party
> disapproved of his [Nehru's] leadership. [Mahavir] Tyagi asked
> Nehru: 'Is this Motilal Lal Nehru's son talking in this strain? There
> is a crisis on the eastern borders and you want to create an internal
> crisis by threatening to resign'. Tyagi later apologized. When
> Nehru continued to defend Menon another member of the CPP
> executive said to Nehru: 'It is Menon today. Tomorrow it will be
> your turn'.

In 1990, there would appear a book by an American political scientist
on Indian decision-making during the 1962 crisis with China.[10]
In 1966, Steven Hoffmann would interview Mahavir Tyagi, and
seventeen years later, he would interview another MP present there,
H.K. Mahatab. Hoffmann would write of this 7 November 1962
meeting:

> . . . Finally Nehru (in the context of a heated discussion) said that
> he would resign if he could not have the ministers he wanted.
> Tyagi then told Jawaharlal Nehru that he should be ashamed to
> call himself the son of Motilal Nehru. It was improper of the
> Prime Minister to threaten this way during an hour of crisis . . .
> Tyagi's comment had implied that Nehru might have to resign,
> too, if he could not abandon Krishna Menon and his policies.
> Mr. Hanumanthaiya [another MP] was more explicit about this
> point, heatedly telling Nehru that it did not matter if he resigned . . .

Subsequently, perhaps late in the evening of 7 November 1962, Nehru forwarded Krishna Menon's resignation to the President:

> I enclose copies of two letters I have received from Shri Krishna Menon offering his resignation from Government. I have already shown you these letters. I propose to write to him accepting his resignation after I learn your wishes in the matter. These wishes have been conveyed to me orally by you already. But I would be grateful if you would kindly repeat them in writing.

This was a curiously worded letter, and what it implied was to be highlighted twenty-seven years later by Radhakrishnan's authoritative biographer, his son, the eminent historian S. Gopal, who was also Nehru's preeminent biographer. Gopal would write:[11]

> In other words, Nehru wished to leave the responsibility for the final decision to the president, with perhaps a subconscious hope for at least delay in, if not abandonment of, Menon's departure. Certainly the recognized procedure of the president acting on the advice of the prime minister was reversed. Radhakrishnan in his reply did not communicate his wishes but took a firm decision; 'As you said, in the circumstances, for the sake of national unity we have to accept Shri Krishna Menon's resignation with regret. On hearing from you a formal announcement will issue from the Rashtrapati Bhavan'.

Nehru would have taken the hint. He wrote to Krishna Menon on 8 November 1962:

> Thank you for your two letters dated the 7th November offering your resignation from the Government. You have already spoken to me about this matter more than once. I appreciate the reasons which have influenced you in coming to this decision.
>
> I should like to express my warm appreciation of the fine work you have done in the Defence Ministry . . . I deeply regret to part with you . . . This is, of course not a parting as both you and I are

dedicated to serve our country in whatever position either of us
may be placed . . . I hope it will be possible in the future to utilize
your high abilities in the cause of the nation. I forwarded your
two letters to the President recommending to him to accept your
resignation. I have just received from him a letter in which he says
that, in the circumstances, we have to accept your resignation with
regret. I am now requesting him to issue a formal announcement
tomorrow . . .

Till his death Krishna Menon would continue to say that he had not
been 'sacked' or 'fired' or 'asked to go'. He would insist that he had
resigned. The evidence does support this fine distinction he drew on
the manner of his departure as defence minister. But it is also true
that many Congress MPs were challenging Nehru. That challenge
intensified after the Soviet Union came out openly on China's side
on 25 October 1962, a position it would, however, nuance a little
later. But the initial Soviet backing of China damaged Krishna Menon
grievously.

A day after Krishna Menon had resigned Nehru wrote to Dr
Rajendra Prasad, the former President of India, giving him an update
on the situation. He added:

> . . . As you know Krishna Menon has resigned. I do not think
> that the propaganda against him was at all justified. But I will not
> go into that. I happen to have been connected with Defence very
> intimately for some time past. For the last five weeks, I have been
> going there daily . . .

Pressure from within the Congress party apart, there was another
factor at work that made Krishna Menon's departure inevitable. Right
from the time Nehru asked for American military assistance, Krishna
Menon was a marked man. There had always been mutual antipathy
between him and the US ambassador in India, John Kenneth Galbraith,
which had been exacerbated after Goa's liberation. Galbraith seized
this opportunity to start a campaign for Krishna Menon's ouster. He
was to later discuss this episode in his memoirs that appeared in 1969.[12]

But Galbraith left out crucial details of what he had done and how he had ensnared the British and the Canadians in his 'plot' to get rid of Krishna Menon as a condition for receiving military assistance. Those details were to be made public for the first time only in 2011 by a noted American scholar of the Cold War—James Hershberg— who excavated American, British and Canadian archives to establish Galbraith's contribution to 'grease Menon's slide from power, just as Nehru grudgingly felt compelled to seek Western military help against the Chinese'.[13] Hershberg's is the most detailed account of the American role in Krishna Menon's exit as defence minister, and I am grateful to him for making available to me the archival material he had collected years ago.

Galbraith had a powerful ally in Washington—not as blunt and direct as the ambassador—but committed to see Krishna Menon go. This was President Kennedy himself. He had met with Krishna Menon a year ago at the White House but now the situation had changed completely. On 26 October 1962, he met with the Indian ambassador to the US, B.K. Nehru. The official US record of that meeting on Krishna Menon was anodyne, but in reality, what Kennedy had told the Indian ambassador was this:

> The President then said that, on a purely personal basis between himself and the Ambassador, and not speaking governmentally, he wished that Krishna Menon were not Defense Minister.

In that conversation, Kennedy had also asked the Indian ambassador whether 'Krishna Menon would continue to be the Grand Moghul presiding over the American military supply line'. During the war, Krishna Menon had tried, till the very end, to avoid seeking military help from the US. On 27 October 1962, Nehru wrote to him:

> In the course of a letter from the President [Radhakrishnan] to me he says:
>
>> USA Ambassador Galbraith was here last evening and said that the USA were willing to supply us with any equipment we

need but that they had not been asked. We should not lose time in getting equipment from any source.

I entirely agree with the President. We have received complaints from our Ambassadors abroad, more especially from London and Paris I think, that they are not being kept informed of what we are trying to get from the respective countries and that we apparently deal directly with the Governments concerned. I think that the Ambassador or High Commissioner should be kept in full touch with the steps we are taking.

The same day Carl Kaysen, a Kennedy aide, sent an 'Eyes Only for Ambassador Galbraith' telegram from the White House:

. . . We here agree with your assessment of the value of getting Menon out . . . We again urge the importance of avoiding the slightest appearance of U.S. initiative and responsibility in removing Menon. Our efforts with Ayub [Ayub Khan, President of Pakistan] will be such as to prepare the way to take advantage of Menon's disappearance without requiring it as a condition for forward motion . . .

On 29 October 1962, Nehru was still very worried and wrote to his defence minister:

. . . From the telegrams that are coming to us you will notice that there is every desire to help in various countries . . . It is not clear to me how far we are taking advantage of this general attitude and offers. We must rather overdo things than underdo them. The immediate need is great. I do not know how I shall explain to Parliament why we have been found lacking in equipment. It is not much good shifting about blame. The fact is that we have been found lacking and there is an impression that we have approached these things in a somewhat amateurish way. I should like to know exactly what we have done or going to do about equipment . . . I suggest that if you are free you might come to see me at 9.30 p.m. tonight at my house.

Before seeing Nehru that night, Krishna Menon finally met with Galbraith in the afternoon. Galbraith had already met Nehru and received a formal request for American military assistance. In his conversation with the US ambassador, Krishna Menon

> reaffirmed request for assistance and said list of requirements would be delivered to Embassy tonight or tomorrow. Stressed urgent need for automatic weapons and long-range mortars.

As the war was raging, Krishna Menon, had, in fact, been speaking with the high commissioners from Canada and the UK for arms and ammunition but with a special request that the aid not be made public. He had the most extensive conversations with Chester Ronning, the Canadian high commissioner, whom he liked and whom he later was to describe as 'a decent fellow'. Ronning's cables back home gave a picture of Krishna Menon, who had all but lost his nerve, never his strong point to begin with.

Krishna Menon had four extended conversations with Ronning in a space of nine days. On the day of the Chinese invasion he was in a 'black mood and engaged in a 'pessimistic and alarming monologue'. Ronning reported:

> QUOTE . . . THE CHINESE HAVE INVADED INDIA IN FORCE AND THREATEN TO SHOOT DOWN OUR AIRCRAFT FLYING OUR OWN TERRITORY NOW OCCUPIED BY THEM. DO YOU REGARD THAT AS SERIOUS? THERE IS NO RPT NO ALTERNATIVE FOR US BUT TO FIGHT AND WE SHALL FIGHT TO DEFEND OUR OWN TERRITORY. WE SHALL DO SO EVEN IF IT MEANS GOING DOWN IN DEFEAT. THE CHINESE HAVE GREATER STRIKING POWER, GREATER RESOURCES AND LOGISTIC ADVANTAGES. THIS PROBLEM WILL NOT RPT NOT BE SOLVED DURING MY LIFETIME. ARROGANT CHINESE AGGRESSORS THREATEN TO OVERRUN THE WHOLE OF INDIA AND ARE ALREADY

IN OCCUPATION OF A LARGE PORTION. THEY HAVE RESORTED TO THE VILEST TYPE OF PROPAGANDA TO ISOLATE US FROM OUR AFRO-ASIAN NEIGHBOURS AND FRIENDS . . . I CANNOT OPEN MY MOUTH TO SAY ANYTHING ABOUT THE SITUATION WITHOUT BEING ATTACKED BY ALL SIDES. WE HAVE ENTERED UPON A WAR WHICH WILL LAST FOR 10 YEARS. UNQUOTE

Krishna Menon then met with Ronning on 22 October 1962 and asked for Canadian transport aircraft. Three days later he expanded this wishlist to cover helicopters and long-range mortars. Thereafter on 29 October 1962, after discussions with officials from both sides on military supplies had been completed, he asked Ronning to stay back. Ronning reported:

MENON IS A HARASSED MAN . . . AND SAID HE WAS BEING ATTACKED FROM ALL SIDES QUOTE INCLUDING MY OWN CABINET COLLEAGUES WHO IN MAKING A SCAPEGOAT OF ME FAIL TO COMPREHEND THAT THE GOVT. AS A WHOLE MUST BE HELD RESPONSIBLE FOR THE MILITARY SETBACK. UNQUOTE. HE COMPLAINED BITTERLY ABOUT QUOTE THE POLITICAL ACTIVITIES OF AMERICANS IN INDIA TO FORCE KRISHNA MENON OUT. UNQUOTE. THESE EFFORTS HE SAID ARE BECOMING INCREASINGLY SUCCESSFUL WITH ALL THOSE WHO WANT INDIA TO BE IN THE AMERICAN POCKET. HE SAID THE CHINESE HAVE SET BACK THE PROGRESS OF SOCIALISM IN INDIA FOR AT LEAST 15 YEARS AND ADDED: QUOTE EVEN IF WE SUCCEED IN ULTIMATELY REACHING A NEGOTIATED SETTLEMENT, INDIA WILL CONTINUE TO BE INTENSELY NATIONALISTIC AND CONTINUE A MILITARY PREPAREDNESS PROGRAMME WHICH WILL DELAY FOR A LONG TIME RAISING THE STANDARD OF LIVING OF THE INDIAN PEOPLE. UNQUOTE.

Parliament convened on 8 November 1962, the session
having been advanced by eleven days after Nehru agreed to a
demand made by opposition leaders. Normally, a minister who
has resigned is allowed to make a personal statement. This is
what, for example, C.D. Deshmukh, Nehru's finance minister,
had done in July 1956. Deshmukh had used that opportunity to
lash out at Nehru and some of his colleagues, who had all heard
him in silence. But Krishna Menon chose to keep quiet. He made
no such statement. In any case, it was hardly the time for him to
speak since there was only a pause in the war. Predictably, his
resignation was widely welcomed both in India and abroad. The
heat was off Nehru, who emerged stronger after Krishna Menon's
departure. But Krishna Menon got hundreds of letters of sympathy
as well, including from those who had been at his receiving end.
On the night of his resignation on 7 November 1962, he got a
letter from his favourite army officer, who too would have to
resign a few weeks hence:

> My dear Minister,
>
> I have just heard the news and don't mind admitting that I could
> not help weeping as a result. The pitiless Destiny! What more can
> I say?
>
> Yours ever,
>
> Bijji Kaul

The navy chief, Admiral Ramdas Katari, wrote a day later:

> I wish to express my deep regret that you have had to vacate your
> office at his critical juncture. I appreciate that, as a politician, you
> are frequently called upon to make symbolic sacrifices at the altar
> of fickle public opinion. At the same time, I am sure that when the
> dust and emotions have settled down your talents and your drive
> will be back in operation in an equally high capacity in the interests

of the country. But what has distressed me beyond measure is the unpleasantness that polluted the atmosphere before the event. I squirmed in shame to behold it. I hope you are given the courage to tide over this temporary period of distress.

Krishna Menon would reply to Katari on 17 November 1959:

> . . . One does not feel too distressed about the changes taking place. I was glad in a way to have an opportunity of being of service both in and by leaving office . . .

Rajni Patel, Russy Karanjia, K.A. Abbas and Balraj Sahni sent him a telegram on 10 November 1962:

> YOU MAY BE OUT OF GOVERNMENT BUT NOT OUT OF OUR THOUGHTS PLEASE COME TO NORTH BOMBAY AND MAKE IT YOUR HEADQUARTER FOR MOBILISING NATIONAL OPINION AGAINST CHINESE AGGRESSION AND INTERNAL REACTION

The same day Winifred Horrabin wrote to him from England:

> This is just one small voice which I hope will reach you. It belongs to someone who well remembers your ceaseless, devoted and self-denying work in London for your beloved country. Work often done in ill-health and poverty, through bitter winters and abuse and vilification. I feel that as much as any brave Indian soldier dying on your country's frontiers you have served your country wonderfully and well in spite of all. If my beloved Frank Horrabin were alive I know he would join his voice with mine in this brief tribute.

Three decades earlier the Horrabins had been active in the India League, and Frank Horrabin's illustrations, arranged by Krishna Menon, had added value to Nehru's books. He would reply to her on 27 December 1962:

I was touched by your very kind letter. It has been years since I have heard from you. I have thought of you ever so often and hoped some day I would see you again. I would not like you to feel that I am depressed or nursing a sense of being injured . . . I enquired about Frank when I was passing through London where I nowadays stay only for a few hours. I learned then that he had passed away . . .

On 10 November 1962, a high-powered National Defence Council, under the chairmanship of Nehru, would be announced. It had many of his cabinet colleagues, serving civil servants and the service chiefs as members. Thimayya and Thorat would be part of this group, as would Indira Gandhi. Conspicuous by his absence was Krishna Menon. His fall could not have been more complete. However, even though the public perception was that he had to quit in disgrace, Krishna Menon would continue to receive messages of solidarity from various people and places. A letter he would receive from a Vijaya Mulay on 16 November 1962 was typical:

You do not know me at all for I am a very ordinary person—a mere nobody. I only know your public image and have long admired from distance, your sincerity and integrity—rare qualities indeed in our present-day politicians. After the recent happenings, I wanted to write to you that the sentiments expressed on the floor of the Parliament by some member or comments of some newspapers are not shared by all. I work for a living and lunchtime in my office is the time when current topics and personalities are discussed. I, therefore, know that most of the people—at least those I know— think that you got a raw deal and you have stood it manfully . . .

He would keep getting brickbats as well. K.C. Agarwal, a student in New Delhi, spoke for many when he wrote to Krishna Menon on 6 November 1962, a day before his resignation:

Perhaps you will try to excuse me, a perfect stranger to you, for thrusting this note upon you. At this critical and challenging juncture, it seems a tragedy of the saddest type that 'personal loyalties' should be given more value than national demands or considerations. Perhaps you will not deny that your handling of the Defence portfolio during these years, have been goody-goody, that you have been attempting to inject yourself and us with a sense of complacency as far as India's Defence requirements were concerned. The results of these have been full of humiliation to us all, as a nation, as the events have shown. However, when practically all the individuals and Political Parties in India have given up personal loyalties and chosen to unite to defend the nation, it is indeed a sad affair that Mr. Nehru should be showing personal loyalty towards you, and that you should be <u>clinging</u> to the post, disregarding the Nation's voice, which says that you are unfit to be minister.

. . . [I]f you have any statesmanship or awareness left in you, then perhaps you will <u>feel</u> the Nation's desire and give up <u>completely</u> and <u>absolutely</u> the ministership and be simply a member of Parliament, or even resign from that and be private citizen.

It was a bold letter from an ordinary citizen. That it reached Krishna Menon was perhaps surprising. That he replied to it patiently was even more surprising, as he did on 17 November 1962:

I am grateful to you for your letter of the 6ᵗʰ November. I note your views. I agree with you that I could be of some service by withdrawing from Government. My position in this matter is set out in the letters written to the Prime Minister which have been published.

On 18 November 1962, Krishna Menon received a handwritten note from Indira Gandhi:

Dear Krishna:

I have tried to contact you but you always seem to be out. Could I have a moment to ask your advice regarding the Citizens Council

that has just been formed. Please ask someone to give me a ring
to let me know what would be a convenient time for you. I hope
you will.

Love

Indu

The Citizens Council had been formed eleven days earlier to 'organise
people's participation on the civilian level in the national defence effort'.
Radhakrishnan was its patron and Indira Gandhi its chairman. It had
twelve members from different walks of life, including independent
India's first army chief, K.M. Cariappa. Indira Gandhi may well have
felt the need to apply a balm on Krishna Menon's wounds.

His friends abroad stood up for him. David and Ruth Glass,
noted academics at the LSE, took umbrage at a London *Times* article
expressing relief at Krishna Menon's resignation and wrote:

> . . . Krishna Menon has attained rare international distinction—
> and will retain it in spite of all setbacks—both as a fiercely
> loyal Indian patriot and as an outstandingly able advocate
> of disarmament. It is true that in these two roles Krishna
> Menon has made many enemies—not least among Western
> journalists . . . There is no reason to be relieved because it may
> be thought that the policies with which Krishna Menon was
> identified—an advocate of India's independent development and
> of international disarmament—are no longer compatible. The
> principles upon which such policies are based are not wrong
> because they appear to be in jeopardy—for reasons which are
> not of India's making . . .

The Chinese attacked a second time on 16 November 1962, two
days after Nehru had turned seventy-three. While 'Indian forces put
up a staunch resistance in Ladakh', this round was to lead to further
disaster in NEFA. General Thapar resigned on 19 November 1962.
Thereafter, China declared a unilateral ceasefire on 21 November

1962, which involved a withdrawal of Chinese troops to the pre-war positions on the NEFA border. The invasion had been building up but the ceasefire and the withdrawal for the Chinese was from a position of strength. Some years later Krishna Menon would speculate on why this happened:[14]

> Why did the Chinese withdraw? Firstly, we killed a lot of their people . . . we did inflict terrible causalities on the enemy . . . Secondly they knew that once we regrouped things would happen . . . Thirdly, the Russians stopped fuel supplies to China . . . No fuel meant no armament . . . Fourthly, public opinion was against China . . . Only one or two small countries supported China . . . The fifth reason was that they may have discovered that we had no desire to take Tibet . . . Also . . . they had achieved what they wanted, namely to discredit Nehru . . . to 'teach us a lesson' and that sort of thing . . .

On 8 December 1962, the conclusions reached by Averell Harriman, President Kennedy's special envoy, who had just visited India, were circulated by the US State Department. There were twelve points, two of which dealt with Krishna Menon directly:

> . . . Indian leadership undergoing changes which should be encouraged. Malevolent influence Krishna Menon finally removed . . .
>   Indian Armed Forces suffered severely under Krishna Menon. Indian Army has shaken up senior commands . . .

Krishna Menon was now only an MP. He was down but not out. His Congress colleagues asked him to come to Bombay and address a public meeting in the suburb of Chembur on 9 December 1962. A crowd of some 60,000 gathered to hear him speak for almost three hours non-stop. That speech was tape-recorded, and in January 1963, it was published as a monograph. It was called 'India and the Chinese Invasion' and is the most detailed statement by him on the subject, apart from what he would say to Brecher a few years later. But it is surprising that in the burgeoning historiography of the Sino-Indian war, it finds no mention whatsoever. In fact, when I brought this 'book' to the attention of India's leading military historian Srinath Raghavan, he expressed complete surprise that such a publication existed. His response is worth quoting:

Thanks so much for giving me a copy of this remarkable document. It's perhaps the only account from VKKM on this crucial episode— and that too so soon after the war. Here are some things that struck me as important.

First, KM [Krishna Menon] clearly shared JN [Jawaharlal Nehru]'s sense that the Chinese had been less than honest and trustworthy on the boundary issue. His comments . . . make this absolutely clear: 'the Chinese Prime Minister, in a way of conduct not worthy of any great statesman . . .' The interesting thing is that KM still felt that a deal should be struck. Here he clearly departed from the consensus amongst JN's colleagues. This is arguably the mark of his realistic approach to world politics.

Second, this speech is perhaps the first public account of the 'forward policy'. [He] outlines the motivations behind the policy, including the hope for a settlement of some kind . . .

Third, KM shared the consensus belief that the Chinese would not embark on a major war against India . . .

Fourth, KM was clearly surprised at the [Indian] withdrawal from Sela (in my opinion, the turning point of the war in NEFA) . . .

Fifth, KM was clearly open to approaching the US for military assistance . . . Which brings up an interesting question: why was Galbraith so keen to secure his exit? To what extent was this move supported by KM's opponents within the government?

Lastly, I was struck by the dignity of his tone throughout this speech. At no point does he display rancour or a sense of injury. He doesn't even defend himself—except on the absurd claim about soldiers not having clothes and shoes.

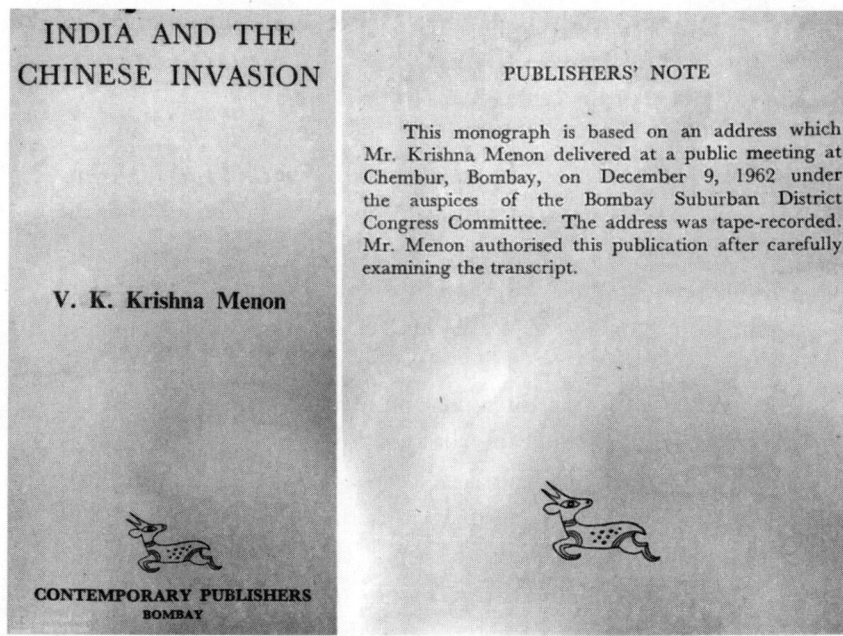

INDIA AND THE
CHINESE INVASION

V. K. Krishna Menon

CONTEMPORARY PUBLISHERS
BOMBAY

PUBLISHERS' NOTE

This monograph is based on an address which
Mr. Krishna Menon delivered at a public meeting at
Chembur, Bombay, on December 9, 1962 under
the auspices of the Bombay Suburban District
Congress Committee. The address was tape-recorded.
Mr. Menon authorised this publication after carefully
examining the transcript.

Krishna Menon's almost unknown book

While Krishna Menon's exit was applauded in the Western world, it evoked a different reaction in the communist camp. On 24 November 1962, the North Vietnamese leader Ho Chi Minh, who was well known to Krishna Menon, told the Chinese charge d'affaires in Hanoi:

Nehru is of the capitalist class, and is also himself an aristocrat. Before Indian independence he was fairly progressive, but the present Nehru is no longer the same. However, among India's ruling circles, he can still be considered a leftist. Right now, the titans of the ruling class are pressurizing him, and have forced him eliminate [Krishna] Menon's post. Since Menon's removal from office, Nehru has been even more isolated.

Krishna Menon had been deposed but he continued to hold British diplomats in thrall. On 15 December 1962, the UK high commissioner in India, Paul Gore-Booth, wrote to Seville Garner of the Commonwealth Relations Office in London on what he called 'the case of Krishna Menon'. Gore-Booth sent Garner a note prepared by one of his colleagues, John Banks:

> A close friend of Mrs. Indira Gandhi's gave me the following account a few days ago of Krishna Menon's 'case history' over the last few years . . .
>
> Menon's troubles began, I was told, when he returned to Delhi from London in 1957. He felt, not unnaturally, out of place—a stranger in India . . . Nevertheless as a Minister Menon performed pretty well for some considerable time . . . From late 1960, however, Menon's psychological difficulties, in which there was now a physical element as well, began to intervene in his work. He asked, I was told, repeatedly that the Prime Minister should relieve him of his office . . .
>
> In October 1960 Mrs. Gandhi consulted a psychiatrist in London about Krishna Menon's case showing him the reports of Menon's doctors. The psychiatrist is said to have commented that a man in his condition should not on any account be holding any position of great responsibility . . .
>
> There is obviously a certain amount of hindsight in all this particularly as Mrs. Gandhi has been repeating the complaint which Krishna Menon has been making recently—namely that the deficiencies revealed by the emergency in the Defence Ministry and the Army were really all the fault of Morarji Desai who had always refused to give Krishna Menon the money he needed . . . But I think the account has generally quite an authentic ring . . .

The identity of this 'close friend of Mrs. Indira Gandhi' was not revealed but my best guess is that it could have been Marie Seton. Such was Krishna Menon's personality that every little conversation in which he figured would find its way into diplomatic communications.

As the fateful year was drawing to a close, Krishna Menon was given a rousing reception in Madras's Marina Beach on 23 December

1962. Tens of thousands of people were present, and the highlight was a poem recited by Kannadasan, one of the all-time greats of Tamil poetry. The English translation, sadly, does not really capture the lyrical beauty and flow of the original Tamil:

Come, Lion of Kerala!

The gold of India, come.
Nehru's comrade, come.
You with the honest heart, come.
Mountain of justice, come.
Wealth of a sharp mind, come.
One of undiminished conviction, come.
Lion of Kerala, come.
The peak of friendship, come.

Unmindful of those who heap abuse you worked without respite.
With your abilities you won the love of the entire motherland.
You set your heart on the right ideology.
Wait, soon a time will come when people will praise you . . .

The scoundrels who will cast aspersion on even pure milk have abused you.
It's opportunist foxes who have slandered you . . .

O warrior, your patriotism is admirable . . .
Your services continue to be required.
Your voice will be heard again.
You will once again rise, O' Lion of Kerala!

It was a fitting end to his official career.

And before the end of the year, the first full-length biography of Krishna Menon would come out. The book had gone to the press just as the Chinese invasion had begun and was published a month later. The author was a noted Hungarian–American academic, and he would, a few years later, write books on Gandhi and Nehru as well.[15]

Emil Lengyel had researched his subject's career fairly extensively. He had also spoken with a number of Krishna Menon's associates, friends and critics in India, the UK and the US as well as interviewed the man himself. Had it come out a few years earlier it may have created a bigger splash. Even so, it evoked considerable interest, with one reviewer observing:

> This biography explains everything, and nothing; it is full of facts, but Krishna Menon remains, in a way, as much a mystery as ever.

Another noted:

> At the moment Menon may be down but it would be a mistake to count him out. His personality is too dynamic, his ambition too sweeping. But it is significant that in her hour of peril India had to cast him aside.

Notes

1. Once in June 2018, when I asked Shankar Bajpai, who had started his foreign service in 1952, how the Americans and the British could know so much of what was happening in New Delhi in the 1950s and 1960s, his reply was 'old boy, whisky'. Krishna Menon, it should be noted, was a strict teetotaller.
2. Dastur (1967).
3. Brecher (1968).
4. Lall (1981).
5. Ananth Krishnan, who was then the Beijing correspondent for *The Hindu*.
6. Subrahmanyam (1987).
7. Palit (1991).
8. Mullik (1970).
9. Kunhi Krishnan (1971).
10. Hoffmann (1990).

11. Gopal (1989).
12. Galbraith (1969).
13. Hershberg (2011).
14. Brecher (1968).
15. Lengyel (1962).

16

Last Seventeen Months with Nehru
(1963–64)

On 9 January 1963, the *Saturday Evening Post*, an American weekly magazine, published an expansive interview with Nehru. Robert Sherrod, its editor, had met the Prime Minister on 27 November 1962 and on 4 December 1962. He wrote:

> My interview took place some time after the sensational firing of Mr. Nehru's acidulous defense minister V.K. Krishna Menon, who had made himself as objectionable to Indian politicians as to United Nations diplomats in New York. Did the Prime Minister lay unpreparedness at Krishna Menon's door?
>
> Mr. Nehru refused to yield an inch insofar as his friend was concerned. 'Krishna Menon is very patriotic, devoted and able. He has some failings. He was very helpful on the Planning Commission—a good economist. It is completely wrong to blame Krishna Menon for army failings. He tried to modernize the army and it is now doing well on his plans. He started a process of modernization with automatic weapons, which is coming to fruition now. Even the British army took four or five years to adopt automatic weapons.'

The immediate post-mortem of India's military debacle in October–November 1962 had revealed that the Chinese had an upper hand, largely because their army had been equipped adequately with semi-automatic rifles. From some time in early 1959, Krishna Menon had been fighting a battle of his own to get India to design and manufacture such rifles. Initially, the army had them imported for field trials from the US but three years later the rifles were rejected by the very same army. Then, orders had been placed in early 1962 with a Belgian company but the rifles were not available when needed most. Eventually, on 12 November 1963, Krishna Menon's successor, Y.B. Chavan, received the first batch of semi-automatic rifles designed and manufactured in India in Ishapore near Calcutta.

Even though he was no longer a minister, Krishna Menon would figure in a well-known book by an American journalist that came out in January 1963. Welles Hangen, in his book titled *After Nehru Who?*, identified eight people who could succeed Nehru—Morarji Desai, Lal Bahadur Shastri, Indira Gandhi, Y.B. Chavan, Krishna Menon, S.K. Patil, Jayaprakash Narayan and Lt General Kaul. Much of the book was written in 1961 and 1962 but passing mention was made of Krishna Menon's departure from Nehru's cabinet. While recognizing him as a pre-eminent figure of the Indian left, Hangen was not at all complimentary about Krishna Menon:[1]

> . . . Now sixty-five and increasingly dependent on drugs to sustain his energy, Menon may even live to see Nehru in his grave. Or the two men may vanish together into the mists of history. But my own feeling is that Menon will outlive his protector. When Nehru is gone, when the mighty banyan tree is removed and Menon is exposed to the pitiless elements, he will make a brave pretense of competing in the open political market by fair means or foul. But when the game is up, as it must soon be, I venture to predict . . . that he will go home to that drab boardinghouse in Camden Town. There you will find him wrapped in cheap scarves, brewing endless cups of tea, and writing mordant articles on the folly of mankind.

Krishna Menon chose to ignore this diatribe. He would prove Hangen wrong and remain active in India over the next eleven years, acquiring a halo after death. As for Hangen he would be killed seven years later while covering the war in Cambodia.

Nehru set the cat among the pigeons in another interview he gave to Milburn Aker, editor of the *Chicago Sun-Times*, which appeared on 4 February 1963. At the end of the hour-long conversation, Aker asked Nehru as they walked out of the room: 'I have read reports that Mr. Menon may return to the government. Are they correct?' Aker went on:

> He [Nehru] smiled and said: 'There is no immediate prospect of Mr. Menon's return. What will take place in the future I cannot say'.

That was enough to fuel fresh feverish talk about Krishna Menon's political future. Diplomatic missions scrambled to find out what was happening and the UK High Commission reported back home:

> Considerable speculation has been caused by Mr. Nehru's remark, in the course of an interview with an American correspondent, that Mr. Menon might after a while return to the Cabinet. Mr. Menon's supporters have organized a speech-making tour for him, mainly in South India, and Mr. Menon's speeches have been on the theme 'one leader, one flag, one nation'. The line now being peddled by the Menonite left is the need for all forces to rally behind the Prime Minister against 'right reaction'.

The speculation would accentuate four months later when the flag-bearer of the left in Nehru's cabinet, K.D. Malaviya, was forced to resign on charges of financial impropriety. Malaviya had been an ardent follower of Krishna Menon and a mentor of sorts to Feroze Gandhi. With him gone the clamour for reinstating Krishna Menon grew louder.

Meanwhile, Krishna Menon would begin to imagine ghosts where none existed. Feeling completely out of sorts, he wrote to Nehru on 7 February 1963:

I was shocked to learn that 'Government' has decided to close down, or indefinitely suspend, the National Defence College. I was very distressed to hear it and I write in the fond hope that you will prevent this happening. This has been built up with great difficulty and took over 3 years to get it going . . . I know my voice is not effective, but in spite of one's handicaps one tries to do things . . . I hope you will save this institution.

The very next day Nehru reassured his erstwhile cabinet colleague:

. . . I referred your letter to the Defence Minister. He has replied to me saying that owing to the great demand for officers due to the Emergency [declared in the wake of the war with China] and the college, it was decided to suspend the College for the present. This decision will, no doubt, be reviewed at the earliest opportunity.

Indeed it was and the National Defence College in New Delhi very soon acquired an international reputation, which it has sustained for over five decades now. It continues to be a very important institution for training of not only senior Indian military officers but also of those from other countries. However, in its portals, Krishna Menon is not exactly a revered name because of the 1962 debacle.

Krishna Menon's sister Janaki Amma had been his emotional anchor for over half a century. She was clearly the one person he had been closest to, the one person in whom he confided completely. She knew all about his women friends. He would badger her for astrological predictions. He had left all his inherited immovable properties to her. For a number of months she had been suffering from cancer in a Bombay hospital and the end came on 24 June 1963. As she lay dying, she asked Krishna Menon what the jeeps scandal was all about, to which he replied: 'I have made some errors in judging people.' He was devastated by her death and shed copious tears as he helped carry the body to the crematorium. Nehru sent him a telegram from Kashmir, where he was on a brief holiday, condoling her demise and recalling how greatly attached Krishna Menon and she had been. Near Calicut is 'Janakikkadu', an eco-tourist destination that gets its name from her to whom this approximately 300 acres of land once belonged. The land was acquired by the Kerala government in 1975.

Even though he had ceased to matter politically, Krishna Menon continued to excite diplomatic interest. Some British papers were speculating about his comeback prompted by the remarks Nehru had made in the *Chicago Sun-Times* interview. On 24 July 1963, Gore-Booth reported back to London:

> Mr. Krishna Menon is, I regret to say, in excellent health and spirits. I met him at the U.A.R. National Day party; he was looking like a rather old-fashioned solicitor's clerk at Brighton, black jacket, stiff white collar and light trousers. We talked theoretically, with the odd barbed remark about Marxism at the end of which Krishna Menon said that the Labour Party would win the next election unless the Tories and their American friends were able to provoke the normal international crisis which would turn things the other way. There are other indications that he is by no means out of action these days.

A year later, when elections were held in the UK, Krishna Menon would be proved right. Labour would win, and his long-time friend Harold Wilson would become Prime Minister.

It had been ten months since Krishna Menon had resigned. Every now and then he would catch up with Nehru but these conversations were desultory and never lasted more than a few minutes. The fact was that Nehru was an extremely sick man. He had, truth be told, been ill since late 1961 but his health took a sharp turn for the worse after November–December 1962. On 12 August 1963, Krishna Menon wrote to Nehru, his longest letter after his resignation:

> I would have asked to see you instead of writing this letter, but for the fact that I know how heavily preoccupied you have been for the last few days. I felt it would be indecent to ask for an appointment . . . It is now nine and a half months or about

since I left the Government. During this period, I have sought to discharge my obligations to the country, both as a member of Parliament and a former member of Government who had till recently the privilege of your confidence to a considerable degree. I have endeavoured to do this with a sense of responsibility and without being involved in the many regrettable squabbles that are rampant. Even in my constituency I have continued to function as best as I can, despite not only the obstructions but humiliations heaped on me. I have felt somewhat relieved to feel that I am able to take all this in my stride and not to become unbalanced in judgment or approach. I thought that it was not only appropriate but also legitimate that I should remind you of my existence and that such services as I can render are fully at your disposal . . .

It is the first time in forty five years or more that I am near unwanted and rendered functionless. I do not complain. In the few occasions you kindly saw me I have tried to convey such sentiments, or views as in my humble opinion and judgment, would supplement or otherwise help you in your vast knowledge and capacity of judgment. It is also known to you that I have made no improper use of these interviews . . .

May I also add that I am a member of the Congress in good standing . . . and a Congress Member of Parliament in good standing. I should also like to add that despite my lack of knowledge of Hindustani . . . I appear to have an appeal to students and young people and also to that strata of our nation which does not go to public meetings or listen to harangues be it Rotary Club, a political or intellectual society.

I have said all this not to write out a testimonial for myself but in order that you may have the facts to make and justify your assessments and decision.

What was Krishna Menon hoping to accomplish with this letter? There was a little bit of the old emotional pressure in it. There was a subtle hint that the Prime Minister had all but forgotten him. But for the most part it was a plea to Nehru to use him not in the government but in the party organization more actively. There was a background to this. The Congress had suffered defeats in three by-elections in June 1963. Three opposition stalwarts had won. All had been close to Nehru in the 1930s and 1940s but had subsequently become his bitterest critics. One—Minoo Masani—was Krishna Menon's chum in the 1930s and another—Rammanohar Lohia—was someone who had admired him at that time. The third—J.B. Kripalani—had been a thorn in Krishna Menon's flesh in the late 1950s.

The Congress was shell-shocked, and it was in this context that Kamaraj, the chief minister of Madras, suggested that he and some other chief ministers should quit and devote themselves full-time to reinvigorating the party. This idea 'appears to have expanded under its own momentum' to cover ministers both at the state and national level. This soon came to be known as the 'Kamaraj Plan', and Kamaraj became the president of the Congress party in early August 1963. The wheel had turned full circle. In the early 1950s, Nehru had asserted the supremacy of the government over the party. Now, he was declaring that the party's interests were paramount.

There was immediate jockeying for power because of the vacancies created in the government. It has to be said in Krishna Menon's favour that he was realistic enough not to ask Nehru for a ministerial position. Instead, his letter offered his services for the party, which was the real underlying motivation for the Kamaraj Plan. Nehru's authoritative biographer, otherwise a caustic critic of Krishna Menon, was forced to concede that 'it would seem that only Krishna Menon took this aspect of the Kamaraj Plan seriously and offered to work and speak on behalf of the Congress'.[2] But that was not to be.

On 5 August 1963, the US, the USSR and the UK signed the Partial Test Ban Treaty in Moscow that barred all nuclear tests except for those conducted underground. Among the most indefatigable campaigners for such an agreement, with Nehru's unstinted backing, was Krishna Menon. He was not completely satisfied since the agreement still left the door open for underground tests and detonations but considered it a step forward nevertheless. Krishna Menon had made his first major speech on nuclear disarmament at the UN on 26 October 1954, and it had drawn wide encomiums. Jules Moch of France had said, 'We all owe Mr. Menon a debt of gratitude and

Vyshinsky who had poured scorn on Krishna Menon two years earlier on his resolution on Korea was sufficiently impressed to ask for the adjournment of the debate so that "we can acquaint ourselves with Mr. Menon's speech".' Krishna Menon would make thirteen major speeches at the UN on disarmament, each of them quite a landmark. The last one was on 21 July 1962, less than four months before his resignation.

Krishna Menon's letter to Nehru appeared to have had one immediate impact. On 19 August 1963, the Lok Sabha began a discussion on the first-ever no-confidence motion against the Nehru government, moved by none other than Kripalani. The debate lasted over twenty hours, and the penultimate speaker defending the Nehru government three days later, after ministers like Morarji Desai and S.K. Patil had said their bit, was Krishna Menon. He had asked to speak just before Nehru answered the no-confidence motion.

Kripalani's attack had been mostly on Krishna Menon and on Nehru's protection of him. So it was natural that Krishna Menon focused on Kripalani's speech, although he directed some barbs at Masani as well. He spoke for over an hour and took Kripalani head on, quoting chapter and verse from Kripalani's earlier speeches in Parliament in which he had bemoaned expenditure on defence. Kripalani had said that defence expenditure was a waste of scarce resources and a betrayal of Gandhian values and principles. Krishna Menon was very effective that day as he demonstrated Kripalani's inconsistency and hypocrisy. He was heckled throughout his speech but he managed to drive home his point forcefully. The result of the vote, however, was never in doubt, and the no-confidence motion was rejected by a huge majority. But Krishna Menon had registered his presence and the fact that he still counted.

A few months later on 12 October 1963, Nehru wrote a 'Secret & Personal' letter to Krishna Menon from Dehra Dun where he was recovering from illness:

> I enclose a note I have drafted in regard to the Punjab affair and Sardar Pratap Singh Kairon. I shall be grateful if you will read through it carefully and comment on it . . .

The note was thirteen pages long and was from Nehru to the President of India, S. Radhakrishnan. Kairon, the chief minister of Punjab, had been accused of corruption by opposition parties in the state, who had also met the President and presented a memorandum containing a number of charges. These charges had actually first surfaced in early 1958, and they had been investigated by a committee of Congressmen who had exonerated Kairon. Thereafter, in a case filed against the state of Punjab, the high court of Punjab had dismissed the petition but the Supreme Court upheld it, passing strictures on Kairon. This added ammunition to those seeking Kairon's ouster. Nehru, after examining the case, recommended to Radhakrishnan that an inquiry be made by a 'high-level judicial authority' into the charges made against Kairon but that he not be asked to resign pending completion of the inquiry.

Krishna Menon gave a seven-page point-by-point comment on Nehru's draft. He harped on the special position of Punjab and the security of India by saying:

> I do not agree with the recommendation you are making to the President . . . If it is your view that it is the leaders of the Opposition that have brought these charges before the President, and some special important attaches to it, it is my submission that they are no more than ordinary petitioners before the President. The proper forum for them is the Punjab Assembly, the Courts, and perhaps the Governor, and not the President . . .
>
>   . . . This is virulent Opposition propaganda. You are being trapped into it . . . You may recall, if one may refer to a personal matter, that when you agreed to my stepping down from the Office of the Defence Minister and you asked me to take on Defence Production, the newspapers and the howling Opposition both within our Party and in the Opposition said: 'We have tasted blood'. This hue and cry will not stop at Pratap Singh Kairon.

He then followed it up a few days later with yet another eight-pager titled 'The Constitutional and Political Implications of the Prime Minister's Decision'. In this, he drew Nehru's attention to the Denning Inquiry, which was in the headlines in the UK. The British Prime Minister, Harold Macmillan, had ordered an inquiry by Lord Denning after the resignation of one of his ministers, John Profumo, who had got himself entangled with a young woman called Christine Keeler, who was, at the same time, involved with a Soviet diplomat stationed in London. Krishna Menon analysed the Denning Inquiry in some detail because 'it furnishes important lessons for us'. He applauded Denning for keeping Britain's larger interests in mind while preparing his report and fixing responsibilities. He ended by saying:

> The problem before the learned Judge who will preside over the enquiry into the charges against the Chief Minister of Punjab will be not to suppress the truth but to find the truth and the whole truth and place all the lessons in their proper perspective before the country.

Thereafter, Krishna Menon met with Kairon and wrote to the Prime Minister twice—on 19 and 20 October 1963. In the second letter he told Nehru:

> . . . As I told you before, I took the Chief Minister to Setalwad. We did not discuss the case. Setalwad and Kairon talked about the Punjab. The Chief Minister, who was quite natural and normal, left a very good impression both of his ability and sincerity as well of his ruggedness. What Setalwad said, partly in fun, was that Kairon should be Chief Minister of Assam or of Assam as well. He also volunteered the statement that he had been greatly impressed by the prosperity in the Punjab and the progress they made all round.
>
> I suggested to you before and I suggest again that it would be appropriate for you to send for Setalwad and have a general talk . . . Three questions at least may be asked of him:
>
> 1. Whether the Central Government have authority to order this inquiry. (The answer would be 'yes')

2. Whether in this case, or in the case of any Chief Minister, it
    is appropriate to take over the inquiry Centrally. (His answer
    would probably be 'no' . . .)
3. Whether such inquiry is best held under the Act of 1952, or
    whether those who have complained should seek their remedy
    at law (I don't know what he would say)

. . . I have written to you on this matter more than once. The
reason is not special pleading for the Chief Minister, who I know
only by official relationship. I am anxious that we do not set
bad constitutional precedents which will boomerang on us. The
President's duty is to function through the Governor. Taking
liberties with the law and the spirit of the Constitution would be
bad. It sets up unhealthy precedents . . .

The proposal before Nehru was to appoint a formal commission of
inquiry under the chairmanship of the former chief justice of India
S.R. Das. Krishna Menon told Nehru that apart from the fact that
Das was 'generally believed to be close to you', to place a former
chief justice in charge of the inquiry 'is to blow the thing out into a
very big size'. Kairon had his admirers as well as critics, and Krishna
Menon belonged to the former category. That he was the only chief
minister to keep silent when Nehru had sought the opinion of all
chief ministers on 6 November 1962 on Krishna Menon's resignation
would have endeared him that much more to the former defence
minister. As it turned out, Nehru disregarded Krishna Menon's
repeated pleadings and persistent advice. The Das Commission of
Inquiry was set up in October 1963. Its report was to be submitted in
June 1964, a few weeks after Nehru's death. Kairon would resign on
21 June 1964 and be assassinated a year later.

On 2 September 1963, Defence Minister Y.B. Chavan tabled a
statement in the Lok Sabha on the NEFA Inquiry report, known to
history as the Henderson Brooks report that still remains classified. The
statement was taken up for discussion seventeen days later. Naturally,
Krishna Menon was the focus of the attack by the Opposition and
Nath Pai led the charge, speaking of the 'alarming, shocking state of

unpreparedness . . . sheer incompetence . . . insane obstinacy and immeasurable responsibility on the part of those who were charged with the defence of the country . . .'. Eyewitness accounts revealed that Krishna Menon was getting worked up by Nath Pai's assault. Then came Frank Antony, who too tore into Krishna Menon and Kaul. Nehru had, on Chavan's suggestion, already decided not to speak and leave everything to the defence minister. But Krishna Menon was visibly agitated and itching to reply to his critics. It turned out that the party's floor managers firmly refused his request. It was just as well.[3]

Earlier in the year, in mid-July 1963, a huge controversy had broken out on the Indian government's decision to allow Voice of America to install at its expense a high-power transmitter that would be used by them as well as All India Radio to relay broadcasts to South East Asia. Krishna Menon had been among those who opposed this and forced an embarrassed Nehru to let the agreement lapse. At about the same time Krishna Menon had expressed his strong opposition to the Anglo-American plans to collaborate with the Indian Air Force for shoring up India's air defences, installing radars and conducting joint exercises. Two months later he was at it again and wrote to the Prime Minister on 11 September 1963:

> I was shocked to read in the press this morning that the United States intends to fire her Nikes in India. The Nike as you know is a nuclear weapon. The ground that this would be for gathering of data is being laid. But this should not deceive us, nor should we be involved in self-deception with the way that the VOA [Voice of America] was a fait accompli resulting in embarrassments . . .
>
> You may remember that when I was in Government, I protested against our agreeing to set up [satellite] tracking stations, over which and the data collected we have no control. I also raised my ineffective voice against placing that programme on our side, in the hands of those who are not greatly concerned about our non-alignment or independence and are also outside normal governmental control.

. . . It would be wrong and grievous to clamp down party discipline or strain loyalties in a matter of this kind. Nuclear war and the abetting of it is a matter of conscience. You may, and perhaps with justification, disregard the personality and self-respect of individuals. But we cannot sell out like this . . .

Krishna Menon's guns were trained fairly and squarely on Homi Bhabha. Amazingly, Nehru replied to this invective the very same day:

I got your letter of the 11th September this morning about the Nike Rocket. I did not connect this with the nuclear weapon at all. The experiments intended are entirely meant for weather research . . . These rockets are sounding rockets, and are not military rockets . . . Nike itself is a booster and is used in the first stage of both the sounding and military rockets. I do not see any harm in our associating ourselves with this. It is essentially a UN scheme and we are being helped in it not only by the US, but also the USSR, France, etc.

The rockets would be launched from Thumba in Kerala, and thereafter, India's space programme would take off.

Another assignment given to Krishna Menon as 1963 was drawing to a close was to draft the foreign policy resolution for the forthcoming Congress session to be held in Bhubaneshwar early in the new year. There was nothing special in this because Krishna Menon had been contributing heavily to such resolutions over the past decade. But this time it was a little different, as he mentioned to Nehru on 20 October 1963:

I would like to see you tomorrow about the Foreign Policy Resolution and to discuss with you its skeleton. As I am now a little outside the context of governmental and your thinking, this is useful.

The Bhubaneshwar session of the Congress party was overshadowed by the paralytic stroke that Nehru suffered on its very first day—8

January 1964. Nehru was not present when Krishna Menon took the stage two days later to speak on the resolution on 'Democracy and Socialism', a subject as close to his heart as foreign policy. As always, *The Hindu* reported on his speech at length the next day:

> . . . The highlight of the debate on the resolution on 'Democracy and Socialism' was the plea made by Mr. V.K. Krishna Menon for the party, in the interests of its own survival, t0 pursue the goal of socialism with its real and basic contents. Mr. Krishna Menon launched a well-argued attack, which, while not appearing to be in downright opposition to the official resolution, yet contained punch and broadsides which the High Command could not let go unanswered without inviting the comment that by its silence it has admitted the weakness of its case. Mr. Krishna Menon said that the present economic base in India was undoubtedly capitalistic and that what the Congress party was seeking to do was build socialism on a capitalistic base . . .

He then went on to define what he meant by true socialism, spoke of concentration of wealth and economic power and monopolies, called for a productivity revolution in agriculture and a massive push for rural industrialization, and advocated nationalization of banks. Other reports of his speech called it 'vigorous' and one that was 'occasionally cheered'. Five years later, Nehru's daughter— aided, abetted and guided by a Krishna Menon acolyte P.N. Haksar—would engineer a split in the Congress party along the lines of the socialist agenda put forward by Krishna Menon at Bhubaneshwar.[4]

Krishna Menon's performance at Bhubaneshwar had not gone unnoticed by the Americans who were paranoid about his return. On 21 January 1964, President Ayub Khan of Pakistan wrote to US President Lyndon B. Johnson 'arguing the necessity for Pakistan to take the Kashmir issue to the UN Security Council'. President Johnson's aides prepared a long brief for him on Ayub Khan's letter, recommending that the US 'back off' from its previous substantive role on the Kashmir issue in the UN Security Council. It called

Pakistan's decision to take the issue to the UN without consulting the US 'ill advised' and did not fail to note:

> Lurking in the background in India will be Krishna Menon, who has always made great political capital by attacking Pakistan. He will be quick to seize upon any opportunity, presented either by apparent Western support of the Pak position, or by too moderate Indian defense, in order to continue to rebuild his political position.

What the Americans feared did happen. The UN Security Council debate on Kashmir took place in February 1964, and for the first time in seven years, Krishna Menon was not in New York defending India's case. Instead, he used the Lok Sabha pulpit as the Americans had feared, as a telegram from Chester Bowles, the US ambassador in New Delhi, back to the State Department in Washington noted on 20 February 1964:

> Krishna Menon has been given a platform and equipped with issue on which he excels. His Feb 14 speech was effective and received reaction from sizeable majority of Lok Sabha. Civil servants . . . who have preached futility of dealing with Pakistan and need for firm line have been strengthened, while moderates are being forced to get on bandwagon.

But the rebuilding of Krishna Menon's political life, which the Americans were mortified about, did not take place. The Krishna Menon era had well and truly passed. He had become a meteor that had crashed.

The week beginning 20 May 1964 would be doubly traumatic for Krishna Menon. A.V. Baliga, his intimate ally in all progressive causes, a key figure in his 1957 and 1962 election campaigns, his doctor who had also looked after his sister, died suddenly on that day in London. The body was flown to Bombay three days later. Krishna Menon was at the airport to receive the coffin and later carried it to Baliga's apartment. At the funeral on 23 May 1964, there were two people who spoke: the veteran thespian Prithviraj Kapoor and Krishna Menon.

Four days later, the man who had projected and protected Krishna Menon for over a quarter of a century himself passed away. Nehru's funeral was held on the evening of 28 May 1964, and a distraught and forlorn Krishna Menon was probably the last person to place a log of wood on the funeral pyre. Quite appropriately from Krishna Menon's point of view, one of Nehru's last letters was to Reginald Sorensen on 1 May 1964:

> I have your letter of the 28th April for which I thank you.
>
> I have been in the habit of addressing a meeting under the auspices of the India League in London whenever I go there. Normally, therefore I would accept your suggestion. But I am not quite sure whether it will be desirable for me to do so. I am very much better but I want to spare myself extra engagements as far as possible. For the present, therefore, I cannot commit myself to any such engagement.

The Commonwealth Prime Ministers were scheduled to meet in London in June 1964, and Sorensen had invited Nehru to speak at the India League, which he had first done in 1935.

After Nehru's funeral, for a few days it appeared that there would be a struggle for the Prime Minister's post between Lal Bahadur Shastri and Morarji Desai. Krishna Menon's name would be dragged in. A quite bizarre story would circulate that he had mobilized all the left-leaning MPs in support of Morarji Desai and the name mentioned as his partner in this enterprise was K.D. Malaviya, who had organized a breakfast meeting of a number of leftist MPs in the Congress party. On 29 May 1964, Dean Rusk, the US secretary of state, who had come to New Delhi for Nehru's funeral, sent a report to President Johnson in which he mentioned a private call he and the US ambassador in India, Chester Bowles, had made on President Radhakrishnan and added:

> ... He believes that the new India will be 'more pro-West than ever'. He believes new government will be constituted very quickly, no later than Saturday, and that Congress Party Parliamentary Group

will probably cast about three hundred votes for Shastri and about one hundred for Morarji Desai. Curious combinations between far right (Morarji Desai) and far left (Krishna Menon) are complicating factor.

Newspaper reports can be discounted but the President of India saying something, and that too in private, cannot be dismissed outright. Radhakrishnan may have been ventilating whatever was in the air but the news had gained so much currency that Malaviya was forced to issue a public statement on 9 June 1964, strongly denying that the leftists were extending support to Morarji Desai. Shastri's definitive biographer[5] would later mention this 'rumour' but not draw attention to its categorical refutation by Malaviya. Krishna Menon, for his part, would vehemently deny any such tie-up with Desai, saying that his presence at Malaviya's breakfast, which had triggered all the speculation, was out of loyalty to a fellow leftist and that at the breakfast he had only spoken of a succession keeping in view constitutional principles.

But there is an intriguing sequel to this supposed Krishna Menon–Morarji joint venture to make the latter Nehru's successor. After he had been declared the leader of the Congress parliamentary party, Shastri called on Radhakrishnan and discussed the inclusion of Krishna Menon in his cabinet as minister of external affairs. The Prime Minister-designate was, however, dissuaded from taking this step by the President. There are three possibilities: The Krishna Menon–Morarji combination was pure gossip; Shastri forgave Krishna Menon for his activities to prop up Morarji Desai; Shastri realized Krishna Menon's positive as well as nuisance value and wanted him as minister of external affairs to signal continuity with Nehru's policies and also to pre-empt Indira Gandhi from staking a claim to that portfolio. Sometimes even archival biographers have to go by their hunches; my hunch from reading Shastri's biography is to go with the third explanation.

A few days after Shastri had taken over as Prime Minister, Bertrand Russell wrote to Krishna Menon on 16 June 1964:

I am greatly disturbed by the situation in South East Asia. I should like to hold a meeting in London for the purpose of discussing a declaration which might be issued by a small international group. The declaration might centre on the reconvening of the fourteen-nation Geneva Conference on Laos, for the purpose of a negotiated settlement for all of Indo-China.

I believe that events are moving very quickly in South East Asia and that it is important for us to speak out now. May I ask if it would be possible for you to come to London and partake in the meeting on July 9? I am also asking M. Claude Bourdet, Dr. Vladimir Dedijer, Signor Riccardo Lombardi, Pastor Martin Niemoeller, Professor Nguyen Van Hieu, Professor Linus Pauling, Professor Jean-Paul Sartre and a spokesman of the Laotian embassy, the Soviet Peace Committee and the Polish Peace Committee.

Krishna Menon had been a key player in the talks on Indo-China in Geneva in 1955 and 1962. Russell's invitation was a recognition of the contributions he had made then. He signed on to Russell's appeal. Two years later in October 1966, Russell would invite Krishna Menon again to join an international tribunal to investigate 'war crimes committed by the United States in Vietnam'. These crimes included, as Russell wrote, 'sustained bombardment of hospitals, schools, sanatoria and leprosaria in North Vietnam and the use of toxic chemicals and poison gas in South Vietnam'. Krishna Menon agreed with Russell wholeheartedly and spoke about it to different audiences in India. But the preoccupation with his re-election prevented him from becoming a member of the tribunal as Russell had wanted.

Krishna Menon and Russell had shared a warm–cold relationship over the decades. On 19 June 1961, Russell had told a prospective biographer of Krishna Menon:

When he [Krishna Menon] was Secretary of the India League and I was President, he did all the work and I merely endorsed his activities . . . I did not know him very well . . .

And even earlier, on 3 January 1955, Krishna Menon had written to Russell:

> I was more than a little distressed . . . that you are under the impression that I had less than warm and respectful feelings and thoughts about you . . . I would like to ask you to accept the assurance of my high regard and affection, as always, for you and also my deep sense of gratitude for your intimate association with the movement for Indian independence and great many other things I believe in . . .

Russell had replied five days later:

> . . . I was very glad indeed to get your friendly letter of January 3. Both on personal and public grounds I did not like to think there could be any coolness between us . . .

In mid-1964, a second biography of Krishna Menon was published in London. For some years T.J.S. George, a young Indian journalist, had been following Krishna Menon around in the hope of writing his life story. George persevered, and by the end of 1963, he had completed the manuscript. On 20 October 1963, Krishna Menon had written to George:

> I have looked at the extracts of letters which you have been able to see as a result of your own initiatives. I have no letters or papers and don't intend to use any. I have, however, no intention of thwarting anyone who exercises initiative. If you have gathered material I will not stand in your way. You are at liberty to use them as far as I am concerned. As a matter of principle I do not authorize any publication. The extracts you have shown me are not taken out of context and you need have no fears that I shall take any action in regard to them either way. You know my views of biographies and autobiographies, especially of living people. Hence my indifference.

George's biography presented an unblemished portrait of the subject in the most adulatory way. No wonder it would receive this review some months later from a highly respected academic in the UK—and an admirer of Krishna Menon:[6]

> The present reviewer first came to know Krishna Menon when he was a St. Pancras Councillor, more than a quarter of a century ago. Upon a youth of 17 he made an indelible impression—not, then, as an Indian nationalist, but as a human personality—erratic, sometimes sacrificing, but always compelling. This reviewer has since always counted himself one of the sparse tribe of Menonites, and has frequently occasioned puzzlement for expressing admiration for a man commonly regarded as a near relation to Lucifer. It was, therefore, with pleasurable anticipation that a jaded reviewer took up this biography. Pleasure soon turned into disappointment. The book is written in Fleet Street style, though the author has undertaken various research among the papers of the India League and elsewhere. The journalese might be overlooked and compensated by serious contributions to knowledge of the subject: but the whole tone and balance of the book make one uneasy. This reads like an attempt to 'promote' Menon in a political come-back. He is presented as a major prophet, a doer of mighty deeds. And those who stand against him are represented as embodying all the vices . . . Those who regard Menon as some sort of devil will not be converted by this attempt to evoke a hero-saint. The truth is much more devious and complex: and much more interesting.

The true Indian that he was, Krishna Menon would have been very gratified by George's biography. The good Britisher that he was, he would have applauded Tinker's review. As far as George is concerned, I asked him whether, in light of all that has come to light after his book originally appeared in 1964, he would revise any of his opinions and views. He replied:

> . . . I'd put in some segments about his needlessly bad temper, the overtly acerbic ways which, once he became a politician, should

have been controlled. I'd also add some humanizing accounts of his lady friends. But I'd emphasise that he was more sinned against than sinning. Even in the Cabinet Morarji would not give an extra rupee to Defence, how then could one organize winter clothing for the troops? How could people hurt the nation because of their aversion to KM [Krishna Menon]? I'd say KM had many faults, but his patriotism was impeccable. Someone should write a book on Morarji—the damage he has done to this country, why Gen. Zia gave him Pakistan's highest civilian honour, etc.

Notes

1. Hangen (1963).
2. Gopal (1984).
3. Pradhan (1998).
4. Ramesh (2018).
5. Srivastava (1995).
6. Tinker (1964).

17

Voice in the Wilderness (1964–66)

Krishna Menon held back for a few months after Shastri had taken over as Prime Minister in June 1964. But on 25 March 1965, while speaking on the budget presented by the finance minister, T.T. Krishnamachari, Krishna Menon shed his reticence and went into attack mode. He criticized the policy to attract foreign investments and bemoaned that the public sector's importance was being heavily diluted. And he returned to his favourite theme of bank nationalization. Krishna Menon and Krishnamachari were good friends but both were known to be strongly abrasive personalities who prided themselves on their socialist credentials. They had both been part of Nehru's inner circle. On 22 August 1962, just a few months before his resignation, Krishna Menon had written a 'Dear T.T.' letter to Krishnamachari:

> I am sorry that my observations at the meeting caused you offence. It was not my intention to treat you with disregard much less to annoy you . . . I might have, indeed I have, expressed myself badly . . . It was not, and is not my intention to cause irritation or claim monopoly of knowledge as I led you to think. However, since that has been the effect, I feel sad about it and hasten to express my regret . . .

Krishnamachari's response had been prompt:

> . . . I assure you that my relations with you would continue to be
> the same as it had been hitherto, as if nothing had happened to
> mar it.

But that day—25 March 1965—Krishna Menon's attack on his budget
was a bit too much for Krishnamachari to take. He retorted that he
yielded to none—not to Krishna Menon certainly—in 'safeguarding
the interests of the country'. He went on to add:

> Mr. Krishna Menon has assumed the role of a Roman Counsel. One
> was reminded of the performance of the characters in Shakespeare's
> Julius Caesar. He played alternately the roles of Brutus, Cassius and
> Mark Antony, willing to wound but afraid to strike.

Krishnamachari had felt particularly peeved because there had been
an assault on his budget from the left, led by Krishna Menon, and also
from the right, led by Minoo Masani. Krishna Menon and Masani had
been fellow socialists in the 1930s but had since parted ways. Now
both had found a common target. The finance minister had the last
word when he said that if only Krishna Menon was finance minister
he would 'realize that nationalization of banks would not open the
floodgates to socialism' and then went on to castigate Krishna Menon
and Masani by saying: '[B]oth these gentlemen were inducted and
inculcated in the spirit of a foreign civilization'.

One foreign leader from the 1950s with whom Krishna Menon
kept in fairly regular touch was President Nasser of Egypt. Krishna
Menon was invited to Cairo for a conference on Palestine in early
April 1965. He hit the headlines on two counts: for his fiery speech
on Palestinian rights, which was along expected lines, but also
for a clash with a Chinese delegate, which was quite unexpected.
Antony Nutting, the junior UK foreign minister who had resigned
in 1956 over Britain's Suez debacle, tried to convince the audience
that the Palestine problem should be resolved through peaceful
means. When Krishna Menon's turn came he exhorted the Arabs

and the Palestinians to take up an armed struggle. He had a very large number of close Jewish friends since the 1930s. He had tried to get asylum in India for Jewish professionals fleeing Europe after the rise of Hitler. As late as 1955 he had argued for Israel's participation at the Afro-Asian Conference at Bandung. But Israel's military misadventure along with Britain and France over the Suez in October–November 1956 had made him change his mind on that country.

The Cairo conference where Krishna Menon was introduced as 'a political legend of Afro-Asian resurgence who had thundered throughout the world as the most articulate spokesman of Nehru's India' hit the headlines for a different reason. Sudhakar Bhat of the *Times of India* reported from Cairo on 3 April 1965:

Mr. V.K. Krishna Menon and the leader of the Chinese youth delegation clashed at a world seminar on the problem of Palestine here. Mr. Menon who has been specially invited for the seminar, drew an analogy between the creation of Israel on Arab land and the forcible occupation of Indian territory by China.

Mr. Menon, however, did not mention China by name but merely said that the attitude of the Arab peoples towards the occupation of Arab land by Zionism should be similar to India's attitude to the occupation of her territory—to resist aggression and to bide their time until they are strong enough to liquidate the aggression. When Mr. Menon had finished, the leader of the Chinese youth delegation came to the rostrum and said Mr. Menon had made an indirect reference to China . . . China, Mr. Liang said, was the victim of aggression and not the aggressor.

Then Mr. Menon walked up to the rostrum and said that having regard to the purpose of the seminar he had taken care not to mention any country by name. He had merely stated that it was the duty of every country to safeguard its frontiers. But China evidently had a guilty conscience . . . China did commit aggression against India and had betrayed India's friendship and had forcibly and illegally occupied 14000 square miles of Indian territory.

Very clearly, what the Chinese had done still rankled. How could it not? It had destroyed not only Krishna Menon but also grievously damaged Nehru, perhaps even hastening his demise. Five years later, Neville Maxwell, an Australian who had been the correspondent of the London *Times* in India in the late fifties and early sixties, would write a book[1] called *India's China War*, which would be very influential in moulding opinion on how the 1962 war was triggered. As the title made clear, India was the aggressor and China was the victim. Henry Kissinger and Chou En-lai would talk about this book in their historic meeting of February 1972. But subsequent scholarship has significantly debunked Maxwell, and the dominant consensus view now is that it is not 'India's China War' but actually 'Mao's India War'.[2] Krishna Menon would make a second visit to Cairo three years later, and in his recollections of men recorded by Michael Brecher, he would speak fondly of his long association with Nasser, going back to Bandung, where they had first met in April 1955.

On 25 May 1965, John Freeman, the UK high commissioner in India, sent a 'Top Secret' message to his Prime Minister, Harold Wilson:

> I was sent for by President Radhakrishnan this morning and asked to inquire from you in conditions of greatest secrecy whether Krishna Menon would be acceptable as Indian High Commissioner in London in place of [Jivraj] Mehta . . . President explained as background for you that he realized Menon's reappointment would not be generally welcomed in British Government circles. But he and Shastri believe that it is most important to get Menon out of India for a long time. And the President holds that by ability and experience Menon is well qualified to hold the London job . . . In other words you are being asked to agree to an appointment which will probably seem rather unattractive in London for the sake of helping Mr. Shastri to banish from India a disturbing and troublesome influence in Indian politics.

I limit my own comment on this to the following points:

(a) the removal of Menon from India would certainly help the Government to take a more moderate line on Pakistan relations and it is at least arguable that Menon's somewhat anti-British influence would be less damaging to Indo-British relations were he in London than it is while he remains a powerful propaganda voice in India.

(b) The President in confiding in us like this has shown a remarkable degree of trust and on this ground alone our interest out here might well be served by responding to his request.

Wilson replied to Freeman six days later:

The proposal of Krishna Menon is a very difficult one. I attach the greatest possible importance to our diplomatic relations between London and New Delhi. Although I fully appreciate the importance of Menon being out of India for a long time nevertheless I am doubtful about any proposal which is likely to militate against close relations between London and New Delhi. I would very much like to talk to Mr. Shastri about it before he comes to a conclusion. Would you therefore explain to the President that I should prefer to hold the question over until the Prime Ministers' Meeting.

Wilson had known Krishna Menon quite intimately for over two decades. But Wilson's Labour Party was different from the Labour Party of Attlee, Morrison, Bevin, Cripps and Bevan, with whom Krishna Menon had been on very friendly terms. In mid-1952, after he had given up his high commissionership, there had been some overtures to Krishna Menon from the Labour Party to contest for the House of Commons as its candidate. But times had changed and just before Freeman had sent the message to Wilson, Krishna Menon had lambasted the British government. He had, on 5 May 1965, attacked Wilson for his pronounced tilt towards Pakistan, saying, 'Britain should be ashamed of itself for its failure to condemn the Pakistani attack in Kutch.' He had reminded Wilson that 'it was British maps and surveys carried out more than 200 years ago which clearly proved that the territory attacked and occupied by Pakistan in Kutch belonged to India and still the United Kingdom advocated a cease-fire without Pakistan vacating aggression'. No wonder the Radhakrishnan–Shastri proposal never went ahead.

Shastri died in Tashkent at 2.15 a.m. on 11 January 1966. In just about eighteen months a second succession battle loomed large on the Congress horizon. It was clear after a few days that there would be only two candidates to succeed him: Morarji Desai and Indira Gandhi. It was also clear that Nehru's daughter had majority support of both the MPs and chief ministers. The challenge, therefore, was more on how to get Desai to withdraw gracefully so as to make her election as the head of the Congress parliamentary party unanimous. On the leadership issue, there was interest outside India as well, and on 18 January 1966, the US ambassador in Pakistan called on President Ayub Khan. In their conversation there was a brief exchange on the Indian succession. The ambassador reported back the next day:

> . . . Ayub indicated considerable reservations about leading candidate Indira Gandhi. He seemed to think she was an extremist who, being a woman, might embark on adventures. While believing she was perhaps better than Morarji Desai, Ayub said he was apprehensive lest she be dominated by Krishna Menon.

But while Ayub Khan was worried about Krishna Menon's influence on Indira Gandhi, Indira Gandhi had a completely different story to tell. Chester Bowles saw her on the morning of 20 January 1966, a day after she had been chosen leader of her party in Parliament. Bowles sent back a report to the State Department after his conversation, covering the subjects that had come up. Two points she made to Bowles were:

> Mrs. Gandhi expressed concern over stories which said had appeared in the US press stating that she leaned towards the USSR and was a close friend of Krishna Menon. She asked for my

personal cooperation in clearing up what she described as a gross misunderstanding . . .

In regard to Krishna Menon the stories of his alleged political connections with her were simply not true. Indeed he had done more to harm her during the past difficult week than any other single individual. He had worked relentlessly for [Gulzarilal] Nanda and had done so in a manner to discredit her personally. While Krishna Menon still had followers among the younger people because of his speaking ability and personal charm, he would have no part in her administration; she had come to look on him as an adversary and not as a friend.

This was a sensational charge Indira Gandhi was levelling against her father's closest friend and against someone who had virtually been part of her family for three decades. Indira Gandhi and Krishna Menon went back to 1935. Her late husband and Krishna Menon too had formed a mutual admiration society for years, and her sons were fond of Uncle Krishna. So why would she have said what she was reported to have said by Bowles? One explanation could be that she was distancing herself from Krishna Menon for purely tactical reasons and out of sheer political expediency. She may well have wanted to build an equation with the US first and foremost, and what better way to begin than by telling the Americans what they wanted to hear about Krishna Menon?

On the other hand, what she had told Bowles could have been true. Independent confirmation comes from Radhakrishnan's authoritative biographer, who wrote:[3]

So Indira Gandhi was Radhakrishnan's choice and he worked for her silently behind the scenes without compromising the dignity of the office. He was surprised when Krishna Menon called on him to urge Nanda's claims but was relieved to find that Kamaraj, the president of the Congress, was not interested in the post and was inclined to favour Mrs Gandhi. That evening Radhakrishnan sent for her, told her that she could not count on Menon and left-wing support . . .

Gulzarilal Nanda, a veteran labour leader, had been sworn in as Prime Minister immediately following Nehru's death and had been asked by Radhakrishnan to continue till the Congress elected a new leader in Parliament. Radhakrishnan had sworn in Nanda a second time as Prime Minister a few hours after Shastri's death, but again with the clear stipulation that this was to continue till the Congress elected its new leader in Parliament.

That Krishna Menon of all people would support Nanda over Indira Gandhi would appear preposterous, even granting the fact that Nanda had founded the Congress Forum of Socialist Action four years earlier. What would have been his motive? Did he feel that Indira Gandhi would not be true to the cause of socialism? Was he aware of the fact that she had met Radhakrishnan on 7 November 1962 and urged the President to save her father from himself by urging him to accept Krishna Menon's resignation speedily?[4] Did he hold her responsible for restricting his unfettered access to Nehru after his resignation? Did he resent the fact that younger people like Dinesh Singh and Asoka Mehta now were playing the role vis-à-vis her of the type he had played with her father? Frankly, it is very hard to say what was going on in Krishna Menon's mind at this point, and he has left no records that might afford a clue. All that can be said is that his behaviour appears inexplicable, given his long and special relationship with both Nehru and Indira Gandhi.

Krishna Menon did not allow much time for Indira Gandhi to settle down. Her first foreign visit as Prime Minister was to Washington to meet with President Johnson in late March 1966. Just a few weeks later Krishna Menon assailed the new government's foreign policy in Parliament, particularly on Vietnam. In a phrase that caught on, he described the policy as 'not even one of drift because drift had a direction' but as 'nothing but flotsam and jetsam'. If ever there was direction, he charged, that came from outside, clearly alluding to the fact that the new Prime Minister was going out of her way to please the Americans. He was, however, careful to compliment her on her impressive 'debut' in foreign affairs with her meeting President Johnson but cautioned that 'personal success is not the same as policy'. He was also very critical of her beseeching

President Johnson for increased supply of wheat; what he had not realized was that the Prime Minister herself had felt humiliated in doing so and had come back determined to make India self-sufficient in foodgrains production at the earliest.

The Americans, for their part, in the initial months of Indira Gandhi's prime ministership, did not want to be seen to be doing anything that would strengthen Krishna Menon's hands. On 27 May 1966, the US Embassy in India cautioned the State Department back home against the US providing military supplies to Pakistan, arguing:

> In the politically charged pre-election atmosphere here this resumption of US military supplies would absolutely foreclose any Indian initiative on the Pak question, undermine the political leadership of Mrs Gandhi and the moderates, greatly strengthen both Krishna Menon and fellow travellers of the left, and the extremists on the right . . .

A month later Indira Gandhi bit the bullet and took the tough and unpopular decision to go ahead with the devaluation of the Indian rupee, which had been on the anvil for well over a year. In July 1966, Krishna Menon joined his critics Morarji Desai and T.T. Krishnamachari in the Congress Working Committee to mount a blistering attack on the decision. Indira Gandhi may have felt entitled that, at least for old times' sake, Krishna Menon would support her. That, however, did not happen. But he did make one concession to her. Unlike others who were bitterly critical, he, while being critical, made constructive suggestions to 'deal with the present situation'.

The year 1966 saw the publication of Walter Crocker's biography of Nehru, the first serious work to appear after the Prime Minister's death two years earlier.[5] It had a foreword by one of the pre-eminent historians of the first half of the twentieth century—Arnold Toynbee. Crocker had been Australia's high commissioner to India in two spells during the fifties and early sixties. His book is perhaps the best work by a foreigner on the Nehru era—sympathetic and insightful on the one hand and critical on the other. He tackled the Nehru–Krishna Menon relationship frontally:

It was Nehru's aloneness combined with his reluctance to be ruthless which gave Krishna Menon the special place he came to occupy from the middle of the fifties. Krishna Menon's position puzzled foreigners when it did not appall them, Indians were as mystified as Americans, and not less disapproving . . . Whether the dislike for Krishna Menon—no figure in Indian public life aroused so much dislike—was justified or not, it is a fair question to ask if for all his merits he had the equilibrium for the role Nehru allowed him . . . It is for psychologists to explain whether Krishna Menon might . . .have served the purpose of expressing Nehru's subconscious mind for him and thus of materializing or getting out of his system certain demonic currents in him.

Notes

1. Maxwell (1970).
2. Gopal (1972) demolishes Maxwell comprehensively and MacFarquhar (1997), Ranganathan and Khanna (2000), Garver (2005) and Raghavan (2006) counter Maxwell's thesis forcefully and persuasively.
3. Gopal (1989).
4. Ibid.
5. Crocker (1966)

18

Out of Congress and Parliament (1967)

Elections were to be held in early 1967, and Krishna Menon had clearly hoped to be renominated as a Congress candidate from the North Bombay constituency. In 1957, there had been no opposition whatsoever to his candidature. Five years later there had been opposition but since Nehru had stood firm Krishna Menon had contested again. But now there was no Nehru, and he was only an ex-minister, one who had had to quit in disgrace, as his opponents and much of the media saw it. For the 1967 elections Krishna Menon's old North Bombay seat had been reconfigured into two: Bombay North-East and Bombay North-West. He applied for the former, and after days of confabulations the Bombay Pradesh Congress Committee rejected his name formally on 5 November 1966. The decision was communicated to the national leadership. In his place, S.G. Barve, a retired ICS officer and then a member of the Planning Commission, was recommended.

The scene then shifted to Delhi. Leading the campaign to deny Krishna Menon the seat was the Bombay strongman S.K. Patil, minister of railways in Indira Gandhi's cabinet. He had been with Krishna Menon in 1957 and 1962. But now he was an implacable foe. On 26 November 1966, Krishna Menon met Indira Gandhi for over an hour, and the next day the *Times of India* reported:

INDIRA FAVOURS MENON FOR BOMBAY SEAT

The Prime Minister today expressed herself strongly in favour of renominating Mr. Krishna Menon from the North-East Bombay constituency for election to the Lok Sabha . . . She disclosed that she left the Congress Central Election Committee yesterday evening under the impression that the decision on this constituency would be postponed. She had made this suggestion at the meeting and also told Mr. Kamaraj [Congress president] about it. She could not stay there beyond 7.30 p.m. on account of another pressing engagement. Now that the Congress president has been entrusted with the decision, it was for him to take the decision. 'I myself had said that the decision should be left to Mr. Kamaraj'. Answering questions . . . the Prime Minister said, 'My own view is that there is no special reason why Mr. Menon should not be given this seat'.

So Indira Gandhi had come out publicly in his favour, even though the Bombay Congress had rejected Krishna Menon's name. It was now all up to Kamaraj. In 1957, he had considered Krishna Menon for a seat in rural Madras. The two were ideologically close. Earlier in the year, in June 1966, both had come out very strongly against Indira Gandhi's decision to devalue the Indian rupee under pressure from the World Bank and Western aid donors. There was no real reason why Kamaraj should have rejected Krishna Menon's name. The two met over the next few days, and finally around 15 December 1966 or so, Kamaraj told Krishna Menon that he could not contest from Bombay North-East because of strong local sentiment against him but that he could contest from some other constituency. Krishna Menon had made his Bombay North-East seat a prestige issue, and in view of what Kamaraj had decided, he wrote to the Congress president on 22 December 1966, severing his association of over three decades with the Congress. He not only quit the Congress but also announced that he would contest the Bombay North-East constituency as an independent candidate. After sending this letter to Kamaraj, he left for Bombay to attend the wedding of S.K. Patil's son.

Krishna Menon's 1962 election had drawn global attention. His 1967 election did not capture international headlines but did evoke a lot of interest nationally. His 1962 election had resulted in a scholarly book by a noted political scientist. His 1967 election would be no less of a watershed and would attract no less scholarly attention in the years to come. In 2010, a noted Princeton University historian[1] would write a book in which Krishna Menon's 1967 election was reckoned to be a turning point in the political transformation of India's financial capital.

In June 1966, Bal Thackeray had started the Shiv Sena in Bombay. That he enjoyed the patronage of the Congress bigwigs in the city cannot be denied because both had a common enemy—communist control over trade unions. But in addition, Thackeray had another target—south Indians who, he proclaimed, had already taken over Bombay, were still coming in droves and were denying locals employment. Krishna Menon's decision to contest from North-East Bombay was a great opportunity for Thackeray to flex his muscle and let his growing cadres loose. Krishna Menon was a double bonanza for this cartoonist-turned-rabble rouser. He was a communist in all but name, or so it was widely believed, and of course he was a south Indian—as dark and wily as the stereotype went. Shiv Sena brigades and communist cadres supporting Krishna Menon clashed frequently.

Barve won but Krishna Menon was by no means humiliated. The Congress and the Shiv Sena worked assiduously to ensure his defeat. But he had certainly given the Congress a scare, losing by some 13,000 votes. Within a few months, however, Barve died suddenly and a by-election was announced. This time the Congress put up Barve's sister, Tarabai Sapre, who had few political credentials, unlike her brother who had been a minister in the state. Krishna Menon again decided to contest as an independent. The by-election saw a repeat of the earlier campaign, with the communists and the Shiv Sena at each other's throats. And this time too Krishna Menon lost, and to make matters worse the margin of defeat had increased to 15,000 votes. 25 April 1967 looked like the end of the political road for him. He had been an MP for fourteen years running, and now he had been defeated twice in a space of two months, the second time by a political novice.

Within five days of his defeat, however, he wrote to the chief minister of Madras, C.N. Annadurai, whose party, the DMK, had just then swept into power:

> I am now writing to ask your advice and support in regard to offering myself as a candidate in the impending by-election in South Madras. I would not consider this much less entertain it, without your full and prior support. I feel that you would consider that my return to Parliament would in a small measure be of service to the country and to Madras. I have publicly declared my support of your government and always have had the enthusiastic and active assistance of the DMK supporters in Bombay.
>
> With your support and endorsement I can win in South Madras. I will do my best to be of service to the Madras state and to further its interests at the Centre. I am as you know, totally and strongly opposed to the Congress and its government as it is today. If there is to be a Congress candidate in South Madras whoever it is I would have no reservations in opposing him fully and vigourously.

Madras South was a seat won by Annadurai himself since he had contested the parliamentary elections. But with him becoming chief minister, a by-election had been necessitated. Krishna Menon had made his case to the person who mattered, but in the end the DMK put up the nephew of one of Annadurai's closest lieutenants as its candidate and won. The lieutenant was M. Karunanidhi, and his nephew was Murasoli Maran. Krishna Menon never stood a chance.

His immediate worry now was to find a roof over his head since he would have to vacate his sprawling official bungalow. He had decided to re-enter the legal profession on a full-time basis to keep himself intellectually busy. But what would he do about the house? He met Indira Gandhi about the house and for other mundane things like getting a passport since for years he had been travelling on a diplomatic one. As luck would have it, in May 1967, the Prime

Minister had appointed as her chief aide a man who was an ardent admirer of Krishna Menon since the mid-1930s. This man would very soon become Indira Gandhi's ideological compass. P.N. Haksar would help Krishna Menon make a relatively smooth transition to the life of a former MP. Most importantly, he found a way of allowing Krishna Menon to retain his house within the extant rules as this exchange between him and Indira Gandhi reveal:[2]

Krishna Menon came to see me.

He is going abroad, first to Cairo for an Afro-Asian Solidarity Conference; next to Stockholm for the Peace Council; then to Tanganyika for a Conference on Apartheid. He says that U Thant [UN secretary general] is very anxious that he should attend this Conference.

This is the first time since Independence he is going abroad as a private citizen. Knowing him you will understand his feelings. He wants help with regard to passport and other formalities and would like our ambassadors informed.

What is the position with regard to his house? He is under the impression that ex-Ambassadors are allowed special consideration . . . Krishna Menon says he is an ex-Ambassador and an Editor.

I think it would be a good thing if you see him and sort out the matter with him.

Indira Gandhi
22.6.67

Secretary

Haksar met Krishna Menon and briefed the Prime Minister exactly a week later:

I saw Shri V.K. Krishna Menon at 8.15 A.M. today. I shall look after him as far as his passport and other formalities are concerned.

As regards the housing problem, this, I am afraid, is a little difficult. Ex-Ambassadors have no special privileges in the matter of housing unless they are Members of Parliament. Editors also do not enjoy any facility. There is a special pool for journalists, but I am sure, Shri Krishna Menon would not like to avail himself of the kind of accommodation which is offered under this pool arrangement.

I understand papers regarding Shri Krishna Menon's housing problem are being personally dealt with by the Minister . . . As far as I can see, the only way in which he can retain his house is to pay commercial rent, which, I believe, will be something like Rs 1300/- per month.

P.M. need not trouble herself about these matters. I am only stating the facts for her information.

P.N. Haksar
29.6.1967

P.M.

Krishna Menon had a curious living arrangement at 19 Teen Murti Marg that had been his official residence since 1956. It became the subject of considerable gossip for years. His private secretary during 1956–62 was Romesh Bhandari, a flamboyant foreign service officer who had known Krishna Menon since the late 1940s. Bhandari, his wife, who belonged to the princely family of Patiala, and their three children all lived with Krishna Menon, and this was to continue till the latter's death. Krishna Menon was attached to the Bhandari children, and there a number of 'Dear Uncle' letters to him from them over the years. The 'Uncle' took great interest in their education. Krishna Menon couldn't have been unaware that such an arrangement would set tongues wagging, because carefully preserved in his archive is an anonymous letter typed sometime in 1973 which made all sorts of insinuations. Be that as it may, I spoke to the eighty-nine-year-old Mrs. Bhandari about her recollections, and her response was: 'Krishna

Menon was [a] much maligned and misunderstood man and I didn't have anything to do with his official life.' Till his death in 2012, Romesh Bhandari, who became foreign secretary in October 1984, spoke and wrote of Krishna Menon in glowing terms, and the study in his farmhouse near New Delhi airport is studded with some wonderful photographs of Krishna Menon.

Marie Seton had first met Krishna Menon in the mid-1930s in London. They went their separate ways thereafter, with Seton writing acclaimed biographies of the Russian film-maker Sergei Eisenstein and the American singer–activist Paul Robeson. She came to India sometime in 1955 at Nehru's invitation to promote the film society movement. She reconnected with Krishna Menon and, in 1958, started researching a book on him. It would have been the very first on him and had generated much interest, including an offer from Dennis Dobson, a leading publisher, who would write to her on 22 July 1958:

> I am most interested in your idea of a book on Krishna Menon which would indeed fit in admirably with our general publishing policy and would form an excellent successor to your Robeson book . . .
>
> The material you have so far collected . . . sounds most exciting and extremely valuable. I am sure . . . what will emerge will be something far more important than just a biography—the story of the rebirth of a great Asian nation, with the personal story one of its creators interweaved into it . . .

She had done extensive homework but reportedly, he threatened to take legal action if she went ahead with her biography of him. She got to know Nehru and Indira Gandhi particularly well. In 1967, her biography of Nehru was published[3] and very large parts of it are actually on Krishna Menon, based on the material she had already collected and the conversations she had had with him over the years. That apart, her book on Nehru shed new light on certain events, such as how much Krishna Menon regretted not having stopped Nehru from embarking on his trip to Colombo on 12 October 1962 when the Indian and Chinese troops were already locked in combat. She also provided a very poignant account of Krishna Menon on the evening when Nehru's last rites were being conducted, where he was the very last person to heave a log into the blaze of the funeral pyre. Contrary to the threat he had made a decade earlier, this time around, when Seton's book on Nehru appeared, Krishna Menon kept quiet. She would continue to be among his greatest champions. In later years she would write a noted biography of Satyajit Ray, and a year before her death in 1985 she would be conferred with the Padma Bhushan award.

On 20 November 1967, the *Statesman* had a special survey of the five years since the Chinese invasion. Three military officers reminisced—Lt General S.P.P. Thorat, General P.N. Thapar and Rear Admiral D. Shankar. But the main scoop for the daily was 'Look Back Without Anger' by 'V.K. Krishna Menon as told to Inder Malhotra'. The daily commented that 'Mr. Menon in his article shows a reticence that does him credit'. After his Bombay speech of 9 December 1962, this was the first time Krishna Menon was saying something on the war with China that had destroyed him politically:

> . . . The Chinese invasion was the first external manifestation of the extraordinary phenomenon we witness in China today; the vanguard movement or Cultural Revolution or whatever it is called first descended upon us . . . I know some people have said that what had come to be known as India's forward policy, the policy of establishing forward posts, was at least partly responsible for converting the situation from one of confrontation to that of armed conflict. I think that this is an entirely wrong view. We never followed any forward policy. A forward policy means our trying to get into someone else's territory, like Lord Curzon tried to do . . . It was China which was following a forward policy in our territory . . . The Chinese had been pushing on their claims forward and forward in the years '54, '55 and '56. We were all the time . . . trying not to look upon it as a major conflict but as something that we could resolve ultimately. From 1958–59 onwards we tried to

do our best to assert ourselves in these areas. And our posts did have the effect of getting back 3000 to 4000 sq. miles out of the 12,000 or 14,000 square miles occupied by China in the Western Region. In the general hullabaloo, this fact is sometimes forgotten.

He then explained why he had remained silent and not defended himself from the vicious attacks that had been mounted on him in 1962 and thereafter:

I cannot say anything about this period without reflecting on my colleagues, without affecting the unity of the country, without aiding the Chinese and without giving out information that may aid them. These reasons still continue . . . I might add that I regard loyalty towards my colleagues, loyalty to certain values of life and proprieties as more important than getting out of any personal embarrassment.

He refuted the allegation that Nehru and he had interfered with operational decisions of the army and put forward, for the first time, the view that what happened in 1962 should not be called a debacle: '[M]ore powerful countries than India have suffered military reverses . . . What really went wrong was the demoralization that set in at the time; that is the type of demoralization the enemy plays upon.' Lessons had been learnt but to him, the most pernicious fallout of 1962 was the growing and dangerous dependence—military and economic—on the West. Indeed, this was the running theme in his election campaign—how the party to which he had once belonged had embraced devaluation, given up non-alignment and opened the floodgates to foreign capital and technology. He would continue to be unapologetic on these themes till his demise.

In 1967, B.M. Kaul would be the first army officer to come out with a memoirs on the 1962 war with China.[4] That was seen universally as an exercise in whitewashing his own culpability for the humiliation that India suffered in NEFA. He had wanted to write his account for quite some time and had informed Nehru about his plans to do so. On 28 September 1963, Nehru had replied:

. . . I have just received your letter of the 26th September. I quite understand your feelings in the matter and I agree with you that at a suitable opportunity you should clear up the misunderstandings that might exist about you. You must realize that at the present moment the attack is not much on you, but much more so on V.K. Krishna Menon and to some extent on me. It is after all I that come in the way of many people's wishes and ambitions. You and Krishna Menon are utilized to attack me . . . When the suitable time comes you can put up some facts as you think necessary before the public . . .

Notes

1. Prakash (2010).
2. Ramesh (2018).
3. Seton (1967).
4. Kaul (1967).

19

Advocate, MP, Peace Crusader (1968–73)

Krishna Menon resumed his legal career and regularly appeared mainly in the Supreme Court and less frequently in different high courts. But electoral politics always beckoned, and there would be one more attempt to get back to Parliament. In March 1968, while the CPM was willing to sponsor his name for the Rajya Sabha from Kerala, its allies in the ruling coalition were unwilling. That effort too having come a cropper, Krishna Menon took on more cases and also became active on the peace circuit internationally through the World Peace Council (WPC), which had been set up by the Soviet Union in 1950 but attracted a large number of progressive writers, scientists and cultural personalities across the world.

Based out of Helsinki, its first president was Frederic Joliot-Curie, the French Nobel laureate in physics. Its moving spirit was Ramesh Chandra, who had been a contemporary of Mohan Kumaramangalam and Rajni Patel in Cambridge in the late 1930s. The trio had been in thrall of Krishna Menon. The causes he crusaded for in the final five years of his life were many, prominent among them being Vietnam, Palestine, nuclear disarmament and an end to apartheid. In 1968, the Syrian government conferred on him its Distinguished Order of Merit for his steadfast support to Arab causes. In 1969, Krishna Menon would be awarded the Joliot-Curie medal of the WPC and thereafter would be a visible presence at the WPC assemblies in Vancouver in

1970, Helsinki and Santiago in 1972, and Warsaw and Moscow in 1973. He would also write regularly for the weekly *Century* that he had launched in 1963, and off and on for another weekly *Mainstream*, which was very much part of the left movement in India.

In early 1968, Brecher's book on Krishna Menon was published. It was and continues to be a unique book. It was based on three weeks of conversation between the two in New Delhi in November–December 1964 and another two weeks in May 1965. The entire conversation was tape-recorded, and Krishna Menon edited the transcript in early 1966. The dialogue between Krishna Menon and Brecher covered an extraordinary range of topics: non-alignment, the Commonwealth, Indo-China, Bandung, Suez, Hungary, Congo, the UN, Goa, China, Pakistan, Kashmir, Ceylon, economic development, Nehru, Shastri and a host of other issues relating to Indian foreign policy and world politics. Brecher had recorded Krishna Menon for some seventeen hours and produced an astonishing book which has not been rivalled since. Not surprisingly the longest section in the book was the conversation on China, and Krishna Menon's recollections covering the period 1949–62 provide an invaluable reference point. He debunked much of what he termed 'propaganda' on the performance of the Indian Army, and his ambivalence on Chou En-lai who so fascinated Henry Kissinger later was clear:[1]

> I cannot make up my mind on Chou En-lai, because the Chou En-lai that I had known was a decent kind of person. I suppose to him it was his country, right or wrong. It is very difficult for me to believe that a man who appeared to be sensitive to argument would be Prime Minister of a country that invaded India. His way of talking about India was not really a party-political one; he did not even subscribe to the views of his colleagues.

For his part, till 1962, there is evidence that Chou En-lai would speak to Indian diplomats of 'my good friend Krishna Menon'. Krishna Menon was pleased with the response that the book received and preserved in his archive is a review of the book that appeared in the *American Political Science Review* in December 1969:

. . . To see how a man of the stature of Menon views his environment, and of even greater consequence, how he arrived at and explains his position on various issues, is fascinating. Once begun, I found the book impossible to put down. This is clearly the principal contribution of the study—an indispensable insight into the mind of a major world leader.

No student of world history of the 1950s can afford not to read Brecher's book. There was only one topic that Krishna Menon did not speak much about and that was Nehru. He refused to 'think aloud' on his long friendship with Nehru. When Brecher persisted, Krishna Menon replied:

It is not because of humility or of an inferiority complex that I avoid the subject. The whole question is too large for me to understand it. As for speaking about nuances of a relationship of a personal nature—since you referred to an obligation to posterity—I would reply that in my mind it could not rise above my own ideas of loyalty in personal relations. I don't discuss these matters with anybody. You may say the world is poorer for my silence; I cannot help it. I think I should keep quiet . . . I think the wisest thing for me to do is keep my mouth shut. That is how I feel . . . I don't think that Panditji's affection for me or my relationship with Panditji affected him in the way you imply. I was neither a buffoon or a Rasputin . . . I don't believe in what is called autobiography; that is what it really comes to. Autobiographies tend to portray the world in a distorted way; you think you made everything because that is all you know!

Soon after Kaul's self-defence of 1967, another book appeared, by an army officer who had fought in the war and been imprisoned by the Chinese.[2] John P. Dalvi's account would debunk Kaul's and also help cement Krishna Menon's notoriety as the main culprit of the military debacle six years earlier. Dalvi was in no doubt that the political decisions had caused the reverses. In 1970, the man who had been the powerful chief of Indian intelligence in the fifties and early sixties, B.N. Mullik, would publish his version[3] of the *The Chinese Betrayal*, in which he would take a different view and absolve Nehru and Krishna Menon of much of the blame. But whether it was Dalvi or Kaul or Mullik, whether it was condemnation of his role or his guilt being absolved, Krishna Menon maintained a studious silence. He had nothing to say when these books appeared.

On 17 May 1968, Krishna Menon was in London to see an idea he had mooted twenty years earlier come to fruition. On that day, the British Prime Minister, Harold Wilson, unveiled a statue of Mahatma Gandhi in Tavistock Square Gardens. Krishna Menon used the occasion to reminisce about someone who had always baffled him:

I have never claimed to be a Gandhian. But there are many in the world while the Mahatma lived—including individuals here—who though not accepting themselves as Gandhians, nevertheless aided the Gandhian ideology, if I may call it such. For some Gandhi was a Mahatma, or saint. He was certainly profoundly influenced by religion. A Hindu, he drew upon the religion of others and respected all . . .

Our history in India indicates that the ideas and ideals that motivated Gandhiji . . . had an ancient lineage. The idea of the renunciation of violent means went back to early times . . . Gandhi offered passive resistance as the method for achieving legitimate ends. His heir, Jawaharlal Nehru, offered the idea that all conflicts could be solved by wise negotiation. This dual political and moral creed offer the alternative to violence . . .

. . . An old British friend of mine—in no way a Gandhian nor a practicing Christian—has told me of the impact made when Gandhi arrived in London for the Round Table Conference. He evoked an unusual thought: My friend said that his arrival here brought thoughts of moral obligation to independent judgment just as at the time Jesus Christ is said to have entered Jerusalem there was moral obligation to try to judge him as a man . . . I think this reaction explains why the Mahatma caused many Britishers to think seriously about India and in a new way . . . I think that in a very positive way Mahatma Gandhi was the liberator of both my people and yours, Mr. Prime Minister.

A year later, in May 1969, Krishna Menon stood as an independent candidate for a by-election in the Midnapur constituency of West Bengal. He was supported in this yet another attempt to get into Parliament by one of his friends from the London days of the mid-1930s. Jyoti Basu was then deputy chief minister of West Bengal, and with the support of the communist and other socialist parties in the state, Krishna Menon won by a comfortable majority. On the same day that he was declared elected—13 May 1969—his old adversary S.K. Patil was also declared elected, having won handsomely in the by-election in Banaskantha in Gujarat. On 16 May 1962, two grand receptions were held in New Delhi to welcome these two stalwarts back to Parliament. One—in honour of Patil—was organized by the Congress party and attended by Indira Gandhi and her entire cabinet. The other—in honour of Krishna Menon—was organized by all the leftist parties. At his function, Krishna Menon demonstrated that two years out of Parliament had not dulled his pungent wit. He was asked by pressmen what he thought of India's future and answered: 'How could anybody say anything about a country which could elect him and Mr. Patil with such big majorities at the same time?' When asked for his reaction to Patil's comeback, Krishna Menon replied:

Mr. Patil is a friend of mine. But politically we are far apart. If I had a vote in Banaskantha I would cast my vote against him. And if he had a vote in Midnapore he would cast his vote against me. But whatever his opinions are, it is all right when he gets into Parliament with the votes of the people. I have nothing personal against him.

The victories of Krishna Menon and Patil were seen as 'symbols of the Right–Left confrontation building up at the Centre with the Prime Minister and her associates adhering to the middle position'. Patil would pass away in 1981, and his memoirs,[4] with a section on Krishna Menon, would appear a decade later. He had written:

In his heyday he [Krishna Menon] was an extraordinary political
figure, though highly controversial. Despite our political differences
he once dropped in on me to inquire about my health. That
naturally moved me. Soon after, he died.

Krishna Menon had redeemed his honour. He had taken on the
Congress which, he felt, had abandoned the path of socialism, and come
out victorious. Ironically, over the next few months, Indira Gandhi,
egged on by P.N. Haksar and a few others, moved the Congress exactly
in the direction that Krishna Menon had advocated. But there was no
place for him in this new Congress. Both Indira Gandhi and Haksar
would always find time for him and would treat him with great respect.
But politically, they kept him at a distance. He would spend more time
travelling abroad and in the Supreme Court than in politics.

Two cases that he appeared in were to be significant—in one he
would be a major figure, and in the other, he would be part of the
supporting cast.

On 9 November 1967, during the course of a press conference
in Trivandrum, the chief minister of Kerala, E.M.S. Namboodiripad,
had said:

. . . Marx and Engels considered the judiciary as instruments of
oppression . . . and even today . . . judges are guided and dominated
by class hatred, class interests and class prejudices, and where the
evidence is between a well-dressed pot-bellied rich man and a poor
ill-dressed and illiterate person, the judge instinctively favours the
former.

Not surprisingly, on 9 February 1968, the Kerala High Court in a
2:1 judgment had held Namboodiripad in contempt of court and
imposed a fine of Rs 1000, failing which he would have to undergo
simple imprisonment of one month. Namboodiripad appealed to
the Supreme Court against the high court judgment and Krishna
Menon argued his case. On 31 July 1970, the Supreme Court
dismissed Namboodiripad's appeal. The ten-page judgment handed
down by the chief justice, M. Hidayatullah, was what made the case

somewhat out of the ordinary. The judgment went in detail into political thought and theory because Krishna Menon had raised these arguments. He first argued that the

> freedom of speech and expression gave immunity to the appellant [Namboodiripad] as all he did was to give expression to the teachings of Marx, Engels and Lenin.

He then argued that

> the appellant has maintained that his philosophy is based upon that of Marx and Engels. Indeed he claims to be descended from the last philosopher and seeks to educate the exploited peoples on the reality behind class oppression. As a Marxist–Leninist he advocates the revolutionary transformation of the State from the coercive instrument of the exploiting classes to an instrument in which the exploited majority can use against these classes. In this transformation, he wishes to make the state wither away and with the state its organs, namely the Legislature, the Executive and the Judiciary also to change. He has justified the press conference as an exposition of his ideology and claims protection under the first clause of Article 19(1) [of the Constitution] which guarantees freedom of speech and expression.

Hidayatullah's judgment began by observing:

> The appellant is only partly right. He and his counsel may be said to have distorted the approach of Marx, Engels and Lenin, and we proceed to explain how . . .

The chief justice, a learned man in his own right, then reviewed at great length all the iconic works of the communist ideology and concluded:

> . . . Indeed in no writing which we have seen or which has been brought to our notice, Marx or Engels has said what the appellant

quotes them as saying. We have summarized into a very small compass, many thousands of words in which these doctrines have been debated from Plekhanov to Lenin, through the thoughts of Kautsky, Kerensky, Lasalle, Belinsky and others who attempted a middle line between the revisionism of Bernstein and the Bolshevik views of Lenin. We have done so because Mr. V.K. Krishna Menon sneered that many people learn about communism through Middleton Murray! . . .

Mr. V.K. Krishna Menon tried to support the action of the appellant by saying that judges are products of their environment and reflect the influences upon them of the society in which they move. He contended that these subtle influences enter into decision making and drew our attention to the writings of Prof. Laski, Justice Cordozo, Holmes and others where the subtle influences of one's upbringing are described . . . But judges do not consciously take a view against the conscience or their oaths. What the appellant wishes to say is that they do . . .

Mr. V.K. Krishna Menon exhorted us to give consideration to the purpose for which the statement was made, the position of the appellant as the head of a state, his sacrifices, his background and his integrity. On the other hand, we cannot ignore the occasion (a press conference), the belief of the people in his word as a Chief Minister and the ready ear which many in his party and outside would give to him . . . Whether he misunderstood the teachings of Marx and Engels or deliberately distorted them is not to much purpose. The likely effect of his words must be seen and they have clearly the effect of lowering the prestige of judges and courts in the eyes of the people.

Krishna Menon lost his case and Namboodiripad had to pay a token fine. His junior N.M. Ghatate recalled to me that when the court adjourned, Hidayatullah remarked to Krishna Menon with a smile on his face that he forced him to read much communist literature that he had never imagined he ever would. The jurist would later write about this case and an earlier encounter in the 1930s with Krishna Menon in his autobiography.[5]

Krishna Menon also appeared on behalf of the Kerala government in the famous bank nationalization case that featured some of the top legal names in the country. Banks had been nationalized by an executive order in July 1969 that later became law. But the legislation had been challenged in the Supreme Court. Seven months later that challenge would be upheld, and Indira Gandhi would be forced to come up with a new law. This would be a case in which Krishna Menon would be joined by one of his acolytes of the 1930s—Mohan Kumaramangalam—who appeared for the state of Tamil Nadu. Both strongly supported the government's stance. Krishna Menon had considered bank nationalization to be an article of faith since the mid-fifties, unlike Indira Gandhi, who got converted in a matter of a few days when faced with a political crisis in early July 1969.[6]

Later in the year, his old friend Mountbatten invited him to deliver the third Nehru Memorial Lecture in London. This was a biannual lecture series started by the ex-viceroy. The first speaker in 1966 had been R.A. Butler, a Tory grandee who came from a family of well-known India hands. In 1968, Mountbatten himself had delivered the lecture in which he reminisced about the events of 1947. When Krishna Menon's turn came on 12 November 1970, he used the opportunity to open up about his association with Nehru but confined his lecture called 'Personal Memories of Jawaharlal Nehru' almost entirely to the pre-1947 period. His parting shot was:

> . . . And I end this by saying that I have taken very good care not to say anything about the post-Nehru period—that is current history—because then you would say I was controversial.

In late December 1970, Indira Gandhi announced that elections to the Lok Sabha were being advanced by a year and would be held in early March 1971. Krishna Menon found it difficult to get his Midnapore seat back again for a second time. So he fished around for a seat in Kerala and announced in early January 1971 that his preference would be for Tellicherry and Palghat, in that order. But he wanted both the CPM and CPI to support him, which proved impossible. Finally, on 13 January 1971, his candidature for the

Trivandrum seat as an independent supported by the CPM was announced. Opposing him would be a candidate belonging to the PSP, who was supported by the CPI as well as by Indira Gandhi's Congress. What a comedown for the man from the pedestal he had placed himself on a decade earlier, when his sister Janaki Amma had told him to stand from the Malabar region where the family had extensive properties and on the assurance that she would ensure his victory. Krishna Menon had retorted that India was a new nation and parochialism and regionalism shouldn't be encouraged. Yet, now in the twilight of his political innings—and indeed of his life—he had returned home to contest an election.

He issued a long appeal to the voters in English which, of course, was translated into Malayalam, but his campaign, as always, was conducted in impeccable English. With support from the communists assured, he won by about 24,000 votes in March 1971. All through his life he had strenuously denied that he was a communist or even a 'fellow traveller'. Yet, without the support of the CPM he could not have even contested, let alone won in 1969 and 1971. Krishna Menon may not have been a communist but the fact remains that communists were for Krishna Menon. It was even more ironic that the very people who had been dismissed from power in 1959 in some measure because of Krishna Menon had now ensured his victory. Indira Gandhi swept the polls with a stupendous majority, which Krishna Menon called 'nothing short of a political avalanche'. He congratulated his old friend for her personal triumph but could not resist saying, 'I have survived the avalanche.'

The new Parliament reconvened in the backdrop of the Pakistani army's brutal crackdown in East Pakistan and a burgeoning refugee crisis in large parts of eastern India. There were calls for military intervention by India. Krishna Menon did not support these calls, but on 27 March 1971 and also four days later, he called for India's recognition of a sovereign, independent Bangladesh, which had been declared in mid-April 1971. Indira Gandhi and Haksar would listen to him, but they had a strategy and game plan of their own which they executed flawlessly.[7] The diplomatic recognition of Bangladesh that Krishna Menon had kept demanding for over five months finally happened in mid–December 1971.

C. Rajagopalachari was turning ninety-three on 10 December 1971. A large number of his friends and admirers in India and abroad collaborated to present him a Festschrift on the occasion. Most of those who contributed to the volume had been critics of some sort or the other of Nehru and his policies. The President of India, V.V. Giri, T.T. Krishnamachari and Mountbatten were three exceptions. Krishna Menon was a fourth, and his recollections of Rajaji were sandwiched between two inveterate Krishna Menon-baiters—B. Shiva Rao and H.V. Kamath. Krishna Menon reminisced:

> . . . The first time I met Mr. C. Rajagopalachari was in 1920 or 1921, quite casually at Mount Road, Madras, outside the Indian Boy Scout Headquarters which was one of the places I functioned . . . My own association with Rajaji, such as it was, was confined to admiration and regard from a distance and an abiding affection and regard which neither the passage of years, nor the vicissitudes of public life, his or mine, have changed . . . At the meeting of the Congress at Hyderabad in the mid–fifties, Rajaji who met me there took upon himself to tell me that I should go into Parliament and be of use to the national field. He said he intended to speak to Panditji about it. I presume he did. I soon found myself in the Rajya Sabha almost entirely of his initiative which had the approval of Panditji . . .

In October 1962, Rajaji had been the first to call for Krishna Menon's resignation. But that very Rajaji had, five years earlier than that, on 25 February 1957, issued a statement on the eve of Krishna Menon's first election in North Bombay:

> Not even Mr. Jawaharlal Nehru's return at the elections certain as it is—is so important as Mr. Krishna Menon's victory in the Bombay elections. After his brave and single-handed fight in the [Security] Council of the United States, united in their hostility to India, if he should by any chance or mishap fail to be returned in Bombay, what would be left of the prestige of India before the world?

While he remained single all his life, Krishna Menon had almost married Barbara Macnamara in 1935. Thereafter, he had had some emotional entanglements, some short-lived and some that had lasted longer. He and Betty-Shields Collins were a pair briefly in 1936 and 1937. Then came his intriguing relationship with Kamala Jaspal, from 1948 till mid-1952. After that, for at least three years, he appears to have been seriously involved with Janet Salamanca, a member of the UN staff. There are well over a 150 letters from her to him during 1953, 1954 and 1955 that survive in his archives and that leave no doubt about their feelings for each other. Subsequently, for a brief while, according to Marie Seton's own admission, she and Krishna Menon, who had been friends for almost a quarter of century, discovered passionate avenues for their friendship. Then came the curious living arrangement with the Bhandari family. But all through, from 1938 onwards, Anna Pollak remained an important presence in his life. His very last letter to her that has survived is dated 26 May 1972 from Brussels:

> A few days ago I received from you a notification about your change of address. It was really kind of you to have remembered and to have sent it.
>
> It is a long time—1939. I was younger, younger! For years you helped me in many ways. It is friendship that lives, whether one meets or not. Writing has become painful to me. I am glad you remain youthful, hopeful and lovely and have made both name and fame. I shall be in London on the 30th or 31st. If you are likely to come to town on the 31st it will be a real pleasure to see you. In case you can't at least telephone. I hope you will come and stay to dinner. As one grows older there is always the feeling that what one does not do one may not have some other time for it!

Pollak would be present at the memorial meeting for Krishna Menon in London on 31 October 1974.

At the stroke of the midnight hour on 15 August 1972, there was a special ceremony in Parliament to celebrate the silver jubilee of India's Independence. Thereafter at the historic Red Fort, over a thousand freedom fighters were specially honoured. One of them was Krishna Menon. For years the charge against him had been that he was not a true freedom fighter since he had never spent time in an Indian jail. But this award washed way that criticism and recognized his contributions to making India free.

As 1972 was drawing to a close, the US and North Vietnam began peace negotiations in Paris. This is what Krishna Menon had been advocating for years. Between 1967 and 1972 especially, he had become a familiar figure in conferences in different parts of the world, calling for an end to the Indo-China war. He had taken a keen interest, despite his declining health, because of the special role he had played in Geneva in 1954 in crafting the peace agreement that had held for almost a decade. He had been a great admirer of Ho Chi Minh and had invited him to India in February 1958, long before Ho had become a global figure.

Krishna Menon paid handsome tributes to Ho on his death on 2 September 1969 saying all that Ho had wanted was that 'the Americans vacate his country'. But Krishna Menon's participation at these conclaves had their downsides as well, as would be noted by Mohit Sen, one of his ardent admirers and a communist intellectual, with reference to a gathering in Paris:[8]

> Krishna Menon was a shadow of his past self—from being a world figure he had come down to the level of a delegate somewhat dependent on the organisers to get an opportunity to let other delegates know he was there. His day had passed and lesser mortals were now important. Some of these persons were obnoxious in brushing him aside. I am reminded of the lines of Shakespeare: 'simians dressed in robes of brief authority'. He should not have come. One of the greats of modern India diminished himself.

Towards the end of 1973, Stephen Xydis, an authority on Cyprus, published his book on that subject, in which Krishna Menon's role at the UN in the 1950s was highlighted.[9] Krishna Menon had achieved quite a feat by his many speeches on Cyprus in New York:

he managed to antagonize all the three parties concerned—the UK, Greece and Turkey. But his position was consistent right from 24 September 1954 when he had first declared that 'Cyprus really was a question of the freedom and independence of the Cypriot people'. He saw Cyprus as a colonial relic and comprising not Greeks and Turks but Cypriots who demanded and deserved political freedom. Mindful of Kashmir perhaps, as he was during the Hungarian crisis in 1956, he never was enamoured by the idea of 'self-determination' being advocated by Greece and Greek Cypriot leaders, most notably Archbishop Makarios, after whom a road would be named in New Delhi years later.

Notes

1. Brecher (1968).
2. Dalvi (1968).
3. Mullik (1971).
4. Patil (1991).
5. Hidayatullah (1980).
6. Ramesh (2018).
7. Ramesh (2018) and Raghavan (2010).
8. Sen (2003).
9. Xydis (1973).

20

The Final Year (1974)

This would be Krishna Menon's last year. He had been in indifferent health for quite some time but had kept himself busy on the lecture circuit for the past few years. Invitations to speak would come from different organizations in India, of course, but he continued to command interest in the US and the UK as well. Every now and then the India League would organize cultural programmes in London to raise funds for its various activities, and Krishna Menon, as its honorary president, would make it a point to be present. The India League had, after India's Independence, taken on a completely new mandate:

> To promote the well-being of independent India and friendly cooperation between the British and Indian peoples and to support that claim on subject peoples to independence.

It had been kept going for years by Bridget Tunnard, a faithful acolyte of Krishna Menon, till her demise in 1971. On 9 March 1974, he attended his very last function, and appropriately enough it was in London. It was a lunch for the 'nightingale of India', Lata Mangeshkar, who was quite a fan of his. She was to sing at Royal Albert Hall on 11, 12 and 14 March 1974 for an India League fundraiser. For a while now, Krishna Menon had been working on establishing a memorial centre in Nehru's name in London for 'contemporary studies of Indian affairs, arts and music' and the famed singer was helping him out. But that very evening Krishna Menon took ill and had to be hospitalized. He returned to India after a week, and thereafter, it was a journey between his residence and the G.B. Pant Memorial Hospital in New Delhi. It was evident that his days had become numbered, for Krishna Menon drew up a will on 26 April 1974. His extensive properties were under litigation. He bequeathed whatever share would accrue to him at the end of the litigation to Janaki Amma's two daughters.

On 5 May 1974, when he was still in hospital, a large number of his friends and admirers gathered to felicitate him on his seventy-eighth birthday. Indira Gandhi sent a message as did a number of others, including Henry Cabot Lodge. Two senior ministers of Indira Gandhi's cabinet—Defence Minister Jagjivan Ram and Minister of External Affairs Swaran Singh—were present and spoke of his contributions to India's self-reliance in the production of defence equipment. Justice Krishna Iyer, then a judge of the Supreme Court, described him as a 'Promethean personality', a 'patriotic pugilist' and a 'human projectile'.

Thirteen days later India carried out its first nuclear test, euphemistically called 'peaceful nuclear explosion'. Soon thereafter, while still in hospital, Krishna Menon sent for Indira Gandhi and reportedly gave her more than a bit of his mind. Krishna Menon was an indefatigable crusader for nuclear disarmament, and one of the most influential voices for it right through the 1950s. Between 1954 and 1962, he had made thirteen major speeches on disarmament at the UN, the last one being less than four months before he resigned. Each of these speeches is considered a landmark, and the one delivered on 2 November 1959 particularly so, in which he ended with a quotation from the *Rubaiyat* of Omar Khayyam:

We must recognize that, as the poet said:

The moving finger writes, and having writ
Moves on: nor all thy Piety nor Wit
Shall lure it back to cancel half a Line
Nor all thy tears wash out a word of it.

Even after China went nuclear in October 1964, Krishna Menon did not change his view—that 'a nuclear bomb is not a weapon of offence or defence; it is a weapon of mass extermination'. He insisted till the very end that the argument against nuclear weapons was not a moral or a political one but 'a common sense view'. India would be accused of using the nuclear reactor set up by Canada in the 1950s for conducting its nuclear test. Eight years earlier this conversation had taken place between him and Brecher:

> Krishna Menon: . . . Once you make the atom bomb you are no longer a non-aligned country. I am not now going into the question of whether India can make it; it is purely a theoretical calculation. What are they going to make it with, the Canadian reactor?
>
> Brecher: According to the agreement between India and Canada they have no right to use the reactor for that purpose.
>
> Krishna Menon: Exactly. And I hope that Canada will stick to it. In that case where will they make it from? The very fact that Dr. Bhabha has made some speeches, which in my view were improper, shows that he has no practical political sense . . .

Immediately following the nuclear test, Canada suspended all cooperation on nuclear matters with India. Krishna Menon may well have applauded that move, so incensed was he with what Indira Gandhi had done on 18 May 1974, in which his one-time protégé P.N. Haksar had played a crucial role.

As Krishna Menon was moving back and forth between his home and hospital, the first of his colleagues published his memoirs. Morarji Desai, who had tangled with him for four years as finance minister, had a whole none-too-flattering chapter on Krishna Menon in his autobiography.[1] There is no doubt that Desai had a difficult task between 1958 and 1962 in managing the country's finances with foreign exchange, especially scarce. On 4 August 1958, he had written to Krishna Menon:

> . . . I got an impression during the last few weeks that you are annoyed with me and therefore I was glad to know the cause of it . . . As you know better than myself the work that is now

assigned to me is full of difficulties. We are passing through a crisis which was inevitable in our circumstances and which we must pass through successfully. Please do not think I want to overlord. I should like to help all Ministries to do their difficult work as smoothly as possible. As the financial position is tight it falls to my lot to see that the available resources are distributed and used among the various Ministries to our best advantage . . .

Fine words without question but the reality was that perhaps the biggest casualty of Desai's conservatism was defence spending. Two factors exacerbated the problem for the armed forces: the lukewarm, if not hostile, chemistry between Desai and Krishna Menon, and the finance minister's own instincts, which were even more pacifist than that of the defence minister. All this changed after the 1962 war when Desai would clear the proposals that he was loath to do before the war with China. In early 1963, when defence officials told Desai that they were planning to build a new factory for manufacturing self-loading rifles, he said, 'Build two.' When told that it would cost Rs 12 crore, his reply was, 'What is money where national security is concerned?' One of the officials left Desai's office wondering whether 'Shri Desai remembered turning down firmly a proposal for Rs 48 lakhs a scant two years earlier'.[2] Desai's obduracy had impacted the availability of heavy mortars as well. As foreign exchange of the order of about Rs 6 crore was not made available in 1961 for purchase, production of mortars and bombs could begin only in December 1962.

On 1 October 1974, Krishna Menon drew up a second will. He had written one on his family movable and immovable properties six months earlier. This will was slightly different.

> I, Vengalil Krishnan Krishna Menon, do hereby execute this Will and Testament which in addition to and apart from the Will I have executed in April 1974 . . .
>
> By this Will I hereby give and bequeath absolutely to the nation, all my properties and interests, movable and immovable (other than my tarwad and tavazhi properties already bequeathed) situated in India, England and elsewhere.

It is my wish and desire that the Prime Minister be pleased
to accept the bequest made herein, on behalf of the Nation, and
employ the same in any manner and whatever purpose she may
deem fit and proper in her absolute discretion . . .

On 4 October 1974, Krishna Menon went back to hospital. We
don't know whether he saw this letter written to him from London
on 29 September 1974 from Granville Eastwood:

I am taking the liberty of writing to you with reference to a book I
am about to write on the life and work of Harold Laski. Knowing,
as I do, something of your association with him I would like to
bring you into the book . . . I understand you were in this country
at the time of Laski's death in 1950 and were a comfort to the
family in their great sorrow . . .

I understand that you have been unwell and hope that you
have now fully recovered. I apologise for troubling you but would
greatly value your help. You'll be glad to know that Mrs Laski is
still very active although, as I think you are aware, her eyesight is
far from good.

But from what we know he asked Indira Gandhi to see him that day
to talk to her about the recently concluded visit of the Shah of Iran.
However, it was only a matter of time, and around 10 p.m. on 5
October 1974, Krishna Menon told his long-time Jeeves, Mahomed
Ali, 'Give me a cup of tea. It may be my last.' And indeed it was. He
suffered a heart attack shortly thereafter, and at 2.15 a.m. on the early
morning of Sunday, 6 October, the world's greatest tea-drinker, who
had guzzled twenty to thirty cups of tea daily for almost half a century,
passed away. His favourite tea supplier was Ismail & Co. in Blackpool,
and he had once written to Ismail way back on 10 September 1951:

You know your tea is my one source of sustenance. Of course, a
lot of other people drink it. However, I must let you know that
tea that has come to me recently has been lousy. Will you kindly
give your personal attention to this and see that no tea is sent to me

that is not the best you can give me. I am sure you won't mind my asking you to do this.

Ismail had immediately responded sheepishly, 'I cannot understand how you came to be sent anything different from what you normally have.'

Krishna Menon's body was brought home, and Indira Gandhi came twice that morning to pay her respects to him. The funeral took place on the evening of 6 October 1974. Present all through was Indira Gandhi with some of her colleagues. That very night, Haksar would go on All India Radio and pay what would perhaps be the best and fairest tribute to Krishna Menon:[3]

. . . There is a tendency in our country to be somewhat inward looking, to say that the struggle for Indian independence was fought and won in India, and undoubtedly it was fought and won in India. But Indian independence was a product of negotiation . . . If those negotiations were made possible then, to a very large extent the preparation of public opinion in Britain and more specifically in the British labour movement, . . . then the credit for the success of these negotiations, so far as the labour movement in Britain is concerned, and not merely the labour movement but liberal movement, intellectual opinion in Britain is concerned, credit must go in all fairness to the life work of Krishna Menon in London through the India League . . .

I am not saying that in Krishna we had a man without flaw. He had his own little foibles, his little weaknesses. But they were nothing compared to the vastness of his intellectual perception . . .

I have examined over a period of years the physiognomy of his critics. There were those who could not bear his proximity to Jawaharlal Nehru. Basically these men and women lacked confidence in themselves and appeared tall because they walked on stilts of office or something else. There were others who turned against him after being beneficiaries of his kindness and patronage; and finally there were those, mostly foreigners, who called him 'abrasive', 'anti-West', 'Fellow traveller' and 'Communist' because he refused to play the diplomatic game according to the rules made by others.

I had occasion to see Krishna in recent years without the halo of office. I found him without rancour. He was troubled but serene. His mind remained alive and he could still come up with devastating comment on men and events. But he was at peace with himself. And that is what most of us would like to feel whenever our days are numbered.

There would be reports of his death in Indian newspapers but the most prominent obituaries were to be carried in the *Guardian,* the London *Times* and the *New York Times* that called him 'Nehru's Alter Ego, Brainstrust, Press Agent, Confidential Adviser and Shock Absorber' and drew attention to his accomplishments as well as his foibles. The *Guardian* called him a 'left-wing maverick', and the London *Times* dubbed him a 'lone wolf' but also added, '[A] remarkable, yet unlikable man who worked untiringly all his life for his country, yet never received a nation's gratitude, or even acceptance.' The *Daily Telegraph* called him an 'Icy Ascetic Who Fell From Grace'. There were letters to the editor in British publications remembering him, and one that appeared in the *New Statesman* signed by eight of his closest associates in the UK was particularly striking:

. . . Most people who knew Krishna well deplored his compulsion to present an unlikable, sarcastic image to the world. It made him enemies of people who even admired his forcefulness and efforts . . . He was his own worst enemy . . . Now that his sharp tongue and irritability is stilled, even many who feared and disliked his personality and opposed him, are likely to remember his uniqueness and impassioned drive . . . There are a few great number of incidents not of public knowledge which illuminate the inner make-up of Krishna Menon. Just one will throw light on his nature. Time and again before Independence, he was bodily thrown out by porters at India House, but when he came in there as the first Indian High Commissioner, he kept on the men who had manhandled him. They had but fulfilled their orders.

In 1956 there were six authors wishing to write books on Krishna Menon, but he poured withering scorn on all of them. He believed history was invariably falsified and the lives of men romanticized. He would give no help to his own posterity. He never kept a diary. A pity, for Krishna Menon had a great deal to do with the making of modern history, not only in terms of Britain and India, but the whole world. We loved him and we love his memory . . . He was in truth as good a Britisher as he was a true Indian.

Sybil Thorndyke Casson	Anthony Greenwood
Elizabeth Collard	James Cameron
Michael Foot	Marie Seton
David & Ruth Glass	Pamela Cullen

Soon after his death an inventory was taken of his house. Over 12,000 books were found, which were donated to different libraries. Hundreds of toys of various types were located, which were given away to children's organizations. A very large number of walking sticks were also discovered, which were taken by various friends of his. The India League organized a memorial meeting for him in London on 31 October 1974. Messages were received from the Prime Ministers of India and the UK, apart from his British friends, including Mountbatten, Listowel, Jennie Lee, Barbara Castle and Palme Dutt. A number of prominent British and Indian personalities including Frida Laski were present. A couple of weeks later, on 18 November 1974, MPs belonging to different political parties led by Indira Gandhi assembled in Parliament in New Delhi to recall the man and his contributions. She went down memory lane, which was quite unusual for her:

> . . . I met him in the nineteen thirties as a student in England. Even then, his personality was a towering one and he managed to rope in every student who had a concern for India's freedom. I have no hesitation in saying that he made us work like slaves . . . All of us young people (and not all were Indians; there were a large number

of Britishers and some other nationalities) did his bidding only too
willingly because he gave us the feeling that we were involved in
a big cause . . .

All of us here know of his sharp intellect, his clear vision and
sheer ability of the man. At a time when he was most unpopular
in some of the countries of the West—and for a large part of
the time he was, though it was not due to any fault in him but
because of his strong advocacy of our cause, which was resented
by most people, his strongly independent stand on India—even
at that time, I happened to meet someone who was fairly high
up in his country's affairs who said: 'I hate your Krishna Menon,
but if I had any difficult problem to solve, he is the person I will
talk to' . . . Had the solution which he had proposed on behalf
of India in the 50s for the India–China situation been accepted,
a great deal of hardship, waste and suffering would have been
avoided . . .

To the very end, in spite of great physical pain, he remained
very clear-headed. In fact, just a week before, he had sent for me—I
got a note, it was very difficult to read, saying that he wanted me
just for a few minutes but he kept me for one whole hour in the
hospital talking about international affairs, domestic affairs and all
kinds of problems, in a very lucid manner . . .

Here was Indira Gandhi confirming what Krishna Menon had always
refused to speak about—namely, his now-forgotten 'swap' formula
to solve the border dispute with China—that China acknowledges
India's claims in the Chumbi Valley and India reciprocates in Aksai
Chin. It is not an exaggeration to say that in the 1950s, it was Krishna
Menon alone who advocated a negotiated settlement to the Sino-
Indian border dispute. Nehru was broadly supportive but he was
hamstrung by the position taken by his senior cabinet colleagues and
indeed by the Indian Parliament itself. The search for a negotiated
settlement continues. If and when that is arrived at, Krishna Menon
would be vindicated.

Of all the tributes that were paid to Krishna Menon after his
death, none could have been more unexpected than the one that

appeared in a daily called *Motherland*, which had been launched in 1970 by the Jan Sangh, an organization that had been bitterly opposed to him all through the fifties and early sixties:

> In Shri Krishna Menon's death the country has lost a controversial politician and a brilliant man . . . Menon was widely blamed to poor performance in the China war . . . But Menon was also the most forceful Defence Minister that this country has had. Shri Menon was a strange amalgam of sweetness and bitterness . . . Menon could be offensive; but he could be extra-kind too. He had something of Voltaire in him, being full of wit, often pungent. He was also the best read politician, and with all his faults, a clean man . . .

Notes

1. Desai (1974).
2. Ram (1997).
3. Ramesh (2018).

21

Life after Death (1974–)

It has been said, 'Few reputations fade more quickly than those of politicians. Often accorded great prominence during their lives, they tend to vanish into oblivion after their deaths.'[1] Krishna Menon certainly did not meet this fate even though he did little to curate his posthumous life. Just eleven days after he passed away, V.R. Krishna Iyer wrote to Indira Gandhi:

> Several respected and responsible friends of late Krishna Menon have been feeling—and I feelingly concur with them—that some principal road or avenue be named after him, the choice of the road having some significance in this context. What I mean is that the place so chosen may be associated with the national services rendered by Krishna Menon such as when he was Defence Minister. In this view, may be the King George's Avenue may be a fitting choice . . .

A while later, King George's Avenue in the heart of Lutyens' Delhi would be renamed Rajaji Marg after C. Rajagopalachari. But the main avenue next to it called Hastings Road was renamed V.K. Krishna Menon Marg. In April, Krishna Iyer took the initiative to set up a Krishna Menon Memorial Society in which Haksar played a leading part. The society would keep Krishna Menon's memory alive for over two decades. Two of his closest British associates—Jennie Lee, the widow of Nye Bevan, and Michael Foot—would deliver the Krishna Menon Memorial lectures in New Delhi in January and October 1976, respectively. Presiding over both of them was Indira Gandhi.

Also in 1975 would come out the first of the memoirs of those who had worked with him. Dharma Vira, an ICS officer, had been with Krishna Menon from April 1951 in the Indian High Commission in London. More importantly, Nehru, with whom Vira had worked earlier, had asked him to make 'certain enquires' about the jeep deals that would besmirch Krishna Menon so very much for ever. These inquiries would be made before Krishna Menon left the High Commission in July 1952. Dharma Vira wrote:[2]

> . . . The Indian Army required a number of jeeps for the defence services. Because of the trouble with Pakistan the British and American governments had banned the supply of jeeps to India and Pakistan. They were not easily available elsewhere. It was then a friend of Krishna Menon, Cleminson who proposed that he could supply jeeps, as good as new, from disposal sources in Europe. Krishna Menon entered into an agreement with this person . . . But Cleminson had no resources of his own. His company had a modest capital of about 100 pounds. So he wanted an advance . . . Some jeeps were delivered but the rub came when the army inspectors turned them down as unsuitable . . . Sometime later, in order the retrieve the position and to set things right, Krishna Menon entered into another deal with Group Captain Searle and another associate of his. They assured that they would procure new jeeps from Belgium provided they were also given the spare parts for these jeeps. They also agreed to adjust the infructuous advance given to the previous contractor in this [new] deal . . . If I remember correctly some five jeeps were all that were delivered . . . This firm also did not have adequate resources . . .
>
> As a *quid pro quo* for the first deal, Krishna Menon had received a substantial cheque from Cleminson, presumably for his India League activities. Krishna Menon's personal integrity had always

been considered to be above reproach; but he was always needing funds for the India League, the India Club, the Students' Hostel, etc. . . . Krishna Menon was pre-occupied with the India League and the hostels. These hostels for Indian students and a restaurant which provided food cheaply engaged his attention . . .

That Cleminson was a shady character seems to be beyond doubt. That Krishna Menon was very close to him is also indubitable. He had, in fact, written to Cleminson on 14 June 1952 when he had been told by Nehru that he had to give up the high commissionership in London. Krishna Menon had been feeling suicidal that day and had written to Nehru, Indira Gandhi, Kamala Jaspal and Bridget Tunnard. He did not forget to reach out to Cleminson as well:

My dear Bob:

You will be grieved to read this but no one will understand it better than you. I have known you for only 12 or 13 years. It has been a friendship I have valued. I know of no occasion when you have regarded it as something sweet or to be made use of. It is odd, is it not, that you of all people should be the victim of this slander and vilification. You have taken it philosophically but one cannot help feel humiliated . . . No one knows the risks you took when I was ill. No one else cared . . . I just wanted to say that your affection and devotion, your care, all have added so much to life and helped to retain faith and endeavour. Please give my love to Nina and father and tell them I am gone in endeavour and not in escape . . . I have had no more devoted friend . . . You are a good fellow, only do not let it get frittered away . . . Laugh even at this, but let us both remember our friendship and love for each other, each to his dying day. Mine now, yours when it comes in the distant future . . . Love to you Bob.

In March 1977, a commemorative plaque of Krishna Menon was unveiled in Camden borough in London.

Heritage plaque, London

A few months later on 17 June 1977, his statue would be installed at Fitzroy Square in London.

Unveiling of Krishna Menon's statue, London, June 1977

Present at both functions—heritage plaque and statue—would be India's high commissioner in the UK, someone whose mother and Krishna Menon had been activists together in the late 1920s and early 1930s and who had quite detested Krishna Menon and had been privy to the US moves to edge Krishna Menon out as a pre-condition for American military assistance in October–November 1962—B.K. Nehru. When the statue was unveiled, Indira Gandhi was no longer Prime Minister but she sent a message for the function as did British Prime Minister James Callaghan. What was somewhat unexpected was the message from Atal Bihari Vajpayee, India's external affairs minister, who had clashed repeatedly with Krishna Menon between 1957 and 1962. He said:

> . . . To the last he [Krishna Menon] remained controversial, reflecting as it were, a mind which rejects the established order and yearns for new and often unattainable horizons of social amity and international understanding. It is but fitting that a memorial statue should be erected in commemoration of this unique personality in the borough, to which he devoted a part of his life.

After 1967, Vajpayee and Krishna Menon had become very good friends. This was because N.M. Ghatate, Vajpayee's closest friend, had become Krishna Menon's junior in his legal practice, drawn to him not so much for his legal skills but by his admiration for the man. Ghatate's doctoral thesis was on disarmament and was based heavily on Krishna Menon's speeches on disarmament at the UN. On Krishna Menon's death, Ghatate would write two articles on the former's contributions to building an indigenous defence industry in India, and quite extraordinarily, these articles appeared in *Organiser*, a publication of the Jan Sangh, the political party to which Vajpayee belonged and which was a virulent critic of Krishna Menon.

This statue of Krishna Menon would have a history of its own. It was stolen in July 1981 and a replacement bust was erected three years later. That too disappeared mysteriously. Finally, a third cast was made. Fed up with what had happened twice earlier, the Camden Council decided to display it in more secure surroundings—at the

Camden Centre, where it can still be seen. The sculptress was Fredda Brilliant, Krishna Menon's friend from the 1930s who had also sculpted Gandhi's statue at Tavistock Gardens. Actually, Brilliant had first sculpted Krishna Menon way back in 1948 and had many years later described her creation:[3]

> The sculpture is unusual in a sense that every quarter of an inch the face changes expression. The full right profile is that of a noble character; a quarter of an inch to the left he smiles, a little further the smile turns to sarcasm, still further towards the front the smile becomes bitter, finally full face is that of a mistrusting man . . . More still further towards the left and the face becomes simpler till finally the left profile is that of a serious intellectual. As a piece of sculpture it is admired by everyone without exception. Lady Mountbatten, who knew Krishna well, said it was the best piece I have done.

Subimal Dutt was Nehru's longest-serving foreign secretary for seven years between 1954 and 1961. In 1977, he would publish an account of his tenure[4] as foreign secretary. He was circumspect about Krishna Menon but most importantly he provided a confirmation of what Krishna Menon had told Brecher over a decade earlier on his contribution to solving the Suez crisis. Krishna Menon's original five-point formula had been:

1. Recognition of the sovereign rights of Egypt.
2. Recognition of the Suez Canal as an integral part of Egypt and as a waterway of international importance.
3. Free and uninterrupted navigation for all nations in accordance with the 1888 Convention.
4. Tolls and charges should be equitable and the facilities of the Canal should be available to all countries without discrimination.
5. The interests of the users of the Canal should receive due recognition.

On 12 October 1956, the foreign ministers of Egypt, UK and France announced a six-point formula as a basis of future negotiations. The UN secretary-general, Dag Hammarskjold, got much of the credit for the breakthrough. Actually all he had done was add one additional point to the Krishna Menon formula: '[I]n case of disputes, any unsolved affairs between the Suez Canal Company and the Egyptian Government would be settled by arbitration.'

In 1978, O. Pulla Reddy, who had been defence secretary for the five years Krishna Menon had been defence minister, published his memoirs.[5] Pulla Reddy had been at the receiving end of one of Krishna Menon's most well-known barbs: 'What sort of an officer are you Pulla Reddy, you neither pull nor are you ready.' Another version of the barb had Krishna Menon say, 'What sort of an officer are you Pulla Reddy, you neither pull nor do you read.' Pulla Reddy described Krishna Menon as an 'institution by himself' who suffered from 'too sharp an intellect', with a style of functioning that was 'highly abrasive and methods of work eccentric by ordinary standards'. He explained the Thimayya resignation episode of August–September 1959 as having been caused by an 'incompatibility of temperament' between Krishna Menon and Thimayya. While praising Krishna Menon for laying great stress on establishing manufacturing facilities within India for defence equipment and for being very sympathetic to the needs of the junior ranks of the three services, Pulla Reddy was very critical of him for favouring Lt General B.M. Kaul to an unwarranted extent, with disastrous consequences for the country.

Four years after Krishna Menon's death, M.O. Mathai's bile-filled memoirs appeared. There was no doubt that he was a powerful figure in Nehru's establishment between 1946 and 1959. There was also no doubt that Krishna Menon and he had been exceedingly close at least till the mid-fifties. Mathai resigned in January 1959 amidst allegations of financial impropriety and Walter Crocker reported to Canberra on 16 May 1959:

. . . For some time these two worked closely together but latterly they fell out and Krishna Menon supplied certain information—

there is reason for believing that even drafted an article—for the Communist press which led off the attack on Mathai.

Mathai took his revenge in his reminiscences which, while being salaciously gossipy, reveal more of the author and his bitterness than of the people he wrote about.

In 1981, Escott Reid's memoirs appeared,[6] in which he devoted a whole chapter to Krishna Menon. Reid was the Canadian high commissioner to India during 1952–57 and would send back many dispatches on 'Nehru's infatuation'. He made the pertinent point that at that time, the more Krishna Menon was attacked, the more Nehru would defend him. But it was also clear from Reid's account that much of the criticism of Krishna Menon was coming from senior ICS officials of the ministry of external affairs, particularly from N.R. Pillai and from members of Nehru's cabinet, especially Morarji Desai, S.K. Patil and T.T. Krishnamachari. In his final report back in April 1957, Reid wrote:

> There is, however, the possibility which cannot be discounted, although at the moment it seems most probable, that Mr. Nehru may be thinking of Mr. Menon as a possible successor. Mr. Nehru has for long had an infatuation for Mr. Krishna Menon. The infatuation has become lately an obsession.

In 1983, the last of the twelve volumes of *The Transfer of Power: 1942–47*, based on official British government records, was published. It had taken thirteen years for the project to be completed, under the direction of the eminent historian Nicholas Mansergh. Before these volumes were available, the widely accepted view was that apart from British government officials in London and New Delhi, a few political leaders of the Congress and the Muslim League were the people involved in the negotiations. The key role of individuals such as V.P. Menon was also known. What the Mansergh volumes would reveal is the critical role played by Krishna Menon in 1946 and 1947, particularly after Mountbatten became viceroy. The extent of his contributions has yet to be fully appreciated because it is a formidable challenge absorbing all that there is in these tomes.

In 1983, Admiral R.D. Katari, who had served as navy chief under Krishna Menon, published his memoirs,[7] in which he described his minister as 'having in abundant measure other traits that go with a high intellect—supreme arrogance on the one hand and, on the other, ill-concealed impatience with those less endowed'. Katari was quite generous in acknowledging that Krishna Menon 'applied himself with single-minded devotion and energy to promoting indigenous production of a variety of defence and allied equipment'. Katari had resigned along with Thimayya in August 1959 over Krishna Menon's style of functioning. He described his meeting with Nehru on the night of 31 August 1959:

> I duly presented myself . . . to be confronted by a grave-looking and sad Prime Minister. In his characteristic style he opened with, 'Well I have received Thimayya's letter of resignation. I understand that you also intend to resign. Is that true'? I told him I was considering doing so. He then remarked that he was grieved that the three Chiefs of Staff should gang up against the Defence Minister. I regretted his use of such an ugly expression and pointed out that if the three of us, individually, were working under such severe disabilities that we found it difficult to function honourably, it could hardly be termed ganging up. I believed he accepted that, and then went on to say that he realized that Krishna Menon was not the easiest men with whom to get on. But, he said, Menon possessed one of the finest intellects that he, Nehru, has come across and it should be utilized for the benefit of the country. At that, I quite spontaneously blurted out, 'But why as Defence Minister, Sir?' I was relieved to find he laughed at that . . . As I was taking my leave at the end of one hour, he revealed that Thimayya had agreed to withdraw his resignation.

A year later Y.D. Gundevia, another foreign service officer who had worked with Krishna Menon, particularly in 1962, published his memoirs, which was quite damaging to Krishna Menon's reputation.[8]

Apart from highlighting his personality quirks and conspiratorial style
of functioning, Gundevia revealed that at the height of the tension
on the India–China border, Krishna Menon was in a state of denial
and tried to create the impression that Pakistan was about to attack
India. He wrote:

> I have never been able to fathom why this nonsense about Pakistan
> troop movements in Murree was fabricated in that crucial week of
> October . . . Did Krishna just think of this meaningless diversion
> on the spur of the moment on hearing that Rajeshwar Dayal
> [India's high commissioner in Pakistan] was in Delhi? Only a week
> later the Chinese were to launch massive attacks on our troops in
> NEFA . . .

Fourteen years later Rajeshwar Dayal would confirm Gundevia's
account in his autobiography.[9] In August 1960, Nehru had agreed
to Hammarskjold's request to have Dayal sent to Congo as a special
envoy of the UN. Congo was to be perhaps one of the very few
occasions when Krishna Menon differed with Nehru and voiced his
differences privately and in the cabinet. Nehru had supported the
dispatch of armed forces under UN aegis, which Krishna Menon had
opposed. Krishna Menon had also opposed the flying out of the first
contingent of Indian troops to Congo by American military aircraft in
March 1961. All along, he had been suspicious of Hammarskjold and
of Western, particularly Belgian motives, and had favoured the path
of negotiations. But at the UN, he had faithfully followed Nehru's
instructions, making forceful speeches and moving constructive
resolutions for much of 1960 and 1961. Indian troops had remained
in Congo for two years.

The year 1984 would also see the completion of S. Gopal's
authoritative three-volume biography of Nehru. Gopal, one of India's
most eminent historians, had unique advantages that made him Nehru's
most authoritative biographer. As the son of S. Radhakrishnan,
India's first Vice President and second President, Gopal had a ringside
view of the Nehru era. He worked in the ministry of external affairs
in the fifties. Later, he had unparalleled access to both the Nehru

archives as well as that of Krishna Menon and of other leaders like Rajagopalachari. His trilogy is distinctive and still stands out. Gopal excoriated Krishna Menon most of the time but his final description of the man was generous:

> Nehru, on 7 November [1962] decided to accept Menon's resignation from the Cabinet . . . But the uncomplaining dignity with which Menon departed from office balanced to an extent his tarnished performance while in power; and his eclipse as a politician enabled him, at long last, to be respected as a personality. To Nehru, who believed that Menon was guiltless of responsibility for the debacle, the resignation was a blow which he accepted in the national cause and not because his own position was threatened. For even a crisis of this dimension [1962 war and its aftermath] did not endanger Nehru's hold on the people.

In 1986, two of India's most distinguished military men, P.C. Lal and S.S.P. Thorat, who had clashed with Krishna Menon in the late fifties and had suffered, published their memoirs. Air Vice Marshal P.C. Lal had been deputed from the Indian Air Force in November 1957 to run the Indian Airlines. But soon, he and Krishna Menon came into serious conflict with each other over the aircraft to be selected for both defence and civilian purposes. Krishna Menon wanted India to manufacture the British twin-engine turbo-prop aircraft made by A.V. Roe & Co. of Manchester (hence its name, Avro). Lal supported the Dutch aircraft Fokker Friendship but 'Krishna Menon's will and enthusiasm prevailed'. Lal, however, had to suffer, and his services were abruptly terminated at the end of his five-year deputation period on 30 September 1962. He would be in limbo till Krishna Menon quit on 7 November 1962. Thereafter, Lal came back to the Indian Air Force and became its chief in July 1969. In his memoirs[10] Lal was, however, fair to Krishna Menon, giving him credit for pushing to establish a tank factory in Avadi near Madras and numerous other indigenous manufacturing facilities. He also admitted that the Avro 'proved to be a reasonably good aircraft which has been used by the IAF [Indian Air Force] for a variety of purposes as also the Indian Airlines'. Lt General Thorat should have taken over from General Thimayya but he had run foul of Krishna Menon because of his proximity to Thimayya. He would be quite discreet in his recollections[11] but for one explosive revelation. Thorat wrote that he had prepared a detailed paper on 9 October 1959, pinpointing how the Chinese would attack India in NEFA and how India should respond to it. He had met Nehru after the NEFA debacle, and the Prime Minister had expressed his great annoyance that 'such an important paper concerning national security written by an Army commander and supported by his Chief' had not been shown to him. Thorat leaves no doubt that Krishna Menon had failed to do so.

From 1986 or thereabouts, the Krishna Menon Society would play an active role in fostering contacts with Chinese academics and research institutions. It linked up with the Chinese Association for International Understanding and the first of these 'non-official' delegations came to India in November 1986. Six months later, Haksar, who was vice president of the society, went to Beijing as the Prime Minister's special envoy. He had been sent by Prime Minister Rajiv Gandhi to signal that India was serious about taking its relationship with China to a higher level. The Prime Minister would make his historic visit to China in December 1988, the first such visit by an Indian head of government after thirty-four years.

In May 1987, one of Krishna Menon's ardent admirers who used to accompany him to the UN in the fifties, R. Venkataraman, became President of India. Thanks to the joint efforts of the society and Venkataraman, in April 1988, a statue of Krishna Menon would be erected at a prominent roundabout in the heart of the nation's capital and formally unveiled by Prime Minister Rajiv Gandhi six months later. Venkataraman, who had been defence minister of India between 1982 and 1984, sent a message on the occasion and referred to Krishna Menon's tenure in the defence ministry:

> . . . Because of his forthrightness, controversy pursued Krishna Menon all through his life. It did not leave him alone in Defence.

But I can say with my knowledge of Defence affairs that the reverses of 1962 were the result of earlier policies, whereas the true evidence of the success of Krishna Menon's efforts is really available in the results of the 1965 and 1971 conflicts when our troops firmly met and repulsed aggression.

Krishna Menon statue in Lutyens' Delhi

As for the statue, Shankar Bajpai, one of India's most distinguished diplomats—the only man to have been ambassador to the US and China and high commissioner to Pakistan and son of Girija Shankar Bajpai—wrote to me on 1 February 2019:

KM [Krishna Menon] must be proving a most interesting biographee. He was undoubtedly brilliant, but how perverse. As I wrote in my review in *The Hindu* of the memoirs of BK Nehru, who couldn't abide him, we owe KM a debt for a number of things, but how can we put memorials for the man who was so singularly responsible for 1962? . . .

However, a statue of his installed in Calicut soon thereafter and unveiled by Venkataraman would not evoke any controversy. Two statues and a major road naming apart, 1988 saw the publication of a third biography of Krishna Menon by a journalist who had been close to him in his final years.[12] The book was published as part of the 'Builders of Modern India' series, and the author had been given privileged access to Krishna Menon's papers. Additionally, he had spoken to a number of people who had worked with Krishna Menon. Perhaps the most significant passage in this book came from an interview the author had conducted with India's strategic affairs guru K. Subrahmanyam, who had told him:

> So far as 1962 events are concerned they are not so much of a political failure as they are military setbacks. It was essentially a command failure. One or two senior people on the spot, whatever might be reasons, in the Armed Forces decided to cover it up and tried to shift all the blame on the politicians. Krishna Menon did have his favourites in the Defence Ministry and that kind of thing did play havoc. I don't agree with the general view that Krishna Menon created divisions and politics in the Indian Army as politics and divisions already existed there. And some people including General Kaul made use of Krishna Menon and it is of course not to the credit of Krishna Menon that he allowed himself to be used.

Three years later, Subrahmanyam's assessment would be corroborated by Major General D.K. Palit, who was director of military operations during the time of the 1962 war.[13] Palit would, of course, be critical of the political leadership but it would be the first time that a senior army man had exposed the abysmal failures of his military brethren, that included not just Lt General B.M. Kaul but a number of others as well. The big plus point of the Palit account was that it was not based on hindsight or memory but was a meticulous record he had prepared at the end of 1962 itself.

Palit's book had just followed that of another army man who had worked intimately with Krishna Menon but in a different area of defence—that of science and production.[14] This account was somewhat unusual in that for once the idiosyncrasies and eccentricities of the former defence minister were not highlighted. Instead, Major General B.D. Kapur wrote chapter and verse about Krishna Menon's yeoman efforts to strengthen the infrastructure for defence research and production of defence equipment in the country. These efforts were very frequently in the face of stiff opposition from the bureaucracy, which Krishna Menon successfully overcame. This must have been the reason why Nehru had, while accepting Krishna Menon's resignation the first time on 31 October 1962, redesignated him as minister of defence production (that included research), but that arrangement had lasted less than a week.

Krishna Menon's birth centenary would be celebrated in Parliament with the President of India, the Vice President of India, Prime Minister and many other political leaders paying handsome tributes to him. Both President Shankar Dayal Sharma and Vice President K.R. Narayanan had known Krishna Menon from his London days in the 1940s. Both were avid fans of his. Nobody mentioned 1962, of course, the one thing that will forever be associated with him. The speeches that day were a reversal of what Shakespeare had Mark Antony say at Caesar's funeral. The birth centenary speeches were proof that at times 'the good that men do lives after them; the evil is oft is interred with their bones'.

But it was left to K. Subrahmanyam, one of his staff officers for a brief while, to write in the *Times of India* three weeks after the birth centenary about Krishna Menon's undoubted contributions but also of his gigantic flaws: '[H]is abysmal judgment of people, his poor appreciation of the role of military power in international politics, his arrogance, overbearing temperament and abrasiveness in dealing with people.' Two years later Narayanan, then President of India, renamed the building of the Indian Society of International Law next to the Supreme Court in Delhi as 'V.K. Krishna Menon Bhawan' and unveiled a bust of his, which greets people as they enter the spacious building.

The mid-1990s also saw a spate of books on Krishna Menon, of which a two-volume account of his London years between 1924 and 1947 by a noted Indian historian[15] and a personal memoir by his grandniece Janaki Ram[16] were the most notable and enduring. Both had been given special access to the Krishna Menon archives. The memoir was particularly notable because it made use of Krishna Menon's many letters to his family and his lady friends. A decade later the same historian would produce another book focused on Krishna Menon's activities during 1932–36.[17]

In 2002, there appeared quite a monumental history of Asians in Britain covering some four centuries.[18] This was a landmark effort based on painstaking archival research and broke new ground. Krishna Menon and the many networks he established with the India League as the pivot in the second quarter of the twentieth century figures prominently in it. The book remains a valuable reference work on the man and the numerous men and women who were in his orbit.

In June 2003, Prime Minister Atal Bihari Vajpayee went to China and both countries decided to appoint one special representative each to begin discussions on a negotiated settlement of the border dispute between the two countries. This was, in many ways, a vindication of Krishna Menon because this was what he had been advocating all along till 1962 and for which he was pilloried in Parliament, most notably by Vajpayee, and in the media.

J.B. Kripalani had been an inveterate foe of Krishna Menon, particularly during the period 1957–62. He was a bitter critic of Nehru as well since 1950 but always took care to qualify that criticism by saying, 'Jawaharlal is my personal friend and I always wish him well.' But he made no such concession to Krishna Menon. Kripalani had written his autobiography in 1982 but that lay unpublished till 2004.[19] Expectedly, Krishna Menon looms large in the book, and the charges that he betrayed India to the Chinese, that he wilfully neglected defence preparedness and that he was communist masquerading as a congressman were repeated.

In 2005, a book based on material in the KGB archives was published, which presented 'evidence' that the Soviet Union was backing Krishna Menon as Nehru's successor in mid-1962 and that his abortive 1967 election bid drew some Soviet financial support.[20] In 2007, a large number of British intelligence files on him were declassified, and he was back in the spotlight. Two years later the authorized history of the MI5 was published, which revealed how British (and Indian) intelligence agencies were obsessed with getting rid of him in 1949 itself.[21]

Also in 2005 came the well-deserved recognition of a relatively lesser-known dimension of Krishna Menon's varied career. Jeremy Lewis published his biography of Allen Lane, the founder of Penguin and Pelican Books, in which he acknowledged the role of Krishna Menon in particularly the latter of the two ventures. There were a couple of hilarious stories of him related to an incident that took place in London in 1935:[22]

> Menon's political enthusiasms and his rapidity as a reader had already been exploited by publishers eager to tap the market for books on current affairs. He had edited a series of Topical Books for Selwyn and Blount, one of the many imprints under the wing of the demented Walter Hutchinson where Robert Lusty remembered him as a 'wild eyed, emaciated limping Indian'. On being told that his half-starved editor was on the verge of death, Lusty hurried round to a garret off Gray's Inn Road and found Menon lying on what looked like a bed of nails. 'I am dying Lusty and I want to see you and say goodbye', Menon told him holding out an emaciated hand and Lusty in return 'muttered some embarrassed good wishes for the journey'.

The story may have been embellished but on 23 April 1970, Sir Robert Lusty, chairman of the Hutchinson Publishing Group, had written to Krishna Menon:

> Please forgive again this voice from your past but I feel I must write once more and urge the writing of an autobiography. This project came afresh to my mind when in Boston a week ago discussing with one of its distinguished publishers whose unwritten autobiography we would very much like to share and yours was one of the foremost. You have so much to say and the ability to write it. Can anything persuade you?

You may incidentally be interested to know my second wife, whom I married nearly seven years ago, was the widow of Dr. Dennis Carroll and thus any book you were to write would be in very friendly hands.

A.P.J. Abdul Kalam was President of India in 2006 when a study he had commissioned over a decade earlier was published.[23] It was called 'Defence Research and Development Organisation (1958–1962)'. The foundations of defence science in India had been laid, at Nehru's personal initiative, by two people: the British nuclear scientist and Nobel laureate P.M.S. Blackett and the noted Indian nuclear physicist D.S. Kothari. Krishna Menon arrived on the scene in April 1957. He knew both Blackett and Kothari well— Blackett from his London years when both were part of the left-wing intellectual circles and had been intimates of Mountbatten and Kothari because of *Nuclear Explosions and Their Effects,* his pioneering analysis which had been published in 1956 as an Indian contribution to the global debate on nuclear disarmament. That analysis had followed a call given in November 1953 at the UN by Krishna Menon that there should be a UN-sponsored study on the 'effect of atomic and hydrogen weapons on populations', but that idea had been shot down by the US and the UK. The Kalam-initiated archival monograph read:

When he took over the reins of the defence ministry, he [Krishna Menon] initiated moves to form the Defence Research and Development Organisation (DRDO) . . . The post of the head of the organization was converted into Scientific Adviser to the Defence Minister instead of being Scientific Adviser to the Ministry of Defence. It appears that even though Shri Krishna Menon had given orders to the Defence Secretary to go ahead with the formation of DRDO in October 1957, this was not given effect to as 'the Chiefs of Staff . . . having a pre-conceived notion on the subject [formation of the DRDO] opposed it and sent a dissenting note to the [defence] Ministry.' On his return from the United Nations at the end of 1957, the Defence Minister held a meeting with top civilian and military officers and the DRDO came into being on 1ˢᵗ January 1958 . . . When it was formed, it appeared as though it had been forced upon the Services by a Defence Minister by his sheer strength of conviction of the necessity of scientists and technologists to be involved with defence weapons and by his influence with the Prime Minister . . .

In 2007, Krishna Menon figured in, of all places, the autobiography of one of Bollywood's greatest stars. In *Romancing with Life*, Dev Anand fondly recalled their close association and had a poignant description of their last meeting in Bombay. The actor may have got his dates mixed up since he wrote that Krishna Menon stood at the gate of his house in Bombay half an hour before midnight and that a few days after their conversation he passed away. This was most unlikely although the encounter described in the memoirs may well have happened a few years earlier. In Anand's words, '[A] shining star on the political firmament suddenly became a political non-entity, like a shooting star fizzling out into nothingness.'

In October 2008, the South African government conferred a special award on Krishna Menon for his contributions to ending apartheid in that country. These contributions had been, of course, largely in the form of thirteen forceful speeches he had delivered at the UN between October 1953 and September 1962. But his association with South Africa had been much deeper. During the India League years he had been in close contact with Dr Yusuf Dadoo and other leaders of the South African Indian community. Later, as high commissioner, he gave considerable support to the South African freedom movement through his close friendship with the South African communist leader Vella Pillay, whose wife worked in the Indian High Commission in London and who, according to British intelligence, was part of the communist network at India House along with others such as P.N. Haksar and Anila Graham—a clear case of completely misplaced paranoia.

In 2010, a doctoral thesis at Oxford University had a significant portion on Krishna Menon and his close association with Laski.[24]

In 2010 and 2011, another British academic using the newly declassified material from British archives published two scholarly articles:[25] '"A Serious Menace to Security": British Intelligence, V.K. Krishna Menon, and the Indian High Commission in London, 1947-1952' and another called 'India's Rasputin? V.K. Krishna Menon and Anglo-American Misperceptions of Indian Foreign Policymaking 1947–1964'. These portray Krishna Menon as less of a villain than he is often made out to be. They reveal the extent of paranoia that the British and American establishments had about Krishna Menon—for the most part needless and misdirected. Four years later Krishna Menon formed a chapter in a book called *Radicals and Reactionaries in Twentieth Century International Thought*, edited by a well-known Australian scholar. The title of the chapter was quite provocative—'Mephistopheles in a Saville Row Suit; V.K. Krishna Menon and the West'.[26]

In October 2013, the Bangladesh government honoured Krishna Menon. Right from the very beginning, eight months prior to its happening, he had advocated diplomatic recognition of Bangladesh by India. He had also called for Bangladesh's admission into the UN at every international forum available to him. That would become a reality just nineteen days before his demise. That Krishna Menon was respected in Bangladesh is evident from a letter that its President, Abu Sayeed Choudhury, had written to him on 17 August 1973:

> I feel very concerned to find in today's newspaper that you have been hospitalized after a sudden illness. I pray to God for your speedy recovery, long life, health and happiness.
>
> Since I came into contact with you in 1959 I have all along admired your abilities. I feel happy to recall your services to the cause of Bangladesh during and after the struggle for liberation. My co-workers were very inspired when you addressed a meeting of ours in London in 1971, although you were in indifferent health.
>
> I shall be anxiously awaiting news of your recovery.

Two years later, a doctoral thesis submitted to Krishna Menon's alma mater shed new light on his thinking, months before the 1962 war with China.[27] What had not been known earlier was that on 10 July 1962, Krishna Menon had met with the departing Chinese ambassador to India, Pan Tzu-li, even as Indian and Chinese troops faced each other in Ladakh. Anton Harder was able to unearth Pan's dispatch back home on that conversation. Harder wrote that 'Krishna Menon suggested . . . that an exchange of territory was feasible' and quoted from the dispatch of 12 July 1962 found in the Chinese archives:

> China's final claims should be stated clearly. Some areas can go to China, at the same time China can make some symbolic concession in other areas, and making modifications in this way we can perhaps solve the problem. In this way India can say to the public some places have been given to China, and China has in other places made concessions. The Aksai Chin road has perhaps a fairly big strategic meaning for China, or is perhaps related to Chinese face, certain places here can go to China (this sentence was not said clearly by Menon).

Pan had also suggested to Krishna Menon that he could perhaps discuss the border issue with Chen Yi when they met up in Geneva later that month. Nehru would be lambasted in Parliament for having Krishna Menon meet with Chen Yi. He had acknowledged that he had asked the defence minister to do so since both he and the Chinese foreign minister would be together for some time. What Harder's thesis showed is that the Chinese may have been looking for some last-minute breakthrough at Geneva in July 1962 which, as we now know, was made impossible by the vehement and vociferous 'we should never negotiate' attitude on display in the Indian Parliament.

In 2016, an eminent political scientist then at King's College, London, told the long story of India,[28] starting with the Buddha in fifty lives, of which number forty-four was the 'Sombre Porcupine', Marie Seton's description of Krishna Menon. The same year India's senior-most diplomat still alive, M.K. Rasgotra, who had worked closely with Krishna Menon at the UN in the fifties, published his memoirs.[29] He was not blind to Krishna Menon's oftentimes needless abrasiveness but provided examples of his contributions at the UN that have all but been forgotten now. He also gave many examples of Krishna Menon's bite and sardonic wit:

> On an earlier occasion in the Security Council [957], the British delegate had the temerity to pick holes in some of the words Menon had used in his speech . . . Menon interrupted him, 'Sir, I can understand your difficulty in understanding what I have said; you picked up your English on the streets of London, I devoted several years of my life to learn it with the care and respect it deserves!'. Derisive laughter silenced the man Sir Pearson Dixon for the rest of the session. At the same meeting when Sir Muhammed Zafarullah Khan [actually it was Sir Feroze Khan Noon] had repeatedly emphasized the urgent necessity of a plebiscite in Kashmir, Menon turned to the chair and exclaimed, 'Plebiscite, Plebiscite, Plebiscite! Sir ask this gentleman whether his country has ever seen a ballot box!'

As recently as in 2018, a noteworthy undergraduate thesis at Cambridge University was entitled 'V.K. Krishna Menon and Indian internationalism in theory and practice, 1947–1962'.[30] Finally, thanks to modern technology, Krishna Menon can also now be seen and heard. The audiovisual library of the UN has eighty-seven items related to him, while eight videos are available on YouTube. Reading about him is one thing but listening to his speeches and press meets and seeing him in action as a proud Indian taking on the might of the Anglo-Saxon world in the 1950s is an altogether different experience.

And so the colourful and cantankerous Krishna Menon, who cultivated the art of ploughing a lonely furrow, who could have 'taught a master class in self-destruction', continues to fascinate and frustrate, inspire and infuriate, be compelling and contradictory, praiseworthy and puzzling and evoke admiration and anger. That was who he was. The narrative arc of his life is certainly not smooth but is certainly captivating.

Notes

1. Anthony Howard, writing of the eminent British politician Richard Crossman.
2. Vira (1975).
3. Brilliant (1986).
4. Dutt (1977).
5. Pulla Reddy (1978).
6. Reid (1981).
7. Katari (1983).
8. Gundevia (1984).
9. Dayal (1998).
10. Lal (1986).
11. Thorat (1986).
12. Madhavan Kutty (1988).
13. Palit (2004).
14. Kapur (1990).
15. Chakravarty (1997).
16. Ram (1997).
17. Chakravarty (2006).
18. Visram (2002).
19. Kripalani (2004).
20. Andrew and Mitrokhin (2005).
21. Andrew (2009).
22. Lewis (2005).
23. Shenoy (2006).
24. Moscovitch (2017).
25. McGarr (2010) and McGarr (2011).
26. Hall (2015).
27. Harder (2015).
28. Khilnani (2016). Inexplicably Nehru is not part of Khilnani's fifty.
29. Rasgotra (2016).
30. Lane (2018).

A Final Word

Ihave always believed that a good biographer should, for the most part, ascertain, not assert. Mine was not to vilify or deify. Mine was to cut through the folklore—both positive and negative—and present the facts as they could be excavated. What I have shown, I hope, is that a man, now remembered only for the debacle of 1962 or for his histrionics at the UN, was intellectually among the most formidable men of his generation, with accomplishments across a wide canvas.

Krishna Menon had two close friends in the British Labour Party—Ernest Bevin and Nye Bevan. He respected the former and was very fond of the latter. Reportedly, when somebody told him that Bevan was his own worst enemy, Bevin's response was: 'Not when I am around, he isn't'. Even though he did have numerous admirers, many people in India and abroad would have had the same response vis-à-vis Krishna Menon. He evoked the strongest sentiments of dislike and like. He was both reviled and applauded at the same time.

That for almost two decades Krishna Menon was singularly responsible for creating and sustaining a climate of opinion in favour of Indian independence in various sections of British society is indubitable. That he almost single-handedly kept the flame of Indian freedom burning across the UK in the 1930s and 1940s is without question. That he played a crucial role in the transfer-of-power negotiations in the months leading up to the end of British rule in India is evident. That he was a hugely impactful envoy for India in the UK between 1947 and 1950 can stand up to scrutiny. That he unravelled many knotty issues at the UN especially between 1952 and 1957 is also clear.

More damaging was his performance as defence minister. He came to that post amidst great expectations and did achieve much in the initial two or three years. These accomplishments in defence research and production have certainly endured and given India a great degree of self-reliance. But it was obvious that he was temperamentally ill-suited for this sensitive assignment, and the country had to pay a heavy price for his personality quirks and work habits. Was Krishna Menon the scapegoat for 1962, the fall guy as it were? His continuation in Nehru's cabinet had become untenable after the war with China began and after the scale of India's reverses became evident. Nehru was able to defuse national anger by reluctantly allowing Krishna Menon to exit. Even Nehru's worst critics like Rajaji demanded only Krishna Menon's resignation and believed that the Prime Minister's continuation in office was essential for rebuilding national morale and strength. It is also beyond doubt that Krishna Menon's animus against three top military officers in particular—Thimayya, Thorat and Manekshaw—cost the country dear. Whether he was Kaul's accomplice in maligning this trio is besides the point, As defence minister, the ultimate responsibility was his and his alone. What Christopher Browning said recently of 'the decisive quality in Neville Chamberlain's personality' could also be said of Krishna Menon: '[H]e stubbornly subordinated the assessment of evidence to the preservation of his own prior convictions.'[1] Even so, the fact remains that Krishna Menon was the only person consistently arguing for a 'deal' with the Chinese to resolve the border dispute, a task in which the two countries have been engaged for seventeen years now.

Krishna Menon did India proud at the height of the Cold War. He argued India's case with passion and eloquence. At a time when the Western powers were ruling the roost, he had the temerity and courage to take them on his terms. But after 1957 or so, his tongue and his manner, barring occasional flashes of constructive engagement, created a negative global image for Nehru and India. For years thereafter, the ghost of Krishna Menon lingered over both the substance and style of Indian diplomacy—needlessly argumentative and combative. And that ghost still lingers.

That he enjoyed a special relationship with Nehru for over a quarter of a century was obvious. They were steeped in the British left traditions. Both were bibliophiles with similar tastes in books. Nehru's friends in the UK were Krishna Menon's as well and vice versa. Both were fiercely Indian but at the same time Anglophones. That Nehru opened up to him like to no one else was evident. He went out of his way to protect Krishna Menon from his own foibles and ultimately paid the price for it. This is part of Indian political history. But why Nehru continued to be loyal after accounting for their remarkable and intense friendship of almost thirty years is puzzling. For years on end, Nehru was unusually forbearing, patient and caring when it came to Krishna Menon. It is not as if he was unaware of Krishna Menon's idiosyncrasies and the havoc he would wreak from time to time. But Nehru felt completely at home with him, and the two were intellectual partners and ideological soulmates in a way that Nehru was with nobody else. They had their differences, often expressed to each other in correspondence, but their bonding was self-evident. Nehru knew Krishna Menon's weaknesses but felt that they were more than compensated for by his indubitable strengths.

Krishna Menon's achievements were gigantic, his failures monumental. His intellectual strengths were awesome, his emotional equilibrium pathetic. He was the delight of his critics, the despair of his admirers. He reached dizzying heights of fame, plumbed depths of notoriety. It is very easy to judge Krishna Menon. He has a long record of pluses and minuses. On what he accomplished, he commands plaudits. On what he botched up, he deserves strictures. But that was not my purpose. What I have tried to do in this narrative is present the man as he emerges from his own writings and from those of his contemporaries. Mine has been a story of the man as he evolved, as he achieved and as he stumbled. Walt Whitman may well have had someone like this mercurial pheno-Menon in mind when he wrote his famous line: 'I am large, I contain multitudes.'

Notes

1.　*New York Review of Books*, 26 September 2019.

A Note on Sources

The sources have been mostly indicated at the appropriate places in the book.

Broadly speaking, all letters to and from Krishna Menon are from his humongous archive at the Nehru Memorial Museum and Library (NMML) in New Delhi unless indicated otherwise. I have made only partial use of what is available in that archive and am pretty sure that it will be used to churn out more books on Krishna Menon. Similarly, the material related to Marie Seton is at NMML as part of the Krishna Menon and Pam Cullen collections.

All letters to and from Nehru are from various volumes of the *Selected Works of Jawaharlal Nehru*, published by the Jawaharlal Nehru Memorial Fund. Letters exchanged between Nehru and his daughter are from *Two Alone, Two Together* edited by Sonia Gandhi (Penguin, 2004). Letters to and from Mahatma Gandhi are from different volumes of the *Collected Works of Mahatma Gandhi* published by the Government of India. Material relating to Vijaya Lakshmi Pandit is from her archive at NMML. Correspondence of Indira Gandhi with Krishna Menon's family members is courtesy of Janaki Ram.

All personal letters from Krishna Menon to his family and his women friends are courtesy of Janaki Ram, who also shared her collection of photographs. Photographs of Krishna Menon with the Bhandari family are courtesy of Madhu Sawhney.

All material used relating to Krishna Menon's meetings with Mountbatten in 1947 are from different volumes of the *Transfer of Power*. The same is the source for correspondence between the viceroys and the secretaries of state for India during 1942–47. All material relating to Krishna Menon's meetings with American officials are from different volumes of the Foreign Relations of the United States (FRUS) series published by the office of the Historian, Department of State, USA. Kissinger's record of his meeting with Krishna Menon is from the John F. Kennedy Presidential Library. Eisenhower's record of his meeting with Krishna Menon is from the Dwight D. Eisenhower Presidential Library and Nixon's from the Richard M. Nixon Presidential Library. The Malcolm Macdonald material is from his archive at Durham University, UK, and the Paul Gore-Booth material is from the National Archives, London. Correspondence of the UK High Commission in New Delhi with the UK government is also from the National Archives, London. Mountbatten's record of his meeting with Sardar Patel is from the Mountbatten archive, University of Southampton. Material relating to M.O. Mathai, B. Shiva Rao, Gopalaswami Ayyangar and General Thimayya are from their respective collections at NMML.

All Scotland Yard and MI5 reports are from the British Library and the Home Department Reports from the National Archives of India. Mountbatten's record of his meeting with Sardar Patel is from the Mountbatten Archives at the University of Southampton. Hammarskjold's letters are from the Kungliga Biblioteket, Stockholm.

A Note of Thanks

$\mathbf{M}$y greatest debt is to the various archives all over the world for giving me access to the material on Krishna Menon. Most notably, the NMML opened up the humungous Krishna Menon collection that had been closed to scholars for well over three decades. I am grateful to Shakti Sinha, director of the NMML, and Swapan Dasgupta, MP, for expediting the decision at my urging.

Janaki Ram, Krishna Menon's grandniece, not only gave me personal letters to and from Krishna Menon but also helped decipher his illegible handwriting. Most importantly, she was always available to answer any query at any moment on her granduncle's multifaceted life.

I thank T.J.S. George for answering questions relating to his 1964 biography of Krishna Menon. Shelley Madhavan Kutty, the wife of another of Krishna Menon's biographers, gave me access to all her late husband's papers that were used to write his book. She also gave me all photographs of Krishna Menon that were in his possession.

I am grateful to N.M. Ghatate, who was Krishna Menon's junior in the latter's post-1967 legal career, for not only his remembrances but also the large amounts of material that he had collected over the years, such as 'The Wit and Wisdom of Krishna Menon', 'Shankar's Cartoons on Krishna Menon', etc.

Madhavan Palat, Geeta Kudaisya and N. Balakrishnan of the Jawaharlal Nehru Memorial Fund, Jaya Ravindran of the National

Archives of India and Jayshree Menon of the Theosophical Society
Archives readily came to my assistance whenever I needed it.

Three people were invaluable sources of information on Indian
political and diplomatic history: Gopal Gandhi, Shankar Bajpai and
Natwar Singh.

A number of academics abroad, including James Hershberg,
Peter Clarke, John Callaghan, Rakesh Ankit, Anton Harder, Paul
McGarr, Brent Moscovitch, Michael Rayner and Ian Hall, have been
generous with their time and responded to my emails promptly.

D. Vijaymohan was always ready to track down people who
had worked with Krishna Menon. Renuka Ray filled gaps in my
knowledge of A.V. Baliga. Archives of *The Hindu* and *Mathrubhumi*
yielded useful material, and I am thankful to both managements.

A.R. Venkatachalapathy took the trouble of translating into
English Kannadasan's tribute to Krishna Menon in Tamil. He,
however, did caution me that no translation can capture the sheer
majesty of the original.

I spent considerable time with Srinath Raghavan and S. Jaishankar
on the subject of Krishna Menon and the 1962 Sino-Indian war
and benefitted greatly from their insights. Shivshankar Menon and
Ramu Damodaran have been constant sources of information and
encouragement.

I thank Friends House, London, Science Museum, London, and
the archives of *Hindustan Times* and *The Hindu* for permission to use
photographs as also the estate of David Low for permission to use his
cartoons.

Nayanjot Lahiri, as always, has been a sounding board and
made many suggestions at various stages of the manuscript. Ranjana
Sengupta and Aditi Muraleedharan have made the book more
readable.

Bibliography

Books

Acheson, Dean. *Present at the Creation*. New York: W.W. Norton & Co, 1970.

Anand, Anita. *The Patient Assassin*. London: Simon and Schuster UK, 2019.

Anand, Mulk Raj. *The Bubble*. New Delhi: Arnold Heinemann, 1984.

Andrew, Christopher and Vasili Mitrokhin. *The Mitrokhin Archive II: The KGB and the World*. London: Allen Lane, 2005.

Andrew, Christopher. *The Defence of the Realm: The Authorized History of the MI5*. London: Penguin UK, 2009.

Ankit, Rakesh. *The Kashmir Conflict: From Empire to the Cold War, 1945–66*. London: Routledge, 2016.

Azad, Maulana Abul Kalam. *India Wins Freedom: The Complete Version*. New Delhi: Orient Blackswan, 1988.

Barnes, Leonard. *Empire or Democracy? A Study of the Colonial Question*. London: Routledge, 1939.

Beers, Laura. *Red Ellen: The Life of Ellen Wilkinson, Socialist, Feminist, Internationalist*. Cambridge: Harvard University Press, 2016.

Brecher, Michael. *India and World Politics: Krishna Menon's View of the World*. Delhi: Oxford University Press, 1968.

Brilliant, Frida. *Biographies in Bronze*. New Delhi: Vikas Publishing House, 1986.

Callaghan, John. *Rajani Palme Dutt: A Study in British Stalinism*. London: Lawrence & Wishart, 1993.

Campbell-Johnson, Alan. *Mission with Mountbatten*. London: Hale, 1951.

Carnall, Geoffrey. *Gandhi's Interpreter*. Edinburgh: Edinburgh University Press, 2010.

Chakravarty, Suhas. *V.K. Krishna Menon and the India League 1925–47*. Vols 1 and 2. New Delhi: Har-Anand Publications, 1997.

Chakravarty, Suhas. *Crusader Extraordinary: Krishna Menon and the India League 1932–1936*. New Delhi: India Research Press, 2006.

Chattopadhyay, Kamaladevi. *Inner Recesses Outer Spaces*. New Delhi: Niyogi, 2014.

Chaudhuri, General J.N. *An Autobiography as Narrated to B.K. Narayan*. New Delhi: Vikas Publishing House, 1978.

Clarke, Peter. *The Cripps Version*. London: Penguin Books, 2002.

Collins, Larry and Dominique Lapierre. *Freedom at Midnight*. New Delhi: Vikas Publishing House, 1975.

Crocker, Walter. *Nehru: A Contemporary's Estimate*. London: George, Allen & Unwin, 1966.

Dalvi, John P. *Himalayan Blunder: The Curtain-Raiser to the Sino-Indian War of 1962*. Bombay: Thacker, 1968.

Darbar, Mrs Gyanvati. *Portrait of a President: Letters of Dr Rajendra Prasad*. Vol. 2. New Delhi: Vikas Publishing House, 1976.

Dastur, Aloo J. *Menon vs. Kripalani: North Bombay Election, 1962*. Bombay: Bombay University Press, 1967.

Dayal, Rajeshwar. *A Life of Our Times*. New Delhi: Orient Longman, 1998.

Desai, Morarji. *The Story of My Life*. Vol. 2. Madras: Macmillan, 1974.

Devika, J. *Her Self: Early Writings on Gender by Malayalee Women, 1898–1938*. Calcutta: Bhatkal and Sen, 2005.

Duff, Sheila Grant. *The Parting of Ways*. London: Peter Owen, 1982.

Dutt, Subimal. *With Nehru in the Foreign Office*. Calcutta: Minerva Associates, 1977.

Eden, Anthony. *Memoirs: Full Circle*. London: Cassell, 1960.

Engerman, David C. *The Price Of Aid: The Economic Cold War in India*. Cambridge: Harvard University Press, 2018.

Galbraith, John Kenneth. *Ambassador's Journal: A Personal Account of the Kennedy Years*. London: Hamish Hamilton, 1969.

George, T.J.S. *Krishna Menon: A Biography*. London: Jonathan Cape, 1964.

Ghosh, Sudhir. *Gandhi's Emissary*. London: Cresset Press, 1987.

Gopal, Sarvepalli, *Jawaharlal Nehru: A Biography*. Vol. 1. Delhi: Oxford University Press, 1975.

Gopal, Sarvepalli. *Jawaharlal Nehru: A Biography*. Vol. 2. Delhi: Oxford University Press, 1979.

Gopal, Sarvepalli. *Jawaharlal Nehru: A Biography*. Vol. 3. Delhi: Oxford University Press, 1984.

Gopal, Sarvepalli. *Radhakrishnan: A Biography*. Delhi: Oxford University Press, 1989.

Gundevia, Y.D. *Outside the Archives*. Hyderabad: Sangam Books, 1984.

Hangen, Welles. *After Nehru Who?* New York: Rupert Hart Davis, 1963.

Hardy, Henry and Mark Pottle, eds. *Building Letters, 1960–1975: Isaiah Berlin*. London: Vintage, 2013.

Heikal, Mohammed H. *Cutting the Lion's Tail: Suez through Egyptian Eyes*. London: Andre Deutsch, 1986.

Hidayatullah, M. *My Own Boswell*. New Delhi: Arnold-Heinemann, 1980.

Hoffmann, Steven A. *India and the China Crisis*. Berkeley and Los Angeles: University of California Press, 1990.

Hough, Richard. *Edwina: Countess Mountbatten of Burma*. London: Weidenfeld and Nicolson, 1985.

Howkins, Adrian. *Frozen Empires: An Environmental History of the Antarctic Peninsula*. Oxford: Oxford University Press, 2016.

Ignatieff, Michael. *Isaiah Berlin: A Life*. London: Vintage, 2000.

Iyer, V.R. Krishna. *Nehru and Krishna Menon*. New Delhi: Konark Publishers, 1993.

Kapur, Major General B.D. *Building a Defence Technology Base*. New Delhi: Lancer International, 1990.

Katari, Admiral R.D. *A Sailor Remembers*. New Delhi: Vikas Publishing House, 1983.

Kaul, Lt. Gen B.M. *The Untold Story*. New Delhi: Allied Publishers, 1967.

Khera, S.S. *India's Defence Problem*. Calcutta: Orient Longman, 1968.

Khilnani, Sunil. *Incarnations: India in 50 Lives*. London: Penguin Random House UK, 2016.

Kirpalani, S.K. *Fifty Years with the British*. Bombay: Orient Longman, 1993.

Kramnick, Isaac and Barry Sheerman. *Harold Laski: A Life on the Left*. London. Hamish Hamilton, 1993.

Kripalani, J.B. *My Times: An Autobiography*. New Delhi: Rupa Publications, 2004.

Kunhi Krishnan, T.V. *Chavan and the Troubled Decade*. Bombay: Somaiya Publications, 1971.

Kutty Madhavan, V.K. *V.K. Krishna Menon*. New Delhi: Publications Division, Government of India, 1988.

Lal, Air Chief Marshal P.C. *My Years with the IAF*. New Delhi: Lancer International, 1986.

Lall, Arthur C. *The Emergence of Modern India*. New York: Columbia University Press, 1981.

Lengyel, Emil. *Krishna Menon*. New York: Walker and Co., 1962.

Lewis, Jeremy. *The Life and Times of Allan Lane*. London: Viking, 2005.

Lloyd, Selwyn. *Suez 1956: A Personal Account*. London: Jonathan Cape, 1978.

Logevall, Fredrik. *Embers of War: The Fall of an Empire and the Making of America's Vietnam*. New York: Random House, 2012.

Lownie, Andrew. *The Mountbattens*. London: Blink Publishing, 2019.

MacFarquhar, Roderick. *The Origins of the Cultural Revolution: The Coming of the Cataclysm 1961–1966*. Vol. 3. New York: Columbia University Press, 1997.

Mansergh, Nicholas (editor-in-chief). *The Transfer of Power*. Vols. 1, 2, 3, 4, 9, 10, 11, 12. London: Her Majesty's Stationery Office, 1970–83.

Masani, Minoo. *Bliss Was It in That Dawn . . .* New Delhi: Arnold-Heinemann, 1977.

Maxwell, Neville. *India's China War.* London: Jonathan Cape, 1970.

Medvedev, Zhores A. and Roy A. Medvedev. *The Unknown Stalin.* New York: I.B. Taurus & Co., 2003.

Menon, K.P.S. *Many Worlds Revisited.* Bombay: Bharatiya Vidya Bhavan, 1965.

Michelson, Bruce. *Mark Twain On the Loose.* Boston: University of Massachusetts Press, 1995.

Millar, T.B., ed. *Australian Foreign Minister: The Diaries of R.G. Casey, 1957–60.* London: Collins, 1972.

Miller, Joan. *One Girl's War.* London: Brandon Books, 1986.

Montagu, Edwin. *An Indian Diary.* London: William Heinemann, 1930.

Moore, R.J. *Churchill, Cripps and India 1939–1945.* Oxford: Oxford University Press, 1979.

Mountbatten, Pamela. *India Remembered.* London: Pavilion Books, 2007.

Mukherjee, Rudrangshu. *Nehru and Bose: Parallel Lives.* New Delhi: Penguin Books, 2014.

Mullik, B.N. *Chinese Betrayal: My Years with Nehru.* Bombay: Allied Publishers, 1971.

Munro, John A. and Alex I. Inglis, eds. *Mike: The Memoirs of the Rt. Hon. Lester B. Pearson, 1948–1957.* Vol. 2. Toronto: University of Toronto Press, 2015.

Nayar, Kuldip. *Beyond The Lines: An Autobiography.* New Delhi: Roli Books, 2012.

Nehru, B.K. *Nice Guys Finish Second.* New Delhi: Penguin Books India, 1997.

Nethercot, Arthur H. *The Last Four Lives of Annie Besant.* London: Rupert Hart-Davis, 1963.

Owen, Nicholas. *The British Left and India.* Oxford: Oxford University Press, 2007.

Palit, Major General D.K. *War in High Himalaya: The Indian Army in Crisis 1962.* London: C. Hurst & Co, 1991.

Palit, Major General D.K. *Musings and Memories*. Vol. 2. New Delhi: Lancer Publishers, 2004.

Pandit, Vijaya Lakshmi. *The Scope of Happiness: A Personal Memoir*. New Delhi: Vikas Publishing House, 1979.

Patil, S.K. *My Years with Congress*. Bombay: Prachure Prakashan Mandir, 1991.

Perkins, Anne. *Red Queen: The Authorised Biography of Barbara Castle*. London: Macmillan, 2003.

Pradhan, R.D. *Debacle to Revival: Y.B. Chavan as Defence Minister, 1962–1965*. New Delhi: Orient Longman, 1998.

Prakash, Gyan. *Mumbai Fables*. New Delhi: HarperCollins, 2010.

Pyarelal. *The Epic Fast*. Ahmedabad: M.M. Bhatt, 1932.

Raghavan, Srinath. *War and Peace in Modern India: A Strategic History of the Nehru Years*. Ranikhet: Permanent Black, 2010.

Raghavan, Srinath. *1971: A Global History of the Creation of Bangladesh*. Cambridge: Harvard University Press, 2013.

Rahman, M.A. *Hungary: An Adventure*. New Delhi: Embassy of Hungary in New Delhi, Balassi Institute, ID Research Ltd/ Publikon Publishers, 2016.

Rajan, M.S. *India in World Affairs, 1954–56*. Bombay: Asia Publishing House, 1963.

Ram, Janaki. *V.K. Krishna Menon: A Personal Memoir*. Delhi: Oxford University Press, 1997.

Ramesh, Jairam. *Indira Gandhi: A Life in Nature*. New Delhi: Simon and Schuster India, 2017.

Ramesh, Jairam. *Intertwined Lives: P.N. Haksar & Indira Gandhi*. New Delhi: Simon and Schuster, 2018.

Ranganathan, C.V. and Vinod C. Khanna. *India and China: The Way Ahead After 'Mao's India War'*. New Delhi: Har-Anand Publications, 2000.

Rao, P. Kodanda. *The Right Honourable V.S. Srinivasa Sastry: A Political Biography*. Bombay: Asia Publishing House, 1963.

Rasgotra, Maharajkrishna. *A Life in Diplomacy*. New Delhi: Penguin Books India, 2016.

Reddy, E.S., ed. *India against Apartheid: Speeches of Krishna Menon at the United Nations*. New Delhi: Sanchar Publishing House, 1994.

Reddy, E.S. and A.K. Damodaran, eds. *Krishna Menon on Kashmir: Speeches at the United Nations*. New Delhi: Sanchar Publishing House, 1992.

Reddy, E.S. and A.K. Damodaran, eds. *Krishna Menon at the United Nations: India and the World*. New Delhi: Sanchar Publishing House, 1994.

Reddy, E.S. and A.K. Damodaran, eds. *Decolonisation, Peace and the United Nations: Krishna Menon Speeches at the United Nations*. New Delhi: Sanchar Publishing House, 1997.

Reddy, O. Pulla. *Autumn Leaves*. Bombay: Bharatiya Vidya Bhavan, 1978.

Reid, Escott. *Envoy to Nehru*. New Delhi: Oxford University Press, 1981.

Sahni, Parikshat. *Non-Conformist: Memories of My Father Balraj Sahni*. New Delhi: Penguin Books, 2019.

Sanghvi, Ramesh. *John F. Kennedy: A Political Biography*. Bombay: The Perennial Press, 1961.

Sen, Mohit. *A Traveller and the Road: The Journey of an Indian Communist*. New Delhi: Rupa & Co., 2003.

Seton, Marie. *Panditji: A Portrait of Jawaharlal Nehru*. London: Dobson Books, 1967.

Shenoy, Ramadas P. *Defence Research and Development Organisation, 1958–1982*. New Delhi: Defence Research and Development Organisation, Ministry of Defence, Government of India, 2006.

Singh, Khushwant. *Truth, Love and a Little Malice*. New Delhi: Penguin Books, 2002.

Sorensen, Reginald W. *My Impression of India*. London: Meridian Books, 1946.

Srivastava, C.P. *Lal Bahadur Shastri*. Delhi: Oxford University Press, 1995.

Straight, Michael. *After Long Silence*. New York: W.W. Norton & Co., 1983.

Thorat, Lt. Gen S.P.P. (Retd). *From Reveille to Retreat*. New Delhi: Allied Publishers, 1986.

Verma, Lt. Gen. S.D. (Retd). *To Serve with Honour*. Dehradun: Natraj Publishers, 1988.

Vira, Dharma. *Memoirs of a Civil Servant*. New Delhi: Vikas Publishing House, 1975.

Visram, Rozina. *Asians in Britain: 400 Years of History*. London: Pluto Press, 2002.

Wolpert, Stanley. *Shameful Flight: The Last Years of the British Empire in India*. New York: Oxford University Press, 2006.

Wolpert, Stanley. *Nehru: A Tryst with Destiny*. New York: Oxford University Press, 1996.

Xydis, Stephen G. Cyprus: *Reluctant Republic*. New York: Mouton & Co., 1973.

Ziegler, Philip. *Mountbatten*. London: Collins, 1985.

Articles in Academic and Other Journals

Barnes, Robert. 2013. 'Between the Blocs: India, the United Nations, and Ending the Korean War'. *Journal of Korean Studies* 18 (2): 263–86.

Gopal, S. 1972. 'Sino-Indian Relations'. *The Round Table* 62 (245): 113–18.

Hershberg, James G. 2012. 'Quietly Encouraging Quasi-Alignment: US–Indian Relations, the Sino-Indian Border War of 1962, and the Downfall of Krishna Menon'. *Eurasia Border Review (Special Issue on China's Post-Revolutionary Borders 1940s–1960s)* 3: 121–57.

McGarr, P.M. 2010. '"A Serious Menace to Security": British Intelligence, V. K. Krishna Menon, and the Indian High Commission in London, 1947–1952'. *The Journal of Imperial and Commonwealth History* 38 (3): 441–69.

McGarr, P.M. 2011. '"India's Rasputin"? V.K. Krishna Menon and Anglo-American Misperceptions of Indian Foreign Policymaking, 1947–1964'. *Diplomacy and Statecraft* 22 (2): 239–60.

Raghavan, Srinath. 2006. 'Sino-Indian Boundary Dispute, 1948–60: A Reappraisal'. *Economic and Political Weekly* 4 (36): 3882–892.

Ramesh, Jairam. 2019. 'The Reorganisation of States and Thereafter'. *IIC Quarterly* 46 (1): 50–65.

Tinker, Hugh. 1964. 'Krishna Menon: A Biography by T.J.S. George', *International Affairs* 40 (4): 753.

Articles in Books

Garver, John W. 'China's Decision for War with India in 1962'. In
Robert S. Ross and Alastair Iain Johnston, eds. *New Approaches to
the Study of Chinese Foreign Policy*. California: Stanford University
Press, 2005.

Hall, Ian. 'Mephistopheles in a Saville Row Suit: V.K. Krishna
Menon and the West'. In Ian Hall, ed. *Radicals and Reactionaries
in Twentieth-Century International Thought*. New York: Palgrave-
Macmillan, 2015.

Articles in Newspapers

Subrahmanyam, K. 'The Real Krishna Menon: Flawed Brilliance
and Super-patriotism'. *The Times of India*, 21 May 1997.

Subrahmanyam, K. 'Indo-Soviet Military Ties: MIG-21 Deal Was a
Watershed'. *The Times of India*, 8 August 1987.

Academic Monographs

Raghavan, Srinath. 'A Missed Opportunity? The Nehru–Zhou Enlai
Summit of 1960'. NMML Occasional Paper, Nehru Memorial
Museum and Library, New Delhi, 2015.

University Dissertations

Harder, Anton. 'Defining Independence in Cold War Asia: Sino-
Indian Relations, 1949-62'. PhD thesis, London School of
Economics and Political Science. 2015.

Lane, Ellie. 'V.K. Krishna Menon and Indian Internationalism in
Theory and Practice, 1947–1962'. Dissertation submitted as
part of the Tripos Examination, Faculty of History, Cambridge
University.

Moscovitch, Brant. 'A "Seedbed" for Post-Colonial Leaders'. PhD
thesis, University of Oxford, 2017.

Index